Economic Growth

Theory and Numerical Solution Methods

Alfonso Novales · Esther Fernández · Jesús Ruiz

Economic Growth

Theory and Numerical Solution Methods

Springer

Professor Alfonso Novales
Dr. Esther Fernández
Dr. Jesús Ruiz
Universidad Complutense
Departamento de Economia Cuantitativa
Campus Somosaguas
28223 Pozuelo de Alarcón (Madrid)
Spain
anovales@ccee.ucm.es
mesferna@ccee.ucm.es
jruizand@ccee.ucm.es

ISBN: 978-3-540-68665-1   e-ISBN: 978-3-540-68669-9

Library of Congress Control Number: 2008929527

Cover design: WMX Design GmbH, Heidelberg

Printed on acid-free paper

9 8 7 6 5 4 3 2 1

springer.com

To our spouses and children,
Charo
Miguel and Miguel Ángel
Rafi and Sergio

Preface

Integrating Growth Theory and Numerical Solutions

Dynamic, stochastic models with optimizing agents have become a standard tool for policy design and evaluation at central banks and governments around the world. They are also increasingly used as the main reference for forecasting purposes. Such models can incorporate general equilibrium assumptions, as it was the case with Modern Business Cycle Theory, or different types of market frictions, in the form of price rigidity or monopolistic competition, as in the New Keynesian Macroeconomics. These models can all be considered as special cases of models of economic growth, and the theoretical and computational methods contained in this book are a first step to get started in this area.

The book combines detailed discussions on theoretical issues on deterministic and stochastic, exogenous and endogenous growth models, together with the computational methods needed to produce numerical solutions. A detailed description of the analytical and numerical approach to solving each of the different models covered in the book is provided, and the solution algorithms are implemented in EXCEL and MATLAB files. These files are provided to illustrate theoretical results as well as to simulate the effects of economic policy interventions. Theoretical discussions covered in the book relate to issues such as the inefficiency of the competitive equilibrium, the Ricardian doctrine, dynamic Laffer curves, the welfare cost of inflation or the nominal indeterminacy of the price level and local indeterminacy in endogenous growth models, among many others. This integration of theoretical discussions at the analytical level, whenever possible, and numerical solution methods that allow for addressing a variety of additional issues that could not possibly be discussed analytically, is a novel feature of this book.

The Audience

This textbook has been conceived for advanced undergraduate and graduate students in economics, as well as for researchers planning to work with stochastic dynamic growth models of different kinds. As described above, some of the applications included in the book may be appealing to many young researchers. Analytical discussions are presented in full detail and the reader does not need to have a specific previous background on Growth theory. The accompanying software has been written using the same notation as in the textbook, which allows for an easy understanding of how each program file addresses a particular theoretical issue. Programs increase in complexity as the book covers more complex models, but the reader can progress easily from the simpler programs in the first chapters to the more complex programs in endogenous growth models or programs for analyzing monetary economies. No initial background on programming is assumed.

The book is self contained and it has been designed so that the student advances in the theoretical and the computational issues in parallel. The structure of program files is described in numerical exercise-type of sections, where their output is also interpreted. These sections should be considered an essential part of the learning process, since the provided program files can be easily changed following our indications so that the reader can formulate and analyze his/her own questions.

Main Ideas

Exogenous and endogenous growth models are thoroughly reviewed throughout the book, and special attention is paid to the use of these models for fiscal and monetary policy analysis. The structure of each model is first presented, and the equilibrium conditions are analytically characterized. Equilibrium conditions are interpreted in detail, with special emphasis on the role of the transversality condition in guaranteeing the stability of the implied solution. Stability is a major issue throughout the book, and a central ingredient in the construction of the solution algorithms for the different models.

Even though this is not a book on economic policy, most of the models considered incorporate a variety of distortionary and non-distortionary taxes, which allow us to address a number of policy issues. Fiscal policy in non-monetary growth economies is considered in Chaps. 2–4 (exogenous growth) and Chaps. 6 and 7 (endogenous growth). Characterizing possible dynamic Laffer effects in endogenous growth models, or the effects of fiscal policy interventions in models with human capital accumulation are some of the issues considered in this first part of the book. Chapters 8 and 9 are devoted to the analysis of monetary economies that incorporate fiscal policy variables and parameters. This allows for a detailed discussion of the interaction between fiscal and monetary policy and their coordinate design. The analysis of each model starts with the characterization of steady state, and a description of the long-run effects of different policy interventions. Stability conditions are then characterized on either linear or log-linear approximations, and the general solution approach is particularized in each case to compute the numerical time series solution to the model under the specific type of policy considered. We are particularly interested in characterizing the effects of a given policy intervention along the transition between steady states. Most models are presented and analysed in continuous and discrete time so that the reader can become familiar with both formulations. Sometimes, a given model is solved under two different approaches, so that the reader can get an even better understanding of the solution techniques.

The illustrations used in the 'Numerical Exercise'-type sections throughout the book discuss a variety of characteristics of the numerical solution to each specific model, including the evaluation of some policy experiments. Most issues considered in these sections, like the details of the numerical simulation of models with technological diffusion or Schumpeterian models under uncertainty are presented for the first time in a textbook, having appeared so far only in research papers.

Brief Description of Contents

The use of rational expectations growth models for policy analysis is discussed in the Introductory chapter, where the need to produce numerical solutions is explained. Chapter 2 presents the neoclassical Solow–Swan growth model with constant savings, in continuous and discrete time formulations. Chapter 3 is devoted to the optimal growth model in continuous time. The existence of an optimal steady state is shown and stability conditions are characterized. The relationship between the resource allocations emerging from the benevolent planner's problem and from the competitive equilibrium mechanism is shown. The role of the government is explained, fiscal policy is introduced and the competitive equilibrium in an economy with taxes is characterized. Finally, the Ricardian doctrine is analyzed. Chapter 4 addresses the same issues in discrete time formulation, allowing for numerical solutions to be introduced and used for policy evaluation. Deterministic and stochastic versions of the model are successively considered.

Chapter 5 is devoted to solution methods and their application to solving the optimal growth model of an economy subject to distortionary and non-distortionary taxes. The chapter covers some linear solution methods, implemented on linear and log-linear approximations: the linear-quadratic approximation, the undetermined coefficients method, the state-space approach, the method based on eigenvalue-eigenvector decompositions of the approximation to the model, and also some nonlinear methods, like the parameterized expectations model and a class of projection methods. Special emphasis is placed on the conditions needed to guarantee stability of the implied solutions.

Chapter 6 introduces some endogenous growth models, in continuous and discrete time formulations. The AK model incorporating fiscal policy instruments is taken as a basis for analysis, both in deterministic and stochastic versions. The possibility of dynamic Laffer curves is discussed. A more general model with nontrivial transition, that includes the AK model as a special case, is also presented. Chapter 7 presents additional endogenous growth models. Stochastic economies with a variety of products, technological diffusion, Schumpeterian growth, and human capital accumulation, are all presented in detail and the appropriate solution methods are explained. Chapters 8 and 9 are devoted to growth in monetary economies. Chapter 8 introduces the basic Sidrauski model and discusses some modelling issues that arise in practical research in these models. The interrelation between monetary and fiscal policy in steady state is also discussed. Special attention is paid to characterize the feasible combinations of fiscal and monetary policies and to the appropriate choice of policy targets. The concept of optimal rate of inflation is introduced. The possibilities for the design of a mix of fiscal and monetary policy in economies with and without distorting taxation are discussed. Conditions for the non-neutrality of monetary policy under endogenous labour supply are examined. The chapter closes with a description of the Ramsey problem that describes the choice of optimal monetary policy. Chapter 9 characterizes the transitional dynamics in deterministic and stochastic monetary economies and presents numerical solution methods for deterministic and stochastic monetary economies. Specific details are provided depending on whether the monetary authority uses nominal interest rates or the rate of growth of money supply as a control variable for monetary policy implementation. Special attention is paid to the possibility of nominal indeterminacy arising as a consequence of the specific design followed for monetary policy. The chapter closes with a presentation of Keynesian monetary models, which are increasingly used for actual policy making. After characterizing equilibrium conditions, a numerical solution approach is discussed in detail.

A more detailed synopsis of the book is provided in Sect. 1.5.

Software

As explained above, MATLAB and EXCEL files are provided to analyze a variety of theoretical issues. EXCEL files are used to compute a single realization of the solution to a given model. That is enough in deterministic economies. There are also MATLAB programs that perform the same analysis. In stochastic economies, however, characterizing the probability distribution of a given statistic through a large number of realizations becomes impossible in a spreadsheet, and it is done in MATLAB programs. All MATLAB and EXCEL files are downloadable from our Web page: www.ucm.es/info/ecocuan/anc/Growth/growthbook.htm

Antecedents and Acknowledgments

Over the years, we have benefited from working through textbooks on Economic Growth and Dynamic General Equilibrium Economies [Barro and Sala-i-Martin (2003), Aggion and Howitt (1999), Stokey and Lucas (1989), Blanchard and Fisher (1998), Lucas (1987), Sargent (1987), Ljunquist and Sargent (2004), Hansen y Sargent (2005), Cooley (1995), Turnovsky (2000), Walsh (1998)], who obviously should not be held accountable for any misconception that might arise in this volume.

We hope to contribute to the huge literature on Economic Growth by the integration of theoretical and computational aspects in the analysis of non-monetary and monetary models of exogenous and endogenous growth. Even though we provide a detailed discussion of a variety of different solution approaches in Chapter 5, we have emphasized the use of variations of the Blanchard and Kahn (1980) approach, in some cases following the applications by Ireland (2004) [see also his Web page: http://www2.bc.edu/~irelandp/programs.html]. Recent textbooks on Computational Methods for Dynamic Economies [Judd (1998), Heer and Maussner (2005), Marimon and Scott eds. (1997), deJong and Dave (2007), Miranda and Fackler

(2002), McCandless (2008)] provide additional reading, in some cases with alternative approaches to model solution.

The idea that any dynamic model has time series implications that can be put to test with actual data has traditionally been a central premise in the graduate programs in Economics at University of Minnesota, and has clearly influenced the conception of this book. Specially important to us were the teachings of Stephen Turnovsky, Tom Sargent and Christopher Sims. In that context, it was easy to understand that advances in Economics should come from iterating between theoretical models and actual data and from there, the need to obtain statistical implications from any model economy.

Previous versions of parts of this book have been used in advanced undergraduate and graduate courses in Economics and Quantitative Finance at Universidad Complutense (Madrid, Spain), City University of Yokohama (Yokohama, Japan) and Keio University (Tokyo, Japan). We appreciate the patience of students working out details of previous drafts. We thank Yoshikiyo Sakai and Yatsuo Maeda for the opportunity to discuss this material while still in process. We are greatly indebted with our friends and colleagues Emilio Domínguez, Javier Pérez and Gustavo Marrero for many useful and illuminating discussions. Finally, our deepest gratitude to our families for their understanding through the long and demanding process of producing this book.

Alfonso Novales
Esther Fernández
Jesús Ruiz

Contents

Chapter 1
Introduction

This is a book on Growth Theory and on the numerical methods needed to fully characterize the properties of most Growth models. In this introductory chapter, we describe the main characteristics of different families of Growth models and their relevance for policy analysis, which is moving leading economic and financial institutions throughout the world to increasingly rely on their use for forecasting as well as for policy evaluation. In particular, we emphasize how the richer structure provided to Growth models by their Microeconomic foundations allows us to address a much broader set of policy issues than in more traditional structural dynamic models. The book gradually builds on by increasing the degree of generality of the models being considered, as explained below. We cover: (a) neoclassical growth under a constant savings rate, (b) optimal growth, (c) numerical solution methods, (d) endogenous growth, and (e) monetary growth. Theoretical discussions on each model are presented, with special attention to characterizing the properties of equilibrium solutions and their use for fiscal policy considerations, while a specific chapter deals with monetary policy issues. Algorithms to solve all models considered are presented, together with EXCEL spreadsheets and MATLAB programs that implement them. Results obtained by these programs are commented in *"Numerical exercise"*-type sections, where some indications are provided on possible modifications of the enclosed programs. The book has been written with the intention that it may be accessible to students without an initial background on Growth Theory or mathematical software. Maintaining the same notation used in the analytical presentations in the book should allow the reader to follow easily the structure of the programs and quickly learn how to adapt them to alternative specifications or theoretical assumptions.

Growth models incorporate very specific assumptions on the structure of preferences, technology, the sources of randomness, and the policy rules followed by the economic authority, and characterize the relationship implied by such a structure between the decisions made by the different agents at each point in time and the information they have available when making their decisions. Under uncertainty, agents' perceptions on the future are an explicit determinant of their actions. Growth models do not make ad-hoc assumptions on the way how expectations influence agents' decisions. Rather, the solution to the optimization problems posed for each agent leads to decision rules for the different agents that incorporate expectations of functions of future variables in a very specific manner. If expectations are assumed to be rational, expectations in the model become endogenous variables, they are fully consistent with the structure of the model, and incorporate agents' perceptions of possible future changes in policy. Doing that, these models are safe from a strong criticism made on a traditional approach to economic policy evaluation by Nobel laureate R.E. Lucas that has been very influential in the last decades. This is the reason why, as we describe below, these models are increasingly being used in the research departments of Central Banks and main international economic institutions to forecast as well as to evaluate the consequences of alternative policy choices.

The counterpart comes from the fact that the type of stochastic control problems that are integrated into a Growth model lack an analytical solution, so they need to be solved following a numerical approach, accompanied by Monte Carlo simulation in the case of stochastic Growth models. The numerical solution to the model then comes in the form of artificial time series that can be analyzed using standard statistical and econometric tools, and the results compared to those obtained in corresponding time series data from actual economies. These are the main issues introduced in this chapter, which are later gradually developed throughout the book. Section 1.1 reviews some statistical concepts using simple time series models, Sect. 1.2 considers some simple dynamic macroeconomic models in which we introduce additional concepts, as well as the fundamentals of the simulation methods that will be used through the book. Section 1.3 introduces the main characteristics of Growth models, in comparison with more traditional dynamic macroeconomic models. This section motivates the convenience to work with Growth models and describes their different types, paying attention to the way they deal with the criticism to more traditional policy evaluation. Section 1.4 explains the need to obtain numerical solutions to Growth models, their potential use, and how this approach has led to changing the type of policy questions we ask and the type of answers we get. This introductory chapter ends up with a synopsis of the book, where a reference is made to the treatment of the issues mentioned along this Introduction.

1.1 A Few Time Series Concepts

Economics is full of statements relating the dynamic properties of key variables. For instance, we may say that inflation is very persistent, that aggregate consumption and GNP experience cyclical fluctuations, or that hours worked and productivity move independently from each other. These statements have direct implications in terms of the time series representations of these variables. Sometimes we are more specific, as when we state that stock exchange returns are white noise, thereby justifying the usual belief that they are *unpredictable*. The unpredictability statement comes from the fact that the forecast of a white noise process, no matter how far into the future, is always the same. That forecast is equal to the mean of the white noise process, which would likely be assumed to be zero in the case of asset returns. If returns are logarithmic, i.e., the first difference of logged market prices, then prices themselves would follow a random walk structure. These properties cannot be argued separately from each other, since they are just two different forms of making the same statement on stock market prices. We may also say at some point that the economy is likely to repeat next year its growth performance from the previous year, which incorporates the belief that annual GNP growth follows a random walk, its best one-step ahead prediction being the last observed value. A high persistence in real wages or in inflation could be consistent with first order autoregressive models with an autoregressive parameter close to 1. We briefly review in this section some concepts regarding basic stochastic processes, of the type that are often used to represent the behavior of economic variables.

1.1.1 Some Simple Stochastic Processes

A stochastic process is a sequence of random variables indexed by time. Each of the random variables in a stochastic process, corresponding to a given time index t, has its own probability distribution. These distributions can be different, and any two of the random variables in a stochastic process may either exhibit dependence of some type or be independent from each other.

A *white noise* process is,

$$y_t = \varepsilon_t, \ t = 1, 2, 3, \ldots$$

where $\varepsilon_t, t = 1, 2, \ldots$ is a sequence of independent, identically distributed zero-mean random variables, known as the *innovation* to the process. A white noise is sometimes defined by adding the assumption that ε_t has a Normal distribution. The mathematical expectation of a white noise is zero, and its variance is constant: $Var(y_t) = \sigma_\varepsilon^2$. More generally, we could consider a *white noise with constant*, by incorporating a constant term in the process,

$$y_t = a + \varepsilon_t, \ t = 1, 2, 3, \ldots$$

with mathematical expectation $E(y_t) = a$, and variance: $Var(y_t) = \sigma_\varepsilon^2$.

The future value of a white noise with drift obeys,

$$y_{t+s} = a + \varepsilon_{t+s},$$

so that, if we try to forecast any future value of a white noise on the basis of the information available[1] at time t, we would have:

$$E_t y_{t+s} = a + E_t \varepsilon_{t+s} = a,$$

---

[1] That amounts to constructing the forecast by application of the conditional expectation operator to the analytical representation of the future value being predicted, where the conditional expectation is formed with respect to the sigma algebra of events known at time t.

because of the properties of the ε_t-process. That is, the prediction of a future value of a white noise is given by the mean of the process. In that sense, a white noise process is *unpredictable*. The prediction of such process is given by the mean of the process, with no effect from previously observed values. Because of that, the history of a white noise process is irrelevant to forecast its future values. No matter how many data points we have, we will not use them to forecast a white noise.

A *random walk with drift* is a process,

$$y_t = a + y_{t-1} + \varepsilon_t, \ t = 1, 2, 3, \ldots \tag{1.1}$$

so that its first differences are white noise. If $y_t = \ln(P_t)$ is the log of some market price, then its return $r_t = \ln(P_t) - \ln(P_{t-1})$, will be a white noise, as we already mentioned. A random walk does not have a well defined mean or variance.

In the case of a *random walk without drift*, we have,

$$y_{t+s} = y_{t+s-1} + \varepsilon_{t+s}, \ s \geq 1$$

so that we have the sequence of forecasts:

$$E_t y_{t+1} = E_t y_t + E_t \varepsilon_{t+1} = y_t,$$
$$E_t y_{t+2} = E_t y_{t+1} + E_t \varepsilon_{t+2} = E_t y_{t+1} = y_t,$$

and the same for all future variables. In this case, the history of a random walk process is relevant to forecast its future values, but only through the last observation. All data points other than the last one are ignored when forecasting a random walk process.

First order autoregressive processes, AR(1), are of the form,

$$y_t = \rho y_{t-1} + \varepsilon_t, \ |\rho| < 1,$$

and can be represented by,

$$y_t = \sum_{s=0}^{\infty} \rho^s \varepsilon_{t-s},$$

the right hand side having a finite variance under the assumption that $Var(\varepsilon_t) = \sigma_\varepsilon^2$ only if $|\rho| < 1$. In that case, we would have:

$$E(y_t) = 0; \ Var(y_t) = \frac{\sigma_\varepsilon^2}{1 - \rho^2}.$$

Predictions from a first order autoregression can be obtained by,

$$E_t y_{t+1} = \rho E_t y_t + E_t \varepsilon_{t+1} = \rho y_t,$$
$$E_t y_{t+2} = E_t(\rho y_{t+1}) + E_t \varepsilon_{t+2} = \rho^2 E_t y_{t+1} = \rho^2 y_t,$$

and, in general,

$$E_t y_{t+s} = \rho^s y_t, \ s \geq 1$$

which is the reason to impose the constraint $|\rho| < 1$. The parameter ρ is sometimes known as the *persistence* of the process. As the previous expression shows, an increase or decrease in y_t will show up in any future y_{t+s}, although the influence of that y_t-value will gradually disappear over time, according to the value of ρ. A value of ρ close to 1 will therefore introduce high persistence in the process, the opposite being true for ρ close to zero.

The covariance between the values of the first order autoregressive process at two points in time is:

$$Cov(y_t, y_{t+s}) = \rho^s Var(y_t), \ s \gtrless 0,$$

so that the linear correlation is:

$$Corr(y_t, y_{t+s}) = \frac{Cov(y_t, y_{t+s})}{Var(y_t)} = \rho^s,$$

which dies away at a rate of ρ. In an autoregressive process with a value of ρ close to 1, the correlation of y_t with past values will be sizeable for a number of periods.

A first order autoregressive process with constant has the representation,

$$y_t = a + \rho y_{t-1} + \varepsilon_t, \ |\rho| < 1.$$

Let us assume by now that the mathematical expectation exists and is finite. Under that assumption, $Ey_t = Ey_{t-1}$, and we have:

$$Ey_t = a + E(\rho y_{t-1}) + E\varepsilon_t = a + \rho Ey_t,$$

so that: $Ey_t = \frac{a}{1-\rho}$. To find out the variance of the process, we can iterate on its representation:

$$
\begin{aligned}
y_t &= a + \rho y_{t-1} + \varepsilon_t = a + \rho(a + \rho y_{t-2} + \varepsilon_{t-1}) + \varepsilon_t \\
&= a(1 + \rho + \rho^2 + \dots + \rho^{s-1}) + \rho^s y_{t-s} \\
&\quad + \left(\rho^{s-1}\varepsilon_{t-s+1} + \dots + \rho^2 \varepsilon_{t-2} + \rho \varepsilon_{t-1} + \varepsilon_t\right),
\end{aligned}
$$

and if we proceed indefinitely, we get

$$y_t = a(1 + \rho + \rho^2 + \dots) + (\dots + \rho^2 \varepsilon_{t-2} + \rho \varepsilon_{t-1} + \varepsilon_t),$$

since $\lim_{s \to \infty} \rho^s y_{t-s} = 0.$[2] Then, taking the variance of this expression:

$$Var(y_t) = Var\left(\dots + \rho^2 \varepsilon_{t-2} + \rho \varepsilon_{t-1} + \varepsilon_t\right) = \sum_{s=0}^{\infty} \rho^{2s} \sigma_\varepsilon^2 = \frac{\sigma_\varepsilon^2}{1 - \rho^2},$$

so that the variance of the y_t-process increases with the variance of the innovation, σ_ε^2, but it is also higher the closer is ρ to 1. As ρ approaches 1, the first order

---

[2] This is the limit of a random variable, and an appropriate limit concept must be used. It suffices to say that the power of ρ going to zero justifies the zero limit for the product random variable.

autoregression becomes a random walk, for which this expression would give an infinite variance. This is because if we repeat for the random walk the same argument we have made here, we get,

$$y_t = a + y_{t-1} + \varepsilon_t = a + (a + y_{t-2} + \varepsilon_{t-1}) + \varepsilon_t$$
$$= as + y_{t-s} + (\varepsilon_{t-s+1} + \dots + \varepsilon_{t-2} + \varepsilon_{t-1} + \varepsilon_t),$$

so that the past term y_{t-s} does not die away no matter how far we move back into the past, and the variance of the sum in brackets increases without bound as we move backwards in time. The random walk process has an infinite variance. Sometimes, it can be assumed that there is a known initial condition y_0. The random walk process can then be represented:

$$y_t = a + y_{t-1} + \varepsilon_t = a + (a + y_{t-2} + \varepsilon_{t-1}) + \varepsilon_t$$
$$= \dots = at + y_0 + (\varepsilon_1 + \dots + \varepsilon_{t-2} + \varepsilon_{t-1} + \varepsilon_t),$$

with $E(y_t) = ta$ and $Var(y_t) = t\sigma_\varepsilon^2$. Hence, both moments change over time, the variance increasing without any bound. However, if we compare in a same graph time series realizations of a random walk together with some stationary autoregressive processes, it will be hard to tell which is the process with an infinite variance.

A future value of the first order autoregression can be represented:

$$y_{t+s} = a + \rho y_{t+s-1} + \varepsilon_{t+s}, \ |\rho| < 1, \ s \geq 1,$$

which can be iterated to,

$$y_{t+s} = a(1 + \rho + \rho^2 + \dots + \rho^{s-1}) + \rho^s y_t + (\rho^{s-1}\varepsilon_{t+1} + \rho^{s-2}\varepsilon_{t+2} + \dots + \varepsilon_{t+s}),$$

so that its forecast is given by,

$$y_{t+s} = a\frac{1 - \rho^s}{1 - \rho} + \rho^s y_t.$$

So, as the forecast horizon goes to infinity, the forecast converges to,

$$\lim E_t y_{t+s} = \frac{a}{1 - \rho},$$

the mean of the process.

1.1.2 Stationarity, Mean Reversion, Impulse Responses

A stochastic process is stationary when the distribution of k-tuples $(y_{t_1}, y_{t_2}, \dots, y_{t_k})$ is the same with independence of the value of k and of the time periods $t_1, t_2, \dots, t_k$ considered. It is a property of any *stationary stochastic process* that the forecast of a future value converges to its mean as the forecast horizon goes to infinity. This is obviously fulfilled in the case of a white noise process. Another characteristic is that any time realization crosses the sample mean often, while a nonstationary process would spend arbitrarily large periods of time at either side of its sample mean. As we have seen above for the first order autoregression, the simple autocorrelation function of a stationary process, made up by the sequence of correlations between any two values of the process, will go to zero relatively quickly, dieing away very slowly for processes close to nonstationarity.

When they are not subject to an stochastic innovation,[3] stationary autoregressive processes converge smoothly and relatively quickly to their mathematical expectation. The y_t-process will converge to $\frac{a}{1-\rho}$ either from above or from below, depending on whether the initial value, y_0, is above or below $\frac{a}{1-\rho}$. The speed of convergence is given by the autoregressive coefficient. When the process is subject to a nontrivial innovation, the convergence in the mean of the process will not be easily observed. This is the case because the process experiences a shock through the innovation process every period, which would start a new convergence that would overlap the previous one, and so on. Under normal circumstances we will just see a time realization exhibiting fluctuations around the mathematical expectation of the process, unless the process experiences a huge innovation, or the starting condition y_0 is far enough from $\frac{a}{1-\rho}$, in units of its standard deviation, $\sqrt{\frac{\sigma_\varepsilon^2}{1-\rho^2}}$.

The property of converging to the mean after any stochastic shock is called *mean reversion*, and is characteristic of stationary processes. In stationary processes, any shock tends to be corrected over time. This cannot be appreciated because shocks to y_t are just the values of the innovation process, which take place every period. So, the process of mean reversion following a shock gets disturbed by the next shock, and so on. But the stationary process will always react to shocks as trying to return to its mean. Alternatively, a non stationary process will tend to depart from its mean following any shock. As a consequence, the successive values of the innovation process ε_t will take y_t every time farther away from its mean.

An alternative way of expressing this property is through the effects of purely transitory shocks or innovations. A stationary process has transitory responses to purely transitory innovations. On the contrary, a nonstationary process may have permanent responses to purely transitory shocks. So, if a stationary variable experiences a one-period shock, its effects may be felt longer than that, but will disappear after a few periods. The effects of such a one-period shock on a nonstationary process will be permanent. A white noise is just an innovation process. The value taken by the white noise process is the same as that taken by its innovation. Hence, the effects of any innovation last as long as the innovation itself, reflecting the stationary of this process. The situation with a random walk is quite different. A random walk takes a value equal to the one taken the previous period, plus the innovation. Hence, any value of the innovation process gets accumulated in successive values of the random walk. The effects of any shock last forever, reflect-

---

[3] That is, if the innovation ε_t has zero variance.

ing the nonstationary nature of this process. In a stationary first order autoregression, any value of the innovation ε_t gets incorporated into y_t that same period. It will also have an effect of size $\rho\varepsilon_t$ on y_{t+1}. This is because $y_{t+1} = \rho y_t + \varepsilon_{t+1}$ so, even if $\varepsilon_{t+1} = 0$, the effect of ε_t would still be felt on y_{t+1} through the effect it previously had on y_t.

This argument suggests how to construct what we know as an *impulse response function*. In the case of a single variables, as with the stochastic processes we consider in this section, that response is obtained by setting the innovation to zero every period except one, in which the impulse is produced. At that time, the innovation takes a unit value.[4] The impulse response function will be the difference between the values taken by the process after the impulse in its innovation, and those that would have prevailed without the impulse. The response of a white noise to an impulse in its own innovation is a single unit peak at the time of the impulse, since the white noise is every period equal to its innovation, which is zero except at that time period. In the case of a general random walk, a zero innovation would lead to a random walk growing constantly at a rate defined by the drift a from a given initial condition y_0. If at time t^* the innovation takes a unit value, the random walk will increase by that amount at time t^*, but also at any future time. So the impulse response is in this case a *step function*, that takes the value 1 at t^* and at any time after that. Consider now a stationary first order autoregression. A unit innovation at time t^* will have a unit response at that time period, and a response of size ρ^s each period $t + s$, gradually decreasing to zero.

Another important characteristic of economic time series is the possibility that they exhibit cyclical fluctuations. In fact, first order autoregressive processes may display a shape similar to that of many economic time series, although to produce regular cycles we need a second order autoregressive processes,

$$y_t = \rho_1 y_{t-1} + \rho_2 y_{t-2} + \varepsilon_t,$$

with ε_t being an innovation, a sequence of independent and identically distributed over time. Using the lag operator: $B^s y_t = y_{t-s}$ in the representation of the process:

$$y_t - \rho_1 y_{t-1} - \rho_2 y_{t-2} = \left(1 - \rho_1 B - \rho_2 B^2\right) y_t = \varepsilon_t.$$

The dynamics of this process is characterized by the roots of its characteristic equation,

$$1 - \rho_1 B - \rho_2 B^2 = (1 - \lambda_+ B)(1 - \lambda_- B) = 0,$$

which are given by:

$$\lambda_+, \lambda_- = \frac{-\rho_1 \pm \sqrt{\rho_1^2 + 4\rho_2}}{2\rho_2}.$$

---

[4] When working with several variables, responses can be obtained for impulses in more than one variable. To make the size of the responses comparable, each innovation is supposed to take a value equal to its standard deviation, which may be quite different for different innovations.

Stationary second order autoregressions have the two roots of the characteristic equation smaller than 1. A root greater than one in absolute size will produce an explosive behavior. A root equal to one also signals nonstationarity, although the sample realization will not be explosive. It will display extremely persistent fluctuations, very rarely crossing its mean, as it was the case with a random walk. This is very clear in the similar representation of a random walk: $(1 - B) y_t = \varepsilon_t$.

Since the characteristic equation is now of second degree, it might have as roots two conjugate complex numbers. When that is the case, the autoregressive process displays cyclical fluctuations. The response of y_t to an innovation ε_t will also display cyclical fluctuations, as we will see in dynamic macroeconomic models below.

1.1.3 Numerical Exercise: Simulating Simple Stochastic Processes

The *Simple simulation.xls* EXCEL book presents simulations of some of these simple stochastic processes. Column A in the Simulations spreadsheet contains a time index. Column B contains a sample realization of random numbers extracted from a $N(0,1)$ distribution. This has been obtained from EXCEL using the sequence of keys: *Tools/Data Analysis/Random Number Generator* and selecting as options in the menu *number of variables* = 1, *observations* = 200, a *Normal* distribution with expectation 0 and variance 1, and selecting the appropriate output range in the spreadsheet.

A well constructed random number generator produces independent realizations of the chosen distribution. We should therefore have in column B 200 independent data points from a N(0,1), which can either be interpreted as a sample of size 200 from a N(0,1) population, or as a single time series realization from a white noise where the innovation follows a N(0,1) probability distribution. The latter is the interpretation we will follow. At the end of the column, we compute the sample mean and standard deviation, with values of 0.07 and 1.04, respectively. These are estimates of the 0 mathematical expectation and unit standard deviation with this sample. Below that, we present the standard deviation of the first and the last 100 observations, of 1.05 and 1.03. Estimates of the variance obtained with the full sample or with the two subsamples seem reasonable. A different sample would lead to different numerical estimates.

Panel 2 contains sample realizations from three different random walks without drift. The only parameter in such processes is the variance of the innovation, which takes values 1, 25 and 100, respectively. At a difference of a white noise, an initial condition is needed to generate a time series for a random walk, because of the time dependence between successive observations, as can be seen in (1.1). The three sample realizations are graphed in the *RandomWalks* spreadsheet. All exhibit extreme persistence, crossing the sample mean just once in 200 observations. We know by construction that these three processes lack a well defined mean and have a time increasing variance. We can always compute sample averages and standard deviations, as shown in the spreadsheet at the end of the series, but it is not advisable to try to interpret such statistics. In particular, in this case, by drawing different realizations for the white noise in column B, the reader can easily check how sample mean and standard deviations may drastically change. In fact, standard deviations are calculated in the spreadsheet for the first and last 100 sample observations, and they can turn out to be very different, and different from the $t\sigma_\varepsilon^2$ theoretical result. The point is we cannot estimate that time-varying moment with much precision.

Panel 3 compares a random walk to three first-order autoregressive processes, with autoregressive coefficients of 0.99, 0.95 and 0.30. As mentioned above, a random walk can be seen as the limit of a first order autoregression, as the autoregressive coefficient converges to 1, although the limit presents some discontinuity since, theoretically, autoregressive processes are stationary so long as the autoregressive coefficient is below 1 in absolute value, while the random walk is nonstationary. The autoregressive processes will all have a well-defined mean and variance, which is not the case for the limit random walk process. The sample time series realizations for the four processes are displayed in the *AR-processes* spreadsheet, where it can be seen that sample differences between the autoregressive process with the 0.99 coefficient and the random walk are minor, in spite of the theoretical differences between the two processes. In particular, the autoregressive process crosses its sample mean in very few occasions. That is also the case for the 0.95-autoregressive process, although its mean reverting behavior is very clear at the end of the sample. On the other hand, the time series realization from the 0.30-autoregressive process exhibits the typical behavior in a clearly stationary process, crossing its sample mean repeatedly.

Panel 4 presents sample realizations from two white noise processes with constant and N(0,1) innovations. As shown in the enclosed graph, both fluctuate around their mathematical expectation, which is the value of the constant defining the drift, crossing their sample means very often. Panel 5 contains time series realizations for two random walk processes with drift. These show in the graph in the form of what could look as deterministic trends. This is because the value of the drifts, of 1.0 and 3.0, respectively, is large, relative to the innovation variance which is of 25 in both cases. If the value of the drift is reduced, or the variance of the innovation increased, the shape of the time series would be different, since the fluctuations would then dominate over the accumulated effect of the drift, as the reader can check by reducing the numerical values of the drift parameters[5] used in the computation of these two columns.

Panel 6 presents realizations of a stationary first order autoregression with coefficient of .90. In the second case we have not included an innovation process, so that it can be considered as a deterministic autoregression. It is interesting to see in the enclosed graph the behavior of a stationary process: starting from an initial condition. In the absence of an innovation, the process will always converge smoothly to its mathematical expectation. That is not the case in the stochastic autoregression, just because the innovation variance, of 25, is large relative to the distance between the initial condition, 150, and the mathematical expectation, 100. The reader can check

---

[5] Or significantly increasing the innovation variance. What are the differences between both cases in terms of the values taken by the process?

how reducing the standard deviation used in column S from 5 to 0.5, the pattern of the time series changes drastically, and the convergence process becomes then evident.

Panel 7 contains realizations for second order autoregressions. The first two columns present sample realizations from stationary autoregressions,

$$\text{Model 1:} \quad y_t = 10 + .6y_{t-1} + .3y_{t-2} + \varepsilon_t, \quad \varepsilon_t \sim N(0,1) \tag{1.2}$$

$$\text{Model 2:} \quad y_t = 30 + 1.2y_{t-1} - .5y_{t-2} + \varepsilon_t, \quad \varepsilon_t \sim N(0,1) \tag{1.3}$$

and are represented in an enclosed graph. The two time series display fluctuations around their sample mean of 100, which they cross a number of times. The second time series, represented in red in the graph can be seen to exhibit a more evident stationary behavior, with more frequent crosses with the mean. The next three columns present realizations for nonstationary second order autoregressions. There is an important difference between them: the first two correspond to processes:

$$\text{Model 3:} \quad y_t = .7y_{t-1} + .3y_{t-2} + \varepsilon_t, \quad \varepsilon_t \sim N(0,1) \tag{1.4}$$

$$\text{Model 4:} \quad y_t = 1.5y_{t-1} - .5y_{t-2} + \varepsilon_t, \quad \varepsilon_t \sim N(0,1) \tag{1.5}$$

that contain exactly a unit root, the second one being stable.[6] The roots of the characteristic equation for Model 3 are 1 and -0.3, while those for Model 2 are 1 and 0.5. The last autoregression

$$\text{Model 5:} \quad y_t = .3y_{t-1} + 1.2y_{t-2} + \varepsilon_t, \quad \varepsilon_t \sim N(0,1) \tag{1.6}$$

has a root greater than one, which produces an explosive behavior. The two roots are -0.95 and 1.25.

The *Impulse responses* spreadsheet contains the responses to a unit shock for the stochastic processes considered above: a random walk, three first-order autoregressions, two stationary second-order autoregressions, and three nonstationary second-order autoregressions. The innovation in each process is supposed to take a zero value in each case for ten periods, to be equal to 1, the standard deviation assumed for the innovation in all cases at $t^* = 11$, and be again equal to zero afterwards. We compare that to the case when the innovation is zero at all time periods. Impulse responses are computed as the difference between the time paths followed by each process under the scenario with a shock at $t^* = 11$, and in the absence of that shock. The first-order autoregressions are supposed to start from an initial condition $y_0 = 100$, when their mathematical expectations is zero, so in the absence of any shock, they follow a smooth trajectory gradually converging to zero at a speed determined by its autoregressive coefficient. The second order autoregressions are assumed to start from $y_0 = y_1 = 100$, which is also their mathematical expectations. So, in the absence of any shock, the processes would stay at that value forever.[7]

---

[6] The two polynomials can be written as $1 - a_1 B - a_2 B^2 = (1 - B)(1 - \lambda B)$, the second root being $1/\lambda$. The reader just need to find the value of λ in each case.

[7] We could have done otherwise, like starting the first-order autoregresisons at their mathematical expectation, and the second-order autoreegressions outside their expected values. The reader can experiment with these changes.

The first graph to the right displays impulse responses for a random walk as well as for the three first order autoregressions considered above, with coefficients 0.99, 0.95 and 0.30. A random walk has the constant, permanent impulse response that we mentioned above when describing this process. The responses of the first order autoregressions can be seen to gradually decrease to zero from the initial unit value. The response is shorter the lower it is the autoregressive coefficient. For high autoregressive coefficients, the process shows strong persistence, which makes the effects of the shock to last longer.

The second graph shows the impulse responses of the two stationary second-order autoregressions. As the reader can easily check, the characteristic equation for Model 1 has roots -0.32 and 0.92, so it is relatively close to nonstationarity. The characteristic equation for Model 2 has roots $0.6 \pm 0.37417i$, with modulus 0.5. This difference shows up in a much more persistent response of Model 1. The complex roots of Model 2 explain the oscillatory behavior of the impulse response of this model.

The third graph displays impulse responses for the three nonstationary second order autoregressions. In the two cases when there is a unit root (Models 3 and 4), the graph shows a permanent response to the purely transitory, one-period shock. The response of Model 5 is explosive because of having one root above 1, and its values are shown on the right Y-axis.

1.2 Structural Macroeconomic Models

In this section we review the main characteristics of structural macroeconomic models, paying special attention to some of the statistics summarizing their properties, since they will also be used to analyze Growth models. Structural models are specified as a system of relationships that include decision rules by economic agents, policy rules, and identities. The first ones are supposed to have originated in an optimizing behavior on the part of economic agents, which is never made explicit. We will focus our attention to dynamic structural models although, to have an appropriate perspective, we nevertheless start with a reference to static macroeconomic models.

1.2.1 Static Structural Models

A linear, static model is made up by a set of equations in which all variables are supposed to refer to the same time period, so that there is no need to use time indexes. Nevertheless, the model is interpreted as relating the values taken by endogenous and exogenous variables at each point in time. A solution to the model is a representation of endogenous variables as functions of structural parameters and exogenous variables only. When such a representation exists, the model can be used to actually compute implied values for endogenous variables as a function of given values for exogenous variables and parameters. A necessary condition for a linear, static model to have a solution is that it must have as many equations as endogenous variables. An example of such a model, in logged variables, is:

$$n = \frac{d_0 + a_2\bar{k} - (w - p)}{1 - a_1},$$
$$n = \eta\,(w - p),$$
$$y = a_0 + a_1 n + a_2\bar{k},$$
$$y = [c_1(1 - \tau)y - c_2(r - \pi^e)] + [i_1 - i_2(r - \pi^e)] + \bar{g},$$
$$\bar{m} - p = m_1 y - m_2 r.$$

The equations in this system are: (a) the demand for labor,[8] increasing in the stock of capital and decreasing in the real wage, (b) the supply of labor, increasing in the real wage, (c) the production function, that determines the supply of goods, (d) the aggregate demand for goods, made up by the private demand for consumption and investment (both inversely related to the real rate of interest), plus government expenditures, which are assumed to be given at $\bar{g}$, and (e) the market clearing condition in the money market, where the supply of real balances is $\bar{m} - p$, with $\bar{m}$ fixed by monetary policy. Market clearing conditions for the labour and goods markets have already been imposed by using the same notation for demand and supply variables. Endogenous variables are $n, y, w - p, p, r$, while exogenous variables are the stock of capital $\bar{k}$, expected inflation, π^e, money supply, $\bar{m}$, and government expenditures, $\bar{g}$. The income tax rate, τ, is one of the parameters of the model, together with input shares in production, or the elasticities in the money demand function.

This model has a recursive structure that allows for a simple analytical solution. The first two equations, labour demand and supply equations, determine the levels of employment and the real wage, the third equation determines the level of output, the equilibrium condition in the goods market determines interest rates, and the equilibrium condition in the money market determines the price level. The solution is:

$$w - p = \omega_0 + \omega_1\bar{k}; \quad n = \eta\omega_0 + \eta\omega_1\bar{k};$$
$$\omega_0 = \frac{d_0}{1 + \eta(1 - a_1)}; \quad \omega_1 = \frac{a_2}{1 + \eta(1 - a_1)};$$
$$y = Y_0 + K_0\bar{k}; \quad Y_0 = a_0 + \frac{a_1 d_0 \eta}{1 + \eta(1 - a_1)}; \quad K_0 = \frac{a_2(1 + \eta)}{a_0 + \frac{a_1 d_0 \eta}{1 + \eta(1 - a_1)}};$$
$$r = \pi^e + \frac{i_1 + \bar{g}}{c_2 + i_2} - R_0 Y_0 - R_0 K_0\bar{k}; \quad R_0 = \frac{1 - c_1(1 - \tau)}{c_2 + i_2};$$
$$p = \bar{m} + m_2\pi^e - (m_1 + m_2 R_0)K_0\bar{k} - (m_1 + m_2 R_0)Y_0 + m_2\frac{i_1 + \bar{g}}{c_2 + i_2}.$$

---

[8] As it would be obtained by a profit-maximizing competitive firm with a Cobb-Douglas technology, $Y = a_0 K^{a_1} L^{a_2}, a_1 + a_2 \leq 1$, represented in logs by the first relationship, with $d_0 = \ln(a_0 a_1)$.

It is immediate to see that an increase of a unit in government expenditures would raise nominal and real interest rates by $\frac{1}{c_2+i_2}$, and the price level by $\frac{m_2}{c_2+i_2}$, with no effect on employment or output. An increase in money supply would raise the price level in the same amount, without affecting any other variable, showing the neutrality of money in this model. Alternative policy exercise could be conducted on the solution without any difficulty, the same way we could explore the potential effects of changes in the elasticity of an input in the aggregate production function, or changes in any elasticity in the consumption, investment or money demand functions. There are two ways to work with this model: (a) the way it is specified, it is better conceived as a long-run model, that is solved under alternative values of exogenous variables and parameters to obtain long-run equilibria values for endogenous variables. When values for endogenous variables are calculated again after introducing some changes in exogenous variables or parameters, we would interpret the result as the equilibrium that would prevail in the economy after those changes have been implemented and enough time has passed for the equilibrium to be restored. From this point of view, the model is silent with respect to short-run adjustments. An alternative use of the model would assume time paths for exogenous variables $\bar{k}, \pi^e$, $\bar{m}, \bar{g}$, and values for structural parameters like the income tax rate, τ, to compute implied time paths for the vector of endogenous variables, $n, y, w - p, p, r$. That way, the implications of this static model could be compared with some statistical properties observed in time series data. In this particular model, a constant stock of capital is a short-run type of assumption, that suggests a preference for the first interpretation. If the model is to be used to relate variables over a long time span, an investment equation should better be added.

In general, a linear static model can be written: $Ay = B + Cx$, where x is the $k \times 1$ vector of exogenous variables, and y is the $n \times 1$ vector of endogenous variables, A is $n \times n$, B is $n \times 1$, and C is $n \times k$. in the previous example: $y = (n, y, w - p, p, r)'$, $x = (\bar{k}, \pi^e, \bar{m}, \bar{g})'$, and

$$
A = \begin{pmatrix}
1 - a_1 & 0 & 1 & 0 & 0 \\
1 & 0 & -\eta & 0 & 0 \\
-a_1 & 1 & 0 & 0 & 0 \\
0 & 1 - c_1(1-\tau) & 0 & 0 & c_2 + i_2 \\
0 & -m_1 & 0 & -1 & m_2
\end{pmatrix} ;
$$

$$
B = \begin{bmatrix} d_0 \\ 0 \\ a_0 \\ i_1 \\ 0 \end{bmatrix} ; \quad
C = \begin{pmatrix}
a_2 & 0 & 0 & 0 \\
0 & 0 & 0 & 0 \\
a_2 & 0 & 0 & 0 \\
0 & c_2 + i_2 & 0 & 1 \\
0 & 0 & -1 & 0
\end{pmatrix} .
$$

Whenever matrix A has full rank, the model has as solution:

$$
y = M + Nx, \text{ with } M = A^{-1}B, \ N = A^{-1}C. \tag{1.7}
$$

Characterizing the solution to a nonlinear static model will usually be much harder. Such model takes the general form: $F(y_t, x_t; \theta) = 0$, with θ representing the vector of parameters, for which a representation like (1.7) will generally not exist. At each point in time, a numerical algorithm to solve nonlinear systems of equations should then be used to obtain the values of endogenous variables as a function of the values of exogenous variables and structural parameters. But a complete nonlinear system[9] of equations may have no solution, or have multiple solutions. In many cases, providing an answer to the question of interest in such a model would require computing a linear, log-linear or polynomial approximation to the $F(y_t, x_t) = 0$ system. The linear model above can be thought of as having this origin.

Stochastic models add random shocks to some equations, taking the form:[10]

$$Ay = B + Cx + D\varepsilon,$$

where ε is the $r \times 1$ vector of exogenous shocks, and D is $n \times r$. If A has full rank, the model has as solution:

$$y = M + Nx + P\varepsilon, \text{ with } M = A^{-1}B, \ N = A^{-1}C, \ P = A^{-1}D. \qquad (1.8)$$

When such a model admits a short-run interpretation, time series can be computed for endogenous variables, contingent on a given scenario for the future evolution of exogenous variables and on some sample realizations for the exogenous shocks, given some values for structural parameters. Sample realizations for the exogenous shocks will be obtained by Monte Carlo simulation, under some assumption on their probability distribution, as it is explained below. Then, the model relates mean values of endogenous and exogenous variables, and the variance of endogenous variables to the variance of exogenous variables and innovations. The model will also have implications regarding the linear correlation coefficients between pairs of variables.[11] The number of innovations in the model, r, will limit the dimensionality of a statistical system that can be analyzed with the variables of the model. For instance, if $r = 1$, then any system with two or more equations, estimated with the time series for exogenous and endogenous variables obtained form the solution procedure outlined above, would have a singular variance-covariance matrix for the random error terms. Specifications of this type have been used to analyze policy design under uncertainty, as in Poole [71], who determined that nominal interest rates should be the preferred policy instrument when monetary or financial shocks (i.e., shocks to the LM-equation) are dominant, money supply being the best control policy when shocks on private or public consumption and investment shocks prevail (i.e., shocks to the IS-equation).

---

[9] A system with as many equations as endogenous variables.

[10] We assume here, for simplicity, that all random shocks are white noise. Extending the model to incorporate possible autoregressive structures for the shocks is straightforward.

[11] If we denote by p_i the i-th row of the $n \times r$ matrix P, then $Var(y_i) = p_i' \Sigma_\varepsilon p_i$, $Var(y_j) = p_j' \Sigma_\varepsilon p_j$, $Cov(y_i, y_j) = p_i' \Sigma_\varepsilon p_j$, and $Corr(y_i, y_j) = \dfrac{p_i' \Sigma_\varepsilon p_j}{\sqrt{p_i' \Sigma_\varepsilon p_i} \sqrt{p_j' \Sigma_\varepsilon p_j}}$, with Σ_ε being the $r \times r$ variance-covariance matrix of vector ε.

1.2.2 Dynamic Structural Models

A dynamic macroeconomic model specifies endogenous variables as functions of *predetermined* variables (lagged endogenous variables), exogenous variables and exogenous shocks:

$$Ay_t = B + Cy_{t-1} + Dx_t + E\varepsilon_t,$$

where variables have the same interpretation as above, except for the $n \times n$ matrix C of coefficients in predetermined variables. This first-order vector autoregressive representation can always be achieved by an appropriate definition of variables.[12] The *short-term solution* to the model would represent current endogenous variables as a function of exogenous variables, predetermined variables and structural parameters, and it would be obtained similarly to the static model, provided matrix A is invertible:

$$y_t = M + Ny_{t-1} + Px_t + Q\varepsilon_t,$$

with $M = A^{-1}B$, $N = A^{-1}C$, $P = A^{-1}D$, $Q = A^{-1}E$.

As a static model, it can be simulated over time for specific trajectories of the exogenous variables, starting from initial conditions for predetermined variables. At a difference from static models, a dynamic macroeconomic model is intended to capture short-run fluctuations in endogenous variables, so that it has long- and short-term implications. The dynamics introduced by the presence of lagged endogenous variables implies that any policy intervention or structural change generally has nontrivial effects over some time period. Hence, these models have richer implications than purely static models, in the form of statistics like: short- and long-run multipliers, cross-correlations or impulse response functions, among others, not unlike those we have already seen in the statistical review of time series in the previous section.

The appropriate concept to analyze the implied *long-run relationships* between the values of endogenous and exogenous variables is that of steady-state, which we introduced below. A steady-state is obtained by setting $y_t = y_{t-1} = y^*$ while setting exogenous shocks to zero $\forall t$, and assuming constant exogenous variables at x^*, and solving the model for y^* as a function of x^*. Steady-state relationships from dynamic models are comparable to static models, which justifies their usual long-run interpretation. When long-run effects are the focus of interest, we just need to compare steady-states before and after a given structural change or policy intervention, that is, for alternative values of structural parameters or exogenous variables. While a static model can also establish that comparison, a dynamic model can describe the *transition*, i.e., the trajectory followed by endogenous variables between the old and the new steady-state. A dynamic model can be used to characterize not the duration of the transition, but also some major characteristics, like the time evolution of the rate of growth of output, interest rates or productivity along the transition. By describing

---

[12] If, for instance, C_t, C_{t-1} and C_{t-2} appear in the model, both, C_t and C_{t-1} will form part of vector y_t, while C_{t-1} and C_{t-2} will be included in vector y_{t-1}. The representation could also be extended easily to accommodate lagged innovation values.

the whole transition, dynamic macroeconomic models allow us to evaluate not only the long-term effects of structural changes and policy interventions, but also the effects along the transition. The policy maker will usually want to take into account the short- and the long-term consequences of any policy intervention. What makes this important is the fact that, as we will repeatedly see throughout this book, it is usually the case in dynamic models that a given policy intervention has effects of different sign on the short- than on the long-term, and either one can prevail, depending on the length of the transition, the size of both types of effects, and the rate of time discount. Hence, focusing on long-term effects alone, as it is done in static models, can easily provide a misleading answer to the policy analysis.

As an example, let us consider the model,

$$C_t = \alpha_1 + \alpha_2 Y_{t-1},$$
$$I_t = \beta_1 + \beta_2 (Y_{t-1} - Y_{t-2}),$$
$$Y_t = C_t + I_t + G_t,$$

where C_t, I_t, Y_t, G_t denote private consumption and investment, output and government expenditures, respectively. The model has three equations and can therefore be used to explain the behavior of three endogenous variables. It seems natural that these should be consumption, investment and output. Moreover, the first equation can be labelled the consumption equation, explaining consumption as a function of last period's output/income. The second equation can be interpreted as determining investment as a function of last period's changes in output, maybe because of adjustment costs of capital. The last equation is the national identity equation in a simple closed economy. This model is known in macroeconomics textbooks as a *multiplier-accelerator* model, since the second (investment) equation captures an acceleration effect in output. The two lags of output in the consumption and investment equations are *predetermined* as of time t, while public expenditures are considered to be *exogenous* to the model.

If we have data for current and future government expenditures, $G_1, G_2, G_3, ...$, as well as initial conditions on output Y_0, Y_{-1}, and parameter values α_1, α_2, β_1, β_2, the model contains enough information to provide us recursively with values for (C_1, I_1, Y_1), (C_2, I_2, Y_2), ... We would start obtaining C_1 from the consumption equation, I_1 from the investment equation, Y_1 from the national income identity, repeating the process for each time period. To do so, we will also need numerical values for the model's parameters, which may have been previously estimated using aggregate macroeconomic time series data. Alternatively, we could generate artificial time series data from the model following the procedure described, starting from some exogenously given initial conditions, and for hypothetical values of the structural parameters.

However, as it is well known, not any model is *identified*. To have the same number of equations as endogenous variables is a necessary, but not sufficient condition for the model to explain the behavior of the variables chosen as endogenous. To understand this, let us now suppose that we chose consumption, output and public expenditures as the endogenous variables. In that case, starting from known parameter values and a given path for investment $I_1, I_2, I_3, \ldots$ as well as initial values Y_0, Y_{-1}, we would again obtain C_1 from the consumption equation, but we would be left with the last equation to obtain values for G_1, Y_1, which is clearly impossible, reflecting the fact that with this choice of endogenous variables, the model would not be identified.

Coming back to the initial choice of endogenous variables, the iterative process we described for that case amounts to substituting the consumption and investment equations into the national income identity, to have the characteristic equation,

$$Y_t - (\alpha_2 + \beta_2)Y_{t-1} + \beta_2 Y_{t-2} = (\alpha_1 + \beta_1) + G_t, \tag{1.9}$$

a second-order difference equation giving the current value of output as a function of its two previous values, as well as the current value of government expenditures. As shown in the next section, the second order polynomial in the left hand side of this equation can display many different types of behavior.

1.2.2.1 Dynamic Behavior of Endogenous Variables

Let us suppose that, starting from initial values for output Y_0, Y_{-1}, government expenditures were fixed at a given value G^*, $G_t = G^* \; \forall t$. Even then, output would not be constant, in general. In fact, we would have:

$$
\begin{aligned}
Y_1 &= (\alpha_2 + \beta_2)Y_0 - \beta_2 Y_{-1} + (\alpha_1 + \beta_1) + G^*, \\
Y_2 &= (\alpha_2 + \beta_2)Y_1 - \beta_2 Y_0 + (\alpha_1 + \beta_1) + G^*, \\
Y_3 &= (\alpha_2 + \beta_2)Y_2 - \beta_2 Y_1 + (\alpha_1 + \beta_1) + G^*,
\end{aligned}
$$

and whether output converges or explodes, i.e., whether it is stable or unstable, and whether it displays oscillations or not, depends just on the values of α_2 and β_2. It is interesting to point out that there is an equilibrium value of output, defined precisely as that level of output such that if the economy started there, it would never move away from it. When it exists, that point is also called the *steady-state* of the system. This equilibrium level can in fact be easily obtained. To do so, we assume output to be constant over time in (1.9), to obtain,

$$Y^* = \frac{(\alpha_1 + \beta_1) + G^*}{1 - \alpha_2},$$

which can be seen to be directly related to the level chosen for government expenditures. Corresponding to these equilibrium values of government expenditures and output there would be associated equilibrium values for private consumption and investment: $C^* = \alpha_1 + \alpha_2 \frac{(\alpha_1 + \beta_1) + G^*}{1 - \alpha_2}$, $I^* = \beta_1$. An economy could stay at equilibrium values G^*, Y^*, C^*, I^* forever.

However, if the economy stays at its equilibrium values, but government expenditures experiences some deviation from its equilibrium value G^*, to a new value G^{**}, the economy would then depart from values Y^*, C^*, I^*. It is then interesting to discuss whether the economy would converge to its new equilibrium value $Y^{**} = \frac{(\alpha_1 + \beta_1) + G^{**}}{1 - \alpha_2}$ or diverge away from it. If the economy converges, it is interesting to know whether it would display oscillations, or it would move along a smooth convergent path.

More specifically, the roots of the characteristic equation are,

$$\lambda_+, \lambda_- = \frac{(\alpha_2 + \beta_2) \pm \sqrt{(\alpha_2 + \beta_2)^2 - 4\beta_2}}{2},$$

so that the general solution to the homogeneous equation,

$$Y_t - (\alpha_2 + \beta_2) Y_{t-1} + \beta_2 Y_{t-2} = 0,$$

is,

$$Y_t = A_1 \lambda_+^t + A_2 \lambda_-^t,$$

showing that if either λ_+ or λ_- were greater than 1 in absolute value, then output will explode. Other possibilities are: (a) λ_+ and λ_- are real, and less than 1 in absolute value. Then output converges monotonically to its new equilibrium, (b) λ_+ and λ_- are conjugate complex numbers, less than 1 in absolute value. Output then converges to its new equilibrium displaying damped oscillations, (c) λ_+ and λ_- are conjugate complex numbers, greater than 1 in absolute value. Output then presents explosive oscillations..

In summary, the solution will be stable if λ_+ and λ_- have both modulus less than 1, while if either one has modulus greater than 1, the solution will be unstable. The characteristic roots are complex if $4\beta_2 > (\alpha_2 + \beta_2)^2$.

The model could have been solved for either one of the other two endogenous variables, consumption and investment. For instance, using the consumption function to eliminate income values from (1.9), we would obtain,

$$C_t - (\alpha_2 + \beta_2) C_{t-1} + \beta_2 C_{t-2} = (\alpha_1 + \alpha_2 \beta_1) + \alpha_2 G_{t-1},$$

with the same characteristic equation as in the case of output, so that consumption will have the same dynamic properties as output in the solution to the model. This is a consequence of consumption being determined by the level of lagged output alone.

1.2.2.2 Dynamic Multipliers

In the response of an endogenous variable to a change in the value of an exogenous variable, we distinguish between the initial effect (the impact multiplier), the response over time (the dynamic multipliers), and the aggregate response over time (the total long-run multiplier). We must also distinguish between the response to a transitory change in an exogenous variable and the response to a permanent change.

In the case of the multiplier-accelerator model, the second order difference output equation can be written,

$$Y_t = (\alpha_2 + \beta_2) Y_{t-1} - \beta_2 Y_{t-2} + (\alpha_1 + \beta_1) + G_t, \qquad (1.10)$$

that in first differences becomes,

$$\Delta Y_t = (\alpha_2 + \beta_2) \Delta Y_{t-1} - \beta_2 \Delta Y_{t-2} + \Delta G_t, \qquad (1.11)$$

as can be seen by subtracting the versions of equation (1.10) corresponding to time t and $t-1$.

This equation clearly shows that the impact multiplier of a change in government expenditures is equal to 1, since any change in G_t translates into a change in output with coefficient 1. Obtaining the dynamic multipliers can be done by numerical simulation. Their analytical computation, is somewhat burdensome, since we need to perform iterative substitutions. We would start by writing (1.11) at time $t+1$,

$$\Delta Y_{t+1} = (\alpha_2 + \beta_2) \Delta Y_t - \beta_2 \Delta Y_{t-1} + \Delta G_{t+1},$$

$$\Delta Y_{t+2} = (\alpha_2 + \beta_2) \Delta Y_{t+1} - \beta_2 \Delta Y_t + \Delta G_{t+2},$$

and substitute (1.11) to obtain,

$$\Delta Y_{t+1} = \left[(\alpha_2 + \beta_2)^2 - \beta_2 \right] \Delta Y_{t-1} - \beta_2 (\alpha_2 + \beta_2) \Delta Y_{t-2}$$
$$+ [\Delta G_{t+1} + (\alpha_2 + \beta_2) \Delta G_t],$$
$$\Delta Y_{t+2} = (\alpha_2 + \beta_2) \left[(\alpha_2 + \beta_2)^2 - 2\beta_2 \right] \Delta Y_{t-1}$$
$$- \beta_2 \left[(\alpha_2 + \beta_2)^2 + \beta_2 \right] \Delta Y_{t-2}$$
$$+ \left[\Delta G_{t+2} + (\alpha_2 + \beta_2) \Delta G_{t+1} + \left[(\alpha_2 + \beta_2)^2 - \beta_2 \right] \Delta G_t \right],$$

where variations in output previous to time t are zero, $\Delta Y_{t-1} = \Delta Y_{t-2} = 0$.

We must distinguish two different cases:

(a) If the change in government expenditures was *permanent*, and of size 2, we would have:

$$\Delta G_t = 2, \ \Delta G_{t+1} = \Delta G_{t+2} = \dots = 0,$$

with an output response,

$$\Delta Y_t = 2, \ \Delta Y_{t+1} = 2(\alpha_2 + \beta_2),$$
$$\Delta Y_{t+2} = 2 \left[(\alpha_2 + \beta_2)^2 - \beta_2 \right], \ \dots$$

(b) On the other hand, if the change in government expenditures was purely *transitory*, lasting for just one period, and was of size 2, we will have,

$$\Delta G_t = 2, \ \Delta G_{t+1} = -2, \ \Delta G_{t+2} = \dots = 0,$$

with an output response,

$$\Delta Y_t = 2, \ \Delta Y_{t+1} = 2\left(\alpha_2 + \beta_2 - 1\right), \ \Delta Y_{t+2} = 2\left[\left(\alpha_2 + \beta_2\right)^2 - \alpha_2 - 2\beta_2\right], \ ...$$

All responses should be scaled according to the size of the change in government expenditures. These algebraic expressions should correspond with the result from the computations made in the accompanying EXCEL book for specific examples. In stable models, responses of endogenous variables to a transitory change in an exogenous variable will go to zero relatively fast. Responses to a permanent shock in an exogenous variable will take endogenous variables gradually from their previous steady-state to the new one. In unstable models, in response to either a transitory or a permanent change in an exogenous variable, endogenous variables will permanently diverge. In larger scale models, characterizing the dynamics can be more complicated, since the *reduced form* equation explaining the behavior of an endogenous variable may well be of order greater than 2, as it was the case in the previous example. This is what happens in the model we discuss below.

It is important to bear in mind that multipliers are very easy to handle in linear models like the one we have considered. In models representing endogenous variables as implicit, nonlinear functions of exogenous variables, multipliers depend on the size of the change considered in the exogenous variables, and they may also depend upon the initial values from which the change is introduced. If the model is nonlinear, we cannot hope to solve anything similar to the characteristic equation, to give us the stability properties of the solution. The best we can do is to obtain the roots of the linearization of the model about a given point, preferable the steady state of the model, if it can be characterized. Unfortunately, stability of the linearized approximation does not guarantee stability of the original, nonlinear model. A second difficulty arises when actually trying to simulate the nonlinear model for given trajectories of the exogenous variables, as in the linear model above, since we will need to solve a nonlinear system of equations each period. As it is well known, even if it is *complete* such a system may have no solution, a single solution, or multiple solutions. Furthermore, the number of solutions may well depend on the range of values of the variables, so that what it is true one period regarding the nature of the solution, may not be true at some other points in time.

1.2.3 Stochastic, Dynamic Structural Models

It is sometimes convenient to specify a stochastic model, in which we explicitly acknowledge that the behavior of each endogenous variable cannot be fully explained by that of the predetermined variables. In that case, we may include random perturbations as additional terms in some or all of the equations. These random variables will follow some specified probability distribution. For simplicity, it can be assumed that they are uncorrelated over time, as well as with each other, although this may not be fully realistic. That way, we would write,

$$C_t = \alpha_1 + \alpha_2 Y_{t-1} + \varepsilon_{1t},$$

$$I_t = \beta_1 + \beta_2 (Y_{t-1} - Y_{t-2}) + \varepsilon_{2t},$$

$$Y_t = C_t + I_t + G_t,$$

where ε_{1t} is the perturbation in the consumption equation, while ε_{2t} is the perturbation in the investment equation. We initially assume $E(\varepsilon_{1t}) = E(\varepsilon_{2t}) = 0$, $E(\varepsilon_{1t}\varepsilon_{1t-s}) = E(\varepsilon_{2t}\varepsilon_{2t-s}) = 0 \ \forall s \neq 0$, $E(\varepsilon_{1t}\varepsilon_{2t-s}) = 0 \ \forall s$, although we will later discuss how to cope with violations of some of these properties.

A shock to the consumption equation, i.e., a change in the value of exogenous innovation ε_{1t}, will have an impact on consumption this period, and also on output, through the aggregate income identity, with no effect on current investment. However, the increase in output at time t would have an effect on consumption, investment and output at time $t + 1$ and beyond. An ε_{2t} shock will have an impact on current investment and output, but not on current consumption. However, dynamic effects will unfold from time $t + 1$ on, as in the case of the ε_{1t} shock. These dynamic reactions are known as the *impulse response functions*, provided the shock takes place in a single period, i.e., that it is a purely transitory shock.

To actually compute numerically the impulse response functions, we start from the steady-state equilibrium values, with all the random perturbations in the model equal to the mean (zero), and assume that one of them takes for one period, a value equal to its standard deviation, with a positive or negative sign, depending on the type of shock we want to analyze. In addition to accumulating the impulse response function, if we want to compute the response to a permanent shock, we can also let the random perturbation take a value equal to its standard deviation from time t on.

That the random perturbations may present some autocorrelation is not hard to handle, since the equation can be quasi-differenced so that the transformed equation has an uncorrelated random error. For instance,

$$C_t = \alpha_1 + \alpha_2 Y_t + \varepsilon_{1t},$$

$$\varepsilon_{1t} = \rho \varepsilon_{1t-1} + a_t,$$

is equivalent to,

$$C_t = \alpha'_1 + \alpha_2 Y_t - \alpha'_2 Y_{t-1} + \rho C_{t-1} + a_t,$$

with $\alpha'_1 = \alpha_1 (1 - \rho)$, $\alpha'_2 = \alpha_2 \rho$, $E(a_t a_{t-s}) = 0 \ \forall s \neq 0$.

A more important difficulty arises when the random perturbations of the different equations are not uncorrelated with each other. We then need to introduce some identifying assumption. A popular method consists on establishing a rank of relevance among endogenous variables, using some ideas on causality. Then, if the random perturbation in the second equation in the ranking, is projected on the random perturbation from the first equation, the residual will be uncorrelated with the latter, and it can be interpreted as the part of ε_{2t} which is not explained by ε_{1t}. The random perturbation in the third equation could be projected on the random perturbations from the first two equations, and the residual would have a similar interpretation, and so on. To actually compute the impulse response functions, each equation in the model (except the first one), must be substituted by a linear combination of those that precede it in the ranking.[13]

1.2.4 Stochastic Simulation

In previous sections we have seen how to simulate the model, generating time series of a pre-specified length for each of the endogenous variables. Necessary inputs for such a simulation are: values for the structural parameters, time series for each of the exogenous variables, as many initial conditions as lagged endogenous variables appear in the model and, in the case of a stochastic model, a time series for each of the exogenous random shocks. We will obtain a numerical value for each variable at each given period. However, we have not fully taken into account the fact that the random shocks in the model follow some specific probability distributions, or that we may have some uncertainty on the values of the parameters in the equations. These facts can be taken into account when performing Monte Carlo simulations.

For instance, to fully exploit the fact that the shock in each equation is a random variable, we simulate the model a large number of times, say 5,000, sampling each time a different time series for each shock. The general approach to simulation consists on generating realizations for the stochastic shocks in the model, and use the model to produce stable time series realizations for all the relevant variables in the economy. That way, a probability distribution for the shocks in the model translates into a probability distribution for the vector of relevant variables. Given that distribution, characterized through a large number of simulations (numerical solutions), we will be ready to compute on our set of realizations, the values of any statistic of interest: (a) output volatility, (b) relative volatility of consumption and investment to output, (c) correlations of consumption investment and interest rates with output, (d) cross correlations among any two variables, (e) estimated coefficients in specific regressions, or (f) responses of a given variable to shocks in any other variable.

We will obtain a different numerical value for any of these statistics in each of the simulations we may run. If we ran 5,000 simulations, say, we would obtain as many values of any of the mentioned statistics, so we will be able to approximate the probability distribution of that statistic through its empirical density. That way, we will be perfectly equipped to answer questions like: what is the probability that in this model, the consumption-output correlation takes a value below 0.92?

Uncertainty on parameter values can also be taken into account by specifying a priori a probability distribution gathering our beliefs on its possible values. For each simulation we would then use a different value for that parameter, chosen at random from its prior probability distribution. There are many probability distributions programmed in most statistical packages, so that almost any type of parameter

---

[13] Which is known as Cholesky identification strategy, from the way how a factor decomposition of the variance-covariance matrix of the original innovations is used to produce the linear transformation of the system of equations.

uncertainty can be accommodated, to obtain simulations. We will just need to specify the numerical values of the parameters characterizing the chosen probability distribution. For instance, we could say that α_2 is Normal(0.85,4), and a numerical value sampled from this distribution can be used in each of the simulations. This is different from the case with no parameter uncertainty, in which the same value of α_2 would be used in all simulations. Parameter uncertainty makes sense when we *calibrate* a model (i.e., when we fix parameter values so that some implied statistics match their average values in time series data), or when the parameters are estimated by econometric methods. Theoretically, the number of simulations to be run should be increased to incorporate the fact that we should run for each parameter value, a large number of model simulations, all sharing the same numerical value for the parameter, but a different realization for the random perturbations.

It would be better to specify a single joint probability distribution for the parameters, as obtained, for example, from the estimation of a simultaneous equations econometric model. However, sampling from that distribution can be more complicated. Besides, if the model has not been previously estimated, the researcher may not have much information on the characteristics of that joint distribution. Nevertheless, the idea in Monte Carlo simulation is to specify as much information as we may have on the sources of uncertainty in the model in the form of probability distributions, to be used in simulation by drawing random realizations for each simulation from those probability distributions.

Even uncertainty over the paths of the exogenous variables can be taken into account this way: suppose we believe that, with probability p, government expenditures will increase at a rate of 1% every period over the simulation horizon, increasing at a rate of 2% with probability $1 - p$. It would be sensible to run two different simulation exercises, with either path for government expenditures, to attach the mentioned probabilities to the resulting empirical frequency distribution for the endogenous variable being considered at a given point in time into the future. The researcher will then have two different empirical distributions for the value of that variable, each one having a given probability of occurring. Alternatively, a single Monte Carlo simulation exercise can be run, using one or the other path for government expenditures, with probabilities p and $1 - p$. This way, we would have a single empirical distribution, possibly with two modes, reflecting the two alternative paths for government expenditures.

1.2.5 Numerical Exercise – Simulating Dynamic, Structural Macroeconomic Models

EXCEL book *Dynamic responses.xls* shows simulation exercises for the dynamic models considered in the previous sections. The *Monotonic* spreadsheet considers a parameterization leading to a second order autoregression for output: $Y_t - .7Y_{t-1} + .1Y_{t-2} = .3 + G_t$, which is stationary, with roots .2 and .5. We consider an initial situation with government expenditures equal to 20 at all time periods, which leads to a steady state value of output of 50.75. We first analyze the effects of a one-period shock in government expenditures, that changes to a level of 21 at t^*, to return to the initial level of 20 afterwards. The output impact multiplier can be seen to be equal to 1, with negative dynamic multipliers afterwards that exactly compensate the initial response. The total long-run multiplier turns out to be zero. This must be the case in a stationary system, as we already know. The response may last longer than the initial shock, but it cannot be permanent. The second exercise looks at the effects of a permanent shock in government expenditures, which are assumed to jump to the level of 21 and stay there forever. The impact multiplier of output is again equal to 1, with positive dynamic multipliers, that make up for a total long-run response of 2.5. The graph to the left shows the output responses to a transitory as well as to a permanent shock in government expenditures. The graph to the right shows the output responses to a transitory shock in government expenditures in this and in the next model, which displays an oscillatory response, as we are about to see.

In the *Oscillatory* spreadsheet, numerical values for the structural parameters are chosen so that the second order autoregression for output is $Y_t - 1.4Y_{t-1} + .8Y_{t-2} = .3 + G_t$, whose characteristic equation has two complex conjugate roots $0.7 \pm 0.55678i$, with modulus of .8. That explains the oscillatory, damped cyclical responses that we see now to a shock in government expenditures. In the case of a permanent shock, the cyclical response takes the process to a new steady state for output above the previous one, while the response to a transitory shock in government expenditures oscillates around the initial steady state for output.

The previous analysis has been performed in models without innovations. We have just changed the value of an exogenous variable, and examined the responses of endogenous variables to that shock. The *Stochastic G* spreadsheet considers a stochastic economy as in the last section, but with a single shock in government expenditures. In the spreadsheet we obtain a time series realization of 100 time observations for G_t out of independent $N(60, 3^2)$ random variable.[14] The equations of the model are used to obtain simulated data for the endogenous variables in the economy. First, we choose two initial values for output, Y_0, Y_{-1}, at its steady-state level.[15] The level of consumption at $t = 1$, C_1 is then obtained from the first equation, and the level of investment from the second equation. Since we already have the whole time sequence for government expenditures, we can now compute the level of output Y_1. Iterating on this scheme, we compute the whole time series for consumption, investment and output. To the right of output we have constructed time series for lagged output. Below the simulated time series data we see sample moments. Government expenditures have a mean of 60.19, with a standard deviation of 2.85. Average consumption is 92.22, with standard deviation of 2.39, average investment is 0.80 and average output is 153.20, with standard deviation of 3.98. Volatility is better indi-

---

[14] Alternatively, we could have considered a process with some inertia for Government expenditures, or even change the model to make the value of Government expenditures to be related to the past level of output, for instance.

[15] The choice of the steady-state level as initial condition is arbitrary. However, in this stochastic version of the model that choice is as good as any other, since the economy is already going to experience fluctuations due to the stochastic component of government expenditures.

cated by the coefficients of variation, which is much higher for investment than for the other variables, a fact consistent with actual data.[16]

Consumption has a linear correlation coefficient of .69 with output, while the correlation of investment with output is lower, of .38. This model is so simple that it is easy to understand the nature of these relationships. From the first equation, the consumption time series has a unit correlation with lagged output, that has a correlation of .69 with current output. This is where the consumption-output correlation comes from. So, with the parameter values considered, the model introduces some persistence in output, as reflected on the correlation of .69 between Y_t and Y_{t-1}. This is also known as the first value of the autocorrelation function of output.[17] This persistence in output is possibly the more interesting feature for the model. It should be noticed that all these numerical values would change for a different realization of the stochastic process for government expenditures. They would also change if we change the stochastic process for government expenditures or any of the equations in the model, but also if we change the value of some structural parameter α_1, α_2, β_1, β_2. Changes in structural parameters will be important so long as they imply noticeable changes in the second order autoregression for output.

To continue illustrating the type of analysis that could be done out of simulated data, we may wonder about the type of consumption-output relationship emerging from this model. The model relates exactly *lagged* output to *current* consumption, but that is not the type of consumption function we are used to think about. The results of estimating such a consumption function, that relates current consumption to current output, are shown below the previous statistics. Because of the reasons already mentioned, we get some explanatory power, with a R^2 coefficient of .48, and an estimated slope of $\hat{\beta} = .42$. The first graph below displays residuals as a function of the explanatory variable, output, with no much evidence of relationship. The graph below shows them as a function of the dependent variable, showing a positive relationship, consequence of the fact that there is a significant component of consumption that remains unexplained by the regression on output and it is therefore included in the regression residuals. The first graph to the right shows residuals as a function of time, with no evidence of persistence. Residuals can be seen to cross their mean value of zero very often. Finally, the graph below shows the consumption-output scatter diagram and the fitted regression line. Time series for the fitted consumption values and the implied residuals are shown to the right of the time series for endogenous variables. Lagged residuals are also displayed and the first order autocorrelation coefficient of .11 is presented at the end of the series.[18] We have included a second spreadsheet *Stochastic G* (2) differing from the previous one only in the sample realization for government expenditures, so that the reader can see what changes can be seen in numerical values of the different statistics as a consequence of the stochastic nature of the model.

---

[16] Notice the difference between computing relative volatility by the ratios of standard deviations or through the ratios of the coefficients of variation, the latter option being preferable.

[17] The autocorrelation function is the sequence of values $Corr(Y_t, Y_{t-s})$, for all s.

[18] This suggests no evidence of residual autocorrelation, a potential source of misspecification in the consumption equation.

The *Multiple shocks* spreadsheet repeats the exercise, this time considering innovations in the consumption and the investment equations, as well as in the stochastic process for government expenditures. The process for government expenditures is the same as in the previous spreadsheets. The linear correlation coefficients of consumption and investment with output are now higher than in previous exercises. This is due to the fact that the consumption innovation affects both, the level of consumption and also the level of output at each time period, so that there is a common stochastic component. The same argument explains the higher correlation between investment and output.

The *Impulse responses* spreadsheet computes responses to transitory and permanent shocks in each of the endogenous variables: consumption, investment and output. These responses are obtained as follows: initially, all variables are supposed to be at their steady-state levels. All innovations take a zero value, so that at all effects it is as if we consider a deterministic model. At some time $t = 0$, an endogenous variable takes a value equal to its steady-state level plus an increase (the impulse), of size equal to one standard deviation, and we compute how all variables evolve from then on. For the size of the impulses, we take standard deviations from the stochastic version in the version of the model when only government expenditures were random.[19] Consumption and output are shown to react strongly to an impulse in consumption. Investment reacts with a one period delay, and the response is very short. Impulses on investment do not have much effect on either consumption or output. Consumption and investment show a strong response to output shocks with a one period delay, the response of investment extending to just one period.

The two previous sections have allowed us to introduce statistical concepts that will be used throughout the book when analyzing numerical solutions to Growth models. We have also advanced some of the fundamentals of Monte Carlo simulations of dynamic models, to show how the statistical and econometric analysis of the set of time series obtained as solution to the model allows us to deduce a much richer set of implications than could be obtained analytically. We now move into describing the main characteristics of Growth models, their evolution following a variety of research interests, how they are equipped to deal with Lucas' criticism on policy evaluation, and how their numerical solutions can be obtained and exploited for policy analysis.

1.3 Why are Economic Growth Models Interesting?

1.3.1 Microeconomic Foundations of Macroeconomics

Growth models try to capture interesting structural, dynamic features of actual economies. As shown throughout the book, Growth models establish implicit relationships between decisions made by economic agents at time t, variables

---

[19] This is arbitrary. We should take an impulse of size equal to one standard deviation of the innovations estimated from actual time series data, since that is the likely single-period fluctuation in each variable.

determined in the past, which are known when time t decisions are made, and current and future exogenous and policy variables. In the case of stochastic models, these relationships will also include expectations of functions of future variables. In turn, these relationships generally have specific implications regarding the rate of growth of the economy. Hence, Growth models can be summarized in the form of dynamic relationships involving variables and expectations of functions at different points in time.

But although Growth models imply dynamic macroeconomic models, their structure is far too rich to be incorporated into the class of models considered in previous sections. Microeconomic foundations lead to very stylized Growth models, where specific and detailed assumptions are made about the behavior of each economic agent (domestic consumers, firms and government, and possibly those of other countries, as well), their objectives, the constraints they face, the information they have, the way each market works, and about the implementation of economic policy. The dynamics of the model are also laid out very carefully, in terms of what is the timing with which different markets open and close, and the specific moment inside each time period in which each decision is made and each trade carried out.[20]

Typically, dynamic optimization problems are solved for each private agent, leading to a collection of aggregate demand and supply schedules for each commodity which, together with specific assumptions on how markets work, lead to the formation of prices. Markets may clear or not, producers of either intermediate or final goods are sometimes assumed to have some monopolistic power, and agents may have access to different information sets. So, a growth model can be analyzed not only under competitive equilibrium assumptions, but under any alternative set of assumptions as well, or under any sort of friction in the working of markets, or asymmetry in the information available to different agents. All that is needed for the model implications to be sorted out is that the whole structure of the economy regarding all these aspects can be specified in full detail. Economic policy enters the model in the form of time paths for variables like tax rates, government expenditures, or the rate of growth of money supply, that are taken as exogenous by private agents when solving their respective optimization problems. That way, the resulting allocation of resources is a function not only of private agents' objective functions and restrictions, but also of the assumptions on the structure of markets and the imposed combination of fiscal and monetary economic policies. In the case of stochastic models, the views of private agents on future policy and on the future evolution of exogenous variables is also a central determinant of their decisions.

Having explicit preferences for private agents, as well as possibly target functions for the economic authority, has as a major implication the possibility of carrying out a normative analysis of policy issues. This emphasis on Microfoundations leads to the somewhat complex structure of Growth models, but also to a significant richness of analysis. All the aspects of the structure of the model are laid out in detail, so that

---

[20] This is, in fact, very important, since the structure and implications of a model may significantly change by just a change in assumptions on the timing of decisions, the arrival of information, or the opening and closing of markets.

we can figure out what is their relevance to explain a given characteristic of the model, or to provide a particular answer to a given policy question.[21]

The significance of this normative approach to economic policy design is evident and yet, such an analysis could not be addressed in the type of structural macroeconomic models we reviewed in the first sections of this Introduction, where objective functions for the different agents: consumers, firms and government, do not play any role. In the simple structural models of Sect. 1.2, it is standard to interpret the first equation as a consumption function that emerges from utility maximization by consumers. Similarly, the second equation could be interpreted as a linear function relating investment to past output as an optimal behavior on the part of profit maximizing firms. Unfortunately, a rigorous analysis of such optimizing behavior is generally inconsistent with such structural dynamic macroeconomic models.

Consider a relatively simple version of a time discounted utility maximization problem by a representative consumer

$$\underset{\{C_t,N_t,K_{t+1}\}_{t=0}^{\infty}}{Max} \sum_{t=0}^{\infty} \beta^t U(C_t, 1-N_t),$$

subject to a budget constraint,

$$(1+\tau^c)C_t + S_t \leq (1-\tau^w)\frac{w_t}{P_t}N_t + [1+(1-\tau^r)r_t]S_{t-1},$$

that displays consumption C_t, leisure (defined as total time, which we normalize to 1 unit, minus hours worked, N_t) and savings S_t, constant tax rates on consumption, labor and capital income τ^c, τ^w, τ^r, the nominal wage, with w_t, the price level, P_t, and the real rate of interest, r_t. In this stylized version of the models analyzed in the book, the conditions determining optimal time-t consumption and leisure decisions are:

$$\frac{\partial U(C_t,1-N_t)}{\partial C_t} = \beta[1+(1-\tau^r)r_{t+1}]\frac{\partial U(C_{t+1},1-N_{t+1})}{\partial C_{t+1}},$$

$$\frac{\frac{\partial U(C_t,1-N_t)}{\partial(1-N_t)}}{\frac{\partial U(C_t,1-N_t)}{\partial C_t}} = \frac{1-\tau^w}{1+\tau^c}\frac{w_t}{P_t}. \tag{1.12}$$

The first equation is an intertemporal relationship that links optimal current and future consumption, while the second is a period-by-period relationship between optimal consumption and leisure (or labor supply). The latter is a labor supply equation, that shows how the optimal labor supply schedule relates nonlinearly the number of hours to the after-tax real wage and the level of consumption.[22]

---

[21] This modelling approach is now commonplace in Macroeconomics. Dynamic models with microeconomic foundations for aggregate economies are often used in Public Finance, Monetary Theory, Labour Economics or International Economics, as they are used in Growth theory. The main difference for the latter is their focus on characterizing the main determinants of short- and long-run growth.

[22] A standard result in intermediate Microeconomics courses.

Even if we assume a relatively simple logarithmic utility function, the first optimization relationship becomes:

$$\frac{1}{C_t} = \beta \left[1 + (1 - \tau^r) r_{t+1}\right] \frac{1}{C_{t+1}}, \tag{1.13}$$

making current consumption to depend on future consumption and on the after-tax rate of return to be obtained the next period on current savings. This makes sense: to maximize time aggregate utility, the consumer must take into account the fact that the consumption decision determines current savings, which will be channeled to firms to invest in physical capital with which to produce output in the future. So, the current consumption/savings decision conditions the future availability of resources and hence, the level of utility. The previous equation describes how the consumer must take these considerations into account by establishing an optimal relationship between current and future consumption. That relationship will depend on policy variables as well as on market determined prices, as it is the case of interest rates. On the other hand, at the aggregate level of the whole economy, given a specific structure for credit markets, interest rates will also depend on consumers' decisions through their influence on the relative demand and supply of credit. This example shows how, even in simple Growth models, current optimal decisions depend on prices and on the future state of the economy in a nonlinear fashion.[23]

In the case of a closed economy in which the government does not exhaust any resource, the stock of capital at the end of period t, K_{t+1}, is obtained as the stock of capital at the beginning of the period, after depreciation[24], $(1 - \delta) K_t$, plus savings, S_t:

$$K_{t+1} = (1 - \delta) K_t + S_t, \tag{1.14}$$

starting from K_0 at the beginning of $t = 0$.

A representative firm maximizing the present value of profits given the available technology, and operating competitively in the markets for inputs and output, would equate the marginal product of each input to its relative price. For instance, under a Cobb-Douglas technology: $Y_t = A_t K_t^\alpha N_t^{1-\alpha}$:

$$(1 - \alpha) A_t \left(\frac{K_t}{N_t}\right)^\alpha = \frac{w_t}{P_t}, \tag{1.15}$$

$$\alpha A_t \left(\frac{N_t}{K_t}\right)^{1-\alpha} = r_t + \delta = \alpha \left(\frac{Y_t}{K_t}\right), \tag{1.16}$$

which transforms (1.13) into:[25]

---

[23] Of course, different utility functions could give raise to different functional forms for the way how current consumption relates to future consumption and interest rates.

[24] With δ being the percent per-period depreciation rate of capital.

[25] In consistency with the utility maximization problem above, we can either assume that there is a single consumer or household in the economy, or interpret labor and capital stock in this equation in per-capita terms.

$$\frac{1}{C_t} = \beta \left[1 + (1 - \tau^r) \left(\alpha \left(\frac{Y_{t+1}}{K_{t+1}} \right) - \delta \right) \right] \frac{1}{C_{t+1}}, \tag{1.17}$$

a sort of consumption function, where consumption depends in a nonlinear fashion on a variety of factors, in addition to future income.

In the type of monetary economies discussed later on in this book, where real balances enter as an argument in the utility function, the following utility maximization condition is obtained:

$$\frac{U_2 \left(C_t, \frac{M_t}{P_t} \right)}{U_1 \left(C_t, \frac{M_t}{P_t} \right)} = (1 + r_t)(1 + \pi_t) - 1, \tag{1.18}$$

where U_1, U_2 denote partial derivatives of the utility function with respect to its two arguments. This is an interesting relationship obtained under utility maximization, that sets the marginal rate of substitution between consumption and real balances, on the left hand side, equal to the nominal rate of interest, on the right hand side. According to this optimality condition, the demand for real balances will exhibit a negative relationship with the real rate of interest and with the rate of inflation, and a positive relationship to the level consumption, capturing a transactions demand aspect of the demand for real balances. So long as the rest of the model generates a positive consumption-income relationship, then real balances will also be positive related to income. Therefore, this relationship is very much in the spirit of the standard money demand function that is usually included in structural macroeconomic models. In fact, that equation is usually rationalized on the basis of utility maximizing consumers who demand real balances for their transactions, as we will assume to be the case when discussing monetary growth models. To be even more specific, let us assume, for the sake of an illustration, that the utility function is logarithmic and separable in its two arguments: $U \left(C_t, \frac{M_t}{P_t} \right) = \ln C_t + \theta \ln \frac{M_t}{P_t}$, $\theta > 0$. Equation (1.18) then becomes: $\frac{\theta C_t}{M_t/P_t} = i_t$, with i_t being the nominal interest rate, that is: $\frac{M_t}{P_t} = \frac{\theta C_t}{i_t}$ which would be consistent with a demand function in logs:

$$\ln \left(\frac{M_t}{P_t} \right) = \beta_0 + \beta_1 \ln C_t + \beta_2 \ln i_t,$$

with specific restrictions on the consumption and interest rate elasticities.

Time-t *state variables* are all those that can influence decision variables at that same time. Some decision variables at time t may become state variables at time $t + 1$. This is usually the case of the stock of productive capital. The change in that stock at time t, investment, will be a *decision variable* which becomes part of the *state variable* at time $t + 1$. The portfolio of assets of the typical consumer is another example. By assuming an optimizing behavior on the part of economic agents, Growth models usually introduce a recursive structure in the decision process followed by each economic agent. Optimizing agents derive decision rules representing the way how decisions are being made each period as a function of the values of state variables. Some of these state variables will be exogenous, and their time evolution will be known before the time paths for decision variables are characterized. Some other state variables will be predetermined variables in the sense defined above, *i.e.*, past decision variables, and they will be obtained recursively, as decision variables are characterized period by period.

All this will be shown in detail in a variety of models throughout the book. The examples in this section are just meant to illustrate the fact that being explicit about the way how economic agents make their decisions, as well as about the structure of preferences and the production technology, takes us quite far away from the sort of dynamic macroeconomic models in the first sections of this Introduction. Advancing on the Microfoundations of economic agents' decisions takes us into relationships where decision or control variables depend on state variables, prices and exogenous variables[26] which are considerably more general than those included in traditional dynamic macroeconomic models. Variables relate in a highly nonlinear manner and there is extensive simultaneity, for which linear dynamic representations will generally be a poor approximation. Not to mention that discussions on efficiency, or questions regarding policy evaluation or optimal policy design can hardly be addressed in standard linear representations.

Summarizing, growth models impose a tight structure on the joint time evolution of the main variables in the economy and the type of dynamic systems summarizing the main characteristics of a growth model are non-linear, and display extensive simultaneity. Non-linearity is essentially unavoidable, at least when we want to consider the model's implications regarding price formation[27] while specifying a explicit structure described above. Extensive simultaneity arises in Growth models because: (a) exogenous shocks spread throughout a model that attempts to explain how the whole economy works, (b) agents usually make simultaneous decisions on several variables, (c) decisions made by an agent (the government decides on the rate of growth of money supply, for instance) condition the decision by another agent (consumers and firms), who takes them as given. The main consequence is that, under uncertainty, the system summarizing the implications of the stochastic Growth model will contain expectations of nonlinear functions of future decision, exogenous and policy variables. That structure is complex enough so that an analytical solution generally does not exist, and the model's implications are better analyzed through statistical and econometric analysis of artificial time series obtained by simulation.

The basic ideas for simulating such a model are similar to those we have already seen in simple linear dynamic macroeconomic models, but the specific structure of Growth models introduces major issues regarding the treatment of expectations as

---

[26] And also on conditional expectations of nonlinear functions of future state and decision variables, in the case of stochastic growth models, as we will see in the next paragraph.

[27] Under endogenous prices, optimization problems solved by economic agents do not have a linear-quadratic structure, implying that their decision rules are non-linear. Since these decisions are part of the system summarizing the model, that system ends up being nonlinear as well.

Sargent's Macroeconomic Theory (1979) contains a variety of partial equilibrium models in which, with exogenous prices, optimization problems have a linear-quadratic structure. In that simple setup, decision rules are linear functions.

well as to guarantee the stability of the obtained solution. However, most statistical concepts are already present in simpler models, and the previous sections can be taken as a quick refresher of statistical fundamentals.

1.3.2 Lucas' Critique on Economic Policy Evaluation

The Microeconomic foundations of Macroeconomic models in general, and Growth models in particular, make explicit the optimization behavior that is supposed to underlie the consumption, investment and other equations that form part of a *structural* macroeconomic model. But possibly the main reason to work with the type of models we consider throughout the book is Lucas' critique. Lucas [57] work was instrumental in pointing out how, under rational expectations, part of the structure of a macroeconomic model depends on the views of private agents on the policy rules being followed by the economic authority now and in the future. The fact that it is agents beliefs that matter, more than the economic policy actually being implemented suggested the importance of the credibility on policy makers, an issue that has been fully incorporated in the way how policy makers interact with the public nowadays. Under the rational expectations view, a policy intervention will only have the desired effects if it is announced and fully understood by private agents.

Another implication is that a change in private agents' views on future policy may easily have market consequences today, even if the change in expectations turns out later on to be unjustified. Obviously, these issues are fundamental for policy analysis. In particular, Lucas' criticism on the way the effects of a policy intervention were analyzed by simulation was devastating, since the structure of the model needs to be changed according to the policy change being considered, so long as we consider that such change will be known and believed by private agents. The standard practice until then, of using the same structural model to simulate the effects of alternative policy choices was shown to be fundamentally inappropriate.

How can we cope with this criticism? Essentially, by not making *ad-hoc* assumptions on either the way how expectations about the future influence agents' current decisions or on the expectations formation mechanism.[28] Structural macroeconomic models sometimes postulate that some decisions, like consumption, saving or investment, depend on expectations of future variables like the rate of inflation or interest rates, on the basis that such dependence emerges from an optimal behavior that is never explicitly specified. To this presumption we can add traditional assumptions on expectations formation, like *adaptive expectations* or *perfect foresight*. These

---

[28] Expectations of future variables or functions of variables appearing in a model need to be treated as new variables, so that a model that includes an explicit role for expectations is not complete without incorporating some kind of assumption on the way agents form their expectations. The assumptions on the expectations formation mechanism play the role of additional equations. They are a crucial part of a stochastic model, as important as the assumptions on the functional form of the utility function or the aggregate production function, and affect the model implications regarding the time behavior for the endogenous variables.

type of mechanisms assume that expectations are formed on the basis of past information,[29] so they can be eliminated from the model right off. Then, policy changes do no affect the structure of the model, and we are back in a situation in which the same model would be used to evaluate alternative policy choices. Lucas' critique applies here with full force.

Growth models are very explicit with the information available to each agent when making decisions, and that has specific implications on the way how expectations enter in the model, characterizing the expectations of which functions are relevant, how far into the future expectations matter, and how those expectations influence agents' decisions. Additionally, a rational agent will form expectations consistent with the agent's perception on the structure of the economy, including future policy rules, and they will be computed using that information. As a consequence, if agents believe that there has been any change in the structure of the model (values of structural parameters, of future exogenous variables or policy rules), the expectations will change in consistency with that change in beliefs. So long as current decisions may depend on expectations of future variables, they will also be affected, and prices and quantities transacted in the markets will also adjust. This is why a different model needs to be used to evaluate the effect of a given policy intervention, if we accept that such intervention will be understood and believed by private agents. By taking into account these effects through a combination of explicit Microeconomic foundations and the assumption of rational expectations, we are not only safe from Lucas' criticism, but we also incorporate into the model the idea that agents beliefs on the future, by themselves, may have a significant impact on the economy.[30]

Under uncertainty, the condition describing how consumption should be optimally distributed over time is an extension of the similar condition (1.13) for the deterministic case,

$$\frac{1}{C_t} = \beta E_t \left(\frac{1 + (1 - \tau^r) r_{t+1}}{C_{t+1}} \right) = \beta E_t \left[\frac{1 + (1 - \tau^r) \left(\alpha \left(\frac{Y_{t+1}}{K_{t+1}} \right) - \delta \right)}{C_{t+1}} \right],$$

to which we have added (1.16). This condition describes how current optimal decisions explicitly depend on expectations about the future, made on the basis of the information available at the time the decision on current consumption is made. The future information which is relevant for the current consumption decision is summarized in either of the expressions in brackets above. This is much more precise that assuming that utility maximization leads to a consumption function in which the current consumption decision depends on current income and expectations of future interest rates. It therefore provides a much richer set of implications that can be tested using actual data.

---

[29] These expectations mechanisms are said to be *backward-looking*, since they are substituted by a function of past variables, agents' views about the future not playing any role.

[30] Alternative specifications for *limited rationality*, in which agents are assumed to form expectations which are partially rational, have been shown to be useful to explain some regularities in actual time series data.

This proposal could conceivable be incorporated into any macroeconomic model, but it is in models with Microeconomic foundations where it is more appropriately implemented. As we have seen in the example, the formulation of specific dynamic, stochastic optimization models for each agent leads naturally to decision rules that include expectations of specific functions of future variables without making the type of ad-hoc assumption on agents' behavior and on the role of expectations that are made in structural macroeconomic models. Being specific about Microeconomic foundations has its own difficulties, like how to deal with agents' heterogeneity,[31] but this is nevertheless also swept under the rug in standard structural macroeconomic models.

Other technical difficulties, like how to handle nonlinear control stochastic models or how to deal with stability of solutions should be welcome, since they allow us to perform policy analysis safely. These are some of the issues discussed throughout this textbook. As described below, this approach has even changed the way we think about policy. We can now establish a mapping between the structure assumed for the model and the results of any policy evaluation exercise. As a consequence, we may identify when is a given policy intervention appropriate, or which particular aspects of the structure of the economy are relevant for a given policy question and which ones are not.

1.3.3 A Brief Overview of Developments on Growth Theory

Let us now briefly summarize some of the main stages in the development of the theory of Economic Growth, to place these issues in perspective, as well as to advance the structure of his textbook.[32] Growth theory started well before Lucas' criticism on policy evaluation, and it was initially conceived to gain some insight into the determinants of the rate of growth of actual economies. The theory of Economic Growth was initially developed at a purely theoretical level, with just a few empirical implications that could attract the interest of researchers. These were mainly related to the implications of exogenous growth models regarding the rate of growth of an economy as well as the convergence in income per capita among a set of countries, that were soon put to test through regression analysis. The neoclassical *Exogenous Growth* model with a constant savings rate, introduced in the seminal papers of Solow [88] and Swan [91] incorporated a constant returns to scale assumption in the production of the final good, which was shown to imply zero long-run growth for per-capita variables. This model is able to explain positive long-term growth in per-capita variables only through some type of *exogenous growth* in productivity. Only that way could the model be made consistent with some regularities observed

---

[31] Significant progress has already been done in dealing with agents' heterogeneity [Rios-Rull [75], Castañeda et al. [19]], although the representative agent framework is still predominant.

[32] This summary is intended to provide an overview to readers unfamiliar with Growth theory. We do not have any pretension of being fully comprehensive.

in actual data.[33] Exogenous growth refers to the fact that such growth is not being produced by either the decisions made by private economic agents, or by any policy intervention. This model is analyzed in Chap. 2 in this textbook, where the main properties of the long-run equilibrium (steady-state) and the transition paths are characterized.

Future developments have taken the broadly denominated Theory of Economic Growth into a variety of branches with noticeably different interests, precisely in part because of the criticism on traditional policy evaluation methods. The current denomination of *Dynamic, Stochastic, General Equilibrium* models (usually referred to by the DSGE initials) includes a wide variety of models with the type of Microeconomic foundations described above. These are essentially Growth models with a zero long-run rate of growth for per-capita variables, possibly after adjusting for exogenous technological growth, and they focus on explaining observed comovements between variables, once growth has been taken out of actual time series data. The reference to general equilibrium, was well justified some years ago, when there was an emphasis in maintaining market clearing and friction free market assumptions. But a large number of new features are gradually being incorporated in mainstream research in Macroeconomics in order to explain some data regularities, that make the models depart from the general equilibrium paradigm. This is why some Exogenous Growth models can be referred to as DSGE models, New Keynesian Phillips Curve models, Business Cycle models, among other denominations, that try to make explicit some of their features or implications.[34] On the other extreme, a wide class of Endogenous Growth models maintain the original motivation of Growth Theory and have made significant advances in explaining how the rate of growth of the economy depends on agents' decisions and policy choices. The reference to Growth theory is increasingly reserved for Endogenous Growth models which, as explained below, make endogenous variables to have a statistical character drastically different from exogenous growth models, with significant implications regarding the effects of policy interventions or structural shocks in both types of models.

Moving one step further, Ramsey [73], Cass [18] and Koopmans [52] among others, brought explicitly into the model a utility maximizing behavior on the part of consumers. That was an important step forward for at least two reasons: first, the assumption in the neoclassical growth model of Solow and Swan that the savings rate was constant over time at an exogenous level essentially precluded the possibility of doing any significant analysis on optimal policy. Under this new modelling

---

[33] As mentioned, the model also had implications regarding the convergence of economies in terms of per-capita income, which developed a huge empirical literature aiming to test such implications that is still very much alive, now in reference to more sophisticated growth models that have been developed since then. Along this line of reasoning, growth theory would not be very different from other areas of economic theory that imply more or less tight restrictions among the joint behavior of variables, that can be reduced to parameter testing in relatively simple econometric models.

[34] Kydland and Prescott [54] *point out: "In other words, modern business cycle models are stochastic versions of neoclassical growth theory. And the fact that business cycle models do produce normal-looking fluctuations adds dramatically to our confidence in the neoclassical growth theory model - including the answers it provides to growth accounting and public finance questions."*

approach, consumers maximized time aggregate utility, making simultaneous decisions every period on consumption and savings which, in turn, provide resources for capital accumulation on the part of firms. And these decisions are taken under an intertemporal optimality criterion. Second, being explicit about the objective functions of private agents, allows for the possibility of bringing into the model a new agent: a benevolent planner who would care about the welfare of consumers and would allocate resources with that goal in mind, without the need of the markets. Explicit objective functions and assumptions on the optimizing behavior of private agents (consumers and firms) allow for addressing very important issues. On the one hand, since we can characterize the allocation of resources emerging from a decentralized market mechanism as well as the one that results from the actions of the benevolent planner, a comparison between them generally allows for discussing the Pareto efficiency of the decentralized mechanism in different setups. On the other hand, we can evaluate consumers' time aggregate welfare under alternative fiscal or monetary policies, which can then be ordered on the basis of the level of welfare they achieve. As an example, normative analysis of this kind to compare alternative types of distortionary taxation in different economic environments remains as one of the more popular policy problems addressed in this framework. More generally, we could attempt to characterize the optimal mixture of consumption and income taxes, or the optimal combination of tax and debt financing, or even combine this with the possibility of money financing. Some of these issues are discussed along the different chapters of this book. Optimal growth is the subject of Chap. 3 where, among other issues, we discuss the efficiency of the competitive equilibrium in different setups, and explain how to establish welfare comparisons among alternative economic policies. These subjects are repeatedly address throughout the different models considered in subsequent chapters.

Theoretical DSGE models developed initially in the work of a large list of very significant authors (R.E. Lucas, T. Sargent, R.J. Barro, E. Prescott, F. Kydland, R. King, R. Phelps, P.M. Romer, among many others), taking advantage of the methodological basis of standard Growth models. DSGE models have had a tremendous influence in emphasizing the Microeconomic foundations of any model that pretends to explain the behavior of macroeconomic aggregates. Because of the impossibility of producing sustained growth unless imposed on the model from some exogenous technological improvement these models, that usually incorporate a constant returns to scale technology, are used to understand the behavior of actual economies as represented in actual, detrended time series data. In fact, different filters aimed to removing different nonstationarity characteristics in actual data, like the Hoddrick–Prescott filter have become standard, and are incorporated even in basic econometric software. We may want to eventually end up by having models that simultaneously explain long-run growth and fluctuations around that trend, but it is unquestionable that the current standard practice of focusing on filtered data has contributed to a huge development in many areas of Macroeconomics, Public Finance, Monetary Theory, Labour Economics or International Economics.

The so-called Real Business Cycle Theory falls into this category by assuming that shocks in productivity are the main source of cyclical fluctuations.

Alternatively, a large variety of models have been proposed with different assumptions on the sources of randomness in the economy or on how markets work, in order to extend traditional theories in these areas as well as to rationalize different empirical regularities. The New Keynesian Theory of the Phillips curve Calvo [15], Gali and Gertler [35], which is now being intensively used in the analysis of a variety of policy issues is another important example in this class. The Microeconomic foundations are carefully laid out, and agents do their best, given the constraints they face. Some producers enjoy some monopoly power and some prices are determined subject to some frictions, which deviates the model from more traditional general equilibrium approaches. Our discussion on Chaps. 3 and 4 can be seen as an introduction to the analysis of DSGE models. Monetary DSGE models are the subject of Chaps. 8 and 9. All the solution methods presented in Chap. 5 are used throughout the book to solve different models, and can be applied to the analysis of DSGE models.

On the other hand, under the denomination of Endogenous Growth models, we have classes of economies in which the rate of growth depends on decisions made by private agents as well as on policy choices. That allows for addressing a broad number of interesting issues regarding either the determinants of growth, or the effects on growth of alternative economic policies. The effect on the long-run rate of growth of the economy of changes in specific tax rates or changes in the rate of growth of money supply can be analyzed in these models. By their own nature these questions could not possibly be addressed in exogenous growth models. A significant peculiarity of endogenous growth models is that, as explained in the corresponding chapter, they imply intrinsic nonstationarity in per-capita variables, which contain a unit root even after eliminating deterministic growth components, as it is sometimes observed in actual data. Therefore, these models may be appropriate to explain empirical nonstationarity characteristics of actual time series data. The non-stationary, unit root per-capita time series emerging from Endogenous Growth models would be consistent with a dynamic macroeconomic model specified in first differences, unless cointegrating relationships are found under the standard tests. But the Endogenous Growth model itself may have implications on cointegration, as was pointed out long ago by King, Plosser and Rebelo [51].[35] Because of the implied nonstationarity, Endogenous Growth models are also special in that a purely transitory structural change or policy intervention has permanent effects, at a difference of exogenous growth models, in which the effects of a purely transitory perturbation may extend to a number of periods, but they would never be permanent.

Endogenous Growth may arise because of constant or increasing returns to scale in the cumulative inputs. The addition of public capital to private capital as a productive input may contribute to aggregate increasing returns and endogenous growth. It can also come about because an economy produces an ever increasing variety of intermediate goods through a process of research and development. Similarly, endogenous growth may come about because successful research leads to intermediate

---

[35] In any event, like in any other Growth model, the relationships among per capita variables emerging from the model will generally be non-linear, and a linear econometric model might be too poor an approximation to them.

goods of improved quality, that substitute for the older goods. A further cause of endogenous growth can be the accumulation of human capital as an input in the technology producing the final good.[36] Endogenous Growth models are presented in Chap. 5, where their main characteristics are shown and the solution methods described in detail.

1.3.4 The Use of Growth Models for Actual Policy Making

A few years ago, Coenen and Wieland [21] described how an increasing number of models had been developed in an attempt to serve as a laboratory for evaluating the performance of alternative monetary and fiscal policy strategies. These authors classified existing models in: (a) small-scale backward looking models, (b) large scale backward-looking models, (c) small-scale models with rational expectations and nominal rigidities, (d) large-scale models of this type, and (e) small models with optimizing agents. Given the significance of Lucas' critique, it is unsurprising that the main international economic and finance institutions in charge of policy making include nowadays macroeconomic models with microfoundations among the set of models they use for policy evaluation and forecasting. An example is the European Central Bank (ECB), that includes[37] the DSGE model by Smets-Wouters [87] in the set of macroeconomic models for the Euro area used for policy making. The statement of the Web page at ECB fits very nicely in this introductory chapter, making reference to the *'recent developments in the construction and simulation of DSGE models that combines rigorous microeconomic derivation of the behavioral equations of macro models which fits the main features of macroeconomic time series. After pointing out as the main difference with respect to more traditional macroeconometric models the way how parameters in structural equations relate to deeper structural parameters in preferences, technology or institutional constraints, three advantages are singled out: (a) the theoretical discipline, (b) the way they deal with Lucas' critique, and (c) the ability to evaluate policy in terms of welfare. The Smets-Wouters model considers three types of agents: consumers, firms and government, and incorporates some real frictions in consumption and investment, as well as some price and wage rigidities, and it is shown to compete favorably with alternative models in forecasting.'*

Additional examples of the use of DSGE models for policy are the New Area-Wide Model (NAWM) at the ECB [Coenen, McAdam and Straub [22]], which focuses in the analysis of fiscal policy. The International Monetary Fund has its

---

[36] Constant returns to scale in the single cumulative input as a reason for positive long-term growth is the characteristic of the AK economy, introduced by Rebelo [74]. An explicit role for public capital as a productive input was proposed by Barro [4]. The model with a variety of intermediate goods is due to Spence [89], Dixit and Stiglitz [31], Ethier [33] and Romer [77, 78]. Uzawa [95], Lucas [60] and Caballé and Santos [13] assigned an explicit role to the stock of human capital in the production of the final good.

[37] As shown in its Web page: http://www.ecb.int/home/html/researcher.en.html.

Global Economy Model (GEM) [Bayoumi, Laxton and Pesenti [8]], and the Federal Reserve Board has an open economy model named SIGMA [Erceg, Guerrieri and Gust [32]]. All of them incorporate recent advances on microfoundations, with some number of nominal and real frictions in an effort to improve their empirical fit both, in the domestic and the international dimension.

1.4 Numerical Solution Methods

We explain in this section the need to compute numerical solutions to Growth models. We address two significant issues: the stability of the obtained solution, and the possible indeterminacy of equilibria. We end up describing how the numerical solutions have led to changing the type of policy questions we raise and the type of answers we get out of macroeconomic models.

Under the assumption of rationality, expectations become endogenous variables, and we can analyze how they are influenced by exogenous shocks affecting the economy, or by the unpredictable component in a policy variable, to mention just two types of interesting questions. Furthermore, under the particular assumption of rationality, expectations errors, for which data can be obtained once we have solved for all variables in the model as well as for the conditional expectations in it, must satisfy clearly specified conditions. Specifically, a rational expectations error cannot have autocorrelation, or exhibit any correlation with variables which were contained in the information set available to agents at time *t*, properties that can be tested for as part of the validation of the numerical solution approach followed.

1.4.1 Why do we Need to Compute Numerical Solutions to Growth Models?

We have described above how the desire to incorporate Microeconomic foundations into models for the aggregate economy leads to Growth models that are made of the interaction of economic agents of different types, each solving a particular dynamic, stochastic optimization problem. We have also seen how the endogenity of prices leads to nonlinear decision rules that involve expectations of functions of future variables, and cannot possibly be reduced to the type of aggregate linear functions usually considered in structural macroeconomic models like those in previous sections. Except by very few exceptions, the nonlinear stochastic systems summarizing the properties of Growth models lack an analytical solution, and the model's implications regarding the behavior of the main variables, their comovements, or their responses to exogenous shocks or to policy interventions, can only be characterized through numerical solutions. Hence, we face the need to obtain numerical solutions, a process which goes significantly beyond the procedures to simulate the linear dynamic macroeconomic models above because of stability and indeterminacy issues, that we address below.

A stochastic, nonlinear dynamic system can be seen as imposing a set of constraints on the multivariate probability distribution of the vector of endogenous (control or decision) time t variables. Such constraints emerge from (a) the analytical structure of the system, (b) the numerical values of the structural parameters in the model, (c) the multivariate probability distribution assumed for the vector of exogenous shocks. The solution to the model can then be seen as that restricted multivariate probability distribution for the vector of endogenous variables. The structure of the model precludes the analytical characterization of that distribution, and Monte Carlo simulation of a given numerical solution method allows us to compute frequency distributions for any statistic of interest, either in steady-state or along the transition. That could either be an statistic from the multivariate distribution of the vector of endogenous variables (like the relative volatility of consumption and investment to output) or, rather, from the joint distribution of time-t state and control variables, like the impulse responses of consumption to an impulse shock in productivity. The estimated frequency distribution can be used to evaluate in probability terms the numerical value of the chosen statistic in actual time series data. Hence, obtaining numerical solutions through Monte Carlo methods allows for a testing approach somewhat different from the one we use in standard econometric models. Numerical solutions can also be used to search for values of structural parameters in growth models providing an acceptable fit of a set of chosen statistical characteristics of actual time series data, an approach exploited in the Simulated Method of Moments estimator.[38, 39]

---

[38] New Econometrics textbooks include some of these methods. As examples, see Canova [16] or De Jong and Dave [27].

[39] These equations can be fitted to data by recently developed econometric methods (Generalized Method of Moments). The idea is that analogous sample moments should not be very different from the theoretical moments implied by the model,

For instance, the stochastic moment condition in page 37, under time-varying taxes, can be written:

$$E_t \left[\frac{1}{C_t} - \beta \left(1 + (1 - \tau_{t+1}) r_{t+1} \right) \frac{1}{C_{t+1}} \right] = 0,$$

which, for any variable Z_t in the information set on which the conditional expectations E_t is formed, it implies:

$$E \left[Z_t \left(\frac{1}{C_t} - \beta \left(1 + (1 - \tau_{t+1}) r_{t+1} \right) \frac{1}{C_{t+1}} \right) \right] = E[h(Z_t, X_t, \theta)] = 0,$$

suggesting that we estimate by solving the optimization problem:

$$\underset{\beta, \delta}{Min} \sum_{t=0}^{\infty} \left[Z_t \left(\frac{1}{C_t} - \beta [1 + (1 - \tau_{t+1}) r_{t+1}] \frac{1}{C_{t+1}} \right) \right]^2,$$

where we have one such condition for each chosen Z_t-variable and each function with a zero conditional expectation.

More generally, the optimization problem:

$$\underset{\theta}{Min} \left[H(Z_t, X_t, \theta) A H(Z_t, X_t, \theta)' \right]$$

1.4.2 Stability

To obtain a numerical solution to a nonlinear, stochastic dynamic system, we need it to be complete, i.e., to have as many equations as decision variables at each point in time. However, the three aspects of the model: (a) nonlinear, (b) stochastic, and (c) dynamic, lead to nontrivial issues regarding such computation. First, a complete nonlinear system is not guaranteed to have a solution, or if it does, there is no guarantee that the solution will be unique. Second, a stochastic system will include expectations of future variables that should be solved consistently with the structure of the model, at least under rational expectations, a maintained assumption throughout this book. Expectations are additional endogenous variables that break down the completeness of the model, and appropriate methods need to be used to obtain a solution.[40] Lastly, an additional issue when solving a dynamic system is the stability of the solution, which is never guaranteed.

In linear dynamic systems, stability can be obtained through conditions on the eigenvalues of the transition matrix in the first-order autoregressive representation of the model. It is not hard to see that in simple models like those in previous sections, these conditions are obtained from stability conditions on lagged coefficients of autoregressive representations for endogenous variables. These, in turn, can be translated into restrictions on admissible values for some structural parameters or for combinations of them. Unfortunately, the numerical solution to a nonlinear dynamic system, which is obtained recursively, providing the values of decision variables each period as a function of state and exogenous variables, will generally produce explosive time trajectories, and we lack the tools to characterize conditions guaranteeing otherwise.

By assuming an optimizing behavior on the part of economic agents, Growth models imply *transversality conditions*. These are limit conditions as time increases, that emerge naturally from those optimization problems, and that are formulated in terms of conditional expectations in the case of stochastic models. Transversality conditions usually impose limits on the rates of growth of state variables which, in turn, impose limits on the range of decisions consistent with stability. They are an intrinsic part of the solution to dynamic optimization problems, and do not have an analogue in dynamic models without an explicit underlying optimization structure. In a growth model, *stability conditions* are relationships between decision and state variables that guarantee that the implied numerical solution fulfills the transversality conditions of the model.

The alternative methods[41] reviewed in Chap. 4 to generate numerical solutions out of stochastic growth models cope with stability in a different manner, and they

---

is solved, where $H(Z_t, X_t, \theta) = (h_1(Z_t, X_t, \theta), h_2(Z_t, X_t, \theta), ..., h_k(Z_t, X_t, \theta))$, with the $h_j(.)$ functions being cross products of Z_t-variables and expressions like the one inside the bracket above, and A is a kxk matrix of weights, which conditions the statistical efficiency of the implied estimates.

[40] For a discussion of analytical solution methods for lineal rational expectations models, see Whiteman [97].

[41] We do not pretend these methods to be superior in any sense to those not covered in the chapter. They have been chosen because of their relative simplicity. An introduction to more complex, but possibly more exact methods, is also provided in that chapter.

provide different degrees of numerical approximation to the true solution. Some methods solve directly the linear or the log-linear approximation to the original model. Some other methods use the approximate stability conditions while keeping some of the nonlinear structure of the original model when computing the numerical solution.

In the absence of *exact stability conditions* for general nonlinear systems that could be added to the model, solution methods achieve a stable solution by adding *approximate stability conditions* to the nonlinear, stochastic or deterministic model. The model needs to be complete to start with because these stability conditions must be obtained from that complete nonlinear system. The obtained solution is an approximation to the true solution because it substitutes the stability conditions for some of the original nonlinear structure of the model. They have a different nature in endogenous than in exogenous growth models. In the latter, they are formulated in terms of per capita variables like consumption or the stock of productive capital, while in endogenous growth models they come out in terms of ratios (sometimes growth rates) of endogenous variables.

1.4.3 Indeterminacy

The solution to a Growth model can display two types of indeterminacy. *Global indeterminacy* refers to the fact that a dynamic general equilibrium model may present multiple steady-states, as in the well known monetary model of Cagan [14]. Since the steady-state is usually the solution to a nonlinear system of equations, multiple solutions might well arise. More generally, in models implying steady-state growth, global indeterminacy refers to the possible existence of multiple balanced growth paths, steady-states in which per capita variables grow at a constant rate. In contrast, *local indeterminacy* arises when given a steady-state or a balanced growth path, there might exist a continuum of trajectories converging to it. We focus here on explaining how local indeterminacy may arise.

A numerical solution algorithm can be seen as a set of rules to choose the values of control or decision variables each period as a function of state variables. Most of these rules will come out of the Growth model, to which we will have added the appropriate stability conditions. Specifically, the latter provide us with the needed dependence between initial decisions and states guaranteeing that transversality conditions are fulfilled. Most often, we have the same number of stability conditions than decision variables. Then the solution to the model is *determinate* but, unfortunately, there is not guarantee of such coincidence. When the number of stability conditions exceeds the number of decision variables, then the system will generally lack a solution, unless some fortunate dependence exists among the relationships emerging from the model and the set of stability conditions, that make some of them redundant.

Finally, when the number of stability conditions falls short of the number of decision variables, we then have some degrees of freedom to choose decision variables. Most of them are related to state variables by the growth model, so that they will

be determinate even in this situation. That will not be the case for expectations variables, that can be considered as decisions made by economic agents, but that are
not explicitly constrained by the theoretical model.[42] Therefore, when the number
of stability conditions is too short, the conditional expectation as of time t of some
function of future variables can be chosen arbitrarily. This is what is known as a
situation in which the solution is *indeterminate*, since any choice of structure for a
given conditional expectation can be made consistent with a solution to the model. It
is important to notice that this is not a characteristic of numerical solution methods
but rather, of the theoretical model itself. In any event, the solution may be indeterminate in some aspects, like those relating to the values taking by some expectations
variables and their associated expectations errors, while being well determined from
the point of view of some other variables or characteristics that define the main object of analysis. In such models, a continuum of solutions exist, and the policy maker
should consider the possibility of making the private sector to select one among the
set of solutions, if such a desired solution exists according to some criterion. Because of the multiplicity of possible solution trajectories, indeterminacy implies a
strong ambiguity regarding policy effects, seriously questioning any normative exercise unless some model specific argument can be made justifying one among the
continuum of potential solutions.

Under indetermination of equilibria, there is at each point in time the need to
choose values for some control variables. The problem is that the choice at time t
does not condition the choice made at any other point in time, so that the economy
can be displaying significant jumps which can sometimes be interpreted as cycles.
In essence, the situation is as if each of this subset of control variables is drawn each
period from a given probability distribution. Indeterminacy can also give raise to
self-fulfilling prophecies: as an example if, for some reason, consumers believe that
future tax rates will rise, they will attempt to reduce the tax base, which may well
lead the government to the need to effectively increase tax rates so as to maintain the
same revenue. That would be a case in which one among the continuum of possible
equilibria is being chosen on the basis of a purely speculative behavior on the part of
consumers.[43] This situation will not arise when the equilibrium is well determined,
since agents then use past information on expectation errors to update their views
on the future of the economy, leaving no role for any unjustified, sudden change in
expectations.

1.4.4 The Type of Questions We Ask and the Conclusions
We Reach

The approach to economic modelling we have described in these sections has had
a tremendous impact on the way we think about the analysis of effects of the dif-

---

[42] Unless we work under the assumption of rational expectations, the model's implications regarding the way agents' expectations relate to state variables are generally hard to derive.

[43] What is called a *bubble equilibrium*.

ferent exogenous shocks in an economy. We can analyze which among the possible shocks is more likely to produce a given statistical characteristic of the solution, or which one is more useful in order for a model to replicate a given statistical regularity observed in actual time series data. Similarly, we can characterize the way how economic policy influences the dynamics of relevant variables, as well as the comovements between them. So, it is not surprising that it is in the normative analysis of economic policy where stochastic, dynamic models with microeconomic foundations have become standard.

As it has already been mentioned, the ability of any dynamic model to provide information not only on the steady-state, but on the transition between steady-states as well, allows us to address the separate characterization of short- and long-run effects of a structural change or a policy intervention. This is a central issue for optimal policy design exercises, which justifies by itself the need to specify very carefully the dynamic structure of the relationships among the variables that are relevant for the question under study.

Even more important, the specific characteristics of Growth models and their numerical solutions allow us to ask questions that could not possibly be addressed in standard dynamic macroeconomic models. This is because the explicit assumptions made by Growth models regarding the objective functions of the different economic agents allow for a normative analysis of a whole variety of issues. Specifically, the welfare effects[44] of any policy intervention or structural change can be nicely addressed in an appropriately chosen exogenous or endogenous Growth model. Evaluating the possible inefficiency introduced by a given policy or market friction also needs a specification for consumer preferences, or a numerical estimation of the compensation that should be introduced to make agents as well of as they would be under the efficient allocation of resources.

But numerical solutions obtained by Monte Carlo simulation allow for evaluating models across many more dimensions than we used to on the basis of analytical solutions. Since we can use the vector time series obtained as solution to the model to compute any univariate or multivariate statistic (like relative volatilities, cross-correlations between any two variables, estimated regressions or VAR representations, impulse response functions, and so on), we can always compare the frequency distribution obtained for that statistic from a Monte Carlo analysis to its estimated from actual data, and see how the model fits the data. Needless to say, this opens the door to the comparison of alternative models on the basis of their ability to replicate a given set of statistics estimated from actual data.[45] Solving Growth models that differ in some structural characteristic, numerical solutions may also point out to the relevance of the different features of the model to explain a given regularity observed in actual data.

---

[44] Welfare should be understood as the discounted time aggregate value of current and future utility. We are thinking here about a set of identical consumers, who live together forever, a usual assumption in growth models.

[45] However, the appropriate approach to use frequency distributions from the alternative models to evaluate in probability terms (or in likelihood terms) their ability to fit the data is still very much open to discussion. And so it is the selection of statistics whose value in actual data should be replicated by the theoretical models considered.

All this has led to a significant change in the type of questions we ask to models, since they can relate to a wide variety of statistical characteristics of the theoretical model that can be estimated from the realizations obtained for the numerical solution, but could not possibly be characterized analytically.

Suppose that fluctuations in the expenditures/output ratio in a given economy can be interpreted as controlled deviations around a pre-announced target level. Should they then be correlated with exogenous supply shocks? [46] This question could be analyzed by solving the model under different positive and negative values for such correlation and computing levels of implied welfare. This would have clear implications on the optimal way to conduct policy. Changes in the expenditure/output ratio to accommodate supply shocks under a maintained correlation with supply shocks would have to come together with changes in a given tax rate (on consumption, labor income or capital income, for instance) to balance the budget.[47] In principle, we should expect that the answer to the optimal correlation question might depend on the type of tax adjustment chosen, so that the answer is two sided: from the point of view of maximizing private agents' welfare, it is optimal to maintain *such* correlation between the expenditures-to-output ratio and supply shocks, and balance the budget every period by adjusting the fluctuations in expenditures with *such* tax rate.

This analysis would make sense even if we believe that the random deviations from a specified target in the expenditures/output ratio is beyond the control of the economic authority, since there would still be a welfare-maximizing correlation between these fluctuations and supply shocks. The theoretical analysis in the previous paragraph would have characterized the optimal expenditure/tax policy. We could then identify separately supply and fiscal shocks in actual data, possibly through an structural VAR type of analysis. The estimated correlation between supply shocks and innovations in the expenditure/output ratio, together with the observation on the type of taxes which are adjusted most often, would give us the extent to which the correlation used in actual policy making departs from the value predicted as optimal by the model.

Beyond this, endogenous growth models allow for analyzing the effects of structural changes or policy interventions on the long-run rate of growth of the economy, a question that would again be generally impossible to analyze in standard dynamic macroeconomic models.

In fact, positive steady-state growth allow endogenous growth models to address a variety of realistic issues that could not possibly arise in economies with zero long-term growth. To mention one covered in this textbook, a dynamic Laffer effect may arise when an economy can afford to lower down taxes while maintaining the same time path for government expenditures that was planned before the tax cut and still have a balanced government budget in an intertemporal sense. How could this be? In

---

[46] Exogebous shocks could be modelled as shocks in productivity, as it is done often throughout the book.

[47] Alternatively, we could consider the possibility of maintaining tax rates unchanged and finance the fluctuations in expenditures by debt management or money injections. Appropriate conditions guaranteing long-run solvency would then have to be imposed, as it is discussed at different points in this textbook.

an endogenous growth economy, the rate of growth may depend on policy variables, like tax rates. When that is the case, a tax cut will lead to increased growth and possibly increased revenues, at least after a number of periods, when the higher growth may have sufficiently increased the income tax base. The tax cut will initially need of issuing some debt, but the increase in revenues may allow for eventually retiring that debt, thereby with a balanced intertemporal government budget constraint.

Together with the change in the type of policy questions we address in growth models, the type of responses we get, even to traditional questions, is now also different. We have seen an example above: characterization of an optimal active expenditure policy that links expenditure fluctuations to supply shocks, may well depend on the strategy for revenue compensation we establish. Conclusions to policy analysis will often be of the sort: "... a standard business cycle model is consistent with the expectations hypothesis of the term structure of interest rates provided monetary shocks are dominant, while having implications contrary to that hypothesis when productivity shocks are the main source of randomness in the economy."[48], or "... if the elasticity of intertemporal substitution is above a critical value, then it is better to adjust labor income taxes over the cycle while maintaining capital income taxes roughly stable, while the opposite is true if the elasticity of intertemporal substitution of consumption is below that value." Fully specified economic structures of the type used in exogenous or endogenous Growth models are likely to lead to such contingent conclusions.

Some researchers view such relativity as a weakness of economic analysis, suggesting that it would better to discuss policy in simpler models, even if missing some interesting economic feature, since they allow for neater conclusions. The opposite is, however, more likely to be true. We may have been too ambitious in attempting to reach statements with absolute validity, regardless of the type of economy being studied. In characterizing optimal policy as a function of the structure of the economy (the source of shocks, the values of structural parameter, etc.) we are aiming at providing our readers a mapping showing the specification of optimal policy appropriate for each economic structure. Did we really believe that a similar kind of policy would be optimum for a variety of widely different economies and for any conceivable policy environment?

A final word to relate to the different statistical properties of variables emerging from exogenous and endogenous growth models. Time series solving a Growth model can always display a deterministic trend because of exogenous growth, in the form of a constant increase in productivity, for instance. This is a deterministic component that can be easily dealt with by appropriate statistical methods. We can take the view that observed trends in per capita variables in actual data are explained by this mechanism and impose on the theoretical model the observed rate of growth.

---

[48] Of course, the type of results reached by Poole [71] in a static setup, that "in the presence of supply shocks it is better to implement a monetary policy aimed to maintaining a given growth rate of money, while leaving interest rates to be determined in the market, the opposite being true if randomness enters mainly through the demand side" is another result typical from the type of analysis described in these sections.

This deterministic trend could be then taken out from both, simulated and actual data, and compare the statistical properties of detrended actual and artificial time series.

A more interesting approach would attempt to explain the rate of growth in per-capita variables sometimes observed in actual data through an endogenous growth model. An advantage is that such model allows for changes in the rate of growth because of policy changes, for instance. But a central implication of endogenous growth models is that per-capita variables have a unit root, even after correcting for the endogenous rate of growth. That leads sometimes to applying some filter to remove this stochastic trend from the time series produced from the model, if such trend is believed not to be present in the data. But the opposite may well happen: often, when working with exogenous growth models that exclude technological growth[49] actual time series data are filtered to eliminate stochastic trends (i.e., unit roots) before comparing them with the artificial time series generated as solution to the theoretical Growth model. An endogenous Growth model would look then very appropriate to match theory to actual data.

1.5 Synopsis of the Book

Chapter 2 presents the neoclassical growth model of Solow and Swan with a constant savings rate. Section 2.2 examines the relationship between the structure of returns to scale in cumulative inputs and the steady-state rate of growth. The impossibility to have positive long-run growth under decreasing returns to scale in the cumulative inputs is shown. Section 2.3 shows the main properties of the model, the dynamics of the economy, the steady-state and the duration of the transition, and characterizes the rates of growth of per capita variables. A special steady-state, the Golden Rule, is introduced. Section 2.4 solves the continuous time, deterministic model. This is a special case, in which an analytical solution exists. The effects of changes in structural parameters are analyzed. The concept of dynamic inefficiency is introduced. Section 2.5 describes and solves the deterministic, discrete-time version of the model, and performs numerical exercises on the effects of changes in structural parameters and on characterizing situations of dynamic inefficiency. Section 2.6 considers the stochastic, discrete-time model, and explains how to obtain numerical solutions.

The problem of optimal growth is considered in Chaps. 3 and 4. The first of these two chapters introduces the continuous time version of the benevolent planner problem. At a difference of Chap. 2, an explicit consideration is made of consumers' preferences, and the savings rate is no longer constant, but rather, the consequence of optimal decisions at each point in time. Optimality (Keynes–Ramsey) condition and transversality conditions are characterized and interpreted in detail. Existence and stability of a unique optimal path is shown, and a numerical exercise is presented

---

[49] And hence, in which per-capita variables display zero growth.

on the long-run effects of changes in structural parameters. Section 2 presents numerical exercises related to the stability and convergence issues discussed in the previous section, paying attention to the relevance of the different structural characteristics of the economy in characterizing the transition path between steady-states. A note of caution is raised about the right way to translate continuous time optimization models into discrete time models. Section 3 show the equivalence between the allocation of resources that emerges from the problem solved by the benevolent planner and from the competitive equilibrium mechanism, showing the Pareto efficiency of the latter. Section 4 describes the competitive equilibrium in an economy with government, and introduces the intertemporal government budget constraint. The so-called problem of the representative agent is introduced. Section 5 discusses the potential inefficiency of the competitive equilibrium with government, and how the inefficiency depends on the type of taxes used and their structure over time. Section 6 is devoted to the Ricardian doctrine, that states the possible irrelevance of the financing tools used by the government, showing that it may not hold under some types of distortionary taxation. Chapter 4 considers the deterministic, discrete time version of the model with and without government. We describe how to solve this model paying special attention to the characterization of stability conditions. Some fiscal policy issues are addressed, describing the way to evaluate the welfare effects of policy changes. Some numerical exercises on characterizing short- and long-term effects of policy changes are presented.

Numerical solution approaches are presented in Chap. 5. The first part of the chapter considers the stochastic optimal growth model of the previous chapter, without taxes. After describing the special cases in which an analytical solution exists, several solution methods are reviewed. The construction of linear and log-linear approximations is explained, and the different methods introduced: the Blanchard and Kahn [10] approach, Uhlig's [94] method of undetermined coefficients, the method based on an eigenvalue-eigenvector decomposition, proposed by Sims [86], and numerical exercises are presented that explain how to implement each of these solution methods and discuss some of the results obtained. The way to deal with stability in each case is explained. The second part of the chapter describes the implementation of the same methods to solve the stochastic optimal growth model with different specification for taxes. Numerical exercises are presented to illustrate the implementation of the methods and to discuss some policy issues. The chapter closes with nonlinear solution methods like the Parameterized expectations method by Marcet [62] and Projection methods. Analytical details of these methods are discussed in their application to some standard Growth models, and programs are again provided to implement these methods.

Endogenous growth models are introduced in Chap. 6. The AK model is examined in detail, first in continuous time, in Sect. 6.1, and after that in its discrete time version, in Sect. 6.2. The absence of transition, the existence of a balanced growth path along which all per capita variables grow at the same constant rate, and the inefficiency of the equilibrium mechanism, are shown. The specific characteristics of dealing with stability in endogenous growth models are analyzed in Sect. 6.3. Section 6.4 shows how transitory policy interventions or structural changes in endogenous growth models have permanent effects. Section 6.5 is devoted to the analysis of dynamic Laffer curves, a possibility which is specific of endogenous growth models, and a numerical exercise is presented to illustrate their occurrence. Section 6.6 describes how to obtain numerical solutions to the stochastic, discrete time version of the AK model, with a numerical exercise illustrating the implementation of the solution method. Section 6.7 considers Barro [4] version of the AK model that includes government expenditures and discusses their effects on the long-run rate of growth of the economy. Section 6.8 introduces the Jones and Manuelli [47] variant of the AK model that generates a non-trivial transition to steady-state. The approach to obtain numerical solutions to this model is described. Section 6.9 is devoted to the stochastic version of the Jones and Manuelli model, describing the transitional dynamics, characterizing the stability conditions, and explaining how to compute numerical solutions, which is illustrated with a numerical exercise.

Chapter 7 reviews some additional mechanisms by which endogenous growth arises. We start in Sect. 7.2 with an economy without capital accumulation in which technological progress shows up in the form of the number of varieties of producer products, possibly differing in quality [Spence [89], Dixit and Stiglitz [31], Ethier [33] and Romer [77, 78]. Technological innovation in these models may lead to either an increase in their number, or in their quality, so the innovation process is key in this economy. These models can be seen to be equivalent to the AK model for an appropriate parameter choice. In particular, except in specific versions of these models there is no transition, per capita variables growing at a constant rate at all points in time after any structural shock or policy intervention. After that, we present in Sect. 7.3 an endogenous growth model by Barro and Sala-i-Martin [5] on technological diffusion between two countries, one being a leader in innovation, as in the model with varieties of producer products, the second one being a follower, that adopts the innovations developed in the leading country. The economy of the follower country displays a non-trivial transition to steady-state. A numerical exercise is presented solving this model and the model of varieties of intermediate goods in the previous section. We then move in Sect. 7.4 to a model economy with *creative destruction* à la Schumpeter [82] following work by Aghion and Howitt [2] and Howitt and Aghion [42], in which endogenous growth arises from improvement in the quality of intermediate goods that is achieved through research and development activities. This model incorporates accumulation of physical capital and displays a nontrivial transition to steady-state. We close in Sect. 7.5 with a detailed discussion of an important model by Uzawa [95] and Lucas [60], of a two-sector economy in which human and physical capital accumulate over time, and where time devoted to education plays an important role, so that the split of time among that devoted to producing the final good, to education (i.e., to human capital accumulation) and leisure is a crucial decision. We include different types of taxes and show that the economy again exhibits a nontrivial transition, and it is an appropriate framework to address interesting questions regarding fiscal policy. The competitive equilibrium is described in detail and the conditions characterizing steady-state are shown. The steady-state is shown to take the form of a balanced growth path. A numerical exercise is presented to compute the steady-state effects of changes in tax rates. Stability conditions are characterized, and a method to compute numerical solutions to the stochastic version of the model is presented, and its implementation is illustrated in a numerical exercise. The potential indeterminacy in this model is shown, and a solution approach is shown for such situation.

Chapter 8 introduces monetary exogenous growth models. The first part of the chapter is devoted to a steady-state (long-run) analysis of monetary policy. Section 8.2 describes the optimal monetary growth model of Sidrauski [84], the steady-state is characterized and the possibilities for monetary policy implementations are analyzed. Special attention is paid to the necessary coordination between fiscal and monetary policy that emerges from the characterization of the long-run equilibrium. Section 8.3 characterizes the optimal steady-state rate of inflation and the welfare cost of inflation. Section 8.4 analyzes two modelling issues: the difference between including either nominal or real debt in the model, and the timing by which real balances enter as an argument into the utility function of the representative consumer. A numerical exercise is presented to illustrate these two issues. Section 8.5 considers monetary policy in the presence of consumption and income taxes. The steady-state is characterized, and a numerical exercise is performed to compute steady-state values for the main variables under alternative policy choices. Fiscal policy is shown not to be neutral. The coordination between fiscal and monetary policy is again discussed. Section 8.6 considers monetary policy under an endogenous labor supply. The possible nonneutrality of monetary policy in different setups is discussed. A numerical exercise is presented, with calculation of the optimal rate of inflation and analyzing the validity of Friedman's rule on the optimality of a zero nominal rate of interest. Section 8.7 considers monetary policy under endogenous labor and distortionary taxation. The Ramsey problem is specified and first order analytical conditions are obtained.

Chapter 9 is devoted to the analysis of the transitional dynamics in monetary growth economies. Section 9.1 characterizes the transitional dynamics, the class of feasible monetary policies, and the short- and long-run neutrality of monetary policy. Section 9.2 analyzes the potential instability of the stock of public debt, and describes a standard way to impose stability by linking the level of lump-sum transfers to consumers to the stock of public debt outstanding each period. Section 9.3 describes the deterministic, discrete-time version of Sidrauski's monetary model under two possibilities, when the monetary authority uses either the nominal rate of interest or the rate of growth of money supply as a control variable. The potential indeterminacy of the price level is discussed. The two alternative policy designs are analyzed in detail in Sects. 9.4 and 9.5. The numerical solution approach for each case is presented. Section 9.6 discusses the results of some numerical exercises on the transitional effects of monetary policy interventions. A full model incorporating money and debt issuing as well as different types of taxes is used to analyze the effects of different policy interventions. Sudden and gradual changes in the rate of growth of money supply are shown to have different effects. Section 9.7 introduces the stochastic version of the monetary growth model. Sections 9.8 and 9.9 consider alternative policy choices, with the monetary authority using either nominal interest rates or money supply growth as control variable for the implementation of monetary policy. The indeterminacy of the price level under a policy of controlling nominal interest rates is again shown. When controlling nominal rates, the monetary authority is assumed to follow a Taylor's rule to implement policy, with different weights assigned to output, inflation, and past interest rates. Numerical exercises are presented to illustrate the implementation of the solution methods in both cases. The chapter closes with a discussion of a New Keynesian monetarist model, of the type which are increasingly being used as one of the reference models in most central banks around the world. These models are characterized by the existence of some monopoly power in some firms, as well as some price frictions. We describe in detail the theoretical foundations and analytically characterize the equilibrium conditions. After that, we present the application of the numerical solution methods introduced in the book to the solution of this model, which allow for the analysis of effects of different policy interventions.

Chapter 2
The Neoclassical Growth Model Under a Constant Savings Rate

2.1 Introduction

We present in this chapter the first growth model, introduced almost simultaneously by R.Solow and S.Swan in two different papers published in 1956. In fact, as we will see, the assumptions embedded in this model imply that, in the long run, and in the absence of technological growth, economies do not grow in per-capita terms. The possibility of aggregate growth arises only from either population growth or growth in factor productivity. Since neither factor is supposed to depend on the decisions of economic agents, this is known as an *exogenous growth* model. There are model economies for which there are steady-states with constant, non-zero growth rates determined by some decisions made by economic agents, like the level of education, or by some policy choices, like a given tax rate. These are known as *endogenous growth models* and will be studied in later chapters.

Per capita income, the most obvious indicator of the state of a given economy, displays two different characteristics in most developed countries: (a) it increases over time, and (b) it experiences cyclical fluctuations around its long-term trend over relatively short periods of time. The Solow–Swan model focuses on explaining the first characteristic, long-term growth, even though, as we have already mentioned, the long-run equilibrium growth rate will be zero unless some conditions are met. Even in versions of the Solow–Swan model implying zero long-run growth, the economy will experience non-zero rates of change in the capital stock per worker or in the level of per-capita income over short periods of time, called *transition* periods. To characterize general conditions under which an economy may display non-zero long-term growth is the goal of the next section.

A stochastic version of growth models is needed if we want the model to reproduce the statistical characteristics of business cyclical fluctuations in actual economies. We will also consider a stochastic version of the Solow–Swan growth model, even though this will still be too simple a model to explain many interesting empirical observations.

2.2 Returns to Scale and Sustained Growth

We start by discussing an important fact: the returns displayed by productive factors in the available aggregate technology will condition the possibilities for the economy to display sustained long-run growth. This initial discussion is of a general nature, although it is made under a set of assumptions defining the Solow–Swan model, to which it applies as a special case.

Assumption 1: The relationship between total output Y_t, and the two production inputs, the stock of physical capital K_t, and labour L_t, at the aggregate level of the economy, can be interpreted as coming from a Cobb–Douglas technology,

$$Y_t = AK_t^\beta L_t^\alpha, \ \alpha, \beta \geq 0,$$

with unrestricted numerical values for the elasticities of the production factors, except that they must be non-negative. A denotes a production scale factor, which affects the productivity of both factors. Changes in A will shift the production frontier. Physical capital tends to accumulate over time through investment. Gross investment I_t has two components: (a) net investment, defined as the variation in the stock of capital, $\dot{K}_t$, and (b) the loss by depreciation D_t:

$$Gross\ Investment \equiv I_t = \dot{K}_t + D_t. \tag{2.1}$$

In the absence of depreciation, the change in capital would be equal to investment. Under positive depreciation, net investment may be positive, or negative, when investment is not enough to replace the loss by depreciation.

Assumption 2: The rate of depreciation of physical capital is constant, δ, so that: $D_t = \delta K_t$.

Assumption 3: Each worker has a unit of time available each period that is supplied inelastically in the labor market. This allows us to identify the number of workers and the supply of labor each period.

Assumption 4: We assume that there is full employment in the economy, so that employment, L_t, and labor supply, N_t, coincide. These first two assumptions allow us to use in what follows total population, N_t, as an input in the production function and write the technology in terms of per capita variables or per-worker variables,

$$\frac{Y_t}{N_t} = A \left(\frac{K_t}{N_t} \right)^\beta N_t^{\alpha+\beta-1}, \ \alpha, \beta \geq 0 \ \Rightarrow \ y_t = Ak_t^\beta N_t^{\alpha+\beta-1}, \tag{2.2}$$

where $y_t = \frac{Y_t}{N_t}, k_t = \frac{K_t}{N_t}$ denote per capita income and physical capital. As we will see, the capital-labor ratio k_t is the key variable determining the evolution over time of this economy.

Assumption 5: There is no government in the economy, which is supposed to be closed to financial or commodity trading with other countries, which implies that aggregate savings and investment are equal to each other every period, $S_t = I_t, \forall t$.

Assumption 6: Additionally, and this is a significant restriction, we assume savings to evolve over time as a constant fraction s of output,

$$Savings \equiv S_t = sY_t.$$

Using Assumption 5 and 6 in (2.1) and dividing by N_t, and using (2.2), we have,

$$sy_t = \frac{\dot{K_t}}{N_t} + \delta k_t = sAk_t^\beta N_t^{\alpha+\beta-1}. \tag{2.3}$$

Assumption 7: We assume that labor force and employment (which are equal to each other at each point in time, by Assumption 2) grow at a constant rate of n,

$$N_t = N_0 e^{nt}.$$

We can now use these assumptions to obtain some properties of Growth models. Taking derivatives with respect to time in the definition of k_t, we have,

$$\dot{k_t} = \frac{\dot{K_t}}{N_t} - \frac{\dot{N_t}K_t}{N_t^2} = \frac{\dot{K_t}}{N_t} - nk_t. \tag{2.4}$$

From equations (2.3) and (2.4), we get,

$$\dot{k_t} = sAk_t^\beta N_t^{\alpha+\beta-1} - (n+\delta)k_t,$$

and, dividing by k_t we obtain the growth rate of the per-worker stock of physical capital, γ_{k_t}:

$$\gamma_{k_t} \equiv \frac{\dot{k_t}}{k_t} = sAk_t^{\beta-1}N_t^{\alpha+\beta-1} - (n+\delta), \tag{2.5}$$

which will change over time with population and with the level of the capital-labor ratio. We also have,

$$\frac{\gamma_{k_t} + (n+\delta)}{sA} = k_t^{\beta-1}N_t^{\alpha+\beta-1}.$$

Taking logs, we get,

$$\ln\left(\frac{\gamma_{k_t} + (n+\delta)}{sA}\right) = (\beta-1)\ln k_t + (\alpha+\beta-1)\ln N_t, \tag{2.6}$$

and taking derivatives with respect to time t, we have,

$$\frac{\dot{\gamma_{k_t}}}{\gamma_{k_t} + (n+\delta)} = (\beta-1)\frac{\dot{k_t}}{k_t} + (\alpha+\beta-1)n, \tag{2.7}$$

where we have used Assumption 7 to imply: $\frac{\dot{N_t}}{N_t} = n$.

We are particularly interested in characterizing a possible state of the economy in which the growth rate of per capita variables[1] can be maintained constant forever. In such a situation, which we will later define more precisely as *steady-state*, the left hand side at (2.6) would be constant. Notice that it is not the levels, but the growth rates of variables like k_t and y_t, that remain constant in steady-state. We will denote them by $\gamma_{k_{ss}}, \gamma_{y_{ss}}$.

Evaluating (2.7) at such steady-state, we get,

$$0 = (\beta - 1)\gamma_{k_{ss}} + (\alpha + \beta - 1)n, \tag{2.8}$$

a condition that any possible steady-state will have to fulfill. It is important to bear in mind that at this point we have not shown existence of such a steady-state, and much less its possible uniqueness. We have only shown that (2.8) is a necessary condition for a steady-state to exist.

We now take logs in (2.3), an expression which is valid at any point in time, to get,

$$\ln s + \ln y_t = \ln(sA) + \beta \ln k_t + (\alpha + \beta - 1)\ln N_t,$$

where $\ln s$ is constant. That taking derivatives with respect to time,

$$\frac{\dot{y}_t}{y_t} = \beta \frac{\dot{k}_t}{k_t} + (\alpha + \beta - 1)n \Rightarrow \gamma_{y_t} = \beta \gamma_{k_t} + (\alpha + \beta - 1)n,$$

so that, in steady-state,

$$\gamma_{y_{ss}} = \beta \gamma_{k_{ss}} + (\alpha + \beta - 1)n, \tag{2.9}$$

which describes the relationship between the growth rates of per capita income and physical capital in a steady-state.

To obtain the relationship with the rate of growth of consumption, we use the global constraint of resources of the economy to show the proportionality between per capita consumption and output:

$$C_t + S_t = Y_t \Rightarrow C_t + sY_t = Y_t \Rightarrow C_t/N_t = (1 - s)Y_t/N_t \Rightarrow c_t = (1 - s)y_t,$$

which implies that both variable grow at the same rate: $\gamma_{c_{ss}} = \gamma_{y_{ss}}$.

Let us now consider some possibilities:

Case 1: Economy with decreasing returns to scale in each production factor, but constant returns to scale on the aggregate,

$$Y_t = AK_t^\beta L_t^\alpha, \quad 0 < \alpha, \beta < 1, \quad \alpha + \beta = 1,$$

In this case, the second term at (2.8) is zero, so that,

$$0 = (\beta - 1)\gamma_{k_{ss}},$$

---

[1] In fact, a steady-state is defined by constant rates of growth of appropriately chosen ratios of variables. In this introductory discussion, it is convenient to define it in terms of per capita variables, although in a later section of this same chapter we need to define it differently.

and since $\beta < 1$, we will necessarily have,

$$\gamma_{k_{ss}} = 0.$$

Hence, if there is any steady state, it will necessarily have to display a zero growth rate for the stock of physical capital per worker. As a consequence of the previous relationships between growth rates, in such an economy all per-capita variables will remain constant in such a steady-state. The constant returns to scale assumption, together with $\gamma_{k_{ss}} = 0$, imply in (2.9) that per-capita income does not grow in steady-state, i.e., $\gamma_{y_{ss}} = 0$ and, as a consequence, $\gamma_{c_{ss}} = 0$. Even though the steady-state condition only allows for a zero steady-state growth rate, that could still be obtained for different levels of per capita variables (k_{ss}, c_{ss}, y_{ss}), leading to multiple steady-states.

Figure 2.1 shows the values of the growth rate of the capital-labor ratio, by illustrating the two functions involved in (2.5). The gap between the two curves provides the growth rate of the capital-labor ratio, which will be positive to the left of the **crossing point**, k_{ss}, and negative to the right of it. That intersection characterizes the steady-state level of the capital-labor ratio. A monotonically decreasing marginal productivity of capital implies uniqueness of that steady-state ratio. To the left of k_{ss} the k_t-ratio will increase, with growth being higher the farther away to the left is the level of k_t. Something similar can be said about the decrease in k_t to the right of k_{ss}.

In fact, this graph shows the *existence and uniqueness* of a zero-growth steady-state in an economy with the assumptions described above. It is particularly important that we have assumed a constant returns to scale production technology together with diminishing returns on the cumulative input, the stock of capital. The graph also illustrates the *stability* of such steady-state, since the economy will converge to it from any position above or below the steady-state capital-labor ratio.

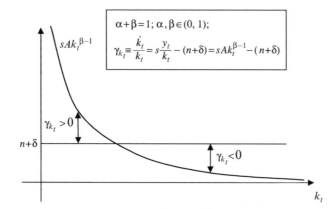

Fig. 2.1 Growth rate of capital-labor ratio: Cobb Douglas technology with constant returns to scale

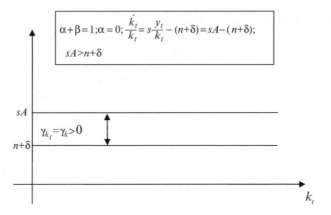

Fig. 2.2 Growth rate of capital-labor ratio: Unit elasticity in cumulative factor

This analysis might suggest that it is not possible to obtain positive growth in steady-state if the technology is of the constant returns to scale type. The next case shows that the opposite is true.

Case 2: Let us now consider constant returns to scale in the aggregate, $\alpha + \beta = 1$, as well as in the cumulative factor, physical capital, $\beta = 1$. We then have $\alpha = 0$, and a linear technology,

$$Y_t = AK_t,$$

usually known as an *AK*-technology, which will be studied in detail in Chap. 5. The second term in (2.8) again becomes zero but, since $\beta = 1$, it is possible to find steady-state situations with $\gamma_{k_{ss}} > 0$ (actually, with $\gamma_{k_{ss}} \neq 0$) as it can be seen in Fig. 2.2. Notice again that this argument does not show existence of a non-zero growth steady-state, but only that such a state is possible.

As we will see in later chapters, a linear technology like this one can generate *endogenous growth*. A possible interpretation of this structural feature comes by considering a second cumulative productive factor, human capital,

$$Y_t = AK_t^{\beta} H_t^{1-\beta},$$

where H_t is a variable including the quality as well as the quantity of labor, i.e., not only the number of workers, but their education level, work experience, and so on. If the two types of capital are assumed to be perfect substitutes, then we would end up with an *AK*-technology[2].

This second case has not considered labor as a second input different from physical capital. In the next case we show the possibility of positive steady-state growth in the presence of both inputs: physical capital and labor.

Case 3: Let us consider constant returns to scale in the cumulative factor, $\beta = 1$, and non-zero returns in the labor factor, $\alpha > 0$, so that we have increasing returns to scale in the aggregate. As shown by (2.7), under these assumptions, steady-state will

---

[2] See Barro and Sala-i-Martin [6], Chap. 4.

only be possible in an economy without population growth, $n = 0$. The second term in (2.8) then again disappears and, since $\beta = 1$, there is the possibility of non-zero growth steady-states, although we cannot prove their existence on general grounds.

An (unproven) general message of this section is that to produce non-zero long-run growth it is necessary to have either constant or increasing returns to scale in the cumulative inputs. Although in this section we have just considered one type of capital, there are interesting models including physical as well as human capital, both accumulating over time. The condition there is that the elasticities of the two capital inputs add up to at least 1, as we already saw in our interpretation of the AK-technology in Case 2.

2.3 The Neoclassical Growth Model of Solow and Swan

This model, introduced by Solow [88]) and Swan [91], describes the time evolution of an economy in which there is growth from some initial, known conditions. The model incorporates the assumptions introduced in the previous section, in a case of decreasing returns in physical capital, but constant returns to scale on the aggregate. As shown in Case 1 above, this economy has a single, stable zero-growth steady-state.

Hence, we consider in this chapter a *closed economy, without government*, so that savings and investment are equal to each other every period, $S_t = I_t$. Firms use physical capital and labor to produce the single consumption commodity, which can either be consumed or accumulated in the form of physical capital. Output is only used as consumption or investment, since there is no public consumption or any exchange with the foreign sector. Physical capital depreciates at a constant rate δ. Consumers are endowed with *a unit of time which supply inelastically* in the labor market.[3] Population N_t grows over time at a constant rate n, so that from an initial population N_0 we have, $N_t = N_0 e^{nt}$. Prices and salaries are fully flexible, so that the economy is always in a state of *full employment*. The full employment assumption, together with eliminating any age structure in the population,[4] makes the labor force and employment to be equal to each other at each point in time so that we will also have, $L_t = L_0 e^{nt}$, which implies $\dot{L}_t = nL_t$. When incorporating to the labor force, each consumer/worker receives an amount of physical capital equal to that owned by each person already in the labor force.

Aggregate savings are a constant proportion of income each period, $S_t = sY_t$ or, in per capita terms, $s_t = sy_t$. There is no reason to believe that this should be an optimal behavior on the part of consumers. In fact, we do not consider any optimizing behavior on the part of economic agents or government in the Solow–Swan model so, the analysis is more positive than normative in character. In the next chapter, we analyze a model where consumption/savings decisions are taken optimally.

---

[3] That would be the case, for instance, if leisure does not enter as an argument in their utility function, which we will not specify in this Chapter.

[4] Consumers are able to work from the moment they are born.

2.3.1 Description of the Model

2.3.1.1 Technology

We assume that at the aggregate level, the available technology can be represented by a first-degree homogeneous production function $Y = F(K_t, N_t)$. As explained above, we identify employment with total population. Derivatives are: F_{K_t}, F_{N_t}, $F_{K_t N_t} > 0$, $F_{N_t N_t}$, $F_{K_t K_t} < 0$ and the Hessian is negative definite, so that F is concave. We further assume: $F(K_t, 0) = F(0, N_t) = 0$, so that we cannot produce anything without using positive amounts of the two inputs, and $\lim_{K_t \to 0} F_{K_t} = \lim_{N_t \to 0} F_{N_t} = \infty$, $\lim_{K_t \to \infty} F_{K_t} = \lim_{N_t \to \infty} F_{N_t} = 0$. These are usually known as Inada conditions.

The more restrictive aspect of this technology is the existence of decreasing returns to scale in each input, which, as we saw in Case 1 in the previous section, precludes the possibility of positive steady-state growth. The aggregate constant returns to scale assumption allows us to write,

$$Y_t = F(K_t, N_t) = N_t F(K_t/N_t, 1) = N_t f(k_t), \tag{2.10}$$

where $k_t = K_t/N_t$ denotes the *per capita stock of productive capital* or *capital-labor ratio*, and $f(k_t) = F(K_t/N_t, 1)$. The assumptions on F imply: $f'(k_t) > 0$, $f''(k_t) < 0$, $f(0) = 0$, $\lim_{k_t \to 0} f' = \infty$, $\lim_{k_t \to \infty} f' = 0$.

The *capital-labor ratio* determines output produced per worker Y_t/N_t and hence, income per worker, so it is reasonable to expect that consumption will also be determined by this capital-labor ratio, which is the key variable in this economy.

The marginal productivity for each input is related to the derivatives of $f(k_t)$. First, taking derivatives with respect to K_t,

$$F_{K_t} = N_t f'(k_t) \frac{\partial k_t}{\partial K_t} = N_t f'(k_t) \frac{1}{N_t} = f'(k_t) > 0, \tag{2.11}$$

where subindices denote partial derivatives. On the other hand, taking derivatives at (2.10) with respect to N_t we get,

$$F_{N_t} = f(k_t) + N_t f'(k_t) \left(\frac{-K_t}{N_t^2} \right) = f(k_t) - k_t f'(k_t). \tag{2.12}$$

Even though it is not implied by the properties of $f(k_t)$, the marginal product of labor must also be positive: $f(k_t) - k_t f'(k_t) > 0$ since otherwise, it would be in the benefit of the firm to reduce employment. Finally, it is simple to check that the concavity of $f(k_t)$ is implied by that of F.

A particular technology satisfying the assumptions above is a Cobb–Douglas production function,

$$F(K_t, N_t) = A K_t^\alpha N_t^{1-\alpha} \quad \text{with } 0 < \alpha < 1,$$

where $A > 0$ indicates the level of technology. Aggregate output can be written,

$$Y_t = AK_t^\alpha N_t^{1-\alpha} = AN_t k_t^\alpha, \tag{2.13}$$

so we are in the setup above, with $f(k_t) = Ak_t^\alpha$. Per-capita output is in this case,

$$y_t = \frac{Y_t}{N_t} = Ak_t^\alpha, \quad 0 < \alpha < 1.$$

Marginal factor productivity for both factors is positive under this technology,

$$F_{K_t} = f'(k_t) = A\alpha k_t^{\alpha-1} > 0,$$
$$F_{N_t} = f(k_t) - k_t f'_t(k_t) = Ak_t^\alpha - k_t A\alpha k_t^{\alpha-1} = (1-\alpha)Ak_t^\alpha > 0.$$

2.3.2 The Dynamics of the Economy

In this simple economy, output (or, equivalently, income) is used either as consumption or in the form of gross investment. The later is used in part to compensate for depreciated capital, and also as net additions to the stock of capital,

$$Net\ investment = \dot{K}_t = \frac{dK_t}{dt} = Gross\ investment - Depreciation$$
$$= I_t - D_t = I_t - \delta K_t,$$

where we have used the assumption on a constant rate δ of physical capital depreciation, independent of the stock of capital, $D_t = \delta K_t$.

So, we have the global constraint of resources:

$$Y_t = C_t + I_t = C_t + \dot{K}_t + \delta K_t,$$

that is,

$$\dot{K}_t = F(K_t, N_t) - C_t - \delta K_t.$$

Dividing by employment,

$$\frac{\dot{K}_t}{N_t} = \frac{F(K_t, N_t)}{N_t} - \frac{C_t}{N_t} - \delta \frac{K_t}{N_t} = f(k_t) - c_t - \delta k_t,$$

and, taking into account that

$$\dot{k}_t = \frac{\dot{K}_t}{N_t} - \frac{\dot{N}_t}{N_t} k_t = \frac{\dot{K}_t}{N_t} + nk_t,$$

we obtain,

$$f(k_t) = c_t + \dot{k}_t + (n+\delta)k_t, \tag{2.14}$$

the identity that describes the uses of income, in per-capita terms: each worker's output is used in part as consumption and as a net addition to the stock of capital, which may be positive or negative. The rest reflects the need to recover the capital lost by depreciation, as well as to provide each new worker with the same units of capital associated to each old worker. The number of workers grows at a rate n, and population growth acts as some sort of depreciation. In fact, it is impossible to disentangle in this model the effects of δ and n.

Since $C_t = (1-s)Y_t$, we can divide by N_t to obtain, in per capita terms,

$$c_t = (1-s) f(k_t),$$

and finally,

$$\dot{k}_t = sf(k_t) - (n+\delta) k_t, \tag{2.15}$$

which is the *law of motion* of the economy, showing how the stock of capital per worker increases in those periods in which savings $sf(k_t)$ exceeds from capital depreciation $(\delta+n)k_t$.

2.3.2.1 Technological Growth

Maintaining the above assumptions on savings, capital formation, population sgrowth and full employment, let us now consider the possibility that there is *exogenous technological growth*, in the form of a variable productivity factor Γ_t, that grows at a constant rate γ:

$$\frac{\dot{\Gamma}_t}{\Gamma_t} = \gamma, \ \forall t.$$

We assume now that the available technology can be represented by an aggregate production function $Y_t = F(K_t, \Gamma_t N_t)$, with $F_{K_t}, F_{\Gamma_t N_t} > 0$, second derivatives: $F_{K_t, \Gamma_t N_t} > 0$, $F_{\Gamma_t N_t, \Gamma_t N_t} < 0$, $F_{K_t, K_t} < 0$ and a negative definite Hessian, so that F is concave. Additionally, $F(K_t, 0) = F(0, \Gamma_t N_t) = 0$, so that we cannot produce anything without using positive amounts of the two inputs, and $\lim_{K_t \to 0} F_{K_t} = \lim_{\Gamma_t N_t \to 0} F_{\Gamma_t N_t} = \infty$, $\lim_{K_t \to \infty} F_{K_t} = \lim_{\Gamma_t N_t \to \infty} F_{\Gamma_t N_t} = 0$.

Introduced this way, technological progress, represented by Γ_t is said to be of the *labor-saving* type, because as Γ_t grows, we will be able to produce a given output with a lower amount of the labour input.[5] The second input in the production function, $\Gamma_t N_t$, is then known as *effective labor*. The more restrictive aspect of this technology is again the existence of decreasing returns to scale in each input, which precludes the possibility of positive steady-state growth.

---

[5] It is also sometimes known as *neutral* in the sense defined by Harrod.

The aggregate constant returns to scale assumption allows us to write,

$$Y_t = F(K_t, \Gamma_t N_t) = \Gamma_t N_t F\left(\frac{K_t}{\Gamma_t N_t}, 1\right) = \Gamma_t N_t f(k_t), \tag{2.16}$$

where $k_t = \frac{K_t}{\Gamma_t N_t}$ denotes *now* the stock of *capital per unit of effective labor*, and $f(k_t) = F(\frac{K_t}{\Gamma_t N_t}, 1)$. The main variables in the economy can be represented in terms of this ratio. For instance, from the last equation, we have output per unit of effective labor:[6]

$$y_t = \frac{Y_t}{\Gamma_t N_t} = f(k_t).$$

An example of such a production function is, $F(K_t, \Gamma_t N_t) = AK_t^\alpha (\Gamma_t N_t)^{1-\alpha}$, with output:

$$Y_t = AK_t^\alpha (\Gamma_t N_t)^{1-\alpha} = A\Gamma_t N_t k_t^\alpha = \Gamma_t N_t f(k_t)$$
$$\text{with } 0 < \alpha < 1 \text{ and } f(k_t) = Ak_t^\alpha,$$

so that, *output per unit of effective labor* is,

$$y_t = \frac{Y_t}{\Gamma_t N_t} = Ak_t^\alpha, \ \ 0 < \alpha < 1.$$

Marginal productivity for each input is again related to the derivatives of $f(k_t)$. First, taking derivatives in (2.16) with respect to K_t,

$$F_{K_t} = \Gamma_t N_t f'(k_t) \frac{\partial k_t}{\partial K_t} = \Gamma_t N_t f'(k_t) \frac{1}{\Gamma_t N_t} = f'(k_t) > 0.$$

On the other hand, taking derivatives in (2.16) with respect to N_t we get,

$$F_{N_t} = \Gamma_t f(k_t) + \Gamma_t N_t f'(k_t) \left(\frac{-\Gamma_t K_t}{(\Gamma_t N_t)^2}\right) = \Gamma_t \left[f(k_t) - k_t f'(k_t)\right].$$

Output is again either consumed or used as gross investment, and we have the same global constraint of resources as before,

$$Y_t = C_t + I_t = C_t + \dot{K}_t + \delta K_t,$$

that is,

$$\dot{K}_t = F(K_t, \Gamma_t N_t) - C_t - \delta K_t.$$

---

[6] The argument in Sect. 2.2, suggests that, under our maintained assumption of decreasing returns to scale, the ratios of physical capital and output per unit of effective labour will experience zero growth in steady-state. In turn, that would imply that per-capita variables like $\frac{K_t}{N_t}$ or $\frac{Y_t}{N_t} = \Gamma_t f(k_t)$ will grow in steady-state at a rate γ_A. These results are shown in the next section.

Dividing by the number of effective units of labor, we have,

$$\frac{\dot{K}_t}{\Gamma_t N_t} = \frac{F(K_t,\Gamma_t N_t)}{\Gamma_t N_t} - \frac{C_t}{\Gamma_t N_t} - \delta \frac{K_t}{\Gamma_t N_t} = f(k_t) - c_t - \delta k_t,$$

where we have used the fact that the homogeneity of degree one of $F(.,.)$ allows us to write: $\frac{F(K_t,\Gamma_t N_t)}{\Gamma_t N_t} = F(\frac{K_t}{\Gamma_t N_t}, \frac{\Gamma_t N_t}{\Gamma_t N_t}) = F(\frac{K_t}{\Gamma_t N_t}, 1) = f(k_t)$. We denote consumption per unit of effective labor by $c_t = \frac{C_t}{\Gamma_t N_t}$. Taking into account that

$$\dot{k}_t = \frac{\dot{K}_t}{\Gamma_t N_t} - \frac{\Gamma_t \dot{N}_t}{\Gamma_t N_t} k_t - \frac{\dot{\Gamma}_t N_t}{\Gamma_t N_t} k_t = \frac{\dot{K}_t}{\Gamma_t N_t} - (n+\gamma) k_t,$$

we get,

$$f(k_t) = c_t + \dot{k}_t + (n+\delta+\gamma) k_t, \tag{2.17}$$

the identity that explores the uses of income, in per-capita terms: each worker's output is used in part as consumption and net additions to the stock of capital. The rest reflects the need to recover the capital lost by depreciation, as well as the need to provide to each new worker with the same capital per units of effective labor owned by each old worker. The number of workers grows at a rate n, while the general level of productivity grows at a rate γ. Again in this model, population growth acts as some sort of depreciation.

Finally,

$$Y_t = C_t + I_t = C_t + S_t = C_t + sY_t,$$

so that, $C_t = (1-s)Y_t$ and, dividing through by $\Gamma_t N_t$ we get, in effective units of labor,

$$c_t = (1-s)f(k_t), \tag{2.18}$$

and

$$\dot{k}_t = sf(k_t) - (n+\delta+\gamma) k_t, \tag{2.19}$$

which is the law of motion of the economy, showing how the stock of capital per unit of effective labor increases in those periods in which per capita savings $sf(k_t)$ exceeds total capital depreciation $(n+\delta+\gamma) k_t$.

2.3.3 Steady-State

Definition 1. In an exogenous growth economy, a *steady-state* is a vector of values for the rates of growth of the main variables (physical capital, output and consumption) in units of effective labor, that if it is ever reached, it can be maintained constant forever.

A steady-state is often referred to as a long-run equilibrium, because of the characteristic of having a constant rate of growth for appropriately defined variables.

Let us consider again the economy's *law of motion* (2.19), from which the growth rate of capital can be written,

$$\gamma_{k_t} = \frac{\dot{k}_t}{k_t} = s\frac{f(k_t)}{k_t} - (n + \delta + \gamma). \tag{2.20}$$

In steady state, γ_{k_t} must be constant, so that $\frac{f(k_t)}{k_t}$ must also be constant. Its time derivative is,

$$\frac{d\left[\frac{f(k_t)}{k_t}\right]}{dt} = \frac{k_t f'(k_t) - f(k_t)}{k_t}\frac{\dot{k}_t}{k_t} \underset{in\ steady\ state}{=} 0.$$

Since $k_t f'(k_t) - f(k_t)$ is the negative of the marginal product of labor, which we assumed to be positive, then we will have in steady state $\frac{\dot{k}_t}{k_t} = 0$, which implies $\dot{k}_t = 0$, and the stock of capital per unit of effective labor will remain constant in steady-state. That, in turn, implies that the stock of productive capital per worker will grow at a rate γ. To see the relationship between the growth rates of income and capital, notice that,

$$\frac{Y_t}{N_t} = F\left(\frac{K_t}{N_t}, \Gamma_t\right) = \frac{K_t}{N_t}F\left(1, \frac{\Gamma_t}{K_t/N_t}\right),$$

and, since $k_t = \frac{K_t}{N_t\Gamma_t}$ is constant in steady-state, output and capital will grow at the same rate. In units of effective labor, these variables grow at a zero rate, while in per capita units they grow at a rate γ. In aggregate terms, they grow at a rate $n + \gamma$. Since consumption is proportional to income, consumption per-capita will also grow at a rate γ, while remaining constant in steady-state in units of effective labor. Even though per-capita variables experience growth in steady-state, since the common growth rate, γ, is exogenous to the model, we say this is an *exogenous growth model*.

Summarizing, steady state is characterized in this economy by $\dot{k}_t = 0$ so that, from (2.19), steady state levels of k_t are solutions to,

$$sf(k_{ss}) - (n + \delta + \gamma)k_{ss} = 0, \tag{2.21}$$

which defines the value of the stock of capital per unit of effective labor in steady state, k_{ss}. The properties of the solution to this equation like its existence and uniqueness, or the way how it is affected by structural parameters, depend on the specific production function assumed. Figure 2.3a shows the possibility of multiple steady-states. The upper graph presents them by the intersection between the $sf(k_{ss})$ curve and the $(n + \delta + \gamma)k_{ss}$ straight line. The lower graph displays the associated time derivatives of the stock of capital per unit of effective labor, as defined by (2.19). However, for standard production functions satisfying the Inada conditions above, (2.21) will have a single non-zero solution, the steady state then being uniquely defined [Fig. 2.3b]. The stock of capital increases to the left of the steady-state, while decreasing to the right of it.

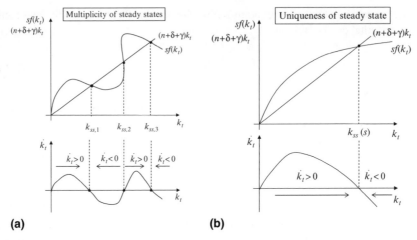

(a)   (b)

Fig. 2.3

Figure 2.3b shows how $k_{ss} = 0$ is another steady-state. It solves equation (2.21) because $f(0) = 0$. At that point, there is zero physical capital, so production is zero and consumption is also zero. There can be no investment, and savings will be zero no matter what the savings rate is, since there are no resources. The economy never leaves this situation, although it has no economic interest.

As an example, let us consider again the Cobb–Douglas production technology $Y_t = F(K_t, \Gamma_t N_t) = AK_t^\alpha (\Gamma_t N_t)^{1-\alpha}, 0 < \alpha < 1$, which can also be represented: $y_t = Ak_t^\alpha, 0 < \alpha < 1$. Steady state is then characterized by,

$$sAk_{ss}^\alpha = (n + \delta + \gamma) k_{ss}.$$

The single solution[7] to that equation is,

$$k_{ss} = \left(\frac{sA}{n + \delta + \gamma} \right)^{\frac{1}{1-\alpha}}, \qquad (2.22)$$

so that the steady-state level of physical capital, in units of efficient labor is higher for higher values of the constant savings rate, while being lower for higher values of either the rate of population growth, the depreciation rate of physical capital, or the rate of growth of productivity. It is also higher the higher the value of the elasticity of physical capital in the production function representing the aggregate technology.

A higher savings rate allows for a more important capital accumulation, leading to a higher stock of physical capital. On the other hand, a higher rate of depreciation detracts more resources from net capital accumulation. Higher population requires more resources to be devoted to provide newborn consumers with the same stock of

---

[7] The equation has another root: $k_{ss} = 0$. This would be a steady-state with zero capital, output and consumption.

physical capital as the already existing consumers. Since we are working with variables in terms of efficient units of labor, technological growth enters the model symmetrically with population growth, so the dependence of steady-state levels with respect to this variable is also negative. Finally, a higher elasticity of physical capital creates a higher incentive for capital accumulation, leading to a higher steady-state level of physical capital.

Output is increasing on the level of physical capital, so that the steady-state levels of output and consumption, in efficient units of labor, y_{ss}, c_{ss}, will also depend on the values of structural parameters, $s, n, \delta, \gamma, \alpha$ as described for k_{ss}. The reader must be careful not to use the (2.18) representation to extrapolate a similar dependence of consumption on the values of structural parameters, because of the presence of the savings rate in that expression. We will get back to this issue in Sect. 2.3.8.

Figure 2.4 shows the dependence of the steady-state on the level of the constant savings rate. An increase in savings rate will raise the slope of the $sf(k_t)$-curve, which will intersect the straight line to the right of the current steady-state. So, the stock of capital per unit of efficient labor will rise and so will do income, investment and consumption. The Figure shows that there is a limit to such a process. When $s = 1$, the $sf(k_t)$-curve coincides with the production function $f(k_t)$, and we have what is known as the *subsistence* steady-state, $\hat{k}$, that in which

$$f\left(\hat{k}\right) = (n + \delta + \gamma)\hat{k}.$$

In the *subsistence* steady-state, so much physical capital has been accumulated, that all output is needed to replace what is lost to physical depreciation as well as to provide new workers with the same stock of physical capital than older workers. There are no resources left for consumption, which is hence equal to zero. Each value of the constant savings rate between 0 and 1 is associated with a steady-state level of capital per unit of labor between 0 and $\hat{k}$. Situations with $k_{ss} > \hat{k}$ are not sustainable as steady states, since they would imply negative consumption.

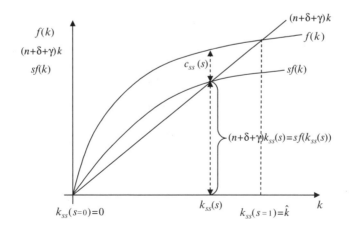

Fig. 2.4 Steady-state as a function of savings rate

2.3.4 The Transition Towards Steady-State

Outside the steady-state the growth rate of the economy is not constant but, rather, it behaves according to (2.20), changing with the level of k_t. We call *transition* the process that unfolds from the starting situation, with a capital stock of k_0, towards the steady-state level.

The first term in that expression, $sf(k_t)/k_t$, is a continuous, decreasing function of k_t which starts at infinity for $k_t = 0$, converging to zero for $k_t = \infty$, as can easily be seen by taking limits. The second term is a constant, represented by a horizontal straight line in Fig. 2.5. Hence, there is some single value of the capital stock for which $sf(k_{ss})/k_{ss} = \delta + n + \gamma$ and so, $\gamma_{k_t} = 0$. The point at which the growth rate of capital per unit of effective labor becomes zero is the single steady-state of the economy, k_{ss}. Since the growth rate γ_{k_t} becomes positive for any stock of capital below the steady-state level, and negative for any capital stock above steady-state, the model implies a monotonic convergence to steady-state so, the *steady-state is globally stable*.

The gap in Fig. 2.5 between the two lines is precisely the growth rate γ_{k_t}, which can be seen to reduce in size as the economy approaches steady-state from either side. As pointed out in Barro and Sala-i-Martin [6], when k_t is relatively low, the average product of capital, $f(k_t)/k_t$, is relatively large, due to the law of diminishing returns. Since consumers save a constant proportion of that product, gross investment per unit of capital, $sf(k_t)/k_t$, which is proportional to the average product of capital, will also be large. With a constant depreciation rate, that will make $\dot{k}_t/k_t$ to be relatively high, and the opposite happens for high levels of k_t. Analytically, changes in γ_{k_t} as the stock of capital changes are given by,

$$\frac{\partial \gamma_{k_t}}{\partial k_t} = s\frac{k_t f'(k_t) - f(k_t)}{k_t^2} < 0,$$

which is negative, since the numerator is equal to minus the marginal product of labor.

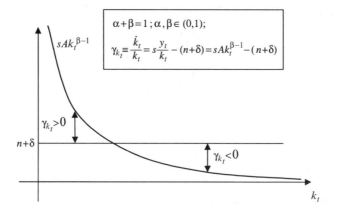

$$\alpha + \beta = 1 \, ; \alpha, \beta \in (0,1);$$

$$\gamma_{k_t} \equiv \frac{\dot{k}_t}{k_t} = s\frac{y_t}{k_t} - (n+\delta) = sAk_t^{\beta-1} - (n+\delta)$$

Fig. 2.5 Steady-state determination under Cobb-Douglas technology

2.3.5 The Duration of the Transition to Steady-State

To have an idea of how fast the economy approaches steady-state, we focus on analyzing $\dot{k}_t$ rather than γ_{k_t}. If we construct the linear approximation of the law of motion for capital around steady-state, we get,

$$
\begin{aligned}
\dot{k}_t &\simeq \left[sf(k_{ss}) - (\delta + n + \gamma) k_{ss} \right] + \left[sf'(k_{ss}) - (\delta + n + \gamma) \right] (k_t - k_{ss}) \\
&= \left[\frac{(\delta + n + \gamma) k_{ss} sf'(k_{ss})}{sf(k_{ss})} - (\delta + n + \gamma) \right] (k_t - k_{ss}) \\
&= (\alpha_k(k_{ss}) - 1)(\delta + n + \gamma)(k_t - k_{ss}),
\end{aligned}
$$

where to obtain the first equality, we have used the fact that, in steady-state $sf(k_{ss}) = (\delta + n + \gamma) k_{ss}$ and where we have defined the elasticity of output with respect to the stock of capital,

$$
\alpha_k(k_t) = \frac{k_t f'(k_t)}{f(k_t)} \in (0, 1).
$$

Under constant returns to scale, $\alpha_k(k_t)$ is also physical capital's share in income distribution. In the Cobb–Douglas production function, $\alpha_k(k_t) = \alpha$, constant. Borrowing from competitive equilibrium ideas, capital would be rented by firms at a price equal to its marginal product, and $\alpha_k(k_t)$ would the proportion of output that would be devoted to pay back to the owners of capital.

Changes in k_t will then be explained by,

$$
\dot{k}_t = -(1 - \alpha_k(k_{ss}))(\delta + n + \gamma)(k_t - k_{ss}) \tag{2.23}
$$

which depends negatively on the distance to steady-state k_{ss}. Hence, the stock of capital per unit of effective labor changes faster initially, when the economy is far from steady state, moving more gradually as the economy approaches its steady-state.[8]

The solution to the differential equation (2.23) is,

$$
k_t - k_{ss} = e^{-(1 - \alpha_k(k_{ss}))(\delta + n + \gamma)t} (k_0 - k_{ss}) = e^{-\mu t} (k_0 - k_{ss}), \tag{2.24}
$$

with $\mu = (1 - \alpha_k(k_{ss}))(\delta + n + \gamma)$. For instance, if we assume that $\alpha_k(k_{ss}) = 1/3$, and $n + \delta + \gamma = 6\%$, then $\mu = 4\%$, so that 4% of the difference between k_t and k_{ss} is closed each period. Half of the initial distance to steady-state would then be closed after 17 periods.

2.3.6 The Growth Rate of Output and Consumption

Because of the global stability of the Solow–Swan model, the model predicts that any economy is either at steady-state, or converging to it. We consider in this section an economy outside steady-state. Because of the global stability of the model, that

---

[8] Notice that this is a result on absolute changes in the stock of capital per unit of effective labor, while the result above was on its rate of growth.

economy will be in a transition phase towards steady-state. Along the transition, the behavior of output is characterized by,

$$\gamma_{y_t} = \frac{\dot{y}_t}{y_t} = \frac{f'(k_t)}{f(k_t)} \dot{k}_t = k_t \frac{f'(k_t)}{f(k_t)} \gamma_{k_t} = \alpha_k(k_t) \gamma_{k_t}. \qquad (2.25)$$

As an example, if the aggregate technology is of the Cobb–Douglas type, then capital's share is $\alpha_k(k_t) = \alpha$, and, along the transition,

$$\gamma_{y_t} = \alpha \gamma_{k_t},$$

the growth rates of income and capital behave similarly, decreasing in magnitude as the economy approaches steady-state.

More generally, we can use (2.20) for γ_{k_t} in (2.25) to get,

$$\gamma_{y_t} = sf'(k_t) - (n + \delta + \gamma) \alpha_k(k_t),$$

so that,

$$\frac{\partial \gamma_{y_t}}{\partial k_t} = \frac{f''(k_t) k_t}{f(k_t)} \gamma_{k_t} - \frac{(n + \delta + \gamma) f'(k_t)}{f(k_t)} (1 - \alpha_k(k_t)),$$

and since $0 \le \alpha_k(k_t) \le 1$, then $\frac{\partial \gamma_{y_t}}{\partial k_t} < 0$ at those points at which $\gamma_{k_t} \ge 0$. If, on the contrary, $\gamma_{k_t} < 0$, then the sign of $\frac{\partial \gamma_{y_t}}{\partial k_t}$ is ambiguous. However, in the proximity of the steady-state, γ_{k_t} will be small, and $\frac{\partial \gamma_{y_t}}{\partial k_t} < 0$. This means that if the economy starts with a capital stock below k_{ss}, both, k_t and y_t will increase, but the rate of growth of income per unit of effective labor, γ_{y_t}, will fall down as we approach steady state, as it is the case with γ_{k_t}. If, on the contrary, the initial stock of capital is above k_{ss}, then k_t and y_t will decrease, but we cannot say anything in general about the behavior of γ_{y_t}. However, once we get close enough to steady-state, γ_{y_t} will gradually increase as the stock of capital keeps falling towards k_{ss}. It may surprise to see that the rate of growth of y_t is increasing in spite of the fact that the stock of capital is falling down to k_{ss}, but it is a negative rate of growth. So, what we have is that as the stock of capital falls down towards steady-state, income per unit of effective labor is falling towards the new steady-state at a decreasing rate. For a relatively high k_t, depreciation is so high that savings and investment are not enough to replace depreciation and hence, the stock of capital decreases and output falls. As the stock of capital decreases from its initially high level, less resources need to be devoted to compensate for depreciation, and income per unit of effective labor falls by a lesser amount, until it stabilizes in its new sustainable steady-state.

On the other hand, since the maintained assumption of this model is,

$$c_t = (1 - s) y_t,$$

then,

$$\gamma_{c_t} = \gamma_{y_t}, \quad \forall t,$$

at any point outside the steady-state. Growth rates of per-capita variables will be equal to the growth rates calculated in this section added by γ, while growth rates for economy-wide aggregates will be the previous ones added by n.

2.3.7 Convergence in the Neoclassical Model

We have so far analyzed the implications of the neoclassical growth model on the evolution of a specific economy. We have characterized the existence of a single steady-state or long-run equilibrium and its dependence on the values of some structural parameters. But the previous discussion has also implications on the comparative evolution of economies from different countries, so long as these can be assumed to fulfill the assumptions characterizing the Solow–Swan model. We are particularly interested on possible implications on whether any two different economies will tend to be more similar to each other over time or rather, differences between them will tend to increase.

We say that two economies *converge in absolute terms* if, starting from a different initial situation in terms of the endowment of physical capital per unit of effective labor, k_0, k'_0, and, hence, in terms of their levels of income per unit of effective labor, the difference between them narrows over time. Let us consider two economies sharing the same values of the structural parameters, s, n, δ, γ, but differing in their initial stocks of capital. The long-run equilibrium (steady-state) levels of physical capital, consumption and income per unit of efficient labor will be the same in both economies. Let us assume that one of them, the *poor economy*, has an initial capital stock k_0^p lower than that of the *rich economy*, k_0^r. Figure 2.6, that presents the determination of both growth rates, shows that the growth rate of the poor economy will be higher than that of the rich economy, so that the respective stocks of capital and,

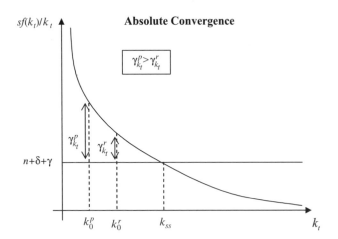

Fig. 2.6

hence, the levels of output (or income) per-unit of effective labor, will become more similar over time, as both converge to the same steady-state level. As a consequence, the neoclassical model implies absolute convergence among countries.

This suggests that a regression like,

$$\gamma_{k_t} = \beta_0 + \beta_1 \ln k_t + u_t, \ \beta_1 < 0,$$

which explains the growth rate of the economy as a function of its current situation, would be an adequate representation of the time series produced by a neoclassical growth model with either time series or cross-section data. Actually, what we have seen as an implication of the Solow–Swan model is that the growth rate depends on the relative distance of income or productive capital from their steady-state values. Hence, a more appropriate representation would be,

$$\gamma_{k_t} = \beta_0 + \beta_1 \left(\ln k_t - \ln k_{ss} \right) + u_t, \tag{2.26}$$

where k_{ss} could be estimated from its expression[9], after having some estimates of the values of structural parameters.

Empirical analysis does not show evidence on this type of convergence, unless we limit our consideration to a set of homogeneous economies (states in the US, OECD countries, province economies in a given country, etc.). One possible reason for that is that a broader set of economies may display substantial differences among their savings rates. In Fig. 2.7, we have labelled as *poor* the economy with the lower savings rate, which implies, as we already know, a lower capital stock and lower per

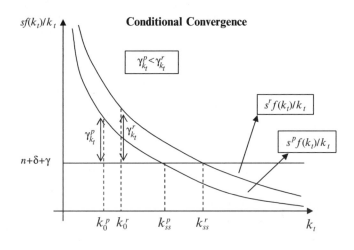

Fig. 2.7

---

[9] It is clear that, being a constant, the correction on physical capital data would not need to be done to estimate the regression, so long as we are careful when interpreting the estimated intercept, although estimates of (2.26) would have a more direct interpretation.

capita income in steady-state. This figure shows that when economic structures are different, it is perfectly possible that the rich country may grow faster then the poor country, if the former is relatively farther away from its steady-state.

This means that empirical analysis should take into account the fact that different countries may have a different steady-state. This is done by conditioning the time evolution of γ_{k_t} on the determinants of steady-state. The result is then known as *conditional convergence*. The neoclassical growth model we have discussed implies that countries with different structural characteristics will experience conditional convergence: once we correct for the fact that the two economies have a different long-run equilibrium, poorer economies should be seen to experience faster growth than richer ones.

The correction is made by adding to the econometric model a vector z_t of variables determining steady-state k_{ss},

$$\gamma_{k_t} = \beta_0 + \beta_1 \ln k_t + \phi \ln z_t + u_t,$$

with ϕ being a vector of the same dimension as z_t. In the neoclassical Solow–Swan model z_t could include the savings rate, depreciation rate, population growth or the output elasticity of physical capital. Sometimes, other indicators as the level of education in the population, expenditures in infrastructures, and so on, are included in z_t, although these are not justified by the Solow–Swan model. In more elaborated models where the savings rate and the rate of technological progress are endogenous, and the role of the government is explicitly considered, there will be an even richer set of variables in z_t.

Similar regressions could be estimated for output per unit of effective labor or for per capita output, if we assume a given value for γ.

2.3.8 A Special Steady-State: The Golden Rule of Capital Accumulation

We remember that steady-state is defined by the relationships,

$$sf(k_{ss}) = (n + \delta + \gamma) k_{ss},$$

$$c_{ss} = f(k_{ss}) - (n + \delta + \gamma) k_{ss},$$

which we have used in the previous section to show that the steady-state stock of productive capital moves in parallel with the level of the savings rate s. That is, for given values of structural parameters $n, \delta, \gamma, \alpha$, the implied steady-state levels of physical capital, output and consumption will depend on the constant value chosen for the savings rate. Since the savings rate affects the stock of capital, and this influences consumption [see (2.18)], it makes sense to ask about the value of the savings rate that would maximize the steady-state level of consumption. That level of savings, and the associated steady-state, are known as the Golden-Rule of capital accumulation.

From the last equation, we see that steady-state consumption will be maximum when $\partial c_{ss}/\partial k_{ss} = 0$, $\partial^2 c_{ss}/\partial k_{ss}^2 < 0$. That happens at the point where,

$$f'(k_{ss}^{GR}) = n + \delta + \gamma, \tag{2.27}$$

that is, the point at which the slope to $f(k)$ is parallel to the straight line $(n+\delta+\gamma)k$. That determines the Golden-Rule level of physical capital in units of efficient labor, k_{ss}^{GR}. The Golden Rule savings rate, s_{GR}, is the value of s for which the function $sf(k)$ intersects the $(n+\delta+\gamma)k$ straight line at k_{ss}^{GR} [see Fig. 2.8].

In the Cobb–Douglas case, $y_t = Ak_t^\alpha$, the Golden Rule condition takes the form,

$$A\alpha k^{\alpha-1} = \delta + n + \gamma,$$

leading to,

$$k_{ss}^{GR} = \left(\frac{\alpha A}{n+\delta+\gamma}\right)^{\frac{1}{1-\alpha}},$$

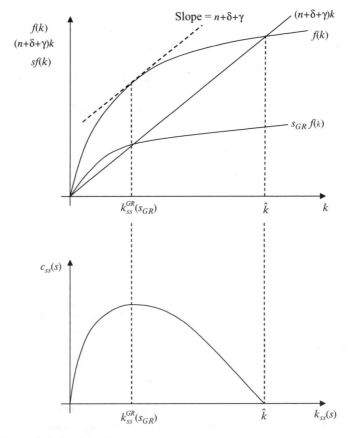

Fig. 2.8 Golden Rule determination

which, by comparison with (2.22) shows that, under this technology, the Golden Rule is *the steady-state arising for a constant savings rate equal to the output elasticity of capital*. Since constant returns to scale lead to a competitive equilibrium allocation with zero profits, and output being distributed to each factor according to their output elasticities, the Golden Rule can also be interpreted as the result of following either the rule: *"Save all capital income"* or, alternatively, *"Consume all labor income"*.

In fact, we now show that this is a general result that does not depend on the available technology, beyond the assumptions made in the Solow–Swan economy. First, notice, that the two statements above are equivalent in this economy because *i*) being a closed economy with no government, what is not consumed it is saved, and *ii*) because the constant returns to scale assumption implies that all output (income) is distributed between the production factors, with no residual profit. Indeed, if we make savings equal to capital income, we have,

$$sY_t = F_{K_t}K_t \Rightarrow sf(k_t) = F_{K_t}\frac{K_t}{\Gamma_t N_t} = f'(k_t)k_t,$$

and, since any steady-state satisfies: $sf(k_{ss}) = (n + \delta + \gamma)k_{ss}$, the condition above implies,

$$f'(k_{ss}^{GR}) = n + \delta + \gamma,$$

so that the only steady state satisfying the described condition is the Golden Rule. This means that in the Golden Rule there are no income transfers between the capital and labor factors. To maintain a steady state with capital above k_{ss}^{GR} there would be a need for a high level of investment, to recover the capital lost to depreciation. That way, it will not be enough with capitalists investing all income they receive as owners of capital, and workers will also have to devote part of their labor income to investment. There will then be an income transfer from workers to the owners of capital. The opposite result would arise in a steady-state below k_{ss}^{GR}.

It would be wrong to interpret the Golden Rule of capital accumulation as an optimal allocation of resources.[10] Since the Golden Rule is the steady-state or long-run equilibrium offering the maximum consumption, it is clear that, unless the utility function of consumers presents a bliss point, the Golden Rule should be preferred to any other possible steady-state. But that is only true if we could place the economy initially at a steady-state of our choice. Unfortunately, that is not the case. The economy is endowed with a given stock of capital per unit of efficient labor, k_0, and its structural characteristics, together with a chosen rate of savings s, will determine the long-run equilibrium. However, to bring the economy to that equilibrium, the economy will go through a transition process, with physical capital converging from k_0 to k_{ss}.

---

[10] The following argument rests on utility comparisons, and we have not specified consumer preferences in this Chapter. It is nevertheless interesting as an introduction to the type of normative analysis that is done in subsequent chapters. In fact, we will address again the suboptimality of the Golden Rule in Chap. 3.

So, suppose that, starting from k_0, consumers choose a savings rate of precisely s_{GR}, the level at which the $sf(k)$-curve intersects the straight line $(n+\delta+\gamma)k$ at k_{ss}^{GR}. The long-run equilibrium or steady-state stock of capital will we k_{ss}^{GR}, but the economy will enter into a *transition* phase towards k_{ss}^{GR} along which it is quite likely that it will have to make some sacrifices in terms of consumption. Once the economy reaches the Golden Rule, consumers will enjoy a higher level of consumption than can be enjoyed at any other steady-state, but it is unclear that the time aggregate level of utility along the whole trajectory would be maximized, precisely because of the initial sacrifice in consumption.

For instance, we could compare utility along the trajectory converging from k_0 to k_{ss}^{GR}, with the one that would be obtained with a savings rate of s_0, the one that would have allowed for maintaining the initial stock of capital k_0, unchanged forever. The result of such comparison is far from obvious, since it depends on: *i*) the magnitude of short-run sacrifices needed to implement a savings rate of s_{GR}, *ii*) the differences between the level of utility provided by the Golden Rule level of consumption, and that corresponding to maintaining a steady-state of k_0, *iii*) the discount applied to future utility, and *iv*) how long it takes for the economy to be in the neighborhood of the Golden Rule, when the savings rate of s_{GR} is implemented.

These effects are far from trivial. To analyze whether consumers' would be better off by staying at their current steady-state or by starting a transition trajectory taking them to the Golden Rule, we need to be able to compute the time series representing the paths followed by the main variables under each scenario, with which to evaluate specific utility functions, as it is done in future chapters.

2.4 Solving the Continuous-Time Solow–Swan Model

2.4.1 Solution to the Exact Model

As in many other models that will be reviewed in future chapters, the time evolution of the stock of capital per worker obeys a nonlinear, first order differential equation, for which a closed form analytical solution generally does not exist. Such a solution exists in the Solow–Swan model, however, and we can find continuous functions of time: $k_t \equiv k(t), y_t \equiv y(t), c_t \equiv c(t), s_t \equiv i_t \equiv s(t) = sy_t$, describing the exact time paths for the capital stock, output, consumption and savings or investment.

We start from the law of motion under a Cobb–Douglas technology,

$$\dot{k}_t = sAk_t^\alpha - (n+\delta+\gamma)k_t, \qquad (2.28)$$

with a steady state defined by $\dot{k}_t = 0$, which leads to,

$$k_{ss} = \left(\frac{sA}{n+\delta+\gamma}\right)^{\frac{1}{1-\alpha}}. \qquad (2.29)$$

If we introduce a new variable $z_t = k_t^{1-\alpha}$, we have $\dot{z}_t = (1-\alpha) k_t^{-\alpha} \dot{k}_t$, and multiplying through (2.28) by $(1-\alpha) k_t^{-\alpha}$, we get,

$$\dot{z}_t = (1-\alpha) sA - (1-\alpha)(n+\delta+\gamma) z_t,$$

a linear differential equation, with solution $z_t = Me^{\mu t} + J$. To find the values of the constants M, μ, J we first write the time derivative $\dot{z}_t = M\mu e^{\mu t}$ which, taken to the equation, yields $\mu = -(1-\alpha)(n+\delta+\gamma)$, $J = \frac{sA}{n+\delta+\gamma}$, so that $z_t = Me^{-(1-\alpha)(n+\delta+\gamma)t} + \frac{sA}{n+\delta+\gamma} = k_t^{1-\alpha}$. The remaining constant will be determined from a boundary condition. In this case, since the starting capital stock k_0 is given, we have at $t = 0$, $k_0^{1-\alpha} = M + \frac{sA}{n+\delta+\gamma}$, so that $M = k_0^{1-\alpha} - \frac{sA}{n+\delta+\gamma}$, and the solution to the original law of motion, finally, satisfies

$$k_t^{1-\alpha} = \left(k_0^{1-\alpha} - \frac{sA}{n+\delta+\gamma} \right) e^{-(1-\alpha)(n+\delta+\gamma)t} + \frac{sA}{n+\delta+\gamma}, \qquad (2.30)$$

from which output, consumption, and investment/savings would be obtained through $y_t = k_t^{\alpha}$, $c_t = (1-s)y_t$, $i_t = s_t = sy_t$. Notice that, as time passes, we have $\lim_{t\to\infty} k_t = \left(\frac{sA}{n+\delta+\gamma} \right)^{\frac{1}{1-\alpha}}$, and the economy converges to steady-state, reflecting the *global stability* of the exact system.

2.4.2 The Linear Approximation to the Solow–Swan Model

Even the simpler growth models have a complex enough structure that prevents from computing an exact analytical solution. As we have just seen, the continuous-time version of the Solow–Swan is an exception. Since we will more often find the opposite situation, we familiarize now the reader with the standard approach of finding an approximation to the model, for which an exact solution can often be found.

Using Taylor's expansion, we can find the linear approximation to (2.19) around steady state k_{ss}. To do so, we need to consider that equation as a function: $\dot{k}_t = \Psi(k_t; \theta)$, where $\theta = (s, A, n, \delta, \alpha)$ is the vector of structural parameters, with a linear approximation:

$$\dot{k}_t \simeq \Psi(k_{ss}; \theta) + \left(\frac{\partial \Psi(k_t; \theta)}{\partial k_t} \right)_{ss} (k_t - k_{ss}) \Rightarrow$$
$$\dot{k}_t \simeq [sf(k_{ss}) - (n+\delta+\gamma)k_{ss}] + [sf'(k_{ss}) - (n+\delta+\gamma)](k_t - k_{ss})$$
$$= [sf'(k_{ss}) - (n+\delta+\gamma)](k_t - k_{ss}), \qquad (2.31)$$

since the constant term is equal to zero. The coefficient of $k_t - k_{ss}$, $sf'(k_{ss}) - (n+\delta+\gamma)$, is negative, since the $sf(k_t)$-curve crosses the $(n+\delta+\gamma)k_t$-line from above. Hence, if we start from below steady-state, the difference $k_t - k_{ss}$ will be negative, and $\dot{k}_t$ will be positive, indicating that physical capital will accumulate and the economy will converge to steady state. If we start from above steady state, the difference $k_t - k_{ss}$ will be positive, so $\dot{k}_t$ will be negative, indicating that physical capital will diminish while the economy gradually converges to steady state. So,

$$k_t < k_{ss} \Rightarrow \dot{k}_t > 0,$$
$$k_t > k_{ss} \Rightarrow \dot{k}_t < 0,$$

and the linearized model is also *globally stable,* the stock of capital converging towards its steady-state level, no matter whether its initial endowment of physical capital, k_0, is above or below steady-state level, k_{ss}.

2.4.2.1 Analytical Solution for the Cobb–Douglas Case

We examine now the special case of a Cobb–Douglas technology. We will have the law of motion for the stock of capital,

$$\dot{k}_t = sAk_t^\alpha - (n + \delta + \gamma)k_t$$
$$\simeq [sAk_{ss}^\alpha - (n + \delta + \gamma)k_{ss}] + [s\alpha Ak_{ss}^{\alpha-1} - (n + \delta + \gamma)](k_t - k_{ss}),$$

which, using the steady state level of the capital-labor ratio k_{ss} characterized in (2.22), leads to,

$$\dot{k}_t \simeq [s\alpha Ak_{ss}^{\alpha-1} - (n + \delta + \gamma)](k_t - k_{ss}) = D(k_t - k_{ss}), \qquad (2.32)$$

with $D = s\alpha Ak_{ss}^{\alpha-1} - (n + \delta + \gamma) = -(1 - \alpha)(n + \delta + \gamma) < 0$, so that the coefficient of $k_t - k_{ss}$ in the linear approximation to the law of motion of the economy is negative, guaranteeing stability of the implied solution, as we have seen in the previous paragraph for the more general case.

This linear approximation in the Cobb–Douglas case (2.32) can be solved analytically. To that end, we try with a linear solution: $k_t = a + be^{\mu t}$ which, plugged into the differential equation (2.32), together with a given initial condition $k(t = 0) = k_0$, leads to,[11]

$$k_t = k_{ss} + e^{Dt}(k_0 - k_{ss}) = (1 - e^{Dt})k_{ss} + e^{Dt}k_0, \qquad (2.33)$$

showing that the stock of capital converges to steady state at a rate D, since taking time derivatives in this expression, we get: $\dot{k}_t/k_t = \frac{d(k_t - k_{ss})/dt}{k_t - k_{ss}} = D$.

---

[11] Substitution of the proposed solution yields, $b\mu e^{\mu t} = Da + Dbe^{\mu t} - Dk_{ss}$ which can hold only if $\mu = D, a = k_{ss}$. Hence, we have: $k_t = k_{ss} + be^{Dt}$. To determine the value of the constant b we use the initial condition: $k_0 = k_{ss} + b$, so that: $b = k_0 - k_{ss}$.

2.4.3 Changes in Structural Parameters

This section is devoted to analyzing the long-run effects, i.e., the effects on steady-state levels of the main variables, of permanent changes in the values of structural parameters. We start by paying special attention to a change in the savings rate, since that is the parameter more easily linked to a policy intervention in this model, and extend the discussion to the remaining structural parameters later on.

2.4.3.1 A Change in Savings Rate

Let us assume that, starting at steady-state, with constant levels of the main variables in units of efficient labor, and a physical capital ratio k_{ss}^1, there is an increase in s, the constant savings rate. Then, the steady-state level of the physical capital ratio would increase to a new level k_{ss}^2, since its level depends positively on the value of the savings rate. A higher savings rate shifts the $sf(k_t)$ upwards, while leaving the $(n+\delta+\gamma)k_t$ function unchanged. Therefore, at k_{ss}^1 we will no longer be at steady-state but rather, to the left of it. As a consequence, right after the increase in savings rate, the stock of capital starts a gradual increase. A similar process is followed by income, $y_t = f(k_t)$, its rate of growth instantaneously jumping and becoming positive at the time of the increase in the rate of savings, and gradually decreasing back to zero as capital and income converge to their new steady-state levels. Later on, when the level k_{ss}^2 is attained, income per unit of efficient labor will again remain constant. Consumption $c_t = (1-s)f(k_t)$ experiences a discontinuity, with an initial fall due to the increase in s. These effects are shown in Fig. 2.9.

With respect to steady-state effects on consumption, we have from (2.17),

$$c_{ss} = f(k_{ss}) - (\delta + n + \gamma)k_{ss},$$

so that,

$$\frac{\partial c_{ss}}{\partial s} = [f'(k_{ss}) - (\delta + n + \gamma)]\frac{\partial k_{ss}}{\partial s},$$

which will be positive so long as,

$$f'(k_{ss}) > \delta + n + \gamma,$$

because $\frac{\partial k_{ss}}{\partial s}$ is always positive, as can be seen in (2.29). Initial consumption will always experience a jump down if a higher savings rate is implemented, but steady-state consumption can be either above or below the steady-state level of consumption with the old savings rate, as we will show in a numerical exercise in Sect. 2.5.4. In fact, an examination of (2.27) shows that steady-state consumption will increase following a rise in savings rate if the initial steady-state had a stock of capital below that associated to the Golden Rule, decreasing otherwise.

Effects following a fall in savings rate are just the opposite of those discussed above.

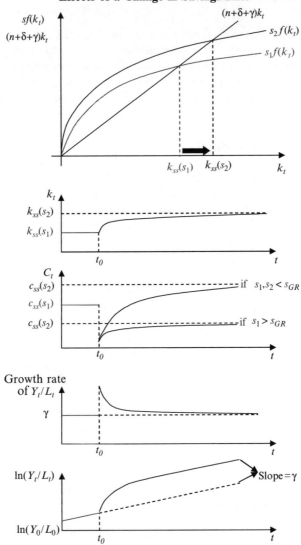

Fig. 2.9

2.4.3.2 Structural Changes

We extend now the analysis of the previous paragraph, to consider the effects of changes in the values of the savings rate, s, the rate of growth of population, n, the rate of depreciation of physical capital, δ, the rate of technological growth, γ, and the output elasticity of capital, α. These effects can be summarized,

$$
\begin{pmatrix}
 & k_{ss} & c_{ss} & y_{ss} & \omega_{ss} & r_{ss} & Y/K & Y/N & \dot{Y}/Y \\
s & + & ? & + & + & - & - & + & 0 \\
n & - & - & - & - & + & + & - & + \\
\delta & - & - & - & - & + & + & - & 0 \\
\gamma & - & - & - & - & + & + & - & + \\
\alpha & + & + & + & + & - & - & + & 0
\end{pmatrix}
$$

where ω_{ss}, r_{ss} denote steady state values of the real wage and the real rate of interest. The reader may be familiar with the standard result that, when a firm takes factor prices as determined outside their control, profit maximization leads to use the production factors to the point where their marginal products equal their respective price. Even though we do not enter at this point in any detailed assumption on the structure of markets for production factors, we use the mentioned properties to justify considering real wages and interest rates defined by,[12]

$$
\omega_t = f(k_t) - k_t f'(k_t),
$$
$$
r_t = f'(k_t),
$$

with similar relationships holding in steady-state. The real rate of interest is inversely related to the steady-state stock of capital, while the real wage is positively related to it:

$$
\frac{\partial r_{ss}}{\partial \eta} = \frac{\partial r_{ss}}{\partial k_{ss}} \frac{\partial k_{ss}}{\partial \eta} = f''(k_{ss}) \frac{\partial k_{ss}}{\partial \eta}
$$
$$
\Rightarrow sign\left(\frac{\partial r_{ss}}{\partial \eta}\right) = -sign\left(\frac{\partial k_{ss}}{\partial \eta}\right), \ \eta = n, \delta, \gamma, s, \alpha
$$
$$
\frac{\partial \omega_{ss}}{\partial \eta} = \frac{\partial \omega_{ss}}{\partial k_{ss}} \frac{\partial k_{ss}}{\partial \eta} = -k_{ss} f''(k_{ss}) \frac{\partial k_{ss}}{\partial \eta}
$$
$$
\Rightarrow sign\left(\frac{\partial \omega_{ss}}{\partial \eta}\right) = sign\left(\frac{\partial k_{ss}}{\partial \eta}\right), \ \eta = n, \delta, \gamma, s, \alpha.
$$

To analyze the effect of a parameter change on consumption and output we use the relationships:

$$
\frac{\partial c_{ss}}{\partial \xi} = (1-s)f'(k_{ss}) \frac{\partial k_{ss}}{\partial \xi} \Rightarrow sign\left(\frac{\partial c_{ss}}{\partial \xi}\right) = sign\left(\frac{\partial k_{ss}}{\partial \xi}\right); \xi = n, \delta, \gamma, \alpha
$$
$$
\frac{\partial c_{ss}}{\partial s} = (1-s)f'(k_{ss}) \frac{\partial k_{ss}}{\partial s} - f(k_{ss}),
$$
$$
\frac{\partial y_{ss}}{\partial \eta} = f'(k_{ss}) \frac{\partial k_{ss}}{\partial \eta}; \ \eta = n, \delta, \gamma, s, \alpha \Rightarrow sign\left(\frac{\partial y_{ss}}{\partial \eta}\right) = sign\left(\frac{\partial k_{ss}}{\partial \eta}\right).
$$

---

[12] This assumption is not a proper element of the Solow–Swan model, which does not leave any role for a profit maximizing behavior on the part of producers of the single good in the economy.

The average product of capital $Y_t/K_t = \frac{f(k_t)}{k_t}$ satisfies: $\frac{\partial (Y_t/K_t)}{\partial k_t} = -\frac{f(k_t) - k_t f'(k_t)}{k_t^2}$ which is negative, since the numerator is equal to the real wage. Hence, average productivity of capital moves contrary to the *capital-labor* ratio. On the other hand, the average product of labor, $\frac{Y_t}{\Gamma_t N_t} = f(k_t)$, moves in the same direction as the capital-labor ratio. Finally, the rate of growth of output (or income) can be written: $\dot{Y}_t/Y_t = \dot{y}_t/y_t + n + \gamma$, its steady-state value being affected just by population growth and the rate of technological progress, since the rate of growth of income per unit of effective labor is zero in steady-state.

As an example, we have already seen that an increase in savings rate raises the steady-state stock of capital and output. The effect on the steady-state level of consumption depends on whether the initial stock of physical capital is above or below the Golden Rule level. The real rate of interest and the average productivity of capital will be lower while the real wage and the marginal product of labor will increase.

A change in savings rate could be thought of as being an economic policy intervention, specially since a higher rate will take the economy to a steady-state with higher per capita income. However, as discussed in the section devoted to the Golden Rule, it is far from clear that the sacrifices needed to place the economy on the path converging to the higher income steady-state are desirable in terms of time aggregate welfare. There is no much more room for policy analysis in the Solow–Swan setup, since it is hard to believe that the depreciation rate of physical capital or the rate of growth of population could be controlled by the government[13].

2.4.4 Dynamic Inefficiency

If we consider an economy at a steady-state situation under a given savings rate, and we want that economy to converge to the Golden Rule, all we need to do is to set the savings rate equal to s_{GR}, since the global stability of the Solow–Swan model guarantees that any economy will converge to the steady-state associated to the prevailing savings rate. Following such change in savings rate, the economy would start a transition, along which the level of consumption will be changing every period, eventually converging to the level achieved at the Golden Rule. However, single-period consumption along the transition might be not only lower than the Golden Rule level, but also lower than the level of consumption at the initial steady-state. This is important, since it is then unclear that consumers' would prefer entering into the transition trajectory taking the economy to the Golden Rule, to staying at the initial steady-state.[14]

As we pointed out at Sect. 2.3.8, factors influencing that comparison are: the magnitude of the utility loss along the transition, the difference in the utility levels

---

[13] Even though in some European countries, tax incentives have recently been introduced in an attempt to increase the birthrate.

[14] The reader should not have much problem thinking about an economy which starts outside steady-state and changes its savings rate to s_{GR}.

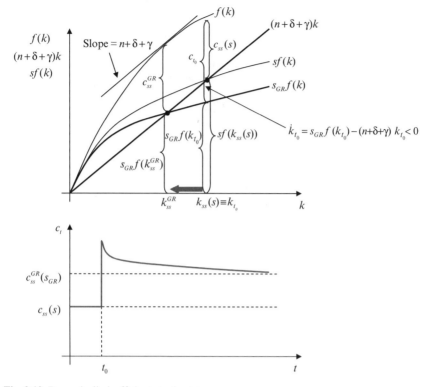

Fig. 2.10 Dynamically inefficient steady-state

at the Golden Rule and at the initial steady-state, the number of periods needed to reach the Golden Rule, the time discount factor applied to future utility. Let us now see how all these effects aggregate. Steady-states to the right of k_{ss}^{GR}, between k_{ss}^{GR} and $\hat{k}$, are *dynamically inefficient*, since starting from either one of them, a decrease in the savings rate starts a trajectory along which, at any time period, per-capita consumption is higher than at the initial state. Starting from either one of these steady-states, consumers would be happy to change the prevailing savings rate to s_{GR} forever.

In Fig. 2.11, suppose we start from a savings rate of s and a steady-state stock of capital equal to $k_{ss}(s)$. If we reduce the savings rate to s_{GR}, then per capita consumption will *immediately jump* from $c_{ss}(s)$ to c_{t_0}, which is higher than c_{ss}^{GR}. This dynamics implies a *gradual decrease* in the stock of capital, from $k_{ss}(s)$ towards k_{ss}^{GR}, which will imply, in turn, that per capita consumption will *gradually decrease* from c_{t_0} towards c_{ss}^{GR}. But c_{ss}^{GR} is still higher than $c_{ss}(s)$, since the Golden Rule is the steady-state with the highest consumption. Therefore, the decrease in the savings rate will have produced a path along which, at each point in time, per capita consumption is higher than the initial consumption level, before the change in savings

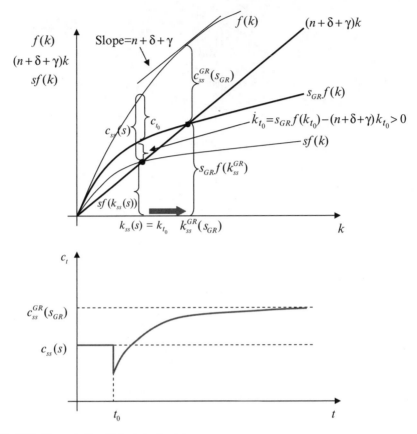

Fig. 2.11 Dynamically efficient steady-state

rate. This is true for any steady state to the right of the Golden Rule, which is why they are said to be *dynamically inefficient*.

The opposite is the case for steady-states to the left of k_{ss}^{GR}. Starting from $k_{ss}(s)$ in Fig. 2.10, a permanent increase in savings rate from s to s_{GR} will produce an immediate fall in consumption from $c_{ss}(s)$ to c_{t_0}. This is lower than initial consumption, $c_{ss}(s)$, and also lower than the level of consumption at the Golden Rule. The new steady-state is given by k_{ss}^{GR}, and the stability of the model implies that the economy starts a trajectory with the stock of capital gradually increasing from $k_{ss}(s)$ to k_{ss}^{GR}. The graph shows how along that trajectory, given the savings rate of s_{GR}, the level of consumption will gradually increase towards c_{ss}^{GR}. We know that c_{ss}^{GR} will be higher than $c_{ss}(s)$, since that is the characteristic defining the Golden Rule among all feasible steady-states. However, along the transition, consumption would have spent some periods below the level of the initial steady state. Hence, it is unclear that when we compute the associated period-by-period utility and aggregate over time its discounted value, we will reach a higher or a lower level than the one that would be obtained at the initial steady-state. We cannot say whether these steady-states are dynamically inefficient or not. An informal argument suggests that it is those steady-states with a low rate of savings which may be dynamically inefficient, since the associated level of consumption might then be very low. As a consequence, even though an increase in savings rate will require consumption sacrifices in the short-run, the opportunity to accumulate physical capital and reach higher levels of output and consumption may compensate for the short-run sacrifices. The elements mentioned in Sect. 2.3.8 will help determine which is the range of values for the saving rate for which a permanent increase may be welfare improving. A numerical examination of this issue is performed in a section below for the discrete time version of the Solow–Swan model, that we introduce next.

2.5 The Deterministic, Discrete-Time Solow Swan Model

2.5.1 The Exact Solution

Theoretical models are built not only to analyze a variety of positive and normative issues, but also to be confronted with actual data, in an attempt to validate their implications. The continuous-time version of the Solow–Swan model can be used to produce time series for physical capital, output, consumption and investment by sampling at discrete points in time, from the continuous time processes obtained from (2.30) and the implied expressions for the remaining variables. Discrete sampling amounts to giving discrete values: $t = 1, 2, 3, \ldots$ to the time index in those expressions. This apparently innocuous procedure is subject, however, to potential pitfalls, that will be illustrated numerically in the next chapter.

An alternative method consists on analyzing directly the discrete version of the Solow–Swan model. To do so, we could think of directly translating the law of motion into discrete time by substituting a time difference $k_{t+1} - k_t$ for the time derivative $\dot{k}_t$, like in:

$$k_{t+1} - k_t = sf(k_t) - (n + \delta + \gamma)k_t. \tag{2.34}$$

Unfortunately, we are about to see that this procedure is also subject to some flaws. If we start from the discrete time analytical representation of all the assumptions characterizing the model, we will end up with a fully justified equation somewhat different from (2.34).

Maintaining the same assumptions on savings, capital formation, population growth and full employment as in the continuous time version of the model, let us now consider the possibility that there is *exogenous technological growth*, in the form of a variable productivity factor Γ_t, that grows at a constant rate γ:

$$\Gamma_t = (1 + \gamma)\Gamma_{t-1} ,$$

from an initial Γ_0 level. The aggregate production function is of the form $Y_t = F(K_t, \Gamma_t N_t)$, with the same assumptions on first and second order derivatives as in the continuous time model. Inada conditions are also assumed to hold. *Effective labor* is again defined as $\Gamma_t N_t$.

Because of the aggregate constant returns to scale assumption we again have,

$$Y_t = F(K_t, \Gamma_t N_t) = \Gamma_t N_t F\left(\frac{K_t}{\Gamma_t N_t}, 1\right) = \Gamma_t N_t f(k_t),$$

where $k_t = \frac{K_t}{\Gamma_t N_t}$ is the stock of *capital per unit of effective labor*, and $f(k_t) = F(\frac{K_t}{\Gamma_t N_t}, 1)$. Output per unit of effective labor is: $y_t = \frac{Y_t}{\Gamma_t N_t} = f(k_t)$. With the Cobb–Douglas specification, $F(K_t, \Gamma_t N_t) = AK_t^\alpha(\Gamma_t N_t)^{1-\alpha}$, $0 < \alpha < 1$, we have the same expressions as in continuous time: $Y_t = AK_t^\alpha(\Gamma_t N_t)^{1-\alpha} = A\Gamma_t N_t k_t^\alpha = \Gamma_t N_t f(k_t)$, with $f(k_t) = Ak_t^\alpha$ and *output per unit of effective labor*: $y_t = \frac{Y_t}{\Gamma_t N_t} = Ak_t^\alpha$.

In the discrete time version of the model investment is defined by: $I_t = K_{t+1} - (1-\delta)K_t$, so the National Income identity becomes,

$$C_t + I_t = C_t + [K_{t+1} - (1-\delta)K_t] = F(K_t, \Gamma_t N_t) = Y_t \Rightarrow$$

$$\Rightarrow \frac{C_t}{\Gamma_t N_t} + \left[\frac{K_{t+1}}{\Gamma_{t+1}N_{t+1}}\frac{\Gamma_{t+1}N_{t+1}}{\Gamma_t N_t} - (1-\delta)\frac{K_t}{\Gamma_t N_t}\right] = \frac{Y_t}{\Gamma_t N_t},$$

which, maintaining the assumption of constant population growth,[15] $N_t = (1+n)^t N_0$, and constant technological growth, $\Gamma_t = (1+\gamma)^t A_0$, leads to the law of motion in per capita variables,

$$c_t + [(1+n)(1+\gamma)k_{t+1} - (1-\delta)k_t] = f(k_t). \tag{2.35}$$

If we again consider a closed economy in which no external sector or government could finance private investment, we will have equality between savings and investment each period $S_t = I_t$, and if we add the crucial assumption of the Solow–Swan model that the savings rate is constant, we have, $S_t = sY_t$,

$$C_t + sY_t = Y_t \Rightarrow C_t = (1-s)Y_t,$$

with a similar relationship in per capita terms, $c_t = (1-s)y_t = (1-s)f(k_t)$, which allows us to write (2.35) as,

$$k_{t+1} = \frac{1}{(1+n)(1+\gamma)}sf(k_t) + \frac{1-\delta}{(1+n)(1+\gamma)}k_t. \tag{2.36}$$

Now we can see the point we raised before. This equation can be written,

$$k_{t+1} - k_t = sf(k_t) - [n + (1+n)\gamma]k_{t+1} - \delta k_t, \tag{2.37}$$

---

[15] Notice the different analytical representation for growth rates, relative to the exponential functions used in the continuous-time version of the model.

which shows some differences with respect to (2.34). The latter was just a rough approximation to the continuous time model, expression (2.37) being the correct discrete-time version of the model.

This difference equation allows us to obtain a numerical solution to the model given an initial condition on the single state variable in the economy, the stock of capital, k_0, a specific functional form for the available technology, $f(k_t)$, and a given parameterization. Indeed, if we assume, for instance, $f(k_t) = Ak_t^\alpha$, then we could substitute the numerical value defining the initial condition on k_0 for k_t in (2.37) to obtain the level of k_1. We would then use k_1 as k_t in the equation, to obtain the level of k_2, and so on. The time series for output would be obtained from $y_t = f(k_t) = Ak_t^\alpha$, investment, which is equal to savings in this closed economy without government would be given by $i_t = s_t = sy_t$, while the time series for consumption would be obtained by: $c_t = (1-s)y_t = y_t - i_t$. This is the *exact solution* to the deterministic, discrete-time version of the Solow–Swan model.

An argument similar to the one we made in the continuous time case, shows that zero is the only possible steady-state rate of growth of the stock of capital per worker. The steady state of this economy is found by making $k_{t+1} = k_t = k_{ss}$,

$$k_{ss} = \frac{1}{(1+n)(1+\gamma)}sf(k_{ss}) + \frac{1-\delta}{(1+n)(1+\gamma)}k_{ss} \Rightarrow \quad (2.38)$$
$$\Rightarrow [n+\delta+(1+n)\gamma]k_{ss} = sf(k_{ss}).$$

Once again, we have one such expression for each possible constant value of the savings rate, each one leading to a different steady-state. For instance, with a Cobb–Douglas technology, $y_t = Ak_t^\alpha$, we would get,

$$k_{ss} = \left(\frac{sA}{n+\delta+(1+n)\gamma}\right)^{\frac{1}{1-\alpha}}, \quad (2.39)$$

slightly different from the expression we obtained in the continuous time formulation of the model. In general, the product $n\gamma$ will be small, so both expressions will lead to a similar steady-state. Since the power is positive, (2.39) shows that the steady-state level of the stock of capital is higher for higher savings rates or higher technology levels, as well as for lower depreciation rates or lower rates of population growth, as in the continuous time case.

2.5.2 Approximate Solutions to the Discrete-Time Model

As the continuous-time model, the discrete-time version of the Solow–Swan economy can be solved exactly through the use of (2.36), as we will show in a section below. That is an exception, since nonlinearities in growth models will usually preclude the existence of an exact solution. To familiarize the reader with that practice, we proceed in this section to obtain the solution to the *linear* and the *quadratic approximations* to the model.

Considering the nonlinear difference equation in (2.36) as a function $k_{t+1} = \Psi(k_t; \theta)$ and using Taylor's expansion and (2.38), the *linear approximation* to that equation around steady-state is,

$$k_{t+1} - k_{ss} = \Psi(k_{ss}) + \left(\frac{\partial \Psi(k_t; \theta)}{\partial k_t} \right)_{ss} (k_t - k_{ss})$$

$$\Rightarrow k_{t+1} \simeq \left(\frac{1}{(1+n)(1+\gamma)} sf(k_{ss}) + \frac{1-\delta}{(1+n)(1+\gamma)} k_{ss} \right)$$

$$+ \left(\frac{1}{(1+n)(1+\gamma)} sf'(k_{ss}) + \frac{1-\delta}{(1+n)(1+\gamma)} \right) (k_t - k_{ss})$$

$$= k_{ss} + \frac{sf'(k_{ss}) + (1-\delta)}{(1+n)(1+\gamma)} (k_t - k_{ss}),$$

which, in the special case of a Cobb-Douglas technology, $f(k_t) = Ak_t^\alpha, 0 < \alpha < 1$, becomes,

$$k_{t+1} \simeq k_{ss} + \frac{s\alpha A(k_{ss})^{\alpha-1} + (1-\delta)}{(1+n)(1+\gamma)} (k_t - k_{ss}) = k_{ss} + D(k_t - k_{ss}), \qquad (2.40)$$

with

$$D = \frac{s\alpha A(k_{ss})^{\alpha-1} + (1-\delta)}{(1+n)(1+\gamma)}$$

$$= \alpha \frac{n + \delta + (1+n)\gamma}{(1+n)(1+\gamma)} + \frac{1-\delta}{(1+n)(1+\gamma)}, \qquad (2.41)$$

where we have used (2.39) to obtain the last expression and, finally, the linear approximation,

$$k_{t+1} - k_{ss} \cong D(k_t - k_{ss})$$

$$= \left[\frac{(1+\alpha n) - (1-\alpha)\delta}{(1+n)(1+\gamma)} + \alpha \frac{\gamma}{1+\gamma} \right] (k_t - k_{ss}). \qquad (2.42)$$

Iterating from an initial condition k_0, we get,

$$k_t = k_{ss} + D^t (k_0 - k_{ss}), \qquad (2.43)$$

which will converge to steady state so long as $|D| < 1, i.e.,$ if:

$$(1-\alpha)(n + \delta + (1+n)\gamma) > 0,$$

which is clearly the case, since $0 < \alpha < 1$. Therefore, under this condition, the linearized system is *stable*. As time passes, the capital stock converges to its steady-state level, k_{ss}, with independence of the initial stock of capital, as we have already shown to happen in the continuous time version of the model.

For a better approximation, we could also use a second order Taylor's expansion to (2.36), by adding to the linear approximation a second order term

$$\frac{1}{2}\left(\frac{\partial^2 \Psi(k_t;\theta)}{\partial (k_t)^2}\right)_{ss}(k_t - k_{ss})^2 = \frac{1}{2}\frac{1}{(1+n)(1+\gamma)}sf''(k_{ss})(k_t - k_{ss})^2,$$

which, in the case of a Cobb–Douglas technology, leads to the approximation,

$$k_{t+1} \simeq k_{ss} + \left[\frac{(1+\alpha n)-(1-\alpha)\delta}{(1+n)(1+\gamma)} + \alpha\frac{\gamma}{1+\gamma}\right](k_t - k_{ss})$$

$$+\frac{1}{2}\frac{\alpha(\alpha-1)}{(1+n)(1+\gamma)}sAk_{ss}^{\alpha-2}(k_t - k_{ss})^2. \tag{2.44}$$

In the numerical exercise in the next section, this approximation is compared to the linear approximation above.

2.5.3 Numerical Exercise – Solving the Deterministic Solow–Swan Model

In the *Discrete* spreadsheet in the *Solow_deterministic.xls* file, time series are obtained for a deterministic, discrete-time version of the Solow–Swan economy from an initial capital stock of $k_0 = 20$. Aggregate technology is supposed to be of the Cobb–Douglas type, with a capital share of $\alpha = 0.36$, and a technological constant $A = 5.0$. Depreciation of physical capital is $\delta = 7.5\%$, savings are 36.0% of output each period, and we assume zero population growth, $n = 0$. Since the savings rate is equal to the output elasticity of capital, the steady-state in this economy will be the Golden Rule.[16] With these parameter values, steady state levels turn out to be: $k_{ss} = 117.94, y_{ss} = 27.85, c_{ss} = 17.82, s_{ss} = i_{ss} = 10.02$. Therefore, the economy starts to the left of the steady-state, with a stock of capital well below the steady-state level. The constant savings rate is relatively high, and capital accumulates quickly because the level of savings initially exceeds from total depreciation expenditures.[17] After 16 periods, the economy has covered half the initial distance to steady-state, with a stock of capital above 70 units. The *Discrete* spreadsheet presents time series for 260 periods, and the discrete time model is solved using the exact solution (2.36), as well as using the solutions to the linear and quadratic approximations (2.43), (2.44) to the discrete-time model. The resulting time series for the stock of capital under the different approaches are reported in the first panel. The time series for output, savings and consumption that are obtained under the exact solution are shown in panel 2, while panels 3 and 4 display the similar time series obtained

---

[16] This is not necessary for the exercise, as the reader may see by changing the value of either the savings rate or the output share of capital.

[17] Which are obtained by adding the depreciation loss to the need to provide new workers with the same stock of capital than the older ones.

under the linear and quadratic approximations to the model. Notice that, according
to the model, output is obtained each period from the stock of capital accumulated
at the end of the previous period. As in subsequent exercises, this is organized in
the spreadsheet by making output to be a function of the stock of capital in the previous row. That is, in the row corresponding to time t we have k_{t+1} and variables
like y_t, c_t. [The same exercise can be reproduced by Matlab file: *Solow_stochastic.m*
by setting the variance parameter *sigmae* to zero] Consumers' preferences do not
play any role in this exercise. Nevertheless, to familiarize the reader with the type of
welfare evaluation that will often be performed in the next chapters, consumers are
supposed to have a constant relative risk aversion utility function, $U(c_t) = \frac{c_t^{1-\sigma}-1}{1-\sigma}$,
with risk aversion coefficient of $\sigma = 3.0$, and a time discount factor $\beta = .95$, and we
compute single-period as well as time-aggregate, discounted utility.

We also present percent errors from the linear and the quadratic approximation,
both for the stock of capital and for consumption. The approximation error for the
capital stock starts around 17% in the initial periods, when the economy is far away
from steady-state, increasing during the first periods up to 40% of the actual value,
and quickly going to zero over time. These clearly excessive errors steam from the
fact that the initial condition is far away from the steady-state, the point around
which we have done the approximations to the law of motion of the economy. The
approximation error for consumption starts at around 6%, and increases in the initial
phase of the transition to steady-state, decreasing to zero as time passes. As can be
seen in the reported time series and the accompanying graph (*Comparing solutions*
spreadsheet), approximation errors for the linear and the quadratic approximations
are very similar, so that the contribution of the quadratic term to the linear approximation is minor.

For the sake of comparison, we also compute in panel 1 the time series that would
be obtained by observing the continuous process at regular intervals of time. We
report time series obtained from the exact solution to the continuous-time model
(2.30), as well as those obtained form the solution to the linear approximation to
that model (2.32). Unfortunately, as we already mentioned, and it will be discussed
in the next chapter, this latter approach of extracting discrete numerical observations from a continuous process is potentially subject to significant pitfalls. In this
case, however, the exact continuous and discrete solutions are very similar to each
other, while the continuous linear approximation is very close to the discrete linear
approximation.

The *Increasing time path* and *Decreasing time path* spreadsheets present two
transition economies. Both share the same parameter values: $\alpha = 0.36$, $A = 3.0$.
$\delta = 7.5\%$, $s = 0.30$, $n = 0.01$, $\gamma = .01$. The implied steady-state is: $k_{ss} = 33.504$,
$y_{ss} = 10.621$, $c_{ss} = 7.435$, $s_{ss} = i_{ss} = 3.186$. Since the savings rate is lower than the
output elasticity of capital, this steady-state falls below the Golden Rule, which is in
this case: $k_{GR} = 44.547$. In the first economy, initial capital is $k_0 = 30.0$, converging to steady-state from below, as it was the case with the economy in the *Discrete*
spreadsheet. The second economy starts from $k_0 = 45.0$, converging to steady-state
from above. In these two exercises, we present in Panel 1 the time series for the stock
of capital, investment, consumption, output and output growth, as well as single

period utility and its discounted value using the exact solution. The last column shows the time series for the stock of capital that would be obtained observing the continuous solution at discrete intervals of time. In Panel 2 we show the full solution obtained from the linear approximation (2.42) to the discrete-time problem, while Panel 3 displays the solution obtained from the discrete quadratic approximation (2.44). Approximation errors are much smaller in these two economies, as a consequence of their relative proximity to steady-state.

2.5.4 Numerical Exercise – A Permanent Change in the Savings Rate

The discrete-time version of the Solow–Swan economy is numerically solved in the *Change_savings.xls* file to simulate the effects of a *permanent increase* in the constant savings rate. The analytical details of this structural change were described in Sect. 2.4.3 [Matlab file: *change_savings.m* performs the same exercise]. Two different parameter structures are analyzed, and in each of the two implied model economies we consider a permanent increase in the savings rate. The exercise is performed twice, to analyze the effects of changes of different size in the savings rate. Effects from a permanent fall could be discussed similarly.

Consumption always falls immediately after the jump in savings rate. In one of the two economies, long-run consumption ends up above its steady-state level before the rise in savings rate, while in the other economy, steady-state consumption after the increase in savings rate is below the steady-state level of consumption for the initial, lower savings rate. As we saw in Sect. 2.4.3, the long-run effect on steady-state consumption of a permanent change in savings rate depends on whether the initial steady-state is above or below the Golden Rule. Steady-state consumption may end up being higher under a higher savings rate because that may allow for a more intense accumulation of capital stock, leading to higher output, which may leave more resources available for consumption, even after providing for the reposition of the stock of capital lost to depreciation.

Assuming a Cobb–Douglas technology, parameter values for the first economy are $\delta = 0.075, n = 0.01, A = 3.0, \alpha = 0.36, \gamma = 0.0$. The population starts at $t = 0$ from an initial value of 100. In the $C - increases(large)$ spreadsheet, the initial savings rate is $s = 0.20$, which is in place until period $t = 11$, when it increases to $s = 0.35$. The steady state stock of capital under the initial savings rate is $k_{ss} = 21.19$, which allows for steady-state output: $y_{ss} = Ak_{ss}^{\alpha} = 9.006$. A percentage of 20% of this, 1.801 units of commodity, are devoted to investment, the remaining 7.205 units of commodity being consumed. The 1.801 units of commodity being invested allow for recovering the depreciation loss of 7.5% of k_{ss}, in addition to providing the 1% new consumers/workers being born every period, with the 21.19 units of steady state capital. In other words, 1.801 is precisely equal to 8.5% of steady-state capital $(n + \delta + \gamma = 0.085)$, as we know it should be the case. Under the new savings rate of $s = 0.35$, the steady-state level of physical capital is 50.80 units, with output: $y_{ss} = Ak_{ss}^{\alpha} = 12.338$. Investment is 35% of output, or 4.318 units of commodity, with consumption equal to 8.020 units of commodity every period in the new steady-state. So, the new, higher savings rate, allows for such an increase in the stock of capital that resources left for consumption after the reposition of depreciated capital are higher than those that could be consumed under the old, lower savings rate of 20%. We assume the representative consumer in the economy has a constant, relative risk aversion utility function on current consumption: $U(c_t) = \frac{c_t^{1-\sigma}-1}{1-\sigma}$, with $\sigma = 3.0$, and a discount factor on future utility of $\beta = 0.95$.

We solve the economy in three ways: first, we provide in Panel 1 the exact solution, obtained from the difference equation (2.36).The second method uses the linear approximation (2.43) to steady-state to obtain the stock of capital as a function of the distance between the previous period stock of capital and the steady-state level [Panel 2]. The third solution approach uses the second order approximation around steady-state (2.44) [Panel 3].

The savings rate is supposed to change at $t = 11$. It is central to the exercise to examine how the stock of physical capital is computed at that period. At that point in time, the economy is no longer in steady state. The new value of the savings rate must be used in equations (2.36), (2.43), (2.44), when computing the exact solution, or the solutions to the linear and quadratic approximations to the model, respectively. Additionally, in (2.43) and (2.44), the steady-state level of capital under the new, higher savings rate must replace the steady-state level obtained under the old savings rate. The value of the D-constant in the linear approximation does not need to be updated in this case, since it is not affected by changes in savings rate. Changes in the rate of depreciation, the output elasticity of capital or population growth would change the value of D.

Graphs under the *Comparing solutions* and *Approximation error* spreadsheets shows that numerical differences among solution methods can be relatively large if the change in savings rate is sizeable. In particular, the quadratic term does not add anything significant to the linear approximation, both being very similar. That is the case in this first simulation, in which the savings rate jumps from 20% to 35%, and the percent approximation error approaches 4% for a few periods after the change, to then gradually decrease towards zero.

In all cases, output is obtained using the analytical representation for the Cobb–Douglas production function, savings is obtained as a proportion of income, investment is equal to savings, and consumption is the proportion of output which is not saved. Growth in per-capita output is also computed under the three solution approaches, and it is displayed in the *Output growth* spreadsheet for the first experiment. Numerical values for single period utility are also reported. These are also discounted and aggregated over time. The resulting level of welfare is 9.804 under the linear approximation and to 9.802 under the exact solution.

Graphs to the right of the simulated data display the time behavior of the main variables after the savings rate increases from 20% to 35%. Growth of output per unit of efficient labor jumps from 0% to 2.2% the period when savings rate increases, smoothly decreasing to zero afterwards.

The $C - increases$ $(small)$ spreadsheet presents an experiment in the same economic structure as above, but with a smaller increase in savings rate, which moves from 30% to 35% at $t = 11$. For the sake of comparison, we have maintained the same ranges in the graphs displaying the responses of the main variables in the spreadsheets that contain the two changes considered in savings rate. It is quite evident that the effects of the 5-point increase in savings considered in the second case are rather smaller than those of the 10-point increase considered in the first analysis.

The $C - decreases$ $(small)$ spreadsheet presents a case in which steady-state consumption decreases following an increase in the savings rate from 30% to 35%. Remaining parameters are $\delta = 2.5\%, n = 1.0\%, A = 5.0, \alpha = 0.25$. The steady state stock of capital under the initial savings rate is $k_{ss} = 149.98$, which allows for steady-state output: $y_{ss} = Ak_{ss}^{\alpha} = 17.50$. A percentage of 30% of these, 5.249 units of commodity, are devoted to investment, the remaining 12.248 units of commodity being consumed. The resources being saved allow for recovering the depreciation loss of 2.5% of k_{ss}, in addition to providing the 1% new consumers/workers being born every period with the 149.98 units of steady state capital. In other words, 5.249 is equal to 3.5% of steady-state capital $(n + \delta + \gamma = 0.035)$. Under the new savings rate of $s = 35\%$, the steady-state level of physical capital is 184.20 units, with output: $y_{ss} = Ak_{ss}^{\alpha} = 18.42$. Investment is 35% of output, or 6.447 units of commodity, with consumption equal to 11.973 units of commodity every period in the new steady-state. So, in this case, the higher savings rate leads to an increase in capital accumulation, but the implied growth in per capita income is not enough to allow for higher steady-state consumption once capital depreciation is accounted for. We maintain the same preferences but consider a discount factor $\beta = 0.90$.

The $C - decreases$ $(large)$ spreadsheet presents the same exercise above, except for a somewhat increase in savings rate, from $s = 30\%$ to $s = 40\%$.

2.5.5 Numerical Exercise – Dynamic Inefficiency

The *Dynamic_inefficiency.xls* file [Matlab file: *Dynamic_inefficiency.m* performs the same exercise] presents the transition trajectories for a number of economies differing in the level of their savings rate. Growth in technology is not considered in this exercise, so $\gamma = 0$. Each economy is supposed to be initially at steady-state. At some point, the savings rate experiences a permanent change, jumping to the level corresponding to the Golden Rule, where it stays forever. As we already know, that level is equal to the output elasticity of physical capital, which is taken to be 0.36 in this exercise. After the change in savings rate, the stock of capital quickly approximates the level corresponding to the Golden Rule. If the savings rate was initially above 0.36, the stock of capital will exponentially decrease after the fall in savings rate, the opposite being the case if the savings rate increases from an initial steady value below 0.36.

After presenting the parameter values in the *Simulations* spreadsheet, we provide the different levels of the savings rate considered, together with their associated

steady-state levels of physical capital and consumption, the single period utility in
the steady-state prior to the change in savings rate and the time aggregate utility
that would obtain by staying at that steady-state, i.e., the time aggregate level of
utility with no change in savings rate. Steady-state consumption is zero for $s = .0$
or $s = 1.0$, so the level of utility cannot be computed in this case for some utility
functions.

Below that, we present time series over 250 periods along the convergence trajectories for the stock of capital. To compute them, we have used the law of motion for
capital after a permanent switch to the Golden Rule of savings, starting from a stock
of capital equal to the steady-state level before the change in savings rate. The panel
below the trajectories for the stock of capital presents the consumption trajectories
in their convergence to the Golden Rule steady-state: $c_t = (1 - s_{GR})y_t = (1 - \alpha)Ak_t^\alpha$.
Below them, we show the discounted levels of utility along the transition, under con-
stant relative risk aversion (CRRA) preferences, $U(c_t) = \frac{c_t^{1-\sigma}-1}{1-\sigma}, \sigma > 0$. A value
$\sigma = 1.00$ is chosen as default to approximate logarithmic differences. Finally, we
aggregate over time the discounted utility series, to compare those sums with the
utility consumers would have by staying at the initial steady-states, with no change
in savings rate. As we can see in Fig. 2.12, the former is higher for all economies
that start with a savings rate above the Golden Rule level. For these economies,
changing from the old savings rate to the Golden Rule rate of savings would be
preferable. The same would be the case for economies starting with a low savings
rate, between .0 and .10 in our numerical exercise. All these are the *dynamically
inefficient steady-states*. Economies with a constant savings rate between .10 and
.36 are not dynamically inefficient.

We should bear in mind that what we have shown in this section is that there
are steady-states which are dominated, in terms of welfare, by trajectories that start

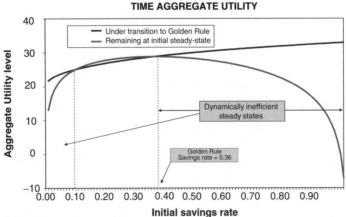

Fig. 2.12 Inefficient steady-states

when the savings rate experiences a once-and-for-all change from its initial level to the level associated with the Golden Rule steady-state. We have not shown in any sense that such trajectories leading to the Golden Rule are optimal in any sense. That is, converging to the Golden Rule is not necessarily the best an economy can do, although we have shown that it is sometimes preferable to staying at the current steady-state. To conclude on optimality, we need an specific analysis which is the object of the next chapter. There, we will characterize the optimal trajectory from any given initial situation. We will also show that, possibly against a first impression, converging to *the Golden Rule* is a suboptimal strategy, in the sense that *it involves too much capital accumulation* early on. The optimal trajectory takes the economy into a trajectory converging to a steady-state with a level of capital below that of the Golden Rule.

2.6 The Stochastic, Discrete Time Version of the Solow–Swan Model

To end the presentation of the constant savings rate growth model, we consider a stochastic version of the Solow–Swan economy that incorporates a random productivity factor. This is only one of the possibilities to make the model stochastic. We consider a technology, $f(k_t) = \theta_t A k_t^\alpha, 0 < \alpha < 1$, where θ_t denotes a *stochastic process* with a known probability distribution. Following the same argument as in the deterministic version of the economy, we find the law of motion,

$$k_{t+1} = \frac{1}{(1+n)(1+\gamma)} s\theta_t A k_t^\alpha + \frac{1-\delta}{(1+n)(1+\gamma)} k_t. \tag{2.45}$$

We assume $E(\theta_t) = 1$ and $Var(\theta_t) = \sigma^2$, although a more general case, with time-varying moments could also be considered. The stochastic properties of the θ_t-process will determine those of the main variables in the economy: output, consumption and investment. In particular, if θ_t displays cycles, as it would be the case if it obeys a second order autoregression with complex roots in its characteristic equation, so will output and consumption.

The same analysis we made of the deterministic, discrete-time version of the model applies to this stochastic case. Hence, we just need to combine the same law of motion for capital (2.36) with the new, stochastic functional form for the technology.

The steady-state in a stochastic economy is obtained assuming that each stochastic processes takes its mean value every single period. In our case, the single stochastic productivity shock would take its mean value of 1, producing the same condition (2.39) characterizing steady state as in the deterministic case. Hence, the steady state levels of the stock of capital, output and consumption in units of efficient labor will be the same as in the deterministic case.

Then, the law of motion of this stochastic economy (2.45) can be approximated around steady state, to obtain,

$$
k_{t+1} = k_{ss} + \left(\frac{1}{(1+n)(1+\gamma)} s\theta_{ss} A\alpha k_{ss}^{\alpha-1} + \frac{1-\delta}{(1+n)(1+\gamma)} \right) (k_t - k_{ss})
$$

$$
+ \frac{1}{(1+n)(1+\gamma)} s\theta_{ss} Ak_{ss}^{\alpha} (\theta_t - \theta_{ss})
$$

$$
= k_{ss} + \left(\frac{n+\delta+\gamma}{(1+n)(1+\gamma)} \alpha + \frac{1-\delta}{(1+n)(1+\gamma)} \right) (k_t - k_{ss})
$$

$$
+ \frac{n+\delta+\gamma}{(1+n)(1+\gamma)} k_{ss} (\theta_t - 1). \tag{2.46}
$$

2.6.1 Numerical Exercise – Solving the Stochastic Solow–Swan Model

Excel file *Solow_stochastic.xls* presents a numerical solution for a stochastic version of the Solow–Swan model [Matlab file *Solow_stochastic.m* performs the same numerical exercise]. We assume that randomness comes in the economy through a productivity shock with a first-order autoregressive structure,

$$
\ln \theta_t = \rho \ln \theta_{t-1} + \varepsilon_t, \quad \varepsilon_t \sim N(0, \sigma_\varepsilon^2), 0 < \rho < 1, \quad \theta_0 = 1,
$$

which is consistent with $\theta_{ss} = 1$. ε_t is the *innovation* in the logged-productivity shock. We consider in this simulation: $\rho = .90, \sigma_\varepsilon = .10$, which imply $E(\ln \theta_t) = 0, Var(\ln \theta_t) = (0.229)^2$. Parameter values are: $s = 0.36, \delta = 0.075, n = 0.0, A = 5.0, \alpha = 0.36$, so the steady-state is the Golden Rule. Technological growth is not considered.[18] This is not necessary for the exercise, and can be changed without any problem. We assume the representative consumer in the economy has a constant, relative risk aversion utility function on current consumption: $U(c_t) = \frac{c_t^{1-\sigma}-1}{1-\sigma}$, with $\sigma = 3.0$, and a discount factor on future utility of $\beta = 0.90$. Deterministic steady-state levels are computed following the expressions in the text. The steady-state stock of capital is 143.41 units, which allows for steady-state production oscillating around 29.88. Two-thirds of this amount is devoted to consumption, as it is approximately the case in developed economies, while the remaining one-third is devoted to investment. The solution starts with a time series realization for the innovation ε_t from a Normal distribution with zero mean and $\sigma_\varepsilon = .10$, obtained with the random number generator included in the *Tools/Data Analysis* tab of EXCEL. Then the implied time series for the logged productivity shock $\ln \theta_t$ is obtained using the autoregressive structure, from an initial condition $\ln \theta_0 = 0$.

---

[18] It would be simple to incorporate it into the simulation, but it would not change the qualitative aspects of the discussion.

The time series for the productivity shock θ_t is then taken to either (2.46) or (2.45), to obtain either an *approximate solution* or an *exact solution* to the model for the stock of physical capital starting from an initial condition k_0. We take as initial condition the steady-state stock of capital, so the generated numerical solution will display fluctuations around steady-state for all variables: stock of physical capital, output, investment and consumption. The production technology is then used to obtain a time series for output, while consumption and savings/investment emerge from the constant-savings rate assumption. The fact that we can generate all the time observations for θ_t without need of computing a single value for k_t reflects the fact that the productivity shock is *exogenous* in this economy.

It is interesting to bear in mind that the structure of the productivity shock will also determine the volatilities of these variables, as well as the correlations among them. Ratios to output, or deviations from an estimated cyclical component can be computed on this simulated data the same way it is usually done in time series analysis of actual data. Sometimes, standard deviations and correlations using these transformations are used to see how a theoretical model matches the data. Main statistics are shown below the simulated time series. The linear approximation is seen to produce time series with statistical properties very similar to those obtained under the exact solution. The relative volatility of consumption to output is similar to the one usually observed in actual data for most economies, which is not the case for the investment volatility, which is well higher than that of output in actual time series data. We also present correlation coefficients between interest rates, consumption and investment, with output.

Unfortunately, this model, where no agent takes any optimal decision, is so simple that the linear correlation coefficients between either consumption or investment and output are 1.0, as a consequence of the fact that the two variables are an exact proportion of output each period, with independence of the fluctuations experienced by the latter variable. For the correlation coefficient to depart from one, we would need different sources of randomness in the two variables considered, which is not the case in this model.

Regression models between some variables, like consumption and output, or investment and output, could also be estimated using the set of time series provided by a numerical solution, the same way it is done with actual data. However, the simplicity of the random element in this model economy would also lead to trivial regressions. An exception is a relationship attempting to relate investment to the real rate of interest. This would be defined by the marginal product of capital, as it has been calculated in the spreadsheet. The nonlinear functions of capital defining these two variables allow for a non-trivial regression, $Investment_t = \alpha + \beta$. *Real interest rate$_t$* $+ u_t$, which is shown below the table of correlation coefficients.

The important point, however, is that although the EXCEL file presents a single time series realization for the endogenous variables, we could conceivably compute as many of these realizations as we wished. The reason is that dealing with a stochastic economy, we could repeat the process starting from a new, different realization for the productivity time series, by using again the random number generator tool of EXCEL. In fact, the *Stochastic*(2),(3) and (4) spreadsheets are identical to the *Stochastic* spreadsheet except by the realization of the productivity shock.[19] By sampling repeatedly from the stochastic process for productivity, we could get a large number of realizations for each statistic of interest, like the relative volatility of consumption to output. A simple example would be the four values for the estimated slope of the investment regression in the different spreadsheets. Computing the numerical value of this statistic for each of 10,000 realizations, say, we could approximate arbitrarily well its probability distribution through the obtained frequency distribution. This should not be surprising. Everything in the model is stochastic, even each sample statistic. The model can be seen as a mapping from the probability structure for the innovation in the productivity shock to the probability distribution of any model characteristic. With actual time series data we have a single sample available, so we can compute a single numerical value for any given statistic, and the interesting point becomes how to compare the single value obtained from actual time series data to the probability distribution estimated from the theoretical model.

2.7 Exercises

Exercise 1. In the (2.29) expression, fix numerical values for three of the parameters A, n, s, α, δ, and discuss how the steady-state value of k_{ss} changes with changes in the remaining parameter. Draw a graph summarizing each of these analyses.

Exercise 2. In the deterministic, discrete-time version of the Solow-Swan economy, assume a Cobb-Douglas technology, with parameter values $\delta = 0.10$, $n = 0.02$, $A = 1, \alpha = 0.33, s = 0.25$, and compute the steady state value of capital. Take an initial value for capital $k_0 < k_{ss}$ and compute the converging path towards steady state. Repeat the exercise for an initial condition $k_0 > k_{ss}$. Repeat the exercise changing the value of one parameter, and draw the trajectories that obtain for different values of that parameter. Numerically obtain the rate of convergence to steady state in each case.

Exercise 3. For a given parameterization, including an initial value of the stock of capital, k_0, and a Cobb-Douglas technology, compare the time series for k_t obtained from propagating the linear approximation (2.40) as well as the exact, nonlinear mechanism.

Exercise 4. Show that the second order linear approximation to the law of motion of the discrete time, deterministic version of the Solow–Swan model around steady state is,

---

[19] The reader can copy the spreadsheet and use the random number generator to write a different realization on top of the old one. All the calculations in the spreadsheet will change, providing a different set of time series for all the variables in the economy. We need to be careful about the fact that EXCEL does not automatically update the regression results.

$$k_{t+1} = k_{ss} + \left(\frac{1}{1+n} sf'(k_{ss}) + \frac{1-\delta}{1+n} \right) (k_t - k_{ss}) + \frac{1}{1+n} sf''(k_{ss})(k_t - k_{ss})^2$$

Solve the model assuming a Cobb-Douglas technology under a given parameterization using this approximation, and compare the implied time series with those obtained from the first order approximation. Would the second order approximation still be the same for the deterministic and stochastic versions of the model?

Chapter 3
Optimal Growth. Continuous Time Analysis

3.1 The Continuous-Time Version of the Cass–Koopmans Model

Maintaining the same structure of the neoclassical growth model of Solow and Swan we have reviewed in the previous chapter, Cass [18] and Koopmans [52] characterized the optimal rate of capital accumulation in order to maximize some social welfare criterion. That amounts to specifying the optimal distribution of output between consumption and savings each period, taking into account the fact that savings decisions provide resources for gross investment, thereby conditioning future production possibilities and growth. We are still in a one-good economy, where the single commodity is produced and can either be consumed or used as an input for future production. The stock of the commodity being used in production is physical capital, which is not reversible. It is subject to some constant rate of depreciation, δ, but it cannot be converted back into consumption.

Other than for this optimality consideration, we maintain all other structural assumptions of the Solow–Swan model, including the one on decreasing returns on the productive factors. As shown in the previous chapter, that precludes the possibility of positive steady-state growth, since we assume at this point that there is no technological progress in the economy. The main difference with the Solow and Swan model is that we now consider that the consumption/savings decision, which determines the physical capital accumulation process and hence, the time evolution of per capita income, is endogenous. The savings rate is therefore no longer constant.

The simplest interpretation of the model would be as an economy populated by identical agents living forever. They all own the same units of physical capital, have access to the same production technology and have the same preferences defined on the stream of current and future consumption. There is continuous population growth, at a rate $n > 0, N_t = N_0 e^{nt}$. Existing consumers give continuously away some resources to endow new agents at birth with the same units of capital they already own. It seems sensible to believe that a benevolent economic planner in this

A. Novales et al., *Economic Growth: Theory and Numerical Solution Methods*, 101
© Springer-Verlag Berlin Heidelberg 2009

economy might be interested in maximizing the time aggregate utility of the typical consumer,

$$\underset{c_t}{Max} \int_0^\infty e^{-\theta t} U(c_t) dt,$$

subject to,

$$\dot{k}_t = f(k_t) - (n+\delta)k_t - c_t, \tag{3.1}$$

and given the initial state of the economy, k_0. As in the previous chapter, lower case variables denote per capita variables, $f(k_t)$ represents the available technology, and subindices t denote functions of time. The restriction in this optimization problem is the law of motion of the stock of physical capital per worker under a time varying savings rate, which we already obtained in the previous chapter. θ is the social rate of time discount, that is, the discount applied to the utility of future consumption. It reflects the rate at which society is willing to substitute future for current utility. We assume the utility function satisfies: $U' > 0, U'' < 0, U'(0) = \infty, U'(\infty) = 0$. Assuming $\theta > 0$, we depart from Ramsey who, interpreting the maximization problem as that solved by a central planner, argued that there was no ethical case for discounting the future [Blanchard and Fischer [11], p. 82].

A second interpretation would correspond to a Robinson Crusoe type of economy, in which a single, infinitely lived agent has access to a production technology. No trading of any type will arise, since there are no other agents in the economy. This single economic agent would maximize time aggregate utility, and the problem would be identical to the one above, with $n = 0$.

The model could still be interpreted as that of an economy with a continuum of generations who live over an infinitesimal time interval, the size of successive generations growing at a rate n. Under this interpretation, an alternative plausible formulation of the planner's problem would use the so-called Benthamite welfare function, in which the felicity function becomes $N_t U(c_t)$, so that the number of family members receiving the given utility level is taken into account. Assuming $N_t = N_0 e^{nt}$, the Benthamite formulation is equivalent to reducing the rate of time preference to $\theta - n$ in our model, because the larger the family at later dates increases the weight given to the utility of the representative individual of a later generation. The results would then be slightly different from those shown in this chapter.

Along our discussion we will follow the first interpretation, making references to the planner's economy and the representative agent living in it. The whole point of the analysis is to characterize the optimal allocation of resources every period between current consumption and savings. The latter will contribute to capital accumulation and to the generation of additional resources in the future. Solving the model amounts to determining the optimal path for the stock of capital starting from an initial level of k_0. Trajectories for all other variables can be obtained as exact functions of the one followed by physical capital.

3.1.1 Optimality Conditions for the Cass–Koopmans Model

The Hamiltonian for the dynamic optimization planner's problem is,

$$H(k_t, c_t, \lambda_t) = e^{-\theta t} \left[U(c_t) + \lambda_t \left(f(k_t) - (n + \delta) k_t - c_t \right) \right],$$

where consumption is the control variable, the stock of capital is the state variable, and the current value multiplier λ_t is the co-state variable. The multiplier has the standard interpretation of being the shadow price of the state variable, k_t: how much would the planner be willing to pay, in utility units, to have one more unit of physical capital per worker at time t.

Since the marginal utility at zero is equal to infinity, the optimal level of consumption will be strictly positive every period, and optimality conditions can be written [see Mathematical Appendix],

$$U'(c_t) - \lambda_t = 0, \tag{3.2}$$

$$f'(k_t) - (n + \delta) - \theta + \frac{\dot{\lambda}_t}{\lambda_t} = 0, \tag{3.3}$$

$$\lim_{t \to \infty} e^{-\theta t} \lambda_t k_t = 0. \tag{3.4}$$

The social value at time t of an additional unit of capital per worker is, along the optimal trajectory, equal to the marginal utility of consumption. This result, which agrees with the nature of λ_t as being the shadow price of capital, is not a hypothesis we have imposed on the model, but rather, a property of its solution.

From (3.2) and (3.3) we get,

$$\frac{dU'(c_t)/dt}{U'(c_t)} = (n + \delta) + \theta - f'(k_t) \tag{3.5}$$

that is,

$$\dot{c}_t = \frac{U'(c_t)}{U''(c_t)} \left[(n + \delta) + \theta - f'(k_t) \right] \tag{3.6}$$

which is known as the *Keynes–Ramsey rule*.

The trajectory solving the previous system of optimality conditions will be optimal from the point of view of a *central planner* having maximization of the representative consumer's welfare as a reasonable goal of economic policy. In the next sections, we analyze whether a *steady state* exists in this economy and if so, whether the optimal trajectory converges to it. Even though the *transition* towards steady-state can last for a long time, economic policy issues have often been analyzed only at steady-state, due to the difficulty of characterizing the behavior of the economy along the transition. Indeed, transition paths are hard to describe analytically, and we will learn later on how to use numerical solution methods to characterize the main properties of transition trajectories to steady-state. Transitions may arise following a policy intervention on an economy which was initially at steady-state, or because a structural change has taken place in such an economy.

3.1.2 The Instantaneous Elasticity of Substitution of Consumption (IES)

Growth models deal with intertemporal consumption and savings decisions. Sacrificing some consumption today allows for higher capital accumulation which, in turn, will lead to higher resources in the future. The main question is then how to optimally distribute a given stream of income over time. Resources can be transferred to the future as explained, while they cannot be brought from the future into the present except in the presence of developed credit markets. When the representative consumer experiences a positive income shock at time t, he/she has a continuum of possibilities, since current consumption can be increased by any fraction of Δy between 0 and 1, saving the rest so as to enjoy higher consumption thereafter. At one end, current consumption would increase by the full size of the income shock, Δy, leaving none of the increase for the future. Alternatively, the income increase will spread over time in the form of higher consumption over a number of periods.

Two related concepts determine the optimal rate at which resources should be transferred over time: the *elasticity of the marginal utility* (EMU) with respect to consumption, i.e., the percent change in marginal utility associated to a one per cent change in the level of consumption,

$$EMU = -\frac{d(\ln(U'(c_t)))}{d(\ln(c_t))} = -\frac{dU'(c_t)}{dc_t}\frac{c_t}{U'(c_t)} = -\frac{c_t U''(c_t)}{U'(c_t)} = \sigma(c_t) > 0.$$

Under a linear utility function, the EMU becomes zero, the marginal utility not changing with the level of consumption although, more generally, the elasticity of the marginal utility of consumption will be a function of the level of consumption.

A related concept, the *intertemporal elasticity of substitution* of consumption, IES, considers the relationship between changes over time in consumption and the size of the implied changes in marginal utility. This is different from a more standard elasticity concept like the EMU, which is intended to compare changes in marginal utility because of a change in the level of consumption at a given point in time:

$$IES = \gamma(c_t) = -\left(\frac{\partial(rate\ of\ change\ in\ U'(c_t))}{\partial(rate\ of\ change\ in\ c_t)}\right)^{-1}$$
$$= -\left(\frac{\partial(\dot{U}'(c_t)/U'(c_t))}{\partial(\dot{c}_t/c_t)}\right)^{-1}.$$

If indifference curves for the representative consumer are close to linear, then marginal utility will be almost constant. As a consequence, the percent change in the marginal utility of consumption will be small, relative to any possible change in the level of consumption, and the intertemporal elasticity of substitution of consumption will be high. In that case, concentrating consumption at a given point in time would not affect the marginal utility by much, so the consumer would be almost indifferent as to when to consume, except for the effect of a possible time discount factor. In response to a positive income shock, consumption would rise by the size of the shock, with no significant increase in capital accumulation coming from saving part of the increase in income.

The opposite will be observed for a low *IES* of consumption, when an increase in consumption would produce a strong fall in marginal utility. Consequently, in that case a positive income shock will generally be followed by a small consumption increase. Most of the rise in income will be saved, leading to further capital accumulation, which will allow for increased consumption thereafter. In this case, consumption is smoother than under a high *IES*, when consumption tends to replicate income fluctuations. Hence, the volatility of consumption will be close to the volatility of income under a high *IES*, while being significantly lower than the volatility of income when the intertemporal elasticity of substitution of consumption is small.

A special case is that of a Constant Relative Risk Aversion (CRRA) utility function,

$$U(c_t) = \frac{c_t^{1-\sigma} - 1}{1 - \sigma}, \ \sigma > 0,$$
(3.7)

which leads to an *elasticity of the marginal utility* of consumption:

$$EMU = \sigma(c_t) = -\frac{c_t U''(c_t)}{U'(c_t)} = -c_t \frac{-\sigma c_t^{-\sigma-1}}{c_t^{-\sigma}} = \sigma,$$

and an *intertemporal elasticity of substitution* of consumption

$$IES = \gamma(c_t) = -\left(\frac{\partial(U'/U')}{\partial(\dot{c}_t/c_t)}\right)^{-1} = -\left(\frac{\partial(-\sigma(\dot{c}_t/c_t))}{\partial(\dot{c}_t/c_t)}\right)^{-1} = 1/\sigma = \frac{1}{EMU},$$

so that both elasticities are then constant, one being the inverse of the other one.

As a special case of our previous remark, it is interesting to see the connection between the value of σ in the CRRA utility and the volatility of consumption. If σ is close to zero, utility is a linear function of the level of consumption and the consumer does not get much compensation from future consumption relative to what he/she misses by sacrificing current consumption. Since the marginal utility is independent of the level of consumption, the consumer is indifferent as to when to consume and the presence of a discount factor will lead to exhausting immediately any unexpected income rise. In this case, there is not much incentive to transfer resources over time through savings and capital accumulation, and consumption will be as volatile as income. Alternatively, when σ is large, changes in consumption over time lead to strong changes in marginal utility. But a volatile marginal utility is contrary to the goal of maximizing the time aggregate level of utility, so the consumer will want changes in consumption to be minimum, preferring to spread out over time the benefits of an unexpected income rise. A similar behavior will arise following an unexpected income shortage. The consumer has a strong incentive to transfer consumption over time, and the consumption path gets smoother, since income fluctuations are smoothed out over time through positive and negative savings.

The inverse relationship between the instantaneous elasticity of substitution of consumption and the elasticity of the marginal utility of consumption can be extended to more general utility functions, although just as an approximation. Let us consider two points in time, $t < s$, $s = t + \Delta t$, with consumption levels c_s, c_t, $c_s = c_t + \varepsilon$, and $\varepsilon \lessgtr 0$, and small relative to c_t.

$$IES^{-1} = \frac{1}{\gamma(c_t)} = -\frac{\partial\left\{\ln\left(U'(c_s)/U'(c_t)\right)\right\}}{\partial\left\{\ln(c_s/c_t)\right\}}$$

$$= -\frac{\partial\left\{\ln\left(U'(c_s)/U'(c_t)\right)\right\}}{\partial\varepsilon}\left(\frac{\partial\ln(c_s/c_t)}{\partial\varepsilon}\right)^{-1}. \tag{3.8}$$

Using Taylor' expansion for the marginal utility of consumption,

$$U'(c_s) = U'(c_t) + U''(c_t)(c_s - c_t) = U'(c_t) + U''(c_t)\varepsilon,$$

that is,

$$\frac{U'(c_s)}{U'(c_t)} = 1 + \frac{U''(c_t)}{U'(c_t)}\varepsilon.$$

Furthermore, $\ln(c_s/c_t) = \ln(1 + \varepsilon/c_t) \simeq \varepsilon/c_t$ and $\ln\left(U'(c_s)/U'(c_t)\right) = \ln\left(1 + \frac{U''(c_t)}{U'(c_t)}\varepsilon\right) \simeq \frac{U''(c_t)}{U'(c_t)}\varepsilon$. Taking derivatives with respect to ε and plugging into (3.8),

$$IES^{-1} = \frac{1}{\gamma(c_t)} \simeq -c_t\frac{U''(c_t)}{U'(c_t)} = EMU.$$

3.1.3 Risk Aversion and the Intertemporal Substitution of Consumption

The parameter σ in the previous family of utility functions may be known to the reader as the *risk aversion parameter*. Indeed, in the theory of decision under uncertainty, *absolute risk aversion* is defined as $ARA(c_t) = -\frac{U''(c_t)}{U'(c_t)}$, while *relative risk aversion* is defined by $RRA(c_t) = -\frac{U''(c_t)}{U'(c_t)}c_t$, just like the elasticity of the marginal utility of consumption. In general, both are functions of the level of consumption. However, for the family of utility functions considered above, the relative risk aversion becomes a constant,

$$RRA = -\frac{U''(c_t)}{U'(c_t)}c_t = \sigma,$$

which is why that family is known as the *constant relative risk aversion* family (*CRRA*) of utility functions.

There is some similarity between the way utility maximization decisions are made under uncertainty at a given point in time, and the way they are made over time, even in the absence of uncertainty. A risk averse consumer with a high value of the σ parameter will dislike facing uncertainty on the level of consumption. When offered a lottery with alternative consumption levels, each with a given probability, he/she will glad to change that lottery for a certain level of consumption, below the expected consumption level provided by the lottery. The difference between them can be interpreted as the *risk* or *insurance premium* the consumer is willing to pay to pass the risk away to someone else. As we have already seen, in a world with no uncertainty, a consumer with a high value of σ will tend to smooth out consumption by spreading the effects of any positive or negative income shock over time. The effect is, in both cases, a less volatile consumption stream than the one implemented by a consumer with a low value of σ, the relative risk aversion coefficient for the *CRRA* family of utility functions, which is then also the inverse of the *IES*.

3.1.4 Keynes–Ramsey Condition

These concepts allow us for an interesting interpretation of the Keynes–Ramsey condition. Using the instantaneous elasticity of substitution of consumption, we can write that condition as,

$$\frac{\dot{c}_t}{c_t} = \gamma(c_t)\left[f'(k_t) - (n+\delta) - \theta\right], \tag{3.9}$$

which shows that *optimal* consumption increases, decreases or stays constant at each point in time, depending on whether the marginal product of physical capital *net* of total depreciation, $f'(k_t) - (n+\delta)$ is greater, lower, or equal to the social rate of time discount, θ.

Let us accept for a while [as we will see in Sect. 3.3] that the equilibrium real rate of interest should be equal to the marginal product of capital net of depreciation: $r_t = f'(k_t) - (n+\delta)$. The intuition for such result is clear, since both capture the real return, i.e., the return in units of the consumption commodity, to two different types of investment: productive and financial investment. The Keynes–Ramsey condition states that if the real rate of interest was equal to the discount rate, then it would be optimal to maintain consumption constant.

On the other hand, when the market valuation of the future, as indicated by r_t, is above the subjective value of time, given by θ, the consumer will find preferable to sacrifice some current consumption, investing the proceeds to enjoy higher future consumption. The consumption path will then be increasing, $\dot{c}_t > 0$. The opposite will be the case when the market valuation of the future is below the subjective value, in which case, the consumer will prefer to maintain current consumption above future consumption, with $\dot{c}_t < 0$.

But by how much would consumers adjust their consumption paths to the gap between the market and the subjective valuation of the future? According to Keynes–Ramsey condition,

$$r_t - \theta = \frac{1}{\gamma(c_t)}\frac{\dot{c}_t}{c_t},$$

which becomes:

$$r_t - \theta = \sigma \frac{\dot{c}_t}{c_t},$$

under *constant relative risk aversion* preferences. For a given spread between r_t and θ, consumption growth will be higher for those consumers with a higher *IES*, in agreement with the discussion in the previous section. Consumers with a low σ have a high intertemporal elasticity of consumption, and they will adjust their paths much more to a given gap between the private and the market valuation of time. The opposite will be the case for consumers with a high σ, who will barely adjust their paths to changes in the difference between the real interest rate and the time discount factor.

3.1.5 The Optimal Steady-State

Since this model shares the same structure than the Solow–Swan model, we already know that whichever steady-states there may be, they will all involve zero growth: $\dot{c}_t = \dot{k}_t = 0$, with the levels of per-capita consumption and income, as well as the capital stock per worker, staying constant over time. Aggregate variables, however, will grow at the same rate than the population, n. We now have two relationships characterizing the time evolution of the economy: (a) the law of motion (3.1), an equation in k_t which we also had in the Solow–Swan model, which acts now as a restriction to the planner's problem, and (b) the Keynes–Ramsey rule (3.9), an equation in $\dot{c}_t$ which is specific to the optimal economic planning problem.

The two equations are of a different character. On the one hand, making $\dot{k}_t = 0$ in the law of motion of the economy, we get,

$$f(k_{ss}) = (n + \delta) k_{ss} + c_{ss},$$

which describes a curve in the (c, k)-plane:

$$c_{ss} = f(k_{ss}) - (n + \delta) k_{ss}, \tag{3.10}$$

which satisfies,

$$\frac{\partial c_{ss}}{\partial k_{ss}} = f'(k_{ss}) - (n + \delta),$$

$$\frac{\partial^2 c_{ss}}{\partial k_{ss}^2} = f''(k_{ss}) < 0.$$

All the points in this curve are consistent with a zero growth rate for the stock of capital. However, (3.10) is the long-run version of just one of the two optimality conditions. The optimizing behavior has additionally provided us with the Keynes–Ramsey condition, so the *optimal steady-state* will be characterized by the per capita levels of physical capital and consumption, k_{ss} and c_{ss} satisfying, in addition to (3.10), equation

$$f'(k_{ss}) = n + \delta + \theta, \tag{3.11}$$

which is obtained by imposing $\dot{c}_t = 0$ in the Keynes–Ramsey condition. The structure of the system is such that equation (3.11) gives us the stock of capital at the optimal steady state, and then (3.10) yields the associated level of consumption. If the production function is concave, the solution is unique.

The Golden Rule, k_{GR}, defined in the previous chapter, was the point on curve (3.10) with the highest level of consumption. The Golden Rule does not solve the planner's problem, since it satisfies just one of the long-run optimality equations, but not the other. From the definition of Golden Rule,

$$f'(k_{GR}) = n + \delta. \tag{3.12}$$

we see that the optimal steady-state has a level of capital below k_{GR} for any $\theta > 0$. Therefore, the optimal steady-state is a point on curve (3.10), to the left of the Golden Rule. As we anticipated in the previous chapter, the Golden Rule involves too much capital accumulation. It allows for a higher level of consumption once steady-state is reached, but it asks for too much consumption sacrifice earlier on. [See Fig. 3.1].

In the planner's problem the savings rate is allowed to vary over time, so that the representative consumer will generally be better off than in a comparable Solow–Swan economy, since the resource allocation in that economy could also be attained in the planner's economy as a special case.

Whether there is more than one of such optimal steady-states and whether the economy converges to any of them from any given initial condition can be discussed by analyzing the behavior of the two (c_t, k_t)-time functions defined by the two differential equations in $\dot{c}_t, \dot{k}_t$, which we do next.

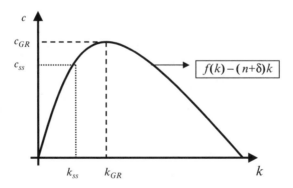

Fig. 3.1 Steady-state relationship between consumption and physical capital

3.1.6 Numerical Exercise: The Sensitivity of Steady-State Levels to Changes in Structural Parameters

The *Steady-state* spreadsheet in the *CK_continuous_time.xls* file shows how steady-state levels differ between economies with different structural parameters. The same analysis can be done through the *CK_c_steady state.m* Matlab file. We consider in all cases an economy with a Cobb–Douglas technology and a constant, relative risk aversion utility function like (3.7). The exercise is designed to display changes in the steady-state levels of the main variables under a permanent change in a single structural parameter, maintaining all the other parameters unchanged. The result can be interpreted either as steady-state differences between two economies differing in the value of a single structural parameter, or as the comparison between final and initial steady state levels for a given economy subject to structural change.

In the latter case, suppose an economy which is at steady-state, in which a permanent change occurs in the value of a structural parameter. After the structural change, the steady-state will be different, so the economy will no longer be in steady state, and a transition period will start, which might take the economy along a convergence path to the new steady-state. Such transition trajectory will be characterized in an exercise below. At this point, we just focus on steady-state changes produced by the permanent change in a structural parameter.

Each panel in the spreadsheet is devoted to analyzing steady-state effects of changes in a specific structural parameter. The initial steady-state is underlined in red in each panel. Under each panel, a graph displays the variation induced in steady-state capital stock and output as a consequence of the change in the structural parameter. A second graph does the same with consumption and single period utility. Under the assumed Cobb–Douglas technology, output follows a behavior parallel to that of the capital stock, and the same can be said for consumption and single period utility, but it is still instructive to see the numerical sensitivity of each pair of variables. A third graph displays the behavior of investment both, in absolute terms, as well as a share of output. The latter characterizes the distribution of resources in the economy, consumption taking the part of output which is not devoted to investment.

We have considered a reasonable range of values for each parameter. By that we mean that the implied steady-state distribution of resources is not very much at odds with what is observed in actual economies. Even though there is always some discussion about what these values should be, we take a conservative position, by considering a wide range of parameter values in each case. The reader will gradually understand how steady-state properties are affected by the values of some structural parameters. In this exercise, it may be specially interesting to pay attention to how (a) the share of output devoted to investment is a linear function of the output elasticity of capital[1], and (b) the optimal distribution of resources between consumption

---

[1] The steady-state stock of capital is $k_{ss} = \left(\frac{\alpha}{n+\delta+\theta} \right)^{\frac{1}{1-\alpha}}$. Under the assumed technology, $y_t = k_t^{\alpha}$, steady-state output and consumption satisfy: $y_{ss} = f(k_{ss}) = k_{ss}^{\alpha}$, $c_{ss} = y_{ss} - (n+\delta)k_{ss}$.

and investment is affected by the depreciation rate of physical capital and, specifically, by how the economy reacts to very high depreciation rates by reducing the stock of capital, rather than by sacrificing too much consumption.

Analyzing further the results, we can see how an increase in the discount applied to future utility decreases the steady-state stock of capital as well as steady-state output. The lower production also leads to a decrease in steady-state consumption and a larger fall in steady-state utility. A higher time discount implies that the consumer cares less about future consumption, which leads him/her to reduce capital accumulation.

A higher value of the output elasticity of capital increases the productivity of this factor, stimulating its accumulation over time. In steady-state, an economy with a higher output share of capital has a higher stock of capital and produces more output, which also allows for higher consumption. Investment is increasing in the output elasticity of capital, moving from an initial share of 14% of output for low elasticity values, to about 20% of output for the higher admissible values of this parameter.

A higher rate of population growth or a higher rate of depreciation of physical capital limit the possibilities for capital accumulation, which is lower in steady-state the higher are either one of these two parameters. As a consequence, steady-state output is also lower for higher depreciation or higher population growth. In our numerical examination, we have taken the depreciation rate to a limit value of 100% which, even if unrealistic, it is nevertheless sometimes used in theoretical models. We would then have full depreciation of physical capital, with the stock of capital being equal to investment every period. A higher depreciation is quickly seen in the figure to take the steady-state stock of capital to very low levels, since many resources are needed to replace what is lost to depreciation, and none would be left for consumption. As shown in the second graph, consumption stabilizes at a strictly positive level. Steady-state investment is low for very low depreciation rates, since then there is not need to make much replacement of physical capital. The investment share of output increases with the rate of depreciation, stabilizing at just below 30% of output. It is interesting to see this stable behavior of investment, as a fraction of output, even when depreciation is complete. This has a direct reflection on consumption stabilizing at just above 70% of output. For large depreciation rates, output would be very low, as shown in the table, and so would be consumption and investment. Reasonable depreciation rates for annual data would be in the 5–15% range. There, investment falls between 17% and 23% of output, the remaining share of output being devoted to consumption.

Finally, the intertemporal elasticity of substitution of consumption or, what is the same, the degree of curvature of the utility function as represented by σ, is

---

So that the investment to output ratio is:

$$1 - \frac{c_{ss}}{y_{ss}} = \alpha \frac{n + \delta}{n + \delta + \theta} = \frac{\alpha}{1 + \frac{\theta}{n+\delta}},$$

smaller than the output share of capital, α. It will approach α only if the rate of time discount is small, relative to total depreciation.

inconsequential for the steady-state allocation of resources, affecting only the level of utility attainable with the steady-state level of consumption, which does not change with the value of this parameter.

3.1.7 Existence, Uniqueness and Stability of Long-Run Equilibrium – A Graphical Discussion

Existence and uniqueness of the optimal steady state are readily seen, since (3.11) determines a unique level of the stock of capital per worker which, taken to (3.10), determines the optimal steady-state level of consumption. Hence, there is a single optimal steady state.

To discuss stability, it is necessary to remember that equations (3.1) and (3.9) characterize the dynamics of the economy. Imposing $\dot{c}_t = 0$ in equation (3.9), we obtain (3.11), that divides the (c,k) space into two regions. To the left of k_{ss}, the marginal product is greater than $f'(k_{ss})$, and hence the function $f'(k) - (n+\delta+\theta)$ will be positive and, as shown in (3.9), consumption will increase. That happens whenever the stock of capital is below its level at the optimal steady state. Furthermore, the rate of growth of consumption will be higher the further below k_{ss} we are. The opposite happens whenever the stock of capital is above the optimal steady-state level, consumption then decreasing at a higher rate the farther away the stock of capital is from the optimal steady state [See Fig. 3.2].

On the other hand, imposing $\dot{k}_t = 0$ in equation (3.1), we obtain $c = f(k) - (\delta+n)k$ that also divides the (c,k) space into two regions. First, we need to characterize the shape of the curve. It goes through the origin, since over that line, $k = 0$ implies $c = 0$. As we saw before, partial derivatives are, $\frac{\partial c}{\partial k} = f'(k) - (\delta+n)$; $\frac{\partial^2 c}{\partial k^2} = f''(k)$, so that the curve is everywhere concave, with a maximum at $f'(k) = (\delta+n)$, i.e., at the Golden Rule. The line crosses the $c = 0$ axis at the non-zero solution to equation $f(k) - (\delta+n)k = 0$. For instance, in the case of a Cobb–Douglas

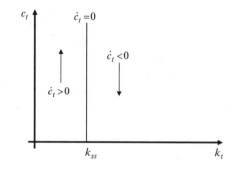

Fig. 3.2 Direction of changes in consumption

technology, that happens at: $Ak^\alpha = (\delta+n)k$, i.e., $k = \left(\frac{A}{n+\delta}\right)^{\frac{1}{1-\alpha}}$, a well defined stock of capital, corresponding to the *subsistence steady-state* of the Solow–Swan economy. Points to the right of this stock of capital are clearly not feasible, since they would imply negative consumption. At any point below the line in the feasible region, we have $c < f(k) - (\delta+n)k$ so that from (3.1) we obtain that $\dot{k} > 0$ and the stock of capital increases. The rate of accumulation of physical capital is higher the farther away we are from the curve. The opposite happens anywhere above the curve, physical capital then decreasing, because of investment being below what would be needed to replace what is lost by depreciation [See Fig. 3.3].

We can then see how the (c,k) space gets split into four regions, as in the *phase diagram* in Fig. 3.4. Starting from a point like A in region I, we move into region II, in the direction of zero capital and high consumption, which is clearly not feasible. As the stock of physical capital decreases, so does output, and it is not possible to maintain an ever increasing level of consumption. The same result would arise starting from point B. If the economy starts at C, then the stock of capital will accumulate and consumption will increase for a while. Indeed, the Keynes–Ramsey

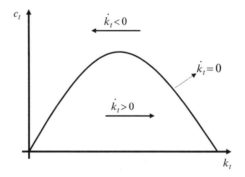

Fig. 3.3 Direction of changes in stock of capital

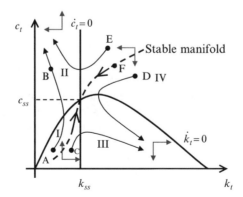

Fig. 3.4 Phase diagram

condition shows that consumption increases everywhere to the left of k_{ss}. However, once it enters into region *III*, consumption will decrease. When it goes to the right of the Golden Rule, condition (3.5) shows that the marginal utility of consumption starts growing faster than θ, while the stock of capital would remain bounded. The transversality condition then fails to hold while the economy converges to the subsistence steady-state of the Solow–Swan economy. It is clear that while being feasible, a trajectory of accumulating capital while bringing consumption to zero cannot possibly be optimum. Starting at *D*, in region *IV* will bring the economy into region *III*, with the same result we just saw, while starting at *E* would eventually bring the economy into region *II*.

It is just when we start from a point like *F* that the rates at which capital accumulates and consumption increases are just adequate to move the economy into the direction of the optimal steady state. If we start from just above or below *F* that will not work, and we will get either unfeasible or suboptimal results. There is a sequence of points like *F* along a curve, called the *stable manifold*. For similar reasons, the stable manifold extends to the left of the optimal steady-state level of capital and below the $\dot{k} = 0$ curve. For each possible level of the stock of capital there is a single level of consumption which is consistent with the economy converging to the optimal steady state. That trajectory is the solution to the planner's problem.

Trajectories converging to the optimal steady state satisfy the transversality condition, since $\lambda_T = \lambda_{ss}, k_T = k_{ss}$ are constant and finite in steady-state, so that,

$$\lim_{T \to \infty} e^{-\theta T} \lambda_{ss} k_{ss} = 0.$$

Since all agents share the same preferences, the resource allocation made by the solution to the planner's problem is also Pareto-optimum, since in it, everybody alive receives the same amount of resources, so that there is no way to increase the level of utility of a given consumer, without decreasing that of another one. On the contrary, any other trajectory will not be Pareto-optimum, since we could improve the level of welfare for each consumer, without decreasing that of a single agent.

3.1.8 Suboptimality of the Golden Rule

We can now take again the discussion on optimality we made when introducing the Golden Rule in the previous chapter. Among all steady-states that can be achieved with alternative values of a constant savings ratio, the Golden Rule is the one providing the highest level of consumption. In principle, achieving the highest possible steady-state level of consumption might seem a sensible goal under monotone preferences. Imposing a constant savings rate s_{GR} will start a *transition path* taking the economy from the initial stock of physical capital k_0 to the Golden Rule level, k_{GR}, as we saw in the previous chapter. But the point is that attaining the Golden Rule might ask for a larger consumption sacrifice along the transition than that needed along the transition path that would take the economy from k_0 to the optimal steady-state level k_{ss}. Since the intertemporal welfare function weights current versus future utility, it is unclear whether converging to k_{GR} might be optimal. Because of this trade-off between the short- and the long-run several issues, like the speed of convergence towards steady-state or the rate of time discount, play a central role in characterizing an optimal path.

In fact, by solving the planner's problem in the previous sections, we have shown that converging to k_{GR} will generally not be optimal. Moreover, since the only difference between the conditions characterizing the optimal steady state k_{ss} and the Golden Rule k_{GR} depends on the rate of time discount θ, we know that the Golden Rule will be the optimal steady-state only when $\theta = 0$, i.e., when future utility is valued as much as current utility. At the Golden Rule, future utility receives too much weight[2], and because of this emphasis on future levels of utility, the Golden Rule involves too much capital accumulation early on.

Rather, optimality requires starting a convergent trajectory leading to the optimal steady state k_{ss}. Analytical expressions for the optimal trajectory would be obtained by integration of the two differential equations (law of motion and Keynes–Ramsey rule) subject to two boundary conditions,

$$k_0 \; given,$$
$$\lim_{T \to \infty} e^{-\theta T} \lambda_T k_T = 0 \quad (transversality \; condition), \tag{3.13}$$

a hard analytical problem. The economy is placed on that trajectory by adequately choosing the initial consumption level c_0. That will determine a specific savings rate at each point in time, converging also to a long-run equilibrium level. Being the solution to the planner's problem, that trajectory guarantees a higher level of welfare than any other alternative path, including the one converging to the Golden Rule steady-state. That is due to the fact that, because of time discount, consumption along the transition gets more weight than steady-state consumption. Once it is reached, the Golden Rule will yield higher utility than the optimal steady-state, but that utility will be heavily discounted in the time aggregate objective function.

3.2 Stability and Convergence

The Keynes–Ramsey condition for an economy with a Cobb–Douglas technology, $y_t = A k_t^\alpha$, $0 < \alpha < 1$, and a constant, relative risk aversion utility function with parameter σ, becomes,

---

[2] Alternatively, it can be said that the utility of future generations receives too much weight. Along the Golden Rule, individuals from successive generations all receive the same weigh in the utility function. However the size of generations grows at a rate n, thereby future generations receiving a higher weight in the planner's objective function.

$$\frac{\dot{c}_t}{c_t} = \frac{1}{\sigma}\left[\alpha A k_t^{-(1-\alpha)} - (n+\delta+\theta)\right],$$

which, for the case $A = 1$, can be written, in terms of the logged variables, as,

$$\frac{d\ln c_t}{dt} = \frac{1}{\sigma}\left[\alpha e^{-(1-\alpha)\ln k_t} - (n+\delta+\theta)\right].$$

On the other hand, the law of motion of the economy (3.1), can also be written in logs,

$$\frac{d\ln k_t}{dt} = e^{-(1-\alpha)\ln k_t} - e^{\ln c_t - \ln k_t} - (n+\delta).$$

In Appendix (3.7) we show that the dynamic system made up by these two differential equations admits the *log-linear approximate representation* around steady state values,

$$\begin{pmatrix} \frac{d\ln c_t}{dt} \\ \frac{d\ln k_t}{dt} \end{pmatrix} = \underbrace{\begin{pmatrix} 0 & -\eta \\ -h & \theta \end{pmatrix}}_{D} \begin{pmatrix} \ln c_t - \ln c_{ss} \\ \ln k_t - \ln k_{ss} \end{pmatrix},$$

with $h = \frac{(1-\alpha)(n+\delta)+\theta}{\alpha} > 0$, $\eta = \frac{1-\alpha}{\sigma}(n+\delta+\theta) > 0$, where the coefficient matrix D has determinant $-\eta h < 0$. Hence, the system admits a saddle point trajectory leading to steady-state. Eigenvalues of the transition matrix are,

$$\mu_1, \mu_2 = \frac{\theta \pm \sqrt{\theta^2 + 4\eta h}}{2},$$

with $\mu_1 > \theta > 0$, while $\mu_2 < 0$.

The continuous-time dynamic system can be written,

$$\dot{x}_t \cong Dx_t.$$

with x being the vector of deviations around steady-state: $x_t = (\ln c_t - \ln c_{ss}, \ln k_t - \ln k_{ss})$ and D the matrix above. The solution to this system is,

$$x_t \cong e^{Dt}x_0. \tag{3.14}$$

Let Γ be the matrix having as columns the right-eigenvectors of D. Then, its inverse matrix, Γ^{-1}, will be the matrix having as rows the left-eigenvectors of D. Using expressions in the Mathematical Appendix for the eigenvectors of a 2×2 matrix,

$$\Gamma = \begin{pmatrix} x_1 & y_1 \\ x_2 & y_2 \end{pmatrix} = \begin{pmatrix} 1 & 1 \\ \frac{-\mu_1}{\eta} & \frac{-\mu_2}{\eta} \end{pmatrix},$$

$$\Gamma^{-1} = \begin{pmatrix} u_1 & v_1 \\ u_2 & v_2 \end{pmatrix} = \frac{\eta}{\mu_1 - \mu_2} \begin{pmatrix} \frac{-\mu_2}{\eta} & -1 \\ \frac{\mu_1}{\eta} & 1 \end{pmatrix}.$$

So, using the results in the Mathematical Appendix on the spectral decomposition of a matrix and the representation of matrix exponential function, we can write the solution (3.14) to the system of differential equations as:

$$x_t \cong e^{Dt} x_0 = \left(\Gamma e^{\Lambda} \Gamma^{-1} \right)^t x_0 = \Gamma e^{\Lambda t} \Gamma^{-1} x_0,$$

that is,

$$
\begin{pmatrix} \ln c_t - \ln c_{ss} \\ \ln k_t - \ln k_{ss} \end{pmatrix} = \frac{\eta}{\mu_1 - \mu_2} \begin{pmatrix} 1 & 1 \\ \frac{-\mu_1}{\eta} & \frac{-\mu_2}{\eta} \end{pmatrix} \begin{pmatrix} e^{\mu_1 t} & 0 \\ 0 & e^{\mu_2 t} \end{pmatrix}
$$
$$
\times \begin{pmatrix} \frac{-\mu_2}{\eta} & -1 \\ \frac{\mu_1}{\eta} & 1 \end{pmatrix} \begin{pmatrix} \ln c_0 - \ln c_{ss} \\ \ln k_0 - \ln k_{ss} \end{pmatrix},
$$

or,

$$\ln c_t - \ln c_{ss} = e^{\mu_1 t} b_{11} + e^{\mu_2 t} b_{12},$$
$$\ln k_t - \ln k_{ss} = e^{\mu_1 t} b_{21} + e^{\mu_2 t} b_{22},$$

with,

$$b_{11} = -\frac{1}{\mu_1 - \mu_2} \left[\mu_2 \left(\ln c_0 - \ln c_{ss} \right) + \eta \left(\ln k_0 - \ln k_{ss} \right) \right],$$

$$b_{12} = \frac{1}{\mu_1 - \mu_2} \left[\mu_1 \left(\ln c_0 - \ln c_{ss} \right) + \eta \left(\ln k_0 - \ln k_{ss} \right) \right],$$

$$b_{21} = \frac{\mu_1}{\left(\mu_1 - \mu_2 \right) \eta} \left[\mu_2 \left(\ln c_0 - \ln c_{ss} \right) + \eta \left(\ln k_0 - \ln k_{ss} \right) \right],$$

$$b_{22} = -\frac{\mu_2}{\left(\mu_1 - \mu_2 \right) \eta} \left[\mu_1 \left(\ln c_0 - \ln c_{ss} \right) + \eta \left(\ln k_0 - \ln k_{ss} \right) \right].$$

The transversality condition (3.13) implies $b_{21} = 0$, because the term $e^{\mu_1 t} b_{21}$ grows at a rate faster than θ. This zero condition amounts to: $\mu_2 \left(\ln c_0 - \ln c_{ss} \right) + \eta \left(\ln k_0 - \ln k_{ss} \right) = 0$, so that stability requires that initial consumption must be chosen by:

$$\ln c_0 = \ln c_{ss} - \frac{\eta}{\mu_2} \left(\ln k_0 - \ln k_{ss} \right). \tag{3.15}$$

Furthermore, notice that this condition also implies: $b_{11} = 0$. Then, using (3.15) in the expressions for b_{12} and b_{22}, we obtain:

$$b_{12} = \frac{1}{\mu_1 - \mu_2} \left[\mu_1 \left(\ln c_0 - \ln c_{ss} \right) - \mu_2 \left(\ln c_0 - \ln c_{ss} \right) \right] = \ln c_0 - \ln c_{ss},$$

$$b_{22} = -\frac{\mu_2}{\left(\mu_1 - \mu_2 \right) \eta} \left[-\frac{\eta \mu_1}{\mu_2} \left(\ln k_0 - \ln k_{ss} \right) + \eta \left(\ln k_0 - \ln k_{ss} \right) \right]$$
$$= \ln k_0 - \ln k_{ss},$$

and the solution finally becomes,

$$\ln c_t - \ln c_{ss} = e^{\mu_2 t}\left(\ln c_0 - \ln c_{ss}\right) = -e^{\mu_2 t}\frac{\eta}{\mu_2}\left(\ln k_0 - \ln k_{ss}\right),$$

$$\ln k_t - \ln k_{ss} = e^{\mu_2 t}\left(\ln k_0 - \ln k_{ss}\right).$$

for a level of c_0 chosen as a function of the initial condition on k_0 according to (3.15).

Hence, if we impose the stability condition to choose initial consumption, then the solution to the system of linear differential equations: $\ln c_t - \ln c_{ss} = e^{\mu_2 t}\left(\ln c_0 - \ln c_{ss}\right)$, implies that the relationship between consumption and the stock of capital is the same at all time periods,

$$\ln c_t = \ln c_{ss} - \frac{\eta}{\mu_2}\left(\ln k_t - \ln k_{ss}\right)\ t = 0, 1, 2, 3, \dots.$$

so that the stability condition holds every period. This is the case because we are working with the linear approximation to the system of differential equations.

As an alternative way to discuss stability, which could be used in systems of any dimensionality, we can write the solution to system (3.14):

$$x_t = \Gamma e^{\Lambda t}\Gamma^{-1}x_0, \tag{3.16}$$

as,

$$z_t = e^{\mu t}z_0, \tag{3.17}$$

after premultiplying in (3.16) by Γ^{-1} and defining $z_t = \Gamma^{-1}x_t$, $t = 0, 1, 2, \dots$ Each element in z_t as a linear combination of deviations from steady-state for both variables, $\ln c_t - \ln c_{ss}$, $\ln k_t - \ln k_{ss}$, and (3.17) shows a set of two equations representing the model. The system will be stable, in the sense of satisfying the transversality condition, only if the elements in the diagonal of Λ, i.e., the eigenvalues of D, are less than θ. But that is only the case for μ_2, as we know and hence, in each equation above there is an explosive term.

The only way to avoid the explosive path is by fixing $z_{1t} = 0\ \forall t$, which amounts to setting to zero each period the inner product of the first row in Γ^{-1} times the vector of variables in deviations from steady-state. That is, we need to set to zero each period the inner product of the left-eigenvector of D associated to the unstable eigenvalue, times the vector of variables in deviations from steady-state. Since that vector is $(-\frac{\mu_2}{\eta}, -1)$, we reach the same stability condition (3.15) as in the previous discussion. Needless to say, had we assumed that μ_1 was the stable eigenvalue, with μ_2 being unstable, we would have concluded the need to set to zero the inner product of the second row of Γ^{-1} (that is, the left-eigenvector associated to the unstable eigenvalue) and the vector of deviations from steady-state. As we will discussed below, we should generally expect a relationship between the number of stability conditions and the number of control or decision variables, since stability

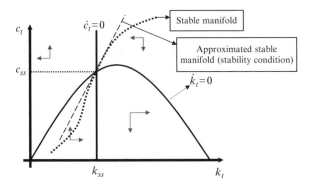

Fig. 3.5 Stability in Cass-Koopmans model

conditions are used when computing a numerical solution to the model, to obtain initial conditions for decision variables (like consumption) as functions of the initial conditions for state variables (like the stock of capital). [See Fig. 3.5].

3.2.1 The Trajectory for Income

Paths for the remaining variables can be obtained from those for the stock of capital and consumption. In the case of output, with our assumptions on technology, we have,

$$y_t = k_t^\alpha \;\Rightarrow\; \ln k_t = \frac{\ln y_t}{\alpha},$$

so that the stock of physical capital and per capita income are proportional to each other at each point in time and, consequently, also in steady-state, so that,

$$\ln k_{ss} = \frac{\ln y_{ss}}{\alpha},$$

so income will grow at the same rate than the stock of capital.

Over time, we will have,

$$\ln y_t - \ln y_{ss} = e^{\mu_2 t} \left(\ln y_0 - \ln y_{ss}\right), \tag{3.18}$$

and finally,

$$\ln y_t = \left(1 - e^{\mu_2 t}\right) \ln y_{ss} + e^{\mu_2 t} \ln y_0, \; \mu_2 < 0,$$

showing that the initial distance to steady-state in terms of income closes down at a rate μ_2, which is therefore the convergence speed to steady-state, whose value increases with the product ηh.

Hence, the rate of growth of income is an inverse function of its initial state: the farther away is an economy from steady-state, the higher will be the growth in income, assuming it starts below steady-state, $k_0 < k_{ss}$. The rate at which the gap between initial capital and consumption and their steady-state values is closed increases with n, δ, θ, and decreases when σ, α increase, as it can be seen by the way how μ_2 depends on these structural parameters. A numerical exercise on the sensitivity of the speed of convergence to changes in structural parameters is performed in the next section.

We can calculate the length of time needed to cover half the distance[3] from the initial capital stock to the steady-state,

$$\ln y_t - \ln y_{ss} = \frac{1}{2}\left(\ln y_0 - \ln y_{ss}\right) \Rightarrow e^{\mu_2 t}\left(\ln y_0 - \ln y_{ss}\right) = \frac{1}{2}\left(\ln y_0 - \ln y_{ss}\right)$$

$$\Rightarrow t = \frac{\ln \frac{1}{2}}{\mu_2}.$$

From the previous expression we also see that any set of economies sharing the same values for the structural parameters $n, \delta, \beta, \theta, \sigma$ will not only converge to the same steady state, but they will do it at a speed inversely related to their initial income. A poor country will grow more rapidly than a rich country with the same steady state. The reason is that, having less capital, the initial productivity of investment is higher. As a consequence, and according to this model, in a cross-section regression of the growth rate of income on initial income, we should have a negative coefficient, as we already saw before.

On the other hand, if two countries converge to different steady-states, we will no longer be able to make any statement about their relative speed of convergence. We should in this case consider the notion of *conditional convergence*, as discussed previously.

The reader is asked in an exercise at the end of the chapter to repeat the analysis on stability and convergence in this section for a general production function.

3.2.2 Numerical Exercise – Characterizing the Transition after a Change in a Structural Parameter

In this exercise we compute numerical values for some characteristics related to the transition of a planner's economy to the optimal steady-state. We make the same assumptions on preferences and technology as in the previous numerical exercise.

3.2.2.1 The Speed of Convergence to Steady-State

We start by examining how the rate at which the economy converges to steady-state changes with changes in the numerical values of structural parameters. This is done

---

[3] Or any other fraction of that distance, of course.

in the *Speed of Convergence* spreadsheet in the *CK_continuous_time.xls* file. We take as benchmark parameter values $A = 1$, $\theta = 0.04$, $\alpha = 0.30$, $n = 0$, $\delta = 0.10$, $\sigma = 2$, we have $h = 0.367$, $\eta = 0.049$, with h, η defined as described in the previous section. With these parameter values, the stable eigenvalue is $\mu_2 = -0.1155$, which gives the rate at which the economy converges to steady-state. The length of time to cover half the distance to steady-state is 6.0, while 12.0 time units would be needed to cover 75% of the initial distance.

In each panel we change the value of a single parameter, maintaining all the others at their benchmark values. The first analysis presents changes in the speed of convergence to steady-state with changes in the discount factor applied to future utility. Underlined in red is the initial situation. For each vector of parameter values we compute the stable eigenvalue, which determines the speed of convergence towards steady-state. Finally, the number of periods needed to close either half the initial gap to steady-state or 75% of it, is obtained. The convergence speed starts at 9.0% when future utility is not discounted, *i.e.*, when it is valued as much as current utility ($\theta = 0$). Convergence to steady-state goes faster for higher values of the discount factor, the relationship between these two variables being essentially linear. When future utility is discounted, more resources are invested to allow for more resources in the future. That way, we can compensate for the heavier discount applied to future utility. As a consequence, the stock of capital accumulates more rapidly, and we have a faster convergence to steady-state.

As the output elasticity of capital increases in the second analysis presented, less capital is needed to produce the same amount of output. There is less incentive to accumulate capital, and the economy moves more slowly towards steady-state. A special case will be considered in chapter 6, when we will allow for a unit value of the output elasticity of capital. The speed of convergence to steady-state goes then to infinity, meaning that the economy jumps immediately to steady-state. In other words, there is no transition to steady-state.

Population growth can be considered as a sort of depreciation of physical capital, so we deal with the next two analysis simultaneously. As depreciation increases, more resources need to be devoted to investment to maintain the stock of capital unchanged. Then, physical capital needs to accumulate more intensively because a larger proportion is lost to depreciation. The higher depreciation and the more intense accumulation of capital go in opposite directions, and our numerical exercise shows how, at least for reasonable parameter values, the second effect dominates, and the economy converges to steady-state faster under higher depreciation.

As the elasticity of intertemporal substitution of consumption increases, the concavity of the assumed CRRA utility function decreases. Agents are relatively indifferent to consumption changes, so it is not surprising that the economy converges faster to steady-state.

3.2.2.2 A First Note of Caution

The next exercise is the first instance in which we compute time series for the endogenous variables in the continuous time version of the Cass–Koopmans economy.

The reader should be aware that this exercise is subject to potential pitfalls. Producing discrete time series out of a continuous-time model amounts to observing the continuous time processes followed by the endogenous variables at equally spaced points in time. By doing that, we miss what is taking place between successive observations, and that could be quite important if our goal is to describe the main characteristics of the vector of endogenous variables, like their volatilities, or the correlation coefficients between pairs of variables. Even more importantly, this limitation is very relevant if we want to compute the level of welfare, defined as the integral of a continuous function of time. It is tempting to compute welfare by aggregating over time the levels of discounted utility computed for each observation period. But that may be a poor approximation to the continuous time integral, as we show in this numerical simulation. To perform a fully justified analysis using discrete time series for the endogenous variables, these must be computed from the discrete-time version of the Cass–Koopmans economy, which we present in a section below.

3.2.2.3 Convergence to Steady State as a Function of the Degree of Risk Aversion

We analyze in this section how the convergence path to steady-state, depends on the concavity of the utility function. We again assume a Cobb-Douglas production technology and a CRRA utility function, so that concavity is characterized by the risk aversion parameter which, as shown in Sect. 3.1.2 is the inverse of the intertemporal elasticity of consumption. These transition trajectories are computed in the *Convergence. Risk aversion* spreadsheet of the *CK_continuous_time.xls* file. Transition paths to steady-state can also be calculated with the *CK_c_transition.m* file.

We examine two economies, differing in their value of σ, the parameter, which determines the concavity of the utility function of their representative agents. As we have seen in the previous sections, the preferences of private agents do not play any role in determining steady state levels, which are therefore the same for both economies. Benchmark parameter values are, $A = 1$, $\theta = 0.04$, $n = 0$, $\delta = 0.10$, $\sigma = 2$, which imply steady state levels for the capital stock, consumption and output, $k_{ss} = 2.9706$, $c_{ss} = 1.0892$, $i_{ss} = .2971$, $y_{ss} = 1.3863$. The degree of concavity of the utility function affects the representation of the linear approximation to steady-state through the value of η and hence, the way how initial consumption is chosen as a function of the initial stock of capital.

Steady-state levels are calculated on the left of the spreadsheet. Below them, we compute the h, η constants and the transition matrix D defined in the *Stability and Convergence* section. After that, we compute the stable and unstable eigenvalues of D, as well as the matrix of right-eigenvectors. The initial condition on the stock of the capital is also assumed to be the same in both economies, capital being 10% above steady-state. The economies then describe smooth decreasing paths converging towards steady-state.

To compute the actual time series, the logged stock of capital is obtained by using the condition that the initial gap to the steady-state is closed at a rate $\mu_2 : \ln k_t - \ln k_{ss} = e^{\mu_2 t} (\ln k_0 - \ln k_{ss})$. Logged-consumption in the initial period is chosen by imposing the stability condition: $\ln c_0 = \ln c_{ss} - \frac{\eta}{\mu_2} (\ln k_0 - \ln k_{ss})$. After that, $\ln c_t - \ln c_{ss} = e^{\mu_2 t} (\ln c_0 - \ln c_{ss})$ is used each period. As we saw in the previous section, this condition guarantees stability. Output is obtained from capital each period using the specification for the production function, and investment is obtained as the difference between output and consumption. Finally, the level of utility as well as its discounted value each discrete time period, are obtained and aggregated over time.

Investment can be seen to follow a different behavior in its convergence to steady-state for the two risk aversion parameter values. Under a less concave utility, investment is relatively low initially, gradually increasing along the convergence to its steady-state level. The opposite happens for a more concave utility, for which investment is higher initially, then decreasing along the convergence path. What happens is that under the less concave utility, agents consume a large part of the amount by which output is initially above its steady state level, investing a relatively low amount of resources. As a consequence, the stock of capital decreases to its steady-state level faster than under the more concave utility. Agents with the latter preferences prefer to invest a greater share of output and maintain a lower consumption than those consumers with the less concave preferences.

It is clear then how distinct degrees of risk aversion determine different convergence paths for all the variables in the economy. After computing discrete time series for all variables, we have obtained time series for single period discounted utility for each agent, and we have aggregated the resulting values at the bottom of each series. According to this exercise, it would look as if maximized welfare is 2.37881 for agent A, and 1.96739 for agent B. These values are not comparable among themselves. They are an estimate of the highest level of welfare that can be achieved by each consumer, given his preferences and his initial stock of capital. It should then be the case that each consumer prefers the optimal consumption trajectory we have computed than the one we have determined for the other type of agent. But that seems not to be the case in this spreadsheet for several reasons that are worthwhile considering. Indeed, to the right of the graphs, we have also computed single period and discounted utility for each agent, under the optimal consumption time series *for the other consumer*. We obtain 2.37227 for agent A, and 1.96852 for agent B, so it would look as if the latter prefers better the consumption trajectory that maximizes welfare for agent A, which would be an obvious inconsistency in our solution. This is a consequence of the fact that each consumption trajectory we report is a log-linear approximation to the optimal consumption trajectory for each of the two values of the risk aversion parameter we have considered. The farther away we start from steady-state, the larger will be the approximation error. On the other hand, if the two consumers are not very different form each other, the approximation error could be enough to explain that one consumer might prefer the approximate optimal consumption trajectory we have computed for the other consumer. In fact, because of the approximation error, none of them is exactly an optimal trajectory for either consumer. Finally, dealing with continuous time as being a discrete variable is an unavoidable source of error that can only be reduced by partitioning the time unit into a large number of observations. The problem cannot be solved by taking care of a single one of these conditions. For instance, if we start very close to steady-state but consumers are not very different from each other, we could still have this paradox. By refining the partition of each time unit we reduce the approximation error, but we do not fully eliminate it.

In the next spreadsheet, *Risk aversion (long horizon)*, we have repeated the exercise, with the same parameterization, this time refining the time interval, which has now a length of 0.025. So, we observe the system 40 times each time period. We consider two consumers with degrees of risk aversion $\sigma = 1.2$ and $\sigma = 10$, and start in each case with a stock of capital 5% above its steady-state level. Welfare is estimated by numerically integrating the discounted utility function over 8000 observations (which amount to 125 time periods), and adding for each observation from that point on the steady-state level of utility. We again compute the level of welfare of each consumer under the consumption trajectory obtained for the other consumer. Discounted utility for agent B is initially larger when calculated for agent A's consumption series, since consumption is higher for agent A. However, as indicated in yellow, at $t = 7.9$, the ordering reverses, and stays that way to infinity. So, as expected, when evaluated between $t = 0$ and $t = \infty$, agent B prefers his own welfare maximizing consumption stream.

The apparent paradox in the previous analysis (*Convergence. Risk aversion*) was due to the three factors we already mentioned: (a) too rough a partition of the time unit, (b) relatively similar consumers, and (c) an initial condition relatively far from steady state. In the *Risk aversion (long horizon)* spreadsheet we have considered even more similar consumers, but started closer to steady state (5% above it) and used a finer partition of the time unit, and the paradoxical result goes away. The reader can check that starting farther away from steady state could again bring the paradoxical result, as it would be the case if we consider still more similar consumers.

3.2.2.4 A Change in Output Elasticity of Capital: Transition Between Steady States

In the *Change in output share of k* spreadsheet in *CK_continuous_time.xls* we present the short- and the long-run effects of a change in the output elasticity of physical capital, from an initial value of $\alpha = 0.30$, to $\alpha = 0.31$. The same analysis can be performed with the *CK_c_change structural parameters.m* MATLAB file. We maintain the same assumptions on preferences and technology as in previous exercises. We assume the economy is initially in steady-state, when the change in output elasticity occurs, and describe what happens from that period on. After describing on the left side of the spreadsheet the benchmark parameter values, $A = 1$, $\theta = 0.04$, $n = 0$, $\delta = 0.10$, $\sigma = 2$, we calculate steady state levels for the capital stock, consumption and output before and after the change in α. The increase in the output elasticity of capital implies a better capacity to produce output, which allows for increases in steady state levels from $k_{ss} = 2.9706$, $c_{ss} = 1.0892$, $i_{ss} = .2971$, $y_{ss} = 1.3863$ to $k_{ss} = 3.1647$, $c_{ss} = 1.1128$, $i_{ss} = .3165$, $y_{ss} = 1.4292$.

The point of the exercise is that even if the economy is initially at steady-state, a change in a structural parameter like the output elasticity of capital, changes the steady-state levels. As a consequence, the economy is no longer at steady-state and, since the system is stable, a transition starts by which the economy converges from its initial situation to the new steady-state. In the spreadsheet we have labelled as $t = 0$ the time at which α changes. The stock of capital at the beginning of $t = 0$ was decided at the end of the previous period, when the structural change was still unknown, so k_t was still at the old steady-state level, defined by $k_{ss} = 2.9706$. Then, α changes, and the economy must position on the stable manifold converging to the new steady-state, $k_{ss} = 3.1647$.

We must now compute the eigenvalues of the transition matrix under the new parameter values, which is why the values in the spreadsheet are slightly different from those in the previous sections. We now have: $h = 0.3516$, $\eta = 0.0483$, with eigenvalues for the coefficient matrix in the log-linear approximation: $\mu_1 = 0.1518$, $\mu_2 = -0.1118$. As in the previous numerical exercises, we do not know the exact representation of the stable manifold that would take the economy towards its new steady-state, but we have a linear approximation for it in the form of the stability condition that links consumption to the stock of capital every period, both in deviations from steady-state. That relationship is again estimated through the left eigenvectors of the matrix of coefficients in the linear approximation to the model, when written as a first order vector autoregression. That is described in the spreadsheet, and the stabilizing constant is estimated at 0.4319, so that the stable manifold can be approximated by,

$$\ln c_t - \ln c_{ss} = 0.4319 \left(\ln k_t - \ln k_{ss} \right),$$

which gives us the level of consumption at $t = 0$.

An increase in the output elasticity of physical capital increases the marginal product for that production factor, creating a strong incentive for capital accumulation. The initial response of the economy is then a large raise in investment together with a fall in consumption. Production increases initially because of the change in technology. Afterwards, the output increase is also due to the larger stock of capital. The consumption recovery is explained by the increase in production. The marginal product of capital gradually diminishes as the economy approaches its new steady-state and, as a consequence, investment decreases somewhat to its new steady-state level. The type of response experienced by investment is known as an *overshooting*, by which the initial reaction of the variable is so large that goes beyond its long-run level, to which it must move later through an adjustment in the opposite direction to the initial change.

3.3 Interpreting the Central Planners's Model as a Competitive Equilibrium Economy

The centralized economy analyzed in previous sections, where a planner makes decisions that imposes on private agents, leads to an allocation of resources that can also be obtained under the competitive equilibrium mechanism in an economy without government. This theoretical equivalence means that an analyst who was given time series for consumption, capital and output extracted from either one of these economies, would not be able to say which one had produced them. Together with the argument in Sect. 3.1.8, this result implies the Pareto efficiency of the competitive equilibrium allocation, which arises because we have not introduced any externality or friction in our model economy.

We assume there are complete financial markets, i.e., any agent can borrow or lend as many units of the consumption commodity as he/she can, at the prevailing rate of interest. There is a set of identical consumers, who are endowed with a unit of labor every period, and derive utility from consumption. Leisure does not enter as an argument in the utility function. The single firm in the economy owns the stock of physical capital, K_t, and uses that factor, together with labor, N_t, to produce the only consumption commodity. It issues some stock, v_t, which is bought by consumers. Each unit of stock gives ownership rights to one unit of capital and yields a real return of r_t. The firm faces competitive markets for inputs and output, so that it treats the real rate of return on capital, r_t, wages, ω_t, and the price of the consumption commodity as given. There is no uncertainty, and the aggregate technology displays constant returns to scale.

3.3.0.5 Consumer's Problem

The representative consumer chooses consumption every period, as well as the units of stock in his/her portfolio, so as to maximize time-aggregate, discounted utility,

$$\underset{c_t,v_t}{Max} \int_0^\infty e^{-\theta t} U(c_t) dt,$$

subject to,

$$\dot{v}_t + c_t = \omega_t + (r_t - n) v_t, \tag{3.19}$$

Initial wealth, v_0, is given, and the consumer takes prices ω_t, r_t as given. The consumer uses salaries, together with the real return on its portfolio, to pay for consumption as well as for the changes in his/her portfolio. If there is a reduction in the size of the portfolio, the consumer will have the proceeds from selling stock as additional resources to pay for consumption. Population growth is subtracted from the real return on assets because of the need to provide newly born consumers each period with the same portfolio as all other consumers.

Maximization of the Hamiltonian,

$$H(c_t, v_t, q_t, \omega_t, r_t) = e^{-\theta t} \left\{ U(c_t) + q_t \left[\omega_t + (r_t - n) v_t - c_t - \tau_t \right] \right\},$$

leads to optimality conditions,

$$state\ equation\ C1\ :\ U'(c_t) = q_t,$$
$$co-state\ equation\ (Euler)\ C2\ :\ \dot{q}_t/q_t = n + \theta - r_t,$$
$$transversality\ condition\ C3\ :\ \lim_{t \to \infty} e^{-\theta t} q_t v_t = 0.$$

Noting that C1 implies $\dot{q}_t = U''(c_t)\dot{c}_t$, we can write C2 as,

$$\frac{\dot{c}_t}{c_t} = \gamma(c_t) \left[r_t - (n + \theta) \right], \tag{3.20}$$

with $\gamma(c_t)$ being the intertemporal elasticity of consumption, $\gamma(c_t) = \frac{U'(c_t)}{U''(c_t)c_t}$. Optimal consumption and savings choices are characterized by $(3.19), (3.20)$ together with the transversality condition C3.

3.3.0.6 The Problem of the Firm

The single firm in the economy maximizes the present value of current and future profits,

$$\underset{K_t, L_t}{MaxV_0} \equiv \int_0^{\infty} e^{-\int_0^t r_s ds} \left[F(K_t, L_t) - \omega_t L_t - (\delta K_t + \dot{K}_t) \right] dt,$$

given the initial stock of capital, K_0, where ω_t denote real salaries. Normalizing the output price to 1, profits are obtained as the difference between output revenues on the one hand, and the aggregate of wage payments and gross investment, on the other. Gross investment is the sum of net investment, $\dot{K}_t$, plus depreciation expenditures.

To solve the optimization problem of the firm, we write the present value of firm's profits V_0 above as,

$$V_0 = \int_0^{\infty} e^{-\int_0^t r_s ds} [F(K_t, L_t) - \omega_t L_t - \delta K_t] dt - \int_0^{\infty} e^{-\int_0^t r_s ds} \dot{K}_t dt. \tag{3.21}$$

To compute the last term, we need to recall the expression for a parametric integral function,

$$I(t) = \int_{a(t)}^{b(t)} f(x, t) dx,$$

whose derivative with respect to the parameter t is given by Leibniz's rule:

$$\frac{dI(t)}{dt} = \int_{a(t)}^{b(t)} \frac{\partial f(x, t)}{\partial t} dx + f(b(t), t) \frac{db(t)}{dt} - f(a(t), t) \frac{da(t)}{dt}.$$

Integrating by parts[4] in: $\int_0^\infty e^{-\int_0^t r_s ds} \dot{K}_t \, dt$, and applying Leibniz's rule, we get:

$$\int_0^\infty e^{-\int_0^t r_s ds} \dot{K}_t dt = \left[e^{-\int_0^t r_s ds} \cdot K_t \right]_0^\infty + \int_0^\infty e^{-\int_0^t r_s ds} r_t K_t \, dt$$

$$= -K_0 + \int_0^\infty e^{-\int_0^t r_s ds} r_t K_t \, dt,$$

where we have applied the transversality condition, $\lim_{t \to \infty} e^{-\int_0^t r_s ds} K_t = 0$.

Therefore, the objective function for the firm (3.21) can be written:

$$V_0 = K_0 + e^{-\int_0^t r_s ds} [F(K_t, L_t) - \omega_t L_t - (r_t + \delta)K_t] \, dt, \qquad (3.22)$$

showing that the trajectories for labor and the stock of capital, $\{K_t, L_t\}_{t=0}^\infty$, maximizing (3.22) are the same as those maximizing single period profits, $F(K_t, L_t) - \omega_t L_t - (r_t + \delta)K_t$. This is the case because decisions at a point in time do not affect any variable entering into the objective function at any other point in time.

To maximize $F(K_t, L_t) - \omega_t L_t - (r_t + \delta)K_t$, the firm chooses K_t, L_t such that,

$$\frac{\partial F(K_t, L_t)}{\partial K_t} = r_t + \delta; \quad \frac{\partial F(K_t, L_t)}{\partial L_t} = \omega_t.$$

We can now use the relationships obtained when discussing the Solow–Swan model, to write conditions above as,

$$F1 : \ \partial F / \partial K_t \equiv f'(k_t) = \delta + r_t, \qquad (3.23)$$

$$F2 : \ \partial F / \partial L_t = f(k_t) - f'(k_t)k_t = \omega_t, \qquad (3.24)$$

which implies that the firm hires workers and capital to the point where marginal products are equal to relative prices ω_t and r_t. Because of the constant returns to scale assumption, single period profits are zero, so that $V_0 = K_0$, showing that the present value of the ownership rights on the firm, i.e., the present value of profits is equal to the initial stock of capital.

Definition 2. Given an initial condition k_0, a competitive equilibrium is a vector of continuous functions of time defined over $(0, \infty)$ $\{c_t^*, k_t^*, \omega_t^*, r_t^*, N_t^*, v_t^*\}_{t=0}^\infty$ such that,

- Given ω_t^*, r_t^*, the time functions c_t^*, v_t^* solve the representative consumer's problem,
- Given ω_t^*, r_t^*, the time functions for capital k_t^* maximizes firm' profits each period,
- The labor market clears, with equality of labor supply and demand. Since labor is supplied inelastically, labor market clearing means that labor demand is equal to total population, $L_t^* = N_t = N_0 e^{nt}$, $\forall t$,

---

[4] To integrate by parts, we define: $u = e^{-\int_0^t r_s ds}$ and: $v = K_t$, so that: $dv = \dot{K}_t dt$, and applying Leibniz's rule: $du = e^{-\int_0^t r_s ds} r_t dt$.

- The units of stock owned by consumers are equal to the stock of capital owned by the firm, $v_t^* = k_t^*$, $\forall t$.

3.3.0.7 Global Constraint of Resources

Taking (3.23) to (3.19) and using the fact that, in equilibrium, $v_t^* = k_t^* \forall t$, we obtain,

$$\dot{k}_t = f(k_t) - (n+\delta)k_t - c_t,$$

which is known as the *global constraint of resources*, and it is precisely the constraint faced by the benevolent planner, that we saw in Sect. 3.1. This is in fact a reflection of Walras' law. As a consequence of equilibrium conditions, that require clearing of the labor market and the market for physical capital, the market for the consumption commodity also clears. That means that total production of the single commodity in the economy is equal, in equilibrium, to the sum of private consumption and gross investment, the latter being the aggregate of net investment and depreciation expenditures,

$$f(k_t) = c_t + [\dot{k}_t + (n+\delta)k_t].$$

3.3.1 The Efficiency of Competitive Equilibrium

In previous sections we have seen two different resource allocation mechanisms: on the one hand, the planner's mechanism, which maximizes social welfare. On the other hand, the competitive equilibrium mechanism, where consumers maximize utility and firms maximize profits taking prices as given. Prices are then determined by market clearing conditions. Interesting questions are:

- Is the competitive equilibrium mechanism able to achieve the same allocation of resources as the one emerging under the planner's mechanism?
- Is a planner needed to achieve efficiency in resource allocation, or can markets achieve efficiency by themselves through the competitive equilibrium mechanism?

The following theorems answer these two questions. Let us start by recalling the optimality conditions for the planner's problem:

$$P1) \; U'(c_t) - \lambda_t = 0,$$

$$P2) \; f'(k_t) - (\delta+n) - \theta + \frac{\dot{\lambda}}{\lambda_t} = 0,$$

$$P3) \lim_{t \to \infty} \lambda_t \, e^{-\theta t} \, k_t = 0.$$

Theorem 1. *Welfare Theorem 1: Let the vector of time functions* $\{c_t^*, k_t^*, N_t^*, r_t^*, \omega_t^*, \gamma_t^*\}$ *be a competitive equilibrium. Then,* $\{c_t^*, k_t^*\}$ *solve the planner's problem. Hence, the resource allocation obtained under the competitive equilibrium is Pareto-efficient.*

Proof. Define $\lambda_t = q_t$, and $C1$ implies $P1$. If we substitute $F1$ into $C2$, we obtain $P2$. Finally, since in competitive equilibrium, $v_t = k_t$, then $C3$ implies $P3$. Hence, the competitive equilibrium time functions for consumption and physical capital solve the planner's problem. The same argument we made above to obtain the global constraint of resources shows that the constraint to the planner's problem is satisfied every period, so the competitive equilibrium allocation of resources as summarized by $\{c_t^*, k_t^*\}$ is a solution to the planner's problem.

Theorem 2. *Welfare Theorem 2: Let* $\{c_t^*, k_t^*\}$ *be a solution to planner's problem (so, it is a Pareto-efficient resource allocation). There are price functions* $\{r_t^*, \omega_t^*\}$ *and time functions for labor and units of stock held* $\{N_t^*, v_t^*\}$ *such that* $\{c_t^*, k_t^*, N_t^*, r_t^*, \omega_t^*, v_t^*\}$ *is a competitive equilibrium.*

Proof. From the given sequence for the stock of capital, let us define prices,

$$\omega_t^* = f(k_t^*) - k_t^* f'(k_t^*), \ \forall t$$

$$r_t^* = f'(k_t^*) - \delta, \ \forall t$$

and time functions,

$$L_t^* = N_t = N_0 e^{nt}, \ \forall t$$

$$v_t^* = k_t^*, \ \forall t.$$

Let us further define a sequence of shadow prices $q_t = U'(c_t^*)$. With these definitions, $C1$ holds by construction. $P2$, together with the definitions of r_t^* and q_t, imply that $C2$ holds. The definitions of v_t^* and q_t, together with $P3$, imply $C3$. Finally, the definitions of r_t^* and ω_t^* imply that $F1$ and $F2$ hold.

Once we introduce the definition of r_t^* into $P2$, we get the competitive equilibrium differential equation for c_t. The law of motion for k_t in competitive equilibrium is the planer's global constraint of resources, so the time functions for consumption and the stock of capital are the solutions to the same system of differential equations as in the benevolent planner's problem. Since the firm is using the same stock of capital and the same labor than under the planner solution, output will be the same. Depreciation is also the same in both solutions, and so is investment, which is equal to savings in this closed economy without government. Hence, the level of output being produced and its decomposition between private consumption and savings are exactly the same as under the planner's solution.

3.4 A Competitive Equilibrium with Government

3.4.1 The Structure of the Economy

We consider again an economy subject to no uncertainty, with an aggregate technology displaying constant returns to scale. We introduce a government of a simple kind, that it cannot directly influence consumers' utility or the production technology. It will, however, take some resources away from the economy, reducing aggregate consumption and investment possibilities. The government finances its activities by issuing bonds paying a certain real return r_t, and by levying per-capita lump-sum taxes τ_t on consumers. We do not consider money in the economy. Consumers are all identical to each other, endowed with a unit of labor every period. Leisure does not enter as an argument in their utility function. The single firm in the economy uses physical capital, K_t, and labor, N_t, to produce the only consumption commodity. The firm is the owner of the stock of physical capital. It issues some stock, v_t, which is bought by consumers. Each unit of stock gives ownership rights to one unit of capital and yields a real rate of return r_t. This must be equal to the return on government bonds since, in the absence of uncertainty, one of the two markets would otherwise disappear.

3.4.1.1 Consumer's Problem

The representative consumer chooses every period consumption and the number of stock and government bonds in his/her portfolio so as to maximize time-aggregate, discounted utility,

$$\underset{c_t,\, a_t}{Max} \int_0^\infty e^{-\theta t} U(c_t)\, dt,$$

subject to,

$$\dot{a}_t + c_t + \tau_t = \omega_t + (r_t - n)\, a_t, \tag{3.25}$$

where $a_t = v_t + b_t$ denotes total assets, the aggregate of stock on the firm, v_t, and government bonds, b_t. Initial wealth, a_0, is given, and the consumer takes real wages and interest rates $\{\omega_t, r_t\}_{t=0}^\infty$ as given.

Maximization of the Hamiltonian,

$$H(c_t, a_t, q_t, \omega_t, r_t) = e^{-\theta t} \left\{ U(c_t) + q_t \left[\omega_t + (r_t - n)\, a_t - c_t - \tau_t \right] \right\},$$

leads to optimality conditions,

$$state\ equation\ C_g1:\ U'(c_t) = q_t,$$
$$co-state\ equation\ (Euler)\ C_g2:\ \dot{q}_t/q_t = n + \theta - r_t,$$
$$transversality\ condition\ C_g3:\ \lim_{t\to\infty} e^{-\theta t} q_t a_t = 0,$$

the last one being the transversality condition for the consumer's problem.

Euler's equation C_g2 is a first order, homogeneous, variable coefficient differential equation which integrates to [see Mathematical Appendix],

$$q_t = q_0 \cdot e^{-\int_0^t (r_s - (n+\theta))ds},$$

so that the transversality condition can be written,

$$\lim_{t\to\infty} e^{-\theta t} q_t a_t = \lim_{t\to\infty} q_0 \cdot e^{-\int_0^t (r_s-n)ds} a_t = 0,$$

or,

$$\lim_{t\to\infty} e^{-\int_0^t (r_s-n)ds} v_t + \lim_{t\to\infty} e^{-\int_0^t (r_s-n)ds} b_t = 0.$$

Unless we allow for a negative stock of government bonds, *i.e.*, for the government to make loans to consumers, both terms will be non-negative, and we must have,

$$\lim_{t\to\infty} e^{-\int_0^t (r_s-n)ds} v_t = \lim_{t\to\infty} e^{-\int_0^t (r_s-n)ds} b_t = 0, \tag{3.26}$$

for the transversality condition of consumer's problem to hold.

It is also interesting to use the consumer's budget constraint to represent the time evolution of his/her portfolio of assets. Using the results in the Mathematical Appendix for non-homogeneous, variable coefficient, first order differential equations, we get,

$$a_t = \left[a_0 + \int_0^t e^{-\int_0^z (r_s-n)ds} (\omega_z - c_z - \tau_z) dz \right] e^{\int_0^t (r_s-n)ds}$$

$$= a_0 e^{\int_0^t (r_s-n)ds} + \int_0^t e^{\int_z^t (r_s-n)ds} (\omega_z - c_z - \tau_z) dz,$$

showing that at each point in time, the stock of assets is the capitalized value of (a) the initial stock of assets, a_0, and (b) past single period differences between wage revenues ω_t and expenditures, $c_t + \tau_t$.

Moving the exponential term to the right to the left hand side and taking limits, we get,

$$\lim_{t\to\infty} e^{-\int_0^t (r_s-n)ds} a_t = a_0 + \lim_{t\to\infty} \int_0^t e^{-\int_0^z (r_s-n)ds} (\omega_z - c_z - \tau_z) dz,$$

the left hand side being equal to zero because of the transversality condition, so we end up with,

$$a_0 = \int_0^\infty e^{-\int_0^z (r_s-n)ds} (c_z + \tau_z - \omega_z) dz,$$

showing that the initial stock of assets allows the consumer to enter into a sequence of future deficits $c_t + \tau_t - \omega_t$, so long as their present value remains below the initial stock of assets. If the present value of future deficits were less than initial assets, the consumer could have increased consumption at some point in time by running a higher deficit, achieving a higher level of welfare. On the other hand, the consumer will not be able to run a sequence of deficits whose discounted present value is above its current stock of assets, since he will not be able to finance its consumption and tax expenditures.

As a matter of fact, any time period can be taken as the initial time, so we can write,

$$a_t = -\int_t^\infty e^{-\int_t^z (r_s - n)ds} \left(\omega_z - c_z - \tau_z \right) dz,$$

which is sometimes called the *forward solution* to the consumer's budget constraint, with an interpretation similar to that of the previous equation.

3.4.1.2 Firm's Problem

The firm chooses sequences of capital stock and employment to maximize the present value of profits,

$$\underset{K_t, N_t}{Max} \int_0^\infty e^{-\int_0^t r_s ds} \left[F(K_t, N_t) - \omega_t N_t - \delta K_t - \dot{K}_t \right] dt,$$

given the initial stock of capital, K_0.

As shown in the previous section, optimality conditions for this problem are,

$$F_g 1: \ \partial F / \partial K_t \equiv f'(k_t) = \delta + r_t,$$
$$F_g 2: \ \partial F / \partial N_t = \omega_t \Leftrightarrow f(k_t) - f'(k_t)k_t = \omega_t.$$

A standard argument can be used to show that the constant returns to scale assumption implies that maximized profits are zero, with total revenues being distributed either in the form of wage payments or as return on issued stock.

3.4.1.3 The Government

The government spends at each point in time G_t units of the consumption commodity which, unfortunately, do not contribute to increase private agents' utility or to improve the available production technology. The government budget constraint is,

$$\dot{B}_t + T_t = r_t B_t + G_t,$$

where the left hand side describes the sources of revenues: issuing debt plus levying lump-sum taxes. The right hand side displays expenditures: interest payments, plus public consumption.

Using lower case letters to denote per capita variables, dividing by population in the government budget constraint and using the relationship

$$\dot{b}_t = \frac{d\left(\frac{B_t}{N_t}\right)}{dt} = \frac{\dot{B}_t}{N_t} - n b_t,$$

we get the government budget constraint in per capita terms,

$$\dot{b}_t = (r_t - n)b_t + g_t - \tau_t, \tag{3.27}$$

where $\tau_t = T_t/N_t$ denote per-capita lump-sum taxes.

A similar analysis to the one we did for the consumer leads to,

$$b_t = \left[b_0 + \int_0^t e^{-\int_0^z (r_s - n)ds} \left(g_z - \tau_z \right) dz \right] e^{\int_0^t (r_s - n)ds}$$

$$= b_0 e^{\int_0^t (r_s - n)ds} + \int_0^t e^{\int_z^t (r_s - n)ds} \left(g_z - \tau_z \right) dz,$$

showing that at each point in time, the stock of outstanding debt is equal to the capitalized value of initial debt, plus the present value of past deficits.

Moving the last exponential term to the left and taking limits,

$$\lim_{t \to \infty} e^{-\int_0^t (r_s - n)ds} b_t = b_0 + \lim_{t \to \infty} \int_0^t e^{-\int_0^z (r_s - n)ds} \left(g_z - \tau_z \right) dz,$$

and using the transversality condition on the left hand side,

$$b_0 = -\int_0^\infty e^{-\int_0^z (r_s - n)ds} \left(g_z - \tau_z \right) dz,$$

showing that the initial debt outstanding requires that the aggregate of the positive and negative budget balances of the government over individual periods must have a positive present value, equal to the initial stock of debt.

Finally, since any time period can be taken as the initial time, we have,

$$b_t = -\int_t^\infty e^{-\int_t^z (r_s - n)ds} \left(g_z - \tau_z \right) dz, \tag{3.28}$$

the *forward solution* to the differential equation for government debt.

So, at each point in time, the present value of current and future government surplus must be equal to current outstanding debt. A current stock of debt below the present value of the sequence of budget surplus would generally be inefficient, because the government would then have some room to decrease taxes, presumably contributing to an increase in consumers' welfare, so the proposed solution would be suboptimal. On the other hand, a level of current debt above the present value of the intertemporal financing capacity of the government would mean that the government will be at some point unable to honor its payment commitments and, consequently, investors will refuse to hold any of that debt.

3.4.2 Feasible Stationary Public Expenditure and Financing Policies

Let us assume that the economy is at time t in steady-state, and that the government wants to follow from then on a policy of constant expenditures and lump-sum taxes in per-capita terms, $g_t = g$, $\tau_t = \tau \ \forall t$. What levels of public consumption and taxes are sustainable in the long-run under this stationary policy?

From the forward solution for the stock of debt, we have,

$$b_t = -\int_t^\infty e^{-\int_t^z (r_s - n)ds} (g_z - \tau_z)\, dz = \int_t^\infty e^{-(r-n)(z-t)} (\tau_z - g_z)\, dz,$$

which, for $t = 0$ implies,

$$b_0 = \int_0^\infty e^{-(r-n)z} (\tau_z - g_z)\, dz = \frac{\tau - g}{r - n},$$

i.e., a fiscal policy is sustainable in steady state if the present value of a single period surplus is equal to the initial stock of debt. If, initially, the government has some debt outstanding, it would only be feasible to sustain a public financing policy with surplus. Policies that are exactly feasible are those that maintain a constant surplus by an amount enough to allow the government to eventually retire its initial debt. There are many other feasible policies, which could consist on initially financing public expenditures by issuing more debt and cutting down taxes to increase them later on, but we have just characterized feasible policies with constant taxes.

3.4.3 Competitive Equilibrium

Definition 3. A competitive equilibrium with government is a vector of continuous functions of time $c_t^*, k_t^*, N_t^*, b_t^*, v_t^*, g_t^*, r_t^*, \tau_t^*, \omega_t^*$, defined on $(0, \infty)$, such that,

- Given $r_t^*, \omega_t^*, \tau_t^*$, the time functions for consumption and assets c_t^*, v_t^*, b_t^* solve consumer's utility maximization problem,
- Given r_t^*, ω_t^*, the time functions for the stock of capital and labor k_t^*, N_t^* solve the firm's profit maximization problem,
- Factor markets clear at each point in time, $v_t^* = k_t^*$, $N_t^* = L_t = L_0 e^{nt}$, all t.
- The government budget constraint (3.27) holds every period,

The following theorem relates the equilibrium level of the real interest rate to the rate at which consumers discount future utility. This relationship was already used in Sect. 3.1.4.

Theorem 3. *If the resource allocation implied by a competitive equilibrium is compatible with the existence of an optimal steady-state, we will have at that point a constant real rate of interest, given by $r^* = \theta + n$. Furthermore, $r^* = f'(k^*) - \delta$.*

Proof. At steady-state, $\dot{q}_t = 0$ which, taken to C_g2, implies a constant interest rate, $r_{ss} = \theta + n$. Condition F_g1, evaluated at steady-state, directly implies the second statement in the theorem.

3.4.4 Global Constraint of Resources

As in the economy without government, we can use equilibrium conditions to consolidate the budget constraints for the consumer and the government into a single, global constraint of resources in the economy, the only constraint a benevolent central planner would face in this economy, similar to (3.1).

Subtracting the government budget constraint from the consumer budget constraint, and taking into account that $\dot{a}_t = \dot{v}_t + \dot{b}_t$, we get

$$g_t + \dot{v}_t + c_t = \omega_t + (r_t - n)v_t,$$

which, using the equilibrium condition $v_t = k_t$, can be written,

$$g_t + \dot{k}_t + c_t = \omega_t + (r_t - n)k_t. \tag{3.29}$$

On the other hand, from profit maximizing conditions F_g1 and F_g2 we get:

$$y_t = f(k_t) = \omega_t + f'(k_t)k_t = \omega_t + (r_t + \delta)k_t,$$

which, taken to (3.29), lead to:

$$g_t + \dot{k}_t + c_t = y_t - (\delta + n)k_t,$$

that is,

$$y_t = c_t + g_t + \dot{k}_t + (\delta + n)k_t, \tag{3.30}$$

which is the *global constraint of resources* in the economy. This constraint is a reflection of Walras' law, showing that the market for the single commodity clears, with output being allocated into private consumption, public consumption, and investment.

3.4.5 The Representative Agent Problem

In the previous section we have characterized the competitive equilibrium allocation by solving optimization problems for the typical consumer and for the single firm in the economy. There are situations in which we can reach the same allocation through a simpler method, which consists on solving a single optimization problem, for the so-called *representative agent* in the economy. This problem is a convenient artificial construction, but it does not represent any specific agent. The household and the productive sectors are consolidated into a single worker-entrepeneur agent, who takes care of production and makes the consumption/savings decisions.[5] Under this approach, two agents are considered in the economy, the government and the representative agent. The budget constraint for the latter includes tax payments, but not government expenditures. The latter appear in the government's budget constraint.[6]

Let us consider an economy with a government that buys a sequence $g_t \geq 0$ of commodity units which finances through lump-sum taxes. We will consider the sequence g_t to be exogenously given. For simplicity, we will also assume that these expenditures do not contribute to production or yield any utility to the consumer. For all practical purposes, we can think that public purchases of the commodity are *'thrown to the sea'*. The government is allowed to issue some debt, $b_t \geq 0$. That way, it can spend more at some points in time than what is collected through the lump-sum tax. The government budget constraint would then be,

$$\dot{b}_t = (r_t - n)b_t + g_t - \tau_t. \tag{3.31}$$

The *representative agent problem* would be,

$$Max_{c_t} \int_0^\infty e^{-\theta t} U(c_t) dt,$$

subject to the sequence of constraints:

$$\dot{b}_t + \dot{k}_t + (\delta + n)k_t + c_t + \tau_t = f(k_t) + (r_t - n)b_t, \tag{3.32}$$

where the paths for $\{\tau_t, r_t\}$, as well as k_0, b_0, are given.

By using state and co-state equations as in optimal control problems solved in previous sections, it is easy to obtain as optimality conditions,

$$\dot{c}_t = \gamma(c_t)\left[(n+\delta) + \theta - f'(k_t)\right], \tag{3.33}$$

$$\dot{c}_t = \gamma(c_t)\left[\theta + n - r_t\right], \tag{3.34}$$

together with (3.32), (3.31) and transversality conditions,

$$\lim_{t \to \infty} e^{-\theta t} U'(c_t) k_t = \lim_{t \to \infty} e^{-\theta t} U'(c_t) b_t = 0. \tag{3.35}$$

The two budget constraints for the consumer and the government imply,

$$c_t + \dot{k}_t + (n+\delta) k_t + g_t = f(k_t). \tag{3.36}$$

---

[5] Turnovsky [93], p.228.

[6] In the simpler situations, the government is supposed to act passively, just taking care of expenditures and revenues. Alternatively, the government may be considered to conduct an optimal policy exercise, thereby designing policy optimally, so a to maximize consumers' welfare. This is the so-called Ramsey Problem, usually subject to technical difficulties.

The solution to the representative agent problem is a vector of time functions (k_t, b_t, c_t) satisfying $(3.33), (3.34), (3.35), (3.32), (3.36)$. It is not hard to show that the allocation of resources implied by this solution (i.e., the centralized solution) coincides with that of the competitive equilibrium mechanism: Plugging $F_g 1$ into $C_g 2$ we get (3.33). Using $C_g 1$ into $C_g 2$ we obtain (3.34). Furthermore, (3.25), together with the profit maximizing conditions $F_g 1$ and $F_g 2$, the equilibrium condition $v_t = k_t$ and the fact that $a_t = b_t + v_t$ lead to (3.32). Plugging $C_g 1$ into $C_g 3$ and using $a_t = b_t + v_t$ we obtain (3.35). Finally, the global constraint of resources characterizing feasible competitive equilibrium allocations is the same as the one for the representative agent problem (3.36). Therefore, the competitive equilibrium allocation can be obtained as the solution to the representative agent problem. Defining factor prices by their marginal products, it is straightforward to show that the resource allocation that emerges as solution to the representative agent problem can be obtained as the competitive equilibrium allocation of an economy where identical consumers and a single firm solve their respective utility and profit maximization problems.

3.5 On the Efficiency of Equilibrium with Government

As explained in Sect. 3.3 the solution to the planner's problem in an economy with identical consumers is Pareto efficient. In this section we discuss the efficiency of the competitive equilibrium allocation under different tax systems, by comparing the implied allocation of resources with that obtained from the planner's problem. Since decisions are determined by marginal rates of substitution that emerge from first order conditions to the optimization problem of each agent, much of what we will do is to compare marginal rates of substitution for the representative agent and for the planner. However, we will see some exceptions to the proposition that the competitive equilibrium allocation can be obtained by solving the associated representative agent problem.

3.5.1 On the Efficiency of Equilibrium Under Lump-Sum Taxes and Debt

In an economy with private and public consumption, a benevolent planner would choose time paths for both types of consumption so as to maximize the time aggregate utility of consumers,[7]

$$\underset{c_t, g_t}{Max} \int_0^\infty e^{-\theta t} U(c_t) dt,$$

---

[7] Note that the planner chooses not only private but also public consumption. On the other hand, at a difference of a government, the planner does not have anything to do with taxes or debt, but only with allocating physical resources in the economy.

subject to the sequence of constraints:

$$c_t + \dot{k}_t + (n+\delta)k_t + g_t = f(k_t),\ c_t \geq 0,\ g_t \geq 0.$$

The Hamiltonian is,

$$H(c_t, k_t, q_t, g_t) = e^{-\theta t}\{U(c_t) + q_t[f(k_t) - (n+\delta)k_t - g_t - c_t]\},$$

and the conditions characterizing the optimal solution,

$$c_t\ :\quad U'(c_t) = q_t, \tag{3.37}$$

$$g_t\ :\quad q_t g_t = 0, \tag{3.38}$$

$$q_t\ :\quad \dot{q}_t/q_t = n + \delta + \theta - f'(k_t), \tag{3.39}$$

$$\lim_{t\to\infty} e^{-\theta t} U'(c_t) k_t = 0.$$

where we have used the fact that the planner chooses not only c_t, but g_t as well.

The general condition for private consumption would be of the type, $c_t \frac{\partial H(.)}{\partial c_t} = 0$, but the assumptions made on the utility function guarantee that the level of consumption must be strictly positive every single period. Hence, condition (3.37) has been obtained under the assumption $c_t > 0, \forall t$. On the other hand, there is nothing in the model that precludes zero public consumption, so the associated optimality condition is (3.38), $g_t \frac{\partial H(.)}{\partial g_t} = 0$. Since we have $U'(c_t) > 0$ for any finite level of consumption, then (3.37) and (3.38) imply $g_t = 0$.

In the previous section we have shown that in an economy where the government finances public purchases of the consumption commodity by raising lump-sum taxes and issuing debt, the competitive equilibrium allocation can be characterized by solving the associated representative agent problem. In spite of their similarity, if the level of public consumption entering the (3.36) condition for the representative agent is strictly positive, the competitive allocation of resources will differ from the planner's allocation. As a consequence, the competitive equilibrium allocation is inefficient except if $g_t = 0, \forall t$. This is because consumers would prefer zero public consumption, if they had a choice.

The competitive equilibrium allocation in a Cass–Koopmans economy with a government which is financed through lump-sum taxes and debt issuing would be efficient if, rather than 'throwing them to the sea', purchases g_t of the consumption commodity by the government were returned to consumers in the form of a lump-sum transfer. The government's budget constraint would remain:

$$\dot{b}_t = (r_t - n)b_t + g_t - \tau_t,$$

while the *representative agent*'s budget constraint would become:

$$\dot{b}_t + \dot{k}_t + c_t + (n+\delta)k_t + \tau_t = f(k_t) + (r_t - n)b_t + g_t,$$

where the consumption units purchased by the government appear as part of the available resources to the private agent. The two budget constraints then imply the global constraint of resources in the economy, and the representative agent problem collapses to the planner's problem with zero public consumption, showing the efficiency of the competitive equilibrium allocation. All we need is to make sure that the sequence of government financing is feasible, i.e., (a) that the government budget constraint holds every period, and (b) that the stock of debt does not violate the transversality condition.

3.5.2 The Inefficiency of the Competitive Equilibrium Allocation Under Distortionary Taxes

The possibility of an inefficient competitive equilibrium allocation is even higher under consumption or income taxes. Under lump-sum taxes, marginal rates of substitution are the same as those without government, the inefficiency coming only from the presence of positive government expenditures not returned to consumers. The presence of income or consumption taxes will generally distort the marginal rates of substitution, making the competitive equilibrium allocation of resources to depart from that solving the planner problem. In summary, there are generally two reasons for inefficiency of the competitive equilibrium under income and consumption taxes: a positive level of government consumption that is 'thrown to the sea', and the presence of distortionary taxes.

To focus on the inefficiency produced by proportional taxation, we will assume that government expenditures are returned to consumers every period as a lump-sum tax. For simplicity, we assume the government is not allowed to issue bonds.

3.5.2.1 The Inefficiency of the Competitive Equilibrium Allocation Under Consumption Taxes

We assume that the government finances public expenditures with a consumption tax,

$$\tau_t^c c_t = g_t. \tag{3.40}$$

The *representative agent* then solves the problem,

$$\underset{c_t}{Max} \int_0^\infty e^{-\theta t} U(c_t) dt,$$

subject to the constraint:

$$\dot{k}_t + (1 + \tau_t^c) c_t = f(k_t) - (n + \delta) k_t + g_t, \tag{3.41}$$

where g_t is the transfer received from the government, equal in size to the revenues obtained from the consumption tax. Maximization of the Hamiltonian:

$$H(c_t, a_t, q_t, \omega_t, r_t) = e^{-\theta t} \{U(c_t) + q_t [f(k_t) - (n + \delta) k_t + g_t - (1 + \tau_t^c) c_t]\},$$

leads to optimality conditions,

$$U'(c_t) = (1 + \tau_t^c) q_t, \tag{3.42}$$

$$\dot{q}_t / q_t = n + \delta + \theta - f'(k_t) \tag{3.43}$$

$$\lim_{t \to \infty} e^{-\theta t} \frac{U'(c_t)}{(1 + \tau_t^c)} k_t = 0, \tag{3.44}$$

From (3.42) and (3.43) we obtain,

$$-\frac{\tau_t^c}{1 + \tau_t^c} \frac{\dot{\tau}_t^c}{\tau_t^c} + \frac{U''(c_t) c_t}{U'(c_t)} \frac{\dot{c}_t}{c_t} = n + \delta + \theta - f'(k_t), \tag{3.45}$$

with $\frac{U''(c_t) c_t}{U'(c_t)}$ being the elasticity of marginal utility. This equation will be different from the one for the planner's problem unless $\dot{\tau}_t = 0, \forall t$, implying that the competitive equilibrium resource allocation will not be Pareto-efficient. The consumption tax is *distortionary* only if the tax rate changes over time, affecting then to the relative price of the consumption commodity over time, while a constant consumption tax rate produces no distortion. It should be clear that adding a lump-sum tax would alter the consumer's budget constraint accordingly, with no change in the optimality conditions. The presence of government debt in the budget constraint would not alter the optimality conditions either. With government debt in the economy, we would just add an optimality condition and a transversality condition, both determining the optimal debt trajectory.

Alternatively, let us assume a constant consumption tax rate. Our assumption that tax revenues are fully returned to consumers as a lump-sum transfer is crucial to obtain the global constraint of resources faced by the benevolent planner from (3.40) and (3.41). The two assumptions together lead to the efficiency of the competitive equilibrium allocation. For that, we just need to show that it can be obtained as the solution to the representative agent problem, since we have just seen the equivalence between the solutions to this and to the planner's problem.

The consumer's problem is now,

$$\underset{c_t, a_t}{Max} \int_0^\infty e^{-\theta t} U(c_t) dt,$$

subject to,

$$\dot{v}_t + (1 + \tau_t^c) c_t = \omega_t + (r_t - n) v_t + g_t, \tag{3.46}$$

where the aggregate of stock on the firm, v_t, is the only asset we consider. Initial wealth, v_0, is given, and the consumer takes real wages and interest rates $\{\omega_t, r_t\}_{t=0}^\infty$ as given. Maximization of the Hamiltonian,

$$H\left(c_t, v_t, q_t, \omega_t, r_t, \tau_t^c\right) = e^{-\theta t}\left\{U(c_t) + q_t\left[\omega_t + (r_t - n)v_t - (1 + \tau_t^c)c_t\right]\right\},$$

leads to optimality conditions,

$$state\ equation\ C_{g\tau}1:\ U'(c_t) = (1 + \tau_t^c)q_t,$$
$$co-state\ equation\ (Euler)\ C_{g\tau}2:\ \dot{q}_t/q_t = n + \theta - r_t,$$
$$transversality\ condition\ C_{g\tau}3:\ \lim_{t\to\infty} e^{-\theta t}q_t v_t = 0.$$

From these, we obtain,

$$-\frac{\tau_t^c}{1+\tau_t^c}\frac{\dot{\tau}_t^c}{\tau_t^c} + \frac{U''(c_t)c_t}{U'(c_t)}\frac{\dot{c}_t}{c_t} = n + \theta - r_t.$$

Now, since the consumption tax does not enter the optimization problem of the firm, the same conditions F_g1 and F_g2 we obtained without the tax, hold again. Plugging them, together with the equilibrium condition $v_t = k_t$, into the consumer's budget constraint, we get the budget constraint for the representative agent problem, (3.41). Equation (3.45) can be obtained using F_g1 and $C_{g\tau}1$ in $C_{g\tau}2$. Finally, the two remaining conditions characterizing competitive equilibrium, the government's budget constraint and the global constraint of resources, are the same as in the representative agent's problem. So, the competitive equilibrium allocation can be obtained as solution to the representative agent's problem, which, under a constant consumption tax, produces the same solution as the planner's problem. The competitive equilibrium allocation is then Pareto-efficient.

3.5.2.2 Leisure in the Utility Function

On the other hand, if we consider *leisure as an argument in the utility function*, then the marginal rate of substitution between consumption and leisure at each point in time t would be *distorted* by the presence of the consumption tax rate even if this was constant over time. It can be shown that, as in the previous case, the resource allocation obtained under the competitive equilibrium mechanism is the same as that from the representative agent's problem. So, in this section we use the latter to illustrate the distortion produced by the consumption tax.

We consider a *representative agent* who has a unit endowment of time every period, and solves the problem,

$$\underset{c_t, l_t}{Max}\ \int_0^\infty e^{-\theta t}U(c_t, h_t)dt,$$

subject to the constraint:

$$\dot{k}_t + (1 + \tau_t^c)c_t = f(k_t, l_t) - (n + \delta)k_t + d_t,$$

where $h_t + l_t = 1$, h_t being the proportion of hours enjoyed as leisure, while l_t denotes the proportion of hours devoted to production.[8] We assume that the utility function satisfies usual assumptions guaranteeing concavity.

Maximization of the Hamiltonian:

$$H\left(c_t, q_t, l_t, h_t, d_t, \tau_t^c\right) = e^{-\theta t} \left\{ U(c_t, h_t) + q_t \left[\begin{array}{c} f(k_t, l_t) - (n+\delta)k_t + d_t \\ -(1+\tau_t^c)c_t \end{array} \right] \right\},$$

leads to optimality conditions,

$$U_c(c_t, h_t) = (1 + \tau_t^c)q_t, \tag{3.47}$$

$$\dot{q}_t / q_t = n + \delta + \theta - \frac{\partial f(k_t, l_t)}{\partial k_t}, \tag{3.48}$$

$$U_h(c_t, h_t) = q_t \frac{\partial f(k_t, l_t)}{\partial l_t}, \tag{3.49}$$

where $U_x(\cdot) = \frac{\partial U(\cdot)}{\partial x}$, $x = c, h$, together with (3.44).

From (3.47) and (3.48) we obtain (3.50), and plugging (3.47) in (3.49), we obtain (3.51):

$$-\frac{\tau_t^c}{1+\tau_t^c}\frac{\dot{\tau}_t^c}{\tau_t^c} + \frac{U_{cc}(c_t, h_t)c_t}{U_c(c_t, h_t)}\frac{\dot{c}_t}{c_t} + \frac{U_{ch}(c_t, h_t)h_t}{U_c(c_t, h_t)}\frac{\dot{h}_t}{h_t} = n + \delta + \theta - \frac{\partial f(k_t, l_t)}{\partial k_t}, \tag{3.50}$$

$$\frac{U_h(c_t, h_t)}{U_c(c_t, h_t)} = \frac{1}{1+\tau_t^c}\frac{\partial f(k_t, l_t)}{\partial l_t}, \tag{3.51}$$

where $U_{cc}(c_t, h_t) = \frac{\partial U_c(c_t, h_t)}{\partial c_t}$, $U_{ch}(c_t, h_t) = \frac{\partial U_h(c_t, h_t)}{\partial c_t}$.

As it was the case in the model without leisure, we see that if the consumption tax remains constant over time, it produces no distortion on the accumulation of capital. However, the last equation shows that, even if the consumption tax rate was constant, it will affect the marginal rate of substitution between consumption and leisure at each point in time. Therefore, the solutions to the representative agent's and the planner's problem will not be the same. The consequence is that even if the competitive equilibrium allocation of resources can be obtained as the solution to the former (which is the case), it will not be Pareto-efficient.

---

[8] The production function has now the form: $Y_t = F(K_t, L_t l_t)$ where $L_t l_t$ is the total number of hours worked. Homogeneity of the production function allows us to normalize,

$$\frac{Y_t}{N_t} = F\left(\frac{K_t}{N_t}, \frac{L_t}{N_t}l_t\right).$$

In equilibrium, $N_t = L_t$, and the production function can be written in per capita terms as, $y_t = F(k_t, l_t)$, where k_t denotes, as usual, the capital-labor ratio.

3.5.2.3 The Inefficiency of the Competitive Equilibrium Allocation Under Income Taxes

Let us assume that the government finances its expenditures with a tax on labor income, at a rate τ_t^w, and a tax on capital income, at a rate τ_t^r. The government's budget constraint will be,

$$g_t = \tau_t^\omega \omega_t + \tau_t^r r_t v_t. \tag{3.52}$$

For simplicity, we will not consider leisure as an argument in the utility function, we will not consider debt issuing, and we will assume that tax revenues are used by the government to purchase g_t units of the consumption commodity that are then returned to consumers as a lump-sum transfer.

The consumer's problem is now,

$$Max_{c_t} \int_0^\infty e^{-\theta t} U(c_t) dt,$$

subject to,

$$\dot{v}_t + c_t = \left(1 - \tau_t^\omega\right) \omega_t + \left((1 - \tau_t^r) r_t - n\right) v_t + g_t, \tag{3.53}$$

where the aggregate of stock on the firm, v_t, is the only asset in the economy. Initial wealth, v_0, is given, and the consumer takes real wages and interest rates $\{\omega_t, r_t\}_{t=0}^\infty$ as given. Maximization of the Hamiltonian,

$$H\left(c_t, v_t, q_t, \omega_t, r_t, \tau_t^c\right) = e^{-\theta t} \left\{ U(c_t) + q_t \left[\begin{array}{c} (1 - \tau_t^\omega) \omega_t + \\ ((1 - \tau_t^r) r_t - n) v_t + g_t - c_t \end{array} \right] \right\},$$

leads to optimality conditions,

$$state\ equation\ C_{g\tau^y} 1:\ U'(c_t) = q_t,$$
$$co-state\ equation\ (Euler)\ C_{g\tau^y} 2:\ \dot{q}_t / q_t = n + \theta - (1 - \tau_t^r) r_t,$$
$$transversality\ condition\ C_{g\tau^y} 3:\ \lim_{t \to \infty} e^{-\theta t} q_t v_t = 0.$$

From these, we obtain,

$$\frac{U''(c_t) c_t}{U'(c_t)} \frac{\dot{c}_t}{c_t} = n + \theta - (1 - \tau_t^r) r_t. \tag{3.54}$$

showing the distortion introduced by tax on capital income. That distortion will remain even if the tax rate was constant over time. As a consequence, the competitive equilibrium allocation of resources will differ from that obtained form the planner's problem, and it will be Pareto-inefficient.

In this case, we cannot consider a representative agent problem whose solution leads to the same allocation of resources than the competitive equilibrium mechanism, except if the tax rates on labor and capital income are the same. To see this, notice that neither tax rate affect the firm's problem, so that conditions $F_g 1$ and $F_g 2$ will still hold. Plugging them, together with the equilibrium condition $k_t = v_t$ into the consumer's budget constraint, we get,

$$c_t + \dot{k}_t = (1 - \tau^{\omega}) \left(f(k_t) - k_t f'(k_t) \right) + (1 - \tau^r) \left(f'(k_t) - \delta \right) k_t - nk_t + g_t, \quad (3.55)$$

which is different from the budget constraint faced by a representative agent subject to a tax on income[9] at a rate τ^y,

$$c_t + \dot{k}_t = (1 - \tau^y) \left(f(k_t) - \delta k_t \right) - nk_t + g_t. \quad (3.56)$$

However, in the special case $\tau^{\omega} = \tau^r = \tau^y$, the two budget constraints, (3.55) and (3.56) would coincide. Nevertheless, as we have already seen, the solution to this problem would differ from the solution to the planner's problem, thereby leading to an inefficient allocation of resources.

Using (3.52), $F_g 1$ and $F_g 2$, together with the equilibrium condition $k_t = v_t$, in (3.55) we get,

$$c_t + \dot{k}_t + (n + \delta) k_t = f(k_t),$$

the global constraint of resources for the planner's problem. This is due to the fact that the government is returning to consumers the revenues raised through the income tax. The only source of inefficiency is then the presence of the income tax. If tax revenues were not fully returned to consumers, then the last argument could not be made, and we would reach a global constraint of the type, $c_t + \dot{k}_t + (n + \delta) k_t + (g_t - d_t) = f(k_t)$, with an additional difference from the planner's problem, which amounts to a second reason for inefficiency of the competitive equilibrium allocation of resources.

Summarizing, the presence of consumption and taxes on factor incomes will alter the marginal rates of substitution with respect to the case of zero tax rates, and the competitive equilibrium allocation will be inefficient. The distortion produced by the consumption tax goes away is the consumption tax rate is constant. Allowing for the government to complement its financing strategy with lump-sum taxes and debt issuing will not alter this basic result. The competitive equilibrium allocation would not be efficient either if the government returned its proceeds to consumers in the form of lump-sum transfers, since the marginal rates of substitution characterizing the competitive equilibrium allocation of resources are distorted by the time varying consumption tax as well as by income tax rates. If the government uses tax revenues to purchase some units of the consumption commodity, g_t, and some of these are not returned to consumers as a lump-sum transfer, we will have a second reason for inefficiency of the competitive equilibrium allocation of resources. The representative agent problem and the planner's problem lead to the same allocation of resources except in the presence of capital income taxes. The competitive equilibrium allocation of resources can be obtained as solution to the representative agent's problem except if factor incomes are subject to different tax rates.

---

[9] By discounting depreciation from output, we are considering depreciation allowances in the tax base. The alternative formulation would be,

$$c_t + \dot{k}_t = (1 - \tau^y) f(k_t) - (n + \delta) k_t + g_t.$$

3.6 The Ricardian Doctrine

3.6.1 The Ricardian Doctrine Under Non-Distorting Taxes

Let us consider again a situation in which the government finances public consumption through a combination of lump-sum taxes and debt issuing. We are going to show that the way how the government splits its revenue raising between taxes and debt issuing is irrelevant in this model, so long as the bond issuing policy be feasible, i.e., so long as the transversality condition holds,

$$\lim_{t \to \infty} e^{-\int_0^t (r_s - n)ds} b_t = 0.$$

This neutrality proposition should be understood in the sense that the competitive process of allocating resources between consumption and investment (or savings) is independent of the way how savings are split between bonds and equities. The irrelevance from the public financing policy in real terms is known as the *Ricardian Doctrine:* consumers are indifferent between paying higher taxes today and maintaining lower debt holdings in their portfolios, or the alternative of paying lower taxes today, to the cost of having to buy a bigger amount of public debt. The reason is that a larger bond emission today will require of more taxes in the future, so that the government can retire the outstanding debt at maturity. According to the Ricardian doctrine, the consumer is indifferent, in terms of present value of disposable income, between both alternatives.

For simplicity, in this section we assume zero population growth ($n=0$). Similarly to our analysis in previous sections, we can integrate the law of motion that for financial assets emerges from the representative consumer budget constraint,

$$\dot{a}_t = \omega_t - c_t - \tau_t + r_t a_t,$$

to have,

$$a_t + \int_t^{\infty} e^{-\int_t^z r_s ds} \omega_z dz = \int_t^{\infty} e^{-\int_t^z r_s ds} (c_z + \tau_z) dz,$$

showing that, each period, the consumer portfolio of assets, plus the present value of his current and future labor income, is equal to the present value of current and future consumption, plus the present value of taxes.

Using (3.28), we get,

$$v_t + \int_t^{\infty} e^{-\int_t^z r_s ds} \omega_z dz = \int_t^{\infty} e^{-\int_t^z r_s ds} (c_z + g_z) dz,$$

showing that the equity issued by the firm, plus the present value of the sequence of current and future wage income, is equal to the present value of the sequences of private and public consumption. Also,

$$\int_t^{\infty} e^{-\int_t^z r_s ds} c_z dz = v_t + \int_t^{\infty} e^{-\int_t^z r_s ds} \omega_z dz - \int_t^{\infty} e^{-\int_t^z r_s ds} g_z dz, \tag{3.57}$$

showing that the feasible consumption sequences are those whose present value does not exceed from the value of current equity holdings, augmented by the present value of labor income, minus the present value of public consumption.

These latter conditions are alternative versions of the *consumer's intertemporal budget constraint.* Existence of perfect capital markets, where the consumer can either borrow or lend as much as he/she wishes, at the current market rate of interest, has allowed us to collapse the sequence of single period budget constraints into the single intertemporal constraint above, without losing any relevant information. Perfect capital markets allow the consumer to distribute over time the present value of current and future income anyway he/she wishes.

It is important to see that neither bonds nor taxes appear in the intertemporal budget constraint, either at a single point in time or in present value. Consumers' decisions are affected by the level of current and future public expenditures, which detracts resources from consumption and investment, as shown in (3.57), but not by the way expenditures are financed, be that through lump-sum taxes or by issuing public debt. This is the Ricardian Doctrine, which is considered part of the neo-classical doctrine, suggesting that it may not be worthwhile to disturb consumers with taxes, since the public deficit can be equally financed by issuing debt. Under the Ricardian Doctrine, no way of financing government expenditures is superior to any other. This result may not hold in economies with finitely lived agents, in some monetary economies, or in the presence of distorting taxation, as we are about to see.

3.6.2 Failure of the Ricardian Doctrine Under Distorting Taxes

In Sect. 3.5.2 we have seen that distortionary taxes (consumption taxes, labor income taxes and capital income taxes) alter the marginal rates of substitution, except in some special cases. The consumption tax is not distortionary if the tax rate is constant over time, and the labor income tax is not distortionary when labor supply is wage-inelastic. In the first case, the consumption tax does not affect the marginal rate of substitution between current and future consumption, so that there is always a time varying lump-sum tax leading to the same consumption path than a constant tax rate on consumption. In the second case, since the labor supply is inelastic, the labor income tax acts as a lump-sum tax. Consequently, it is always possible to find a lump-sum tax producing the same consumption path that it is obtained under the labor income tax.

Since the consumption tax and the labor income tax can be substituted by a lump-sum tax, the Ricardian equivalence holds in both cases. In all remaining situations, there is no lump-sum tax leading to the same consumption trajectory than the distortionary tax. This is because, at a difference of the lump-sum tax, distortionary taxes change the intertemporal marginal rate of substitution of consumption over time, or the marginal rate of substitution between consumption and leisure at a given point in time. We show next that the Ricardian equivalence fails indeed to hold in such situations.

Let us assume that the consumer faces taxes on consumption, capital income and labor income, at rates $\tau_t^c, \tau_t^r, \tau_t^\omega$. Let $\{c_t', a_t'\}$ be the paths for consumption and total assets chosen by the private agent under distortionary taxes, $\tau=(\tau_t^c, \tau_t^\omega, \tau_t^r)$. So, they satisfy the representative consumer budget constraint:

$$\dot{a}_t' + (1 + \tau_t^c)c_t' = (1 - \tau_t^\omega)\,\omega_t + (1 - \tau_t^r)\,r_t a_t',$$

where total financial assets are,

$$a_t' = b_t + v_t',$$

with v_t' being the equity issued by the firm. We allow for the possibility that the path for public debt, b_t, be the same than under the lump-sum tax system. Distortionary taxes and the stock of debt must satisfy the government budget constraint,

$$\dot{b}_t = r_t b_t + g_t - \left(\tau_t^c c_t' + \tau_t^\omega \omega_t n_t' + \tau_t^r r_t a_t'\right),$$

where n_z' denotes employment. This budget constraint can be written,

$$\dot{b}_t = (1 - \tau_t^r)\,r_t b_t + g_t - I_t,$$

where $I_t = \tau_t^c c_t' + \tau_t^\omega \omega_t n_z' + \tau_t^r r_t v_t'$ denotes total revenues.

Solving this first order differential equation [see Mathematical Appendix], we get,

$$b_t = -\int_t^\infty e^{-\int_t^z (1-\tau_s^r)r_s ds}\,(g_z - I_z)\,dz, \tag{3.58}$$

while if we integrate the consumer's budget constraint, we get,

$$a_t' = -\int_t^\infty e^{-\int_t^z (1-\tau_s^r)r_s ds}\left[\left(1 - \tau_z^\omega\right)\omega_z n_z' - \left(1 + \tau_z^c\right)c_z'\right]dz.$$

Substituting a_t' by $b_t + v_t'$ and using (3.58):

$$v_t' = -\int_t^\infty e^{-\int_t^z (1-\tau_s^r)r_s ds}\left[\left(1 - \tau_z^\omega\right)\omega_z n_z' - \left(1 + \tau_z^c\right)c_z' - g_z + I_z\right]dz,$$

and using the definition of I_t,

$$v_t' + \int_t^\infty e^{-\int_t^z (1-\tau_s^r)r_s ds}\omega_z n_z' dz = \int_t^\infty e^{-\int_t^z (1-\tau_s^r)r_s ds}\left(g_z + c_z' - \tau_z^r r_z v_z'\right)dz,$$

which can be written,

$$\int_t^\infty e^{-\int_t^z (1-\tau_s^r)r_s ds}c_z' dz = v_t' + \int_t^\infty e^{-\int_t^z (1-\tau_s^r)r_s ds}\omega_z n_z' dz$$
$$- \int_t^\infty e^{-\int_t^z (1-\tau_s^r)r_s ds}\left(g_z - \tau_z^r r_z v_z'\right)dz.$$

The equation illustrates very clearly the failure of the Ricardian equivalence proposition to hold whenever $\tau_t^r \neq 0$, because of the last term at the right hand side of the equation. But even more importantly, the Ricardian proposition will not hold even if $\tau_t^r = 0$, because consumers' decision on consumption, leisure and private assets will then be distorted relative to the case of a pure lump-sum tax. The point is that distortionary taxes other than τ_t^r appear implicitly in the previous equation through the consumption, labor and asset holding decisions, which is the reason behind the failure of the Ricardian equivalence proposition.

3.7 Appendix

3.7.1 Appendix 1 – Log-linear Approximation to the Continuous Time Version of Cass–Koopmans Model

By a log-linear approximation we understand an approximate representation of the economy which is linear in logged variables. We obtain in this appendix the log-linear representation of the two differential equations characterizing Cass–Koopmans model, for the case of a Cobb–Douglas technology, $y_t = k_t^\alpha$,

$$\frac{d\ln c_t}{dt} = \frac{1}{\sigma}\left[\alpha e^{-(1-\alpha)\ln k_t} - (n+\delta+\theta)\right], \tag{3.59}$$

$$\frac{d\ln k_t}{dt} = e^{-(1-\alpha)\ln k_t} - e^{\ln c_t - \ln k_t} - (n+\delta). \tag{3.60}$$

Since in steady-state, $\frac{d\ln c_t}{dt} = \frac{d\ln k_t}{dt} = 0$, steady-state levels of consumption and physical capital must satisfy,

$$e^{-(1-\alpha)\ln k_{ss}} = \frac{n+\delta+\theta}{\alpha} \Rightarrow k_{ss} = \left(\frac{\alpha}{n+\delta+\theta}\right)^{\frac{1}{1-\alpha}},$$

$$e^{\ln c_{ss} - \ln k_{ss}} = e^{-(1-\alpha)\ln k_{ss}} - (n+\delta) = \frac{n+\delta+\theta}{\alpha} - (n+\delta)$$

$$= \frac{(1-\alpha)(n+\delta)+\theta}{\alpha} \equiv h > 0,$$

and we can build the linear approximation of the two equations around steady-state using Taylor's expansion, and using the fact that,

$$\frac{d}{d\ln k_t}\left(e^{-(1-\alpha)\ln k_t}\right) = -(1-\alpha)e^{-(1-\alpha)\ln k_t},$$

$$\frac{d}{d\ln k_t}\left(e^{\ln c_t - \ln k_t}\right) = -e^{\ln c_t - \ln k_t},$$

$$\frac{d}{d\ln c_t}\left(e^{\ln c_t - \ln k_t}\right) = e^{\ln c_t - \ln k_t},$$

so we have, for (3.59),

$$\frac{d\ln c_t}{dt} \simeq -\frac{1}{\sigma}\alpha(1-\alpha)e^{-(1-\alpha)\ln k_{ss}}(\ln k_t - \ln k_{ss}),$$

where,

$$-\frac{1}{\sigma}\alpha(1-\alpha)e^{-(1-\alpha)\ln k_{ss}} = -\frac{1-\alpha}{\sigma}(n+\delta+\theta) \equiv -\eta < 0,$$

so we finally have,

$$\frac{d\ln c_t}{dt} = -\eta(\ln k_t - \ln k_{ss}),$$

while for (3.60) we have,

$$\frac{d\ln k_t}{dt} \cong -e^{\ln c_{ss}-\ln k_{ss}}(\ln c_t - \ln c_{ss})$$

$$-\left[(1-\alpha)e^{-(1-\alpha)\ln k_{ss}} - e^{\ln c_{ss}-\ln k_{ss}}\right](\ln k_t - \ln k_{ss})$$

$$= -h(\ln c_t - \ln c_{ss}) - \left[(1-\alpha)\frac{n+\delta+\theta}{\alpha} - h\right](\ln k_t - \ln k_{ss})$$

$$= -h(\ln c_t - \ln c_{ss}) + \theta(\ln k_t - \ln k_{ss}),$$

with a matrix representation,

$$\begin{pmatrix}\frac{d\ln c_t}{dt} \\ \frac{d\ln k_t}{dt}\end{pmatrix} \cong \begin{pmatrix} 0 & -\eta \\ -h & \theta \end{pmatrix}\begin{pmatrix}\ln c_t - \ln c_{ss} \\ \ln k_t - \ln k_{ss}\end{pmatrix}.$$

3.7.2 Appendix 2 – An Alternative Presentation of the Equivalence Between the Planner's and the Competitive Equilibrium Mechanisms in an Economy Without Government

In Sect. 3.4 we showed the equality between the resource allocations achieved under the competitive equilibrium and under the planner's mechanisms in an economy without government. There, we assumed that the firm was the owner of the stock of capital, hiring labor to produce output. In the alternative presentation in this appendix, we assume that consumers are the owners of physical capital, so the firm must hire that productive factor from them, with the real rate of interest being the rental price.

We will assume that there are complete markets in the economy. There is a set of identical consumers, who are endowed with a unit of labor every period and have preferences on consumption. Leisure does not enter as an argument in the utility function. The single firm in the economy uses physical capital, K_t, and labor, N_t, to produce the only consumption commodity in the economy. The firm issues some stock, v_t, which is bought by consumers. Each unit of stock gives ownership rights to one unit of capital and yields a real return of r_t. The firm faces competitive markets for inputs and output, treating the real return on capital, r_t, real wages, ω_t, and the price of the consumption commodity as given. There is no uncertainty, and the aggregate technology displays constant returns to scale.

Each consumer uses all his savings to purchase productive capital. The aggregate budget constraint for all consumers is,

$$C_t + S_t = \omega_t N_t + r_t K_t.$$

Since this is a closed economy with no government, gross investment is equal to savings,

$$S_t = I_t = \dot{K}_t + \delta K_t,$$

and we get,

$$C_t + \dot{K}_t + \delta K_t = \omega_t N_t + r_t K_t,$$

which, following an argument similar to that in the previous chapter, can be written in per capita terms as,

$$c_t + \dot{k}_t + (n + \delta) k_t = \omega_t + r_t k_t. \tag{3.61}$$

The representative consumer takes prices $\{\omega_t, r_t\}_{t=0}^{\infty}$ as given, and chooses consumption and investment to solve the problem,

$$\underset{c_t, k_t}{Max} \int_0^{\infty} e^{-\theta t} U(c_t) dt,$$

subject to (3.61), and given k_0.

Maximization of the Lagrangian,

$$L(c_t, k_t, \lambda_t, \omega_t, r_t) = e^{-\theta t} [U(c_t) + \lambda_t (\omega_t + r_t k_t - c_t - (n + \delta) k_t)],$$

leads to optimality conditions,

$$C_a 1 : \ e^{-\theta t} U'(c_t) = \lambda_t,$$
$$C_a 2 : \ \dot{\lambda}_t / \lambda_t = \delta + n - r_t + \theta,$$
$$C_a 3 : \ \lim_{t \to \infty} e^{-\theta t} \lambda_t k_t = 0.$$

Combining $C_a 1$ and $C_a 2$ we get,

$$\frac{\dot{c}_t}{c_t} = \gamma(c_t) [r_t - (n + \delta + \theta)], \tag{3.62}$$

with $\gamma(c_t)$ being the *intertemporal elasticity of substitution of consumption*, $\gamma(c_t) = \frac{U'(c_t)}{U''(c_t) c_t}$. Optimal consumption and savings choices are characterized by (3.61), (3.62), together with the transversality condition $C_a 3$.

The single firm in the economy maximizes the present value of its cash-flow stream,

$$\underset{K_t, L_t}{Max} \int_0^{\infty} e^{-\int_0^t r_s ds} \left[F(K_t, L_t) - \omega_t L_t - r_t K_t \right] dt,$$

given the initial stock of capital, K_0.

Notice the difference between the problems for the consumer and the firm in this appendix and those considered in previous sections. Now, the firm does not own the stock of capital, so it must rent it at a price r_t. On the other hand, since the consumer owns the stock of capital, he must also support the cost of depreciation, as it shows in his budget constraint. In previous sections, the firm was the owner of the capital stock and it had to bear the cost of depreciation. Then, the firm maximized the present value of profits, as opposed to maximizing the present value of the cash-flow stream when it does not own the stock of capital.

Optimality conditions for this problem are,

$$F_a 1 : \partial F / \partial K_t \equiv f'(k_t) = r_t, \tag{3.63}$$

$$F_a 2 : \partial F / \partial N_t = f(k_t) - f'(k_t) k_t = \omega_t, \tag{3.64}$$

which implies that the firm hires workers and capital to the point where marginal products are equal to ω_t and r_t.

Definition 4. Given an initial condition k_0, a competitive equilibrium is a vector of continuous functions of time, defined over $(0, \infty)$ $\{c_t, k_t, \omega_t, r_t, N_t\}_{t=0}^{\infty}$ such that,

- Given price functions ω_t, r_t, the time functions c_t, k_t solve the representative consumer's problem,
- Given price functions ω_t, r_t, the time function for capital k_t maximizes firm' profits each period,
- The labor market clears, with equal supply and demand of labor. Since labor is supplied inelastically, this means that labor demand is equal to total population, $L_t = N_t$,
- The market for physical capital clears, the stock of capital owned by consumers being equal to the stock of capital the firm wants to rent.

For a competitive equilibrium allocation, $(3.61), (3.62), (3.63)$, and (3.64) all hold. Plugging (3.63) and (3.64) into (3.61) we get,

$$c_t + \dot{k}_t + (n + \delta) k_t = f(k_t), \tag{3.65}$$

the equilibrium condition in the market for the consumption commodity. It states that produced output is equal to consumption plus total gross investment. So, Walras' law holds: market clearing in the markets for labor and physical capital imply market clearing in the market for the consumption commodity.

Theorem 4. *The resource allocation achieved under the competitive mechanism and the planner's mechanism, are the same.*

Proof. Let us assume that the vector of time functions $\{c_t, k_t, \omega_t, r_t, N_t\}$ is a competitive equilibrium. As we have just seen, then (3.65) holds. Furthermore, substituting (3.64) in (3.62) we get,

$$\frac{\dot{c_t}}{c_t} = \gamma(c_t)\left[f'(k_t) - (n + \delta + \theta)\right]. \tag{3.66}$$

But (3.65) and (3.66) are precisely the differential equations characterizing the time paths $\{c_t, k_t\}$ in the planner's allocation, so that the resource allocation emerging under the competitive equilibrium allocation coincides with that obtained under the centralized resource allocation mechanism, for a same initial condition k_0.

Let us now consider an initial stock of capital k_0 and the solution to the planner's problem, $\{c_t, k_t\}$. So, these two time functions satisfy (3.65) and (3.66), and a function λ_t can be defined by (3.2) so that (3.3) and (3.4) also hold. From them, let us define time functions for real wages and interest rates $\{\omega_t, r_t\}$ through (3.63), (3.64) and introduce an auxiliary variable q_t by $q_t = \lambda_t$. Then, the first and second conditions in the definition of a competitive equilibrium hold by construction. Finally, since the $\{c_t, k_t\}$-functions solving the planner's problem include the aggregate stock of capital in the economy and the whole population, then, defining prices as indicated, we guarantee that the labor market and the market for productive capital, both clear. Hence, the resource allocation solving the planner's problem can be achieved as the one emerging in a competitive equilibrium, so long as prices are defined as above.

3.8 Exercises

Exercise 1. In the Steady-state spreadsheet, contained in the CK_continuous_time. xls file, change the benchmark parameter values and check how the graphs displaying the sensitivity of steady-state levels to structural parameters change. Are the results you obtain what you expected?

Exercise 2. In the Speed of convergence spreadsheet, contained in the CK_ continuous_time.xls file, change the benchmark parameter values and check how the graphs displaying the sensitivity of steady-state levels to structural parameters change. Are the results you obtain what you expected?

Exercise 3. In the continuous time Cass–Koopmans model, assume there is a government that purchases some of the units of output produced in the economy with the revenues obtained taxing consumption at a rate τ^c and levying income taxes at a rate τ^y. The government does not issue any debt. The utility function of consumers is of the CRRA family. The available technology exhibits constant returns to scale in physical capital and labor. Show that the transition matrix in the log-linear approximation to the model does not depend on either one of the tax parameters, so that the stability condition is the same as that in Sect. 3.2. Notice that once the government decides on the values of the tax rates on consumption and income, public expenditures are endogenously determined.

Exercise 4. Discuss the stability of the Cass–Koopmans model using a linear approximation to the model around steady-state under the assumption of a production technology using physical capital and labor inputs and displaying constant returns to scale. To do so, use Taylor's expansion in Keynes–Ramsey's rule as well as in the budget constraint, to obtain linear approximations representing $\dot{c}_t$ *and* $\dot{k}_t$ as functions of $c_t - c_{ss}$ *and* $k_t - k_{ss}$, and examine the eigenvalues of that linear representation.

Chapter 4
Optimal Growth. Discrete Time Analysis

4.1 Discrete-Time, Deterministic Cass–Koopmans Model

In this chapter we present the discrete time version of some of the issues discussed in the previous chapter. We introduce a government in the economy, and define and characterize the competitive equilibrium. The intertemporal government budget constraint, the relationship between the competitive equilibrium allocation and that of the benevolent planner mechanism, and the Ricardian doctrine, can be all analyzed in discrete-time in a similar fashion as we have done in the continuous time version of the model. Dealing with all the details of the discrete time version of the Cass–Koopmans economy is very instructive in order to be able to formulate alternative, more complex growth models, as well as to perform policy analysis, as we do towards the end of the chapter. It is particularly important to get familiar with the formulation and use of the transversality condition and with the characterization of stability conditions. As we will see below, stability conditions are crucial to generate a numerical solution for this model in the form of a set of time series for the endogenous variables.

The discrete time formulation also allows us to consider a stochastic version of the economy, as we do in the following chapter. This is important, since a stochastic version of the economy is needed to characterize the influence of exogenous shocks on the trajectories followed by the endogenous variables, their volatilities, correlations with other variables, or any other statistic.

4.1.1 The Global Constraint of Resources

In line with the continuous time version of the model, we maintain for the discrete time version a gross population rate of growth equal to n, and a linear depreciation rate for physical capital equal to δ.

The global constraint of resources in the economy is,

$$C_t + K_{t+1} - (1 - \delta)K_t = F(K_t, N_t),$$

which states that consumption plus investment is equal to output each period. This is because we consider a closed economy, with no government. The stock of capital chosen at the end of period t is denoted by K_{t+1}, and it will be used in production at time $t + 1$. Dividing by population, which is equal to employment because of the maintained assumption on full employment, we get,

$$\frac{C_t}{N_t} + \frac{K_{t+1}}{N_{t+1}}\frac{N_{t+1}}{N_t} - (1 - \delta)\frac{K_t}{N_t} = \frac{F(K_t, N_t)}{N_t} = F\left(\frac{K_t}{N_t}, 1\right) = f(k_t),$$

where $k_t = \frac{K_t}{N_t}$, and we have used the constant returns to scale property of the aggregate production technology, as we did in the Solow-Swan model. We thus have the global constraint of resources in per capita terms,

$$c_t + (1 + n)k_{t+1} - (1 - \delta)k_t = f(k_t),$$

which can be written in the form of the *law of motion for the stock of capital* per worker,

$$k_{t+1} = \frac{1}{1+n}[f(k_t) + (1 - \delta)k_t - c_t] = h(k_t, c_t), \tag{4.1}$$

the stock of capital at the end of each period being a nonlinear function of last period's capital and the current period level of consumption.

As in continuous time, the *intertemporal elasticity of substitution* of consumption considers changes in marginal utility between two different points in time, as opposed to changes in marginal utility between two different levels of consumption at a given point in time, as it is the case with the *EMU*. Given two points in time t and $s, s > t, s = t + \Delta t$, the *intertemporal elasticity of substitution of consumption IES* in discrete time is defined as the inverse of the ratio between the percent change in the slope of the indifference curve and the percent change in consumption between t and s:

$$IES = \gamma(c_t) = -\left(\frac{\partial \ln(\text{rate of change in } U')}{\partial \ln(\text{rate of change in } c)}\right)^{-1}$$

$$= -\left[\frac{\partial \{\ln(U'(c_s)/U'(c_t))\}}{\partial \{\ln(c_s/c_t)\}}\right]^{-1}$$

$$\simeq -\left[\frac{\Delta(U'(c_s)/U'(c_t))}{\Delta(c_s/c_t)} \cdot \frac{c_s/c_t}{U'(c_s)/U'(c_t)}\right]^{-1}.$$

In discrete time, the logarithmic rate of change is used to approximate the time derivative. With a CRRA utility, the *EMU*, which maintains the same definition as with continuous time, is equal to σ, while for the *IES* we have,

$$IES = \gamma(c_t) = -\left[\frac{\partial\left\{\ln\left(U'(c_s)/U'(c_t)\right)\right\}}{\partial\left\{\ln(c_s/c_t)\right\}}\right]^{-1}$$

$$= -\left[\frac{\partial\left\{\ln\left(c_s^{-\sigma}/c_t^{-\sigma}\right)\right\}}{\partial\left\{\ln(c_s/c_t)\right\}}\right]^{-1} = -\left[\frac{\partial\left\{-\sigma[\ln(c_s)-\ln(c_t)]\right\}}{\partial\left\{\ln(c_s)-\ln(c_t)\right\}}\right]^{-1}$$

$$= 1/\sigma = \frac{1}{EMU},$$

the same inverse relationship we found in the continuous time version of the model.

4.1.2 Discrete-Time Formulation of the Planner's Problem

The benevolent planner chooses sequences of consumption and physical capital to solve the problem,

$$\max_{\{c_t,k_{t+1}\}_{t=0}^{\infty}} \sum_{t=0}^{\infty} \beta^t U(c_t),$$

subject to (4.1), given the initial capital stock, k_0.

The discounted Lagrangian for this problem is,

$$L(\{c_t,k_{t+1},\lambda_t\}) = \sum_{t=0}^{\infty} \beta^t \left[U(c_t)+\lambda_t\left[\begin{array}{c} f(k_t)-c_t-(1+n)k_{t+1} \\ +(1-\delta)k_t \end{array}\right]\right],$$

in which the terms involving k_{t+1} are,

$$\ldots + \beta^t \left\{U(c_t)+\lambda_t\left[f(k_t)-c_t-(1+n)k_{t+1}+(1-\delta)k_t\right]\right\}$$
$$+\beta^{t+1}\left\{U(c_{t+1})+\lambda_{t+1}\left[f(k_{t+1})-c_{t+1}-(1+n)k_{t+2}+(1-\delta)k_{t+1}\right]\right\}+\ldots$$

Necessary conditions for optimality are obtained by taking derivatives in the Lagrangian with respect to c_t and k_{t+1},

$$\beta^t\left(U'(c_t)-\lambda_t\right) = 0,\ t = 0,1,2,3,\ldots \tag{4.2}$$

$$-\beta^t\lambda_t(1+n)+\beta^{t+1}\lambda_{t+1}\left(f'(k_{t+1})+1-\delta\right) = 0,\ t = 0,1,2,3,\ldots \tag{4.3}$$

where we have assumed interior solutions, i.e., $c_t,k_{t+1} > 0,\ \forall t$. Excluding the possibility of zero consumption in the optimality conditions, we get the equality between marginal utility and the shadow price of capital each period.

Substituting (4.2) in (4.3), we obtain the Keynes-Ramsey condition for the discrete-time version of the planner's economy, also known as *Euler equation*:

$$U'(c_t)(1+n) = \beta U'(c_{t+1})\left[f'(k_{t+1})+1-\delta\right]. \tag{4.4}$$

Under a *CRRA* utility, the condition becomes,

$$\frac{c_{t+1}^{\sigma}}{\beta c_t^{\sigma}} = \frac{f'(k_{t+1}) + 1 - \delta}{1 + n},$$

the left hand side being the marginal rate of substitution of consumption between t and $t + 1$. For logarithmic preferences $(\sigma = 1)$, the condition further simplifies to,

$$\frac{c_{t+1}}{\beta c_t} = \frac{f'(k_{t+1}) + 1 - \delta}{1 + n}.$$

From the second optimality condition for successive time periods we get,

$$\frac{\lambda_{t+1}}{\lambda_t} = \frac{1 + n}{\beta \left(f'(k_{t+1}) + 1 - \delta \right)},$$

the *co-state equation* in discrete time.[1]

4.1.3 The Optimal Steady-State

In steady-state, we will have $\lambda_t = \lambda_{t+1}$, and,

$$f'(k_{ss}) = \frac{1 + n}{\beta} - 1 + \delta. \tag{4.5}$$

Redefining the discount factor as $\beta = \frac{1}{1+\theta}$, (4.5) can be written

$$f'(k_{ss}) = n + \theta + \delta + n\theta,$$

very similar to the condition obtained in the continuous time version of the model, specially taking into account that the product $n\theta$ will usually take a very small value. Once again, we see that the optimal steady-state falls to the left, i.e., with lower capital than the Golden Rule, showing that the suboptimality of the Golden Rule arises from too much capital accumulation early on, that is, from a too high savings rate.

In steady-state, the law of motion for capital becomes,

$$c_{ss} = f(k_{ss}) - (n + \delta)k_{ss},$$

---

[1] Which, by redefining the discount factor as $\beta = \frac{1}{1+\theta}$, can be written,

$$\frac{\lambda_{t+1} - \lambda_t}{\lambda_t} = \frac{n + \theta + \delta + n\theta - f'(k_{t+1})}{f'(k_{t+1}) + 1 - \delta},$$

in terms of the rate of change of the Lagrange multiplier, so that it can be compared to the similar condition in the continuous time model.

the same functional relationship as in the continuous time version of the model. Hence, the relationship can again be represented by a concave curve in the (c,k)-space, with a maximum at $f'(k) = n + \delta$, and a zero at the subsistence level of capital, at which $f(k_{ss}) = (n+\delta)k_{ss}$. The only change with respect to the continuous time analysis is that (4.5) leads to a stock of capital slightly to the left of the level determined for the continuous time version of the model. However, the product $n\delta$ should be expected to be small, and so will be the difference between the two steady-states.

4.1.4 The Dynamics of the Model: The Phase Diagram

To analyze the dynamics of the model, let us consider again the Keynes-Ramsey condition, for the case of CRRA preferences,

$$c_{t+1} = c_t \left[\frac{\beta}{1+n} \left(f'(k_{t+1}) + 1 - \delta \right) \right]^{1/\sigma} = g(k_t, c_t), \tag{4.6}$$

and the budget constraint,

$$k_{t+1} = \frac{1}{1+n} \left[f(k_t) + (1 - \delta) k_t - c_t \right] = h(k_t, c_t), \tag{4.7}$$

a system of two equations giving us the laws of motion for consumption and capital, $k_{t+1} = h(k_t, c_t)$, $c_{t+1} = g(k_t, c_t)$.[2]

As in continuous time, the so-called *phase diagram* is constructed on the basis of two curves, relating k_t to c_t. Each curve corresponds to one of the two zero-change cases: $k_{t+1} = k_t$ (the budget constraint), $c_{t+1} = c_t$ (the Keynes-Ramsey condition).

First, we impose $c_{t+1} = c_t$ in (4.6) to get a curve characterized by,

$$f'(k_{t+1}) = \frac{1+n}{\beta} - (1 - \delta), \tag{4.8}$$

which is, in fact, an implicit relationship between k_t and c_t because of the dependence of k_{t+1} on these two variables, as shown in the budget constraint. Notice that $\frac{1+n}{\beta} - (1 - \delta) > 0$ because the marginal product of capital must be positive for any positive capital stock. To write this relationship as a curve in the (c_t, k_t)-space, we make the total differential of (4.8) equal to zero:

$$f''(k_{t+1}) \frac{\partial k_{t+1}}{\partial k_t} dk_t + f''(k_{t+1}) \frac{\partial k_{t+1}}{\partial c_t} dc_t = 0, \tag{4.9}$$

---

[2] The $g(k_t, c_t)$ function is obtained after using the budget constraint to eliminate k_{t+1}.

and we obtain the slope of the curve by:

$$\frac{\partial c_t}{\partial k_t} = -\frac{\partial k_{t+1}/\partial k_t}{\partial k_{t+1}/\partial c_t},$$

where partial derivatives must be computed from (4.8), that is:

$$\frac{\partial c_t}{\partial k_t} = -\frac{\partial k_{t+1}/\partial k_t}{\partial k_{t+1}/\partial c_t} = -\frac{\frac{1}{1+n}(f'(k_t)+1-\delta)}{-1/(1+n)} = f'(k_t)+1-\delta, \qquad (4.10)$$

which is therefore a positive relationship in the (c_t, k_t)-space, because $f'(k_t) + 1 - \delta > 0, \forall k_t$.

From (4.7) and (4.8) the equation for the $g(k_t, c_t)$-curve itself is:

$$k_{t+1} = \frac{1}{1+n}[f(k_t)+(1-\delta)k_t-c_t] = (f')^{-1}\left(\frac{1+n}{\beta}-(1-\delta)\right).$$

This line will have a negative intercept with the vertical axis at $k_t = 0$, because at that point we would have: $f'\left(-\frac{c_t}{1+n}\right) = \frac{1+n}{\beta} - (1-\delta) > 0$, and the marginal product function is defined only over the positive real line. The curve has a positive slope, as shown by (4.10), and along it, $c_t \to \infty$ as $k_t \to \infty$. So, it will cross the horizontal axis, and it will do it only once, because of the strict concavity of f.

For any point to the right of the line described by (4.8) there is a point on that line with the same value of k_t and a higher c_t, for which $f'(k_{t+1}) = \frac{1+n}{\beta} - (1-\delta)$. So, if the point to the right of the line as a lower c_t and the same k_t, its value of $\frac{1}{1+n}[f(k_t)+(1-\delta)k_t-c_t]$ will be higher, and the marginal product will be lower than on the line, where it was equal to $\frac{1+n}{\beta} - (1-\delta)$. Hence, at that point to the right of the line, $f'(k_{t+1}) < \frac{1+n}{\beta} - (1-\delta)$ and, according to the Keynes-Ramsey condition, we will have $c_{t+1} < c_t$, and the opposite happens at any point to the left of the (4.8)-line.

On the other hand, when $k_{t+1} = k_t$, the budget constraint gives us,

$$c_t = f(k_t) - (\delta+n)k_t,$$

an increasing and concave function. Consumption is higher at any point above the curve than it is on the curve, so that $c_t > f(k_t) - (\delta+n)k_t$, which, taken to the budget constraint, it implies: $k_{t+1} < k_t$. The opposite happens at any point below the curve. Hence, we have the phase diagram shown in the graph, which describes the existence of a single stable manifold taking the economy to the optimal steady-state, as it was the case in the continuous time version of the economy. [See Fig. 4.1].

The final sections of the chapter are devoted to the numerical computation of a trajectory converging to the steady-state from a given initial condition, in an economy with taxes.

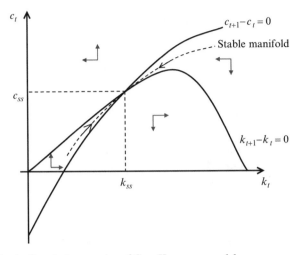

Fig. 4.1 Stability in discrete-time version of Cass-Koopmans model

4.1.5 Transversality Condition in Discrete Time

The transversality condition for the infinite horizon problem is obtained by taking limits in the similar condition for the finite horizon problem. The finite horizon problem is,

$$\underset{\{c_t,k_{t+1}\}_{t=0}^{T}}{Max} \sum_{t=0}^{T} \beta^t U(c_t),$$

subject to the same sequence of budget constraints up to time T,

$$k_{t+1} = \frac{1}{1+n}[f(k_t) + (1-\delta)k_t - c_t],$$

having as Lagrangian,

$$L(\{c_t, k_{t+1}, \lambda_t\}) = \sum_{t=0}^{T} \beta^t \{U(c_t) + \lambda_t [f(k_t) - c_t - (1+n)k_{t+1} + (1-\delta)k_t]\},$$

with first-order conditions,

$$\beta^t [U'(c_t) - \lambda_t] = 0, \ t = 0, 1, 2, 3, \ldots$$

$$-\beta^t \lambda_t (1+n) + \beta^{t+1} \lambda_{t+1} [f'(k_{t+1}) + 1 - \delta] = 0, \ t = 0, 1, 2, 3, \ldots$$

and a transversality condition which is obtained when taking derivatives of the Lagrangian with respect to the stock of capital with the highest time index, k_{T+1},

$$-\beta^T \lambda_T (1+n) \le 0, \ and \ \beta^T \lambda_T k_{T+1} (1+n) = 0.$$

This condition implies that at the end of the maximization period, either the consumer does not want to maintain any capital stock or its value, as measured by its shadow price, will be zero. Usually, it will be the case that $k_{T+1} = 0$.

The transversality condition for the infinite horizon problem is obtained by taking limits in the one for the finite horizon problem, to obtain,

$$\lim_{T \to \infty} \left[-\beta^T \lambda_T (1+n) \right] \le 0, \text{ and } \lim_{T \to \infty} \beta^T \lambda_T k_{T+1} = 0.$$

Taking into account the relationship between discount factors for the continuous and discrete time problems: $\beta \approx e^{-\theta}$, we see the equivalence between the formulation of the transversality condition in both cases.

4.1.6 Competitive Equilibrium with Government

4.1.6.1 The Government

As we did in the continuous time analysis, we now introduce a government in the competitive equilibrium model of an economy with a firm and identical consumers, maintaining the assumption that there is no uncertainty. We assume that the government consumes G_t units of the commodity each period, an exogenous sequence which is not linked to the aggregate level of income for the whole economy. To finance these expenditures, the government can either issue bonds or levy non-distortionary, lump-sum taxes.

The government's budget constraint is:

$$G_t + r_t B_t = T_t + B_{t+1} - B_t, \ \forall t = 0, 1, 2, \dots.$$

with B_t being the stock of public debt outstanding at time t. These were issued and purchased by the private sector at time $t - 1$. r_t is the rate of return paid at time t on bonds issued at time $t - 1$, which is announced and known before hand.

The government budget constraint in per capita terms, is:

$$g_t + r_t b_t = \tau_t + (1+n)b_{t+1} - b_t, \ \forall t = 0, 1, 2, \dots. \tag{4.11}$$

with $\tau_t = \frac{T_t}{N_t}$.

Our goal is to characterize in this economy the allocation of resources emerging under the competitive equilibrium mechanism, and the way how this distribution of resources depends on the level of public consumption.

4.1.6.2 The Problem of the Household

The consumer is allocated with a unit of time every period. Under the assumption that consumption is the only argument in his/her utility function, the unit of time is supplied inelastically in the labor market.

We denote by v_t the units of firm's stock owned by the representative consumer, while a_t denotes total financial assets (public debt plus firms' stock):

$$a_t = b_t + v_t. \tag{4.12}$$

The consumer's budget constraint at time t is:

$$c_t + (1+n)a_{t+1} - a_t + \tau_t = \omega_t + r_t a_t, \tag{4.13}$$

so that the following optimization problem is solved each period:

$$\underset{\{c_t, b_t, v_t\}_{t=0}^{\infty}}{Max} \sum_{t=0}^{\infty} \beta^t U(c_t),$$

subject to (4.12), (4.13), and given a_0.

The discounted Lagrangian for this problem is:

$$L(\{c_t, a_{t+1}, b_t, v_t, \lambda_t, \mu_t\}) = \sum_{t=0}^{\infty} \beta^t U(c_t)$$

$$+ \sum_{t=0}^{\infty} \beta^t \lambda_{1t} \left[\omega_t + (1+r_t)a_t - c_t - (1+n)a_{t+1} - \tau_t \right]$$

$$+ \sum_{t=0}^{\infty} \beta^t \lambda_{2t} \left[a_t - b_t - v_t \right].$$

with first order conditions:

$$c_t : \quad U'(c_t) = \lambda_{1t}, \tag{4.14}$$

$$b_t : \quad \beta^t \lambda_{2t} \le 0, \ \beta^t \lambda_{2t} b_t = 0, \tag{4.15}$$

$$v_t : \quad \beta^t \lambda_{2t} \le 0, \ \beta^t \lambda_{2t} v_t = 0, \tag{4.16}$$

$$a_{t+1} : \quad (1+n)\lambda_{1t} = \beta \lambda_{1t+1}(1+r_{t+1}) - \lambda_{2t}. \tag{4.17}$$

If the consumer demands a positive number of bonds and stock ($b_{t+1}, v_{t+1} > 0$), then $\lambda_{2t} = 0$. Plugging this condition, together with (4.14) into (4.17), we get:

$$(1+n)U'(c_t) = \beta U'(c_{t+1})(1+r_{t+1}). \tag{4.18}$$

The transversality condition is :

$$\lim_{t \to \infty} \beta^t \lambda_{1t} a_{t+1} = 0 \iff \lim_{t \to \infty} \beta^t \lambda_{1t}(b_{t+1} + v_{t+1}) = 0, \tag{4.19}$$

which will hold only if:

$$\lim_{t \to \infty} \beta^t \lambda_{1t} b_{t+1} = 0, \tag{4.20}$$

$$\lim_{t \to \infty} \beta^t \lambda_{1t} v_{t+1} = 0, \tag{4.21}$$

since $b_{t+1} > 0$ and $v_{t+1} > 0$.

We can obtain a more intuitive representation for the transversality conditions by noting that optimality conditions imply $(1+n)\,\lambda_{1t} = \beta\,\lambda_{1t+1}\,(1+r_{t+1})$, which leads to the first order difference equation: $\lambda_{1t+1} = \frac{(1+n)\lambda_{1t}}{\beta(1+r_{t+1})}$. Iterating backwards on this equation, we get:

$$\lambda_{1t} = \frac{(1+n)^t}{\beta^t \Pi_{s=1}^t (1+r_s)}\lambda_{10}.$$

Plugging this result into (4.20) and (4.21) we finally obtain the conditions:

$$\lim_{t \to \infty} \frac{(1+n)^t}{\Pi_{s=1}^t (1+r_s)} b_{t+1} = 0, \tag{4.22}$$

$$\lim_{t \to \infty} \frac{(1+n)^t}{\Pi_{s=1}^t (1+r_s)} v_{t+1} = 0. \tag{4.23}$$

4.1.6.3 The Problem of the Firm

The single firm uses labor and physical capital as factors to produce the single good in the economy. The firm owns the stock of physical capital, and pays a wage ω_t to the L_t workers hired at time t. The firm chooses the amount of physical capital and the number of workers to use every period in production in order to maximize the discounted present value of profits:

$$\underset{\{K_t,\,L_t\}}{Max}\ V_0 = F(K_0, L_0) - \omega_0 L_0 - \delta K_0 - (K_1 - K_0)$$

$$+ \sum_{t=1}^{\infty} \frac{1}{\Pi_{s=1}^t (1+r_s)} [F(K_t, L_t) - \omega_t L_t - \delta K_t - (K_{t+1} - K_t)],$$

where single period profits are defined as the difference between output revenues and the aggregate of wage payments and gross investment. Being the owner of capital, the firm takes care of depreciation expenditures.

The present value of profits can be written,

$$\underset{\{K_t,\,L_t\}}{Max}\ V_0 = F(K_0, L_0) - \omega_0 L_0 - \delta K_0$$

$$+ \sum_{t=1}^{\infty} \frac{1}{\Pi_{s=1}^t (1+r_s)} [F(K_t, L_t) - \omega_t L_t - \delta K_t]$$

$$- (K_1 - K_0) - \sum_{t=1}^{\infty} \frac{1}{\Pi_{s=1}^t (1+r_s)} [K_{t+1} - K_t].$$

But,

$$
\begin{aligned}
(K_1 - K_0) &+ \sum_{t=1}^{\infty} \frac{1}{\prod_{s=1}^{t}(1+r_s)} [K_{t+1} - K_t] \\
&= \left[K_1 + \frac{K_2}{1+r_1} + \frac{K_3}{(1+r_1)(1+r_2)} + \cdots \right] \\
&\quad - \left[K_0 + \frac{K_1}{1+r_1} + \frac{K_2}{(1+r_1)(1+r_2)} + \cdots \right] \\
&= -K_0 + K_1 \frac{r_1}{1+r_1} + K_2 \frac{r_2}{(1+r_1)(1+r_2)} + \cdots \\
&= -K_0 + \sum_{t=1}^{\infty} \frac{r_t K_t}{\prod_{s=1}^{t}(1+r_s)}.
\end{aligned}
$$

Therefore, the objective function for the firm becomes:

$$
V_0 = F(K_0, L_0) - \omega_0 L_0 + (1-\delta)K_0 + \sum_{t=1}^{\infty} \frac{1}{\prod_{s=1}^{t}(1+r_s)} \left[\begin{matrix} F(K_t, L_t) - \omega_t L_t \\ -(r_t + \delta)K_t \end{matrix} \right].
$$

Note that, at time $t = 0$, the firm chooses the amount of work, but not the stock of capital K_0, which is exogenously given. We can see that V_0 is no longer a dynamic function, in the sense that each term depends only on variables determined at time t. There is no connection between decisions made at time t and future profits. Therefore, the first order conditions for the profit maximization problem coincide with those for the static problem of profit maximization for a single period:

$$
r_t + \delta = \frac{\partial F(K_t, L_t)}{\partial K_t} = f'(k_t), \quad t = 1, 2, 3 \ldots \tag{4.24}
$$

$$
\omega_t = \frac{\partial F(K_t, L_t)}{\partial L_t} = f(k_t) - k_t f'(k_t), \quad t = 0, 1, 2, 3 \ldots \tag{4.25}
$$

where small case letters denote again per capita variables.

4.1.6.4 Competitive Equilibrium

A competitive equilibrium is a vector of time series: $\{c_t, k_t, g_t, b_t, v_t, L_t, N_t, \omega_t, r_t, \tau_t\}_{t=0}^{\infty}$, such that:

1. Given prices and taxes $\{\omega_t, r_t, \tau_t\}_{t=0}^{\infty}$, then $\{c_t, a_t, b_t, v_t\}_{t=0}^{\infty}$ solve the problem of the representative consumer.
2. Given prices $\{\omega_t, r_t\}_{t=0}^{\infty}$, then $\{k_t, L_t\}_{t=0}^{\infty}$ solve the firm's problem.
3. Factor markets are in equilibrium, $v_t = k_t$, $N_t = L_t$, $\forall t$.
4. The set of time series $\{g_t, r_t, b_t, \tau_t\}_{t=0}^{\infty}$ satisfy the government budget constraint every period.
5. The transversality conditions $(4.22), (4.23)$ hold.

Once again, the fact that the competitive equilibrium allocation satisfies the government's as well as the consumer's budget constraints, implies that the market for the single commodity in the economy is in equilibrium:

$$c_t + (1+n)k_{t+1} - (1-\delta)k_t + g_t = f(k_t). \tag{4.26}$$

with total output being distributed among private and public consumption, and investment. This represents the *global constraint of resources* in the economy.

4.1.6.5 The Optimal Steady State

The optimal steady state is a dynamic, competitive equilibrium in which per capita variables remain constant over time: $c_{t+1} = c_t = c_{ss}$, $k_{t+1} = k_t = k_{ss}$. Being exogenously chosen by the government, public per capita consumption must also remain constant for a steady state to exist.

The steady state rate of interest is determined from condition (4.18), particularized at steady-state:

$$r_{ss} = \frac{1}{\beta} - 1.$$

Plugging this result into (4.24), again particularized at steady-state, we obtain that the steady-state stock of capital satisfies:

$$f'(k_{ss}) = \frac{1}{\beta} - 1 + \delta,$$

showing that the steady-state stock of capital is independent from public consumption, while being affected by the time discount factor and the depreciation rate of capital. Besides, it takes the same value as in the economy without government, so that the presence of government expenditures does not affect the capital accumulation process, at least in the long-run.[3]

From (4.26), we get steady-state consumption:

$$c_{ss} = f(k_{ss}) - (n+\delta)k_{ss} - g_{ss},$$

where it can be seen how public consumption crowds out private consumption.

Steady-state real wages are obtained from (4.25):

$$\omega_{ss} = f(k_{ss}) - k_{ss}f'(k_{ss}).$$

Finally, if the government chooses exogenously a path for public debt, b_{ss} $\forall t$, then the lump-sum tax must be determined from the government budget constraint so as to finance public expenditures and interest payments:

$$\tau_{ss} = g_{ss} + r_{ss}b_{ss}.$$

---

[3] Remember the equivalence: $\beta = \frac{1}{1+\theta}$.

4.1.6.6 The Representative Agent Problem

As in continuous time, the competitive equilibrium allocation in an economy with consumers and firms solving their respective optimization problems can be characterized as the optimal allocation for a *representative consumer-entrepreneur agent*,[4]

$$\underset{\{c_t,b_{t+1},k_{t+1}\}_{t=0}^{\infty}}{Max} \sum_{t=0}^{\infty} \beta^t U(c_t),$$

subject to,[5]

$$c_t + (1+n)k_{t+1} - (1-\delta)k_t + (1+n)b_{t+1} - \tau_t = f(k_t) + (1+r_t)b_t. \qquad (4.27)$$

Optimality conditions for this problem are,

$$(1+n)U'(c_t) = \beta U'(c_{t+1})(1+r_{t+1}),$$
$$(1+n)U'(c_t) = \beta U'(c_{t+1})(1-\delta+f'(k_{t+1})),$$

$$\lim_{t\to\infty} \frac{(1+n)^t}{\prod_{s=1}^{t}(1+r_s)}(b_{t+1}+k_{t+1}) = 0.$$

together with (4.27).

The competitive equilibrium allocation is characterized by these same conditions, together with the government budget constraint (4.11) and the consumption commodity market clearing condition (4.26).

A proof analogous to that in Sect. 3.5 can be made to show that the competitive equilibrium allocation in this economy is not efficient if the government implements positive expenditures, $g_t > 0$, unless they are returned to consumers as a lump-sum transfer.

4.2 Fiscal Policy in the Cass–Koopmans Model

4.2.1 The Deterministic Case

Let us consider an economy in which the private sector (consumers and the firm) is modeled as a representative composite worker-entrepreneur. That is, we consider that the whole private sector can be represented as a single representative agent interested in maximizing his/her time aggregate welfare, with preferences represented by a constant relative risk aversion utility function, with parameter $\sigma > 0$. The agent has access to a technology to produce consumption commodity using

---

[4] The proof is analogous to that in Sect. 3.4.

[5] Where it can be seen that, at a difference of the planner's problem, government expenditures do not appear.

labor and capital as inputs. The single good in the economy can either be consumed or saved in the form of physical capital. The production technology is represented by a function with decreasing returns to scale in each of the two production factors, but constant returns to scale in the aggregate.

The government implements a time sequence of expenditures, which do not affect the production technology or the utility of the representative agent. Using the expression we introduced previously, public consumption is 'thrown to the sea'.[6] Government expenditures are financed through taxes on output and consumption, at flat rates, τ_t^y, τ_t^c. We assume that government expenditures are decided every period on the basis of tax revenues, so as to keep a balanced budget. This is the only source of revenues: the government does not print any money, and there is not bond issuing. The single-period government budget constraint is,

$$g_t = \tau_t^y y_t + \tau_t^c c_t, \ t = 0, 1, 2, 3, \dots \tag{4.28}$$

Note that government expenditures are not exogenously given in this model. Being determined by tax revenues, they will change with consumption and output.

In Sect. 3.5.2 we discussed in the continuous time version of the competitive equilibrium allocation can be obtained as the solution to the representative agent's problem when the tax rate on labor income and capital income is the same, τ^y. We use this result to characterize the competitive equilibrium allocation of an economy operating under consumption and income taxes by solving the simpler optimization problem of the representative agent.

With population growth equal to n, and a linear depreciation rate for physical capital equal to δ, the budget constraint of the representative agent is,

$$(1 + \tau_t^c) c_t + (1 + n) k_{t+1} - (1 - \delta) k_t = \left(1 - \tau_t^y\right) f(k_t), \tag{4.29}$$

where we have used the constant returns to scale property to write the aggregate production technology $Y_t = F(K_t, N_t)$ in per capita terms as $y_t = f(k_t)$.

The representative agent solves the problem,

$$\underset{\{c_t, k_{t+1}\}_{t=0}^{\infty}}{Max} \sum_{t=0}^{\infty} \beta^t \frac{c_t^{1-\sigma} - 1}{1 - \sigma},$$

subject to (4.29) and given the initial capital stock, k_0.

The Lagrangian for this problem is,

$$L(\{c_t, k_{t+1}, \lambda_t\}) = \sum_{t=0}^{\infty} \beta^t \left[\frac{c_t^{1-\sigma} - 1}{1 - \sigma} + \lambda_t \left[\begin{array}{c} \left(1 - \tau_t^y\right) f(k_t) - (1 + \tau_t^c) c_t \\ - (1 + n) k_{t+1} + (1 - \delta) k_t \end{array} \right] \right].$$

We assume in what follows that the constant returns to scale production function is of the Cobb-Douglas type, so that per capita output can be written,

$$y_t = f(k_t) = A k_t^{\alpha}, \ 0 < \alpha < 1.$$

---

[6] As a consequence, the competitive equilibrium allocation will not be efficient.

Necessary conditions for optimality are obtaining by taking derivatives in the Lagrangian with respect to c_t and k_{t+1}, to obtain, assuming interior solutions $(c_t, k_{t+1} > 0, \forall t)$,

$$\beta^t \left[c_t^{-\sigma} - \lambda_t \left(1 + \tau_t^c \right) \right] = 0, \tag{4.30}$$

$$-\beta^t \lambda_t (1+n) + \beta^{t+1} \lambda_{t+1} \left[\left(1 - \tau_{t+1}^y \right) A \alpha k_{t+1}^{\alpha - 1} + 1 - \delta \right] = 0. \tag{4.31}$$

We also have the transversality condition,

$$\lim_{t \to \infty} \beta^t \lambda_t k_{t+1} = 0.$$

Condition (4.30) can also be written,

$$\frac{c_t^{-\sigma}}{1 + \tau_t^c} = \lambda_t,$$

which, substituted in (4.31) leads to,

$$c_{t+1} = \left[\frac{\beta}{1+n} \frac{1 + \tau_t^c}{1 + \tau_{t+1}^c} \left[\left(1 - \tau_{t+1}^y \right) A \alpha k_{t+1}^{\alpha - 1} + 1 - \delta \right] \right]^{\frac{1}{\sigma}} c_t, \tag{4.32}$$

the version of the Keynes-Ramsey condition under income and consumption taxes. This condition is the extension of the standard equality, at each point in time, between the marginal rate of substitution of consumption and the marginal product of capital net of taxes and depreciation, that relationship changing over time as a function of possible changes in the consumption tax rate.

4.2.1.1 Solving the Representative Agent Problem

For an initial condition k_0, and given time series for $\{\tau_t^c, \tau_t^y\}$, a competitive equilibrium is a set of real functions $\{c_t, k_{t+1}\}$ defined on $(0, \infty)$, such that: (1) given τ_t^c, τ_t^y the vector of functions $\{c_t, k_{t+1}\}$ solves the utility maximization problem of the representative agent, (2) the commodity market clears, and (3) the budget constraint (4.28) for the government is satisfied in every period. The competitive equilibrium allocation will not be efficient because a positive level of public consumption is 'thrown to the sea', and because there is distortionary taxation in the economy. This can be shown by an argument parallel to that in Sect. 3.5.

Together with the transversality condition, the budget constraint (4.29) satisfied with equality and the Keynes-Ramsey condition (4.32) form a system of non-linear difference equations characterizing the optimal time paths for physical capital and consumption, starting from an initial condition k_0. We could think of solving this system of equations directly. Even though it is a system of two non-linear equations each period for which no analytical solution exists, values for consumption and capital stock for every period can be obtained using any numerical solution algorithm for nonlinear systems included in a mathematical computer library. The budget constraint is a relationship between c_t and k_{t+1}, given k_t, while the Keynes-Ramsey condition relates c_{t+1} and k_{t+1}, given c_t. This suggests that starting form the initial condition k_0, a given choice of initial consumption c_0 would allow us to compute k_1 from the budget constraint, to then obtain c_1 from Keynes-Ramsey condition, and the procedure could be iterated to obtain full time series for both variables. The trouble is that, with all probability, the obtained solution would not converge to steady state, due to the fact that we would not be imposing any stability condition. Such condition is necessary to guarantee that the transversality condition will hold. If initial consumption could be chosen arbitrarily, as described in the previous paragraph, we could have a continuum of solutions, since any possible choice of initial consumption would start a trajectory taking the economy to steady state. That is a characteristic of *globally stable* systems. The phase diagrams discussed for the continuous and the discrete time version of the model show that the planner's problem has a *saddle-point structure*, characterized by the existence of a single stable manifold, *i.e.*, a single trajectory converging to steady-state. The economy will be on a stable path, converging to steady state only if initial consumption is chosen appropriately, and there is a single choice guaranteeing stability. That specific choice of initial consumption is determined by the stability condition we discuss next.

4.2.1.2 Stability

A stability condition will guarantee that the set of time series for the relevant variables obtained as a solution to the representative agent problem, converges to steady-state levels. To characterize such condition, we start by constructing the linear approximation to the system around steady-state. With a production technology displaying decreasing returns to scale in the cumulative factor (physical capital), the only growth rate which is sustainable on the long-run is zero, as we saw in chapter 2. Hence, in steady-state, per capita variables will stay constant, $c_t = c_{ss}$, $k_t = k_{ss}$, $y_t = y_{ss}$, $\forall t$.

For simplicity, we assume the government uses constant income and consumption tax rates,

$$\tau_t^y = \tau^y, \ \tau_t^c = \tau^c, \ \forall t.$$

This assumption is more strict than needed, but it should be clear that existence of a zero growth rate steady state requires of a sufficiently stable behavior of tax rates.

Taking these assumptions to (4.32), we obtain the steady state level of physical capital,

$$k_{ss} = \left[\frac{(1 - \tau^y) A \alpha}{\frac{1+n}{\beta} - (1 - \delta)} \right]^{\frac{1}{1-\alpha}},$$

a function of the tax rate on income, which is not affected by the tax rate on consumption. Hence, consumption taxes do not affect the long-run process of physical capital accumulation. Plugging this expression into the budget constraint, we get,

$$c_{ss} = \frac{1}{1+\tau^c}\left[(1-\tau^y)Ak_{ss}^\alpha - (n+\delta)k_{ss}\right].$$

We can now approximate the first order conditions around steady-state. We first write the budget constraint,

$$k_{t+1} - \frac{1-\tau^y}{1+n}Ak_t^\alpha - \frac{1-\delta}{1+n}k_t + \frac{1+\tau^c}{1+n}c_t = 0, \qquad (4.33)$$

and consider it as a function $G(k_{t+1}, c_{t+1}, k_t, c_t) = 0$, whose linear approximation is,

$$(k_{t+1} - k_{ss}) - \left[\frac{1}{1+n}\left((1-\tau^y)A\alpha k_{ss}^{\alpha-1} + 1 - \delta\right)\right](k_t - k_{ss})$$
$$+ \frac{1+\tau^c}{1+n}(c_t - c_{ss}) = 0.$$

From the expression for k_{ss} we see that the first bracket is equal to $\frac{1}{\beta}$, so that we get,

$$k_{t+1} - k_{ss} = \frac{1}{\beta}(k_t - k_{ss}) - \frac{1+\tau^c}{1+n}(c_t - c_{ss}). \qquad (4.34)$$

On the other hand, considering the optimality condition for the representative agent problem, (4.32), as a function $F(k_{t+1}, c_{t+1}, k_t, c_t) = 0$, it can be approximated by,

$$c_{t+1} - c_{ss} = \frac{1}{\sigma}\Omega_{ss}^{\frac{1}{\sigma}-1}\left[\frac{\beta}{1+n}(1-\tau^y)A\alpha(\alpha-1)k_{ss}^{\alpha-2}\right]c_{ss}(k_{t+1} - k_{ss})$$
$$+ \Omega_{ss}^{\frac{1}{\sigma}}(c_t - c_{ss}),$$

where Ω_{ss} denotes the bracketed expression in (4.32), $\Omega_{ss} = \frac{\beta}{1+n}((1-\tau^y)A\alpha k_{ss}^{\alpha-1} + 1 - \delta)$. Particularizing (4.32) at steady-state, we get: $\Omega_{ss} = 1$.

So we have,

$$(c_{t+1} - c_{ss}) - \frac{1}{\sigma}\frac{\beta}{1+n}(1-\tau^y)A\alpha(\alpha-1)k_{ss}^{\alpha-2}c_{ss}(k_{t+1} - k_{ss}) = c_t - c_{ss}. \quad (4.35)$$

These two approximations can be written in matrix form,

$$\begin{pmatrix} 1 & 0 \\ -\frac{1}{\sigma}\frac{\beta}{1+n}(1-\tau^y)A\alpha(\alpha-1)k_{ss}^{\alpha-2}c_{ss} & 1 \end{pmatrix}\begin{pmatrix} k_{t+1} - k_{ss} \\ c_{t+1} - c_{ss} \end{pmatrix}$$
$$= \begin{pmatrix} \frac{1}{\beta} & -\frac{1+\tau^c}{1+n} \\ 0 & 1 \end{pmatrix}\begin{pmatrix} k_t - k_{ss} \\ c_t - c_{ss} \end{pmatrix}, \qquad (4.36)$$

which can be abbreviated,

$$B_0 z_{t+1} = B_1 z_t,$$

where $z_t = (k_t - k_{ss}, c_t - c_{ss})$, and B_0, B_1 are the 2x2 coefficient matrices in (4.36). Since B_0 is invertible,

$$B_0 = \begin{pmatrix} 1 & 0 \\ M & 1 \end{pmatrix} \Rightarrow B_0^{-1} = \begin{pmatrix} 1 & 0 \\ -M & 1 \end{pmatrix},$$

with,

$$M = -\frac{1}{\sigma} \frac{\beta}{1+n} (1-\tau^y) A\alpha (\alpha - 1) k_{ss}^{\alpha-2} c_{ss} > 0.$$

And we can also write the linear approximation to the optimality conditions of the model with taxes as,

$$\begin{pmatrix} k_{t+1} - k_{ss} \\ c_{t+1} - c_{ss} \end{pmatrix} = \begin{pmatrix} \frac{1}{\beta} & -\frac{1+\tau^c}{1+n} \\ -\frac{1}{\beta}M & 1+M\frac{1+\tau^c}{1+n} \end{pmatrix} \begin{pmatrix} k_t - k_{ss} \\ c_t - c_{ss} \end{pmatrix}$$

$$= \begin{pmatrix} d_{11} & d_{12} \\ d_{21} & d_{22} \end{pmatrix} \begin{pmatrix} k_{t-1} - k_{ss} \\ c_{t-1} - c_{ss} \end{pmatrix}. \tag{4.37}$$

where the 2×2 matrix of coefficients $D = \begin{pmatrix} d_{11} & d_{12} \\ d_{21} & d_{22} \end{pmatrix}$, has as characteristic equation,

$$\mu^2 - (d_{11} + d_{22})\mu + (d_{11}d_{22} - d_{12}d_{21}) = 0,$$

with roots,

$$\mu = \frac{(d_{11} + d_{22}) \pm \sqrt{(d_{11} + d_{22})^2 - 4(d_{11}d_{22} - d_{12}d_{21})}}{2}.$$

Using the discussion in the Mathematical Appendix and following an argument similar to the one used in Sect. 3.2, we use the spectral decomposition of D, $D = \Gamma\Lambda\Gamma^{-1}$ and expressions for the matrix of right eigenvectors and its inverse $\Gamma = \begin{pmatrix} x_1 & y_1 \\ x_2 & y_2 \end{pmatrix}$, $\Gamma^{-1} = \begin{pmatrix} u_1 & v_1 \\ u_2 & v_2 \end{pmatrix}$ to represent the dynamics of the solution as,

$$\begin{pmatrix} k_t - k_{ss} \\ c_t - c_{ss} \end{pmatrix} = \Gamma\Lambda\Gamma^{-1} \begin{pmatrix} k_{t-1} - k_{ss} \\ c_{t-1} - c_{ss} \end{pmatrix}$$

$$= \begin{pmatrix} x_1 & y_1 \\ x_2 & y_2 \end{pmatrix} \begin{pmatrix} \mu_1 & 0 \\ 0 & \mu_2 \end{pmatrix} \begin{pmatrix} u_1 & v_1 \\ u_2 & v_2 \end{pmatrix} \begin{pmatrix} k_{t-1} - k_{ss} \\ c_{t-1} - k_{ss} \end{pmatrix}, \tag{4.38}$$

where, in terms of parameter values, $x_1 = 1$, $x_2 = \frac{\mu_1 - d_{11}}{d_{12}}$; $y_1 = 1$, $y_2 = \frac{\mu_2 - d_{11}}{d_{12}}$; $u_1 = \frac{\mu_2 - d_{11}}{\mu_2 - \mu_1}$, $v_1 = -\frac{d_{12}}{\mu_2 - \mu_1}$; $u_2 = -\frac{\mu_1 - d_{11}}{\mu_2 - \mu_1}$ and $v_2 = \frac{d_{12}}{\mu_2 - \mu_1}$.

Iterating over time, we get the full trajectory from starting values k_0, c_0,

$$
\begin{pmatrix} k_t - k_{ss} \\ c_t - k_{ss} \end{pmatrix} = \Gamma \Lambda^t \Gamma^{-1} \begin{pmatrix} k_{t-1} - k_{ss} \\ c_{t-1} - k_{ss} \end{pmatrix}
$$

$$
= \begin{pmatrix} x_1 & y_1 \\ x_2 & y_2 \end{pmatrix} \begin{pmatrix} \mu_1^t & 0 \\ 0 & \mu_2^t \end{pmatrix} \begin{pmatrix} u_1 & v_1 \\ u_2 & v_2 \end{pmatrix} \begin{pmatrix} k_0 - k_{ss} \\ c_0 - k_{ss} \end{pmatrix}.
$$

The characteristic equation for this system satisfies the conditions described in the Mathematical Appendix on models with a saddle point structure, so that the two roots satisfy: $|\mu_1| > 1/\sqrt{\beta}$, $|\mu_2| < 1$. For reasons that will become clear shortly, we call μ_2 the *stable eigenvalue*, μ_1 being the *unstable eigenvalue*[7].

The matrix product in the previous expression is:

$$
\begin{aligned}
k_t - k_{ss} &= x_1 \mu_1^t \left[u_1 (k_0 - k_{ss}) + v_1 (c_0 - c_{ss}) \right] \\
&\quad + y_1 \mu_2^t \left[u_2 (k_0 - k_{ss}) + v_2 (c_0 - c_{ss}) \right], \\
c_t - c_{ss} &= x_2 \mu_1^t \left[u_1 (k_0 - k_{ss}) + v_1 (c_0 - c_{ss}) \right] \\
&\quad + y_2 \mu_2^t \left[u_2 (k_0 - k_{ss}) + v_2 (c_0 - c_{ss}) \right].
\end{aligned}
$$

The transversality condition on the capital stock is,

$$
\lim_{t \to \infty} \beta^t \frac{1}{1 + \tau^c} k_t c_t^{-\sigma} = \lim_{t \to \infty} \beta^t k_t = 0,
$$

where we have used the fact that consumption will not go to zero along the optimal trajectory. Since $|\beta \mu_1| > 1$ while $|\beta \mu_2| < \beta$, the transversality condition will hold only if the coefficient on the unstable eigenvalue, μ_1, in the equation for $k_t - k_{ss}$ is set equal to zero. But, as shown above, $x_1 = 1$, so that it is the bracketed term accompanying μ_1^t which must be zero. In the consumption equation, the same condition must hold, because x_2 depends on the values of the structural parameters, and cannot be chosen to be zero:

$$
u_1 (k_0 - k_{ss}) + v_1 (c_0 - c_{ss}) = 0, \tag{4.39}
$$

---

[7] The rate of growth along the solution is clearly related to the absolute values of the μ_1, μ_2 roots. The critical rate of growth below which the solution is stable is model–specific. The requirement for a well–defined solution to exist is that the objective function remains bounded, which will require upper bounds on its variable arguments. Those bounds will depend on the functional form of the objective function. Sometimes, as in the Cass–Koopmans model, transversality conditions take care of that. In other cases, transversality conditions may be needed for feasibility or optimality even when the objective function is bounded, so that extra upper bounds on growth rates will then need to be added, to guarantee that transversality conditions hold. Note that a linear approximation to the set of first order conditions for the representative agent problem amounts to a linear-quadratic approximation to that problem. Hence, given a quadratic approximation to the objective function (i.e., $\sum_{t=0}^{\infty} \beta^t U(c_t) \simeq \sum_{t=0}^{\infty} \beta^t (a\tilde{c}_t^2 + b\tilde{c}_t + d)$, where $\tilde{c}_t = c_t - c_{ss}$), it is clear that the sum will converge for solutions of the type $\tilde{c}_t = \mu^t \tilde{c}_0$, only if $|\mu| < 1/\sqrt{\beta}$.

so that stability requires that initial consumption c_0 be chosen by:

$$c_0 - c_{ss} = -\frac{u_1}{v_1}(k_0 - k_{ss}) = \frac{\mu_2 - d_{11}}{d_{12}}(k_0 - k_{ss}).$$

If the initial consumption choice is made according to this stability condition, then the dynamics of the system thereafter is given by,

$$k_t - k_{ss} = y_1 \mu_2^t [u_2(k_0 - k_{ss}) + v_2(c_0 - c_{ss})], \qquad (4.40)$$
$$c_t - c_{ss} = y_2 \mu_2^t [u_2(k_0 - k_{ss}) + v_2(c_0 - c_{ss})], \qquad (4.41)$$

so that,

$$c_t - c_{ss} = \frac{y_2}{y_1}(k_t - k_{ss}) = \frac{\mu_2 - d_{11}}{d_{12}}(k_t - k_{ss}), \qquad (4.42)$$

where we can see that stability requires that the same condition between capital stock and consumption, in deviations from steady state levels, must hold at each point in time as at time 0. This is the *stability condition* we were looking for. Additionally, it is easy to see that, even though we have not imposed them explicitly, conditions (4.40) and (4.41) will also hold at time $t = 0$.

Consequently, the dynamics of the system can be simplified to,

$$k_t - k_{ss} = \mu_2^t [y_1(u_2(k_0 - k_{ss}) + v_2(c_0 - c_{ss}))] = \mu_2^t (k_0 - k_{ss}),$$
$$c_t - c_{ss} = \frac{\mu_2 - d_{11}}{d_{12}}\mu_2^t (k_0 - k_{ss}) = \mu_2^t (c_0 - c_{ss}),$$

showing that both, consumption and the stock of capital smoothly converge from their initial values to their steady state levels along this linear approximation.

The numerical solution to the model could be computed from the linear approximation, using the stability condition to calculate initial consumption, c_0. This is because of the property above that the linear approximation will satisfy the stability condition at any time period, if it is imposed at $t = 0$. However, the linear approximation may be a crude approximation to the nonlinear economy, so this procedure is not advisable. As an alternative, we could solve using one of the two equations in the linear approximation, together with the stability condition, at any time period. A better approach is to use each period the stability condition and the nonlinear global constraint of resources (4.29). That way, we preserve some of the nonlinearity in the original model. The solution so obtained will, in fact, be seen to converge towards steady-state. The condition not being used will not hold exactly each period. On the other hand, if a solution is obtained directly from the two non-linear conditions, without imposing stability at any point, the resulting time series will eventually diverge away from steady-state. That would be the case because we would not be taking proper care of the transversality condition. It is important to realize that the potential instability issues do not have anything to do with the stochastic nature of the problem, arising also in deterministic economies like the one considered in this chapter.

In more complex deterministic models, the stability conditions can be seen as picking the *stable* initial values for the decision variables as functions of the exogenous initial values of the state variables. If we have less stability conditions than decision variables in the system[8], we will only be able to solve the model as a function of a given, arbitrary, starting value for one or more decision variables[9], and they will all be stable. Since any such an arbitrary choice will produce stable paths converging to steady-state, the solution is *indeterminate*, in the sense of Benhabib and Perli [9] and Xie [98]. The system is then said to be *globally stable*. On the other hand, the system does not have a solution when there are more independent stability conditions than control variables to be chosen. The stable subspace will then reduce to the steady state, if it exists, and the economy will be globally *unstable*, getting into divergent paths as soon as it experiences even slight deviations from steady state. Finally, the solution will be *unique* when the set of stability conditions can be used to represent all the control variables as functions of state and exogenous variables, the system of equations having a unique solution. In the previous model we have one state variable and one decision variable, so one stability condition produces a unique solution.

To obtain a solution to this model, in the form of a set of time series for the relevant variables, we proceed as follows,

1. Give numerical values to structural parameters, β, δ, A, α, n, σ, as well as to the initial condition, k_0, and policy parameters, τ^y, τ^c,
2. Obtain steady state levels for physical capital and consumption, k_{ss}, c_{ss},
3. Numerically evaluate the transition matrix in (4.37), and compute its eigenvalues and eigenvectors,
4. Starting from k_0, use the stability condition to obtain the value for initial consumption, c_0, placing the economy on the trajectory converging to steady-state,
5. Obtain k_1 from the budget constraint, and c_1 from the stability condition. Repeat the process for every time period t.

As we have already mentioned, a numerical solution computed from the two nonlinear equations, the budget constraint and the Keynes-Ramsey rule, will be explosive. As seen above, that would require an arbitrary choice of initial consumption, with no hope that the solution might be stable. The model can be solved applying each period the stability condition, together with the budget constraint. The Keynes-Ramsey condition, which is not being used to compute the solution, will not hold exactly, reflecting the numerical approximation error produced by having used an approximation to the stability condition. The model could also be solved imposing the stability condition at each period and using either one of the equations in the linear approximation to the model. Although we have shown above that the linear

---

[8] After using equations that involve only contemporaneous values of decision variables (as it may be the case with some identities) to eliminate some of these decision variables from the problem.

[9] Initial consumption, in the Cass–Koopmans economy considered in this chapter. We will get back to this issue in the Mathematical Appendix.

approximation expands the stability condition towards the future, it is interesting to point out that if we impose the stability condition just in the initial period and use the equations in the linear approximation to compute the solution, it will converge to steady-state, but it will eventually end up by abandoning it.

4.2.2 Numerical Exercise – Solving the Deterministic Competitive Equilibrium with Taxes

In the *CK_Taxes_deterministic.xls* file we solve the deterministic, discrete time version of the representative consumer's problem, in an economy where the government makes some nonzero consumption each period, financed with the proceeds from consumption and income taxes, as characterized in the previous section. The same analysis can be implemented using MATLAB file *CK_d_transition.m*. This exercise is extremely important to understand the role of stability conditions when computing numerical solutions for deterministic and stochastic optimization problems, like those involved in planner problems or when characterizing the competitive equilibrium allocation of resources.

Benchmark values for structural parameters are, $A = 1$, $\beta = .90$, $\alpha = .33$, $n = .0$, $\delta = .07$, $\sigma = 0.50$, and tax rates: $\tau_c = 20.0\%$, $\tau_y = 12.478\%$. Under this parameterization, steady state levels are $k_{ss} = 2.007$, $c_{ss} = 0.801$, $y_{ss} = 1.258$, and government revenues: $g_{ss} = 0.3172$. Steady state investment is equal to the difference between disposable income and consumption $i_{ss} = (y_{ss} - \tau_y y_{ss} - \tau_c c_{ss}) - c_{ss} = .1405$. This figure is equal to $(\delta + n)k_{ss}$, the aggregate of the depreciation loss of physical capital, plus what must be given away to the consumers being born every period to maintain constant the stock of capital per worker, nk_{ss}, as it should be to make the steady state sustainable.

Below the benchmark parameter values and tax rates, steady-state levels for the main endogenous variables are shown in the first columns of the spreadsheet. Below them, the reader can find the numerical values for the elements of the transition matrix in the linear approximation to the model, as well as its eigenvalues and eigenvectors, used to estimate the linear approximation to the stable manifold for the competitive equilibrium under the chosen parameterization. The M-constant in the spreadsheet is the same as in the previous section. With the mentioned benchmark parameter values, the approximate stability condition is estimated at,

$$c_t - c_{ss} = 0.2868(k_t - k_{ss}), \ \forall t.$$

The first case considered in Panel 1 presents an economy with an initial stock of capital equal to the steady-state level, $k_0 = k_{ss}$. Then, we choose per capita consumption from the stability condition, which positions the economy on the stable manifold. But, since the stock of capital is at its steady-state level, the economy is positioned right at steady-state, with $k_0 = k_{ss}$, $c_0 = c_{ss}$. After the initial period, we use the budget constraint to find next period's stock of capital, and the

Keynes-Ramsey condition to find the associated level of consumption. Since the economy starts right at steady-state, the implied numerical solution is trivial, the economy never leaving the steady-state. Notice that some relationship other than Keynes-Ramsey condition needs to be used to calculate initial consumption c_0, because of the dependence on previous period consumption in that equation.

The second case in Panel 1 considers an economy which starts to the left of the optimal steady-state, i.e., with a stock of capital below that of steady-state. As in the previous case, the stability condition is used to compute c_0, and the full nonlinear structure of the economy is used as the propagation mechanism from $t = 0$ on. We use sequentially the budget constraint, an equation of the form $k_{t+1} = f(k_t, c_t)$ to find end-of-period capital, and Keynes-Ramsey condition, which has the form $c_{t+1} = f(k_{t+1}, c_t)$ to find the level of consumption next period. So, starting from k_0, the stability condition gives us c_0, the budget constraint provides us with k_1, the Keynes-Ramsey condition with c_1, and we iterate over time. Since we start to the left of the steady-state, the linear approximation to the stability condition chooses a level of consumption below that of steady-state. From that point on, capital stock and consumption increase, as it should be the case in order to converge to steady state. However, after some point in time shown in red in the spreadsheet, the economy changes its direction, with the stock of capital decreasing and consumption increasing above the steady-state level. In terms of the stability graph, we have moved from the lower-left region to the upper-left region and, as indicated in the enclosed graph, the economy moves toward the vertical axis, with decreasing capital and ever increasing consumption, a clearly unfeasible situation, which has a clear reflection in the numerical solution. This happens because we have not positioned the economy on the stable manifold except at $t = 0$, being outside it for the remaining periods.

One might think that the previous situation arises because we have started far from steady-state. The third case in Panel 1 starts again to the right and below steady-state, but very close to it, using again the stability condition to obtain initial consumption, and the full nonlinear structure of the economy as the propagation mechanism from that point on. Once again, the economy starts moving in the right direction towards the steady-state, but it reaches a point where the stock of capital falls quickly to zero. The only difference with the previous case is that it takes longer to depart from the convergent trajectory. In fact, the reader can check that the same result arises by arbitrarily choosing the initial level of consumption, *i.e.*, the level in cells M24 or P24.

Panel 2 exploits the linear approximation to the model, losing the information contained in the nonlinearity aspects of the economy. Both, the stock of capital and consumption are obtained from the linear approximation (4.34) to the model. However, initial consumption cannot be obtained that way, so the stability condition is used just at $t = 0$, to choose c_0. In the first case, initial capital is at steady-state level, so our mechanism positions the economy at steady-state, which is never left. In the second case, the economy starts with a stock of capital below that of steady-state. From then on, (4.37) propagates the system forwards into the future. The use of the fully linearized system takes the economy to steady-state, so long as we use the stability condition to compute initial consumption. The accompanying graph shows smooth, gradual transition paths for the stock of capital and consumption. As shown in the third case, starting farther away from steady-state just requires more periods for convergence, but stability prevails. The only problem in this panel is that purely numerical approximation errors in EXCEL throw the trajectories away from steady-state after having been arbitrarily close to it for a large number of periods. The size of errors clearly depends on how far is the initial condition from steady-state.

We compute in Panel 3 the numerical solution using again the linear approximation to the model, as we did in Panel 2. The difference is that we now use the stability condition every period, not just at time 0, to obtain the consumption time series. We obtain the same time series for consumption and capital as in Panel 3, where we used the stability condition just at $t = 0$, for the same initial condition, The third column computes the consumption times series again, but using the other equation in the linear approximation, rather than the stability condition. The point is that the linear approximation cannot be used to compute initial consumption, so the stability condition is used instead to obtain c_0. But then, as we saw in the previous section, the stability condition will hold forever, so it is not surprising that the two linear approaches to computing consumption in this panel produce the same stable solution. After the consumption time series, we present the percent approximation error in consumption and physical capital from using the linear approximation to the model rather than its nonlinear structure, as reflected in the Keynes-Ramsey condition and the budget constraint. Approximation errors become negligible after a finite number of periods.

In Panel 4, the stability condition is used at all time periods to obtain the level of per capita consumption, while the budget constraint is used to obtain end-of-period stock of capital, as $k_{t+1} = f(k_t, c_t)$. This mechanism would leave the economy at steady-state if it started from there, as shown in the first situation considered. In the second case, the economy starts from a stock of capital below steady-state. The stability condition guarantees convergence to steady-state, no matter what the initial stock of capital is. There is an unavoidable numerical approximation error in the fact that we use as stability condition that of the linearly approximated system. However, the solution is in this case a better approximation to the true solution than that found in Panel 2 when starting from the same initial stock of capital, since in that case, we did not use any of the true, nonlinear structure the model, as we do in this Panel 4.

To the far right we present a first graph comparing the trajectories obtained under the linear approximation in Panel 3 and the more nonlinear solution in Panel 4. A second graph shows the smooth converging paths for consumption and the stock of capital, as well as the trajectory that would follow the stock of capital if we started farther away from steady-state. The consumption trajectories calculated under the stability condition or using the Keynes-Ramsey condition, and the levels of utility provided by them, are seen to be very similar to each other. In the '%-deviation in C' column we show the percent difference between the level of per capita consumption that would arise from the exact calculation provided by the

Keynes-Ramsey condition, and the level that is obtained under the stability condition to the linear approximation to the model. These alternative consumption trajectories are shown in the last graph. When the economy starts close to steady-state, the approximation error is small, of 0.50%, becoming negligible after just 6 periods. The last case in Panel 4 considers an economy starting farther away from steady-state. That does not have any substantial implications regarding convergence, except for the fact that it takes longer to reach the steady state and that the numerical approximation error in consumption is initially rather large, but again becomes negligible after very few periods.

4.2.3 Numerical Exercise – Fiscal Policy Evaluation

In the excel file *CK_solution_changes_in_tax.xls,* we use the model introduced in the previous section to analyze the effects of different changes in government's fiscal policy. The *Steady State* spreadsheet shows long-run effects, while the *Transition* spreadsheet contains short- and also long-run effects. In all cases, we compute the welfare effects of policy changes. We start in this section by presenting the measure we use to evaluate welfare effects, as used by Lucas [59].

4.2.3.1 Measuring Welfare Effects

We measure the welfare effect, ΔW, of a fiscal policy change as the additional consumption which should be given to the representative consumer each period along the old consumption path, to make him indifferent between the old policy and the new one. A negative value of ΔW would mean that there is a welfare loss associated to the fiscal reform. We measure the consumption compensation as a percentage of the level of output prior to the fiscal reform. We further assume that the tax change takes place on a steady-state economy.

Let c_{ss}^I, y_{ss}^I denote steady-state consumption and output under the initial tax policy, while c_t^N denotes period's t consumption under the new fiscal policy. Tax reform is implemented at $t = 0$, when the economy is at steady state. Rather than staying at c_{ss} forever, the economy will start a transition towards the new steady-state, with a consumption trajectory denoted by c_t, $t = 0, 1, 2, \ldots$ The effect on welfare is thus measured as $\Delta W = 100 \frac{\Delta c}{y_{ss}^I}$.

The consumption compensation Δc must satisfy:

$$\sum_{t=0}^{\infty} \beta^t \frac{\left(c_{ss}^I + \Delta c\right)^{1-\sigma} - 1}{1 - \sigma} = \sum_{t=0}^{\infty} \beta^t \frac{\left(c_t^N\right)^{1-\sigma} - 1}{1 - \sigma}.$$

Defining $\eta = \frac{\Delta c}{c_{ss}^I}$, we can write, $\Delta W = 100 \frac{\eta c_{ss}^I}{y_{ss}^I}$, and the previous equation becomes:

$$\sum_{t=0}^{\infty} \beta^t \frac{\left((1+\eta) c_{ss}^I\right)^{1-\sigma} - 1}{1-\sigma} = \sum_{t=0}^{\infty} \beta^t \frac{\left(c_t^N\right)^{1-\sigma} - 1}{1-\sigma},$$

which implies a level of η:

$$\eta = \frac{\left[(1-\beta)(1-\sigma)\left(\sum_{t=0}^{\infty} \beta^t \frac{\left(c_t^N\right)^{1-\sigma}-1}{1-\sigma}\right) + 1\right]^{\frac{1}{1-\sigma}}}{c_{ss}^I} - 1,$$

and,

$$\Delta W = 100. \left(\frac{\left[(1-\beta)(1-\sigma)\left(\sum_{t=0}^{\infty} \beta^t \frac{\left(c_t^N\right)^{1-\sigma}-1}{1-\sigma}\right) + 1\right]^{\frac{1}{1-\sigma}}}{c_{ss}^I} - 1\right) \frac{c_{ss}^I}{y_{ss}^I}. \qquad (4.43)$$

If the analysis is restricted to long-run effects, then $c_t^N = c_{ss}^N$, and η then becomes:

$$\eta = \frac{c_{ss}^N}{c_{ss}^I} - 1,$$

so that,

$$\Delta W_{ss} = \frac{\eta c_{ss}^I}{y_{ss}^I} \cdot 100 = \left(\frac{c_{ss}^N}{c_{ss}^I} - 1\right) \frac{c_{ss}^I}{y_{ss}^I} \cdot 100. \qquad (4.44)$$

Structural parameter values are given on the left side of the *Steady State* spreadsheet: $A = 1$, $\beta = .90$, $\alpha = .33$, $n = .0$, $\delta = .07$, $\sigma = 0.50$. Three questions are analyzed in that spreadsheet: *i*) the long-run effects of a change in the income tax rate, keeping constant the consumption tax rate (in fact, we assume $\tau^c = 0$), *ii*) the long-run effects of a change in the consumption tax rate, keeping constant the income tax rate (specifically, we assume $\tau^y = 0$). In both cases, we can see that tax revenues and hence, public consumption, both change. Finally, we analyze the long-run effects of simultaneous changes in both tax rates keeping tax revenues constant.

4.2.3.2 Long-Run Effects of a Tax Reform

In Panel 1 in the *Steady-state* spreadsheet we start from a situation with zero consumption taxes, and compute changes in the capital stock, private and public consumption, production, after-tax income, and the weight of public consumption on total output, as the consumption income tax rate increases from zero, while keeping the income tax rate fixed at zero. We also compute the welfare cost of that tax increase. A similar study is performed in Panel 2. In that case, it is the income tax rate which starts at zero and gradually increases, while the consumption tax stays at zero. In all cases, we use the steady-state expressions for capital stock and consumption characterized in the previous section. The same analysis can be implemented with the *CK_d_long run tax changes.m* MATLAB file. Output is $y_{ss} = f(k_{ss}) = Ak_{ss}^{\alpha}$, investment: $i_{ss} = (n+\delta)k_{ss}$, revenues are $\tau_c c_{ss} + \tau_y y_{ss}$, utility: $U_{ss} = \frac{c_{ss}^{1-\sigma}-1}{1-\sigma}$, and disposable income: $y_{ss}^d = (1-\tau_y)y_{ss}$. Welfare cost is obtained from (4.44).

Below the numerical results we present some graphs summarizing these two analysis. The blue line shows steady-state responses of different variables to changes in the income tax rate, while the red line shows the response to changes in the consumption tax rate. An increase in the consumption tax has no long-run effect on the accumulation process for physical capital and hence, on the long-run stock of capital. As a consequence, steady-state output and investment do not change either. Steady-state investment is obtained by applying the depreciation rate anf population growth to the steady-state stock of capital. Tax revenues increase, which allows for a raise in public consumption. The latter crowds out private consumption in a one-to-one basis, since there is no change in output or investment. This substitution reduces consumers' utility level. The welfare cost of the consumption tax increases monotonically with the tax rate.

The main difference between an increase in either tax rate is the way they affect productivity, which is not affected by a consumption tax. An increase in the income tax rate produces a reduction in the after tax marginal product of labor, which discourages capital accumulation and leads to a reduction in the steady-state levels of the stock of capital and output. The lower disposable income leads to a reduction in private consumption and utility. For similar tax rates, the negative effect on growth and welfare of an income tax is greater than that of a consumption tax. It is interesting to notice that tax revenues do not increase monotonically with an income tax, being highest when income taxes are of about 67%, and decreasing for higher income tax rates. This is what is known as Laffer's curve. In spite of this reduction in revenues for higher tax rates, the share of public consumption in production is always increasing. The welfare cost again increases monotonically with the income tax rate.

At a difference of the analysis in Panels 1 and 2, we consider in Panels 3 and 4 the real effects produced by simultaneous tax changes that keep tax revenues constant. We consider two levels of revenues: 0.317 and 0.550. Results for both cases are jointly summarized in a set of graphs below the numerical calculations. To characterize the association between both tax rates, we write the budget constraint for the economy with taxes in steady-state:

$$(1+\tau^c)c_{ss} + (n+\delta)k_{ss} = (1-\tau^y)Ak_{ss}^{\alpha},$$

that is,

$$c_{ss} = y_{ss} - (\tau^y y_{ss} + \tau^c c_{ss}) - (n+\delta)k_{ss} = y_{ss} - g_{ss} - (n+\delta)k_{ss},$$

and solve in (4.28) for τ^c:

$$\tau^c = \frac{g_{ss} - \tau^y y_{ss}}{y_{ss} - g_{ss} - (n+\delta)k_{ss}}.$$

To obtain the first tax combination, we assume that there are not income taxes, and compute how large should the consumption tax rate be in order to allow for financing the predetermined level of expenditures. For instance, when expenditures are 0.317 and the income tax rate is zero, the consumption tax rate must be of 37.1%. To compute alternative tax combinations, we successively increase the income tax rate in intervals of 5%, and compute the consumption tax rate needed to finance the predetermined level of expenditures. We can see that the increase in revenues produced by the raise in income taxes leads to consumption tax rate cuts. As the income tax raises, implied revenues from this tax alone could be even higher than public expenditures, which leads to the need to implement negative consumption taxes, i.e., the government would then be subsidizing purchases of the consumption commodity. This is the case, for instance, when public expenditures are 0.317 and the income tax rate is 30% or higher.

When the government introduces a tax reform by reducing the consumption tax at the cost of increasing the income tax so as to maintain constant revenues, the stock of capital decreases, since the after-tax marginal product of capital is now lower. Since the firm owns a lower stock of the production factor, output falls. The reduction in after-tax income because of the higher income tax leads to a reduction in private consumption, in spite of the fact that the consumption tax is now lower. The level of utility consequently, diminishes. Hence, the consumer would prefer a tax mixture with zero income taxes. The welfare cost of fully eliminating the consumption tax by income taxes is increasing and convex. That is, starting from a situation where public expenditures are fully financed by consumption taxes, the welfare cost of increasing the income tax from 0% to 10% is more than twice the cost of increasing the tax rate from 0% to 5%. Notice that, even though tax revenues remain constant, they decrease, as a percentage of output, as the government uses more intensively the income tax relative to the consumption tax.

When we repeat the analysis for a level of public expenditures of 0.550 we see that, in order to maintain revenues unchanged, an increase in income taxes may need to come together with an increase in the consumption tax. For instance, when $\tau^y = 0.65$, then $\tau^c = 0.135$, while when $\tau^y = 0.70$, then $\tau^c = 0.183$. This is the case because, from the point of view of the income tax, we are in the decreasing region of Laffer's curve. The qualitative effects of tax changes are similar to those of the previous analysis, except for output and the stock of capital, which are now monotonically decreasing in the income tax rate. It is particularly striking the fact that the welfare cost of replacing the consumption tax by the income tax in a given amount is the same, with independence of the level of public expenditures (tax revenues).

The reader can use positive tax rates where these have been set to zero in Panels 1 and 2 in the spreadsheet, and check that the results shown in the graphs change as expected.

4.2.3.3 Short- and Long-Run Effects of a Tax Reform Experiment

In the *Transition* spreadsheet, we start by characterizing the short- and the long-run effects of a permanent increase in either tax rate, keeping the other tax rate constant, with implied changes in steady-state tax revenues. The same analysis can be done with the *CK_d_long_short run tax changes.m* MATLAB file. In Panel 1, the consumption tax rate is raised from 20.0% to 22.0%, while the income tax rate stays at 12.48%. Government revenues increase from 0.317 to 0.330. In Panel 2, the income tax rate is raised from 12.48% to 14.48%, the consumption tax rate staying at 20.0%. Government revenues then increase from 0.317 to 0.335. Finally, we characterize in panel 3 the short- and long-run effects of an increase in the income tax rate, accompanied of a reduction in the consumption tax from 20.0% to 17.32%, so that steady-state government revenues and expenditures remain constant at 0.317. Along the transition, however, government revenues change, initially increasing with the tax rise, and converging afterwards to their steady-state level before the tax change. Tax reform is implemented at $t = 10$. Structural parameter values are the same as in the steady-state analysis described above. To compute short-term effects we need to obtain the transition paths for the endogenous variables, as they converge from the initial steady state to the new one, after the change in tax rates takes place. To do so, we implement the numerical solution method described in the previous section.

Below the description of each policy experiment, we report steady state levels for the endogenous variables before and after the tax change, as well as the transition matrix for the linear approximation and the stabilizing constant needed to relate consumption to the stock of capital, as described in the previous section. We do this twice, before and after the change in tax rates. We use the stability condition obtained under the initial steady state right until the period of the tax change, when we switch to the stability condition obtained under the new steady state.

The first tax reform consists of an increase in the consumption tax from 20% to 22%, while keeping the income tax fixed at 12.48%. The stock of capital, the level of output and after-tax income remain unchanged, in the short- as well as in the long-run. Consumption decreases in the period when the tax change is introduced, to the steady-state level associated to the new tax rate. This translates into a permanent fall in utility from period $t = 10$ on. All effects following a change in consumption taxes take place in a single period, as can be seen in the graphs below the numerical computations. The elasticity of consumption to changes in the consumption tax rate is below one, which implies that consumption tax revenues increase at $t = 10$, remaining at their new level from then on. The welfare cost of the mentioned increase in the consumption tax rate amounts to 1.04% of initial production in the form of additional consumption every period.

In the second tax experiment, the income tax rate increases from 12.48% to 14.48%, while keeping the consumption tax constant at 20%. Effects are displayed in the graphs below the numerical computations, with the τ_c-constant label. As a consequence of the tax hike, the after-tax marginal productivity of capital decreases, and so does the accumulation of physical capital. This translates into a fall in the level of production starting at $t = 11$, since production at the time the tax reform is introduced, $t = 10$, is determined by the stock of capital chosen at $t = 9$, under the initial tax rates. Production then converges to its new steady-state level which, as already explained, is lower than before the tax increase. After-tax income decreases from $t = 10$, leading to a reduction in private consumption and utility. Tax revenues increase drastically at the time of the tax increase, in spite of the fact that revenues obtained from the consumption tax, decrease. In the following periods, tax revenues decrease somewhat, converging to their new steady-state level, which is above the initial level of revenues. Something similar happens with the output share of public expenditures. We find that the welfare cost of this tax reform amounts to an additional consumption of 1.66% of initial output every period. We again get the result that a change in the income tax has a more negative effect on welfare that a change in the consumption tax having the same effect on revenues.

In the last experiment, a consumption tax cut to 17.425% is introduced so that government revenues remain constant in the long-run when the income tax rate is raised from 12.48% to 14.48%. Effects of this policy experiment are displayed in the graphs below panel 2, with the τ_c-adjusting label. Consumption is seen to increase at the time of the tax reform, decreasing afterwards while it converges to its new steady-state level. Steady-state consumption is below the initial steady-state but, as expected, it is above the one obtained when the consumption tax did not adjust to maintain constant revenues. There are now two effects on consumption: a positive one, from the reduction in the consumption tax, and a negative one, because the increase in the income tax reduces disposable income. We can see that the first effect dominates in the short-run, so consumption initially increases, while the second effect is stronger in the long-run, since the steady-state level of consumption is lower after the tax reform. This behavior of consumption also leads to an increase in single period utility in the short-run, decreasing thereafter to end below its initial steady-state level. Aggregating over time, we see that the welfare cost of this tax reform amounts to an additional consumption of 0.24% of initial production, less than the welfare cost we obtained when the consumption tax was kept constant. Notice that even though tax revenues remain unchanged in the long-run, they increase in the short-run and stay above their initial steady-state level for a number of periods.

In order to maintain tax revenues unchanged in the short- as well as in the long-run, then we would need to allow for changes in the consumption tax along the transition of the economy between steady-states. We would then have to redefine the vector of variables in the model to include the consumption tax next to the stock of capital and consumption in period t. The transition matrix would then be of dimension 3×3. Computing the numerical solution for a model of that kind would amount to characterizing approximate stability conditions and using them, together with part of the nonlinear structure of the model, to compute time series for the endogenous variables in the economy. A general discussion on stability follows in the next section.

4.3 Appendices

4.3.1 A Reformulation of the Stability Condition for the Deterministic Version of the Model

Condition (4.42) is the approximate linear representation of the stable manifold for this problem, which we characterized graphically in previous sections, and it is called the *stability condition* of the system.[10] This condition imposes orthogonality between the row of Γ^{-1} associated to the unstable eigenvalue, and the vector of initial deviations with respect to steady-state $(k_0 - k_{ss}, c_0 - c_{ss})$. In fact, the row of Γ^{-1} associated to the unstable eigenvalue of D, μ_1, is: $(u_1, v_1) = \frac{d_{12}}{\mu_2 - \mu_1}(\frac{\mu_2 - d_{11}}{d_{12}}; -1)$, where we have skipped the proportionality constant when imposing the orthogonality condition: $(u_1, v_1)'(k_0 - k_{ss}, c_0 - c_{ss}) = 0$.

That the stability condition satisfying the transversality condition can be written this way is not casual. The linear approximation to the deterministic, dynamic system (4.36) can be written,

$$B_0 \tilde{x}_{t+1} = B_1 \tilde{x}_t,$$

with $\tilde{x}_t$ the vector of deviations around steady-state. In the tax reform analysis in the previous section, $\tilde{x}_t = (k_t - k_{ss}, c_t - c_{ss})$.

Provided B_0 is invertible, we have,

$$\tilde{x}_{t+1} = B_0^{-1} B_1 \tilde{x}_t = D\tilde{x}_t,$$

and using the spectral decomposition of D:

$$\tilde{x}_{t+1} = D\tilde{x}_t = \Gamma \Lambda \Gamma^{-1} \tilde{x}_t , \qquad (4.45)$$

or,

$$\tilde{z}_{t+1} = \Lambda \tilde{z}_t ,$$

after premultiplying in (4.45) by Γ^{-1} and defining $\tilde{z}_t = \Gamma^{-1} \tilde{x}_t$. Each element in $\tilde{z}_t$ is a linear combination of deviations from steady-state for all variables in $\tilde{x}_t$. By repeated substitutions, taking into account the diagonal structure of Λ, we get,

$$\tilde{z}_t = \Lambda^t \tilde{z}_0 ,$$

a system of linear equations which will be stable, in the sense of satisfying the transversality conditions, only if the elements in the diagonal of Λ, i.e., the eigenvalues of D are less than $1/\sqrt{\beta}$.

In the tax reform analysis, the system is 2x2, and each element in $\tilde{z}_t$ is a linear combination of deviations from steady-state for both variables, $k_t - k_{ss}, c_t - c_{ss}$. We have already shown that, in that system, the μ_1-eigenvalue has absolute value greater than 1 so the system becomes explosive.

---

[10] Even though we did not compute it that way. Rather, we obtained the linear approximation to the model, and obtained the exact stability condition for this approximated model.

The only way to avoid the explosive path is by fixing $\tilde{z}_{1t} = 0\ \forall t$, which amounts to setting to zero each period the inner product of the first row in Γ^{-1} (which is the left- eigenvector associated to the explosive eigenvalue) times the vector of variables in deviations from steady state. Needless to say, had we assumed that μ_1 was the stable eigenvalue, with μ_2 being unstable, we would have concluded the need to set to zero the inner product of the second row of Γ^{-1} and the vector of deviations from steady-state.

Some observations are worthwhile at this point:

- There are infinite linear trajectories passing through the optimal steady state, all having the form: $c_t - c_{ss} = b(k_t - k_{ss})$ for a certain range of slope values, b. If we choose c_t each period to satisfy any one of these conditions, given the stock of capital k_t chosen at the end of the previous period, the economy will converge to the optimal steady state. The solution procedure described in the previous section can be seen as selecting, among all those linear trajectories, the one approximating better the true model, at least in a neighborhood of the optimal steady-state, since it is not possible to characterize that stable manifold analytically. In fact, in the numerical exercises we present in EXCEL files, we check the amount by which the Keynes-Ramsey condition, not used in the generation of the solution, is not fulfilled by the numerical solution. The stable root takes care that the law of motion for the stock of capital takes k_t in the right direction, towards k_{ss}, so we obtain stable time series for the stock of capital as well as for consumption. However, these time series would satisfy just part of the model, the budget constraint, but not the Keynes-Ramsey condition.

- The discussion in this section generalizes to more general models, as we will have a chance to see in subsequent chapters. In general, we will have a vector $\tilde{x}_t$ of q variables in deviations with respect to steady-state, r of which will be control or decision variables, the remaining $q - r$ being state variables. In the Cass–Koopmans model, $r = 1, q = 2$, with consumption as the single control or decision variable, and the stock of capital as the state variable. For the model to have a single stable solution, it is necessary to have as many stability conditions as control variables, r, so that the matrix of coefficients D in the first order vector autoregression (4.45) will need to have $q - r$ stable eigenvalues, i.e., less than $1/\sqrt{\beta}$ in absolute value, and r unstable eigenvalues, and the rows of matrix Γ^{-1} associated to the unstable eigenvalues will provide us with stability conditions, just like we have done in the Cass–Koopmans model.

- As we will see in the next chapter, in stochastic models, stability conditions generate a set of relationships between stochastic shocks to the model and expectation errors, which can be interpreted as approximating the way rational expectations errors depend on the innovations to the exogenous stochastic processes. Additionally, these relationships allow the researcher to generate time series for the expectations errors from the time series for the exogenous processes once the model has been solved. In turn, these time series can be used for implementing rationality tests on the expectations errors: zero mean, no serial correlation, and lack of correlation with any variable contained in the information set available to the agent when forming their expectations. If the numerical solution is a good approximation to the true solution, the expectations data should not fail these rationality tests. Unfortunately, this type of validation of the numerical solution is not very often implemented in practice.

4.3.2 The Intertemporal Government Budget Constraint

We present in this section an intertemporal analysis of the government budget constraint, following the lines of the presentation we made on the continuous time version of the model. The reader will recognize that the qualitative results we reach and the expressions we obtain are similar to those we obtained in Sect. 3.4. Familiarization with the analytic details of this presentation is needed to discuss more general questions relating to government financing in discrete time models. For simplicity, we assume zero population growth ($n = 0$).

4.3.2.1 Government Budget Constraint

We can rewrite (4.11) as:

$$b_{t+1} = g_t + (1+r_t)b_t - \tau_t, \tag{4.46}$$

and for the following period:

$$b_{t+2} = g_{t+1} + (1+r_{t+1})b_{t+1} - \tau_{t+1},$$

and the two expressions together lead to:

$$b_{t+2} = g_{t+1} + (1+r_{t+1})[g_t + (1+r_t)b_t - \tau_t] - \tau_{t+1},$$

so that the present value of the level of debt outstanding at period $t+2$, is:

$$\frac{b_{t+2}}{(1+r_{t+1})(1+r_t)} = \frac{g_{t+1} - \tau_{t+1}}{(1+r_{t+1})(1+r_t)} + \frac{g_t - \tau_t}{(1+r_t)} + b_t.$$

Repeating the process for the stock of debt outstanding at time $t+3$, we get:

$$b_{t+3} = g_{t+2} + (1+r_{t+2})b_{t+2} - \tau_{t+2}$$

$$= g_{t+2} + (1+r_{t+2})[g_{t+1} + (1+r_{t+1})[g_t + (1+r_t)b_t - \tau_t.] - \tau_{t+1}]$$

$$- \tau_{t+2},$$

so that the present value of debt outstanding at time $t+3$ is:

$$
\frac{b_{t+3}}{(1+r_{t+2})(1+r_{t+1})(1+r_t)} = \frac{g_{t+2} - \tau_{t+2}}{(1+r_{t+2})(1+r_{t+1})(1+r_t)}
$$
$$
+ \frac{g_{t+1} - \tau_{t+1}}{(1+r_{t+1})(1+r_t)} + \frac{g_t - \tau_t}{(1+r_t)} + b_t.
$$

Repeating the process T times, we obtain that the present value of debt outstanding at time $t + T + 1$:

$$
\frac{b_{t+T+1}}{\prod_{s=0}^{T}(1+r_{t+s})} = \sum_{j=0}^{T} \frac{g_{t+j} - \tau_{t+j}}{\prod_{s=0}^{j}(1+r_{t+s})} + b_t.
$$

Taking limits on T:

$$
\lim_{T\to\infty} \frac{b_{t+T+1}}{\prod_{s=0}^{T}(1+r_{t+s})} = \sum_{j=0}^{\infty} \frac{g_{t+j} - \tau_{t+j}}{\prod_{s=0}^{j}(1+r_{t+s})} + b_t = 0, \tag{4.47}
$$

and using the fact that the transversality condition implies: $\lim_{T\to\infty} \frac{b_{t+T+1}}{\prod_{s=0}^{T}(1+r_{t+s})} = 0$, we get,

$$
b_t = \sum_{j=0}^{\infty} \frac{\tau_{t+j} - g_{t+j}}{\prod_{s=0}^{j}(1+r_{t+s})},
$$

so that, in each period, the present value of current and future government budget surplus must be equal to the stock of debt outstanding.

Likewise, it is possible to write equation (4.47) as,

$$
\sum_{j=0}^{\infty} \frac{g_{t+j}}{\prod_{s=0}^{j}(1+r_{t+s})} + b_t = \sum_{j=0}^{\infty} \frac{\tau_{t+j}}{\prod_{s=0}^{j}(1+r_{t+s})}, \tag{4.48}
$$

showing that, each period, the present value of the stream of current and future government expenditures, added to the current stock of debt outstanding, must be equal to the present value of current and future tax revenues.

Alternatively, we could have integrated the government budget constraint towards the past. Then, the stock of public debt at time t could be written:

$$
b_t = g_{t-1} + (1+r_{t-1})b_{t-1} - \tau_{t-1},
$$

which, plugged into (4.46), allows us to obtain the level of debt outstanding in period $t+1$,

$$
b_{t+1} = g_t + (1+r_t)[g_{t-1} + (1+r_{t-1})b_{t-1} - \tau_{t-1}] - \tau_t.
$$

Repeating the process a number of times, we get:

$$
b_{t+1} = (g_t - \tau_t) + \sum_{j=1}^{t} \left[\prod_{s=0}^{j-1}(1+r_{t-s})(g_{t-j} - \tau_{t-j}) \right] + \prod_{s=0}^{t}(1+r_{t-s})b_0, \tag{4.49}
$$

showing that the stock of debt outstanding at the end of period t is the result of capitalizing: i) the initial stock of debt, and ii) the government budget deficit or surplus from previous periods. This latter effect can be either negative or positive each time period t, so that each period, the stock of debt can be either above or below initial debt, b_0.

4.3.2.2 Sustainable Steady-State Expenditures and Financing Policies

Steady-state is a dynamic, competitive equilibrium, along which per capita variables remain constant over time. In particular, $r_t = r_{ss}$, $g_t = g_{ss}$, $\tau_t = \tau_{ss}$ must remain constant. We want to characterize steady-state feasible fiscal policies. The steady-state version of the present value government budget constraint, integrated towards the past (4.49), is:

$$b_{t+1} = (1+r)^{t+1} b_0 + \sum_{j=0}^{t} (1+r)^j (g - \tau)$$

$$= (1+r)^{t+1} b_0 + (g - \tau) \left[\frac{(1+r) - (1+r)^{t+1}}{1 - (1+r)} \right]$$

$$= (1+r)^{t+1} b_0 + \frac{g - \tau}{r} \left[(1+r)^{t+1} - (1+r) \right].$$

But b_{t+1} must satisfy the transversality condition (4.22):

$$\lim_{t \to \infty} \frac{1}{(1+r)^t} b_{t+1} = 0,$$

which is equivalent to:

$$\lim_{t \to \infty} \frac{1}{(1+r)^t} \left[(1+r)^{t+1} b_0 + \frac{g - \tau}{r} \left[(1+r)^{t+1} - (1+r) \right] \right] = 0, \Leftrightarrow$$

$$(1+r) \lim_{t \to \infty} \left[b_0 + \frac{g - \tau}{r} \left[1 - (1+r)^{-t} \right] \right] = 0, \Leftrightarrow$$

$$b_0 + \frac{g - \tau}{r} \left[1 - \lim_{t \to \infty} (1+r)^{-t} \right] = 0, \Leftrightarrow$$

$$b_0 = \frac{\tau - g}{r}.$$

Only if $b_0 = \frac{\tau - g}{r}$ will the transversality constraint hold. In fact, any steady-state policy involving a period-by-period budget surplus in an amount $\tau - g \geq rb_0$ will be *feasible*. In the absence of initial debt outstanding, the only feasible policy would be one of maintaining a balance government budget forever. With strict inequality, the transversality condition will be violated, with $\lim_{t \to \infty} \frac{1}{(1+r)^t} b_{t+1} < 0$. That would be a feasible, albeit suboptimal steady-state fiscal policy, since the government could have afforded running larger deficits at some point, presumably leading to an increase in consumers' welfare.

4.4 Appendix 2: The Ricardian Proposition Under Non-Distortionary Taxes in Discrete Time

We use now the discrete time representation to show that the Ricardian proposition holds in the Cass–Koopmans economy under non-distortionary taxation. The proposition states that the way how government expenditures, g_t, are financed is irrelevant, provided that the bond issuing policy associated to each alternative financing strategy be feasible, *i.e.*, that the transversality condition (4.19) holds. This implies that the distribution of resources between consumption and savings implied by the competitive equilibrium mechanism is independent of the way how savings are split into government bonds and firm's stock.

The irrelevance of government financing is known as the Ricardian doctrine: consumers are indifferent between paying higher taxes today and holding a lower stock of debt in their portfolio, or paying less taxes today, but being forced to hold more debt in their portfolios. As we have seen in previous sections, in the absence of uncertainty and with perfect capital markets, the sequence of single-period budget constraints can be integrated in a time aggregated present value budget constraint, this being the only constraint faced by the consumer. A similar consideration holds for the sequence of single-period government budget constraints. Joint consideration of both intertemporal constraints leads to the Ricardian proposition.

We now proceed to integrating the consumer budget constraint towards the future. For simplicity, we assume zero population growth ($n = 0$). From (4.13) we obtain:

$$a_{t+1} = (1+r_t)a_t + (\omega_t - \tau_t - c_t). \tag{4.50}$$

Analogously,

$$a_{t+2} = (1+r_{t+1})a_{t+1} + (\omega_{t+1} - \tau_{t+1} - c_{t+1}). \tag{4.51}$$

Plugging (4.51) into 4.50), we get:

$$\frac{a_{t+2}}{(1+r_{t+1})(1+r_t)} = \frac{\omega_{t+1} - \tau_{t+1} - c_{t+1}}{(1+r_{t+1})(1+r_t)} + \frac{\omega_t - \tau_t - c_t}{(1+r_t)} + a_t.$$

After T substitutions,

$$\frac{a_{t+T+1}}{\Pi_{s=0}^{T}(1+r_{t+s})} = \sum_{j=0}^{T} \frac{\omega_{t+j} - \tau_{t+j} - c_{t+j}}{\Pi_{s=0}^{j}(1+r_{t+s})} + a_t,$$

and, by continuous substitutions,

$$\lim_{T \to \infty} \frac{a_{t+T+1}}{\prod_{s=0}^{T}(1+r_{t+s})} = \sum_{j=0}^{\infty} \frac{\omega_{t+j} - \tau_{t+j} - c_{t+j}}{\prod_{s=0}^{j}(1+r_{t+s})} + a_t = 0,$$

since the transversality condition holds. From this expression, we get:

$$\sum_{j=0}^{\infty} \frac{\omega_{t+j}}{\prod_{s=0}^{j}(1+r_{t+s})} + a_t = \sum_{j=0}^{\infty} \frac{\tau_{t+j} + c_{t+j}}{\prod_{s=0}^{j}(1+r_{t+s})}, \tag{4.52}$$

showing that each period, the stock of assets held by the consumer, plus the present value of his/her current and future labor income, must be equal to the present value of current and future consumption, plus the present value of taxes.

Combining the budget constraints for the government (4.48) and the consumer (4.52), both integrated towards the future, we get:

$$\sum_{j=0}^{\infty} \frac{g_{t+j} - \omega_{t+j}}{\prod_{s=0}^{j}(1+r_{t+s})} + b_t - a_t = -\sum_{j=0}^{\infty} \frac{c_{t+j}}{\prod_{s=0}^{j}(1+r_{t+s})} \Leftrightarrow$$

$$\sum_{j=0}^{\infty} \frac{\omega_{t+j}}{\prod_{s=0}^{j}(1+r_{t+s})} + v_t = \sum_{j=0}^{\infty} \frac{c_{t+j} + g_{t+j}}{\prod_{s=0}^{j}(1+r_{t+s})},$$

so that the present value of the stock issued by the firm, plus the present value of the sequence of current and future labor income, must be equal to the present value of public and private consumption:

$$\sum_{j=0}^{\infty} \frac{c_{t+j}}{\prod_{s=0}^{j}(1+r_{t+s})} = \sum_{j=0}^{\infty} \frac{\omega_{t+j}}{\prod_{s=0}^{j}(1+r_{t+s})} + v_t - \sum_{j=0}^{\infty} \frac{g_{t+j}}{\prod_{s=0}^{j}(1+r_{t+s})},$$

showing that the feasible sequences of consumption are those whose present value remains below the sum of current holdings of firm's stock plus the present value of labor income, net of the present value of public consumption. In this latter expression, neither bonds nor taxes appear, either at a given point in time, or in present value form. That means that consumer's decisions are affected by the level of current and future government expenditures, but not by the way how these are financed, be that by issuing debt or through lump-sum taxes.

4.5 Exercises

Exercise 1. In the discrete time version of the Cass–Koopmans economy, show the inefficiency of the competitive equilibrium mechanism by showing that the implied allocation of resources does not coincide with the one that is obtained from the planner's problem when there is a government that purchases g_t units of the consumption commodity which are 'thrown to the sea', financing them with a lump-sum tax and debt issuing. Start by showing that the competitive equilibrium allocation can be obtained as the solution to a representative agent problem. Repeat the exercise for an economy in which the government uses a consumption tax at a rate τ^c, and taxes all income at the same tax, τ^y. Identify the several reasons for inefficiency of the competitive equilibrium allocation in this economy.

Exercise 2. In the discrete time version of the Cass–Koopmans economy, show the inefficiency of the competitive equilibrium mechanism by showing that the implied allocation of resources does not coincide with the one that emerges from the planner's problem when there is a government that purchases g_t units of the consumption commodity which are returned to consumers as a lump-sum transfer, financing them with a consumption tax, a capital income tax, and issuing debt. Identify the several reasons for that inefficiency. Explain why it is not possible to characterize the competitive equilibrium allocation through a representative agent problem in this economy.

Exercise 3. In the deterministic version of the Cass–Koopmans economy, suppose that the production function has constant returns to scale and the utility function is $U(c_t) = ln\ c_t$. There is a government that implements a lump-sum transfer to consumers, financed by a consumption tax. Suppose that the government keeps constant the level of the lump-sum transfer along the transition, so that it is the tax rate that gets adjusted over time.

- Set up the set of equations characterizing the resource allocation under the competitive equilibrium mechanism
- Notice that, since Walras' law holds, it is not necessary to impose the budget constraint of the consumer and yet, the competitive equilibrium allocation satisfies that equation. Notice that the system made up by the Euler equation and the equation characterizing equilibrium in the market for the consumption commodity also characterizes the time paths for consumption and capital. Hence, the time path for both variables is independent of monetary policy instruments. Once consumption and capital have been determined, the consumption tax rate can be solved from the government budget constraint.
- Choose a set of parameters and calculate implied steady state values for consumption, capital and output.
- Choose arbitrary initial conditions for the stock of capital and consumption and get time series for these variables using the two non-linear conditions: the global resources constraint and the Keynes–Ramsey condition. Check that the resulting time series will be explosive, because of not having imposed any stability condition.
- With the same initial conditions, solve the model using the linear approximation. Check that the solution is again unstable.
- Characterize the stability condition for the model under the chosen parameterization. Generate time series for the relevant variables using the stability condition and either one of the equations in the linear approximation. Check that we obtain convergence, no matter which of the equation in the linear approximation is used. Also, check that the other equation in the linear approximation holds.

- Solve the model using the stability condition and either the global resources constraint or the Keynes–Ramsey condition. Check that the obtained time series are stable in either case. Check that the condition not being used, is not satisfied by the set of time series we have obtained.
- Solve the model using the two non-linear conditions: the global resources constraint and the Keynes–Ramsey condition, after having imposed the stability condition at $t = 0$, *to compute* $c_0, c_0 = \phi k_0$. Check that the solution is unstable.
- Solve the model using conditions $k_t - k_{ss} = (k_0 - k_{ss}) \mu_2^t$, $c_t - c_{ss} = (c_0 - c_{ss}) \mu_2^t$, after having imposed the stability condition at $t = 0$ to compute c_0. Check that the implied time series are stable. Check that stability arises even without imposing stability at $t = 0$.

In the next two exercises, the ratio of government expenditures to output (G/Y), rather than government expenditures themselves, are kept constant.

Exercise 4. In the discrete-time version of the Cass–Koopmans economy, consider a Cobb-Douglas production function with constant returns to scale and a utility function with a constant intertemporal elasticity of substitution of consumption. The government tax consumption and income from the representative agent, using the revenues to purchase the single good produced in the economy.

1. Characterize analytical expressions for steady state values for consumption, the stock of capital, output and government expenditures. Show in a graph how these values depend on each of the two tax rates. Let us assume that the tax rate on consumption is initially 0.2 while the income tax rate is 0.15. Compute the welfare long-term gains or losses, in terms of consumption, from a permanent change in either one of the two tax rates.
2. Characterize different combinations of tax rates on consumption and income that can be used to finance in steady-state the same ratio of government expenditures/output than with $\tau^c = 0.2$ *and* $\tau^y = 0.15$. Compute steady-state values obtained under each of these fiscal policies for each variable in the economy. What is among them the tax policy that maximizes utility while maintaining the ratio of expenditures/output? (second-best policy)
3. Assume now that initial tax rates are $\tau^c = 0.2$ *and* $\tau^y = 0.15$. Characterize the short- and long-term effects from a change in each of the two tax rates.
4. Assume that initial tax rates are $\tau^c = 0.2$ *and* $\tau^y = 0.15$. The government modifies tax policy while maintaining ratio of government expenditures/output constant in steady-state. Characterize the short- and long-term effects from an increment in each tax rate. Do ratio of government expenditures/output remain constant during the transition to the new steady-state? What type of change in tax rates should the government introduce to maximize time-aggregate discounted utility while maintaining steady-state government expenditures/output ratio constant?

Exercise 5. In the discrete-time version of the Cass–Koopmans economy, consider a Cobb-Douglas production function with constant returns to scale and a utility function with a constant intertemporal elasticity of substitution of consumption. Consider a time discount parameter of $\beta = 0.99$, a depreciation rate $\delta = 0.025$, zero population growth, $n = 0$, output elasticity with respect to capital of 0.33 and an intertemporal elasticity of substitution of consumption $1/\sigma = 1/3$. The government tax consumption and income from the representative agent, using the revenues to purchase the single good produced in the economy.

1. Let us assume that the tax rate on consumption is $\tau^c = 0.2$ while the tax rate on income is $\tau^y = 0.30$. Characterize steady-state levels for private and public consumption, the stock of capital, output and utility. What is the composition of aggregate demand in this economy?

2. Starting from the previous situation, let us assume that the government reduces the tax rate on income to $\tau^y = 0.25$, while adjusting the tax rate on consumption so that the steady-state level of tax revenues/output ratio remains constant. Characterize and provide an interpretation for the short- and long-term effects of fiscal policy on private consumption, output, investment, public expenditures, the stock of capital, and the utility level. What are the computed welfare gains when (a) only long-term effects are taken into account, (b) when short-term effects are also taken into account?

3. So long, we have assumed that the government tax at the same rate income from labor and from renting capital. Let us now assume that both revenue sources are taxed differently, while maintaining the consumption tax in the model. Characterize the steady-state in this economy and discuss the effects of a reduction in government expenditures. (Hint: write and solve the decentralized competitive general equilibrium problem).

Chapter 5
Numerical Solution Methods

5.1 Numerical Solutions and Simulation Analysis

To learn about the causes of aggregate fluctuations is one of the basic goals of Macroeconomics. One of the main characteristics of aggregate fluctuations is that business cycles are neither regular nor predictable. Because of that, most economists consider that there are different shocks impinging on the economy, which are different in nature and intensity. These shocks do not follow a known pattern. Observed fluctuations in actual economies are the result of such shocks and the propagation mechanisms associated to them. There are different schools of thought in Macroeconomics whose main difference relates to the type of specific shocks which are accountable for economic fluctuations as well as in the description of their propagation mechanisms.

The simplest model to explain aggregate fluctuations is the stochastic version of the Cass–Koopmans economy, whose deterministic version has been studied in the previous chapter. We can consider that the economy is subject to a productivity shock, although alternative shocks could also be considered. This would be a supply type of shock, although it does not need to be the only source of randomness in the economy. An example of a demand shock would be a given variable in the utility function that evolves over time according to a given stochastic process. In this chapter we will consider just supply shocks, since they are the most often used in the literature.

As we are about to see, agents take decisions under uncertainty on the basis of their expectations on future values of nonlinear functions of state and decision variables. To assume rationality implies that those expectations cannot be made to follow arbitrary processes over time. They become endogenous variables, and they need to be determined jointly with the rest of the endogenous variables in the model when computing a numerical solution.

Dynamic, stochastic general equilibrium models (DSGE models) do not usually have analytical solution, except in some cases like the model in McCallum [65] which we describe at the beginning of this chapter. In general, DSGE models will have to be analyzed through numerical solutions using simulation analysis.

The goal of this chapter is to familiarize the reader with the basic details of some of the main methods to obtain numerical solutions to the type of stochastic, growth models discussed along the book. The methods we present can be used to find stable solutions for any system of stochastic, nonlinear difference equations. The optimization problems we are introducing to characterize either the behavior of the different economic agents operating under a competitive equilibrium mechanism, or the decisions on resource allocation made by a benevolent planner, all lead to such a system of equations, so numerical solutions can be found for them using the methods we are about to discuss. When solving these models, it is crucial to be aware of the fact that a stable solution, i.e., a solution in which per capita variables do not explode too fast, cannot be found unless we impose on the solution the appropriate *stability conditions*. Lack of stability does not arise because of excessive fluctuations around steady state in a stochastic economy. In fact, if the right stability conditions are imposed, fluctuations around steady-state will be stable no matter how wide they are. Given its importance, we will emphasize how stability is dealt with under each solution approach. The method introduced in the previous chapter to characterize the dynamic evolution of the deterministic version of the Cass–Koopmans economy is just a special case of the more general collection of methods we present in this chapter.

Computing a *numerical solution* to set of equations summarizing the main properties of a model economy is just the first step in *model simulation*. A numerical solution is a set of time series, one for each relevant variable in the model economy, satisfying each period all the conditions in the model. Simulation is a procedure by which a numerical solution is found for each specific time series realization of the vector stochastic process of the exogenous shocks affecting the economy. By reproducing a large number of these sample realizations, we can approximate arbitrarily well the probability distribution of the vector stochastic process of endogenous variables.

Once a specific sample realization for the vector of state and decision variables has been obtained, we can then summarize the properties of their joint distribution in the form of standard statistics: sample means, standard deviations, coefficients of variation, simple and partial autocorrelation functions, correlation coefficients between pairs of variables, regression coefficients, cross correlation functions, vector autoregressive representations (VAR), impulse responses in a subset of variables, decompositions of variance, spectral density matrices, etc. For each of these point statistics we will obtain as many realizations as numerical solutions we get for the model, i.e., as many as sample realizations we draw in our simulations from the probability distribution for the exogenous random shocks.

To simulate a model, we first need to assign numerical values to its structural parameters. Then simulation allows us to characterize the model's properties, which the researcher will want to compare with their analogue, computed from actual data. Before that, he/she will have selected a set of such characteristics as relevant for the question under analysis. The comparison could be established in terms of mean values, or through probability statements. There is, hence, some sense in which the artificial economy is estimated and tested, since after the mentioned comparison, we will conclude wether or not the model is adequate to explain the issue in mind.

Stochastic properties for the endogenous variables in the model depend on three assumptions: (a) the structure of the model, (b) the values assumed for the structural parameters, (c) the law of motion for the exogenous shocks. In this chapter, we focus on (b) and (c).

We start the chapter by reviewing two simple growth model that admit a closed form analytical solution. This is not often the case, and it is the simplicity of the model, because of some specific assumptions, that allow for a closed form solution to exist. We introduce them as baseline models for comparison, as well as to familiarize the reader with the widespread need for numerical solutions. The second part of the chapter considers a simple, stochastic version of the planner's problem introduced in the previous chapter. The only random component of the model will come around again through a technology shock. We will use this model to illustrate a variety of numerical solution approaches, even though some of them will not be used anywhere else in the book. However, understanding the details of their implementation in this simple setup will allow the reader to design their application in more complex economic environments. In the third part of the chapter, we consider a stochastic version of the representative agent's problem with consumption and income taxes, which is solved under two of the approaches discussed previously. The numerical solution to the model is used to undergo some analysis concerning the design of optimal fiscal policy. Along the chapter, we do not discuss calibration or parameter estimation. The interested reader can consult the books by DeJong and Dave [27] or Canova [16].

5.2 Analytical Solutions to Simple Growth Models

We present in this section two benevolent planner models having analytical solution. This is the case because the assumption of full depreciation of capital every period eliminates much of the dynamics in the model, investment being equal to the stock of capital every period.

5.2.1 A Model with Full Depreciation

A simple growth model that admits an analytical solution is considered in McCallum [65]. We consider an economy with a single good, which can be either consumed or saved in the form of productive physical capital. In a closed economy, private investment and savings coincide, and gross investment is equal to the aggregate of net investment and depreciation replacement. Thus, we have,

$$C_t + S_t = Y_t,$$
$$S_t = I_t,$$
$$K_{t+1} = (1 - \delta) K_t + I_t.$$

Preferences of the representative consumer in the economy can be represented through a constant relative risk aversion utility function,

$$U(C_t) = \frac{C_t^{1-\sigma} - 1}{1 - \sigma}, \quad \sigma > 0.$$

We also assume that the technology for the production of the single good in the economy, $Y_t = \theta_t K_t^\alpha$, is stochastic, due to the presence of an exogenous, stochastic productivity factor θ_t, an *i.i.d.* random variable with $E(\theta_t) = 1$. The state of the technology evolves over time according to the law of motion,

$$\ln(\theta_t) = \rho \ln(\theta_{t-1}) + \varepsilon_t, \ \varepsilon_t, \underset{iid}{\sim} N(0, \sigma_\varepsilon^2),$$

where a constant is not needed, precisely because of the assumption on $E(\theta_t)$. Under the assumed autoregressive process, $\ln(\theta_t)$ has an unconditional probability distribution which has expectation zero and variance $\frac{\sigma_\varepsilon^2}{1-\rho^2}$. Conditional on information up to time $t - 1$ it has a Normal distribution (so long as ε_t is Normal) with $E_{t-1}(\ln(\theta_t)) = \rho \ln(\theta_{t-1})$, $Var_{t-1}(\ln(\theta_t)) = \sigma_\varepsilon^2$, a smaller variance than that of the unconditional distribution.

Investment takes one period to be productive: at time t, decisions are made on c_t and k_{t+1}. Hence, output at time t depends on k_t, the decision on physical capital made the previous period.

We assume that population does not grow and we normalize total population to be equal to one, so per capita variables and aggregate variables are the same. From now on, all variables are expressed in terms per capita.

In what follows, we consider a special case characterized by two conditions, both important for the model to have an analytical solution: (a) capital fully depreciates every period, $\delta = 1$, so that the stock of capital available for production at time $t + 1$ is equal to investment at time t : $K_{t+1} = I_t$, $k_{t+1} = I_t/N$ ($N = 1$ being population size), and (b) utility is of the logarithmic type, $\sigma = 1$.

A representative agent in the economy chooses consumption and end of period stock of capital to maximize its time aggregated, discounted, constant relative risk aversion utility function, subject to the technological possibilities and an initial condition on the stock of capital:

$$\underset{\{c_t, k_{t+1}\}_{t=0}^\infty}{Max} E_0 \sum_{t=0}^\infty \beta^t \ln(c_t)$$

subject to: $\quad c_t + k_{t+1} = \theta_t k_t^\alpha,$ \hfill (5.1)

$$\ln(\theta_t) = \rho \ln(\theta_{t-1}) + \varepsilon_t, \ \varepsilon_t, \underset{iid}{\sim} N(0, \sigma_\varepsilon^2),$$

$$c_t, k_t > 0, \ given \ k_0, \theta_0.$$

The Lagrangian for this utility maximization problem is (in the case $\sigma = 1$),

$$L\left(\{c_t, k_t, \lambda_t\}_{t=0}^{\infty}\right) = E_0 \sum_{t=0}^{\infty} \beta^t \left[\ln(c_t) + \lambda_t \left(\theta_t k_t^{\alpha} - c_t - k_{t+1}\right)\right],$$

with first order conditions,

$$\frac{1}{c_t} = \lambda_t, \; t = 0, 1, 2, \ldots \tag{5.2}$$

$$\lambda_t = \beta \alpha E_t \left(\theta_{t+1} \lambda_{t+1} k_{t+1}^{\alpha-1}\right), \; t = 0, 1, 2, \ldots, \tag{5.3}$$

together with the budget constraint, $c_t + k_{t+1} = \theta_t k_t^{\alpha}$, $t = 0, 1, 2, \ldots$ For each time t, these two equations, together with the budget constraint, form a system giving us the optimal values of c_t, k_{t+1}, λ_t, as functions of the two states of the economy, θ_t, k_t.

From (5.2) and (5.3) we get,

$$\frac{1}{c_t} = \alpha \beta E_t \left(\frac{\theta_{t+1} k_{t+1}^{\alpha-1}}{c_{t+1}}\right), \; t = 0, 1, 2, \ldots. \tag{5.4}$$

A linear guess for the optimal decision rules, of the type:

$$c_t = a\theta_t k_t^{\alpha},$$
$$k_{t+1} = b\theta_t k_t^{\alpha},$$

plugged into (5.4) leads to,

$$\frac{1}{a\theta_t k_t^{\alpha}} = \alpha E_t \left(\frac{\beta \theta_{t+1} k_{t+1}^{\alpha-1}}{a\theta_{t+1} k_{t+1}^{\alpha}}\right) = \frac{\alpha \beta}{ab\theta_t k_t^{\alpha}}, \; t = 0, 1, 2, \ldots,$$

which implies that: $b = \alpha \beta$.

Taking the optimal decision rules to the representative agent's budget constraint leads to,

$$a\theta_t k_t^{\alpha} + b\theta_t k_t^{\alpha} = \theta_t k_t^{\alpha},$$

which implies that: $a = 1 - \alpha\beta > 0$.

So, in this special case, we get a closed form solution:

$$c_t = (1 - \alpha\beta)\,\theta_t k_t^{\alpha} = (1 - \alpha\beta)y_t, \; t = 0, 1, 2, \ldots, \tag{5.5}$$
$$k_{t+1} = \alpha\beta\theta_t k_t^{\alpha} = \alpha\beta y_t, \; t = 0, 1, 2, \ldots$$

The steady state for this model is obtained by assuming c_t, k_t, λ_t are constant over time, equal to $c_{ss}, k_{ss}, \lambda_{ss}$, and the random productivity shock takes its expected value of one every period. That way, we get,

$$\theta_{ss} = 1, \; k_{ss} = (\alpha\beta)^{\frac{1}{1-\alpha}}, \; y_{ss} = (\alpha\beta)^{\frac{\alpha}{1-\alpha}}, \; c_{ss} = (1 - \alpha\beta)y_{ss}.$$

5.2.2 A Model with Leisure in the Utility Function

Let us denote labor by l_t, and normalize available time to one unit. If we include leisure $1 - l_t$ into a separable logarithmic utility function,

$$U(c_t, n_t) = v \ln c_t + (1 - v) \ln(1 - l_t), \ 0 < v < 1,$$

and labor in the production technology for the single good in the economy,

$$y_t = \theta_t k_t^{\alpha} l_t^{1-\alpha},$$

the problem of the representative agent becomes,

$$\underset{\{c_t, k_{t+1}, n\}_{t=0}^{\infty}}{Max} \ E_0 \sum_{t=0}^{\infty} \beta^t \left[v \ \ln c_t + (1 - v) \ \ln(1 - l_t) \right]$$

subject to,

$$c_t + k_{t+1} = \theta_t k_t^{\alpha} l_t^{1-\alpha}, \ c_t, k_t > 0, \tag{5.6}$$

and given k_0, with Lagrangian,

$$L(\{c_t, k_t, l_t, \lambda_t\}_{t=0}^{\infty}) = E_0 \sum_{t=0}^{\infty} \beta^t \left[\begin{matrix} (v \ \ln c_t + (1 - v) \ \ln(1 - l_t)) \\ + \lambda_t \left(\theta_t k_t^{\alpha} l_t^{1-\alpha} - c_t - k_{t+1} \right) \end{matrix} \right],$$

and first order conditions,

$$\frac{v}{c_t} = \lambda_t, \tag{5.7}$$

$$\frac{1 - v}{1 - l_t} = (1 - \alpha) \lambda_t \theta_t k_t^{\alpha} l_t^{-\alpha}, \tag{5.8}$$

$$\lambda_t = \alpha \beta E_t \left(\lambda_{t+1} \theta_{t+1} k_{t+1}^{-(1-\alpha)} l_{t+1}^{1-\alpha} \right), \tag{5.9}$$

$$c_t + k_{t+1} = \theta_t k_t^{\alpha} l_t^{1-\alpha}. \tag{5.10}$$

With a logarithmic utility function and full depreciation, the income and substitution effects of a wage rate change just offset each other, leaving the leisure choice unaffected [King, Plosser, Rebelo [51], McCallum [65]]. As a consequence, labor will be constant along the optimal trajectory, $l_t = l$, and an examination of the global constraint of resources (5.10) suggests that c_t and k_{t+1} will be proportional to the product $\theta_t k_t^{\alpha}$, that is,

$$c_t = a \theta_t k_t^{\alpha}, \ k_{t+1} = b \theta_t k_t^{\alpha}. \tag{5.11}$$

First, we use (5.7) to write (5.9),

$$\frac{v}{c_t} = \alpha \beta E_t \left(\frac{v}{c_{t+1}} \theta_{t+1} k_{t+1}^{-(1-\alpha)} l_{t+1}^{1-\alpha} \right),$$

and using our guess (5.11),

$$\frac{v}{a\theta_t k_t^\alpha} = \alpha\beta E_t \left(\frac{v\theta_{t+1}k_{t+1}^{-(1-\alpha)}l_{t+1}^{1-\alpha}}{a\theta_{t+1}k_{t+1}^\alpha} \right) = \alpha\beta \frac{vl^{1-\alpha}}{ab\theta_t k_t^\alpha},$$

where we have used the fact that, in our guess, labor is constant over time. Equation above implies,

$$b = \alpha\beta l^{1-\alpha}.$$

Using again twice our guess in (5.10) we get,

$$a = (1 - \alpha\beta)l^{1-\alpha}.$$

Finally, taking these expressions for a and b to (5.7)–(5.8), we get a constant equilibrium level of labor,

$$l = \frac{(1-\alpha)v}{(1-\alpha)v + (1-v)(1-\alpha\beta)}.$$

Hence, we have shown our guess to be right. In this special example, consumption and physical capital fluctuate according to,

$$c_t = (1 - \alpha\beta)l^{1-\alpha}\theta_t k_t^\alpha = (1-\alpha\beta)y_t,$$
$$k_{t+1} = \alpha\beta l^{1-\alpha}\theta_t k_t^\alpha,$$

experiencing fluctuations due to the presence of the technology shock in both decision rules.

Since the optimal level of employment is constant over time, steady-state employment is also equal to that level. Steady-state levels for the remaining variables are:

$$\theta_{ss} = 1, \ k_{ss} = l(\alpha\beta)^{\frac{1}{1-\alpha}}, \ y_{ss} = l(\alpha\beta)^{\frac{\alpha}{1-\alpha}}, \ c_{ss} = (1-\alpha\beta)y_{ss}.$$

Steady-state levels for the stock of capital, consumption and output are different in the two economies we have just analyzed, because of the presence of labor in the production function in the second model. Since time series for the main variables experience fluctuations around steady-state levels, single period values for a given variable are different in the two models. However, relative fluctuations, i.e., percent fluctuations relative to steady-state, are the same in both economies. As a consequence, coefficients of variation, cross-correlations with output as well as the way how output is split between consumption and investment (which is equal to the stock of capital in this economy) are the same in both economies. This is a reflection of the fact that under logarithmic preferences and full depreciation, adding leisure separably as an input in the utility function does not contribute to the ability of the model to explain business cycle fluctuations. We have seen that in such model, labor supply turns out to be inelastic, which is the implicit assumption made when leisure does not enter as an argument in the utility function. In fact the latter model is obtained as a special case of the more general model that includes leisure as an argument in the utility function, when $\upsilon = 1$, as the reader can easily check using the *Simple-models.xls* spreadsheet.

5.2.3 Numerical Solutions of the Growth Model Under Full Depreciation

In *Simple_models.xls* we present a sample realization for each of the two economies considered in this section. The *McCallum* spreadsheet contains the model without leisure in the utility function, while the *McCallum with leisure* spreadsheet contains the model with leisure as an argument in the utility function. We consider a production function: $y_t = \theta_t A k_t^{\alpha}$, with $A = 1$, a logarithmic utility function by assuming $\sigma = 1.0$ in: $U(c_t) = \frac{c_t^{1-\sigma}-1}{1-\sigma}$, full depreciation, $\delta = 1$, and zero population growth, $n = .0$. Benchmark parameter values are: $\rho = .90, \alpha = .33, \beta = .90, \sigma_\varepsilon = .01$. Steady-state levels are computed using the expressions in this section under the box displaying parameter values. We start by using the random number generator in Excel to produce a sample realization with 538 observations for the innovation in the first order autoregression for the logged productivity shock. To that end, we simulate a N(0,1) random variable which is then multiplied by σ_ε. From that, the productivity shock itself is readily obtained. After that, time series for the stock of capital, output and consumption are obtained by using expressions for the analytical solution in the two models. Finally, relative fluctuations are calculated as the difference between the time series for each variable and its steady-state level, as a percentage. Graphs displaying the obtained time series for consumption and capital, together with that for output, are shown. The strong output correlations of consumption and the stock of capital implied by these models are evident in the graphs. We also present graphs for the relative deviations in some variables around steady-state levels. Similar graphs are obtained in the *McCallum with leisure* spreadsheet, where a time graph, as well as a scatter diagram of relative deviations on capital stock and output are displayed.

Below the time series, we present sample mean, standard deviation and volatility relative to output for each variable. The coefficient of variation is also shown, which allows for some volatility comparisons across variables. The decomposition of output between consumption (70.3%) and investment (29.7%) is also calculated. Notice that, under full depreciation, investment and the stock of capital are the same each period. Finally, the cross correlation function between each variable and output is calculated. The cross-correlation of output with itself is obviously symmetric, since it reduces to the simple autocorrelation for output. All these figures should be expected to experience some changes if we use a different sample realization of the productivity shock, as the reader can easily check as an exercise.

5.3 Solving a Simple, Stochastic Version of the Planner's Problem

To illustrate the similarities and differences among different solution methods, we use the stochastic version of the standard Brock–Mirman growth model [Brock, W.A. and L.J. Mirman [12]], represented by the planner´s problem[1],

$$\underset{\{c_t, k_{t+1}\}_{t=0}^{\infty}}{Max} \quad E_0 \sum_{t=0}^{\infty} \beta^t U(c_t) = E_0 \sum_{t=0}^{\infty} \beta^t \frac{c_t^{1-\sigma} - 1}{1-\sigma},$$

for some $\sigma > 0$, where a constant relative risk aversion time separable utility function has been assumed. The discounted, time aggregate utility function is maximized subject to the global constraint of resources,

$$c_t + k_{t+1} - (1-\delta) k_t = \theta_t k_t^{\alpha}, \ 0 < \alpha < 1, \tag{5.12}$$

given k_0.

The law of motion of the stochastic productivity is supposed to be,

$$\ln \theta_t = \rho \ln \theta_{t-1} + \varepsilon_t, \ 0 < \rho < 1, \ \varepsilon_t \underset{iid}{\sim} N(0, \sigma_\varepsilon^2), \text{ given } \theta_0, \tag{5.13}$$

and the Lagrangian for the optimization problem is,

$$L(\{c_t, k_t, \theta_t\}_{t=0}^{\infty}) = E_0 \sum_{t=0}^{\infty} \beta^t \left[\frac{c_t^{1-\sigma} - 1}{1-\sigma} + \lambda_t \left(\begin{array}{c} \theta_t k_t^{\alpha} - c_t - k_{t+1} \\ + (1-\delta) k_t \end{array} \right) \right]$$

for which optimality conditions are, under the assumption that $c_t > 0$, since an infinite marginal utility at the origin implies that consumption will be strictly positive every period, and $k_{t+1} > 0$,

$$c_t^{-\sigma} = \lambda_t,$$
$$\lambda_t = \beta \ E_t \left[\lambda_{t+1} \left(\alpha \theta_{t+1} k_{t+1}^{\alpha-1} + 1 - \delta \right) \right],$$

together with (5.12).

Eliminating the Lagrange multiplier we get,

$$c_t^{-\sigma} = \beta \ E_t \left[c_{t+1}^{-\sigma} \left(\alpha \theta_{t+1} k_{t+1}^{\alpha-1} + 1 - \delta \right) \right], \tag{5.14}$$

together with the transversality condition,

$$\lim_{t \to \infty} E_0 \left(\beta^t \lambda_t k_{t+1} \right) = \lim_{t \to \infty} E_0 \left(\beta^t c_t^{-\sigma} k_{t+1} \right) = 0.$$

---

[1] There is no externality of any kind in this model, so welfare theorems apply, and the solution to the planner's problem leads to the same allocation of resources as the competitive equilibrium. This, in turn, can be obtained as the solution to the representative agent problem.

Steady state level for per-capita variables are given by,

$$k_{ss} = \left(\frac{\alpha\beta}{1 - \beta\left(1 - \delta\right)} \right)^{\frac{1}{1-\alpha}},$$ (5.15)

$$c_{ss} = \left(\frac{\alpha\beta}{1 - \beta\left(1 - \delta\right)} \right)^{\frac{\alpha}{1-\alpha}} - \delta \left(\frac{\alpha\beta}{1 - \beta\left(1 - \delta\right)} \right)^{\frac{1}{1-\alpha}},$$ (5.16)

where we have already used $\theta_{ss} = 1$.

In the next sections we discuss different approaches to finding a numerical solution to optimization problems like the one considered in this section. A first approach is to construct the best *linear-quadratic approximation* to the optimization problem we want to solve. A linear-quadratic problem has a quadratic objective function and linear constraints. Consequently, decision rules are linear and hence, very simple to use for data generation. The drawback is that we solve a problem different from the one we originally had posed. The *undetermined coefficients* method by H. Uhlig, *Blanchard and Kahn's* method and the *eigenvalue-eigenvector decomposition* method proposed by C.A. Sims use a log-linear approximation to the optimality conditions for the original optimization problem. So, they use the actual, non-linear structure of the model, although they approximate the set of first-order conditions. As discussed in the previous chapter, stability conditions are needed in order to obtain non-explosive paths for the endogenous variables, and the different solution methods differ essentially in the way stability conditions are imposed on the numerical solution. Alternatively, a linear approximation to the optimality conditions, rather than a log-linear approximations, could be used to produce the solution. This will generally be analytically simpler, although approximation errors will be larger.

The previous methods are said to be linear, since they end up using linear systems to relate control to state variables. After introducing the planner's problem with taxes, we will present two nonlinear solution methods: (a) the *parameterized expectations method,* that uses again the first order conditions to the original problem, but approximates the conditional expectations that appear in the first order conditions by exponential polynomials, and (b) the *class of projection methods,* that parameterize the decision rules or control equations as polynomial functions of state variables.

5.3.1 Solving the Linear-Quadratic Approximation to the Planner's Problem

To implement this simple solution method (Kydland and Prescott [53], Díaz-Giménez, J. [30]), we start by substituting (5.12) into the utility function, to obtain,

$$U\left(k_{t+1}, k_t, \ln\theta_t\right) = \frac{\left(\theta_t k_t^\alpha + \left(1 - \delta\right) k_t - k_{t+1}\right)^{1-\sigma} - 1}{1 - \sigma}.$$

The quadratic approximation around steady-state to the utility function above can be written,

$$U(k_{t+1}, k_t, \ln\theta_t) \simeq U(z_{ss}) + \frac{\partial U}{\partial z_t}\Big|_{z_t=z_{ss}}(z_t - z_{ss})$$

$$+ \frac{1}{2}(z_t - z_{ss})'\left(\frac{\partial^2 U}{\partial z_t \partial z_t'}\Big|_{z_t=z_{ss}}\right)(z_t - z_{ss}),$$

where $z_t = (k_{t+1}, k_t, \ln\theta_t)$, which amounts to,

$$U(c_t) = U(k_{t+1}, k_t, \ln\theta_t) \cong U(k_{ss}, k_{ss}, \ln\theta_{ss})$$

$$+ \frac{\partial U}{\partial k_{t+1}}\Big|_{(k_{ss}, k_{ss}, \ln\theta_{ss})}(k_{t+1} - k_{ss}) + \frac{\partial U}{\partial k_t}\Big|_{(k_{ss}, k_{ss}, \ln\theta_{ss})}(k_t - k_{ss})$$

$$+ \frac{\partial U}{\partial \ln\theta_t}\Big|_{(k_{ss}, k_{ss}, \ln\theta_{ss})}(\ln\theta_t - \ln\theta_{ss}) + \frac{1}{2}(z_t - z_{ss})'\left(\frac{\partial^2 U}{\partial z_t \partial z_t'}\Big|_{(k_{ss}, k_{ss}, \ln\theta_{ss})}\right)(z_t - z_{ss})$$

$$= B_1(k_{t+1} - k_{ss}) + B_2(k_t - k_{ss}) + B_3(\ln\theta_t - \ln\theta_{ss})$$

$$+ \frac{1}{2}(z_t - z_{ss})'\left(\frac{\partial^2 U}{\partial z_t \partial z_t'}\Big|_{(k_{ss}, k_{ss}, \ln\theta_{ss})}\right)(z_t - z_{ss})$$

where,

$$U(k_{ss}, k_{ss}, \ln\theta_{ss}) = \frac{(k_{ss}^\alpha - \delta k_{ss})^{1-\sigma} - 1}{1 - \sigma},$$

and after some tedious algebra, we get the gradient vector,

$$\frac{\partial U}{\partial k_{t+1}} = (\theta_t k_t^\alpha + (1-\delta)k_t - k_{t+1})^{-\sigma}(-1)$$

$$\Rightarrow B_1 \equiv \frac{\partial U}{\partial k_{t+1}}\Big|_{(k_{ss}, k_{ss}, \ln\theta_{ss})} = -(k_{ss}^\alpha - \delta k_{ss})^{-\sigma},$$

$$\frac{\partial U}{\partial k_t} = (\theta_t k_t^\alpha + (1-\delta)k_t - k_{t+1})^{-\sigma}(\alpha\theta_t k_t^{\alpha-1} + 1 - \delta)$$

$$\Rightarrow B_2 \equiv \frac{\partial U}{\partial k_t}\Big|_{(k_{ss}, k_{ss}, \ln\theta_{ss})} = \frac{1}{\beta}(k_{ss}^\alpha - \delta k_{ss})^{-\sigma} = -B_1\frac{1}{\beta},$$

$$\frac{\partial U}{\partial \ln\theta_t} = (\theta_t k_t^\alpha + (1-\delta)k_t - k_{t+1})^{-\sigma}\left(e^{\ln\theta_t}k_t^\alpha\right)$$

$$\Rightarrow B_3 \equiv \frac{\partial U}{\partial \ln\theta_t}\Big|_{(k_{ss}, k_{ss}, \ln\theta_{ss})} = (k_{ss}^\alpha - \delta k_{ss})^{-\sigma}k_{ss}^\alpha = -B_1 k_{ss}^\alpha,$$

where we have used the identity $e^{\ln \theta_t} = \theta_t$ to obtain $\frac{\partial U}{\partial \ln \theta_t} = \frac{\partial U}{\partial \theta_t} \frac{\partial \theta_t}{\partial \ln \theta_t} = \frac{\partial U}{\partial \theta_t} \theta_t$,
as well as the two facts: $[\theta_t k_t^\alpha + (1-\delta) k_t - k_{t+1}] \mid_{(k_{ss}, k_{ss}, \ln \theta_{ss})} = k_{ss}^\alpha - \delta k_{ss}$, and
$(\alpha \theta_t k_t^{\alpha-1} + 1 - \delta) \mid_{(k_{ss}, k_{ss}, \ln \theta_{ss})} = 1/\beta$.

The elements of the Hessian $\left(\frac{\partial^2 U}{\partial z_t \partial z_t'} \Big|_{(k_{ss}, k_{ss}, \ln \theta_{ss})} \right)$ are,

$$\frac{\partial^2 U}{\partial k_{t+1}^2} = -\sigma \left(\theta_t k_t^\alpha + (1-\delta) k_t - k_{t+1} \right)^{-\sigma-1}$$

$$\Rightarrow A_{11} \equiv \frac{\partial^2 U}{\partial k_{t+1}^2} \mid_{(k_{ss}, k_{ss}, \ln \theta_{ss})} = -\sigma \left(k_{ss}^\alpha - \delta k_{ss} \right)^{-\sigma-1}$$

$$= \sigma B_1 \frac{1}{k_{ss}^\alpha - \delta k_{ss}}.$$

$$\frac{\partial^2 U}{\partial k_{t+1} \partial k_t} = \sigma \left(\theta_t k_t^\alpha + (1-\delta) k_t - k_{t+1} \right)^{-\sigma-1} \left(\alpha \theta_t k_t^{\alpha-1} + 1 - \delta \right)$$

$$\Rightarrow A_{12} \equiv \frac{\partial^2 U}{\partial k_{t+1} \partial k_t} \mid_{(k_{ss}, k_{ss}, \ln \theta_{ss})} = \frac{\sigma}{\beta} \left(k_{ss}^\alpha - \delta k_{ss} \right)^{-\sigma-1}$$

$$= -\frac{A_{11}}{\beta}.$$

$$\frac{\partial^2 U}{\partial k_{t+1} \partial \ln \theta_t} = \sigma \left(\theta_t k_t^\alpha + (1-\delta) k_t - k_{t+1} \right)^{-\sigma-1} e^{\ln \theta_t} k_t^\alpha$$

$$\Rightarrow A_{13} \equiv \frac{\partial^2 U}{\partial k_{t+1} \partial \ln \theta_t} \mid_{(k_{ss}, k_{ss}, \ln \theta_{ss})}$$

$$= \sigma \left(k_{ss}^\alpha - \delta k_{ss} \right)^{-\sigma-1} k_{ss}^\alpha = -A_{11} k_{ss}^\alpha.$$

$$\frac{\partial^2 U}{\partial k_t^2} = -\sigma \left(\theta_t k_t^\alpha + (1-\delta) k_t - k_{t+1} \right)^{-\sigma-1} \left(\alpha \theta_t k_t^{\alpha-1} + 1 - \delta \right)^2$$

$$+ \left(\theta_t k_t^\alpha + (1-\delta) k_t - k_{t+1} \right)^{-\sigma} \alpha (\alpha - 1) e^{\ln \theta_t} k_t^{\alpha-2}$$

$$\Rightarrow A_{22} \equiv \frac{\partial^2 U}{\partial k_t^2} \mid_{(k_{ss}, k_{ss}, \ln \theta_{ss})} = -\frac{\sigma}{\beta^2} \left(k_{ss}^\alpha - \delta k_{ss} \right)^{-\sigma-1}$$

$$+ \left(k_{ss}^\alpha - \delta k_{ss} \right)^{-\sigma-1} \alpha (\alpha - 1) k_{ss}^{\alpha-2}$$

$$= A_{11} \left(\frac{1}{\beta^2} - \frac{\alpha (\alpha - 1) k_{ss}^{\alpha-2}}{\sigma} \right).$$

$$\frac{\partial^2 U}{\partial k_t \partial \ln \theta_t} = -\sigma \left(\theta_t k_t^\alpha + (1-\delta) k_t - k_{t+1}\right)^{-\sigma-1} e^{\ln \theta_t} k_t^\alpha \times \left(\alpha \theta_t k_t^{\alpha-1} + 1 - \delta\right)$$

$$+ \left(\theta_t k_t^\alpha + (1-\delta) k_t - k_{t+1}\right)^{-\sigma} \alpha e^{\ln \theta_t} k_t^{\alpha-1}$$

$$\Rightarrow A_{23} \equiv \frac{\partial^2 U}{\partial k_t \partial \ln \theta_t} \bigg|_{(k_{ss},k_{ss},\ln \theta_{ss})} = A_{11} \frac{k_{ss}^\alpha}{\beta} - B_1 \alpha k_{ss}^{\alpha-1}.$$

$$\frac{\partial^2 U}{\partial \ln \theta_t^2} = -\sigma \left(\theta_t k_t^\alpha + (1-\delta) k_t - k_{t+1}\right)^{-\sigma-1} \left(e^{\ln \theta_t} k_t^\alpha\right)^2$$

$$+ \left(\theta_t k_t^\alpha + (1-\delta) k_t - k_{t+1}\right)^{-\sigma} e^{\ln \theta_t} k_t^\alpha$$

$$\Rightarrow A_{33} \equiv \frac{\partial^2 U}{\partial \ln \theta_t^2} \bigg|_{(k_{ss},k_{ss},\ln \theta_{ss})} = -\sigma \left(k_{ss}^\alpha - \delta k_{ss}\right)^{-\sigma-1} k_{ss}^{2\alpha}$$

$$+ \left(k_{ss}^\alpha - \delta k_{ss}\right)^{-\sigma} k_{ss}^\alpha = k_{ss}^\alpha \left(A_{11} k_{ss}^\alpha - B_1\right),$$

and we have the approximation to the utility function,

$$U\left(k_{t+1}, k_t, \ln \theta_t\right) \cong \text{Constants} + (B_1, B_2, B_3) \begin{pmatrix} k_{t+1} - k_{ss} \\ k_t - k_{ss} \\ \ln \theta_t - \ln \theta_{ss} \end{pmatrix}$$

$$+ \frac{1}{2} \left(k_{t+1} - k_{ss}, k_t - k_{ss}, \ln \theta_t - \ln \theta_{ss}\right)$$

$$\times \begin{pmatrix} A_{11} & A_{12} & A_{13} \\ A_{12} & A_{22} & A_{23} \\ A_{13} & A_{23} & A_{33} \end{pmatrix} \begin{pmatrix} k_{t+1} - k_{ss} \\ k_t - k_{ss} \\ \ln \theta_t - \ln \theta_{ss} \end{pmatrix},$$

which is quadratic, so that we can impose the *certainty-equivalence principle*[2]. Hence, we initially ignore the stochastic nature of the problem, to impose the first order condition,

$$\frac{\partial U}{\partial k_{t+1}} = 0,$$

which implies,

$$0 = \beta^t \left[B_1 + A_{11}\widetilde{k}_{t+1} + A_{12}\widetilde{k}_t + A_{13} \ln \theta_t\right]$$

$$+ \beta^{t+1} \left[B_2 + A_{22}\widetilde{k}_{t+1} + A_{12}\widetilde{k}_{t+2} + A_{23} \ln \theta_{t+1}\right]$$

---

[2] The certainty-equivalence principle is also know as the separation principle, since it states that in linear-quadratic problems (optimization problems with quadratic objective functions subject to linear constraints) we can separate the control problem from the estimation problem. That implies that we need to solve just the deterministic version of the problem, to then add conditional expectations in the decision rules in front of any term involving future decision or control variables.

where tildes denote deviations with respect to steady-state values and we have used that $\ln\theta_{ss} = 0$, or,

$$\beta A_{12}\tilde{k}_{t+2} + (A_{11} + \beta A_{22})\tilde{k}_{t+1} + A_{12}\tilde{k}_t = -A_{13}\ln\theta_t - \beta A_{23}\ln\theta_{t+1}$$

$$\Rightarrow \tilde{k}_{t+1} + \frac{A_{11} + \beta A_{22}}{\beta A_{12}}\tilde{k}_t + \frac{1}{\beta}\tilde{k}_{t-1} = -\frac{A_{13}}{\beta A_{12}}\ln\theta_{t-1} - \frac{A_{23}}{A_{12}}\ln\theta_t,$$

where we have used the fact that $B_1 + \beta B_2 = 0$.

The lag operator B can be used to write the polynomial on the left hand side of the equation as: $\left(1 + \frac{A_{11} + \beta A_{22}}{\beta A_{12}}B + \frac{1}{\beta}B^2\right)\tilde{k}_{t+1}$. This polynomial can be factored as $(1 - \mu_1 B)(1 - \mu_2 B)$, the two roots μ_1, μ_2, being related through $\mu_1 + \mu_2 = -\frac{A_{11} + \beta A_{22}}{\beta A_{12}}$, $\mu_2 = \frac{1}{\mu_1\beta}$. They are defined by,

$$\mu_1, \mu_2 = \frac{-\frac{A_{11} + \beta A_{22}}{\beta A_{12}} \pm \sqrt{\left(\frac{A_{11} + \beta A_{22}}{\beta A_{12}}\right)^2 - 4\frac{1}{\beta}}}{2\frac{1}{\beta}}$$

Since $-\frac{A_{11} + \beta A_{22}}{\beta A_{12}} = 1 + \frac{1}{\beta} - \frac{\beta}{\sigma}\alpha(\alpha-1)k_{ss}^{\alpha-2} > 0$, we can use the argument in section *Systems with a saddle path property* in the Mathematical Appendix to show that one root falls inside the unit interval, $0 < \mu_1 < 1$, while the second root $\mu_2 > 1/\beta$, so that the equation as,

$$(1 - \mu_1 B)(1 - \mu_2 B)\tilde{k}_{t+1} = -\frac{A_{13}}{\beta A_{12}}\ln\theta_{t-1} - \frac{A_{23}}{A_{12}}\ln\theta_t,$$

whose solution can be represented,[3]

$$(1 - \mu_1 B)\tilde{k}_{t+1} = -\frac{A_{13}}{\beta A_{12}}\frac{1}{1 - \mu_2 B}\ln\theta_{t-1} - \frac{A_{23}}{A_{12}}\frac{1}{1 - \mu_2 B}\ln\theta_t$$

$$\equiv \frac{A_{13}}{\beta A_{12}}\sum_{i=1}^{\infty}\frac{1}{\mu_2^i}\ln\theta_{t-1+i} + \frac{A_{23}}{A_{12}}\sum_{i=1}^{\infty}\frac{1}{\mu_2^i}\ln\theta_{t+i}.$$

Up to this point we have solved the optimal deterministic control problem. Application of the certainty equivalence principle amounts to taking conditional expectations in the optimal decision rule above. Expectations are taken conditional on the information available at time t, on the basis of which the decision on $\tilde{k}_{t+1}$ is made. We get,

---

[3] We are using the fact that, for $\mu_2 > 1$, $\frac{1}{1 - \mu_2 B} = -\frac{1}{\mu_2 B - 1} = -\frac{B^{-1}}{\mu_2 - B^{-1}} = -\frac{B^{-1}}{\mu_2}\frac{1}{1 - \frac{1}{\mu_2}B^{-1}}$
$= -\frac{B^{-1}}{\mu_2}\sum_{s=0}^{\infty}\frac{1}{\mu_2^s}B^{-s} = -\sum_{s=1}^{\infty}\frac{1}{\mu_2^s}B^{-s}$, so that $\frac{1}{1 - \mu_2 B}X_t = -\sum_{s=1}^{\infty}\frac{1}{\mu_2^s}X_{t+s}$.

$$(1 - \mu_1 B)\tilde{k}_{t+1} = \frac{A_{13}}{\beta A_{12}} \sum_{i=1}^{\infty} \frac{1}{\mu_2^i} E_t (\ln \theta_{t-1+i}) + \frac{A_{23}}{A_{12}} \sum_{i=1}^{\infty} \frac{1}{\mu_2^i} E_t (\ln \theta_{t+i})$$

$$= \frac{A_{13}}{\beta A_{12}} \sum_{i=1}^{\infty} \frac{1}{\mu_2^i} \rho^{i-1} \ln \theta_t + \frac{A_{23}}{A_{12}} \sum_{i=1}^{\infty} \frac{1}{\mu_2^i} \rho^i \ln \theta_t$$

$$= \left(\frac{A_{13}}{\beta A_{12}} \frac{1}{1 - \frac{\rho}{\mu_2}} + \frac{A_{23}}{A_{12}} \frac{\rho}{1 - \frac{\rho}{\mu_2}} \right) \frac{1}{\mu_2} \ln \theta_t,$$

and, finally,

$$\tilde{k}_{t+1} = \mu_1 \tilde{k}_t + \frac{1}{\mu_2 - \rho} \frac{A_{13} + \beta \rho A_{23}}{\beta A_{12}} \ln \theta_t,$$

an equation that allows us to generate data for $\tilde{k}_t$ and, from that time series, data for k_t.

As we can see, the decision rule we have used for the stock of capital is linear, as opposed to the way how we generate consumption data from the stock of capital through the budget constraint, which incorporates a non-linear technology. It is also important to notice that we can obtain the whole time series for the stock of capital without need of computing any consumption data point, showing the sequential nature of the problem and also the fact that *the stock of capital is exogenous relative to the consumption decision.*

The *Simple_planner_problem.xls* file computes a single sample realization for the planner's problem without taxes, using the linear-quadratic approximation described in this section and a benchmark parameterization that we will consider in illustrations of other solution methods. We consider a production function: $y_t = \theta_t A k_t^\alpha$, with $A = 1$, a risk aversion parameter $\sigma = .5$, a depreciation rate, $\delta = .1$, and zero population growth, $n = .0$, and benchmark parameter values: $\rho = .90, \alpha = .33, \beta = .90, \sigma_\varepsilon = .01$. Time series for the stock of capital, consumption, output and investment are obtained using the expressions presented above. Below the time series realizations we present standard statistics: mean, standard deviation, coefficient of variation, relative volatility to output, correlation coefficient with output, and the cross-correlation function with output for lags from -2 to $+2$. We also present graphs displaying the sample realizations for pairs of endogenous variables.

The *lq.m* MATLAB program also computes a single numerical realization from the solution to the planner's model using an extension of the method described in this section to the case when consumption and income taxes are considered. The optimal growth model or planner's model is discussed in the second part of this chapter. The interested reader can set the two tax rates to zero in the initial section of the program on parameter values, to obtain the numerical realization of the solution to the model without taxes we have just analyzed. The *methods.m* MATLAB program can be used to compute an arbitrarily large number of sample realizations using the linear-quadratic approximation among a variety of alternative solution methods that we describe in this chapter, after setting consumption and income taxes to zero. If the reader does not feel comfortable with MATLAB programming, staying with a single realization may be enough for a while. Each run of the MATLAB program will change the sample realization of the productivity shock, producing numerical values for the statistics for the main variables different from those obtained with previous realizations.

In this section we have solved the linear-quadratic problem that approximates best the original problem we are interested on. So, we have computed the exact solution to an approximate problem. In the alternative methods described in the next sections, we consider different approximations to the optimality conditions of the original optimization problem.

5.3.2 The Log-Linear Approximation to the Model

We now proceed to describe how to compute a log-linear approximation to the simple growth model introduced above. This type of approximation will be used in the next sections. In this approach, we start from the optimality conditions to the representative agent problem (5.12), (5.14) and (5.13):

$$c_t + k_{t+1} - (1-\delta)k_t = \theta_t k_t^\alpha, \ 0 < \alpha < 1,$$

$$c_t^{-\sigma} = \beta \ E_t \left[c_{t+1}^{-\sigma} \left(\alpha \theta_{t+1} k_{t+1}^{\alpha-1} + (1-\delta) \right) \right],$$

$$\ln \theta_t = \rho \ \ln \theta_{t-1} + \varepsilon_t, \ 0 < \rho < 1, \ \varepsilon_t \underset{iid}{\sim} N(0,\sigma_\varepsilon^2), \text{ given } \theta_0.$$

To construct the *log-linear approximation* to the model, we start by using identities like: $x_t = e^{\ln x_t}$, $c_t^{-\sigma} = e^{-\sigma \ln c_t}$ and introduce auxiliary variables: $\tilde{x}_t \equiv \ln(x_t/x_{ss})$, which are differences in logged values of the original variables with respect to their steady-state levels. Another useful identity is $x_t = x_{ss} e^{\tilde{x}_t}$, which is approximated by: $x_t = x_{ss} e^{\tilde{x}_t} \simeq x_{ss}(1+\tilde{x}_t)$. Additional approximations used are of the type, (a) $x_t^{-\sigma} = x_{ss}^{-\sigma} e^{-\sigma \tilde{x}_t} \simeq x_{ss}(1-\sigma \tilde{x}_t)$, (b) $x_{t+1} z_{t+1} \simeq x_{ss}(1+\tilde{x}_{t+1}) z_{ss}(1+\tilde{z}_{t+1}) \simeq x_{ss} z_{ss}(1+\tilde{x}_{t+1}+\tilde{z}_{t+1})$.

This allows us to write condition (5.12),

$$0 = c_{ss} e^{\tilde{c}_t} + k_{ss} e^{\tilde{k}_{t+1}} - \theta_{ss} e^{\tilde{\theta}_t} k_{ss}^\alpha e^{\alpha \tilde{k}_t} - (1-\delta) k_{ss} e^{\tilde{k}_t},$$

$$0 \cong c_{ss}(1+\tilde{c}_t) + k_{ss}\left(1+\tilde{k}_{t+1}\right) - \theta_{ss} k_{ss}^\alpha \left(1+\alpha \tilde{k}_t + \tilde{\theta}_t\right)$$
$$- (1-\delta) k_{ss}\left(1+\tilde{k}_t\right),$$

$$0 \cong [c_{ss} + k_{ss} - \theta_{ss} k_{ss}^\alpha - (1-\delta)k_{ss}] + c_{ss}\tilde{c}_t + k_{ss}\tilde{k}_{t+1} - \theta_{ss} k_{ss}^\alpha \alpha \tilde{k}_t$$
$$- (1-\delta) k_{ss}\tilde{k}_t - \theta_{ss} k_{ss}^\alpha \tilde{\theta}_t,$$

where the first bracket is equal to zero, because the budget constraint holds every period so, in particular, it also holds in steady-state. Adding the fact that $\theta_{ss} = 1$ and dividing through k_{ss} we get,

$$0 \cong \frac{c_{ss}}{k_{ss}}\widetilde{c}_t + \widetilde{k}_{t+1} - \left(\alpha k_{ss}^{\alpha-1} + 1 - \delta\right)\widetilde{k}_t - k_{ss}^{\alpha-1}\widetilde{\theta}_t,$$

and using the steady-state relationship $\alpha k_{ss}^{\alpha-1} + 1 - \delta = \frac{1}{\beta}$, we get,

$$0 \cong \frac{c_{ss}}{k_{ss}}\widetilde{c}_t + \widetilde{k}_{t+1} - \frac{1}{\beta}\widetilde{k}_t - \frac{1}{\alpha}\left(\frac{1}{\beta} - 1 + \delta\right)\widetilde{\theta}_t. \qquad (5.17)$$

Condition (5.14) can be written as,

$$c_{ss}^{-\sigma} e^{-\sigma\widetilde{c}_t} = \beta E_t \left[c_{ss}^{-\sigma} e^{-\sigma\widetilde{c}_{t+1}} \left(\alpha\theta_{ss} e^{\widetilde{\theta}_{t+1}} k_{ss}^{\alpha-1} e^{(\alpha-1)\widetilde{k}_{t+1}} + (1-\delta) \right) \right]$$

$$= \beta \left(c_{ss}^{-\sigma} \alpha\theta_{ss} k_{ss}^{\alpha-1} \right) E_t \left(e^{-\sigma\widetilde{c}_{t+1}} e^{\widetilde{\theta}_{t+1}} e^{(\alpha-1)\widetilde{k}_{t+1}} \right)$$

$$+ \beta c_{ss}^{-\sigma} (1-\delta) E_t \left(e^{-\sigma\widetilde{c}_{t+1}} \right)$$

$$\Rightarrow c_{ss}^{-\sigma} (1 - \sigma\widetilde{c}_t) = \beta \left(c_{ss}^{-\sigma} \alpha\theta_{ss} k_{ss}^{\alpha-1} \right) E_t \left[\left(\begin{array}{c} 1 - \sigma\widetilde{c}_{t+1} + \widetilde{\theta}_{t+1} + \\ (\alpha-1)\widetilde{k}_{t+1} \end{array} \right) \right]$$

$$+ \beta c_{ss}^{-\sigma} (1-\delta) E_t (1 - \sigma\widetilde{c}_{t+1})$$

$$\Rightarrow 0 \cong \left[c_{ss}^{-\sigma} - \beta \left(c_{ss}^{-\sigma} \alpha\theta_{ss} k_{ss}^{\alpha-1} \right) - \beta(1-\delta)c_{ss}^{-\sigma} \right] - c_{ss}^{-\sigma}\sigma\widetilde{c}_t$$

$$+ \beta \left(c_{ss}^{-\sigma} \alpha\theta_{ss} k_{ss}^{\alpha-1} \right) E_t \left(\sigma\widetilde{c}_{t+1} - \widetilde{\theta}_{t+1} + (1-\alpha)\widetilde{k}_{t+1} \right)$$

$$+ \beta c_{ss}^{-\sigma} (1-\delta) \sigma E_t \widetilde{c}_{t+1},$$

where, again, the constant has been set to zero because it is the steady-state representation of Euler equation, so,

$$-\sigma\widetilde{c}_t + \beta \left(\alpha\theta_{ss} k_{ss}^{\alpha-1} \right) E_t \left(\sigma\widetilde{c}_{t+1} - \widetilde{\theta}_{t+1} + (1-\alpha)\widetilde{k}_{t+1} \right) + \beta(1-\delta)\sigma E_t \widetilde{c}_{t+1} \cong 0. \qquad (5.18)$$

Finally, the law of motion of the technology shock can be written as,

$$\widetilde{\theta}_{t+1} + \ln\theta_{ss} \cong \rho\widetilde{\theta}_t + \rho\ln\theta_{ss} + \varepsilon_{ss} e^{\widetilde{\varepsilon}_{t+1}}$$

$$\Rightarrow E_t\widetilde{\theta}_{t+1} \cong \rho\widetilde{\theta}_t, \qquad (5.19)$$

since $\ln\theta_{ss} = 0$, $\varepsilon_{ss} = 0$.

Substituting (5.19) in (5.18):

$$0 \cong \sigma\widetilde{c}_t - \sigma E_t(\widetilde{c}_{t+1}) + [1 - (1-\delta)\beta]\rho\widetilde{\theta}_t - [1 - (1-\delta)\beta](1-\alpha)\widetilde{k}_{t+1} \cong 0, \qquad (5.20)$$

since $\alpha k_{ss}^{\alpha-1} + 1 - \delta = \frac{1}{\beta}$.

5.3.3 The Blanchard–Kahn Solution Method for the Stochastic Planner's Problem. Log-Linear Approximation

This solution method (Blanchard and Kahn [10]) uses the log-linear approximation obtained in the previous section. Equations (5.17) and (5.20) can be written in matrix form:

$$\underbrace{\left[\begin{array}{cc} \left(\frac{1}{\beta}-(1-\delta)\right)(1-\alpha) & \frac{1}{\beta}\sigma \\ 1 & 0 \end{array}\right]}_{A} \underbrace{\left[\begin{array}{c} \tilde{k}_{t+1} \\ E_t\tilde{c}_{t+1} \end{array}\right]}_{E_t s^0_{t+1}}$$

$$= \underbrace{\left[\begin{array}{cc} 0 & \frac{1}{\beta}\sigma \\ \frac{1}{\beta} & -\frac{c_{ss}}{k_{ss}} \end{array}\right]}_{B} \underbrace{\left[\begin{array}{c} \tilde{k}_t \\ \tilde{c}_t \end{array}\right]}_{s^0_t} + \underbrace{\left[\begin{array}{c} \left(\frac{1}{\beta}-(1-\delta)\right)\rho \\ \left(\frac{1}{\beta}-(1-\delta)\right)\frac{1}{\alpha} \end{array}\right]}_{C} \tilde{\theta}_t,$$

that is,

$$E_t s^0_{t+1} = D s^0_t + F \tilde{\theta}_t, \tag{5.21}$$

where $D = A^{-1}B$ and $F = A^{-1}C$.

This solution approach starts from the observation that the D matrix has one stable eigenvalue, the other one being unstable, which allows the solution to the optimization problem to be unique, characterized by the stable manifold. Our strategy is to find an analytical approximation to that manifold in a neighborhood of the steady-state, and use that approximation to produce time series for the relevant variables in the economy. Without loss of generality, we will denote $|\mu_1| < 1$ and $|\mu_2| > 1/\beta$. The orthogonal decomposition for D is $D = \Gamma\Lambda\Gamma^{-1}$. Premultiplying (5.21) by $\Gamma^{-1} = \left[\begin{array}{cc} u_1 & v_1 \\ u_2 & v_2 \end{array}\right]$, we get:

$$\Gamma^{-1}E_t s^0_{t+1} = \Lambda\Gamma^{-1}s^0_t + \Gamma^{-1}F\tilde{\theta}_t,$$

that is,

$$\left[\begin{array}{cc} u_1 & v_1 \\ u_2 & v_2 \end{array}\right]\left[\begin{array}{c} \tilde{k}_{t+1} \\ E_t\tilde{c}_{t+1} \end{array}\right]$$

$$= \left[\begin{array}{cc} \mu_1 & 0 \\ 0 & \mu_2 \end{array}\right]\left[\begin{array}{cc} u_1 & v_1 \\ u_2 & v_2 \end{array}\right]\left[\begin{array}{c} \tilde{k}_t \\ \tilde{c}_t \end{array}\right] + \underbrace{\left[\begin{array}{cc} u_1 & v_1 \\ u_2 & v_2 \end{array}\right]\left[\begin{array}{c} F_1 \\ F_2 \end{array}\right]}_{Q}\tilde{\theta}$$

$$\Rightarrow \left\{\begin{array}{ll} \underbrace{u_1\tilde{k}_{t+1} + v_1 E_t\tilde{c}_{t+1}}_{E_t s^1_{1,t+1}} = \mu_1\underbrace{(u_1\tilde{k}_t + v_1\tilde{c}_t)}_{s^1_{1,t}} + Q_1\tilde{\theta}_t & \text{[A]} \\[2em] \underbrace{u_2\tilde{k}_{t+1} + v_2 E_t\tilde{c}_{t+1}}_{E_t s^1_{2,t+1}} = \mu_2\underbrace{(u_2\tilde{k}_t + v_2\tilde{c}_t)}_{s^1_{2,t}} + Q_2\tilde{\theta}_t & \text{[B]} \end{array}\right.$$

where $Q_1 = u_1 F_1 + v_1 F_2$, $Q_2 = u_2 F_1 + v_2 F_2$.

Equation [A] provides us with a stable solution for the conditional expectation $E_t s^1_{1,t+1}$, while equation [B] yields an unstable solution for the conditional expectation $E_t s^1_{2,t+1}$ because of the autoregressive coefficient being greater than one in absolute value. To get a stable solution for equation [B], we need to solve it forwards. The equation can be written as, $E_t s^1_{2,t+1} = \mu_2 s^1_{2,t} + Q_2 \tilde{\theta}_t$. Solving for $s^1_{2,t}$ we get:

$$s^1_{2,t} = \frac{1}{\mu_2} E_t s^1_{2,t+1} - \frac{Q_2}{\mu_2} \tilde{\theta}_t, \qquad (5.22)$$

where $-1 < \frac{1}{\mu_2} < 1$.

Writing (5.22) at time $t + 1$:

$$s^1_{2,t+1} = \frac{1}{\mu_2} E_{t+1} s^1_{2,t+2} - \frac{Q_2}{\mu_2} \tilde{\theta}_{t+1}. \qquad (5.23)$$

Substituting (5.23) into (5.22) and applying the law of iterated expectations, together with the fact that $E_t \tilde{\theta}_{t+j} = \rho^j \tilde{\theta}_t$, we get:

$$s^1_{2,t} = \frac{1}{\mu_2^2} E_t s^1_{2,t+2} - \left(1 + \frac{\rho}{\mu_2}\right) \frac{Q_2}{\mu_2} \tilde{\theta}_t. \qquad (5.24)$$

Writing (5.22) at time $t + 2$:

$$s^1_{2,t+2} = \frac{1}{\mu_2} E_{t+2} s^1_{2,t+3} - \frac{Q_2}{\mu_2} \tilde{\theta}_{t+2}, \qquad (5.25)$$

and substituting (5.25) into (5.24) and applying again the law of iterated expectations as well as the fact that $E_t \tilde{\theta}_{t+j} = \rho^j \tilde{\theta}_t$, we get:

$$s^1_{2,t} = \frac{1}{\mu_2^3} E_t s^1_{2,t+3} - \left(1 + \frac{\rho}{\mu_2} + \left(\frac{\rho}{\mu_2}\right)^2\right) \frac{Q_2}{\mu_2} \tilde{\theta}_t. \qquad (5.26)$$

Repeating the substitution process for infinite periods and taking limits, we would finally get the forward solution to equation [B],

$$s^1_{2,t} = \underbrace{\lim_{j \to \infty} \frac{1}{\mu_2^j} E_t s^1_{2,t+j}}_{=0} - \frac{Q_2}{\mu_2} \tilde{\theta}_t \underbrace{\sum_{j=0}^{\infty} \left(\frac{\rho}{\mu_2}\right)^j}_{\frac{\mu_2}{\mu_2 - \rho}} = \frac{Q_2}{\rho - \mu_2} \tilde{\theta}_t, \qquad (5.27)$$

which provides us with the *stability condition* for the optimization problem of the representative agent:

$$s^1_{2,t} = \frac{Q_2}{\rho - \mu_2} \tilde{\theta}_t.$$

The stability condition relates $s^1_{2,t}$, a linear combination of the state and the control variable, to the productivity shock $\tilde{\theta}_t$. The definition of $s^1_{2,t} = u_2 \tilde{k}_t + v_2 \tilde{c}_t$ can be used to write the stability condition above as:

$$\tilde{c}_t = -\frac{u_2}{v_2}\tilde{k}_t + \frac{Q_2/v_2}{\rho - \mu_2}\tilde{\theta}_t, \tag{5.28}$$

which relates the decision variable at each point in time, $\tilde{c}_t$, to the two state variables, $\tilde{k}_t, \tilde{\theta}_t$, all in logs and in deviations with respect to steady state levels.

Using now the stability condition in equation [A]:

$$u_1\tilde{k}_{t+1} + v_1 E_t\left[-\frac{u_2}{v_2}\tilde{k}_{t+1} + \frac{Q_2/v_2}{\rho - \mu_2}\tilde{\theta}_{t+1}\right]$$

$$= \mu_1\left[u_1\tilde{k}_t + v_1\left(-\frac{u_2}{v_2}\tilde{k}_t + \frac{Q_2/v_2}{\rho - \mu_2}\tilde{\theta}_t\right)\right] + Q_1\tilde{\theta}_t.$$

Since $\tilde{k}_{t+1}$ is a time $t-$decision, we have: $E_t\tilde{k}_{t+1} = \tilde{k}_{t+1}$. Solving for $\tilde{k}_{t+1}$ and applying the expectations operator on $\tilde{\theta}_{t+1}$, we get:

$$\tilde{k}_{t+1} = \mu_1\tilde{k}_t + \underbrace{\left(\frac{Q_1 - \frac{\rho-\mu_1}{\rho-\mu_2}\frac{Q_2 v_1}{v_2}}{u_1 - v_1 u_2/v_2}\right)}_{G}\tilde{\theta}_t, \tag{5.29}$$

which gives us the solution for the logged capital stock at each point in time t, in deviations from steady-state, given a realization for the productivity shock. Using (5.13), (5.29) and (5.28), we can represent the solution to the log-linearized system in matrix form,

$$\begin{cases}\begin{bmatrix}\tilde{k}_{t+1} \\ \tilde{\theta}_{t+1}\end{bmatrix} = \begin{bmatrix}\mu_1 & G \\ 0 & \rho\end{bmatrix}\begin{bmatrix}\tilde{k}_t \\ \tilde{\theta}_t\end{bmatrix} + \begin{bmatrix}0 \\ 1\end{bmatrix}\varepsilon_{t+1} & \text{[E1]} \\[2em] \tilde{c}_t = \begin{bmatrix}-\frac{u_2}{v_2} & \frac{Q_2/v_2}{\rho-\mu_2}\end{bmatrix}\begin{bmatrix}\tilde{k}_t \\ \tilde{\theta}_t\end{bmatrix} & \text{[E2]}\end{cases},$$

with $G = \frac{Q_1 - \frac{\rho-\mu_1}{\rho-\mu_2}\frac{Q_2 v_1}{v_2}}{u_1 - v_1 u_2/v_2}$. which is known as a *state-space representation*, with [E1] being the *state equation* and [E2] the *observation equation*.

Given $\tilde{k}_0$ and specific values for the structural parameters, together with a sample realization for the productivity innovation, $\{\varepsilon_t\}_{t=0}^T$, time series for $\{\tilde{k}_{t+1}, \tilde{\theta}_t\}_{t=0}^T$ can be readily obtained from [E1]. The consumption time series $\{\tilde{c}_t\}_{t=0}^T$ can then be obtained from [E2]. We could also use recursively the law of motion of the technology shock, together with the nonlinear global constraint of resources and the stability condition [E2], to obtain $\{\tilde{k}_{t+1}, \tilde{\theta}_t, \tilde{c}_t\}_{t=0}^T$, given $\tilde{k}_0$ and $\{\varepsilon_t\}_{t=0}^T$.

The *CK_solution_BK.xls* file computes a single sample realization for the planner's problem with taxes, using an extension of the approach described in this section, which will be presented in detail in the second part of the chapter. There, we analyze some numerical results obtained under the benchmark parameterization used along the chapter. The interested reader may use at this point that spreadsheet to obtain time series for the stock of capital, consumption, output and investment by setting the two taxes to zero in the second box to the left of the *Stochastic-BK* spreadsheet ($\tau_c = \tau_y = .0$). The *Revenues* series will of course be then equal to zero each period. Seven alternative parameterizations are used in the file, in order to analyze the effect of parameter changes on volatility and cross-correlations among variables, as it will be discussed in the second part of the chapter. The *Stochastic-BK(2)* spreadsheet implements the same analysis on a different sample realization for the productivity shock, so that the reader can appreciate how numerical values of the main statistics change with the sample realization of the productivity shock.

Expressions programmed in the file appear more complex than those in this section because they correspond to the economy with consumption and income taxes, to be described later on. The same can be said for the *Blanchard Kahn.m* MATLAB program, which computes a single numerical realization from the solution to the planner's model with taxes using the extension of the Blanchard–Kahn's approach described in this section. The interested reader can set the two tax rates to zero in the initial section of the program on parameter values, to obtain the numerical realization of the solution to the model without taxes we have just analyzed. The *methods.m* MATLAB program can be used to compute an arbitrarily large number of sample realizations using the Blanchard–Kahn's approach among a variety of alternative solution methods.

A computationally more efficient solution method, which reaches the same time numerical time series than Blanchard–Kahn's is Uhlig's method, which we describe in the next section.

5.3.4 Uhlig's Undetermined Coefficients Approach. Log-Linear Approximation

This approach (Uhlig [94]) starts from the log-linear approximation of the conditions characterizing the solution ((5.17) and (5.20) obtained above):

$$0 \cong \alpha_1 \widetilde{c}_t + \alpha_2 \widetilde{k}_{t+1} + \alpha_3 \widetilde{k}_t + \alpha_4 \widetilde{\theta}_t, \tag{5.30}$$

$$0 \simeq \beta_1 \widetilde{c}_t + \beta_2 E_t \widetilde{c}_{t+1} + \beta_3 \widetilde{\theta}_t + \beta_4 \widetilde{k}_{t+1}, \tag{5.31}$$

with $\alpha_1 = \frac{c_{ss}}{k_{ss}}$, $\alpha_2 = 1$, $\alpha_3 = -\frac{1}{\beta}$, $\alpha_4 = -\frac{1}{\alpha}\left(\frac{1}{\beta} - 1 + \delta\right)$, $\beta_1 = \sigma$, $\beta_2 = -\sigma$, $\beta_3 = [1 - (1 - \delta)\beta]\rho$, $\beta_4 = -[1 - (1 - \delta)\beta](1 - \alpha)$.

The fact that there are two state variables in this economy $\widetilde{\theta}_t$, $\widetilde{k}_t$, suggests that the two decision variables, $\widetilde{c}_t, \widetilde{k}_{t+1}$ should be, each period, functions of the two states,

$$\widetilde{k}_{t+1} = \eta_{kk}\widetilde{k}_t + \eta_{k\theta}\widetilde{\theta}_t, \tag{5.32}$$

$$\widetilde{c}_t = \eta_{ck}\widetilde{k}_t + \eta_{c\theta}\widetilde{\theta}_t,$$

and also, taking conditional expectations as of time t,

$$E_t \widetilde{k}_{t+1} = \eta_{kk} \widetilde{k}_t + \eta_{k\theta} \widetilde{\theta}_t,$$

$$E_t \widetilde{c}_{t+1} = \eta_{ck} E_t \widetilde{k}_{t+1} + \eta_{c\theta} E_t \widetilde{\theta}_{t+1} = \eta_{ck} \left(\eta_{kk} \widetilde{k}_t + \eta_{k\theta} \widetilde{\theta}_t \right) + \eta_{c\theta} \rho \widetilde{\theta}_t$$

$$= \eta_{ck} \eta_{kk} \widetilde{k}_t + \left(\eta_{ck} \eta_{k\theta} + \eta_{c\theta} \rho \right) \widetilde{\theta}_t,$$

which taken to the log-linear approximation (5.30)–(5.31) gives us,

$$0 = \alpha_1 \left(\eta_{ck} \widetilde{k}_t + \eta_{c\theta} \widetilde{\theta}_t \right) + \alpha_2 \left(\eta_{kk} \widetilde{k}_t + \eta_{k\theta} \widetilde{\theta}_t \right) + \alpha_3 \widetilde{k}_t + \alpha_4 \widetilde{\theta}_t,$$

$$0 = \beta_1 \left(\eta_{ck} \widetilde{k}_t + \eta_{c\theta} \widetilde{\theta}_t \right) + \beta_2 \left[\eta_{ck} \eta_{kk} \widetilde{k}_t + \left(\eta_{ck} \eta_{k\theta} + \eta_{c\theta} \rho \right) \widetilde{\theta}_t \right]$$

$$+ \beta_3 \widetilde{\theta}_t + \beta_4 \left(\eta_{kk} \widetilde{k}_t + \eta_{k\theta} \widetilde{\theta}_t \right),$$

and for these equations to hold we need to have,

$$0 = \alpha_1 \eta_{ck} + \alpha_2 \eta_{kk} + \alpha_3, \tag{5.33}$$

$$0 = \alpha_1 \eta_{c\theta} + \alpha_2 \eta_{k\theta} + \alpha_4, \tag{5.34}$$

$$0 = \beta_1 \eta_{ck} + \beta_2 \eta_{ck} \eta_{kk} + \beta_4 \eta_{kk}, \tag{5.35}$$

$$0 = \beta_1 \eta_{c\theta} + \beta_2 \left(\eta_{ck} \eta_{k\theta} + \eta_{c\theta} \rho \right) + \beta_3 + \beta_4 \eta_{k\theta}. \tag{5.36}$$

From (5.33), we have,

$$\eta_{ck} = -\frac{\alpha_2 \eta_{kk} + \alpha_3}{\alpha_1}, \tag{5.37}$$

which taken to (5.35) yields,

$$0 = -\beta_1 \frac{\alpha_2}{\alpha_1} \eta_{kk} - \frac{\beta_1}{\alpha_1} \alpha_3 - \beta_2 \left(\frac{\alpha_2 \eta_{kk} + \alpha_3}{\alpha_1} \right) \eta_{kk} + \beta_4 \eta_{kk}$$

$$\Rightarrow 0 = \beta_1 \alpha_3 + \left(\beta_1 \alpha_2 + \beta_2 \alpha_3 - \beta_4 \alpha_1 \right) \eta_{kk} + \beta_2 \alpha_2 \eta_{kk}^2,$$

a quadratic equation in η_{kk} which must be solved to obtain the value of this parameter. Equation (5.37) will then give us the value of η_{ck}. These two, taken to (5.34) and (5.36) will provide us with the values of $\eta_{c\theta}$ and $\eta_{k\theta}$. Only one of the roots of the quadratic equation in η_{kk} is less than one.[4] That is the *stable* root, since η_{kk} is the coefficient of $\widetilde{k}_t$ in equation (5.32), which gives us the time path for $\widetilde{k}_{t+1}$. The other root would clearly produce an explosive path for $\widetilde{k}_t$, and it is not used. This

---

[4] Using the definitions of the α and β coefficients, the second degree equation in η_{kk} can be written: $\sigma \left[\eta_{kk}^2 - \left(1 + \frac{1}{\beta} + \frac{[1-(1-\delta)\beta](1-\alpha)}{\sigma} \frac{c_{ss}}{k_{ss}} \right) \eta_{kk} + \frac{1}{\beta} \right] = 0$ and an argument similar to that used in section *Systems with a saddle path property* in the Mathematical Appendix can be used to show that one of the roots is greater than $1/\beta$, while the other root is less than one.

is the way *stability* is imposed in this solution approach. After tedious algebra, the solution for the elasticities with respect to the technology shocks are,

$$\eta_{k\theta} = -\frac{(\beta_1 + \rho\beta_2)\,\alpha_4 - \alpha_1\beta_3}{\beta_1\alpha_2 - \beta_2\,(\alpha_1\eta_{ck} - \alpha_2\rho) - \beta_4\alpha_1},$$

$$\eta_{c\theta} = -\frac{\alpha_2\eta_{k\theta} + \alpha_4}{\alpha_1}.$$

Once we have the four η-parameters, generating the time series for the stock of capital, consumption and output is straightforward.

The *Simple_planner_problem.xls* file computes a single sample realization for the planner's problem without taxes, following the undetermined coefficients method as described in this section, with the same benchmark parameterization considered with other solution methods. Time series for the stock of capital, consumption, output and investment are obtained using the expressions presented in this section. The *uhlig.m* MATLAB program also computes a single numerical realization from the solution to the planner's model using an extension of the method described in this section to the case when consumption and income taxes are considered. The interested reader can set the two tax rates to zero in the initial section of the program on parameter values, to obtain the numerical realization of the solution to the model without taxes we have just analyzed. As it was the case with the Blanchard–Kahn's approach, the *methods.m* MATLAB program can be used to compute an arbitrarily large number of sample realizations using the undetermined coefficients method among a variety of alternative solution methods.

5.3.5 Sims' Eigenvalue-Eigenvector Decomposition Method Using a Linear Approximation to the Model

The previous two numerical solution methods (Uhlig's undetermined coefficients method and Blanchard–Kahn's method) could be implemented on a linear approximation to the optimality conditions of the stochastic planner's problem. Linear approximations are somewhat easier to obtain analytically, but they lead to larger approximation errors than log-linear approximations. The reason is that the latter produce stability conditions which are linear in the logs of the main variables in the economy, so that they are nonlinear in the levels of the original variables. Allowing for nonlinearity in the relationships between control and state variables reduces somewhat the numerical errors of linear approximations.

To familiarize the reader with both approximations to the planner's problem, we describe the method in this section [Sims [86]] using the linear approximation, although a log-linear approximation would be preferable, for the same reasons described in the previous paragraph. In fact, we describe its implementation on the log-linear approximation at the end of the section. A linear approximation was also used in the previous chapter to solve the deterministic version of the planner's problem with taxes, so that the linear approximation considered here can be seen as the extension to the stochastic case, of the solution approach there.

The dynamics of the model could be summarized in the system formed by the Euler condition:

$$\frac{1}{c_t^\sigma} = \beta E_t \left[\frac{1}{c_{t+1}^\sigma} \left(\alpha \theta_{t+1} k_{t+1}^{\alpha-1} + 1 - \delta \right) \right] \tag{5.38}$$

together with the global constraint of resources,

$$c_t + k_{t+1} - (1-\delta) k_t \leq f(\theta_t, k_t) = \theta_t k_t^\alpha, \ 0 < \alpha < 1 \tag{5.39}$$

with θ_t being a random shock to productivity, having a lognormal distribution characterized by,

$$\ln(\theta_t) = \rho \ln(\theta_{t-1}) + \varepsilon_t, \ \varepsilon_t \underset{iid}{\sim} N\left(0, \sigma_\varepsilon^2\right), \ given \ \theta_0,$$

and given the initial capital stock, k_0.

We also have the transversality condition,

$$\lim_{t \to \infty} \beta^t E_0 \left(\lambda_t k_{t+1} \right) = 0, \tag{5.40}$$

which clearly shows the additional difficulty we face in this stochastic model: the optimality condition above involves the conditional expectation of a nonlinear function of state and decision variables, for which we do not have a closed form analytical expression.

The linear approximation to the global constraint of resources is,[5]

$$0 = (k_{t+1} - k_{ss}) - \left[\alpha \theta_{ss} k_{ss}^{\alpha-1} + 1 - \delta \right] (k_t - k_{ss})$$
$$+ (c_t - c_{ss}) - k_{ss}^\alpha \theta_{ss} (\ln \theta_t - \ln \theta_{ss}),$$

which simplifies to:

$$0 = (k_{t+1} - k_{ss}) - \frac{1}{\beta} (k_t - k_{ss}) + (c_t - c_{ss}) - k_{ss}^\alpha \theta_{ss} (\ln \theta_t - \ln \theta_{ss}),$$

because of the steady-state equality: $1 = \beta \left(\alpha \theta_{ss} k_{ss}^{\alpha-1} + 1 - \delta \right)$.

On the other hand, we take into account that the conditional expectation of a given function can be written: $E_t g_{t+1} = g_{+1} - \xi_{t+1}$, $E_t \xi_{t+1} = 0$, an identity that defines the expectations error ξ_{t+1} as the difference between the realized value of the function at time $t+1$ and the expectation formed at time t.[6] The steady-state value of the expectations error is equal to zero: $\xi_{ss} = 0$. In this model, if we take as function $g_{t+1} = \frac{1}{c_{t+1}^\sigma} \left(\alpha \theta_{t+1} k_{t+1}^{\alpha-1} + 1 - \delta \right)$, we can follow the same argument

---

[5] Note that $\theta_{t+1} = e^{\ln \theta_{t+1}}$, so that $\frac{\partial \theta_{t+1}}{\partial \ln \theta_{t+1}} = e^{\ln \theta_{t+1}} = \theta_{t+1}$.

[6] A similar expression applies to any future expectation, the higher time index showing up in the definition of function $g(.)$: $E_t g_{t+k} = g_{t+k} - \xi_{t+k}$, with $E_t \xi_{t+k} = 0$.

as in the previous chapter, to obtain the linear approximation to (5.38) around the deterministic steady-state:

$$0 = (c_{t+1} - c_{ss}) - \frac{1}{\sigma}(\Omega_{ss})^{\frac{1}{\sigma}-1} c_{ss}\beta\alpha(\alpha-1)\theta_{ss}k_{ss}^{\alpha-2}(k_{t+1} - k_{ss})$$

$$- (\Omega_{ss})^{\frac{1}{\sigma}}(c_t - c_{ss}) - \frac{1}{\sigma}(\Omega_{ss})^{\frac{1}{\sigma}-1} c_{ss}\beta\alpha\theta_{ss}k_{ss}^{\alpha-1}(\ln\theta_{t+1} - \ln\theta_{ss})$$

$$+ \beta\frac{c_{ss}}{\sigma}\Omega_{ss}^{1/\sigma}\xi_{t+1},$$

where $\Omega_{ss} = \beta\left[\alpha\theta_{ss}k_{ss}^{\alpha-1} + 1 - \delta - \xi_{ss}\right] = 1$, so that the linear approximation can be simplified to,

$$(c_{t+1} - c_{ss}) - \frac{1}{\sigma}c_{ss}\beta\alpha(\alpha-1)\theta_{ss}k_{ss}^{\alpha-2}(k_{t+1} - k_{ss})$$

$$- (c_t - c_{ss}) - \frac{1}{\sigma}c_{ss}\beta\alpha\theta_{ss}k_{ss}^{\alpha-1}(\ln\theta_{t+1} - \ln\theta_{ss}) + \beta\frac{c_{ss}}{\sigma}\xi_{t+1} = 0.$$

Finally, the law of motion for the technology shock does not need a linear approximation, because of our choice of $\ln\theta_t$, rather than θ_t, as the relevant variable. So, using again the fact that $\theta_{ss} = 1$, $\ln\theta_{ss} = 0$, we have,

$$\ln\theta_{t+1} - \ln\theta_{ss} = \rho(\ln\theta_t - \ln\theta_{ss}) + \varepsilon_t,$$

and we can represent the full system in matrix form,

$$A\begin{pmatrix} k_{t+1} - k_{ss} \\ c_{t+1} - c_{ss} \\ \ln\theta_{t+1} - \ln\theta_{ss} \end{pmatrix} = B\begin{pmatrix} k_t - k_{ss} \\ c_t - c_{ss} \\ \ln\theta_t - \ln\theta_{ss} \end{pmatrix} + \Phi\begin{pmatrix} \varepsilon_{t+1} \\ \xi_{t+1} \end{pmatrix},$$

$$\text{with } A = \begin{pmatrix} 1 & 0 & 0 \\ M & 1 & M\frac{k_{ss}}{\alpha-1} \\ 0 & 0 & 1 \end{pmatrix};$$

$$B = \begin{pmatrix} \frac{1}{\beta} & -1 & Ak_{ss}^{\alpha} \\ 0 & 1 & 0 \\ 0 & 0 & \rho \end{pmatrix}; \Phi = \begin{pmatrix} 0 & 0 \\ 0 & -\beta\frac{c_{ss}}{\sigma} \\ 1 & 0 \end{pmatrix},$$

and $M = -\frac{1}{\sigma}c_{ss}\beta\alpha(\alpha-1)\theta_{ss}k_{ss}^{\alpha-2}$.

We have,

$$A^{-1} = \begin{pmatrix} 1 & 0 & 0 \\ -M & 1 & -M\frac{k_{ss}}{\alpha-1} \\ 0 & 0 & 1 \end{pmatrix};$$

$$A^{-1}B = \begin{pmatrix} \frac{1}{\beta} & -1 & k_{ss}^{\alpha} \\ -M\frac{1}{\beta} & M+1 & -M\left(k_{ss}^{\alpha}+\rho\frac{k_{ss}}{\alpha-1}\right) \\ 0 & 0 & \rho \end{pmatrix};$$

$$A^{-1}\Phi = \begin{pmatrix} 0 & 0 \\ -M\frac{k_{ss}}{\alpha-1} & -\beta\frac{c_{ss}}{\sigma} \\ 1 & 0 \end{pmatrix},$$

so that the dynamics of the system can be represented as,

$$\begin{pmatrix} k_{t+1}-k_{ss} \\ c_{t+1}-c_{ss} \\ \ln\theta_{t+1}-\ln\theta_{ss} \end{pmatrix} = \begin{pmatrix} \frac{1}{\beta} & -1 & k_{ss}^{\alpha} \\ -M\frac{1}{\beta} & M+1 & -M\bar{\kappa} \\ 0 & 0 & \rho \end{pmatrix} \begin{pmatrix} k_t-k_{ss} \\ c_t-c_{ss} \\ \ln\theta_t-\ln\theta_{ss} \end{pmatrix}$$

$$+ \begin{pmatrix} 0 & 0 \\ -M\frac{k_{ss}}{\alpha-1} & -\beta\frac{c_{ss}}{\sigma} \\ 1 & 0 \end{pmatrix} \begin{pmatrix} \varepsilon_{t+1} \\ \xi_{t+1} \end{pmatrix},$$

where $\bar{\kappa} = \left(k_{ss}^{\alpha}+\rho\frac{k_{ss}}{\alpha-1}\right)$, with the transition matrix, i.e., the matrix of autoregressive coefficients, having one root equal to ρ, which is less than one. The other two roots are those of the upper 2×2 submatrix. Its characteristic equation is: $\mu^2 - \left[\frac{1}{\beta}+(M+1)\right]\mu + \frac{1}{\beta} = 0$, and the argument in section *Systems with a saddle path* in the Mathematical Appendix shows that one of the roots is above $1/\beta$ while the other is below one. The single root above $1/\beta$ is unstable, while the other two roots are stable. The eigenvector associated to the unstable eigenvalue defines the single stability condition in this system, in the form of a linear relationship between deviations from steady-state of consumption, capital and the technology shock.

The spectral representation for the autoregressive coefficient matrix,

$$\begin{pmatrix} \frac{1}{\beta} & -1 & k_{ss}^{\alpha} \\ -M\frac{1}{\beta} & M+1 & -M\left(k_{ss}^{\alpha}+\rho\frac{k_{ss}}{\alpha-1}\right) \\ 0 & 0 & \rho \end{pmatrix} = \Gamma\Lambda\Gamma^{-1},$$

can be used to transform the model,

$$\Gamma^{-1}\begin{pmatrix} k_{t+1}-k_{ss} \\ c_{t+1}-c_{ss} \\ \ln\theta_{t+1}-\ln\theta_{ss} \end{pmatrix} = \Lambda\Gamma^{-1}\begin{pmatrix} k_t-k_{ss} \\ c_t-c_{ss} \\ \ln\theta_t-\ln\theta_{ss} \end{pmatrix}$$

$$+ \Gamma^{-1}\begin{pmatrix} 0 & 0 \\ -M\frac{k_{ss}}{\alpha-1} & -\beta\frac{c_{ss}}{\sigma} \\ 1 & 0 \end{pmatrix} \begin{pmatrix} \varepsilon_{t+1} \\ \xi_{t+1} \end{pmatrix}.$$

Defining a vector of transformed variables, $\tilde{z}_t = \Gamma^{-1} \begin{pmatrix} k_t - k_{ss} \\ c_t - c_{ss} \\ \ln \theta_t - \ln \theta_{ss} \end{pmatrix}$, we get,

$$\tilde{z}_{t+1} = \Lambda \tilde{z}_t + Q \begin{pmatrix} \varepsilon_{t+1} \\ \xi_{t+1} \end{pmatrix}, \qquad (5.41)$$

with $Q = \begin{pmatrix} q_{11} & q_{12} \\ q_{21} & q_{22} \\ q_{31} & q_{32} \end{pmatrix} = \Gamma^{-1} \begin{pmatrix} 0 & 0 \\ -M\frac{k_{ss}}{\alpha - 1} & -\beta\frac{c_{ss}}{\sigma} \\ 1 & 0 \end{pmatrix}.$

For the autoregressive system in $\tilde{z}_t$ to be stable, we need to eliminate in (5.41) the equation corresponding to the row of Λ associated to the single unstable eigenvalue of the coefficient matrix. Without loss of generality, let us assume that we have ordered eigenvalues decreasingly along the diagonal of Λ, so that the unstable eigenvalue is the (1,1) element in Λ. If we represent by γ^{ij} the (i,j)-element in Γ^{-1}, we will impose the condition:

$$\tilde{z}_{1t} = \gamma^{11}(k_t - k_{ss}) + \gamma^{12}(c_t - c_{ss}) + \gamma^{13} \ln \theta_t = 0, \ \forall t, \qquad (5.42)$$

a constraint imposing a linear dependence between deviations from steady state in the stock of capital, consumption, and the logged productivity shock. In that sense, it is similar to (5.28), the stability condition we derived following the Blanchard–Kahn approach.

The previous condition amounts to,

$$q_{11}\varepsilon_{t+1} + q_{12}\xi_{t+1} = 0, \ \forall t. \qquad (5.43)$$

describing an approximate linear relationship between the expectations error ξ_{t+1} and the single exogenous shock in the model, ε_{t+1}, at each point in time.

To actually compute a numerical solution, we start by producing a time series for the technology shock. Then a strategy similar to the deterministic case, always imposing the stability condition as part of the solution algorithm, will provide us with a set of stable time series solving the model. There are some differences, however, in that the stability condition involves the productivity shock, so we should do the following:

1. Parameterize the model and find eigenvalues and eigenvectors of the transition matrix of the linear approximation, written as a first order vector autoregression,
2. Generate a time series for the technology shock from its assumed stochastic process. Assuming Normality for the innovation ε_t will give us a lognormal technology shock.
3. Use the stability condition to obtain initial consumption, c_0, from the initial capital stock k_0, and get k_1 from the global constraint of resources. Iterate on this step to generate full time series for the stock of capital and consumption.
4. Use Euler's equation to compute rational expectations errors. In this model, with a single Euler condition, expectations errors ξ_{t+1} are obtained as the difference

between $\frac{1}{c_{t+1}^\sigma}\left(\alpha\theta_{t+1}k_{t+1}^{\alpha-1}+1-\delta\right)$ and $\frac{1}{\beta c_t^\sigma}$. Rationality tests can then be run on the ξ_t-time series.

The last step is clearly specific of stochastic models, and it is crucial. We are assuming that agents form expectations rationally, meaning that they make an efficient use of the available information. As a consequence, a rational expectations error must fulfill three conditions: (a) have zero mean, (b) be serially uncorrelated, besides (c) being uncorrelated with any variable contained in the information set available to the agent at the time the conditional expectation was made. The latter condition may be tricky sometimes, since time indices may be misleading, as it is the case with the stock of capital k_{t+1}, a variable which is decided at time t, so that it satisfies, $E_t k_{t+1} = k_{t+1}$. As with previous solution methods, the *methods.m* MATLAB program can be used to compute an arbitrarily large number of sample realizations from the solution to the planner's problem using Sims' eigenvalue-eigenvector approach.

5.3.5.1 Numerical Exercise: Solving the Stochastic Representative Agent's Model Through the Eingenvector-Eigenvalue Decomposition Approach

Numerical solutions for the planner's problem without taxes using the eigenvalue-eigenvector decomposition are obtained in *CK_stochastic.xls*. The four simulations presented differ in the value of the risk aversion parameter as well as in the autoregressive coefficient for the productivity shock. At the left side of the spreadsheet we present computations needed to estimate the stability condition, which will be used to produce the value of consumption each period (decision or control variable) as a function of the productivity shock and the stock of capital available at the beginning of the period (the two state variables).

Starting from a capital stock at the level of the deterministic steady-state, and given a sample realization for the productivity shock, the (k_0, θ_0)-pair is used to obtain c_0. The global constraint of resources is then used to compute k_1, and the process is iterated over time to. Output is obtained each period from the stock of capital available at the beginning of the period and the productivity shock, and investment is calculated as the difference between output and consumption. Once we have time series data for all variables, the expectations error is calculated as the difference between the realized value of the function inside the conditional expectation, $\frac{1}{c_{t+1}^\sigma}\left(A\alpha\theta_{t+1}k_{t+1}^{\alpha-1}+1-\delta\right)$ and its expectation as of time t, $\frac{1}{\beta c_t^\sigma}$.

The benchmark parameterization used is $\beta = 0.90$, $\alpha = 0.33$, $\delta = 0.07$, $\sigma_\varepsilon = 0.001$. Simulation 1.1 uses $\sigma = 1.50$, $\rho = 0.90$, simulation 2.1 uses $\sigma = 1.50$, $\rho = 0.99$, and the last two simulations use $\sigma = 5.0$ with $\rho = 0.90$ and $\rho = 0.99$, respectively. The spreadsheet can accommodate values other than $A = 1$, $n = .0$, which have been used throughout the previous section.

As usual, below the time series, we compute steady-state values, standard deviations and coefficients of variation for the main variables, as well as their contemporaneous and cross-correlations with output, and the percent decomposition of output between consumption and investment. We also present in the spreadsheet rationality tests for the expectations error, i.e., for the forecast error associated to the expectation of the nonlinear function of state and decision variables appearing in the Keynes–Ramsey condition. In spite of the widespread use of numerical solution methods for linear and nonlinear models under the assumption that economic agents form their expectations rationally, this hypothesis is seldom subject to test. This is unfortunate, because failure to satisfy rationality should preclude using a particular sample solution for economic policy analysis or any other use. So, this should be taken as a necessary, although not sufficient condition, to accept that the numerical approximation necessarily involved in any solution method is acceptable.

We suggest implementing two types of test: on the one hand, if agents use the available information rationally, expectations errors should not have information in common with variables which were known at the time the expectation was formed. This means that the correlation between the expectations error and variables in the information set at time t should be zero. With a sample size of $T = 538$, the standard deviation for each of these correlations can be approximated by $1/\sqrt{T} = .043$, so none of the correlations shown in the table are statistically significant.

Contemporaneous correlations between the rational expectation error and variables in the information set

	c_t	y_t	i_t	k_t
S1.1	.003	.007	.017	.000
S2.1	−.057	−.057	−.048	−.057
S3.1	.015	.016	.017	.013
S4.1	.040	.040	.039	.041

The second test examines the expectations error autocorrelation function, which should not be significant at any lag, since that would suggest somewhat systematic patterns in the errors, against the assumption of an efficient use of the available information. With a sample size of $T = 538$, the standard deviation for each value of the autocorrelation function of the expectations error can again be approximated by $1/\sqrt{T} = .043$, so again none of the autocorrelations violate this condition.

Sample autocorrelation function for the rational expectations error

Lag	0	1	2	3	4	5	6
S1.1	1.0	−.024	−.014	.027	.017	−.050	.037
S2.1	1.0	−.007	.008	.053	.038	−.031	.056
S3.1	1.0	−.027	−.016	.026	.016	−.051	.036
S4.1	1.0	−.028	−.012	.033	.020	−.051	.038

Even though the autocorrelation function of the expectations error, as well as its correlations with time t variables have turned out not to be significant for the sample realization of the productivity innovation in the Excel file, that may not be the case for different sample realizations, as the reader may easily check by generating alternative time series from an independent $N(0,1)$ distribution on top of the one in the spreadsheet. Finally, an statement would have to be made on the values of these statistics once a large number of sample realizations, 5,000 say, have been obtained. We would then have that same number of estimates for each of the statistics in the previous tables, and the analyst would have to conclude on their individual and global significance. The MATLAB programs provided with this textbook produce that large number of realizations for each variable in the model, from which a frequency distribution can be obtained for any statistic. That is different from the numerical exercises provided in Excel files, in which a single realization is provided in most cases for a given parameterization. In this case, we just want the reader to fully understand the process of computing time series realization for all variables in the model.

5.3.5.2 Solving the Planner's Problem with the Eigenvalue-Eigenvector Decomposition Under a Log-Linear Approximation

As it is the case with the other methods, the eigenvalue-eigenvector decomposition can also be used on a log-linear approximation. The reader is asked in an exercise at the end of the chapter to check that such an approximation takes the form:

$$
A \begin{pmatrix} \ln k_{t+1} - \ln k_{ss} \\ \ln c_{t+1} - \ln c_{ss} \\ \ln \theta_{t+1} - \ln \theta_{ss} \end{pmatrix} = B \begin{pmatrix} \ln k_t - \ln k_{ss} \\ \ln c_t - \ln c_{ss} \\ \ln \theta_t - \ln \theta_{ss} \end{pmatrix} + \Phi \begin{pmatrix} \varepsilon_{t+1} \\ \xi_{t+1} \end{pmatrix}, \tag{5.44}
$$

$$
A = \begin{pmatrix} 1 & 0 & 0 \\ \left(\frac{1}{\beta} - (1-\delta)\right)(1-\alpha) & \frac{\sigma}{\beta} & -\left(\frac{1}{\beta} - (1-\delta)\right) \\ 0 & 0 & 1 \end{pmatrix};
$$

$$
B = \begin{pmatrix} \frac{1}{\beta} & -\frac{c_{ss}}{k_{ss}} & \left(\frac{1}{\beta} - (1-\delta)\right)\frac{1}{\alpha} \\ 0 & \frac{\sigma}{\beta} & 0 \\ 0 & 0 & \rho \end{pmatrix}; \Phi = \begin{pmatrix} 0 & 0 \\ 0 & -\beta \\ 1 & 0 \end{pmatrix}.
$$

Pre-multiplying the log-linear approximation (5.44) by the inverse of matrix A would lead to a first order autoregressive representation for the vector of variables in deviations with respect to steady-state. The same steps described to obtain the solution using the linear approximation can then be followed to obtain the numerical solution using the approximation above. The resulting time series will not be the same under both approximations even if the same sample realization was used for the technology shock.

The *methods.m* file contains a main MATLAB program solving the planner's problem under consumption and income taxes by different solution methods: the linear-quadratic approximation, Uhlig's undetermined coefficients method, Blanchard–Kahn's method, the eigenvalue-eigenvector decomposition implemented on either the linear or the log-linear approximation to the model, and the parameterized expectations method that we introduce below.

5.4 Solving the Stochastic Representative Agent's Problem with Taxes

In this second part of the chapter we consider a more complex economy, including consumption and income taxes, which will allow us to perform some exercises dealing with optimal fiscal policy design. For the sake of an illustration, we also allow for nonzero population growth and a level of technology A different from 1. Most expressions in these sections reduce to their analogue in the first part of the chapter if we set taxes and population growth to zero, and the technology level to 1. We will again assume that productivity is random, the production function being of the form, $y_t = \theta_t A k_t^\alpha$, where θ_t follows a stationary stochastic process. There would be alternative ways of making the representative agent's problem stochastic, but the solution could always be obtained by simple adaptation of the procedures we outline in the previous sections.

Under constant consumption and income taxes, the government's budget constraint is,

$$\tau^c c_t + \tau^y y_t = g_t$$

while the stochastic version of the representative agent's problem considered in the previous chapter becomes,

$$\underset{\{c_t, k_{t+1}\}_{t=0}^\infty}{Max} E_0 \left[\sum_{t=0}^\infty \beta^t \frac{c_t^{1-\sigma} - 1}{1 - \sigma} \right]$$

subject to: $(1 + \tau^c)c_t + (1 + n)k_{t+1} - (1 - \delta)k_t \leq (1 - \tau^y)\theta_t A k_t^\alpha$,   (5.45)

given k_0, with $\ln \theta_t = \rho \ln \theta_{t-1} + \varepsilon_t$, $\varepsilon_t \underset{iid}{\sim} N(0, \sigma_\varepsilon^2)$. The population rate of growth is n.

The Lagrangian for this optimization problem is,

$$L(\{c_t, k_{t+1}, \theta_t\}_{t=0}^\infty) = \sum_{t=0}^\infty \beta^t \left\{ \frac{c_t^{1-\sigma} - 1}{1 - \sigma} + \lambda_t [(1 - \tau^y)\theta_t A k_t^\alpha \right.$$

$$\left. -(1 + \tau^c)c_t - (1 + n)k_{t+1} + (1 - \delta)k_t] \right\},$$

with first order conditions,

$$c_t^{-\sigma} = (1+\tau^c)\lambda_t \tag{5.46}$$

$$(1+n)\lambda_t = \beta E_t \left\{ \lambda_{t+1} \left[(1-\tau^y)\theta_{t+1} A \, \alpha k_{t+1}^{\alpha-1} \right. \right. \tag{5.47}$$
$$\left. \left. +(1-\delta) \right] \right\},$$

$$\lim_{t\to\infty} E_0 \beta^t \lambda_t k_{t+1} = 0,$$

where a conditional expectation operator has been written in front of all terms involving future values of state or decision variables.

Hence, given tax rates τ^c, τ^y, and a realization for the productivity shock, $\{\theta_t\}_{t=0}^\infty$, the solution to the optimization problem is a set of time series $\{c_t, k_{t+1}, y_t, g_t\}_{t=0}^\infty$ satisfying,

(a) The budget constraint,

$$(1+\tau^c)c_t + (1+n)k_{t+1} - (1-\delta)k_t = (1-\tau^y)\theta_t A \, k_t^\alpha, \tag{5.48}$$

(b) The law of motion for the productivity shock,

$$\ln\theta_t = \rho\ln\theta_{t-1} + \varepsilon_t, \ \varepsilon_t \underset{iid}{\sim} N(0,\sigma_\varepsilon^2),$$

(c) The government's budget constraint, $\tau^c c_t + \tau^y y_t = g_t$, and

(d) The Euler equation, which is obtained by using (5.46) to eliminate the Lagrange multiplier in (5.47):

$$(1+n)\frac{c_t^{-\sigma}}{1+\tau^c} = \beta \, E_t \left[\frac{c_{t+1}^{-\sigma}}{1+\tau^c} \left((1-\tau^y)\alpha\theta_{t+1} A \, k_{t+1}^{\alpha-1} + (1-\delta) \right) \right], \tag{5.49}$$

where the consumption tax rate, being constant over time, can be eliminated. Therefore, it does not distort the allocation of resources over time. This set of stochastic, dynamic equations fully characterize the time evolution of the economy in per capita terms.

The deterministic steady state is attained when $c_t = c_{t+1} = c_{ss}$, $k_t = k_{t+1} = k_{ss}$, $y_t = y_{t+1} = y_{ss}$, $\theta_t = \theta_{t+1} = 1$, $\varepsilon_t = \varepsilon_{t+1} = 0$ so that we get from (5.49):

$$1+n = \beta \left[(1-\tau^y)\alpha A k_{ss}^{\alpha-1} + 1 - \delta \right], \tag{5.50}$$

which leads to:

$$k_{ss} = \left[\frac{(1-\tau^y)\alpha A}{\frac{1+n}{\beta} - (1-\delta)} \right]^{\frac{1}{1-\alpha}}, \tag{5.51}$$

decreasing in τ^y but independent of τ^c. The steady-state stock of capital increases with the output elasticity of capital, α, the time discount factor β and the level of technology A, while decreasing with n and δ. The same parameter dependence holds for output, which is given by:

$$y_{ss} = A\, k_{ss}^{\alpha}.$$

Finally, from (5.48) we get the steady state level of consumption:

$$c_{ss} = \frac{k_{ss}}{1+\tau^c}\left[(1-\tau^y)Ak_{ss}^{\alpha-1} - (n+\delta)\right]. \tag{5.52}$$

which is inversely related to the tax rate on consumption. This condition also shows that consumption expenditures are independent of τ^c. The consumption tax implies a split of total expenditures between actual consumption and consumption taxes.

5.4.1 The Log-Linear Approximation

Following the same steps as in the model without taxes, we leave as an exercise for the reader to show that the loglinear approximation to the Euler condition is,

$$0 = \frac{1+n}{\beta}\sigma\tilde{c}_t - \frac{1+n}{\beta}\sigma E_t\tilde{c}_{t+1} + \left(\frac{1+n}{\beta} - (1-\delta)\right)\left(\rho\tilde{\theta}_t - (1-\alpha)\tilde{k}_{t+1}\right), \tag{5.53}$$

while the log-linear approximation to the budget constraint (5.48) is:

$$(1+\tau^c)\frac{c_{ss}}{k_{ss}}\tilde{c}_t + (1+n)\tilde{k}_{t+1} = \frac{1+n}{\beta}\tilde{k}_t + \left(\frac{1+n}{\beta} - (1-\delta)\right)\frac{1}{\alpha}\tilde{\theta}_t, \tag{5.54}$$

where tildes denote deviations in logged variables with respect to steady-state values.

Equations (5.53) and (5.54) can be written in matrix form:

$$\underbrace{\begin{bmatrix} \left(\frac{1+n}{\beta} - (1-\delta)\right)(1-\alpha) & \frac{1+n}{\beta}\sigma \\ 1+n & 0 \end{bmatrix}}_{A}\underbrace{\begin{bmatrix} \tilde{k}_{t+1} \\ E_t\tilde{c}_{t+1} \end{bmatrix}}_{E_t s_{t+1}^0}$$

$$= \underbrace{\begin{bmatrix} 0 & \frac{1+n}{\beta}\sigma \\ \frac{1+n}{\beta} & -(1+\tau^c)\frac{c_{ss}}{k_{ss}} \end{bmatrix}}_{B}\underbrace{\begin{bmatrix} \tilde{k}_t \\ \tilde{c}_t \end{bmatrix}}_{s_t^0} + \underbrace{\begin{bmatrix} \left(\frac{1+n}{\beta} - (1-\delta)\right)\rho \\ \left(\frac{1+n}{\beta} - (1-\delta)\right)\frac{1}{\alpha} \end{bmatrix}}_{C}\tilde{\theta}_t.$$

The Blanchard–Kahn's method, and the undetermined coefficients method can be applied on this approximation. The *Blanchard Kahn.m* and *uhlig.m* MATLAB programs compute a single sample realization from each of them for the model above, as explained in the first part of the chapter. We now describe the implementation details just for the Blanchard–Kahn's method.

5.4.2 Numerical Exercise: Solving the Stochastic Representative Agent's Model with Taxes Through Blanchard and Kahn's Approach. Log-Linear Approximation

The same argument in section (5.3.3) can be followed to show that there is again one unstable eigenvalue above $1/\beta$, and one stable eigenvalue below 1. We start by computing $D = A^{-1}B, F = A^{-1}C$. Then, eigenvalues for D are obtained and matrix Γ having as columns the right eigenvectors of D is inverted. Vector Q is defined by $Q = \Gamma^{-1}F$, and we reach the same expression for the stability condition,

$$\hat{c}_t = -\frac{u_2}{v_2}\tilde{k}_t + \frac{Q_2/v_2}{\rho - \mu_2}\hat{\theta}_t, \qquad (5.55)$$

as in the case with no taxes, where (u_2, v_2) is the row of Γ^{-1} associated to the unstable eigenvalue. We will again have a *state-space representation*,

$$\begin{cases} \begin{bmatrix} \tilde{k}_{t+1} \\ \hat{\theta}_{t+1} \end{bmatrix} = \begin{bmatrix} \mu_1 & G \\ 0 & \rho \end{bmatrix}\begin{bmatrix} \tilde{k}_t \\ \hat{\theta}_t \end{bmatrix} + \begin{bmatrix} 0 \\ 1 \end{bmatrix}\varepsilon_{t+1} & \text{[E1]} \\ \hat{c}_t = \begin{bmatrix} -\dfrac{u_2}{v_2} & \dfrac{Q_2/v_2}{\rho-\mu_2} \end{bmatrix}\begin{bmatrix} \tilde{k}_t \\ \hat{\theta}_t \end{bmatrix} & \text{[E2]} \end{cases},$$

with $G = \dfrac{Q_1 - \frac{\rho-\mu_1}{\rho-\mu_2}\frac{Q_2 v_1}{v_2}}{u_1 - v_1 u_2/v_2}$, where [E1] is the *state equation* and [E2] the *observation equation*, although the numerical values of μ_1, μ_2, Q_1, Q_2, u_1, v_1, u_2, v_2, G will generally depend on the values of the population rate growth, the level of technology and the consumption and income tax rates.

The *Stochastic-BK* spreadsheet in *CK_solution_BK.xls* presents a numerical simulation of the solution to the representative agent's problem using the Blanchard–Kahn approach. Benchmark parameter values used in simulation #1, are $A = 1$, $\beta = .90$, $\alpha = .33$, $n = .0$, $\delta = .07$, $\sigma = 1.50$, $\rho = .90$, $\sigma_\varepsilon = .01$, and tax rates: $\tau_c = 20.0\%$, $\tau_y = 12.478\%$. Under this parameterization, steady state levels are $k_{ss} = 2.007$, $c_{ss} = 0.801$, $y_{ss} = 1.258$. Steady state investment is equal to the difference between disposable income and consumption $i_{ss} = (y_{ss} - \tau_y y_{ss} - \tau_c c_{ss}) - c_{ss} = .1405$ which, since $n = 0$, is equal to the depreciation loss of physical capital, δk_{ss}, as it should be to make the steady state sustainable. Following the same notation as in the previous section, the A, B, C matrices are calculated, as well as $D = A^{-1}B$, $F = A^{-1}C$. Then, eigenvalues for D are obtained and matrix Γ having as columns the right eigenvectors is inverted. Eigenvalues and eigenvectors are calculated following the expressions in the Matrix Algebra section of the Mathematical Appendix. Vector Q is obtained as $\Gamma^{-1}F$, and the coefficients for the stability condition (5.55) are obtained, together with the G constant in the state-space representation.

The first data column gives the sample realization from the random number generator for a $N(0, 1)$ distribution, and the second column takes those figures as the realization for the innovation in the technology process, corrected by the desired standard deviation. Using the assumed first order autoregressive stochastic process and the sample realization for the innovation, a time series for the technology shock is obtained. Equation (5.54) is used to obtain a time series for the stock of capital, and the stability condition gives us the time series for consumption. To generate these time series, it is important to remember that in the previous section, tildes denote deviations in logged per capita variables with respect to their steady-state levels.

The way how initial conditions are chosen and the time conventions followed to generate the time series, are crucial to maintain the right model dynamics. The first entry for the stock of capital, associated to $t = 0$, is the stock of capital which will be available for production at time $t = 1$. In our standard notation, this is $\tilde{k}_1$, but the convention followed in the spreadsheet is that data are written at the time the corresponding decisions are being made. So, in the row for $t = 1$ we compute the values of decision variables $\tilde{k}_2, \hat{c}_1$, both as function of the states $\tilde{k}_1$ (which is in the $t = 0$ row), and $\hat{\theta}_1$, according to (5.55) and (5.54) and then, we produce the data for y_1, i_1. Output is obtained using the representation of the aggregate technology, and investment comes as the difference between disposable income and consumption. Finally, we compute tax revenues for each period. The reader should make sure to understand the way how these time relationships are entered into the spreadsheet. On top of the time series data we present graphs of the capital stock, consumption and investment, each of them compared with output. We display time graphs as well as scatter diagrams. We will produce simulations obtained under different parameterizations, and some results are summarized in the tables below.

Below the set of time series, we present sample statistics for the variables in the economy. Since they are calculated with a single realization, these numerical values must be understood as being random draws from the probability distribution for the corresponding population statistics. We compute sample means, standard deviations, coefficients of variation, and contemporaneous correlation with output as well as cross correlations with output at lags from -3 to 3, for the innovation in the technology process, the technology shock itself, consumption, the stock of capital, output, investment and tax revenues. The convention we follow is that for negative lags the variable under consideration is lagged, while output is lagged for positive lags. As a further summary of statistical properties, we estimate of each simulation a least-squares regression of per capita consumption on disposable income.

Since we start with the steady-state capital stock at time $t = 0$ and the solution is stable, the time series for all variables display fluctuations around their respective steady-state, so the sample means provide an estimate of steady state values, and that is the case across all simulations. Estimation errors may generally be larger in simulations producing more volatility, as a general consequence of the statistical problem of estimating a sample mean.

Volatility is a central characteristic of models intended to explain business cycle characteristics. The stock of capital is the variable with the highest sample standard deviation, but that does not mean that it is highly volatile, since each variable fluctuates around a different sample mean. In fact, coefficients of variation indicate that, as it is the case in most growth models designed to display cyclical fluctuations, it is investment the more volatile variable, while the remaining variables have more comparable coefficients of variation. Consumption is somewhat less volatile than output in all parameterizations, another robust empirical fact in most developed economies. Below the contemporaneous correlations with output, we show the output decomposition in consumption, investment and public expenditures (or tax revenues). Consumption amounts to about two thirds of output, as it is approximately the case in most developed economies.

Coefficients of variation for different parameterizations

σ	ρ	σ_ε	θ_t	c_t	y_t	i_t	k_t	g_t
S1 : 1.5	.90	.01	2.3%	2.8%	3.3%	8.7%	3.5%	3.0%
S2 : **0.5**	.90	.01	2.3%	3.1%	3.9%	13.4%	5.4%	3.4%
S3 : **5.0**	.90	.01	2.3%	2.7%	3.1%	7.0%	2.8%	2.9%
S4 : 1.5	.90	**.05**	12.0%	14.7%	17.2%	44.3%	18.4%	15.8%
S5 : 1.5	**.99**	.01	3.7%	4.9%	5.2%	8.5%	5.0%	5.1%
S6 : 1.5	.90	**.002**	0.5%	0.6%	0.7%	1.7%	0.7%	0.6%
S7 : 1.5	**.50**	**.10**	11.6%	9.7%	15.2%	69.7%	15.8%	11.9%

Relative to the first simulation, **S1**, simulation **S2** considers a less concave utility function, while maintaining the values of all other parameters. As expected from the discussion on the intertemporal elasticity of substitution of consumption in the previous chapter, this variable becomes more volatile for a more linear utility function, as it is the case with output. The increase in volatility in investment and the stock of capital is larger. The opposite happens in simulation **S3**, which increases the concavity of the utility function, with the consequence of less volatile variables. However, the decrease in volatility relative to the first simulation is minor. Decreasing concavity reduces the correlations with output, which increase when the utility function is more concave (except for capital stock). The next table shows correlations with output of the main variables in the economy.

Contemporaneous correlations with output

σ	ρ	σ_ε	c_t	y_t	i_t	k_t	g_t
S1 : 1.5	.90	.01	.969	1.00	.834	.886	.993
S2 : **0.5**	.90	.01	.924	1.00	.791	.918	.984
S3 : **5.0**	.90	.01	.981	1.00	.851	.870	.996
S4 : 1.5	.90	**.05**	.969	1.00	.840	888.	.993
S5 : 1.5	**.99**	.01	.991	1.00	.849	.934	.998
S6 : 1.5	.90	**.002**	.968	1.00	.833	.885	.993
S7 : 1.5	**.50**	**.10**	.838	1.00	.870	.770	.975

There are two ways how the technology shock may become more volatility: the more obvious is to increase the variance of the innovation, as we do in simulation **S4**. An alternative is to increase the coefficient of the autoregressive process, which increases the persistence as well as the variance of the technology shock, even if the variance of the innovation of that process stays the same, as we do in simulation **S5**. Their effects are quite different, as can be appreciated in the values of the sample statistics as well as in *Consumption* the graph that presents all consumption time series together. The graphs of the main variables, shown on the upper part of the spreadsheet also illustrate noticeable differences. Increasing the variance of the innovation increases volatility in a quite obvious manner, while increasing volatility through a greater persistence of the process does not produce what we would call a more volatile consumption process. The sample variance increases in this case because the increased persistence makes the consumption process not to cross its sample mean often, staying at one side of that value for a large number of periods. This is what increases the sample variance under such high persistence. Simulation **S4** shows an excessively high coefficient of variation for output relative to actual data, because of the persistent position at a given side of the mean value, with no mean crossing. The same observation applies to simulation **S7**, this time because of a too large innovation variance.

On the opposite side, reducing the innovation variance as in simulation **S6** stabilizes all series, not only in terms of a lower sample variance, but also in terms of the observed sample range. Under the smaller innovation variance, sample averages are more precise estimates of steady-state values. The graphs for the consumption, investment and output series for this simulation, shown in the spreadsheet on top of the data, clearly show variables smoothly oscillating around their central value. The reader will notice the evident differences between the graphs for this case and those for the previous simulations. Finally, we increase variance in simulation **S7** while reducing persistence. This is the opposite of what we did in simulation **S4**. We use a combination of parameters (standard deviation for the innovation and persistence parameter) such that the variance of the random productivity process itself (labelled *theta* in the spreadsheet) is the same in both cases. In spite of sharing the same innovation variance, the volatility of consumption and output as measured by the coefficients of variation is larger in simulation **S4**, while investment is more volatile in simulation **S7**. However, the type of high volatility that arises in simulation **S7** is very unlike that observed in actual time series data, so the parameterization of the stochastic process for the technology shock in this case would not seem appropriate.

Examination of the *Consumption* graph having the respective sample variances in mind will also show the reader the very distinct shapes that can generate relatively large variances, and also that identifying variance with volatility is not always justified. Simulations **S4** and **S5** have both large variance, with high coefficients of variation for consumption, for instance, and the time behavior of this variable is rather different between both cases.

Changes in σ_ε^2 have a smaller impact on contemporaneous correlations with output than changes in ρ.

The Stochastic-BK(2) spreadsheet contains results obtained with the same **S1** to **S7** parameterizations, but a different sample realization of the innovation in the productivity process. Comparing the estimated statistics in both spreadsheets, the reader will appreciate some numerical differences, due to the fact that a different sample realization for the productivity innovation is used. Numerical values for the parameters are the same. It is important to bear in mind that the numerical solutions in the Excel files we present are in most cases just a single sample realization for each parameterization. Actually, a large number of such realizations, 5,000 say, should be generated for each parameterization. That way, we can compute the value of each single statistic 5,000 times, with which we can compute the frequency distribution for that statistic. That will be a quite precise estimate of the unknown probability distribution for that statistic, and probability statements can then be obtained as desired. In particular, probability statements on the significance of each single statistic can readily be obtained. The *methods.m* MATLAB program provided with this text, and the library that is associated with it, produce precisely that large number of sample realizations for each variable in the model, from which frequency distributions for any statistic can be obtained.

5.4.3 Numerical Exercise: Computing Impulse Responses to a Technology Shock. Log-Linear Approximation

The *BK-impulse* spreadsheet in the *CK-solution_BK.xls* file presents impulse responses to a transitory, one period technology shock for the benchmark parameterization used in the previous numerical exercise, that illustrated the Blanchard–Kahn solution approach. Notice that we compute responses to an instantaneous, single period increase in the innovation ε_t to the stochastic process, rather than in the technology shock θ_t itself. A single period innovation ε_t will translate into a sequence of shocks in technology, because of the persistence of the stochastic process $\ln \theta_t = \rho \ln \theta_{t-1} + \varepsilon_t$. Precisely this autoregressive structure would seriously difficult to think of a single-period shock in θ_t, which is not the case considered here.

What we do is to assume that the innovation ε_t in the productivity process is equal to zero every period, with all variables at their deterministic steady-state values, until at some point in time, ε_t takes a positive value. To normalize the analysis, it is a standard practice to assume that value is one standard deviation, .01 according to our parameterization. After that, the innovation is again equal to zero forever. This impulse, a one-period shock, produces a time reaction in the technology shock θ_t extending to a large number of periods, until it gradually gets back to zero again. The same equations used to solve the model in the previous exercise are used to generate time series for consumption, investment and output taking the generated time series for the technology shock. A first way to compute impulse responses is by taking the difference between the value of a given variable at any point in time after the shock, and its value prior to the shock.[7] Output displays the largest instantaneous response, followed by consumption. The response of consumption is bigger after a few periods. The response of capital stock gradually builds up over time, as an accumulation of the single period responses of investment. Revenues are a linear combination of output and consumption, so their time shape combines those of the two variables.

---

[7] Later on we will introduce a different approach to compute impulse responses.

All responses converge to zero, as a reflection of the stability of the system: the effect of a purely transitory shock may be felt for a number of periods, depending on the persistence of the exogenous stochastic processes impinging on the economy, but they must be transitory. The fact that the responses converge all to zero means that the steady-state is unchanged by the one period technology innovation, as it should be expected. These are, however, unnormalized responses, and are not appropriate to discuss which is the variable that experiences the largest reaction to a technology shock. The reason is that a .05 response, say, may be small for output, and large for investment. To normalize responses, it is customary to put them in units of their respective standard deviations. This is very reasonable, since the standard deviation measures the average fluctuation experienced by a variable. However, standard deviations should not be computed on the process of responding to a shock, which is a transition process displaying the convergence to the new steady-state. Rather, we should estimate them from a numerical solution obtained under the same parameterization. This is the one used for simulation **S1** in the *Stochastic_BK* spreadsheet in *CK_solution_BK.xls*, from where we borrow the values of the sample standard deviations, although acknowledging that they have been estimated with a single realization of the numerical solution.[8] With this normalization, we see in the graph to the right a largest response by investment, of about 0.50 standard deviations, while the maximum responses by consumption and output are of 0.20 and 0.30 standard deviations. The difference is that the largest output reaction is immediate, which is not the case for consumption.

In the second panel, to the right, we compute step responses, i.e., the reaction of each variable to a permanent one-standard deviation increase in the innovation technology. Unnormalized responses are interesting now because they give us the size of permanent effects. What happens is that the permanent shock of one standard deviation, 0.01, in the technology innovation alters steady-state levels, in the amount shown in the spreadsheet and the graph: output increases by 0.23 units in the long-run (a 18.6% increase), consumption by 0.14 units (17.8%), investment by 0.03 units (a 23.7% increase) and revenues (and hence, government expenditures) by 0.06 units (18.2%). The sum of the long-run increments in the last three variables amounts to that in output. The steady-state stock of capital increases by 0.48 units (a 23.8% increase). Normalized responses tell us that these are large increments, of about 6 standard deviations for the stock of capital, output, consumption and revenues, and of about 3 standard deviations in investment. These responses may look large, but the permanent increase of 0.01 units in ε_t amounts to adding a constant to the process for $\ln\theta_t$. The assumed Cobb–Douglas technology: $y_t = A\theta_t k_t^\alpha$, can be written in logs: $\ln y_t = \ln A + \ln\theta_t + \alpha\ln k_t$, so the permanent increase in the productivity shock amounts to an 1% increase in the level of productivity, with A moving from 1.0 to 1.01. The *BK impulse response.m* program does the same exercise described in this section.

---

[8] Notice that if we change the value of any structural parameter, these standard deviations would have to be estimated again.

5.4.4 Numerical Exercise: Solving the Stochastic Representative Agent's Model with Taxes Through the Eigenvector and Eigenvalue Decomposition Approach. Linear Approximation

We use in this section the eigenvalue-eigenvector decomposition to solve the representative agent's problem with taxes, whose optimality conditions are $(5.49), (5.48)$. We leave as an exercise for the reader to check, following an argument similar to that in $(5.3.5)$ that the linear approximation to (5.49) is:

$$0 = (c_{t+1} - c_{ss}) - \frac{1}{\sigma} c_{ss} \frac{\beta}{1+n} (1 - \tau^y) A\alpha (\alpha - 1) \theta_{ss} k_{ss}^{\alpha-2} (k_{t+1} - k_{ss})$$

$$- (c_t - c_{ss}) - \frac{1}{\sigma} c_{ss} \frac{\beta}{1+n} (1 - \tau^y) A\alpha \theta_{ss} k_{ss}^{\alpha-1} (\ln \theta_{t+1} - \ln \theta_{ss}) + \frac{\beta}{1+n} \frac{c_{ss}}{\sigma} \xi_{t+1},$$

while that for (5.48) is:

$$0 = (k_{t+1} - k_{ss}) - \frac{1}{\beta} (k_t - k_{ss}) + \frac{1+\tau^c}{1+n} (c_t - c_{ss})$$

$$- \frac{1-\tau^y}{1+n} A k_{ss}^{\alpha} \theta_{ss} (\ln \theta_t - \ln \theta_{ss}).$$

We can represent the full system in matrix form,

$$A \begin{pmatrix} k_{t+1} - k_{ss} \\ c_{t+1} - c_{ss} \\ \ln \theta_{t+1} - \ln \theta_{ss} \end{pmatrix} = B \begin{pmatrix} k_t - k_{ss} \\ c_t - c_{ss} \\ \ln \theta_t - \ln \theta_{ss} \end{pmatrix} + \Phi \begin{pmatrix} \varepsilon_{t+1} \\ \xi_{t+1} \end{pmatrix},$$

with:

$$A = \begin{pmatrix} 1 & 0 & 0 \\ M & 1 & M\frac{k_{ss}}{\alpha-1} \\ 0 & 0 & 1 \end{pmatrix}; \quad B = \begin{pmatrix} \frac{1}{\beta} & -\frac{1+\tau^c}{1+n} & \frac{1-\tau^y}{1+n} A k_{ss}^{\alpha} \\ 0 & 1 & 0 \\ 0 & 0 & \rho \end{pmatrix};$$

$$\Phi = \begin{pmatrix} 0 & 0 \\ 0 & -\frac{\beta}{1+n} \frac{c_{ss}}{\sigma} \\ 1 & 0 \end{pmatrix},$$

and $M = -\frac{1}{\sigma} c_{ss} \frac{\beta}{1+n} (1 - \tau^y) A\alpha (\alpha - 1) \theta_{ss} k_{ss}^{\alpha-2}$.

We have,

$$A^{-1} = \begin{pmatrix} 1 & 0 & 0 \\ -M & 1 & -M\frac{k_{ss}}{\alpha-1} \\ 0 & 0 & 1 \end{pmatrix};$$

$$A^{-1}B = \begin{pmatrix} \frac{1}{\beta} & -\frac{1+\tau^c}{1+n} & \frac{1-\tau^y}{1+n}Ak_{ss}^\alpha \\ -M\frac{1}{\beta} & \frac{1+\tau^c}{1+n}M+1 & -M\left(\frac{1-\tau^y}{1+n}Ak_{ss}^\alpha + \rho\frac{k_{ss}}{\alpha-1}\right) \\ 0 & 0 & \rho \end{pmatrix};$$

$$A^{-1}\Phi = \begin{pmatrix} 0 & 0 \\ -M\frac{k_{ss}}{\alpha-1} & -\frac{\beta}{1+n}\frac{c_{ss}}{\sigma} \\ 1 & 0 \end{pmatrix},$$

with a transition matrix,

$$\begin{pmatrix} \tilde{k}_{t+1} \\ \tilde{c}_{t+1} \\ \ln\tilde{\theta}_{t+1} \end{pmatrix} = \begin{pmatrix} \frac{1}{\beta} & -\frac{1+\tau^c}{1+n} & \frac{1-\tau^y}{1+n}Ak_{ss}^\alpha \\ -M\frac{1}{\beta} & \frac{1+\tau^c}{1+n}M+1 & -M\hat{k} \\ 0 & 0 & \rho \end{pmatrix} \begin{pmatrix} \tilde{k}_t \\ \tilde{c}_t \\ \ln\tilde{\theta}_t \end{pmatrix}$$

$$+ \begin{pmatrix} 0 & 0 \\ -M\frac{k_{ss}}{\alpha-1} & -\frac{\beta}{1+n}\frac{c_{ss}}{\sigma} \\ 1 & 0 \end{pmatrix} \begin{pmatrix} \varepsilon_{t+1} \\ \xi_{t+1} \end{pmatrix},$$

where $\tilde{k}_t \equiv k_t - k_{ss}$, $\tilde{c}_t \equiv c_t - c_{ss}$, $\ln\tilde{\theta}_t \equiv \ln\theta_t - \ln\theta_{ss}$, $\hat{k} \equiv \left(\frac{1-\tau^y}{1+n}Ak_{ss}^\alpha + \rho\frac{k_{ss}}{\alpha-1}\right)$.
We obtain the spectral representation for the autoregressive coefficient matrix,

$$\begin{pmatrix} \frac{1}{\beta} & -\frac{1+\tau^c}{1+n} & \frac{1-\tau^y}{1+n}Ak_{ss}^\alpha \\ -M\frac{1}{\beta} & \frac{1+\tau^c}{1+n}M+1 & -M\left(\frac{1-\tau^y}{1+n}Ak_{ss}^\alpha + \rho\frac{k_{ss}}{\alpha-1}\right) \\ 0 & 0 & \rho \end{pmatrix} = \Gamma\Lambda\Gamma^{-1},$$

and we follow the procedure described in 5.3.5 to estimate the stability condition, which will allow us to obtain the level of consumption compatible each period with the predetermined stock of capital and the realization of the productivity shock.

A numerical solution to this model following the procedure above is described in *CK_stochastic_taxes.xls*. The benchmark parameterization used is $A = 1$, $\beta = 0.90$, $\alpha = 0.33$, $n = 0$, $\delta = 0.07$, $\sigma = 1.50$, $\rho = 0.90$, $\sigma_\varepsilon = 0.001$, and tax rates: $\tau_c = 20.0\%, \tau_y = 15.0\%$. Under this parameterization, steady state levels are $k_{ss} = 1.921$, $c_{ss} = 0.767$, $i_{ss} = 0.134$, $y_{ss} = 1.240$. Under the benchmark parameterization, the stability condition is estimated, $c_t = c_{ss} + 0.2868(k_t - k_{ss}) + 0.3087\ln\theta_t$, but the numerical values of the coefficients in this condition change with the parameterization. Consumption and the stock of capital must be positively related along this condition, as can be seen in the stability graph we discussed in the previous chapter. They either increase or decrease simultaneously as they approach their steady-state values. The stable manifold lies along the first and third quadrants. If the economy is in the first one, $k_t - k_{ss}$ and $c_t - c_{ss}$ will both be positive, and we move towards steady-state by simultaneously reducing their positive values to zero. If the economy falls in the third quadrant, both differences will then be negative, and we move towards steady-state by simultaneously reducing the absolute values of those differences.

We start by generating the time series for the technology shock, which does not need of any other information, reflecting its exogenous nature. Then, starting from an initial condition for the capital stock, which we take to be that the initial capital stock is at its steady-state level, $k_0 = k_{ss}$, the stability condition is used to choose initial consumption so as to place the economy on the stable manifold or, at least, on the linear approximation to it. That implies a choice for investment (output minus consumption minus public expenditures) and hence, a given level for the stock of capital at the end of the period, which is obtain from the single period budget constraint. By using the budget constraint, we keep some of the nonlinear structure of the original model, thereby obtaining a better numerical approximation.

Below the set of time series, we present sample statistics for the variables in the economy. Since they are calculated with a single realization, these numerical values must be understood as being random draws from the probability distribution for the corresponding population statistics. The variables considered are the innovation in the technology process, the technology shock itself, consumption, the stock of capital, output, investment and tax revenues, for which we compute sample means, standard deviations, coefficients of variation, and contemporaneous as well as cross correlations with output at lags from -2 to $+2$. The convention we follow is that for negative lags the variable under consideration is lagged, while output is lagged for positive lags.

We also compute two other parameterizations, considering a higher tax on consumption $\tau_c = 30\%$ while maintaining the income tax at $\tau_y = 15\%$, and a higher tax on income $\tau_y = 20\%$ with the original consumption tax of $\tau_c = 20\%$. Simulations S1 and S3 share the consumption tax. The capital stock time series is the same in simulations S1 and S2, which share the same income tax. Obviously, the same is the case for the output time series. Consumption is proportionally lower in S2 because of the higher consumption tax. However, consumption expenditures, i.e., the aggregate of real consumption and the consumption tax, are the same in S1 and S2. Consequently, the investment time series is also the same in both simulations. Increasing the income tax in S3 introduces some distortions. The *Output, Consumption*, and *Investment* graphs display the time series obtained for these variables in the three simulations.

Coefficients of variation, cross-correlations with output and the decomposition of output in private consumption, investment and public investment, are invariant to changes in the consumption tax. On the other hand, the increase in the income tax lowers steady-state levels of the stock of capital, output and consumption with minor changes in volatility, except for the lower volatility of investment. A larger proportion of output goes now into investment and public expenditures, while a lower proportion is devoted to consumption. Cross-correlations with output increase slightly.

We also present in the spreadsheet rationality tests for the expectations error, as explained when solving the model without taxes by this solution method. With a sample size of $T = 538$, the standard deviation for each of the correlations between the expectations error and variables in the information set at time t, or autocorrelations can be approximated by $1/\sqrt{T} = .043$, so none of the correlations shown in the table are statistically significant.

Contemporaneous correlations between the rational
expectation error and variables in the information set

c_t	y_t	i_t	k_t	g_t	g_t/y_t
.012	.013	.019	.006	.014	$-.018$

The second test examines the expectations error autocorrelation function, which should not be significant at any lag, since that would suggest somewhat systematic patterns in the errors, against the assumption of an efficient use of the available information. Since the sample realization for the innovation in the productivity shock is the same in the three simulations, the expectations errors for any two of the three simulations have correlation equal to one. Hence, we present the sample autocorrelation function for just one of the simulations. The fourth lag in the sample autocorrelation functions in the table is the only one violating this condition. It would be hard to explain why this might arise, but there not being any significance in any other lag, we do not take this as a serious evidence against rationality.

Sample autocorrelation function for the rational
expectations error

Lag	0	1	2	3	4	5	6
S1	1.0	.009	$-.031$	$-.052$	.114	$-.029$	$-.022$

The analysis in *CK_stochastic_taxes_structural_parameters.xls* uses as benchmark parameterization $A = 1$, $\beta = 0.90$, $\alpha = 0.33$, $n = 0$, $\delta = 0.07$, $\sigma_\varepsilon = 0.001$. Simulation 1.1 uses $\sigma = 1.50$, $\rho = 0.90$, simulation 2.1 uses $\sigma = 1.50$, $\rho = 0.99$, and the last two simulations use $\sigma = 5.0$ with $\rho = 0.90$ and $\rho = 0.99$. The sample realization for the innovation in the productivity shock is the same as that in the previous analysis, which helps producing an autocorrelation function for the expectations error very similar to the one in the table above.

Contemporaneous correlations between the rational
expectation error and variables in the information set

	c_t	y_t	i_t	k_t	g_t	g_t/y_t
S1.1	.012	.014	.015	.010	.014	$-.012$
S2.1	$-.019$	$-.019$	$-.017$	$-.019$	$-.019$	.005
S3.1	.009	.012	.017	.001	.011	$-.019$
S4.1	.042	.042	.040	.045	.042	$-.027$

The contemporaneous correlations between the expectations error and variables known at time t are not significant for this sample realization, although a more complete analysis using a large number of realizations should be done.

5.5 Nonlinear Numerical Solution Methods

Functional equations are a well known instrument in dynamic analysis in Economics. Bellman's equation is an example of a functional fixed-point equation. Euler's equation, that arises as an optimality condition in the control problems we are discussing in this book is another example of a functional equation. Functional equations are hard to solve because the unknown is not a vector in $\mathbb{R}^n$, but a function whose domain contains an infinite number of points. In general, functional equations lack closed solutions, and cannot be solved exactly.

Up to this point, we have discussed how to solve these functional equations through linear methods. In this section, we will describe and analyze briefly two nonlinear numerical solution methods: (a) the parameterized expectations approach by den Haan and Marcet [28], Marcet and Lorenzani [63], and (b) a class of solution methods known as Weighted Residual Methods or Projection Methods, to which we will find accurate approximate solutions. A good textbook where these methods can be studied in more detail is Judd [48]. Books discussing nonlinear and other methods are Marimon and Scott [64], Miranda and Fackler [68], Adda and Cooper [1], Ljunqvist and Sargent [56], Heer and Mausoner [41], Canova [16], or DeJong and Dave [27].

5.5.1 *Parameterized Expectations*

The parameterized expectations method was introduced in den Haan and Marcet [28]. In this solution method, each conditional expectation in the optimality conditions is represented by an exponential polynomial function of the state variables. The parameters in these polynomial representations are estimated using time series data generated from an initial parameter choice, as explained below.

The optimality condition involving conditional expectations in the basic growth model is,

$$c_t^{-\sigma} = \beta \, E_t \left[c_{t+1}^{-\sigma} \left(\alpha \theta_{t+1} k_{t+1}^{\alpha-1} + 1 - \delta \right) \right], \qquad (5.56)$$

and we parameterize that conditional expectation as a polynomial function of the two states of the economy,

$$E_t \left[c_{t+1}^{-\sigma} \left(\alpha \theta_{t+1} k_{t+1}^{\alpha-1} + 1 - \delta \right) \right] = \Psi(k_t, \theta_t, a) = a_1 k_t^{a_2} \theta_t^{a_3}, \qquad (5.57)$$

where a denotes the parameter vector $a = (a_1, a_2, a_3)$. The steady state of this model has been calculated previously: (5.15)–(5.16).

The solution method starts by giving values to σ_ε and ρ and obtaining a time series of data for the innovation in the productivity process. We also need to choose initial values a_1^0, a_2^0, a_3^0 to the a_1, a_2, a_3-parameters. This solution approach requires a numerical convergence procedure, which is not always well behaved, so that the choice of starting parameter values is crucial.

It is standard to use as initial conditions a_1^0, a_2^0, a_3^0 the values of these parameters under full depreciation, $\delta = 1$, and logarithmic utility, $\sigma = 1$. As shown in Sect. 5.2.1, the stochastic model has then a closed form analytical solution, given by (5.5). Under these assumptions, we get, from (5.57) and (5.56):

$$\beta^{-1} c_t^{-1} = a_1 k_t^{a_2} \theta_t^{a_3},$$

and using (5.5):

$$\frac{1}{\beta (1 - \alpha\beta) \theta_t k_t^{\alpha}} = a_1 k_t^{a_2} \theta_t^{a_3},$$

from where we obtain:

$$a_1 = \frac{1}{\beta (1 - \alpha\beta)},$$
$$a_2 = -\alpha,$$
$$a_3 = -1.$$

To estimate the parameters in $\Psi(.)$ when depreciation is not complete and/or utility is not logarithmic, a gradual procedure needs to be implemented. First, only the $\delta = 1$ assumption is relaxed slightly, making $\delta = .90$, say, and using the previous values as initial conditions: $a_1^0 = \frac{1}{\beta(1-\alpha\beta)}$, $a_2^0 = -\alpha, a_3^0 = -1$. Then, we solve the non-linear estimation problem,[9]

$$S\left(a^0\right) = \underset{a^0}{Arg\,min}\; E\left[\left(c_{t+1}\left(a^0\right)\right)^{-\sigma} \left(\frac{\alpha\theta_{t+1}\left(k_{t+1}\left(a^0\right)\right)^{\alpha-1} + 1 - \delta}{a_1 k_t\left(a^0\right)^{a_2}\theta_t^{a_3}} \right) - 1 \right]^2,$$
(5.58)

to find the a^0-vector that minimizes the mean square of adjustment errors. In this expression we have made explicit the dependence of the capital stock and consumption series on the parameter values being used in the expectations polynomial. Once we have an a_0-vector, the conditional expectation disappears from the model, and the variables can be propagated over time using the law of motion for k_t (the global constraint of resources), and the law of motion for θ_t together with the relationship,

$$c_t^{-\sigma} = \beta\Psi\left(k_t, \theta_t, a\right) = \beta a_1 k_t \left(a^0\right)^{a_2} \theta_t^{a_3}.$$
(5.59)

This is how it works: starting from $\{k_0, \theta_0\}$, (5.59) gives us c_0, and the law of motion for capital, i.e., the global constraint of resources, gives us k_1 which, taken to (5.59) together with θ_1, allows us to obtain c_1 and k_2, and so on. Hence, the initial parameter values a^0 allow us to produce time series consumption and physical capital. Those time series will not satisfy (5.56) exactly, and the point is to iterate on vector a so as to minimize the sample average of those errors, as

---

[9] Initially, the σ parameter may be set up to 1, but that might change in subsequent iterations, as explained below.

indicated at (5.58). Being the difference between the value of the nonlinear function whose conditional expectation appears in (5.56) and the numerical value of the polynomial representing the conditional expectation itself, these can be interpreted as expectations errors. In fact, however, the differences include expectations errors plus the error in specifying the representation for the conditional expectation.

The nonlinear estimation procedure can be implemented through a Gauss–Newton algorithm. To that end, we need to estimate a linear regression from the initial *residuals* on the components of the gradient of the function to be fitted, $\Psi(k_t, \theta_t, a)$. The estimated coefficients in that regression are the corrections to introduce on the initial estimates of $a = (a_1, a_2, a_3)$, to obtain new values, and the procedure is iterated until convergence.

In our model the gradient of $\Psi(k_t, \theta_t, a)$ is,

$$\frac{\partial \Psi}{\partial a} = \begin{pmatrix} \frac{\partial \Psi}{\partial a_1} \\ \frac{\partial \Psi}{\partial a_2} \\ \frac{\partial \Psi}{\partial a_3} \end{pmatrix}_{a^0 = (a_1^0, a_2^0, a_3^0)} = \begin{pmatrix} k_t^{a_2^0} \theta_t^{a_3^0} \\ a_1^0 k_t^{a_2^0} \theta_t^{a_3^0} \ln k_t \\ a_1^0 k_t^{a_2^0} \theta_t^{a_3^0} \ln \theta_t \end{pmatrix}.$$

Each of these elements is a time series that can be evaluated, as a function of the initial estimations. The initial *residuals* are defined as,

$$\hat{u}_t^0 = c_{t+1}^{-\sigma} \left(\alpha \theta_{t+1} k_{t+1}^{\alpha-1} + 1 - \delta \right) - c_t^{-\sigma}$$
$$= c_t^{-\sigma} \left(\theta_t \alpha k_t^{\alpha-1} + 1 - \delta \right) - \Psi(k_{t-1}, \theta_{t-1}, a^0),$$

and we estimate the regression,

$$\hat{u}_t^0 = \left(\frac{\partial \Psi}{\partial a} |_{a^0} \right)' b + v_t,$$

where b is a 3×1-vector, to then introduce the correction,

$$a^{i+1} = a^i + \hat{b}, \tag{5.60}$$

and the process starts again until the convergence criteria are fulfilled. Den Haan and Marcet [28] suggest working with a different sequence, $\tilde{a}$, which is obtained using the correction scheme,

$$\tilde{a}^{i+1} = \lambda a^i + (1 - \lambda) a^{i+1},$$

for some $0 < \lambda < 1$ chosen beforehand, where a^{i+1} is first obtained from (5.60).

Once vector a^0 has been found, we allow for a slight variation in σ from its initial value $\sigma = 1$ in the direction of the desired value of σ, using as initial conditions in each step the a^0-vector obtained for the previous value of σ. The process is repeated several times until we reach the a^0-vector associated to the desired value of σ.

To estimate this model, an alternative procedure consists on using as initial conditions the numerical a^0-vectors reported by Den Haan and Marcet [28] for several depreciation rates, and start changing values for the structural parameters, one at a time, as desired. The MATLAB routines provided with this book estimate the expectations polynomial and solve the model allowing for departures from the $\sigma = 1$ value used by Den Haan and Marcet for the risk aversion parameter. That possibility has not been considered in this section either. It also allows for a consumption and an income tax, not considered in their paper. The method is implemented in Matlab programs *marcet.m, marcet1.m, marcet2.m. Marcet.m* estimates the parameters in the exponential polynomial used to approximate the conditional expectation in the model, *marcet1.m* solves the planer's problem using the *fminunc.m* MATLAB minimization routine, while *marcet2.m* does the same using a Gauss–Newton algorithm.

Finally, we remind the reader that *methods.m* is a main MATLAB program solving the planner's problem under consumption and income taxes by different solution methods: the linear-quadratic approximation, Uhlig's undetermined coefficients method, Blanchard–Kahn's method, the eigenvalue-eigenvector decomposition implemented on either the linear or the log-linear approximation to the model, and the parameterized expectations method.

5.5.2 Projection Methods

In this section we describe solution methods based on projections that use interpolation techniques. A good reference for these methods is McGrattan [67]. After a general description of these methods, we will particularize them to the solution of deterministic and stochastic versions of the optimal Cass–Koopmans growth model.

The goal of this type of problems is to find a function $C : \mathbb{R}^m \longrightarrow \mathbb{R}^n$ satisfying a functional equation $F(C) = 0$, where $F : D_1 \longrightarrow D_2$ with D_1 and D_2 being function spaces. In our case, C is a vector of decision or control variables which are functions of the state variables, and this vector must satisfy the set of first order conditions for the optimization problem we consider. In the case of the Cass–Koopmans model, C includes the consumption decision, which is a function of the two state variables in the economy, the stock of capital K and the structural shock θ. The solution will therefore be a function: $C(K, \theta) : \mathbb{R}^2 \longrightarrow \mathbb{R}$, satisfying the Euler equation for the problem under the assumption of rational expectations.

Since finding function C is generally impossible, our goal is to find an approximation $C^d(x; \mu)$ defined on $x \in \Omega$, with x being the vector of state variables, that depends on a finite dimensional parameter vector $\mu = (\mu_1, \mu_2, ..., \mu_d)'$. The method of weighted residuals assumes that C^d is a finite linear combination of a family of previously chosen *basis functions* $\Psi_i(x)$:

$$C^d(x; \mu) = \Psi_0(x) + \sum_{i=1}^{d} \mu_i \Psi_i(x) \qquad (5.61)$$

Families of basis functions are usually quite simple:

- Monomials: $\Psi_0(x) = 1, \Psi_i(x) = x^i, i = 1, 2, ..., d$
- A family of orthogonal polynomials.[10] An example is the family of Chebychev polynomials:

$$\Psi_0(x) = 1, \Psi_1(x) = x, \ \Psi_i(x) = 2x\Psi_{i-1}(x) - \Psi_{i-2}(x), i = 2, 3, ..., d$$

These polynomials are defined on the interval $[-1,1]$. If the domain of a state variable x is [a,b], the transformation $z = 2\frac{x-a}{b-a} - 1$ is applied before computing Chebychev polynomials.[11]

These polynomials are more useful than monomials for a large choice of the number of basis functions, d. The reason is that for large d, it is hard to distinguish between x^d and x^{d+1}, which implies that the approximation provided by the $C^d(x;\mu)$ function will barely improve with an additional basis function of type x^{d+1}. However, this is not the case with orthogonal polynomials since, precisely because of their orthogonality, they can be easily distinguished from each other.

- Finite element methods, that use piecewise linear functions, also called polynomial splines:

$$\Psi_i(x) = \frac{x - x_{i-1}}{x_i - x_{i-1}} \text{ for } x \in [x_{i-1}, x_i] \qquad (5.62)$$

$$= \frac{x_{i+1} - x}{x_{i+1} - x_i} \text{ for } x \in [x_i, x_{i+1}]$$

$$= 0 \text{ otherwise}$$

for a pre-specified grid of x_i-points on the range of sample values of variable x.

Let us now define *residual equation*, $R(x;\mu)$ defined by the functional equation evaluated at the approximate solution $C^d(x;\mu)$:

$$R(x;\mu) = F\left(C^d(x;\mu)\right) \qquad (5.63)$$

---

[10] Let $\Psi_i(x), \Psi_j(x)$ be two polynomials from a same family of basis functions. The two polynomials are said to be orthogonal to each other if there is a weighting function $W(x)$ such that:

$$\int_a^b W(x)\Psi_i(x)\Psi_j(x)dx = 0, \forall i \neq j.$$

A family of polynomials is said to be orthogonal if any two polynomials in the family are orthogonal to each other. The weighting function that makes Chebychev polynomials orthogonal to each other, is: $W(x) = \frac{1}{\sqrt{1-x^2}}$.

[11] Stable solutions will always have control and state variables moving in a bounded space. The [a,b] interval can be chosen allowing for relatively wide fluctuations around steady-state. Violation of that assumed range by the numerical solution may point out to potential instability problems. Otherwise, the range can be widened and the solution algorithm implemented again.

The problem is to choose the vector μ so that the residual equation $R(x;\mu)$ is as close to zero as possible, in the sense of a weighted integral:

$$\int_\Omega \phi_i(x)R(x;\mu)dx = 0, \; i = 1,2,...,d \tag{5.64}$$

with $\phi_i(x)$ being the *weight functions*. These functions can take different forms, and the procedure followed to find the $\mu_1,...,\mu_d$ coefficients will be different in each case. According to the choice of weight functions, we will have the following methods:

1. *Least squares method*, defined by $\phi_i(x) = \frac{\partial R(x;\mu)}{\partial \mu_i}$. This set of weights can be interpreted as first order conditions to the problem:

$$\underset{\mu}{Min} \int_\Omega [R(x;\mu)]^2 dx$$

2. *Collocation method*, defined by $\phi_i(x) = \delta(x - x_i)$, with δ being *Dirac delta function*. This set of weighting functions makes the residual function to be zero at d points: $x_1, x_2, ..., x_d$, called *collocation points*:

$$R(x_i;\mu) = 0, \; i = 1,2,..,d$$

3. *Galerkin method*, defined by $\phi_i(x) = \Psi_i(x)$. This method forces the residual function to be orthogonal to each basis function.

5.5.2.1 Solving the Deterministic Cass–Koopmans Optimal Growth Model

The Ramsey–Cass–Kopmans optimal growth model was studied in Chap. 2, where we saw that the model can be summarized in the optimization problem:

$$\underset{\{c_t,k_{t+1}\}}{Max} \sum_{t=0}^{\infty} \beta^t \frac{c_t^{1-\sigma} - 1}{1-\sigma}, \; \sigma > 0$$

subject to:

$$(1+n)k_{t+1} - (1-\delta)k_t + c_t = Ak_t^\alpha, \; \alpha, \delta \in (0,1), \; A > 0, n \geq 0,$$

given k_0.

The Euler condition for this problem is:

$$\beta \frac{[c(k_t)]^\sigma \left\{ \alpha A \left[\frac{1}{1+n}(Ak_t^\alpha - (1-\delta)k_t - c(k_t)) \right]^{\alpha-1} + (1-\delta) \right\}}{\left[c\left(\frac{1}{1+n}(Ak_t^\alpha - (1-\delta)k_t - c(k_t)) \right) \right]^\sigma} - 1 = 0. \tag{5.65}$$

Our goal is to find the $c(k_t)$ function satisfying the functional equation (5.65). Since that is not possible, we will find the vector of coefficients μ such that the function $C^d(k_t;\mu)$ approximately satisfies that functional equation.

To that end, we are going to use the *Collocation method*.

- **Step1:** Implementation of the algorithm starts by computing the values x_i of the state variable that we want to use to define the Dirac delta functions. These are the points at which the Collocation method will force the Residual functional to be exactly zero, providing us then with the values of the μ-coefficients. We first choose the relevant range of values for the state variable k, on which we want to approximate the function $C^d(k_t;\mu)$. Let that interval be $k \in [k_{min}, k_{max}]$, where $k_{min} = k_{ss}(1-\lambda), k_{max} = k_{ss}(1+\lambda)$, where k_{ss} is the steady-state level of k and $\lambda \in (0,1)$. The value chosen for λ determines the range on which we approximate the decision rule. We want to cover a wide range, but the algorithm is based on an approximation around steady-state, which suggests choosing a moderate value of λ. We then choose the x_i points in this interval to be the *Chebychev nodes*, which are defined as:

$$k_i = \frac{k_{max} + k_{min}}{2} + \frac{k_{max} - k_{min}}{2} \cos\left(\frac{d-i+0.5}{d}\pi\right), \ i = 1,2,...,d$$

where we compute a number of nodes equal to d, the highest order of the polynomial function we plan to use in the $C^d(k_t;\mu)$ approximation. Chebychev nodes are not equally spaced: they are closer to each other at both ends of the interval, and more disperse[12] towards the center of the interval.[13]

- **Step 2:** We choose as basis functions Chebychev[14] polynomials $\Psi_{i-1}(.)$, so that:

$$C^d(k;\mu) = \sum_{i=1}^{d} \mu_i \Psi_{i-1}\left(\hat{k}\right) \tag{5.66}$$

where the original state variable, k, has been transformed so that $\hat{k} = 2\frac{k-k_{min}}{k_{max}-k_{min}} - 1$ takes values in $[-1,1]$.

- **Step 3:** We evaluate the residual functional (5.65) at each Chebychev node:

$$R(k_i;\mu) = \frac{\beta \left[C^d(k_i;\mu)\right]^\sigma \left[\alpha A (k_i')^{\alpha-1} + (1-\delta)\right]}{\left[C^d(k_i';\mu)\right]^\sigma} - 1,$$

---

[12] Let us suppose that $k_{min} = 0$ and $k_{max} = 100$, and that we choose $d = 10$. Chebychev nodes are then: 0.62, 5.45, 14.65, 27.30, 42.18, 57.82, 72.70, 85.35, 94.55 and 99.38.

[13] According to Rivlin's theorem, *'Chebychev node polynomial interpolants are very nearly optimal polynomial approximants'*.

[14] Using Chebychev nodes and Chebychev polynomials is just one among the many alternative choices available. Chebychev nodes have been shown to provide a superior approximation than alternatives like equally-spaced nodes. Similarly, to compute the approximated decision rule, we could use monomials, splines or a family of orthogonal polynomials other than Chebychev polynomials.

$$i = 1, 2, ..., d$$

$$\text{where } k'_i = \frac{1}{1+n} \left(Ak_i^\alpha - (1 - \delta)k_i - C^d(k_i; \mu) \right).$$

This way, we have d equations in d unknowns: $\mu_1, \mu_2, ..., \mu_d$. We have reduced the problem of finding a function $C^d(k_i; \mu)$, to the problem of finding a zero to this nonlinear system of d equations and d unknowns.

- **Step 4:** Once we have the values of the μ-coefficients, we can compute the approximation to the policy function: $c = C^d(k; \mu)$ and hence the value of the Residual functional over the whole range of values of the state variable k. By construction, the functional will be zero on Chebychev nodes, but not elsewhere. The number of basis functions (Chebychev polynomials) used to construct $C^d(k; \mu)$ is increased if a chosen tolerance level, like 10^{-5}, is violated at some point over the range of k, and the algorithm is then implemented again. To perform this exercise, a relatively fine grid of equally spaced values of k is used. Once the $C^d(k; \mu)$ functional provides us with a good enough approximation for some order d, we can represent the decision rule as a curve in the (c, k)-plane.

  We know from Chapter 4 that when $n = 0, \delta = 1, \sigma = 1$, there is an analytical solution to the optimization problem which has the form: $c = (1 - \alpha\beta)Ak^\alpha$. Therefore, we can compare the goodness of fit of the C^d-function by comparing the exact to the approximate solution. In general, the optimization problem will not have an exact solution, but the goodness of fit of the approximation can still be evaluated by computing the magnitude of the residual equation at points in the $[k_{max}, k_{min}]$-interval. Under the collocation approach, the residual equation will be exactly zero at the interpolation nodes, but it will not be equal to zero, in general, at any other point of the interval above.

- **Step 5:** Simulation: (a) Given an initial value for the stock of capital k_0, we compute $c_0 = C^d(k_0; \mu)$, (b) Given $\{c_0, k_0\}$ and using the constraint of resources, we obtain: $k_1 = \frac{1}{1+n} \left[Ak_0^\alpha + (1 - \delta)k_0 - c_0 \right]$, (c) Given k_1, we compute $c_1 = C^d(k_1; \mu)$, and repeat the procedure.

5.5.2.2 The Stochastic Cass–Koopmans Optimal Growth Model

In this section we illustrate the application of projection methods to the stochastic optimal growth model. As an alternative to the collocation method used to approximate the decision rule in the deterministic version of the model, we will use Galerkin's method to approximate the decision function in the stochastic version of the model.

The stochastic optimal growth model can be summarized in the optimization problem:

$$\underset{\{c_t, k_{t+1}\}}{Max} E_0 \sum_{t=0}^{\infty} \beta^t \frac{c_t^{1-\sigma} - 1}{1 - \sigma}, \quad \sigma > 0$$

subject to:

$$(1+n)k_{t+1} - (1-\delta)k_t + c_t = A\theta_t k_t^\alpha, \ \alpha \in (0,1), \delta \in [0,1], \ A > 0, n \geq 0$$
$$\ln\theta_t = \rho \ln\theta_{t-1} + \varepsilon_t, \ |\rho| < 1, \varepsilon_t \underset{iid}{\sim} N(0,\sigma_\varepsilon^2)$$

given k_0.

The Euler condition for this problem is:

$$\beta E_t \left\{ \frac{[c(k_t,\theta_t)]^\sigma \left\{ \alpha A(k_{t+1})^{\alpha-1}\theta_{t+1} + (1-\delta) \right\}}{[c(k_{t+1},\theta_{t+1})]^\sigma} \right\} - 1 = 0 \qquad (5.67)$$

where $k_{t+1} = \frac{1}{1+n}(\theta_t A k_t^\alpha - (1-\delta)k_t - c(k_t,\theta_t))$, $\theta_{t+1} = \exp(\rho\ln\theta_t + \varepsilon_{t+1})$, and we need to find a function $c(k_t,\theta_t)$ satisfying the functional equation (5.67). That is, we must find the vector of coefficients μ such that the approximating function $C^d(k_t,\theta_t;\mu)$ makes (5.67) to be as close to zero as possible.

Since ε follows a Normal distribution, θ can take any value between 0 and ∞, so that it does not have a compact support. If we transform θ into $z = \tanh(\ln\theta)$, this new z variable falls in the interval $[-1,1]$. Notice that the hyperbolic tangent function (tanh) can also be expressed:

$$z = \tanh(\ln\theta) = \frac{e^{\ln\theta} - e^{-\ln\theta}}{e^{\ln\theta} + e^{-\ln\theta}} = \frac{\theta^2 - 1}{\theta^2 + 1}$$

which implies: $\theta = \sqrt{\frac{1+z}{1-z}}$. With this transformation, we can write the approximating function as:

$$C^d(k,z;\mu) = \sum_{i=1}^{d} \mu_i \Psi_i(k,z).$$

On the other hand, the autoregressive process for the structural shock can be written:

$$z_t = \tanh\left(\rho \tanh^{-1}(z_{t-1}) + \sqrt{2}\sigma_\varepsilon \upsilon_t\right)$$

where $\upsilon_t = \frac{\varepsilon_t}{\sqrt{2}\sigma_\varepsilon}$, $E(\upsilon_t) = 0$, $Var(\upsilon_t) = 1/2$, and $\tanh^{-1}(.)$ is the hyperbolic arc tangent function. If we denote by J the Jacobian of the transformation of ε_t into υ_t, the density function for υ is obtained: $g(\upsilon) = \frac{1}{|J|}f(\varepsilon) = \frac{1}{1/\sqrt{2}\sigma_\varepsilon} \frac{1}{\sqrt{2}\sqrt{\pi}\sigma_\varepsilon} e^{-\frac{\varepsilon^2}{2\sigma_\varepsilon^2}} = \frac{1}{\sqrt{\pi}}e^{-\upsilon^2}$. The interest of this transformation becomes evident below.

Solving this stochastic problem requires us to face two additional difficulties, as compared with the deterministic problem:

1. We have additional state variables in the form of exogenous random variables, and the set of basis functions would in principle be made up by the products of each element in the set of basis functions for k: $[\Psi_0(k), \Psi_1(k), ..., \Psi_{d_k}(k)]$ by all the elements in the set of basis functions for z: $[\Psi_0(z), \Psi_1(z), ..., \Psi_{d_z}(z)]$. But the

implied number of elements grows very quickly with the orders d_k, d_z, and would the number of equations to be solved for the μ-coefficients.

To maintain the problem tractable, we use the so-called *set of complete polynomials*, instead of all the products of basis functions for k and z. For instance, if we choose as basis functions the monomials $\{k^i\}_{i=0}^{d_k}$ and $\{z^j\}_{j=0}^{d_z}$, the complete set of basis functions that we could use in the case $d_k = d_z = 2$ would be $\{1, k, z, k^2, z^2, zk\}$ instead of $\{1, k, z, k^2, z^2, zk, z^2k, zk^2, z^2k^2\}$, with 6 coefficients, less than the 9 polynomials we would obtain through all cross products. If $d_k = d_z = 3$, we would need to compute 10 coefficients, rather than 16, and so on. The same reduction in dimensionality would be achieved with any other choice of basis functions.

2. The second difficulty comes from the need to evaluate a conditional expectation. Given the $N(0, 1/2^2)$ distribution for υ, such expectation can be written as:

$$\frac{1}{\sqrt{\pi}} \int_{-\infty}^{\infty} \frac{\left[C^d(k, z; \mu)\right]^{\sigma}}{\left[C^d(k', z'; \mu)\right]^{\sigma}} \left(\alpha A (k')^{\alpha-1} \sqrt{\frac{1+z'}{1-z'}} + (1-\delta)\right) e^{-\upsilon^2} d\upsilon$$

where:

$$k' = \frac{1}{1+n} \left[Ak^a \sqrt{\frac{1+z}{1-z}} + (1-\delta) - C^d(k, z; \mu)\right], \text{ and}$$

$$z' = \tanh\left(\rho \tanh^{-1}(z) + \sqrt{2}\sigma_\varepsilon \upsilon\right).$$

We approximate the value of this integral using an *m-point quadratic rule*. This is a rule by which abscissae and weights can be obtained to obtain a good numerical approximation to certain integral functions, $e^{-\upsilon^2}$ being one of them [See Press et al. [72]]. The transformation of ε into υ is justified by leading to the specific functional form for the integrand above. The abscissae are the values of υ_M on the $[-\infty, \infty]$ interval on which the integral is evaluated, while $\omega_M, M = 1, 2, ..., m$ are the weights being applied to each of those values to approximate the integral by the expression:

$$R(k, z; \mu) \simeq \frac{\beta}{\sqrt{\pi}} \sum_{M=1}^{m} \frac{\left[C^d(k, z; \mu)\right]^{\sigma}}{\left[C^d(k', z'_M; \mu)\right]^{\sigma}}$$

$$\times \left(\alpha A (k')^{\alpha-1} \sqrt{\frac{1+z'_M}{1-z'_M}} + (1-\delta)\right) \omega_M - 1$$

where $z'_M = \tanh\left(\rho \tanh^{-1}(z) + \sqrt{2}\sigma_\varepsilon \upsilon_M\right)$.

Press et al. [72] suggest using the *Gauss–Hermite quadratic rule,* which is based on Hermite polynomials:[15] $\Phi_0(x) = 1, \Phi_1(x) = x, \Phi_i(x) = 2x\Phi_{i-1}(x)$

---

[15] Note the similarity, but also the differences, with respect to Chebychev polynomials.

$-i\Phi_{i-2}(x), i = 2,3,\ldots$. These are orthogonal polynomials with respect to the e^{-v^2} weights: $\int_{-\infty}^{\infty} e^{-x^2}\Phi_i(x)\Phi_j(x) = 0, i \neq j$. Abscissae are then obtained as the roots of the m-th Hermite polynomial: $x_1, x_2, \ldots, x_m$, while the weights are the solution to the system:

$$
\begin{pmatrix}
\Phi_0(x_1) & \cdots & \Phi_0(x_m) \\
\Phi_1(x_1) & \cdots & \Phi_1(x_m) \\
\cdots & \cdots & \cdots \\
\Phi_{m-1}(x_1) & \cdots & \Phi_{m-1}(x_m)
\end{pmatrix}
\begin{pmatrix}
\omega_1 \\
\omega_2 \\
\cdots \\
\omega_m
\end{pmatrix}
=
\begin{pmatrix}
\int_{-\infty}^{\infty} e^{-x^2}\Phi_0(x)dx \\
0 \\
\cdots \\
0
\end{pmatrix},
$$

where $\int_{-\infty}^{\infty} e^{-x^2}\Phi_0(x)dx = \sqrt{\pi}$.

5.5.2.3 Implementation of Galerkin's Method

Once we have made decision on how to solve these two difficulties, to implement *Galerkin's method* we need to make two last choices: (a) the number and type of basis functions for each state variable that we will use to compute the complete set of polynomials, (b) the grid of points in the space of state variables, the (k,z)-space in this case, on which we want to compute the Residual functional. Here, we need to decide first on the number of points in that grid, and then on a way to select them on the product space of values for the state variables.

1. **Step 1:** We choose the set of Chebychev polynomials as basis functions for each state variable, and compute a *complete set of polynomials*. For instance,

   (a) if $d_k = d_z = 2$, we choose: $C^{d=6}(k,z;\mu) = \sum_{i=1}^{6} \mu_i \Psi_i(\hat{k},z)$, with $\Psi_1(\hat{k},z) = 1$, $\Psi_2(\hat{k},z) = \Psi_1(\hat{k})$, $\Psi_3(\hat{k},z) = \Psi_1(z)$, $\Psi_4(\hat{k},z) = \Psi_2(\hat{k})$, $\Psi_5(\hat{k},z) = \Psi_2(z)$, $\Psi_6(\hat{k},z) = \Psi_1(\hat{k})\Psi_1(z)$, where $\Psi_i(\hat{k})$, $\Psi_i(z)$ are Chebychev polynomials for $\hat{k}$ and z, with $\hat{k} = 2\frac{k-k_{min}}{k_{max}-k_{min}} - 1$.
   (b) if $d_k = d_z = 3$, we choose: $C^{d=10}(k,z;\mu) = \sum_{i=1}^{10} \mu_i \Psi_i(\hat{k},z)$, where $\Psi_1(\hat{k},z)$ to $\Psi_6(\hat{k},z)$ are the same as in the previous example, and $\Psi_7(\hat{k},z) = \Psi_3(\hat{k})$, $\Psi_8(\hat{k},z) = \Psi_3(z)$, $\Psi_9(\hat{k},z) = \Psi_2(\hat{k})\Psi_1(z)$, $\Psi_{10}(\hat{k},z) = \Psi_1(\hat{k})\Psi_2(z)$, and so on.
2. **Step 2:** We consider the following intervals: $k \in [k_{min}, k_{max}]$, where $k_{min} = k_{ss}(1-\lambda)$, $k_{max} = k_{ss}(1+\lambda)$, $\lambda \in (0,1)$; $\ln(\theta) \in [-\frac{2}{1-\rho}\sigma_\varepsilon, \frac{2}{1-\rho}\sigma_\varepsilon]$, i.e., an interval of two standard deviations around its mathematical expectation of zero, and choose points in these intervals as Chebychev nodes, with orders d_k, d_z:

$$
k_i = \frac{k_{max}+k_{min}}{2} + \frac{k_{max}-k_{min}}{2}\cos\left(\frac{d_k-i+.5}{d_k}\pi\right),
$$

with $i = 1,2,\ldots,d_k$

$$
\ln\theta_j = \frac{2}{1-\rho}\sigma_\varepsilon\cos\left(\frac{d_z-i+.5}{d_z}\pi\right), \quad j = 1,2,\ldots,d_z
$$

$$
z_j = \tanh(\ln\theta_j), \quad j = 1,2,\ldots,d_z
$$

3. We compute the abscissae and weights $(v_M, \omega_M, M = 1, 2, ..., m)$ for an *m-point Gauss–Hermite quadrature* as explained above, and approximate the expectation integral by:

$$\frac{\beta}{\sqrt{\pi}} \sum_{M=1}^{m} \frac{[C^d(k_i, z_j; \mu)]^\sigma}{[C^d(k', z'_M; \mu)]^\sigma} \left(\alpha A(k')^{\alpha-1} \sqrt{\frac{1+z'_M}{1-z'_M}} + (1-\delta) \right) \omega_M^{-1}, \text{ where } k' = \frac{1}{1+n}$$

$\left[Ak^\alpha \sqrt{\frac{1+z}{1-z}} + (1-\delta) - C^d(k, z; \mu) \right]$, and $z' = \tanh(\rho \tanh^{-1}(z) + \sqrt{2}\sigma_\varepsilon v_M)$. In fact, this is done at the same time the system of d Residual functional equations is solved:

$$0 = \sum_{i=1}^{d_k} \sum_{j=1}^{d_z} \left\{ \Psi_D(k_i, z_j; \mu) \left[\frac{\beta}{\sqrt{\pi}} \sum_{M=1}^{m} \frac{[C^d(k_i, z_j; \mu)]^\sigma}{[C^d(k', z'_M; \mu)]^\sigma} \right. \right.$$
$$\left. \left. \times \left(\alpha A(k')^{\alpha-1} \sqrt{\frac{1+z'_M}{1-z'_M}} + (1-\delta) \right) \omega_M - 1 \right] \right\}, \quad (5.68)$$
$$D = 1, 2, ..., d$$

where[16] $\Psi_D(k_i, z_j; \mu)$, $D = 1, 2, ..., d$, is each of the d polynomials in the complete set of basis functions previously chosen. This system of d equations will provide us with μ-coefficients: $\mu_1, \mu_2, ..., \mu_d$, and we will have the approximation to the decision rule:

$$C^d(k, z; \mu) = \sum_{D=1}^{d} \mu_D \Psi_D(k, z; \mu)$$

As in the deterministic model, we can evaluate the goodness of fit of the approximation provided by this function by analyzing the residual equation for a relatively fine grid of (k, z)-pairs.

Finally, we can simulate the solution as follows: (a) Given k_0, θ_0, we can obtain: $z_0 = \tanh(\ln \theta_0)$, c_0 from the approximating function $c_0 = C^d(k_0, z_0; \mu)$, and k_1 from the global constraint of resources:

$$k_1 = \frac{1}{1+n} [\theta_0 A k_0^\alpha + (1-\delta)k_0 - c_0],$$

and (b) A single draw from a Normal distribution with expectation 0 and variance σ_ε^2 provides us with the value of ε_1. We can then compute $\theta_1 : \theta_1 = \exp(\rho \ln \theta_0 + \varepsilon_1)$, and $z_1 = \tanh(\ln \theta_1)$, $c_1 = C^d(k_1, z_1; \mu)$, k_2 from the global constraint of resources, and iterate on this procedure.

---

[16] In general, we compute μ by solving a system of equations of the form: $\int_\Omega W_i(x)R(x; \mu)dx = 0$, $i = 1, 2, ..., d$. In particular, Galerkin's method consists on choosing as weights the basis polynomials: $W(x) \equiv \Psi(x)$, which in this case will be the complete set of polynomials for (k, z).

5.5.2.4 Numerical Exercise: Solving the Deterministic and Stochastic Optimal Growth Model by Projection Methods

Deterministic optimal growth model

Matlab program *coll_cheb.m* computes a numerical solution to the optimal growth model using the Collocation method and Chebychev polynomials. Parameter values are: $\alpha = 0.36$, $\beta = 0.96$, $\sigma = 1.5$, $\delta = 0.1$, $n = 0$, $A = 1$, which can be changed, as desired. The program starts with three basis functions ($d = 3$), but iterates until a number of basis functions is found providing a satisfactory approximation. Initial values of the μ-coefficients are: $\mu_0 = 0, \mu_1 = c_{ss}, \mu_2 = 0.1\frac{k_{ss}}{c_{ss}}$, taken from DeJong and Dave [27]. Given the definition of $C^d(k;\mu)$, this choice leads to an initial approximation: $c = C^d(k;\mu) = c_{ss} + 0.1\frac{k_{ss}}{c_{ss}}$. The system of nonlinear equations defined at each of the Chebychev nodes is solved, to obtain the values of the μ-coefficients.

By construction, the Residual functional will be equal to zero at each of the Chebychev nodes. But, in order to have a well-defined decision rule, we want the Residual functional to be as close to zero as possible on the whole range of values of the state variable k. The following block of equations in the program chooses an equally spaced 100-point grid on the range of values of k on which to compute the numerical value of the Residual functional for the vector of μ-coefficients previously obtained. The number of basis functions is then increased while the tolerance bound is violated at some point of the grid, and the algorithm implemented again with the increased value of d. The program uses a default tolerance bound of 10^{-7}.[17]

Once we have the $C^d(k;\mu)$ function approximating the decision rule, we compute time series, using this function to obtain the value of consumption each period. To display some transition, the initial condition for the stock of capital is set 10% above its steady-state level. The final graph presents: (a) the approximated policy function $c(k) \equiv C^d(k;\mu)$, (b) the values of the Residual functional on the grid of values for the state variable k, (c) the time series for consumption and capital, smoothly converging to their steady-state levels form the initial conditions in this deterministic version of the model. Under a choice of parameter values: $\sigma = 1.0, \delta = 1.0, n = 0$, the model has an analytical solution, and a graph compares in that case the exact and approximate solutions in a scatter diagram, showing the close similarity between them.

Stochastic optimal growth model

Programs *g_cheb_s_3.m*, *g_cheb_s_4.m* and *g_cheb_s_5.m* compute a numerical solution to the stochastic version of the optimal growth model using 3, 4 and 5 basis functions, respectively, for each of the state variables, k and z. At a difference of the deterministic case, now we do not perform iterations on this order to improve the fit of the approximating polynomial function. Values for structural parameters are as in

---

[17] This can be easily changed in the program.

the deterministic case, adding a 0.90 autoregressive coefficient for the productivity shock, and a 0.001 standard deviation for the innovation in that process.

These programs follow the steps described above for the stochastic optimal growth model, with the μ-coefficients obtained by Galerkin's method, using a complete set of Chebychev polynomials as basis functions and an m-point Gauss–Hermite quadrature to compute the numerical approximation to the expectation integral. Chebychev nodes are used in the range of values defined for the state variables to evaluate the decision rule that appears in the expectation integral. The number of values of each state variable to construct the grid is arbitrary, and it does not need to be the same for both variables. The programs show where the default choice for this number can be changed. The more points are chosen to construct the grid the better will be the polynomial approximation to the decision rule, albeit with increased computational cost. The *herm.m* program computes numerical values for Hermite polynomials which are then used to compute the abscissae and weights of the m-point Gauss–Hermite quadrature. The choice of initial values for the μ-parameters is important, specially the first ones.[18] Values provided in the program have been obtained by running a few iterations that used the μ-coefficients from the deterministic problem as initial guess. The *Cds_3, Cds_4.m* and *Cds_5.m* Matlab functions compute the value of the decision variable c through the approximating function C^d, given a set of μ-parameters. The *res.m* program is used, as in the deterministic problem, to compute numerical values for the residual at the chosen points of the grid, and the program calls the Matlab *fsolve.m* routine to solve for the values of the μ-coefficients. Once we have them, the *Cds_3, Cds_4.m* and *Cds_5.m* Matlab functions are again used to compute the value of the approximated decision rule on a relatively fine grid of points in the sample space.

Once we have the μ-coefficients, the approximating function C^d is used to evaluate the optimal decision rule on a finer grid of values in the (k,z)-space of state variables, than that used to compute the m-point Gauss–Hermite quadrature. The final graph shows the approximated decision rule, the values of the Residual functional in the (k,z)-space, and the time series realizations for consumption and physical capital. Changing the program to produce an arbitrary number of sample realizations for the μ-coefficients already obtained is straightforward.

5.6 Appendix – Solving the Planner's Model Under Full Depreciation

The conditions characterizing the stochastic, dynamic equilibrium in McCallum's model are:

$$\frac{\beta^t}{c_t} = \alpha E_t \left(\frac{\beta^{t+1} \theta_{t+1} k_{t+1}^{\alpha-1}}{c_{t+1}} \right), \tag{5.69}$$

---

[18] This may be the most sensitive parte of the numerical algorithm for the projection method, and finding initial values can sometimes be tricky. It is strongly advisable to start solving simplified versions of the model, to gain some insight into appropriate initial values for the μ-coefficients.

$$c_t + k_{t+1} = \theta_t k_t^\alpha. \tag{5.70}$$

From (5.70) we get:

$$\frac{\theta_{t+1}}{c_{t+1}} = \frac{1}{k_{t+1}^\alpha} + \frac{k_{t+2}}{c_{t+1} k_{t+1}^\alpha}.$$

Substituting this expression in (5.69), we get:

$$\frac{1}{c_t} = \alpha\beta \frac{1}{k_{t+1}} E_t \left(1 + \frac{k_{t+2}}{c_{t+1}}\right).$$

The previous expression can be written:

$$X_t = \alpha\beta + \alpha\beta E_t (X_{t+1}), \tag{5.71}$$

where $X_t = \frac{k_{t+1}}{c_t}$.

Equation (5.71) shifted one period to the future becomes:

$$X_{t+1} = \alpha\beta + \alpha\beta E_{t+1} (X_{t+2}). \tag{5.72}$$

If we take conditional expectations as of time t and applying the law of iterated expectations:

$$E_t (X_{t+1}) = \alpha\beta + \alpha\beta E_t (X_{t+2}).$$

If we shift one period forward (5.72) and take conditional expectations in the resulting expression, we obtain:

$$E_t (X_{t+1}) = \alpha\beta + (\alpha\beta)^2 + (\alpha\beta)^2 E_t (X_{t+3}).$$

Repeating the process indefinitely, we obtain:

$$E_t (X_{t+1}) = \alpha\beta \sum_{i=0}^{\infty} (\alpha\beta)^i + \lim_{T \to \infty} (\alpha\beta)^T E_t (X_{t+T}),$$

where $\lim_{T \to \infty} (\alpha\beta)^T E_t (X_{t+T}) = 0$ because $\alpha\beta < 1$. Therefore,

$$E_t (X_{t+1}) = \frac{\alpha\beta}{1 - \alpha\beta}. \tag{5.73}$$

Using (5.73) in (5.71), we get:

$$X_t = \frac{\alpha\beta}{1 - \alpha\beta}.$$

Since $X_t = \frac{k_{t+1}}{c_t}$, we obtain from the previous expression:

$$c_t = \frac{1 - \alpha\beta}{\alpha\beta} k_{t+1}. \tag{5.74}$$

Using (5.74) in (5.70), we get:

$$k_{t+1} = \theta_t \alpha \beta k_t^\alpha, \tag{5.75}$$

and substituting this expression in (5.74):

$$c_t = \theta_t (1 - \alpha\beta) k_t^\alpha. \tag{5.76}$$

Expressions (5.75) and (5.76) coincide with those obtained in the section.

5.7 Exercises

Exercise 1. Solve the simple model with full depreciation considered in Sect. 5.2 with and without leisure in the utility function, for A = 3, and n = 0.01. Maintain other parameter values as in that section. Generate a sample realization for the productivity shock with $\rho = 0.9$, and a Normal innovation with $\sigma_\varepsilon = 0.01$. Starting from an initial capital stock equal to the steady-state level, compute time series for the stock of capital, consumption and output. Obtain the main statistics used to characterize business cycle properties: mean, standard deviation and coefficient of variation for each series, as well as cross-correlations with output at up to ±2 lags. Using the same realization for the productivity shock, repeat the exercise in the model which includes leisure as an argument in the utility function.

Exercise 2. Obtain the analytical details of the log-linear quadratic approximation to the planner's problem without taxes.

Exercise 3. Obtain the analytical details for implementation of the eigenvector-eigenvalue decomposition on a linear approximation to the planner's problem without taxes for A ≠ 1 and n > 0.

Exercise 4. Obtain the analytical details for implementation of the eigenvector-eigenvalue decomposition on a log-linear approximation to the representative agent's problem without taxes. Compute sample realizations for the main variables using the linear and the log-linear approximations and compare the time series obtained. (Note: For this exercise to be meaningful, the same sample realization for the productivity shock needs to be used. That is easily done in Excel. Using MATLAB, it will be necessary to first save the sample realization for the productivity shock used with one of the approximations, to then load it into the program computing the other approximation to the model).

Exercise 5. Show that the log-linear approximation to the representative agent's problem with consumption and income taxes is as described in Sect. 5.3.5.

Exercise 6. Show that the linear approximation to the economy with taxes is as described in Sect. 5.4.4.

Exercise 7. Repeat exercise 4 considering consumption and income taxes in the economy.

Exercise 8. Obtain the analytical details of the linear-quadratic approximation to the planner's problem with positive income and consumption taxes. Obtain numerical solutions for this model using the same parameter values as those considered in the CK_solution_BK.xls file.

Exercise 9. In the discrete-time version of the Cass–Koopmans economy, consider a Cobb–Douglas production function with constant returns to scale and a utility function with a constant intertemporal elasticity of substitution of consumption. Consider a time discount parameter of $\beta = 0.99$, a depreciation rate $\delta = 0.025$, *zero population growth, $n = 0$,* output elasticity with respect to capital of 0.33 and an intertemporal elasticity of substitution of consumption $1/\sigma = 1/3$. The government levies a tax of 20% on consumption as well as a tax of 15% on income from the representative agent, using the revenues to purchase the single good produced in the economy.

1. Let us assume that there is uncertainty in the economy due to the fact that productivity follows a random process, satisfying the assumptions specified in this chapter. Characterize the response of the different variables to a transitory change in productivity of size equal to one standard deviation of that process. Let us assume that the coefficient in the first-order autoregression for the productivity shock is 0.95, and the standard deviation for the innovation is 0.01, and interpret the obtained results.
2. Do 5 simulation of 101 periods each. Characterize the following properties of an economic cycle: volatility for output and for each component of aggregate demand, as well as correlations of each of these variables with output.
3. Let us assume that fiscal policy consists of an 25% income tax, together with a consumption tax, in such a way that tax revenues in steady-state is the same as before the tax change. Repeat the analysis in point 1, using the same realization for the innovation to used in point 1. What do you see in the results?

Exercise 10. Consider the same model as in the previous exercise, and suppose that the government implements a constant public expenditures policy. The income tax rate changes over time so that the budget constraint holds as an equality each time period. Compute a sample realization for the productivity shock and for the main variables in the model, and estimate their cyclical properties, under the assumption that in steady-state, the income tax rate is 15% and the consumption tax rate is 20%. For the same realization of the productivity shock, suppose now that the consumption tax rate is 25% while the income tax rate adjusts every period so that tax revenues remain constant at their steady-state level. Compare the paths for the main variables and the estimated values for the main statistics with those obtained in the first case. **(advanced)**

Exercise 11. In the Cass–Koopmans model with consumption and income taxes, consider that the government chooses one of the two tax rates as well as the level of public expenditures, as in the previous exercise. There are two sources of uncertainty: a productivity shock, and a shock on the level of public expenditures. Both shocks are uncorrelated. Should public expenditures be cyclic or anticyclic in order to maximize welfare? (**advanced**)

Exercise 12. Check that for a given sample realization of the productivity shock, the numerical solutions provided by the Blanchard–Khan and Uligh methods are identical.

Chapter 6
Endogenous Growth Models

6.1 The *AK* Model

The *AK* model, introduced by Rebelo [74], is characterized by a constant returns to scale technology, linear in physical capital

$$Y_t = AK_t,$$

with A representing the constant average and marginal productivity of capital, and K_t the aggregate stock of capital. As we saw in Chap. 2, aggregate constant returns to scale in the cumulative inputs is a necessary condition for endogenous growth. This assumption is a violation of the Inada condition $\lim_{K_t \to \infty} F'(K_t) = 0$, which is assumed to hold in neoclassical growth models under decreasing returns to scale.

We consider an economy populated with identical consumers, who are the owners of the production inputs and have an infinite life span. The number of individuals is N_t, which increases over time at an exogenous rate n, $N_t = e^{nt} N_0$. They all have the same preferences, which depend only on the amount consumed of the single commodity in the economy, and an identical production ability. Since leisure does not affect the level of utility, labor is inelastically supplied. We assume the labor market to be in equilibrium every period. Since we do not consider any difference between population and labor supply, employment is equal to population: $L_t = N_t$.

In per worker terms, this technology can be written

$$Y_t/L_t = AK_t/L_t \Rightarrow \tilde{y}_t = A\tilde{k}_t.$$

Hence, $\tilde{k}_t$ denotes the number of machines per worker in the economy at time t, equal to the per capita stock of physical capital. As we will see below, an important difference between the models in this chapter and those analyzed previously is that per capita variables display constant non-zero growth in steady-state.[1] For analytical

---

[1] In presence of technological growth, per-capita variables grow in steady-state in exogenous growth model, but there is no growth when variables are considered in units of efficient labor. Introducing technological growth in the *AK* model, variables in units of efficient labor would still display non-zero growth in steady-state.

convenience, we will sometimes work with normalized per capita variables, that are obtained from the original variables after extracting from them the effect of the endogenous, constant rate of growth. In what follows we denote with tildes, $\tilde{c}_t, \tilde{k}_t, \tilde{y}_t$, per capita variables that grow in steady-state while denoting without tildes, c_t, k_t, y_t, the variables obtained after taking out from the former their growth trends.[2]

Under constant relative risk aversion preferences, the planner's problem is to maximize the discounted, time aggregate utility of the typical consumer, subject to the aggregate constraint of resources in the economy,

$$\max U_0 = \int_0^\infty e^{-\theta t} \frac{\tilde{c}_t^{1-\sigma} - 1}{1 - \sigma}, \quad \sigma > 0$$
$$\text{subject to } d\tilde{k}_t/dt = A\tilde{k}_t - (n+\delta)\tilde{k}_t - \tilde{c}_t, \text{ and given } \tilde{k}_0, \quad (6.1)$$

with Hamiltonian

$$H = e^{-\theta t} \left(\frac{\tilde{c}_t^{1-\sigma} - 1}{1 - \sigma} + \lambda_t \left[A\tilde{k}_t - (n+\delta)\tilde{k}_t - \tilde{c}_t \right] \right),$$

and first order conditions,

$$\text{order condition: } \frac{\partial H}{\partial \tilde{c}_t} = 0 \Rightarrow \tilde{c}_t^{-\sigma} = \lambda_t \Rightarrow \tilde{c}_t = \lambda_t^{-1/\sigma}, \quad (6.2)$$

$$\text{co-state equation: } \dot{\lambda}_t = \theta\lambda_t - e^{\theta t}\frac{\partial H}{\partial \tilde{k}_t} \Rightarrow$$
$$\dot{\lambda}_t = \lambda_t [\theta - A + (n+\delta)], \quad (6.3)$$
$$\text{transversality condition: } \lim_{T\to\infty} e^{-\theta T}\lambda_T \tilde{k}_T = 0,$$

which imply a growth rate for consumption

$$\gamma_{\tilde{c}_t} = \frac{d\tilde{c}_t/dt}{\tilde{c}_t} = -\frac{1}{\sigma}\frac{\dot{\lambda}_t}{\lambda_t} = -\frac{1}{\sigma}(\theta + \delta + n - A) = \gamma_{\tilde{c}}, \quad \forall t, \quad (6.4)$$

which happens to be constant over time, $\gamma_{\tilde{c}}$. Consumption will actually grow if $A > \theta + \delta + n$, decreasing otherwise.

The dependence of the growth rate of consumption from structural parameters can be written

$$\gamma_{\tilde{c}}\sigma + \theta = A - (\delta + n),$$

with the standard interpretation that the cost of one unit less of consumption at time t is equal to the benefit of saving that unit in the form of physical capital. Specifically, the rate of growth is higher for lower values of θ and σ, that raise the willingness to save, and for a higher productivity A.

---

[2] Without loss of generality, we will not use this convention with Hamiltonian or Lagrange multipliers.

According to (6.4), the optimal time evolution of consumption is

$$\tilde{c}_t = \tilde{c}_0 e^{\gamma_{\tilde{c}}t} = \tilde{c}_0 e^{-\frac{1}{\sigma}(\theta+\delta+n-A)t},$$

while (6.1) gives us the growth rate for physical capital,

$$\gamma_{\tilde{k}_t} = \frac{d\tilde{k}_t/dt}{\tilde{k}_t} = A - (n+\delta) - \frac{\tilde{c}_t}{\tilde{k}_t}, \quad \forall t . \tag{6.5}$$

6.1.1 Balanced Growth Path

At this point, we remember the notion of *steady state:*

Definition. Steady state is a trajectory along which all the relevant per capita variables either stay constant or grow at a constant rate.

Hence, in steady-state $\gamma_{\tilde{k}}$ is constant, but that can only happen in (6.5) if $\tilde{k}_t$ grows at the same constant rate than $\tilde{c}_t$, i.e., $\gamma_{\tilde{k}} = \gamma_{\tilde{c}} = -\frac{1}{\sigma}(\theta+\delta+n-A)$. Furthermore, since the technology is linear, $\tilde{y}_t$ will also have to grow in steady state at the same rate than per capita consumption and physical capital: $\gamma_{\tilde{y}} = \gamma_{\tilde{k}} = \gamma_{\tilde{c}}$. So, the steady-state takes the form of a *balanced growth* path, with all per capita variables growing at the same constant rate, $\gamma = -\frac{1}{\sigma}(\theta+\delta+n-A)$.

On the other hand, from (6.3) we have that along the optimal trajectory for consumption and the stock of capital,

$$\lambda_t = \lambda_0 e^{-(A-(\delta+n)-\theta)t},$$

and the transversality condition becomes

$$\lim_{T\to\infty} e^{-\theta T} \lambda_0 e^{-(A-(\delta+n)-\theta)T} \tilde{k}_T = \lim_{T\to\infty} \lambda_0 e^{-(A-\delta-n)T} \tilde{k}_T = 0, \tag{6.6}$$

which imposes an upper bound of $A - \delta - n$ on the rate of growth of the stock of physical capital per worker.

6.1.2 Transitional Dynamics

We show in this section that the *AK* model lacks any transitional dynamics. So far, we have shown that the steady-state for this economy takes the form of a *balanced growth* path, with all per capita variables growing at the same constant rate. We will now show that physical capital and output grow at the same rate than consumption at any point in time. The argument consists on integrating the global constraint of resources forwards, using the transversality condition as terminal condition. This will lead to a linear relationship between per capita consumption and physical capital every period, from which the equality of growth rates is immediate.

Having already shown that consumption grows at the same rate every period, we will then have that all per capita variables grow at a constant rate at all time periods, so the economy is always on steady-state. Furthermore, from our previous argument, that steady-state will take the form of a balanced growth path, with the same, constant rate of growth for per capita variables at all time periods.

We already know from (6.4) that consumption grows at a constant rate $\gamma_{\tilde{c}} = (A - \delta - n - \theta)/\sigma$ no matter whether the economy is at steady-state or not. Multiplying the differential equation (6.1) through by $e^{-(A-\delta-n)t}$ and integrating between 0 and any arbitrary time T, we have,

$$\int_0^T \left[\frac{d\tilde{k}_t}{dt} - (A - \delta - n)\tilde{k}_t \right] e^{-(A-\delta-n)t} dt = -\tilde{c}_0 \int_0^T e^{[\gamma_{\tilde{c}} - (A-\delta-n)]t} dt.$$

Integrating by parts the first term on the left-hand side,

$$\int_0^T \frac{d\tilde{k}_t}{dt} e^{-(A-\delta-n)t} dt = \left[e^{-(A-\delta-n)t}\tilde{k}_t \right]_0^T$$

$$+ \int_0^T (A - \delta - n)\tilde{k}_t e^{-(A-\delta-n)t} dt,$$

so that

$$e^{-(A-\delta-n)T}\tilde{k}_T - \tilde{k}_0 = -\tilde{c}_0 \frac{1}{\gamma_{\tilde{c}} - (A - \delta - n)} \left(e^{[\gamma_{\tilde{c}} - (A-\delta-n)]T} - 1 \right).$$

Multiplying through by $e^{(A-\delta-n)T}$, and taking into account that $\gamma_{\tilde{c}} - (A - \delta - n) = (A - \delta - n)\frac{1-\sigma}{\sigma} - \frac{\theta}{\sigma}$, we have, at any point in time:

$$\tilde{k}_T = Me^{(A-\delta-n)T} - \frac{\tilde{c}_0}{\gamma_{\tilde{c}} - (A - \delta - n)} e^{\gamma_{\tilde{c}}T}$$

$$= Me^{(A-\delta-n)T} + \frac{\tilde{c}_0}{\phi} e^{(A-\delta-n-\theta)\frac{T}{\sigma}}, \quad (6.7)$$

where $M = \tilde{k}_0 + \frac{\tilde{c}_0}{\gamma_{\tilde{c}} - (A-\delta-n)}$, $\phi = (A - \delta - n) - \gamma_{\tilde{c}}$.

If we now take (6.7) to the transversality condition (6.6), we have

$$\lim_{T \to \infty} \lambda_0 e^{-(A-\delta-n)T}\tilde{k}_T = \lim_{T \to \infty} \left(\lambda_0 M + \frac{\tilde{c}_0}{\phi} \lambda_0 e^{[\frac{A-\delta-n-\theta}{\sigma} - (A-\delta-n)]T} \right) = 0,$$

for which the following two conditions must hold: (1) $M = 0$, (2) $(A - \delta - n) \times (1 - \sigma) < \theta$.

The first condition, in turn, implies

$$\gamma_{\tilde{c}} = (A + \delta + n) - \frac{\tilde{c}_0}{\tilde{k}_0} \Rightarrow \tilde{c}_0 = \tilde{k}_0 [(A - \delta - n) - \gamma_{\tilde{c}}] = \phi \tilde{k}_0,$$

defining a link between the initial levels of consumption and physical capital. But taking $M = 0$ to (6.7), which applies to any point in time, we have

$$\tilde{k}_t = \frac{\tilde{c}_0}{\phi} e^{(A-\delta-n-\theta)\frac{t}{\sigma}} = \frac{1}{\phi}\tilde{c}_t, \quad \forall t,$$

showing that the same relationship between the initial values of physical capital and consumption holds at all points in time. This is an important relationship that guarantees that the stock of capital does not grow too quickly. It also implies that physical capital and consumption grow *every period* at the same constant rate $\tilde{k}_t = \tilde{k}_0 e^{\gamma_{\tilde{c}} t}$. As a consequence, so does output,

$$\gamma_{\tilde{c}} = \gamma_{\tilde{k}} = \gamma_{\tilde{y}} = \gamma.$$

A lower consumption growth would allow for more capital accumulation, but with lower time aggregate utility. A more rapid consumption growth would lead to less intense capital accumulation which would in turn be unable to provide enough resources so as to maintain the rate of growth of consumption.

Since all per capita variables grow at a constant rate at all time periods, *the economy is always in steady state*. Starting from an initial condition $\tilde{k}_0$, the economy jumps immediately to the steady-state, per capita variables growing at a rate γ at all time periods. Following any structural change or a policy intervention that changes γ,[3] the economy will jump immediately from the old to the new steady-state with the new growth rate, since there is no transition between steady states.

To end this section let us make two comments on convergence in economies with an *AK* production technology. First, since the rate of growth of output is constant at all time periods, two countries differing in any parameter $A, \delta, \theta, n, \sigma$ will permanently grow at different rates.

Second, economic growth is independent from income, so a relatively poor economy will not grow faster than a richer one. Therefore, there is neither absolute nor conditional convergence among *AK* economies.

6.1.3 Boundedness of Time-Aggregate Utility

Aggregate utility over a finite interval of time $(0, T)$ is

$$U_0 = \int_0^T e^{-\theta t} \frac{\tilde{c}_t^{1-\sigma} - 1}{1 - \sigma} \, dt.$$

If the integrand grows too quickly, U_0 would grow with T without bound, and the welfare maximization problem would become meaningless. To avoid this situation, some restriction among structural parameters may be needed.

---

[3] In this simple version of the *AK* economy policy interventions do not directly affect the rate of growth, which depends on the values of $A, n, \delta, \theta, \sigma$. Later on, we will see that policy choices may also affect growth.

Since $\tilde{c}_t$ grows at a rate γ, we have

$$U_0 = \int_0^T e^{-\theta t} \frac{(c_0 e^{\gamma t})^{1-\sigma} - 1}{1-\sigma} \, dt.$$

The constant term in the utility function has as integral

$$-\int_0^T e^{-\theta t} \frac{1}{1-\sigma} dt = \frac{1}{\theta} \frac{1}{1-\sigma} e^{-\theta t} |_0^T = \frac{1}{\theta} \frac{1}{1-\sigma} \left(e^{-\theta T} - 1 \right),$$

which remains bounded when $T \to \infty$ for any values of the structural parameters. On the other hand, the term in consumption integrates to

$$\frac{1}{\gamma(1-\sigma) - \theta} \frac{c_0^{1-\sigma}}{1-\sigma} \left(e^{[\gamma(1-\sigma)-\theta]T} - 1 \right),$$

which will remain bounded as T grows provided[4]

$$\theta > \gamma(1-\sigma),$$

which using the expression for the rate of growth: $\gamma = (A - \delta - n - \theta)/\sigma$, can be seen to hold if and only if

$$\theta > (1-\sigma)(A - \delta - n), \tag{6.8}$$

meaning that, if $\sigma < 1$, the discount rate must be relatively large for welfare to be bounded.[5] On the other hand, if $\sigma > 1$, then any value of the discount rate leads to a bounded time aggregate utility, so long as growth is positive, i.e., if $A > \theta + \delta + n$. In this endogenous growth economy, when $\sigma < 1$, welfare can become unbounded for a sufficiently large level of productivity, in which case, there would not be much need for a planner. That economy would be able to produce enough resources to allow for consumption to grow over time in such a way that time aggregate utility becomes infinite.

6.2 The Discrete Time Version of the Model

As in previous chapters, we now develop the model in discrete time formulation. Qualitative results will be the same as in the continuous time version but, as discussed in Chap. 3, discrete time should be used for numerical simulations.

---

[4] A quite natural condition, that requires that the rate of growth of the consumption argument in the single period utility function be lower than the rate of time discount, θ.

[5] But this is exactly the same condition (2) we obtained before to guarantee that the transversality condition will hold, although the latter also requires the linear relationship between consumption and capital we characterized in the previous section.

The constraint of resources at the level of the whole economy is, in discrete time,

$$C_t + (K_{t+1} - (1-\delta)K_t) \leq Y_t \Rightarrow K_{t+1} = AK_t - C_t + (1-\delta)K_t,$$

which, in per capita terms, amounts to,

$$\tilde{k}_{t+1} = \frac{1}{1+n}\left(A\tilde{k}_t - \tilde{c}_t + (1-\delta)\tilde{k}_t\right). \tag{6.9}$$

Assuming that the preferences of the typical consumer can be represented by a constant relative risk aversion utility function

$$U(\tilde{c}_t) = \frac{\tilde{c}_t^{1-\sigma} - 1}{1-\sigma}, \quad \sigma > 0,$$

the problem solved by the *representative agent* is[6]

$$\max U_0 = \sum_{t=0}^{\infty} \beta^t \frac{\tilde{c}_t^{1-\sigma} - 1}{1-\sigma}, \tag{6.10}$$

subject to the constraint of resources (6.9) and the structure of the production technology: $\tilde{y}_t = A\tilde{k}_t$.

The optimization problem of the representative consumer is (6.10), subject to (6.9) and $\tilde{c}_t, \tilde{k}_{t+1} \geq 0$, with $\tilde{k}_0$ given. The Lagrangian of the problem is

$$L = \sum_{t=0}^{\infty} \beta^t \left(\frac{\tilde{c}_t^{1-\sigma} - 1}{1-\sigma} - \lambda_t \left[(1+n)\tilde{k}_{t+1} - A\tilde{k}_t + \tilde{c}_t - (1-\delta)\tilde{k}_t \right] \right),$$

with optimality conditions,[7]

$$\frac{\partial L}{\partial \tilde{c}_t} = 0 \Rightarrow \tilde{c}_t^{-\sigma} = \lambda_t, \quad t = 0, 1, 2, \ldots,$$

$$\frac{\partial L}{\partial \tilde{k}_{t+1}} = 0 \Rightarrow -(1+n)\lambda_t + \beta(A+1-\delta)\lambda_{t+1} = 0,$$

$$\text{for } t = 0, 1, 2, \ldots,$$

Transversality Condition: $\lim_{t \to \infty} (1+n)\beta^t \lambda_t \tilde{k}_{t+1} = 0.$

---

[6] Since there are no taxes, money or any public expenditures in this simple version of the *AK* economy, the planner's problem is the same as that of the representative agent.

[7] As usual, the transversality condition comes from taking derivatives in the finite horizon version of the Lagrangian with respect to $\tilde{k}_{T+1}$, and imposing the condition,

$$\lim_{T \to \infty} \beta^T \tilde{k}_{T+1} \frac{\partial L}{\partial \tilde{k}_{T+1}} = 0,$$

the partial derivative of the Lagrangian with respect to the last period's stock of capital being equal to λ_T.

These conditions lead to

$$\lambda_t = \frac{1}{\beta}\frac{1+n}{A+1-\delta}\lambda_{t-1} = \left(\frac{1+n}{\beta(A+1-\delta)}\right)^t \lambda_0,$$

$$\tilde{c}_t = \left(\beta\frac{A+1-\delta}{1+n}\right)^{1/\sigma}\tilde{c}_{t-1} = \left(\beta\frac{A+1-\delta}{1+n}\right)^{t/\sigma}\tilde{c}_0, \qquad (6.11)$$

where per capita consumption $\tilde{c}_t$ can be seen to grow at a constant gross rate every period

$$1+\gamma_{\tilde{c}_t} = 1+\gamma_{\tilde{c}} = \left(\beta\frac{A+1-\delta}{1+n}\right)^{1/\sigma},$$

which is actually positive if $A+1-\delta > \frac{1+n}{\beta}$, being negative otherwise.

Condition (6.11) shows that the marginal rate of substitution between current and future consumption is equal, under the optimal solution, to the marginal product of capital, net of depreciation[8]: $\frac{\tilde{c}_t^{\sigma}}{\beta\tilde{c}_{t-1}^{\sigma}} = \frac{A+1-\delta}{1+n}$. In other words, capital is accumulated to the point where the relative preference for current versus future consumption is equal to the net return of using an additional unit of physical capital in production.

From the global constraint of resources, the growth rate of physical capital in a given period is

$$1+\gamma_{\tilde{k}_t} = \frac{\tilde{k}_{t+1}}{\tilde{k}_t} = \frac{1}{1+n}\left(A+(1-\delta) - \frac{\tilde{c}_t}{\tilde{k}_t}\right),$$

which will be constant if and only if $\tilde{c}_t$ and $\tilde{k}_t$ grow at the same rate at all time periods. Therefore, a constant growth of physical capital requires that its rate of growth be the same as that of per capita consumption

$$\gamma_{\tilde{k}} = \gamma_{\tilde{c}}.$$

Furthermore, the AK−technology implies that per capita income satisfies a similar property

$$1+\gamma_{\tilde{y}} = \frac{\tilde{y}_t}{\tilde{y}_{t-1}} = \frac{\tilde{k}_t}{\tilde{k}_{t-1}} = 1+\gamma_{\tilde{k}} = 1+\gamma_{\tilde{c}} = \left(\beta\frac{A+1-\delta}{1+n}\right)^{1/\sigma},$$

so that the three variables, consumption, physical capital and output stay on a *balanced growth path* from the initial time, growing at the same constant rate in all time periods. We will refer to this common growth rate as γ. The economy is therefore at steady-state at all time periods, and there is no transition to steady-state, as we already saw in the continuous time version of the model. Following any policy intervention or any structural change that might alter the steady-state rate of growth,

---

[8] This would be physical depreciation as well as the loss of resources due to providing the newly born with the same stock of capital as owned by existing workers.

the economy will start growing at the new rate in the very first period after the policy intervention. The same comments we made in Sect. 6.1.2 on the fact that the AK model implies neither absolute nor conditional convergence could be made here.

6.2.1 The Transversality Condition and Bounded Utility

The transversality condition corresponding to the previous optimization problem is, in steady-state:

$$\lim_{t\to\infty}(1+n)\beta^t\lambda_t\tilde{k}_{t+1} = 0$$

$$\Rightarrow \lim_{t\to\infty}\beta^t\left(\frac{1+n}{\beta(A+1-\delta)}\right)^t\left(\beta\frac{A+1-\delta}{1+n}\right)^{(t+1)/\sigma}\lambda_0\tilde{k}_0 = 0,$$

which will be the case so long as

$$\lim_{t\to\infty}\left(\frac{1+n}{A+1-\delta}\right)^t\left(\beta\frac{A+1-\delta}{1+n}\right)^{t/\sigma} = \lim_{t\to\infty}\beta^{t/\sigma}\left(\frac{A+1-\delta}{1+n}\right)^{\frac{1-\sigma}{\sigma}t} = 0,$$

which will happen provided,[9]

$$\left(\frac{A+1-\delta}{1+n}\right)^{1-\sigma} < \frac{1}{\beta}, \tag{6.12}$$

which places an upper bound on the rate of growth: $1+\gamma < 1/\beta^{\frac{1}{1-\sigma}}$ when $\sigma < 1$, or a lower bound, $1+\gamma > 1/\beta^{\frac{1}{1-\sigma}}$ when $\sigma > 1$.

It is interesting to note that, as in the continuous time version of the model, the condition guaranteeing that the transversality condition holds, (6.12), is the same condition guaranteeing that maximized welfare remains finite. Indeed, once we know the growth rate of consumption, welfare can be written

$$\sum_{t=0}^{\infty}\beta^t\frac{\tilde{c}_t^{1-\sigma}-1}{1-\sigma} = \sum_{t=0}^{\infty}\beta^t\frac{\left(\beta\frac{A+1-\delta}{1+n}\right)^{\frac{1-\sigma}{\sigma}t}c_0^{1-\sigma}-1}{1-\sigma}$$

$$= \frac{c_0^{1-\sigma}}{1-\sigma}\sum_{t=0}^{\infty}\left[\beta\left(\frac{A+1-\delta}{1+n}\right)^{1-\sigma}\right]^{\frac{t}{\sigma}} - \frac{1}{1-\sigma}\sum_{t=0}^{\infty}\beta^t,$$

which will be bounded so long as condition (6.12) holds. Positive growth at the same time than bounded welfare requires here that either: $\frac{1+n}{\beta} < A+1-\delta < \frac{1+n}{\beta^{1/(1-\sigma)}}$, if $\sigma < 1$, or just the left hand inequality, if $\sigma \geq 1$.

---

[9] The similarity between restriction (6.12) and the analogue constraint we found in the continuous time version of the model is evident.

6.2.2 Absence of Transitional Dynamics: Relationship Between the Stock of Physical Capital and Consumption

As in the continuous time version, it is not hard to show that this economy is always in steady state so that, following any structural change or policy intervention, there is not transitional dynamics between steady-states. The argument will be the same as in the continuous time version of the model, by integrating the global constraint of resources subject to the transversality condition as a terminal condition.

First of all, (6.11) shows that per capita consumption grows at a constant rate every period. With regards to the stock of capital, we have from (6.9)

$$\tilde{k}_{t+1} = \frac{A+1-\delta}{1+n}\tilde{k}_t - \frac{1}{1+n}c_0\left(\beta\frac{A+1-\delta}{1+n}\right)^{t/\sigma}, \tag{6.13}$$

a non-homogeneous difference equation, with characteristic root $\mu = \frac{A+1-\delta}{1+n}$, so that the solution to the homogeneous part of the equation is: $\tilde{k}_t = M\left(\frac{A+1-\delta}{1+n}\right)^t$, for a given constant M to be determined from boundary conditions. A particular solution to the full equation may adopt the form, $\bar{\bar{k}}_t = H\left(\beta\frac{A+1-\delta}{1+n}\right)^{t/\sigma}$, for a particular constant H.

Plugging this analytical expression into (6.13) we get

$$H = \frac{c_0}{(A+1-\delta)-(1+n)\left(\beta\frac{A+1-\delta}{1+n}\right)^{1/\sigma}},$$

so that the complete solution to the non-homogeneous equation is

$$\tilde{k}_t = M\left(\frac{A+1-\delta}{1+n}\right)^t + H\left(\beta\frac{A+1-\delta}{1+n}\right)^{t/\sigma}.$$

To determine the remaining constant, M, we take this expression to the transversality condition,[10]

$$\lim_t \beta^t\lambda_t\tilde{k}_{t+1} = \lim_{t\to\infty}\beta^t c_0^{-\sigma}\left(\beta\frac{A+1-\delta}{1+n}\right)^{-t}\left[M\left(\frac{A+1-\delta}{1+n}\right)^{t+1}\right.$$
$$\left.+H\left(\beta\frac{A+1-\delta}{1+n}\right)^{(t+1)/\sigma}\right]$$
$$= c_0^{-\sigma}\lim_{t\to\infty}\left[M\frac{A+1-\delta}{1+n}+H\beta^{\frac{t+1}{\sigma}}\left(\frac{A+1-\delta}{1+n}\right)^{t\frac{1-\sigma}{\sigma}+\frac{1}{\sigma}}\right]$$

---

[10] When it is not needed, in what follows we skip the $1+n$ factor from the transversality condition.

$$= c_0^{-\sigma} \left[\lim_{t\to\infty} \left(M\frac{A+1-\delta}{1+n} \right) + H \left(\beta\frac{A+1-\delta}{1+n} \right)^{\frac{1}{\sigma}} \right.$$

$$\left. \times \lim_{t\to\infty} \left[\beta \left(\frac{A+1-\delta}{1+n} \right)^{1-\sigma} \right]^{\frac{t}{\sigma}} \right].$$

The condition that guarantees a bounded level of welfare also implies that the last term in this expression converges to zero, so that the transversality condition will hold if, in addition to that condition, we have $M = 0$, implying an equilibrium path for physical capital is

$$\tilde{k}_t = \frac{1}{(A+1-\delta) - (1+n)\left(\beta\frac{A+1-\delta}{1+n}\right)^{1/\sigma}} \left(\beta\frac{A+1-\delta}{1+n}\right)^{t/\sigma} c_0,$$

which, using (6.11) can also be written

$$\tilde{k}_t = \frac{1}{(A+1-\delta) - (1+n)\left(\beta\frac{A+1-\delta}{1+n}\right)^{1/\sigma}} \tilde{c}_t = \phi\tilde{c}_t,$$

or

$$\tilde{c}_t = [(A+1-\delta) - (1+n)(1+\gamma)]\,\tilde{k}_t, \quad t = 0,1,2,\dots.$$

Hence, as in the continuous time version of the model, we again have two necessary conditions for the transversality condition to hold. One of them also guarantees boundedness of the time aggregate utility function. The second condition imposes a linear relationship between per capita consumption and physical capital at each point in time, so that the two variables grow at the same rate. Since consumption grows at a constant rate at all time periods, so does physical capital, and the steady state takes the form of a balanced growth path.

6.3 Stability in the *AK* Model

We apply in this section the same arguments as in previous chapters to characterize stability conditions for the *AK* economy. As described in previous chapters, imposing the appropriate stability conditions is crucial in order to obtain acceptable solutions. This is now specially important because of the growing nature of per capita variables in the *AK* economy. The linearity of the *AK* model makes unnecessary to compute any further approximation on which to discuss stability. Because of that, we obtain as the single stability condition for this model exactly the same relationship between per capita consumption and capital that we obtained above for the transversality condition to hold. This is just a reflection of the fact that stability conditions restrict the time paths of the main variables so that the transversality condition holds.

In terms of detrended variables c_t, k_t, defined by

$$\widetilde{c}_t = (1+\gamma)^t c_t, \quad \widetilde{k}_t = (1+\gamma)^t k_t,$$

the optimality conditions we found in the previous section for the optimization problem of the representative agent can be written

$$c_{t+1} = c_t, \tag{6.14}$$

$$k_{t+1} = \frac{A+1-\delta}{(1+n)(1+\gamma)} k_t - \frac{1}{(1+n)(1+\gamma)} c_t, \tag{6.15}$$

or, in matrix form

$$\begin{pmatrix} c_{t+1} \\ k_{t+1} \end{pmatrix} = \begin{pmatrix} 1 & 0 \\ -\frac{1}{(1+n)(1+\gamma)} & \frac{A+1-\delta}{(1+n)(1+\gamma)} \end{pmatrix} \begin{pmatrix} c_t \\ k_t \end{pmatrix} = B \begin{pmatrix} c_t \\ k_t \end{pmatrix}. \tag{6.16}$$

As we can see, in this deterministic version of the model, optimal detrended consumption will remain constant, thereby getting an extreme form of the *consumption smoothing* property, while the stock of physical capital will evolve according to (6.15).

Since the transition matrix B of this system is lower triangular, its eigenvalues are just the diagonal elements, 1 and $\frac{A+1-\delta}{(1+n)(1+\gamma)}$, the latter being greater than 1, if the transversality condition is to be satisfied, as shown in (6.12). The unit eigenvalue is characteristic of endogenous growth models, in which per capita variables display non-zero growth along the steady state, which adopts the form of a balanced growth path. The unit eigenvalue shows up in the form of a unit root in the determination of optimal consumption above. The second eigenvalue, being greater than 1, will provide us with a stability condition. Since k_0 is given and c_0 is free, that structure guarantees a well-determined solution, provided we choose initial consumption on the stable path, as we saw in the Cass–Koopmans model. The associated eigenvectors are, respectively, $\begin{pmatrix} \phi \\ 1 \end{pmatrix}$ and $\begin{pmatrix} 0 \\ 1 \end{pmatrix}$, where ϕ is the same constant as in the previous section: $\phi = A + 1 - \delta - (1+n)(1+\gamma)$, as can be seen by solving the systems

$$\begin{pmatrix} 1 & 0 \\ -\frac{1}{(1+n)(1+\gamma)} & \frac{A+1-\delta}{(1+n)(1+\gamma)} \end{pmatrix} \begin{pmatrix} x \\ 1 \end{pmatrix} = 1 \begin{pmatrix} x \\ 1 \end{pmatrix},$$

that defines the first eigenvalue and eigenvector, and

$$\begin{pmatrix} 1 & 0 \\ -\frac{1}{(1+n)(1+\gamma)} & \frac{A+1-\delta}{(1+n)(1+\gamma)} \end{pmatrix} \begin{pmatrix} y \\ 1 \end{pmatrix} = \frac{A+1-\delta}{(1+n)(1+\gamma)} \begin{pmatrix} y \\ 1 \end{pmatrix},$$

that defines the second eigenvalue and eigenvector, having normalized the eigenvectors to have a unit second component.[11]

The spectral decomposition of the transition matrix B, is $B = \Gamma \Lambda \Gamma^{-1}$, where Λ is the diagonal matrix made up by the two eigenvalues, 1 and $\frac{A+1-\delta}{(1+n)(1+\gamma)}$, while matrix Γ has as columns the right eigenvectors: $\begin{pmatrix} \phi & 0 \\ 1 & 1 \end{pmatrix}$, with inverse matrix $\begin{pmatrix} \frac{1}{\phi} & 0 \\ -\frac{1}{\phi} & 1 \end{pmatrix}$.

Using this decomposition, the autoregressive representation can be iterated to

$$\begin{pmatrix} c_t \\ k_t \end{pmatrix} = B^t \begin{pmatrix} c_0 \\ k_0 \end{pmatrix} = (\Gamma \Lambda \Gamma^{-1})^t \begin{pmatrix} c_0 \\ k_0 \end{pmatrix} = \Gamma \Lambda^t \Gamma^{-1} \begin{pmatrix} c_0 \\ k_0 \end{pmatrix}$$

$$= \begin{pmatrix} \phi & 0 \\ 1 & 1 \end{pmatrix} \begin{pmatrix} 1 & 0 \\ 0 & \left(\frac{A+1-\delta}{(1+n)(1+\gamma)}\right)^t \end{pmatrix} \begin{pmatrix} \frac{1}{\phi} & 0 \\ -\frac{1}{\phi} & 1 \end{pmatrix} \begin{pmatrix} c_0 \\ k_0 \end{pmatrix}$$

$$= \begin{pmatrix} c_0 \\ \frac{c_0}{\phi} - \left(\frac{A+1-\delta}{(1+n)(1+\gamma)}\right)^t \left(\frac{c_0}{\phi} - k_0\right) \end{pmatrix}, \qquad (6.17)$$

which could in principle be used to produce time series for consumption and capital. However, the initial optimal level of consumption, c_0 is still unknown, since consumption is a decision variable and c_0 must be chosen optimally as a function of the initial state of the economy.

Using the representation for the per capita stock of physical capital from (6.17), we can see that the transversality condition holds if and only if

$$\lim_{t \to \infty} \beta^t \lambda_t \widetilde{k}_{t+1} = \lim_{t \to \infty} \beta^t \widetilde{c}_t^{-\sigma} \widetilde{k}_{t+1}$$

$$= \lim_{t \to \infty} \left(\left(\beta (1+\gamma)^{-\sigma}\right)^t c_0^{-\sigma} (1+\gamma)^{t+1} k_{t+1} \right)$$

---

[11] There is nothing specific of the normalization we use. In fact, if we normalized the eigenvectors to have unit norm, these would be $\begin{pmatrix} \frac{\phi}{\sqrt{1+\phi^2}} \\ \frac{1}{\sqrt{1+\phi^2}} \end{pmatrix}$ and $\begin{pmatrix} 0 \\ 1 \end{pmatrix}$, and the system could be written

$$\begin{pmatrix} c_t \\ k_t \end{pmatrix} = \begin{pmatrix} \frac{\phi}{\sqrt{1+\phi^2}} & 0 \\ \frac{1}{\sqrt{1+\phi^2}} & 1 \end{pmatrix} \begin{pmatrix} 1 & 0 \\ 0 & \left[\frac{A+1-\delta}{(1+n)\gamma}\right]^t \end{pmatrix} \begin{pmatrix} \frac{1}{\phi}\sqrt{(1+\phi^2)} & 0 \\ -\frac{1}{\phi} & 1 \end{pmatrix} \begin{pmatrix} c_0 \\ k_0 \end{pmatrix}$$

$$= \begin{pmatrix} c_0 \\ \frac{1}{\phi}c_0 + \left(k_0 - \frac{c_0}{\phi}\right) \left[\frac{A+1-\delta}{(1+n)\gamma_{ss}}\right]^t \end{pmatrix},$$

the same representation we obtained before, so the same argument could be made to characterize the single stable trajectory. Normalizing the eigenvectors to have their second component equal to one would again give raise to the same characterization of stability.

$$
= \frac{c_0^{1-\sigma}(1+\gamma)}{\phi} \lim_{t\to\infty} \left(\beta(1+\gamma)^{1-\sigma}\right)^t
$$

$$
+ \left(k_0 - \frac{c_0}{\phi}\right) c_0^{-\sigma} \lim_{t\to\infty} \left\{ \left[\beta(1+\gamma)^{-\sigma}\right]^t (1+\gamma)^{t+1} \right.
$$

$$
\left. \times \left(\frac{A+1-\delta}{(1+n)(1+\gamma)}\right)^{t+1} \right\}
$$

$$
= \frac{c_0^{1-\sigma}(1+\gamma)}{\phi} \lim_{t\to\infty} \left(\beta(1+\gamma)^{1-\sigma}\right)^t
$$

$$
+ \left(k_0 - \frac{c_0}{\phi}\right) \frac{A+1-\delta}{1+n} c_0^{-\sigma}
$$

$$
\times \lim_{t\to\infty} \left(\beta(1+\gamma)^{-\sigma}\right)^t \left(\frac{A+1-\delta}{1+n}\right)^t
$$

$$
= 0, \tag{6.18}
$$

where we have used: $\widetilde{c}_t = (1+\gamma)^t c_t$, $\widetilde{c}_0 = c_0$, $\widetilde{k}_{t+1} = (1+\gamma)^{t+1} k_0$ and (6.17). Since $\beta(1+\gamma)^{1-\sigma}$ is less than 1 under condition (6.12), the first limit in the previous expression is equal to zero. On the other hand, for the second limit we have

$$
\lim_{t\to\infty} \left(\beta(1+\gamma)^{-\sigma}\right)^t \left(\frac{A+1-\delta}{1+n}\right)^t = \lim_{t\to\infty} \left((1+\gamma)^{-\sigma}\beta\frac{A+1-\delta}{1+n}\right)^t = 1,
$$

where we have used the expression for the steady-state rate of growth: $1+\gamma = \left(\beta\frac{A+1-\delta}{1+n}\right)^{\frac{1}{\sigma}}$. Therefore, the second limit in (6.18) will be zero if and only if $c_0 = \phi k_0$. This condition characterizes the only equilibrium trajectory along which the transversality condition holds. Together with (6.15), this relationship implies: $k_t = k_0$ for all t, so that the proportionality between detrended consumption and capital $c_t = \phi k_t$ holds at any point in time.

As in the Cass–Koopmans model, to eliminate the unstable trajectories that violate the transversality condition it is enough to choose appropriately the initial level of consumption, $c_0 = \phi k_0$. We refer to this as the *stability condition,* which selects the only *stable* trajectory satisfying equilibrium conditions. We have just shown that, as it is the case in the general discussion in Chap. 3 for exogenous growth models, this condition amounts to making equal to zero at all time periods the cross product of the left eigenvector[12] associated to the unstable eigenvalue, i.e., the second eigenvalue, $\left(-\frac{1}{\phi}\ 1\right)$, and the column vector of variables $\begin{pmatrix} c_t \\ k_t \end{pmatrix}$.

Summarizing, we have been able to find a stable solution to the system because of the existence of an eigenvalue greater than one in absolute value since then, the associated eigenvector determines the unstable direction. Eliminating this direction

---

[12] Remember that the left eigenvectors are obtained as the *rows* in the inverse of the matrix that has the right eigenvectors as columns.

at all time periods, we find the initial consumption value guaranteeing stability of the implied solution. The stability condition is in this case a necessary but not sufficient condition for the transversality condition to hold.

6.4 Effects from Transitory Changes in Policy Parameters

We show in this section that policy interventions, even if transitory, produce permanent effects in the *AK*-economy. This runs contrary to the implication in an exogenous growth model, like the standard Cass–Koopmans model, where transitory interventions have purely transitory effects. In the Cass–Koopmans model, the effects may be longer lasting than the own policy intervention, but they are not permanent in any case.

We maintain the same assumptions on preferences and technology, but we now assume that the government raises income taxes at a rate τ_t. The government uses tax revenues to finance some lump-sum transfers to consumers, $\tilde{g}_t$. Government expenditures are therefore endogenous, being a function of output, as opposed to a case when government expenditures are given, and the tax rate adjust each period so that tax revenues equal expenditures at each point in time. The budget constraint of the representative agent would now be

$$(1+n)\tilde{k}_{t+1} = (1-\tau_t)A\tilde{k}_t - \tilde{c}_t + (1-\delta)\tilde{k}_t + \tilde{g}_t, \qquad (6.19)$$

and the Lagrangian for the utility maximization problem is

$$L = \sum_{t=0}^{\infty} \beta^t \left\{ \frac{\tilde{c}_t^{1-\sigma}-1}{1-\sigma} - \lambda_t \left[(1+n)\tilde{k}_{t+1} \right. \right.$$

$$\left. \left. - (1-\tau_t)A\tilde{k}_t + \tilde{c}_t - (1-\delta)\tilde{k}_t - \tilde{g}_t \right] \right\},$$

with optimality conditions

$$\frac{\partial L}{\partial \tilde{c}_t} = 0 \Rightarrow \tilde{c}_t^{-\sigma} - \lambda_t = 0, \quad t = 0,1,2,\ldots,$$

$$\frac{\partial L}{\partial \tilde{k}_{t+1}} = 0 \Rightarrow -(1+n)\lambda_t + \beta\left((1-\tau_{t+1})A+1-\delta\right)\lambda_t = 0,$$

$$\text{for } t = 0,1,2,\ldots,$$

and transversality condition,

$$\lim_{T\to\infty} \beta^T \lambda_T \tilde{k}_{T+1} = 0,$$

leading to the optimality condition

$$\frac{\tilde{c}_{t+1}}{\tilde{c}_t} = \left[\beta \frac{(1-\tau_{t+1})A+1-\delta}{1+n}\right]^{1/\sigma},$$

which, together with the global constraint of resources,

$$(1+n)\tilde{k}_{t+1} = A\tilde{k}_t - \tilde{c}_t + (1-\delta)\tilde{k}_t,$$

provide us with a system of two non-linear difference equations in $\tilde{c}_t, \tilde{k}_t$.

The first equation shows that consumption grows at a time varying rate:

$$1 + \gamma_{\tilde{c}_{t+1}} = \frac{\tilde{c}_{t+1}}{\tilde{c}_t} = \left[\beta \frac{(1-\tau_{t+1})A+1-\delta}{1+n}\right]^{1/\sigma}$$

from the initial period. The growth rate depends negatively on the proportional tax rate on income, which originates the *endogenous growth* denomination of this economy, since policy decisions affect growth.

6.4.1 A Policy Intervention

We consider now the effects in the *AK* economy of a transitory policy intervention. For simplicity, we will assume the tax policy

$$\tau = \tau_0, \quad t \neq t^*, \tag{6.20}$$
$$\tau = \tau_1, \quad t = t^*, \quad \tau_0 < \tau_1,$$

where the income tax rate is increased for just one period t^*, being constant in all other periods. A similar analysis could be used to discuss the effects of changes in the tax rate which are maintained over a finite number of periods but, for simplicity, we consider here a single-period policy intervention.

Under a fiscal policy that maintains a constant tax rate we can consider a possible steady-state, with all per capita variables growing at a constant rate. Furthermore, as it is the case without taxes, there is no transitional dynamics in the economy, so any change in the rate of growth is achieved immediately, with no gradual adjustments. As a consequence, the higher tax rise will lower the rate of growth of per capita variables at time t^*, the rate of growth returning to its value prior to the policy intervention as soon as the tax rate returns at time $t^* + 1$ to its starting value of τ_0.

We maintain the assumption of a constant relative risk aversion utility function. In the absence of policy intervention we would have a rate of growth $1 + \gamma^0 = \left[\beta \frac{(1-\tau_0)A+1-\delta}{1+n}\right]^{1/\sigma}$, and if denote by $\{\tilde{k}_t^0, \tilde{c}_t^0\}$ and $\{\tilde{k}_t^1, \tilde{c}_t^1\}$ the optimal trajectories for physical capital and consumption without the transitory policy intervention or under the policy intervention, respectively, we have

$$\tilde{k}_t^0 = (1+\gamma^0)^t k_0,$$
$$\tilde{c}_t^0 = (1+\gamma^0)^t c_0 = (1+\gamma^0)^t \left((1-\tau_0)A + 1 - \delta - (1+n)(1+\gamma^0)\right) k_0.$$

Under the policy intervention, we will have

$$\tilde{k}_t^1 = (1+\gamma^0)^t k_0, \quad t < t^*,$$
$$\tilde{k}_t^1 = (1+\gamma^0)^{t-1}(1+\gamma^1) k_0, \quad t \geq t^*,$$

where we have used the fact that the tax rate is changed for just one period, the duration of the policy intervention. In that expression, $1 + \gamma^1 = \left[\beta \frac{(1-\tau_1)A+1-\delta}{1+n}\right]^{1/\sigma}$ is smaller than $1 + \gamma^0$, as a consequence of the rise in tax rates, so that physical capital will be *permanently* lower after the tax raise.

We also have the consumption path:

$$\tilde{c}_t^1 = \tilde{c}_t^0 = (1+\gamma^0)^t \left[(1-\tau_0)A + 1 - \delta - (1+n)(1+\gamma^0)\right] k_0, \quad t < t^*,$$

$$\tilde{c}_t^1 = \frac{1+\gamma^1}{1+\gamma^0} \tilde{c}_t^0$$

$$= (1+\gamma^0)^{t-1}(1+\gamma^1) \left[(1-\tau_0)A + 1 - \delta - (1+n)(1+\gamma^0)\right] k_0, \quad t \geq t^*.$$

The difference between the trajectories after and before the tax rise is

$$\frac{\tilde{k}_t^1}{\tilde{k}_t^0} = \frac{\tilde{c}_t^1}{\tilde{c}_t^0} = 1, \quad t < t^*;$$

$$\frac{\tilde{k}_t^1}{\tilde{k}_t^0} = \frac{\tilde{c}_t^1}{\tilde{c}_t^0} = \frac{1+\gamma^1}{1+\gamma^0} < 1, \quad t \geq t^*,$$

showing that, in fact, a permanent effect is produced on the levels of per capita variables following a single-period policy intervention.

6.4.2 A Comparison with the Cass–Koopmans Economy

Let us now consider for comparison the effects of a similar policy intervention on an economy of the Cass–Koopmans type. We again consider a single period change in the tax rate. With a budget constraint for the representative consumer,

$$(1+n)k_{t+1} = (1-\tau_t)f(k_t) - c_t + (1-\delta)k_t + g_t, \quad (6.21)$$

where $f(k_t)$ fulfills the standard Inada properties, and relative risk aversion preferences, we have first order conditions,

$$\frac{c_{t+1}}{c_t} = \left[\frac{\beta}{1+n}\left((1-\tau_{t+1})f'(k_{t+1})+1-\delta\right)\right]^{1/\sigma}, \tag{6.22}$$

together with (6.21) and the transversality condition $\lim_{t\to\infty}\beta^t c_t^{-\sigma} k_{t+1} = 0$.

From (6.22), the steady-state of this economy under a constant tax rate τ is given by

$$f'(k_{ss}(\tau)) = \frac{\frac{1+n}{\beta} - (1-\delta)}{1-\tau},$$

$$c_{ss}(\tau) = (1-\tau)f(k_{ss}(\tau)) - (n+\delta)k_{ss}(\tau),$$

with $k_{ss}(\tau)$ and $c_{ss}(\tau)$ both decreasing in the tax rate τ.[13]

Let us suppose that the government has been running a policy of income taxes at a rate τ_0. The economy will then be on a trajectory smoothly converging to $k_{ss}(\tau_0)$, either increasing towards that value (if k_0 happens to be below $k_{ss}(\tau_0)$), or decreasing, otherwise. As we saw in previous chapters, given k_0, the planner will choose an initial level of consumption on the convergence manifold, and trajectories for c_t, k_t would start from those initial values to converge towards $c_{ss}(\tau_0), k_{ss}(\tau_0)$.

Now, suppose that at time t^* there is a transitory change in τ, as in (6.20). Given the previous period values k_{t^*}, c_{t^*-1}, the current period values k_{t^*+1}, c_{t^*} will be given by the *stability condition* we characterized in Chap. 4, with $\tau = \tau_1$, and (6.21),

$$k_{t^*+1}(\tau_1) = \frac{(1-\tau_0)f(k_{t^*}) - c_{t^*}(\tau_1) + (1-\delta)k_{t^*}}{1+n}. \tag{6.23}$$

If the economy was accumulating capital towards its steady-state, the stock of capital k_{t^*+1} could either be above or below k_{t^*}, depending on the size of the change in tax rate. The value of c_{t^*} from the stability condition will guarantee that (k_{t^*+1}, c_{t^*}) is on the new stable manifold, which will be different from that at time t^*-1. Consumption c_{t^*} can also fall either above or below c_{t^*-1}. At time t^*+1, the laws of motion (6.22), (6.23) for k_{t^*+2} and c_{t^*+1} will again involve τ_0, rather than τ_1. Steady state values will again be $c_{ss}(\tau_0), k_{ss}(\tau_0)$, and the value of c_{t^*+1} will be on the stable manifold converging now from the current position to the same steady-state we had before the policy intervention. The levels of consumption and capital will be different at each point in time from those that would have prevailed without the policy intervention, but their trajectories converge to the same steady-state. Hence, those differences will decrease over time.[14]

---

[13] To show this, first notice that the marginal product of capital changes directly with the tax rate. Furthermore,

$$\frac{\partial c^*(\tau)}{\partial \tau} = \frac{\partial k^*(\tau)}{\partial \tau}\left((1-\tau)f'(k^*(\tau))-\delta\right) - f(k^*(\tau)) < 0.$$

The sign of this expression comes from $\frac{\partial k^*(\tau)}{\partial \tau} < 0$ and $(1-\tau)f'(k^*(\tau))-\delta > 0$, since the latter is the marginal product of capital net of taxes and depreciation, which will coincide in equilibrium with the real interest rate in the economy, which must be positive.

[14] For any $\varepsilon > 0$, there is always a time period t_ε such that $t > t_\varepsilon \Rightarrow |(k_t^0/k_t^1) - 1| < \varepsilon$.

6.5 Dynamic Laffer Curves

An increase in tax rates, implemented on a low level of taxes, should be expected to lead to an increase in tax revenues. However, in a static setup, the Laffer curve captures the possibility that a raise on an already high level of the tax rate might actually lower revenues. That could be the case because the decrease produced in the after tax rate of return on capital might discourage capital accumulation sufficiently so that an implied lower level of income, subject to the higher tax, could give raise to lower tax revenues. Hence, the Laffer curve may display a typical inverted-U shape, revenues increasing with the tax rate up to a given level, above which revenues will fall if tax rates are further raised.

In a dynamic framework, Ireland [43] used an AK model to analyze the possibility that income tax rates could be lowered down while the government being able to finance a given stream of public expenditures. In that setup, the Laffer curve relates the *present value* of tax revenues to the level of the tax rate, while the *present value* of government expenditures is kept constant. It is clear that for that to be the case, we must lower the tax rate associated to a distortionary tax, since only then the rate of growth of the economy might positively respond to the decrease in taxes. The lower tax rates will produce budget deficits in the short-run, which will require to issue some debt for a number of periods. If the economy grows faster because of the decrease in the tax rate, then the additional resources produced over the long-run might allow the government to retire the debt issued to finance the short-run budget imbalance. This is because the present value of tax revenues have in fact increased after the tax cut. This possibility is the analog, in an intertemporal framework, of the decreasing part of the Laffer curve.[15]

We consider a linear AK technology, $Y_t = AK_t$, $A > 0$, a standard rule for capital accumulation: $K_{t+1} = (1 - \delta)K_t + I_t$, and a $CRRA$ utility function with parameter $\sigma > 0$ and a discount factor $\beta \in (0,1)$. At each time period t, the government charges a proportional income tax τ_t and gives each consumer a lump-sum transfer of $\tilde{g}_t = G_t/N_t$ units of commodity. The government can finance a given deficit each period by issuing discounted, one-period bonds, in an amount B_{t+1}. Each bond is sold at a price $1/R_t$ in terms of the period-t consumption commodity, thereby giving the owner the claim to one unit of consumption at time $t + 1$. R_t is then the real rate of return between time t and $t + 1$, and it is known with certainty at time t.

Defining per capita government debt $b_t = B_t/N_t$, the budget constraint for the representative agent is

$$(1 - \tau_t)A\tilde{k}_t + (1 - \delta)\tilde{k}_t + b_t + \tilde{g}_t \geq \tilde{c}_t + (1 + n)\tilde{k}_{t+1} + (1 + n)b_{t+1}/R_t. \quad (6.24)$$

Consumers takes their initial stocks of physical capital, and bonds, $k_0, b_0 > 0$, as well as the sequences $\{\tau_t, \tilde{g}_t, R_t\}_{t=0}^{\infty}$ as given when maximizing their lifetime aggregate utility subject to the sequence of budget constraints (6.24).

---

[15] The reader can find in Novales and Ruiz [69] the analysis of dynamic Laffer effects in an endogenous growth model with human capital accumulation.

First order conditions for the representative agent problem are

$$\tilde{c}_t : \tilde{c}_t^{-\sigma} = \lambda_t,$$

$$\tilde{k}_{t+1} : \beta^t (1+n) \lambda_t = \beta^{t+1} \lambda_{t+1} [(1 - \tau_{t+1}) A + (1 - \delta)],$$

$$b_{t+1} : \beta^t (1+n) \lambda_t \frac{1}{R_t} = \beta^{t+1} \lambda_{t+1},$$

together with the transversality condition,[16]

$$\lim_{T \to \infty} (1+n)^{T+1} \frac{\tilde{k}_{T+1} + b_{T+1}/R_T}{\prod\limits_{s=0}^{T-1} R_s} = 0,$$

which can be written,

$$\tilde{c}_t^{-\sigma} = \frac{\beta}{1+n} \tilde{c}_{t+1}^{-\sigma} R_t,$$

$$R_t = (1 - \tau_{t+1}) A + 1 - \delta,$$

and growth can be written,

$$1 + \gamma_t = \left(\frac{\beta R_t}{1+n} \right)^{1/\sigma}.$$

As we already know, the stock of capital and output will also grow at the same constant rate than consumption, provided the tax rate is kept constant over time. As we can see, the growth rate depends on policy decisions through the income tax rate, reflecting again the endogenous growth nature of the model. We have also characterized above the equilibrium real rate of return on bonds as a function of structural and policy parameters.

The government commits itself to providing for a sequence $\{g_t\}_{t=0}^{\infty}$ of transfers to consumers. The government constraint is

$$\tau_t A \tilde{k}_t + (1+n) b_{t+1}/R_t \geq \tilde{g}_t + b_t, \tag{6.25}$$

with the terminal condition,[17]

$$\lim_{T \to \infty} (1+n)^{T+1} \frac{b_{T+1}/R_T}{\prod\limits_{s=0}^{T-1} R_s} \leq 0. \tag{6.26}$$

We consider the following tax experiment: the economy starts from a unit stock of physical capital: $k_0 = 1$, and is subject to a constant income tax rate up to a given

---

[16] The presence of the product of real interest rates in the denominator of this fraction is due to solving backwards for the Lagrange multiplier that usually appears in the transversality condition.

[17] To eliminate the possibility of non-zero Ponzi games.

time: $\tau_t = \tau^0, \forall t$. For simplicity, we will also assume that, initially, there is zero debt outstanding, and that debt is never issued: $b_t = 0, \forall t$. These assumptions imply

$$1 + \gamma^0 = \left(\beta \frac{\left(1 - \tau^0\right) A + 1 - \delta}{1 + n} \right)^{1/\sigma},$$

$$\tilde{k}_t^0 = \left(1 + \gamma^0\right)^t, \tag{6.27}$$

so that the *balanced growth path* for government transfers is

$$\tilde{g}_t = \tau^0 A \tilde{k}_t = \tau^0 A \left(1 + \gamma^0\right)^t. \tag{6.28}$$

The question is whether the government could use a lower constant tax rate, $\tau^1 < \tau^0$ and still finance the same path for government expenditures $\{\tilde{g}_t\}_{t=0}^{\infty}$ characterized by (6.28). The change in taxes takes place at some point in time that we can consider, without loss of generality, to be $t = 0$. As described by Ireland [43] the reduction in the marginal tax rate from τ^0 to τ^1 has three effects on the government's budget constraint: (a) a direct effect decreasing total tax revenues, (b) the lower tax rate increases the rate of capital accumulation as can be seen by comparing (6.27) with (6.29). This effect increases the tax base and hence, total revenues, (c) the lower tax rate increases the real rate of interest (6.30), thereby decreasing the present value of the government futures receipts and expenditures.

The same argument we made above shows that, under the alternative tax rate we would have trajectories for capital and interest rates

$$1 + \gamma^1 = \left(\beta \frac{\left(1 - \tau^1\right) A + 1 - \delta}{1 + n} \right)^{1/\sigma},$$

$$\tilde{k}_t^1 = \left(1 + \gamma^1\right)^t, \tag{6.29}$$

$$R_t^1 = R^1 = \left(1 - \tau^1\right) A + 1 - \delta. \tag{6.30}$$

The terminal condition on government debt will be satisfied only if

$$\sum_{t=0}^{\infty} (1 + n)^t \frac{1}{\prod_{s=0}^{t-1} R_s^1} \left(\tau^1 A \tilde{k}_t^1 - \tilde{g}_t \right) \geq 0, \tag{6.31}$$

which defines the set of feasible fiscal policies, i.e., the set of combinations of tax rates and government expenditures that would allow for eventually retiring any debt outstanding as of the time of the change in the tax rate. It is a single *intertemporal budget constraint*, that we have obtained by *integrating* the sequence of single-period constraints (6.25) under the terminal condition (6.26). The condition just states that for a fiscal policy to be *feasible* all we need is that the present value, as of the time of the tax change, of the sequence of tax revenues should be greater than that of the sequence of government expenditures. The condition adopts a simpler form because of our assumption of zero initial debt. Otherwise, the condition would state that the present value of current and future government surplus should be at least equal to the initial stock of debt, b_0.

Using the levels for k_t^1 and R_t^1 given by (6.29), (6.30), as well as the pre-specified $\{\tilde{g}_t\}_{t=0}^{\infty}$ path, it is easy to see that the intertemporal government budget constraint will hold under the alternative income tax rate τ^1 if and only if

$$\sum_{t=0}^{\infty} \frac{\tau^1 A \left(1+\gamma^1\right)^t - \tau^0 A \left(1+\gamma^0\right)^t}{(R^1)^t (1+n)^{-t}} \geq 0. \tag{6.32}$$

Since along the balanced growth path: $1 + \gamma^1 < R^1/(1+n)$,[18] we have: $\sum_{t=0}^{\infty} \frac{\tau^1 A (1+\gamma^1)^t}{(R^1)^t(1+n)^{-t}} = \tau^1 A \sum_{t=0}^{\infty} \left(\frac{1+\gamma^1}{R^1/(1+n)}\right)^t = \frac{\tau^1 A R^1}{R^1 - (1+n)(1+\gamma^1)}$ and since $1 + \gamma^0 <$ $1 + \gamma^1 < R^1/(1+n)$, $\sum_{t=0}^{\infty} \frac{\tau^0 A (1+\gamma^0)^t}{(R^1/(1+n))^t} = \tau^0 A \sum_{t=0}^{\infty} \left(\frac{1+\gamma^0}{R^1/(1+n)}\right)^t = \frac{\tau^0 A R^1}{R^1 - (1+n)(1+\gamma^0)}$. Hence, condition (6.32) holds if and only if

$$\frac{\tau^1 A R^1}{R^1 - (1+n)(1+\gamma^1)} - \frac{\tau^0 A R^1}{R^1 - (1+n)(1+\gamma^0)} \geq 0. \tag{6.33}$$

The answer to the question we raised on the possibility of a tax rate cut can be obtained from (6.33). Any value of τ^1 satisfying that inequality will be a feasible alternative income tax rate, below the initial τ^0, while being consistent with the intertemporal government budget constraint.

6.5.1 Numerical Exercise on Dynamic Laffer Curves

The *DynamicLaffer.xls* file contains the results of a fiscal policy experiment along the lines of the previous section. Parameter values are: $A = 0.165$, $\beta = 0.988$, $\delta = 0.10$, $\sigma = 1.0001$, $n = 0$. The initial income tax rate of $\tau = 20.0\%$ is consistent with annual growth of 2.0%, and a real interest rate of 3.2%. The first column considers possible permanent tax cuts of different size. The first entry corresponds to totally eliminating the income tax, so it is the largest cut. The last entry corresponds to the no-change case. The next two columns display the final real interest rate and rate of growth. The *sum1, sum2* columns contain the numerical values of the two terms in (6.33).

---

[18] Indeed, from the transversality condition, we have

$$\lim_{t\to\infty} \beta^t \, \lambda_t \tilde{k}_{t+1} = 0 \Leftrightarrow \lim_{t\to\infty} \beta^t \tilde{c}_t^{-\sigma} \tilde{k}_{t+1} = 0 \Leftrightarrow \lim_{t\to\infty} \left(\beta \left(1+\gamma^1\right)^{1-\sigma}\right)^t = 0$$

$$\Leftrightarrow \beta \left(1+\gamma^1\right)^{1-\sigma} < 1 \Leftrightarrow 1+\gamma^1 < R/(1+n),$$

since $1 + \gamma^1 = \left(\frac{\beta R^1}{1+n}\right)^{1/\sigma}$.

The effect on the budget, L, is obtained as the difference between these two terms. Positive values correspond to feasible tax cuts. These are tax cuts that stimulate growth by enough so that the increased future tax revenues allow for retiring the debt which is initially issued to cover the budget deficits that arise for a number of periods after the tax cut. Obviously, small tax cuts appear as having a lesser effect on the present value budget constraint, and lead to negative budget effects. So, those tax cuts are not feasible. As shown in the graph, with the chosen parameterization, the income tax rate can be cut down all the way to 7.6%, but it could not be brought below that level without violating the present value government budget constraint.

The effects on steady-state growth are shown in the next column, relative to initial annual growth. These are increasing in the size of the tax cut. A tax cut to 13.8% increases annual growth by 1.0%, while the largest feasible tax cut increases growth by 2.0%. Effects on growth and on the present value government budget deficit of a variety of tax cuts are illustrated in the *Budget and growth* graph, where we can see how tax rates below 7.6% would have a negative effect on the present value budget, thereby not being feasible. On the other hand, the growth effect would be largest for the total elimination of the income tax, decreasing almost linearly for smaller tax cuts.

After this initial steady-state analysis that characterizes the feasible range for income tax cuts, we present below the transitional dynamics analysis for a permanent tax cut from 20.0% to 17.0%. The first panel (left, *Before reform*) contains time series for the stock of physical capital and for the size of the lump-sum transfers under the initial parameter values, with no change in taxes. The second panel (right, *After reform*) presents time series after the tax change, that is assumed to take place at $t = 0$. As explained in the previous section, the size of the lump-sum transfer is maintained the same as without the tax change, since the point of the exercise is precisely the possibility of financing the same expenditures with lower taxes. Output is obtained from the stock of capital, using the *AK*-technology, while consumption is calculated using the stability condition.

Tax revenues are obtained from income data, and the deficit is the difference between government expenditures (the lump-sum transfer to consumers) and tax revenues. Budget deficits are largest immediately after the tax cut, decreasing thereafter. After a number of periods, 34 in this exercise, the government obtains a budget surplus, as a consequence of the more rapid growth in the tax base. Debt will accumulate, starting from the initial zero stock, for two reasons: to cover the current period deficit, and to pay interest on outstanding debt. Per capita debt is calculated dividing by the population rate of growth. The spreadsheet then shows deficit and debt as a proportion of output. Debt increases up to almost 72% of output, 45 periods after the tax cut, decreasing thereafter. In fact, 84 periods after the tax cut, the government could give resources away to the private sector. The final columns provide information on single period utility as well as on time aggregate, discounted utility.

The *Deficit and debt* graph displays the time evolution of deficit and debt, both as a percentage of output, following the tax cut. The change in sign in both variables after the number of periods mentioned in the previous paragraph is apparent.

The reader is encouraged to consider the feasibility of tax cuts for different parameterizations, which can be easily analyzed using this same Excel file.

6.6 Solving the Stochastic, Discrete Time Version of the *AK* Model

We now consider the discrete time version of the *AK* model under stochastic productivity,

$$\widetilde{y}_t = \theta_t A \widetilde{k}_t,$$

with a law of motion for the productivity shock,

$$\ln \theta_t = \rho \ln \theta_{t-1} + \varepsilon_t, \tag{6.34}$$

with $\varepsilon_t \underset{iid}{\sim} N\left(0, \sigma_\varepsilon^2\right)$, as we assumed in the stochastic version of the Cass–Koopmans economy. Each possible random realization of the productivity shock will lead to a realization of the vector stochastic process of the main variables in the economy. As with previous models, the model translates the probability distribution for the productivity shock into a probability distribution for this vector stochastic process. However, we must bear in mind that the dimension of implied randomness cannot be larger than the number of stochastic shocks in the economy, which is just one in this case.

Maintaining the assumption of constant relative risk aversion preferences for the representative consumer, the use of random Lagrange multipliers as we did in previous chapters allow us to obtain optimality conditions given the starting level of physical capital,[19]

$$\widetilde{c}_t^{-\sigma} = \frac{\beta}{1+n} E_t \left[\widetilde{c}_{t+1}^{-\sigma} \left(A\theta_{t+1} + 1 - \delta \right) \right], \tag{6.35}$$

together with the global constraint of resources,

$$\widetilde{c}_t + (1+n)\widetilde{k}_{t+1} - (1-\delta)\widetilde{k}_t = A\theta_t \widetilde{k}_t, \tag{6.36}$$

and the transversality condition,

$$\lim_{t \to \infty} (1+n)\beta^t \widetilde{c}_t^{-\sigma} \widetilde{k}_{t+1} = 0.$$

---

[19] As explained in Chap. 5, random Lagrange multipliers lead to a formulation of first order conditions involving conditional expectations.

To obtain a numerical solution to the model, i.e., a set of time series realizations for the main variables in this economy over a period of time, we start from a choice of values for the structural parameters, $\{n, \rho, \sigma_\varepsilon^2, \sigma, \delta, A, \beta\}$, as well as for the initial stock of capital. A time series of the chosen length can be obtained for the productivity shock from (6.34) before we generate data for any other variable, reflecting the fact that the productivity shock is *exogenous*. When choosing structural parameter values, it is important to remember the conditions we impose on the level of productivity in order to have a bounded level of welfare and the transversality condition to hold.

We have already seen that in the steady state of the deterministic *AK* model economy, per capita variables grow at a constant rate. Furthermore, since growth rates are the same for all variables, the ratios of any two variables will stay constant in steady state. In the stochastic version of the economy, such ratios will experience fluctuations around the constant values that characterize the deterministic steady-state. Most endogenous growth models can be written in ratios of the relevant variables in such a way that a standard steady-state, characterized by constant levels of the main per capita variables, can be defined for the transformed economy.

In particular, in the *AK* economy, we define auxiliary variables,

$$1 + \gamma_{t+1} = \frac{\widetilde{k}_{t+1}}{\widetilde{k}_t}, \quad x_t = \frac{\widetilde{c}_t}{\widetilde{k}_t},$$

which help transforming (6.35) into

$$\frac{1}{\beta} = E_t \left[\left(\frac{\widetilde{k}_{t+1}}{\widetilde{k}_{t+1}} \frac{\widetilde{k}_t}{\widetilde{k}_t} \frac{\widetilde{c}_{t+1}}{\widetilde{c}_t} \right)^{-\sigma} \frac{1}{1+n} (A\theta_{t+1} + 1 - \delta) \right]$$

$$= E_t \left[\left(\frac{x_{t+1}}{x_t} (1 + \gamma_{t+1}) \right)^{-\sigma} \frac{1}{1+n} (A\theta_{t+1} + 1 - \delta) \right]. \tag{6.37}$$

On the other hand, from the global constraint of resources we have an expression for the rate of growth

$$1 + \gamma_{t+1} = \frac{\widetilde{k}_{t+1}}{\widetilde{k}_t} = \frac{1}{1+n} \left(A\theta_t - \frac{\widetilde{c}_t}{\widetilde{k}_t} + 1 - \delta \right) \tag{6.38}$$

$$= \frac{1}{1+n} (A\theta_t - x_t + 1 - \delta),$$

where we have used in (6.37) the fact that, being known at time t, $\widetilde{c}_t$ can be taken in and out of the time-t conditional expectation operator.

In the case of no uncertainty, $\theta_t = 1$ for all t, and we could ignore the conditional expectations operator E_t. In steady-state, with $\gamma_{t+1} = \gamma_t = \gamma$, $x_{t+1} = x_t = x_{ss}$, we would have, from these two equations

$$1 + \gamma = \left(\beta \frac{A + 1 - \delta}{1 + n} \right)^{1/\sigma},$$
$$x_{ss} = A + 1 - \delta - (1 + n)(1 + \gamma),$$

which are, of course, the same as in the deterministic version of the model. In the stochastic economy, the ratio of consumption to capital will in fact experience fluctuations induced by the time variation in the technology shock, and the actual growth rate of per capita variables will also fluctuate over time. The next section explains how to obtain a numerical solution to this model through a linear approximation to the set of first order conditions.

6.6.1 A Linear Approximation to the Stochastic AK Model

We provide in this section the analytical details of solving the stochastic, discrete-time version of the *AK* economy using the eigenvalue-eigenvector decomposition on a linear approximation to the model. However, any of the methods discussed in the chapter on numerical solution methods could be used as an alternative either on this linear approximation, or on a log-linear approximation to the set of first order conditions. This is proposed as an exercise at the end of the chapter.

Given a time series realization for $\ln \theta_t$, (6.37) and (6.38) form a system of two difference equations in γ_{t+1}, x_t, which could conceivably be used to obtain time series for these two variables. However, since these two equations are nonlinear, we need to obtain first a linear approximation. First, we rewrite (6.37) as

$$\frac{1}{\beta} = \left(\frac{x_{t+1}}{x_t} \frac{A\theta_t - x_t + 1 - \delta}{1 + n} \right)^{-\sigma} \frac{1}{1 + n} (A\theta_{t+1} + 1 - \delta) - v_{t+1}, \qquad (6.39)$$

where v_{t+1} denotes the expectations error, defined by:

$$v_{t+1} = \left(\frac{x_{t+1}}{x_t} (1 + \gamma_{t+1}) \right)^{-\sigma} \frac{1}{1 + n} (A\theta_{t+1} + 1 - \delta)$$

$$- E_t \left[\left(\frac{x_{t+1}}{x_t} (1 + \gamma_{t+1}) \right)^{-\sigma} \frac{1}{1 + n} (A\theta_{t+1} + 1 - \delta) \right].$$

To construct the linear approximation to this equation we define an auxiliary function:

$$F = \left(\frac{1}{1 + n} \frac{x_{t+1}}{x_t} (A\theta_t - x_t + 1 - \delta) \right)^{-\sigma} \frac{1}{1 + n} (A\theta_{t+1} + 1 - \delta),$$

to have[20]

$$\frac{\partial F}{\partial x_{t+1}} = -\sigma \frac{1}{x_t} \frac{A\theta_t - x_t + 1 - \delta}{1+n} \left(\frac{x_{t+1}}{x_t} \frac{A\theta_t - x_t + 1 - \delta}{1+n} \right)^{-\sigma-1}$$

$$\times \frac{1}{1+n} (A\theta_{t+1} + 1 - \delta),$$

$$\frac{\partial F}{\partial x_t} = \sigma \frac{1}{1+n} \frac{x_{t+1}}{x_t} \left[1 + \frac{A\theta_t - x_t + 1 - \delta}{x_t} \right]$$

$$\times \frac{1}{1+n} \left(\frac{x_{t+1}}{x_t} \frac{A\theta_t - x_t + 1 - \delta}{1+n} \right)^{-\sigma-1} (A\theta_{t+1} + 1 - \delta),$$

$$\frac{\partial F}{\partial \ln \theta_{t+1}} = \left(\frac{x_{t+1}}{x_t} \frac{A\theta_t - x_t + 1 - \delta}{1+n} \right)^{-\sigma} \frac{1}{1+n} A\theta_{t+1},$$

$$\frac{\partial F}{\partial \ln \theta_t} = -\sigma \left(\frac{1}{1+n} \right)^2 \frac{x_{t+1}}{x_t} A\theta_t$$

$$\times \left(\frac{x_{t+1}}{x_t} \frac{A\theta_t - x_t + 1 - \delta}{1+n} \right)^{-\sigma-1} (A\theta_{t+1} + 1 - \delta),$$

and using the steady-state relationships

$$F_{ss} = \frac{1}{\beta}, \quad \frac{A\theta_{ss} - x_{ss} + 1 - \delta}{1+n} = 1 + \gamma, \quad \frac{A\theta_{ss} + 1 - \delta}{1+n} = \frac{1}{\beta} (1+\gamma)^\sigma,$$

we can rewrite (6.39) as

$$\frac{1}{\beta} \simeq \frac{1}{\beta} - \frac{\sigma}{\beta x_{ss}} (x_{t+1} - x_{ss}) + \frac{\sigma}{\beta(1+\gamma)} \left(\frac{1}{1+n} + \frac{1+\gamma}{x_{ss}} \right) (x_t - x_{ss})$$

$$+ \frac{A}{1+n} (1+\gamma)^{-\sigma} \ln \theta_{t+1} - \frac{A}{1+n} \frac{\sigma}{\beta(1+\gamma)} \ln \theta_t - v_{t+1}, \tag{6.40}$$

so that from (6.40) and (6.34), we get the matrix system

$$\begin{pmatrix} \frac{\sigma}{\beta x_{ss}} & -\frac{A}{1+n}(1+\gamma)^{-\sigma} \\ 0 & 1 \end{pmatrix} \begin{pmatrix} x_{t+1} - x_{ss} \\ \ln \theta_{t+1} \end{pmatrix}$$

$$= \begin{pmatrix} \frac{\sigma}{\beta(1+\gamma)} \left(\frac{1}{1+n} + \frac{1+\gamma}{x_{ss}} \right) & -\frac{A}{1+n} \frac{\sigma}{\beta(1+\gamma)} \\ 0 & \rho \end{pmatrix} \begin{pmatrix} x_t - x_{ss} \\ \ln \theta_t \end{pmatrix} + \begin{pmatrix} -v_{t+1} \\ \varepsilon_{t+1} \end{pmatrix},$$

which is of the form

$$\Gamma_0 z_{t+1} = \Gamma_1 z_t + \xi_{t+1} \Rightarrow z_{t+1} = (\Gamma_0^{-1} \Gamma_1) z_t + \Gamma_0^{-1} \xi_{t+1}, \tag{6.41}$$

---

[20] Taking again into account the fact that $\frac{\partial F}{\partial \ln \theta_{t+1}} = \frac{\partial F}{\partial \theta_{t+1}} \theta_{t+1}$. Additionally, $\theta_{ss} = 1$, so that $\ln \theta_{ss} = 0$.

where z_t is the vector of variables $z_t = (x_t - x_{ss}, \ln \theta_t)'$, and the elements of the Γ_0, Γ_1 matrices are just functions of the values of the structural parameters. As usual, we will define stability conditions using the rows in the inverse of the matrix of eigenvectors for $\Gamma_0^{-1}\Gamma_1$ to impose the orthogonality conditions between eigenvectors associated to unstable eigenvalues[21] of $\Gamma_0^{-1}\Gamma_1$ and the vector of variables z_t. In this case, with x_t a 'decision' variable and θ_t a state variable, we should expect to have a single unstable eigenvalue, i.e., a single stability condition, of the form[22]:

$$m_1 (x_t - x_{ss}) + m_2 \ln \theta_t = m_1 \left(\frac{\tilde{c}_t}{\tilde{k}_t} - x_{ss} \right) + m_2 \ln \theta_t = 0, \quad \forall t.$$

To that extent, we will use the rows corresponding to the eigenvectors associated to unstable eigenvalues.

But the system has a simple enough structure so that the single stability condition can be characterized analytically. The structure of the matrices for the linear approximation to the AK economy (6.41) is

$$\Gamma_0 = \begin{pmatrix} a & b \\ 0 & 1 \end{pmatrix}, \quad \Gamma_1 = \begin{pmatrix} m & n \\ 0 & \rho \end{pmatrix},$$

so that, the eigenvalues of $(\Gamma_0^{-1}\Gamma_1)'$ are obtained solving the characteristic equation

$$\begin{vmatrix} \frac{m}{a} - \lambda & \frac{n - \rho b}{a} \\ 0 & \rho - \lambda \end{vmatrix} = 0,$$

which has a root $\lambda_1 = \rho$, positive and less than 1. The economy will have a saddle point structure if the other root of the characteristic equation is above one in absolute value. That root is

$$\lambda_2 = \frac{m}{a} = \frac{x_{ss}}{1+\gamma} \left(\frac{1}{1+n} + \frac{1+\gamma}{x_{ss}} \right) = \frac{1}{1+n} \frac{x_{ss}}{1+\gamma} + 1,$$

which is, indeed, greater than 1. Hence, the system in normalized variables has a saddle-point structure, with a single trajectory leading to a unique steady-state of the system. If we normalize eigenvectors to have a first component equal to one, the matrix of associated eigenvectors is

$$\Phi = \begin{pmatrix} 1 & 1 \\ 0 & -\frac{m - \rho a}{n - \rho b} \end{pmatrix} \Rightarrow \Phi^{-1} = \begin{pmatrix} 1 & \frac{n - \rho b}{m - \rho a} \\ 0 & -\frac{n - \rho b}{m - \rho a} \end{pmatrix},$$

so that the stability condition can be added to the model by imposing

---

[21] Those with absolute size above $\frac{1}{\sqrt{\beta}}$.

[22] Note that the ratio $\frac{c_t}{k_t}$ can be written with the growth trend or without it $\frac{\tilde{c}_t}{\tilde{k}_t}$ since the growth rates of both variables are the same.

$$\left(\frac{\tilde{c}_t}{\tilde{k}_t} - x_{ss}\right) + \frac{n-\rho b}{m-\rho a}\ln\theta_t = 0, \quad \forall t \Leftrightarrow \left(\frac{\tilde{c}_t}{\tilde{k}_t} - x_{ss}\right) + \frac{n-\rho b}{m-\rho a}\ln\theta_t = 0,$$

where $\tilde{c}_t = (1+\gamma)^t c_t$, and $\tilde{k}_t = (1+\gamma)^t k_t$, which can be used together with (6.36), to solve the model.

Given a time series for $\ln\theta_t$, and an initial condition for k_0, we can use the stability condition above to obtain c_0, and obtain k_1 from the global constraint of resources, $k_1 = \frac{1}{(1+n)(1+\gamma)}[A\theta_0 k_0 + (1-\delta)k_0 - c_0]$, and the process is repeated for every time period.[23] The expectations error υ_{t+1} can be computed from (6.39), once time series for all variables have already been obtained. The time series obtained by this procedure should satisfy the statistical properties of a rational expectations error: zero mean, lack of autocorrelation, and zero correlation with variables in the information set at the time the conditional expectation was made. All of them can be tested for as suggested by den Haan and Marcet [28].

The original level variables would be obtained by applying the steady state growth rate to the no growth variables we have just obtained, i.e.,

$$\tilde{q}_t = (1+\gamma)^t q_t,$$

where $q_t = c_t, k_t, y_t$. However, they clearly experience exponential growth, so its time evolution over long periods of time is not very interesting.

6.6.2 Numerical Exercise: Solving the Stochastic AK Model

The solution approach we have just described is implemented in the *AKModel.xls* Excel file. A single realization of the main detrended variables is obtained, i.e., after extracting the constant rate of endogenous growth. The consumption to capital ratio, or the period-to-period rates of growth of each of these variables, remain quite stable over time. On the other hand, even after extracting the rate of endogenous growth, per capita variables follow unit root processes, as explained in previous sections, which is quite apparent in the graph representations for the per capita variables *consumption, capital* and *output*. The same variables are also shown including the endogenous growth, but the implied time series are not very interesting, being dominated by what appears as an exponential growth.

On the right panel, we solve the model as a special case of a more complex model as it is explained in sections below. This approach uses a log-linear approximation to the model, producing very similar numerical results. The MATLAB file

---

[23] Again, either the version with growth or the one without growth of the global constraint of resources, could be used to obtain the stock of capital. Alternatively, that constraint could be used to obtain time series for the rate of growth of capital,

$$1 + \gamma_{k_t} = \frac{1}{(1+n)(1+\gamma_{ss})}\left[A\theta_t + (1-\delta)k_t - \frac{c_t}{k_t}\right],$$

to obtain the time series for capital itself, afterwards: $k_{t+1} = \frac{1+\gamma_{k_t}}{1+\gamma}k_t$.

AKStochastic.m, also computes a single realization of the *AK* economy with stochastic productivity using the linear approximation of the previous paragraph. The number of observations can be chosen at the beginning of the file. The program produces graphs for the realizations of the main variables in the economy, after discounting their deterministic endogenous growth component. The *mAKStochastic.m* file computes a number of sample realizations chosen by the user at the beginning of the program and displays a summary of the sample distributions for some interesting statistics, like volatilities and correlations between variables.

6.7 An Endogenous Growth Model with Productive Public Expenditures: Barro's Model

Barro [4] introduced a version of the *AK* model including the services provided by public expenditures $\widetilde{g}_t$ as an additional productive input

$$\widetilde{y}_t = A\widetilde{k}_t^\alpha \widetilde{g}_t^{1-\alpha}, \quad 0 < \alpha < 1.$$

The presence of the services provided by public expenditures can be rationalized under full depreciation of public capital. Then, public expenditures becomes equal to public investment, which would substitute for public capital as a second input in the aggregate technology. We would then have a technology with decreasing returns to scale in each of the two inputs, private and public capital, but constant returns to scale in the aggregate.

The government follows a balanced-budget policy every period and raises proportional income taxes at a rate τ, which determines the level of public expenditures,[24]

$$\widetilde{g}_t = \tau\widetilde{y}_t = \tau A\widetilde{k}_t^\alpha \widetilde{g}_t^{1-\alpha} \Rightarrow \widetilde{g}_t = (\tau A)^{1/\alpha}\widetilde{k}_t. \tag{6.42}$$

Public expenditures accumulate over time because they are proportional to private capital, which is a cumulative input.

From (6.42) the production function can be written as a version of the standard *AK* model

$$\widetilde{y}_t = A\widetilde{k}_t^\alpha (\tau A)^{\frac{1-\alpha}{\alpha}} \widetilde{k}_t^{1-\alpha} = \left(\tau^{1-\alpha}A\right)^{\frac{1}{\alpha}}\widetilde{k}_t,$$

and consequently, as we show below, this model also lacks transitional dynamics.

Maintaining the assumption of a *CRRA* utility function, the Lagrangian for the representative agent problem is

$$L = \sum_{t=0}^\infty \beta^t \left\{ \frac{\widetilde{c}_t^{1-\sigma}-1}{1-\sigma} - \lambda_t \left[(1+n)\widetilde{k}_{t+1}\right. \right.$$
$$\left.\left. - (1-\tau)A\widetilde{k}_t^\alpha \widetilde{g}_t^{1-\alpha} + \widetilde{c}_t - (1-\delta)\widetilde{k}_t\right]\right\},$$

---

[24] Again, government expenditures become endogenous because of the structure of the financing policy.

with optimality conditions

$$\tilde{c}_t^{-\sigma} = \lambda_t,$$
$$(1+n)\lambda_t = \beta\lambda_{t+1}\left[(1-\tau)A\alpha\tilde{k}_{t+1}^{\alpha-1}\tilde{g}_{t+1}^{1-\alpha} - (1-\delta)\right],$$

that, using (6.42) lead to the Euler equation

$$1+\gamma_{\tilde{c}_{t+1}} \equiv \frac{\tilde{c}_{t+1}}{\tilde{c}_t} = \left(\beta\frac{(1-\tau)\alpha A^{\frac{1}{\alpha}}\tau^{\frac{1-\alpha}{\alpha}} + (1-\delta)}{1+n}\right)^{\frac{1}{\sigma}}.$$

We will use this condition together with the global constraint of resources

$$(1+n)\tilde{k}_{t+1} = (1-\tau)A\tilde{k}_t^{\alpha}\tilde{g}_t^{1-\alpha} - \tilde{c}_t + (1-\delta)\tilde{k}_t, \tag{6.43}$$

and the transversality condition $\lim_{t\to\infty}(1+n)\beta^t\lambda_t\tilde{k}_{t+1} = 0$, where λ_t is the Lagrange multiplier associated to the global constraint of resources.

The Euler condition shows that the rate of growth of consumption $\tilde{c}_t$ is constant over time. Since public expenditures are proportional to private capital every period, both inputs share the same growth rate at all points in time. Besides, from (6.43), we have

$$\frac{\tilde{c}_t}{\tilde{k}_t} = (1-\tau)A\left(\frac{\tilde{k}_t}{\tilde{g}_t}\right)^{\alpha-1} + (1-\delta) - (1+n)(1+\gamma_{k_{t+1}}).$$

Since $\frac{\tilde{k}_t}{\tilde{g}_t} = \frac{1}{(\tau A)^{\frac{1}{\alpha}}}$ is constant, there is a *balanced growth path* equilibrium with consumption and physical capital growing at the same rate, which makes the ratio $\frac{\tilde{c}_t}{\tilde{k}_t}$ to be constant. So, we have, $\gamma_c = \gamma_k = \gamma_g = \gamma$ and the steady state is of the *balanced growth path* class, with all per capita variables growing at the same constant rate in all time periods.

In terms of detrended, no-growth variables, c_t, k_t, defined by $\tilde{c}_t = (1+\gamma)^t c_t$, $\tilde{k}_t = (1+\gamma)^t k_t$, we have: $c_{t+1} = c_t$, and the system above can be written

$$\begin{pmatrix} c_{t+1} \\ k_{t+1} \end{pmatrix} = \begin{pmatrix} 1 & 0 \\ -\frac{1}{(1+n)(1+\gamma)} & \frac{(1-\tau)A^{\frac{1}{\alpha}}\tau^{\frac{1-\alpha}{\alpha}}+(1-\delta)}{(1+n)(1+\gamma)} \end{pmatrix}\begin{pmatrix} c_t \\ k_t \end{pmatrix} = B\begin{pmatrix} c_t \\ k_t \end{pmatrix},$$

the transition matrix B having eigenvalues 1 and $\eta = \frac{(1-\tau)A^{\frac{1}{\alpha}}\tau^{\frac{1-\alpha}{\alpha}}+(1-\delta)}{(1+n)(1+\gamma)}$, the latter being greater than one. To show this, we consider the transversality condition

$$\lim_{t\to\infty}(1+n)\beta^t\tilde{\lambda}_t\tilde{k}_{t+1} = \lim_{t\to\infty}(1+n)\beta^t\tilde{c}_t^{-\sigma}\tilde{k}_{t+1}$$

$$= \lim_{t\to\infty}(1+n)\beta^t(1+\gamma)^{-\sigma t}\tilde{c}_0^{-\sigma}(1+\gamma)^t(1+\gamma)\tilde{k}_0$$

$$= (1+n)(1+\gamma)\tilde{c}_0^{-\sigma}\tilde{k}_0\lim_{t\to\infty}\left[\beta(1+\gamma)^{1-\sigma}\right]^t = 0,$$

which will hold only if $\beta(1+\gamma)^{1-\sigma} < 1$, which amounts to

$$1+\gamma < \frac{(1+\gamma)^{\sigma}}{\beta} = \frac{(1-\tau)\alpha A^{\frac{1}{\alpha}}\tau^{\frac{1-\alpha}{\alpha}} + (1-\delta)}{1+n} < \eta,$$

showing that the second eigenvalue of the transition matrix above is, indeed, greater than one, since $\gamma > 0$.

Following the same argument as in Sect. 6.2.2, the solution to the dynamic system is

$$k_t = \left[\frac{1}{(1+n)(1+\gamma)(\eta-1)}\right]c_0 + \left(k_0 - \frac{1}{(1+n)(1+\gamma)(\eta-1)}c_0\right)\eta^t.$$

Since $\eta > 1$, the solution for k_t will be explosive unless $c_0 = (1+n)(1+\gamma)(\eta-1)k_0$, a condition which eliminates the unstable path. Along the implied solution, the no-growth versions of consumption and private capital will remain constant at their initial values, for all t. The same happens with public expenditures, which are proportional to private capital, so this economy also lacks any transitional dynamics.

As we can see, once we eliminate the trend produced by the constant rate of growth, models that generate endogenous growth usually have an eigenvalue equal to one and as many eigenvalues greater than one in absolute value as control variables, in order to have a saddle point structure.[25] In the particular case of an endogenous growth model with a single state and a single control variable like the one discussed so far, the unstable eigenvalue allows for determination of equilibrium, while the unit eigenvalue produces lack of transitional dynamics.

6.8 Transitional Dynamics in Endogenous Growth: The Jones and Manuelli Model

The models presented in the previous sections lack transitional dynamics with constant growth rates over time. Jones and Manuelli [47] present an economy that experiences transitional dynamics with endogenous growth. These authors consider a technology that combines a standard constant returns to scale technology with labor and capital inputs, with an AK technology,

$$\widetilde{Y}_t = A\widetilde{K}_t + G\left(\widetilde{K}_t, \widetilde{N}_t\right) = A\widetilde{K}_t + B\widetilde{K}_t^{\alpha}\widetilde{N}_t^{1-\alpha}.$$

Alternatively, $G\left(\widetilde{K}_t, \widetilde{N}_t\right)$ could be any technology satisfying the properties of the standard neoclassical production function (decreasing marginal productivity in each

---

[25] The remaining eigenvalues, if any will be smaller than one in absolute value. In the two models considered, there is a control variable and a single state variable, so an eigenvalue is equal to one and the other one is greater than one in absolute value.

input, constant returns to scale on the aggregate, and the Inada conditions). However, the previous production function violates one of the Inada conditions, since the marginal product of capital converges to a non-zero, positive constant A when the stock of physical capital increases without bound. The AK-component of the production function will produce endogenous growth, while the other component will generate richer dynamics than the models analyzed in previous sections.

The planner solves the time aggregate utility maximization problem, facing a global constraint of resources in per capita terms,

$$(1+n)\widetilde{k}_{t+1} = A\widetilde{k}_t + B\widetilde{k}_t^{\alpha} - \widetilde{c}_t + (1-\delta)\widetilde{k}_t. \tag{6.44}$$

Assuming a constant relative risk aversion utility function, first order conditions for the maximization of the Lagrangian are

$$\widetilde{c}_t^{-\sigma} = \lambda_t,$$

$$(1+n)\lambda_t = \beta\left(A + B\alpha\widetilde{k}_{t+1}^{\alpha-1} + (1-\delta)\right)\lambda_{t+1}.$$

From these, we get the Euler equation

$$1+\gamma_{c_{t+1}} \equiv \frac{\widetilde{c}_{t+1}}{\widetilde{c}_t} = \left(\beta\frac{A + \alpha B\widetilde{k}_{t+1}^{\alpha-1} + (1-\delta)}{1+n}\right)^{\frac{1}{\sigma}}, \tag{6.45}$$

that shows a time varying rate of growth of per capita consumption that depends on the stock of capital.

Given $\widetilde{k}_0$, optimality conditions are summarized by (6.44), (6.45) and the transversality condition

$$\lim_{t\to\infty}(1+n)\beta^t\widetilde{c}_t^{-\sigma}\widetilde{k}_{t+1} = 0.$$

To analyze the dynamics of the model, we define auxiliary variables, $z_t = \widetilde{y}_t/\widetilde{k}_t$, $x_t = \widetilde{c}_t/\widetilde{k}_t$, which should display zero growth along a balanced growth steady-state. In terms of the auxiliary variables we have

$$z_t = A + B\widetilde{k}_t^{\alpha-1} \Rightarrow B\widetilde{k}_t^{\alpha-1} = z_t - A, \tag{6.46}$$

while the rate of growth of per capita physical capital can be obtained dividing through the global constraint of resources by $\widetilde{k}_t$,

$$(1+n)(1+\gamma_{k_{t+1}}) = A + B\widetilde{k}_t^{\alpha-1} - x_t + (1-\delta) \tag{6.47}$$

$$\Rightarrow 1+\gamma_{k_{t+1}} = \frac{z_t - x_t + (1-\delta)}{1+n}.$$

We can now write a system summarizing the dynamics of this economy in variables displaying zero growth in steady-state. First, we use (6.46) in the identity $\widetilde{k}_{t+1}^{\alpha-1} = \widetilde{k}_t^{\alpha-1}(1+\gamma_{k_{t+1}})^{\alpha-1}$ to obtain

$$z_{t+1} = A + (z_t - A) \left(\frac{1+n}{z_t - x_t + (1-\delta)} \right)^{1-\alpha}, \tag{6.48}$$

where we have used expression (6.47) for the rate of growth of capital. Secondly, dividing through (6.45) by $\tilde{k}_{t+1}$ and using the fact that $\frac{\tilde{c}_t}{\tilde{k}_{t+1}} = \frac{\tilde{c}_t}{\tilde{k}_t} \frac{\tilde{k}_t}{\tilde{k}_{t+1}} = \frac{\tilde{c}_t}{\tilde{k}_t} \frac{1}{1+\gamma_{k_{t+1}}}$ together with (6.46) and (6.47), we get

$$x_{t+1} = x_t \frac{1+n}{z_t - x_t + (1-\delta)} \left(\beta \frac{A + \alpha (z_{t+1} - A) + 1 - \delta}{1+n} \right)^{1/\sigma}. \tag{6.49}$$

Numerical solutions to this model economy will be obtained below from the system made up by (6.48) and (6.49).

6.8.1 Steady-State

The steady-state equilibrium will be reached when $\tilde{c}_t$, as well as $\tilde{k}_t$, grow at a constant rate. But, as in previous sections, the global constraint of resources implies that consumption and capital must grow at the same rate in steady state. Besides, from expression (6.45) for $1+\gamma_{c_t}$ we see that such a limit growth rate must be

$$1 + \gamma = \left(\beta \frac{A + (1-\delta)}{1+n} \right)^{\frac{1}{\sigma}}, \tag{6.50}$$

since, with positive growth, $\tilde{k}_{t+1}^{\alpha-1} \to 0$ when $t \to \infty$. Steady-state growth will actually be positive for sufficiently high levels of productivity: $A + (1-\delta) > \frac{1+n}{\beta}$. We first evaluate (6.48) and (6.49) at steady-state to obtain steady-state values of z_t, x_t:

$$z_{ss} = A,$$

$$x_{ss} = x_{ss} \frac{1+n}{z_{ss} - x_{ss} + (1-\delta)} \left(\beta \frac{A + \alpha (z_{ss} - A) + 1 - \delta}{1+n} \right)^{1/\sigma},$$

so that,

$$A - x_{ss} + (1-\delta) = (1+n) \left(\beta \frac{A+1-\delta}{1+n} \right)^{1/\sigma}$$

$$\Rightarrow A - x_{ss} + (1-\delta) = (1+n)(1+\gamma)$$

$$\Rightarrow x_{ss} = A + (1-\delta) - (1+n)(1+\gamma).$$

Plugging now the steady-state values x_{ss}, z_{ss} in (6.47) we get the same steady-state rate of growth as in (6.50).

Furthermore, to guarantee that growth is actually positive, the transversality condition implies that the parameters must satisfy the condition,

$$\lim_{t\to\infty}(1+n)\beta^t\tilde{\lambda}_t\tilde{k}_{t+1}=0 \Rightarrow \text{(in steady state) } \beta\,(1+\gamma)^{1-\sigma} < 1.$$

6.8.2 Solving the Deterministic Version of Jones and Manuelli's Model Through a Linear Approximation

To produce a numerical solution, we linearize (6.48), (6.49) around steady state. To do so, let us denote

$$f(z_{t+1},x_{t+1},z_t,x_t) = (z_{t+1}-A) - (z_t-A)\left(\frac{1+n}{z_t-x_t+(1-\delta)}\right)^{1-\alpha},$$

$$g(z_{t+1},x_{t+1},z_t,x_t) = x_{t+1}-x_t\frac{1+n}{z_t-x_t+(1-\delta)}$$
$$\times\left(\beta\frac{A+\alpha\,(z_{t+1}-A)+1-\delta}{1+n}\right)^{1/\sigma},$$

so that

$$\frac{\partial f}{\partial z_{t+1}} = 1$$

$$\frac{\partial f}{\partial z_t} = -\left(\frac{1+n}{z_t-x_t+(1-\delta)}\right)^{1-\alpha} - (z_t-A)(1-\alpha)$$
$$\times\frac{1+n}{[z_t-x_t+(1-\delta)]^2}\left(\frac{1+n}{z_t-x_t+(1-\delta)}\right)^{-\alpha};$$

$$\frac{\partial f}{\partial x_{t+1}} = 0$$

$$\frac{\partial f}{\partial x_t} = -(z_t-A)(1-\alpha)\left(\frac{1+n}{z_t-x_t+(1-\delta)}\right)^{-\alpha}$$
$$\times\frac{1+n}{[z_t-x_t+(1-\delta)]^2};$$

$$\frac{\partial g}{\partial z_{t+1}} = -x_t\frac{1+n}{z_t-x_t+(1-\delta)}\frac{1}{\sigma}\frac{\beta\alpha}{1+n}$$
$$\times\left(\beta\frac{A+\alpha\,(z_{t+1}-A)+1-\delta}{1+n}\right)^{\frac{1}{\sigma}-1};$$

$$\frac{\partial g}{\partial z_t} = -x_t\frac{1+n}{[z_t-x_t+(1-\delta)]^2}\left(\beta\frac{A+\alpha\,(z_{t+1}-A)+1-\delta}{1+n}\right)^{1/\sigma};$$

$$\frac{\partial g}{\partial x_{t+1}} = 1;$$

$$\frac{\partial g}{\partial x_t} = -\left(\frac{1+n}{z_t - x_t + (1-\delta)} + x_t \frac{1+n}{[z_t - x_t + (1-\delta)]^2}\right)$$

$$\times \left(\beta \frac{A + \alpha(z_{t+1} - A) + 1 - \delta}{1+n}\right)^{1/\sigma};$$

but in steady-state: $z_{ss} = A$, $\frac{1+n}{z_t - x_t + (1-\delta)} = \frac{1}{1+\gamma}$, so that the partial derivatives become

$$\left.\frac{\partial f}{\partial z_{t+1}}\right|_{ss} = 1; \quad \left.\frac{\partial f}{\partial z_t}\right|_{ss} = -\frac{1}{(1+\gamma)^{1-\alpha}};$$

$$\left.\frac{\partial f}{\partial x_{t+1}}\right|_{ss} = 0; \quad \left.\frac{\partial f}{\partial x_t}\right|_{ss} = 0;$$

$$\left.\frac{\partial g}{\partial z_{t+1}}\right|_{ss} = -\frac{x_{ss}}{1+\gamma}(1+\gamma)\frac{1+n}{A + (1-\delta)}\frac{1}{\beta\sigma}\frac{\beta\alpha}{1+n}$$

$$= -[A + (1-\delta) - (1+n)(1+\gamma)]\frac{1}{A + (1-\delta)}\frac{\alpha}{\sigma}$$

$$= -\frac{\alpha}{\sigma}\left(1 - \frac{(1+n)(1+\gamma)}{A + (1-\delta)}\right);$$

$$\left.\frac{\partial g}{\partial z_t}\right|_{ss} = -\frac{x_{ss}}{(1+n)(1+\gamma)} = -\frac{A + (1-\delta)}{(1+n)(1+\gamma)} + 1;$$

$$\left.\frac{\partial g}{\partial x_{t+1}}\right|_{ss} = 1;$$

$$\frac{\partial g}{\partial x_t} = -\frac{1}{1+\gamma}\left(1 + \frac{x_{ss}}{(1+n)(1+\gamma)}\right)(1+\gamma)$$

$$= -\frac{A + (1-\delta)}{(1+n)(1+\gamma)};$$

and we have the linearized system:

$$\begin{pmatrix} 1 & 0 \\ \kappa_1 & 1 \end{pmatrix}\begin{pmatrix} \hat{z}_{t+1} \\ \hat{x}_{t+1} \end{pmatrix} = \begin{pmatrix} \frac{1}{(1+\gamma)^{1-\alpha}} & 0 \\ \frac{x_{ss}}{(1+n)(1+\gamma)} & \frac{A+(1-\delta)}{(1+n)(1+\gamma)} \end{pmatrix}\begin{pmatrix} \hat{z}_t \\ \hat{x}_t \end{pmatrix},$$

or, equivalently,

$$\begin{pmatrix} \hat{z}_{t+1} \\ \hat{x}_{t+1} \end{pmatrix} = \begin{pmatrix} \frac{1}{(1+\gamma)^{1-\alpha}} & 0 \\ \kappa_2 & 1 + \frac{x_{ss}}{(1+n)(1+\gamma)} \end{pmatrix}\begin{pmatrix} \hat{z}_t \\ \hat{x}_t \end{pmatrix},$$

where $\hat{z}_t = z_t - A$, $\hat{x}_t = x_t - x_{ss}$, $x_{ss} = (A + 1 - \delta) - (1 + n)(1 + \gamma)$, $\kappa_1 = \frac{\alpha}{\sigma}\left(1 - \frac{(1+n)(1+\gamma)}{A+(1-\delta)}\right)$, and $\kappa_2 = \frac{\alpha}{\sigma}\left(\frac{x_{ss}}{A+1-\delta}\right)\frac{1}{(1+\gamma)^{1-\alpha}} + \frac{x_{ss}}{(1+n)(1+\gamma)}$.

Eigenvalues of the previous system are $\frac{1}{(1+\gamma)^{1-\sigma}}$ and $1+\frac{x_{ss}}{(1+n)(1+\gamma)}$. The first eigenvalue will be less than one whenever steady-state growth is positive, i.e., $A+(1-\delta) > \frac{1+n}{\beta}$. On the other hand, it is not hard to see that the second eigenvalue is above 1. The transformed model does not display endogenous growth, since we do not have an eigenvalue equal to one. On the contrary, it has the saddle point structure we need to solve, since z_0 is an exogenous state variable[26] while x_t is a control variable whose initial value x_0 needs to be chosen optimally.

The solution to the system is

$$z_t - A = \left[(1+\gamma)^{\alpha-1} \right]^t (z_0 - A), \tag{6.51}$$

$$x_{t+1} - x_{ss} = \kappa_2 \left[(1+\gamma)^{\alpha-1} \right]^t (z_0 - A) + \Omega \left(x_t - x_{ss} \right), \tag{6.52}$$

where

$$\Omega = 1 + \frac{x_{ss}}{(1+n)(1+\gamma)}.$$

The solution for the dynamic equation (6.52) is given by

$$x_t - x_{ss} = \frac{\kappa_2 (z_0 - A)}{(1+\gamma)^{\alpha-1} - \Omega} \left[(1+\gamma)^{\alpha-1} \right]^t$$

$$+ \Omega^t \left[(x_0 - x_{ss}) - \frac{\kappa_2 (z_0 - A)}{(1+\gamma)^{\alpha-1} - \Omega} \right].$$

Since $\Omega > 1$, to guarantee stability we must impose the condition

$$x_0 = x_{ss} + \frac{\kappa_2}{(1+\gamma)^{\alpha-1} - \Omega} (z_0 - A).$$

Thus, given k_0, we can compute the value for z_0. The system will evolve over time on its stable trajectory if and only if the initial condition for the control variable x_t fulfills the previous condition, starting from its steady-state value, corrected by $\frac{\kappa_2}{(1+\gamma)^{\alpha-1} - \Omega} (z_0 - A)$. For any initial k_0, the value for z_0 will always be different from its steady-state level of A, since $z_0 = A + Bk_0^{1-\alpha}$, eventually converging to it so long as the economy follows its stable trajectory.

---

[26] As a consequence of the fact that k_0 is given and so is y_0 which is a function of just k_0.

6.9 The Stochastic Version of Jones and Manuelli Model

To have a stochastic version of the Jones–Manuelli growth model, we consider the production technology:

$$\tilde{Y}_t = \theta_t \left(A\tilde{K}_t + B\tilde{K}_t^\alpha \tilde{N}_t^{1-\alpha} \right),$$

or, in per capita terms:

$$\tilde{y}_t = \theta_t \left(A\tilde{k}_t + B\tilde{k}_t^\alpha \right),$$

where θ_t is a productivity shock, that obeys the stochastic process:

$$\ln \theta_t = \rho \ln \theta_{t-1} + \varepsilon_t, \quad |\rho| < 1, \quad \varepsilon_t \underset{iid}{\sim} N(0, \sigma_\varepsilon^2).$$

The problem for the representative agent is

$$\max_{\{\tilde{c}_t, \tilde{k}_{t+1}\}} E_0 \sum_{t=0}^{\infty} \beta^t \frac{\tilde{c}_t^{1-\sigma} - 1}{1-\sigma}$$

subject to

$$(1+n)\tilde{k}_{t+1} - (1-\delta)\tilde{k}_t + (1+\tau^c)\tilde{c}_t = (1-\tau^y)\theta_t \left(A\tilde{k}_t + B\tilde{k}_t^\alpha \right) + \tilde{g}_t, \qquad (6.53)$$

and given $\tilde{k}_0$. Relative to the previous section, we have introduced proportional consumption and income taxes in addition the productivity shock. As in previous sections, the government is supposed to use tax revenues to finance lump-sum transfers to consumers ($\tilde{g}_t$).

The Lagrangian for this problem is

$$L = E_0 \sum_{t=0}^{\infty} \beta^t \frac{\tilde{c}_t^{1-\sigma} - 1}{1-\sigma} + \beta^t \lambda_t \left[(1-\tau^y)\theta_t \left(A\tilde{k}_t + B\tilde{k}_t^\alpha \right) + \tilde{g}_t \right.$$
$$\left. - (1+n)\tilde{k}_{t+1} + (1-\delta)\tilde{k}_t - (1+\tau^c)\tilde{c}_t \right].$$

with first order conditions:

$$\tilde{c}_t^{-\sigma} = \lambda_t(1+\tau^c), \qquad (6.54)$$

$$(1+n)\lambda_t = \beta E_t \left[\lambda_{t+1} \left((1-\tau^y)\theta_{t+1} \left(A + \alpha B\tilde{k}_{t+1}^{\alpha-1} \right) + 1 - \delta \right) \right], \qquad (6.55)$$

together with the transversality condition $\lim_{T \to \infty} (1+n)\beta^{T+t} E_t \tilde{c}_{t+T}^{-\sigma} \tilde{k}_{t+T+1} = 0$.

From conditions (6.54) and (6.55) we obtain the stochastic Euler or Keynes–Ramsey condition:

$$(1+n)\tilde{c}_t^{-\sigma} = \beta E_t \left[\tilde{c}_{t+1}^{-\sigma} \left((1-\tau^y)\theta_{t+1} \left(A + \alpha B\tilde{k}_{t+1}^{\alpha-1} \right) + 1 - \delta \right) \right]. \qquad (6.56)$$

6.9.1 Deterministic Balanced Growth Path

Along the deterministic *Balanced Growth Path* (BGP in what follows) we have $\theta_t = \theta_{ss} = 1$, $\forall t$, $\tilde{c}_{t+1}/\tilde{c}_t = 1 + \gamma_c$, $\tilde{k}_{t+1}/\tilde{k}_t = 1 + \gamma_k$, $\tilde{y}_{t+1}/\tilde{y}_t = 1 + \gamma_y$, where γ_c, γ_k, γ_y are constants. From (6.53) we also have, along the BGP

$$\left(\frac{\tilde{c}_t}{\tilde{k}_t}\right) = -\frac{\left[(1+\gamma_k)(1+n) - (1-\delta) - (1-\tau^y)\left(A + B\tilde{k}_t^{\alpha-1}\right)\right]}{(1+\tau^c)}. \tag{6.57}$$

Taking into account that the capital stock will grow along the BGP at a constant, positive rate, we have $\lim_{t\to\infty}\tilde{k}_t^{\alpha-1} = 0$, and (6.57) implies that the ratio $\frac{\tilde{c}_t}{\tilde{k}_t}$ eventually becomes constant, since the left-hand side at (6.57) is constant. That, in turn, means that the long-run growth rates of consumption and physical capital are the same. Therefore,

$$\left(\frac{\tilde{c}_t}{\tilde{k}_t}\right)_{ss} = \frac{1}{1+\tau^c}\left[(1-\tau^y)A + (1-\delta) - (1+\gamma_k)(1+n)\right], \tag{6.58}$$

while the linear technology implies that $\left(\frac{\tilde{y}_t}{\tilde{k}_t}\right)_{ss} = A$, so that in the long-run, output and capital will also grow at the same rate.

From (6.56) we have

$$1 + \gamma = \left[\frac{\beta}{1+n}\left((1-\tau^y)A + 1 - \delta\right)\right]^{1/\sigma}, \tag{6.59}$$

an extension of the condition in Sect. 6.8, to an economy with taxes.

6.9.2 Transforming the Model in Stationary Ratios

Consider the transformation:

$$z_t = \frac{\tilde{y}_t}{\tilde{k}_t} = \theta_t\left(A + B\tilde{k}_t^{\alpha-1}\right), \tag{6.60}$$

$$x_t = \frac{\tilde{c}_t}{\tilde{k}_t}, \tag{6.61}$$

so that, as we saw in the deterministic case: $z_{ss} = A$, and $x_{ss} = \frac{1}{1+\tau^c}[(1-\tau^y)A + (1-\delta) - (1+\gamma)(1+n)]$.

From the definition (6.60), we have that $\tilde{k}_t = \left(\frac{z_t/\theta_t - A}{B}\right)^{1/(\alpha-1)}$. Hence,

$$\frac{\tilde{k}_{t+1}}{\tilde{k}_t} = \left(\frac{\frac{z_t}{\theta_t} - A}{\frac{z_{t+1}}{\theta_{t+1}} - A}\right)^{1/(1-\alpha)}. \tag{6.62}$$

Using the budget constraint for the representative agent, together with (6.60), (6.61) and (6.62), we have

$$(1+n)\left(\frac{\frac{z_t}{\theta_t}-A}{\frac{z_{t+1}}{\theta_{t+1}}-A}\right)^{1/(1-\alpha)} = (1-\tau^y)z_t + (1-\delta) - x_t(1+\tau^c), \qquad (6.63)$$

or,

$$z_{t+1} = \theta_{t+1}\left\{A + \left(\frac{z_t}{\theta_t}-A\right)\right. \qquad (6.64)$$

$$\left.\times \left[\frac{1+n}{(1-\tau^y)z_t + (1-\delta) - x_t(1+\tau^c)}\right]^{(1-\alpha)}\right\}.$$

Using Keynes–Ramsey condition, together with (6.60), (6.61) and (6.62), we have

$$x_t^{-\sigma} = \frac{\beta}{1+n}E_t\left[\left(\frac{z_t/\theta_t - A}{z_{t+1}/\theta_{t+1} - A}\right)^{-\sigma/(1-\alpha)} x_{t+1}^{-\sigma}\right.$$

$$\left.\times \left[(1-\tau^y)((1-\alpha)A\theta_{t+1} + \alpha z_{t+1}) + 1 - \delta\right]\right],$$

and finally, using (6.63)

$$\left(\frac{x_t(1+n)}{(1-\tau^y)z_t + (1-\delta) - x_t(1+\tau^c)}\right)^{-\sigma}$$

$$= \frac{\beta}{1+n}E_t\left[x_{t+1}^{-\sigma}((1-\tau^y)((1-\alpha)A\theta_{t+1} + \alpha z_{t+1}) + 1 - \delta)\right] \qquad (6.65)$$

Expressions (6.64) and (6.65) completely characterize the dynamics of this model. Notice that in a typical AK economy, $B = 0$, and we would have: $z_t = \theta_t A$ in the stochastic version of the economy, or just $z_t = A$ in the deterministic version, $\forall t$, and (6.65) would define by itself the dynamics of the consumption to capital ratio.

6.9.3 The Phase Diagram of the Deterministic Version of the Jones–Manuelli Model: Transitional Dynamics

We can write expression (6.64) in its deterministic version, more conveniently:

$$z_{t+1} - z_t = (z_t - A) \qquad (6.66)$$

$$\times \left\{\left[\frac{1+n}{(1-\tau^y)z_t + (1-\delta) - x_t(1+\tau^c)}\right]^{(1-\alpha)} - 1\right\}.$$

From here, we can obtain pairs of values for z and x for which the z variable remains unchanged, $z_{t+1} = z_t$. That will be the case whenever

$$z_t = A \tag{6.67}$$

or whenever $\left[\dfrac{1+n}{(1-\tau^y)z_t + (1-\delta) - x_t(1+\tau^c)} \right]^{(1-\alpha)} = 1$, i.e., when

$$x_t = \frac{1}{1+\tau^c} [(1-\tau^y)z_t - n - \delta]. \tag{6.68}$$

We can write the deterministic version of (6.65) more conveniently:

$$\left(\frac{x_{t+1}}{x_t} \right)^\sigma = \left(\frac{1+n}{(1-\tau^y)z_t + (1-\delta) - x_t(1+\tau^c)} \right)^\sigma \tag{6.69}$$
$$\times \frac{\beta}{1+n} [(1-\tau^y)(A + \alpha(z_{t+1} - A)) + 1 - \delta].$$

From this expression, we can obtain pairs of values for z and x for which the x variable remains unchanged, $x_{t+1} = x_t$. That will be the case whenever:

$$1 = \left(\frac{1+n}{(1-\tau^y)z_t + (1-\delta) - x_t(1+\tau^c)} \right)^\sigma \frac{\beta}{1+n} \tag{6.70}$$
$$\times \left[(1-\tau^y) \left(A + \alpha(z_t - A) \right. \right.$$
$$\times \left. \left(\frac{1+n}{(1-\tau^y)z_t + (1-\delta) - x_t(1+\tau^c)} \right)^{(1-\alpha)} \right) + 1 - \delta \right].$$

The steady-state will be characterized by the intersection of either one of the two curves (6.67), (6.68) with curve (6.70). The Matlab program *dfase.m* computes the representation for the three curves in a (z, x)-plane. It can be noticed that (6.68) and (6.70) intersect for a negative, not feasible value of z_t, while the intersection of (6.67) with (6.70) provides us with a well defined steady-state.

The graph also displays the transitional dynamics for z and x for a given parameterization and an initial value of the state variable z, once an approximate solution has been obtained following the steps described in the next paragraph. Such representation is captured in the Fig. 6.1, where the arrows indicate the directions of movements in z and x when they are outside steady-state. If the economy is on the (6.68)-line, a marginal increase in x keeping constant z, will lead to an increase in z as time advances, since the right-hand side of (6.66) takes a higher value. The opposite would happen for a marginal decrease in x. Therefore, above the (6.68)-line, z increases over time and, above that line, z decreases over time. If the economy is on the (6.70)-line, a marginal increase in z keeping x constant, will lead to a decrease in x as time advances, since the right-hand side at (6.69) takes a lower value. The

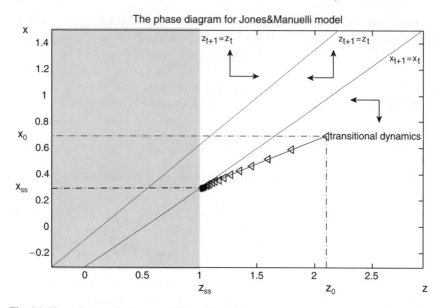

Fig. 6.1 Phase diagram for Jones and Manuelli model

opposite would happen for a marginal decrease in z. Hence, above the (6.70)-line, x increases over time while below that line, x decreases over time. Notice that z can never be below its steady-state level.

6.9.4 Computing the Dynamics: Log-Linear Approximation

Let us define the ratios $\hat{z}_t = \ln(z_t/A)$, $\hat{x}_t = \ln(x_t/x_{ss})$. We write (6.64) in a more convenient fashion:

$$0 = -e^{\ln z_{t+1}} + e^{\ln \theta_{t+1}}\left\{A + \left(e^{\ln z_t - \ln \theta_t} - A\right)\right. \tag{6.71}$$

$$\left. \times \left[\frac{1+n}{(1-\tau^y)e^{\ln z_t} + (1-\delta) - e^{\ln x_t}(1+\tau^c)}\right]^{1/(1-\alpha)}\right\}.$$

from which we get the log-linear approximation:

$$\hat{z}_{t+1} = (1+\gamma)^{\alpha-1}\hat{z}_t + \hat{\theta}_{t+1}, \tag{6.72}$$

where $\hat{\theta}_{t+1} = \ln \theta_{t+1}$, indicating that in such approximation, $\hat{z}_t$ follows an autoregressive process, which will be of order 1 if θ_t is a white noise, or of order 2 if θ_t follows a first order autoregressive process.

We can now write (6.65)

$$0 = E_t \left\{ -\left(\frac{e^{\ln x_t}(1+n)}{(1-\tau^y)e^{\ln z_t} + (1-\delta) - e^{\ln x_t}(1+\tau^c)} \right)^{-\sigma} \right.$$
$$\left. + \frac{\beta}{1+n} e^{-\sigma \ln x_{t+1}} \left[(1-\tau^y)((1-\alpha)Ae^{\ln \theta_{t+1}} + \alpha e^{\ln z_{t+1}}) + 1 - \delta \right] \right\},$$

from which we obtain its log-linear approximation:

$$0 = E_t \begin{bmatrix} \sigma \left(\frac{x_{ss}(1+n)}{(1-\tau^y)A+(1-\delta)-x_{ss}(1+\tau^c)} \right)^{-\sigma-1} \\ \times \left(\frac{x_{ss}(1+n)((1-\tau^y)A+(1-\delta)-x_{ss}(1+\tau^c))+x_{ss}(1+n)x_{ss}(1+\tau^c)}{((1-\tau^y)A+(1-\delta)-x_{ss}(1+\tau^c))^2} \right) \hat{x}_t \\ -\sigma \left(\frac{x_{ss}(1+n)}{(1-\tau^y)A+(1-\delta)-x_{ss}(1+\tau^c)} \right)^{-\sigma-1} \\ \times \left(\frac{x_{ss}(1+n)(1-\tau^y)A}{((1-\tau^y)A+(1-\delta)-x_{ss}(1+\tau^c))^2} \right) \hat{z}_t \\ -\sigma \frac{\beta}{1+n} x_{ss}^{-\sigma} ((1-\tau^y)A + 1 - \delta) \hat{x}_{t+1} \\ + \frac{\beta}{1+n} x_{ss}^{-\sigma} (1-\tau^y)A(1-\alpha) \hat{\theta}_{t+1} \\ + \frac{\beta}{1+n} x_{ss}^{-\sigma} (1-\tau^y)A\alpha \hat{z}_{t+1} \end{bmatrix}.$$

Taking into account steady-state expressions, this latter expression can be written

$$0 = \frac{\sigma}{\beta}(1+\gamma)^{2\sigma-1}\hat{x}_t - \left(\sigma(1+\gamma)^{\sigma-1} - \beta\alpha(1+\gamma)^{\alpha-1} \right)$$
$$\times \frac{(1-\tau^y)A}{1+n}\hat{z}_t + \beta\frac{(1-\tau^y)A}{1+n}\rho\hat{\theta}_t - \sigma(1+\gamma)^\sigma E_t\hat{x}_{t+1},$$

and if we solve for $\hat{x}_t$:

$$\hat{x}_t = \beta(1+\gamma)^{1-\sigma}E_t\hat{x}_{t+1}$$
$$+ \left(\sigma(1+\gamma)^{\sigma-1} - \beta\alpha(1+\gamma)^{\alpha-1} \right)$$
$$\times \frac{(1-\tau^y)A}{(1+n)\sigma}\beta(1+\gamma)^{1-2\sigma}\hat{z}_t \qquad (6.74)$$
$$-\beta^2 \frac{(1-\tau^y)A}{(1+n)\sigma}(1+\gamma)^{1-2\sigma}\rho\hat{\theta}_t.$$

Leu us now define:

$$\varphi_1 = \beta(1+\gamma)^{1-\sigma},$$
$$\varphi_2 = \left(\sigma(1+\gamma)^{\sigma-1} - \beta\alpha(1+\gamma)^{\alpha-1} \right) \frac{(1-\tau^y)A}{(1+n)\sigma}\beta(1+\gamma)^{1-2\sigma},$$
$$\varphi_3 = -\beta\frac{(1-\tau^y)A}{(1+n)\sigma}\beta(1+\gamma)^{1-2\sigma}\rho.$$

Notice that if $\sigma > 1$, then $\varphi_1 \in (0,1)$ and hence, we can solve forwards the dynamic equation that incorporates conditional expectations (6.74). Besides, this condition for φ_1 must hold to guarantee that the utility function is bounded, as it can be seen by applying the transversality condition in steady-state.

Under the definitions above, (6.74) can be written more compactly

$$\hat{x}_t = \varphi_1 E_t \hat{x}_{t+1} + \varphi_2 \hat{z}_t + \varphi_3 \hat{\theta}_t. \tag{6.75}$$

so that, applying the law of iterated expectations and solving (6.74) forwards, we get

$$\hat{x}_t = \varphi_2 \sum_{j=0}^{\infty} \varphi_1^j E_t \hat{z}_{t+j} + \frac{\varphi_3}{1 - \varphi_1 \rho} \hat{\theta}_t. \tag{6.76}$$

We now proceed to compute $\sum_{j=0}^{\infty} \varphi_1^j E_t \hat{z}_{t+j}$ given (6.72):

Step 1: we compute $E_t \hat{z}_{t+j}$:

$$j = 0 : E_t \hat{z}_t = \hat{z}_t;$$
$$j = 1 : E_t \hat{z}_{t+1} = E_t \left[(1+\gamma)^{\alpha-1} \hat{z}_t + \hat{\theta}_{t+1} \right] = (1+\gamma)^{\alpha-1} \hat{z}_t + \rho \hat{\theta}_t;$$
$$j = 2 : E_t \hat{z}_{t+2} = E_t \left[(1+\gamma)^{\alpha-1} \hat{z}_{t+1} + \hat{\theta}_{t+2} \right] \Rightarrow$$

$$E_t \hat{z}_{t+2} = \left[(1+\gamma)^{\alpha-1} \right]^2 \hat{z}_t + \rho \hat{\theta}_t \left[(1+\gamma)^{\alpha-1} + \rho \right]$$

$$j = 3 : E_t \hat{z}_{t+3} = E_t \left[(1+\gamma)^{\alpha-1} \hat{z}_{t+2} + \hat{\theta}_{t+3} \right] \Rightarrow$$

$$E_t \hat{z}_{t+3} = \left[(1+\gamma)^{\alpha-1} \right]^3 \hat{z}_t + \rho \hat{\theta}_t \left[\left((1+\gamma)^{\alpha-1} \right)^2 + (1+\gamma)^{\alpha-1} \rho + \rho^2 \right]$$

so that, for a generic j we have

$$E_t \hat{z}_{t+j} = E_t \left[(1+\gamma)^{\alpha-1} \hat{z}_{t+j-1} + \hat{\theta}_{t+j} \right]$$
$$= \left[(1+\gamma)^{\alpha-1} \right]^j \hat{z}_t + \rho \hat{\theta}_t \left[\left((1+\gamma)^{\alpha-1} \right)^{j-1} \right.$$
$$+ \left((1+\gamma)^{\alpha-1} \right)^{j-2} \rho + \cdots + \left((1+\gamma)^{\alpha-1} \right) \rho^{j-2} + \rho^{j-1} \right]$$
$$= \left[(1+\gamma)^{\alpha-1} \right]^j \hat{z}_t + \frac{1}{(1+\gamma)^{\alpha-1} - \rho}$$
$$\times \left(\left((1+\gamma)^{\alpha-1} \right)^j - \rho^j \right) \hat{\theta}_t.$$

Step 2: compute $\sum_{j=0}^{\infty} \varphi_1^j E_t \hat{z}_{t+j}$:

$$\sum_{j=0}^{\infty} \varphi_1^j E_t \hat{z}_{t+j} = \sum_{j=0}^{\infty} \varphi_1^j \left\{ \left[(1+\gamma)^{\alpha-1} \right]^j \hat{z}_t + \frac{1}{(1+\gamma)^{\alpha-1} - \rho} \right.$$
$$\times \left. \left(\left((1+\gamma)^{\alpha-1} \right)^j - \rho^j \right) \hat{\theta}_t \right\}$$

$$
= \hat{z}_t \left\{ \sum_{j=0}^{\infty} \left[\varphi_1 (1+\gamma)^{\alpha-1} \right]^j \right\} + \hat{\theta}_t \frac{1}{(1+\gamma)^{\alpha-1} - \rho}
$$

$$
\times \left\{ \sum_{j=0}^{\infty} \left[\varphi_1 (1+\gamma)^{\alpha-1} \right]^j - \sum_{j=0}^{\infty} \left[\varphi_1 \rho \right]^j \right\}
$$

$$
= \frac{\hat{z}_t}{1 - \varphi_1 (1+\gamma)^{\alpha-1}} + \frac{\hat{\theta}_t}{(1+\gamma)^{\alpha-1} - \rho}
$$

$$
\times \left[\frac{1}{1 - \varphi_1 (1+\gamma)^{\alpha-1}} - \frac{1}{1 - \varphi_1 \rho} \right].
$$

so that the consumption to physical capital ratio is

$$
\hat{x}_t = \frac{\varphi_2 \hat{z}_t}{1 - \varphi_1 (1+\gamma)^{\alpha-1}} + \hat{\theta}_t \left[\frac{\varphi_2}{(1+\gamma)^{\alpha-1} - \rho} \right. \tag{6.77}
$$

$$
\left. \times \left(\frac{1}{1 - \varphi_1 (1+\gamma)^{\alpha-1}} - \frac{1}{1 - \varphi_1 \rho} \right) \frac{\varphi_3}{1 - \varphi_1 \rho} \right],
$$

and (6.72), (6.77) fully characterize the dynamic evolution of this economy.

6.9.5 Numerical Exercise: Solving the Jones and Manuelli Model

A single realization for the stochastic Jones and Manuelli economy can be obtained using *AK_JMs.m,* and the time series for the main variables in the economy are displayed. Program *mAK_JMs.m* can be used to produce an arbitrary number of realizations from the solution to this economy. Average statistics for the main variables across the set of realizations are then reported in a table. Single or multiple realizations for the *AK* model can be obtained from these two programs by setting $B = 0$.

6.9.6 The Stochastic AK Model as a Special Case

If $B = 0$, then $z_t = \theta_t A$, $\hat{z}_t = \hat{\theta}_t$, so we just need to characterize the time evolution of $\hat{x}_t$ to solve the stochastic version of the *AK* model with taxes. Then, (6.65) becomes

$$
\left(\frac{x_t (1+n)}{(1 - \tau^y) A \theta_t + (1 - \delta) - x_t (1 + \tau^c)} \right)^{-\sigma}
$$

$$
= \frac{\beta}{1+n} E_t \left[x_{t+1}^{-\sigma} \left((1 - \tau^y) A \theta_{t+1} + 1 - \delta \right) \right],
$$

with a log-linear approximation:

$$0 = E_t \left[\sigma(1+\gamma)^{2\sigma-1} \frac{1}{\beta} \hat{x}_t - \sigma(1+\gamma)^{\sigma-1} \frac{(1-\tau^y)A}{1+n} \hat{\theta}_t \right.$$
$$\left. - \sigma(1+\gamma)^{\sigma} \hat{x}_{t+1} + \frac{\beta}{1+n}(1-\tau^y)A\hat{\theta}_{t+1} \right],$$

and if we solve for $\hat{x}_t$:

$$\hat{x}_t = \beta(1+\gamma)^{1-\sigma} E_t \hat{x}_{t+1} + \left(\sigma(1+\gamma)^{\sigma-1} - \beta\rho \right)$$
$$\times \frac{(1-\tau^y)A}{(1+n)\sigma} \beta(1+\gamma)^{1-2\sigma} \hat{\theta}_t.$$

If we solve this equation forwards, by applying the law of iterated expectations, we obtain the time evolution of the consumption to capital ratio:

$$\hat{x}_t = \frac{\varphi_2'}{1-\varphi_1\rho} \hat{\theta}_t, \tag{6.78}$$

where $\varphi_2' = \left(\sigma(1+\gamma)^{\sigma-1} - \beta\rho \right) \frac{(1-\tau^y)A}{(1+n)\sigma} \beta(1+\gamma)^{1-2\sigma}$, since $\varphi_1 = \beta(1+\gamma)^{1-\sigma} \in (0,1)$.

Once we have time paths for $\hat{z}_t$ and $\hat{x}_t$, we can compute those for z_t and x_t:

$$z_t = A e^{\hat{z}_t},$$
$$x_t = x_{ss} e^{\hat{x}_t}.$$

The time path for $\tilde{k}_t$ can then be obtained recursively from the budget constraint

$$\tilde{k}_{t+1} = \frac{(1-\tau^y)z_t + (1-\delta) - x_t(1+\tau^c)}{1+n} \tilde{k}_t, \quad \text{with } \tilde{k}_0 \text{ given.}$$

The time path for the no-growth stock of capital k_t can be obtained

$$k_t = (1+\gamma)^{-t} \tilde{k}_t,$$

while the time paths for $\tilde{c}_t$ and c_t can be obtained

$$\tilde{c}_t = x_t \tilde{k}_t,$$
$$c_t = x_t k_t.$$

6.10 Exercises

Exercise 1. In the discrete-time version of the AK economy, where consumers face income taxes, show that all per capita variables grow at the same constant rate in steady-state, and also that there is no transitional dynamics.

Represent the effects of income taxes on the steady-state values of consumption and capital through a phase diagram. What would be the difference in that diagram if the government would finance expenditures through consumption taxes?

Show that a permanent policy intervention in the Cass–Koopmans economy will have permanent effects, since it will generally have an effect on the steady-state.

Show that any numerical solution with parameter values violating the boundedness condition (6.12) would produce explosive trajectories.

Once we have computed a time series realization for all relevant variables, an interesting exercise consists on computing responses of the main variables to an impulse in the technology innovation. That is computed by giving a unit value to ε_0, followed by $\varepsilon_t = 0$, $\forall t \geq 1$. Check how these responses will clearly show that a transitory shock has permanent effects.

Exercise 2. Describe the analytical details of solving the stochastic, discrete-time version of the *AK* model by using a log-linear approximation and: (a) Uhlig's undetermined coefficients method, (b) parameterized expectations, (c) the eigenvalue-eigenvector decomposition.

Chapter 7
Additional Endogenous Growth Models

7.1 Introduction

In this chapter we review some additional mechanisms by which endogenous growth arises. We start with an economy without capital accumulation in which technological progress shows up in the form of the number of varieties of producer products, possibly differing in quality [31, 33, 76, 78, 89].[1] Technological innovation in these models may lead to either an increase in their number, or in their quality, so the innovation process is key in this economy. These models can be seen to be equivalent to the *AK* model for an appropriate parameter choice. In particular, except in specific versions of these models there is no transition, per capita variables growing at a constant rate at all points in time after any structural shock or policy intervention. After that, we present a model of technological diffusion between two countries, one being a leader in innovation, as in the model with varieties of producer products, the second one being a follower, that adopts the innovations developed in the leading country. The economy of the follower country displays a non-trivial transition to steady-state. We then present a model economy with *creative destruction* à la Schumpeter [82] in which growth is driven endogenously by attempts to improve the quality of existing goods through innovation. This model incorporates accumulation of physical capital and displays a nontrivial transition to steady-state. We close with an important model, that of a two-sector economy in which human and physical capital accumulate over time, and where time devoted to education plays an important role, so that the split of time among that devoted to producing the final good, to education (i.e., to human capital accumulation) and leisure is a crucial decision. This model again exhibits a nontrivial transition, and it is an appropriate framework to address interesting questions regarding fiscal policy. Furthermore, this model can also give raise of indeterminacy of equilibrium, which we discuss in a separate section.

---

[1] Other models consider endogenous growth in economies with a variety of consumer products. Since the treatment is relatively similar to that of models with a variety of products, we do not include those models here.

A. Novales et al., *Economic Growth: Theory and Numerical Solution Methods,*
© Springer-Verlag Berlin Heidelberg 2009

7.2 A Variety of Producer Products

7.2.1 The Economy

7.2.1.1 The Final Good Sector

At a difference of the economies considered in previous chapters, we now follow Romer [77, 78][2] to consider a set of different firms, each specialized in the production of an intermediate good, and a single firm producing the single final good in the economy.[3] The latter behaves competitively in the markets for inputs and output. New intermediate goods are discovered through research, which is undergone at a fixed cost in terms of unit of the final good. When a firm decides to engage at a point in time into research activities, it will be able to develop a new intermediate good, which will then be allowed to produce as a single monopolist forever. Monopoly rents are the incentive firms need to spend in research and development. This process is not subject to any uncertainty. At a difference from other models considered in this book, there is not accumulation of physical capital in this model. Intermediate goods are discovered at a cost in terms of units of the final good, and the final good is produced from labour and from the intermediate goods. The only state variable in this model is the number of intermediate goods available at each point in time.

The final good is produced according to the production function:

$$\tilde{Y}_t = AL_t^{1-\alpha} \int_0^{\tilde{N}_t} x_{jt}^\alpha \, dj,$$

where $0 < \alpha < 1$, $\tilde{Y}_t$ denotes the output of the final good at time t, while L_t and x_{jt} denote the labor input and the amount used of the j-th intermediate good, $j \in (0, \tilde{N}_t)$.[4] The production output $\tilde{Y}_t$ can be used either for consumption, for the production of intermediate goods or for the research and development needed for the invention of further intermediate goods. From now on, we assume for simplicity a constant labor supply, $L_t = L, \forall t$.

Additive separability makes the marginal product for each of the $\tilde{N}_t$ intermediate goods to be independent of the quantities employed of the others. Then, a new type

---

[2] Previous studies by Spence [89], Dixit and Stiglitz [31] and Ethier [33] all consider the benefits of a variety of products. Spence [89] and Dixit and Stiglitz [31] considered a utility function defined on the set of consumption commodities as arguments, while Ethier [33] used a setup similar to that in Romer [77, 78]. The latter included a variety of productive inputs in the context of technological change and economic growth.

[3] This is a simplifying assumption, equivalent to having a set of identical firms producing the final good.

[4] The number of varieties will grow at a rate γ_{N_t} from its initial value N_0. This means that we have to consider N_t to be a continuous variable taking values on the positive real line. As an exception, we will use the N-notation for the number of intermediate goods in an economy with constant population L.

of product is neither a direct substitute for nor a direct complement with products that already exist. Since marginal products become infinite at $x_{jt} = 0$, the firm has an incentive to use all of them in production. We interpret x_{jt} as being purchases of nondurable goods and services, so that the only state variable is the number of product varieties at each point in time, $\tilde{N}_t$.[5]

The profit maximizing problem for the producer of the final good is

$$\max_{x_{jt}} \tilde{Y}_t - w_t L - \int_0^{\tilde{N}_t} P_{jt} x_{jt} dj,$$

where w_t is the wage rate and P_{jt} the price of the j-th intermediate good. We assume that the producer of the final good behaves competitively, taking factor prices as given, which leads to profit maximizing conditions

$$x_{jt} = L \left(\frac{A\alpha}{P_{jt}} \right)^{\frac{1}{1-\alpha}}, \quad j \in [0, \tilde{N}_t], \quad t = 0, 1, 2, \dots \tag{7.1}$$

$$\tilde{w}_t = (1 - \alpha) \frac{\tilde{Y}_t}{L}, \quad t = 0, 1, 2, \dots \tag{7.2}$$

that determine demand schedules for the quantity of each intermediate good, as well as for labour.

7.2.1.2 The Sectors for the Intermediate Goods

We assume that the inventor of good j, which is also its producer, retains perpetual monopoly rights over the production and sale of that good.[6] Each intermediate good costs one unit of the final good to produce, so that the present value of the returns from discovering the j-th intermediate good is

$$V_t = \sum_{s=t}^{\infty} \frac{1}{\prod_{l=0}^{s-t}(1 + r_{t+l})} [P_{js}(x_{js}) - 1] x_{js},$$

where x_{jt} is the quantity produced at time t and we have made explicit the dependence of the monopoly price from the quantity produced. The fixed cost of discovering a new good can then be recovered only if the sales price is greater than the marginal cost of production, which we have assumed to be equal to one, over some period of time.

---

[5] Alternatively, x_{jt} could be considered as the flow of services provided by a vector of durable intermediate goods subject to some depreciation. But we would then have to keep track of the quantities of each of intermediate good available at the firm each time period, which complicates the analysis significantly.

[6] See Chap. 6 in Barro and Sala-i-Martin [6] for a model with random duration of monopoly rights.

Because of the nondurable nature of the intermediate goods, there is no possible accumulation of stocks. Furthermore, the demand function for intermediate goods lacks any intertemporal features, so profit maximization for the monopolist producing each intermediate good becomes a sequence of static problems, each maximizing profit at a single point in time, taking the aggregate demand for the intermediate good as given,

$$\max_{P_{jt}} (P_{jt} - 1) x_{jt},$$

where x_{jt} is the demand of the j-th intermediate good by the firm producing the final good.

So the j-th monopolist solves

$$\max_{P_{jt}} (P_{jt} - 1) L \left(\frac{A\alpha}{P_{jt}} \right)^{\frac{1}{1-\alpha}},$$

which has as solution

$$P_{jt} = P = \frac{1}{\alpha} > 1.$$

Monopoly prices impose a mark-up of $\frac{1-\alpha}{\alpha} > 0$ over the cost of production, which we have assumed to be equal to 1. Monopoly prices for intermediate goods are all the same because we have assumed that they enter symmetrically into the production function of the final consumption commodity, and they are also constant over time.

Monopoly profits are

$$\pi_t = L\alpha^{\frac{2}{1-\alpha}} \frac{1-\alpha}{\alpha} A^{\frac{1}{1-\alpha}},$$

constant over time.

Taking factor prices to the profit maximizing condition for the producer of the final good, we obtain the quantity demands of each intermediate good on the part of the final producer:

$$x_{jt} = L \left(\frac{A\alpha}{1/\alpha} \right)^{\frac{1}{1-\alpha}} = LA^{\frac{1}{1-\alpha}} \alpha^{\frac{2}{1-\alpha}} = x, \quad j \in (0, \tilde{N}_t), \ t = 0, 1, 2, \ldots, \quad (7.3)$$

which is the same for all intermediate goods, and constant over time, because of the assumption of a constant labour supply. This is also the quantity produced of the j-th intermediate good at time t.

Output for the firm producing the final good is then given by

$$\tilde{Y}_t = AL^{1-\alpha} \int_0^{\tilde{N}_t} x_{jt}^{\alpha} dj = AL^{1-\alpha} \tilde{N}_t x^{\alpha} = A^{\frac{1}{1-\alpha}} \alpha^{\frac{2\alpha}{1-\alpha}} L\tilde{N}_t = \frac{1}{\alpha^2} \tilde{N}_t x, \quad (7.4)$$

which has a similar structure to the technology of the AK model, with the number of varieties of intermediate goods here playing the role of the stock of physical capital.

This expression shows that for fixed L, output grows at the same rate than $\tilde{N}_t$. Therefore, endogenous growth will arise in output because of the expansion in the number of product varieties, $\tilde{N}_t$. The idea is that the diminishing returns in individual intermediate goods can be avoided by spreading resources among a larger variety of producer products, rather than increasing the production of existing intermediate goods. In other words, because of the diminishing returns, new resources should be better devoted to increase the number of varieties, $\tilde{N}_t$, than to increase the quantity produced of each one of them, x_{jt}.

7.2.1.3 Interest Rate Determination

Taking now monopoly prices and the quantities of each intermediate good to the expression for present value of returns, we get

$$V_t = LA^{\frac{1}{1-\alpha}} \alpha^{\frac{2}{1-\alpha}} \frac{1-\alpha}{\alpha} \sum_{s=t}^{\infty} \frac{1}{\prod_{l=0}^{s-t}(1+r_{t+l})},$$

which is going to help us to determine equilibrium rates.

We assume that the fixed cost to create a new intermediate good is constant, at η units of the final product. If the existing commodities would make easier to come up with new developments, we could have a cost to develop new products decreasing with the number of commodity types, $\tilde{N}_t$. On the other hand, if new ideas are hard to produce once a number of commodities have already been developed, the cost should be increasing with $\tilde{N}_t$. The assumption of a fixed cost independent of the value of $\tilde{N}_t$ seems then acceptable on average. It is also consistent with a constant rate of growth of output, as we see next.

To rationalize the incentives needed for expenditures in research and development (R&D), we additionally assume that there are no barriers to entry into the invention business. That means that anybody can pay the cost η of research and development to obtain V_t. Then, an equilibrium exists[7] only if $V_t = \eta$, so that

$$\eta = LA^{\frac{1}{1-\alpha}} \alpha^{\frac{2}{1-\alpha}} \frac{1-\alpha}{\alpha} \sum_{s=t}^{\infty} \frac{1}{\prod_{l=0}^{s-t}(1+r_{t+l})}$$

and the equilibrium present value of returns to invention then happens to be constant over time, $V_t = V_{t+1} = \eta$.

The relationship between the present value of returns at two different points in time, $t+1$ and t can be written

---

[7] If $V_t < \eta$, then no resources would be devoted to further invention, and the number of goods would remain constant over time. On the other hand, if $V_t > \eta$, then investing in R&D provides positive profits, so an infinite amount of resources would be devoted to that activity, and we could not possibly have an equilibrium.

$$V_{t+1} = \left(V_t - LA^{\frac{1}{1-\alpha}} \alpha^{\frac{2}{1-\alpha}} \frac{1-\alpha}{\alpha} \frac{1}{1+r_t} \right) (1+r_t),$$

which using $\eta = V_t = V_{t+1}$, leads to

$$\eta = \eta \left(1 + r_t \right) - LA^{\frac{1}{1-\alpha}} \alpha^{\frac{2}{1-\alpha}} \frac{1-\alpha}{\alpha},$$

and, finally,

$$r_t = \frac{1}{\eta} LA^{\frac{1}{1-\alpha}} \alpha^{\frac{2}{1-\alpha}} \frac{1-\alpha}{\alpha} = \frac{1-\alpha}{\alpha} \frac{1}{\eta} x = r, \tag{7.5}$$

which is constant over time under the assumption of a constant labour supply.

7.2.1.4 The Problem of the Representative Household

We assume that there is a constant number L of households, endowed with a unit of time, which will be supplied inelastically to firms, because leisure does not enter into the utility function. This is consistent with the assumption above on a constant labor input of L in the production of the final good. The representative household maximizes time aggregate discounted utility over an infinite horizon

$$\max_{\{\tilde{c}_t, \tilde{a}_{t+1}\}} U_0 = \sum_{t=0}^{\infty} \beta^t \frac{\tilde{c}_t^{1-\sigma} - 1}{1-\sigma},$$

having the opportunity to save each period at a constant return of r, and being supplied with 1 unit of labor each period. For simplicity, we assume zero population growth, $n = 0$. The single period budget constraint is

$$\tilde{c}_t + \tilde{a}_{t+1} = \tilde{w}_t + (1+r)\tilde{a}_t.$$

The Lagrangian is

$$L(\tilde{c}_t, \tilde{a}_{t+1}, \lambda_t) = \sum_{t=0}^{\infty} \beta^t \left(\frac{\tilde{c}_t^{1-\sigma} - 1}{1-\sigma} - \lambda_t \left[\tilde{c}_t + \tilde{a}_{t+1} - \tilde{w}_t - (1+r)\tilde{a}_t \right] \right),$$

with utility maximizing conditions

$$\frac{\partial L}{\partial \tilde{c}_t} = 0 \Rightarrow \tilde{c}_t^{-\sigma} = \lambda_t, \quad t = 0, 1, 2, \ldots,$$

$$\frac{\partial L}{\partial \tilde{k}_{t+1}} = 0 \Rightarrow -\beta^t \lambda_t + \beta^{t+1}(1+r)\lambda_{t+1} = 0, \quad t = 0, 1, 2, \ldots,$$

$$\text{Transversality Condition}: \ \lim_{t \to \infty} \beta^t \tilde{c}_t^{-\sigma} \tilde{a}_{t+1} = 0,$$

leading to

$$\tilde{c}_{t+1} = [\beta(1+r)]^{1/\sigma}\,\tilde{c}_t, \quad t = 0,1,2,\ldots$$

with the implication that, under the equilibrium mechanism, utility-maximizing per-capita consumption $\tilde{c}_t$ grows at a constant rate at all time periods

$$1 + \gamma_{\tilde{c}} = (\beta(1+r))^{1/\sigma} = \beta^{1/\sigma}\left(1 + \frac{1}{\eta}LA^{\frac{1}{1-\alpha}}\alpha^{\frac{2}{1-\alpha}}\frac{1-\alpha}{\alpha}\right)^{1/\sigma}, \quad (7.6)$$

which is actually positive if $1 + r > \frac{1}{\beta}$, being negative otherwise.

7.2.1.5 The Aggregate Constraint of Resources

Aggregate consumption must satisfy the economy-wide global constraint of resources

$$\tilde{C}_t = \tilde{Y}_t - \eta\left(\tilde{N}_{t+1} - \tilde{N}_t\right) - \tilde{N}_t x. \quad (7.7)$$

Since η is the unit cost of increasing the number of intermediate goods, the term $\eta\left(\tilde{N}_{t+1} - \tilde{N}_t\right) = \eta\gamma_{\tilde{N}_t}\tilde{N}_t$ above is the cost of innovation at time t. Resources devoted to R&D allow for increasing the number of product varieties to be used in production next period. The $\tilde{N}_t x$ term captures the resources spent on the production of intermediate goods at time t.

From the profit maximization conditions: $(1 - \alpha)\tilde{Y}_t = Lw_t$, and using equation (7.4), $\tilde{Y}_t = \frac{1}{\alpha^2}\tilde{N}_t x$, we have

$$\tilde{C}_t + \eta\tilde{N}_{t+1} = (1-\alpha)\tilde{Y}_t + \alpha\tilde{Y}_t + \eta\tilde{N}_t - \tilde{N}_t x = L\tilde{w}_t + \frac{1}{\alpha}\tilde{N}_t x + \eta\tilde{N}_t - \tilde{N}_t x,$$

so that

$$\tilde{c}_t + \frac{\eta}{L}\tilde{N}_{t+1} = \tilde{w}_t + \frac{\eta}{L}\tilde{N}_t + \frac{1-\alpha}{\alpha}\frac{1}{L}\tilde{N}_t x,$$

and using (7.5), we have

$$\tilde{c}_t + \frac{\eta}{L}\tilde{N}_{t+1} = \tilde{w}_t + \frac{\eta}{L}(1+r)\tilde{N}_t.$$

Comparing with the individual household budget constraint, we see that, in equilibrium, period t savings are

$$\tilde{a}_{t+1} = \frac{\eta}{L}\tilde{N}_{t+1}.$$

7.2.1.6 The Balanced Growth Path

The transitional dynamics of the model can be analyzed by an argument very similar to the one used in the *AK* model. From (7.7) and (7.4)

$$\tilde{C}_t = \frac{1}{\alpha^2}\tilde{N}_t x - \eta\tilde{N}_{t+1} + \eta\tilde{N}_t - \tilde{N}_t x = \frac{1-\alpha^2}{\alpha^2}x\tilde{N}_t - \eta\tilde{N}_{t+1} + \eta\tilde{N}_t,$$

so that the number of intermediate goods satisfies the difference equation

$$\tilde{N}_{t+1} = \left(1 + \frac{1-\alpha^2}{\alpha^2}\frac{x}{\eta}\right)\tilde{N}_t - \frac{(1+\gamma_{\tilde{c}})^t}{\eta}\tilde{c}_0, \tag{7.8}$$

which has a particular solution of the form: $\tilde{N}_t = B(1+\gamma_{\tilde{c}})^t$, while the homogeneous equation has a solution of the form: $\tilde{N}_t = D\left(1+\frac{1-\alpha^2}{\alpha^2}\frac{x}{\eta}\right)^t$, for specific constants B, D. To find B, we substitute the proposed solution in the difference equation, to have: $B(1+\gamma_{\tilde{c}})^{t+1} = \left(1+\frac{1-\alpha^2}{\alpha^2}\frac{x}{\eta}\right)B(1+\gamma_{\tilde{c}})^t - \frac{(1+\gamma_{\tilde{c}})^t}{\eta}\tilde{c}_0$, so that: $B = \frac{c_0}{\eta}\frac{1}{\left(1+\frac{1-\alpha^2}{\alpha^2}\frac{x}{\eta}\right)-(1+\gamma_{\tilde{c}})}$. Hence, the general solution to (7.8) will have the form

$$\tilde{N}_t = D\left(1+\frac{1-\alpha^2}{\alpha^2}\frac{x}{\eta}\right)^t + \frac{c_0}{\eta}\frac{1}{\left(1+\frac{1-\alpha^2}{\alpha^2}\frac{x}{\eta}\right)-(1+\gamma_{\tilde{c}})}(1+\gamma_{\tilde{c}})^t. \tag{7.9}$$

At $t=0$, we have: $\tilde{N}_0 = D + \frac{c_0}{\eta}\frac{1}{\left(1+\frac{1-\alpha^2}{\alpha^2}\frac{x}{\eta}\right)-(1+\gamma_{\tilde{c}})}$, from which we get the value of the constant D: $D = \tilde{N}_0 - \frac{c_0}{\eta}\frac{1}{\left(1+\frac{1-\alpha^2}{\alpha^2}\frac{x}{\eta}\right)-(1+\gamma_{\tilde{c}})}$. Hence, the behavior of $\tilde{N}_t$ gets characterized by

$$\tilde{N}_t = \left(\tilde{N}_0 - \frac{c_0}{\eta}\frac{1}{\left(1+\frac{1-\alpha^2}{\alpha^2}\frac{x}{\eta}\right)-(1+\gamma_{\tilde{c}})}\right)\left(1+\frac{1-\alpha^2}{\alpha^2}\frac{x}{\eta}\right)^t$$
$$+\frac{c_0}{\eta}\frac{1}{\left(1+\frac{1-\alpha^2}{\alpha^2}\frac{x}{\eta}\right)-(1+\gamma_{\tilde{c}})}(1+\gamma_{\tilde{c}})^t.$$

The transversality condition requires: $\lim_{t\to\infty}\beta^t\tilde{c}_t^{-\sigma}\tilde{a}_{t+1} = 0$. For this condition to hold, we need

$$\lim_{t\to\infty}\beta^t(1+\gamma_{\tilde{c}})^{-t\sigma}\tilde{c}_0^{-\sigma}\frac{\eta}{L}\left(\tilde{N}_0 - \frac{c_0}{\eta}\frac{1}{\left(1+\frac{1-\alpha^2}{\alpha^2}\frac{x}{\eta}\right)-(1+\gamma_{\tilde{c}})}\right)$$
$$\times\left(1+\frac{1-\alpha^2}{\alpha^2}\frac{x}{\eta}\right)^{t+1} + \lim_{t\to\infty}\beta^t(1+\gamma_{\tilde{c}})^{-t\sigma}\tilde{c}_0^{-\sigma}\frac{\eta}{L}\frac{(1+\gamma_{\tilde{c}})^{t+1}}{\eta}\tilde{c}_0 = 0. \tag{7.10}$$

Using the expressions for the rate of growth (7.6) and research effort (7.3), it is straightforward to see that $\beta(1+\gamma_{\tilde{c}})^{-\sigma}\left(1+\frac{1-\alpha^2}{\alpha^2}\frac{x}{\eta}\right) > 1$, so that for the transversality condition to hold we will need

$$\lim_{t\to\infty}\left(\tilde{N}_0-\frac{c_0/\eta}{\left(1+\frac{1-\alpha^2}{\alpha^2}\frac{x}{\eta}\right)-(1+\gamma_{\tilde{c}})}\right)\left[\frac{\beta\left(1+\frac{1-\alpha^2}{\alpha^2}\frac{x}{\eta}\right)}{(1+\gamma_{\tilde{c}})^\sigma}\right]^t=0,$$

$$\lim_{t\to\infty}\left[\beta\left(1+\gamma_{\tilde{c}}\right)^{1-\sigma}\right]^t=0,$$

each condition guaranteeing that one of the two limits at (7.10) is equal to zero. The second condition holds if

$$\left(1+\frac{1}{\eta}LA^{\frac{1}{1-\alpha}}\alpha^{\frac{2}{1-\alpha}}\frac{1-\alpha}{\alpha}\right)^{1-\sigma}<\frac{1}{\beta},$$

a restriction among the values of structural parameters that also guarantees bounded welfare, as it can be shown following an argument similar to the one we used for the *AK* model. The first condition requires

$$c_0=\eta\left[\left(1+\frac{1-\alpha^2}{\alpha^2}\frac{x}{\eta}\right)-(1+\gamma_{\tilde{c}})\right]\tilde{N}_0,$$

and tells us how to choose initial consumption as a function of the state variable, the initial number of intermediate goods, so that the implied solution is stable, in the sense of satisfying the transversality condition. It is, therefore, a *stability condition*, that once again, relates a control to a state variable.

This condition implies a time behavior for $\tilde{N}_t$:

$$\tilde{N}_t=\frac{1}{\left(1+\frac{1-\alpha^2}{\alpha^2}\frac{x}{\eta}\right)-(1+\gamma_{\tilde{c}})}(1+\gamma_{\tilde{c}})^t\frac{c_0}{\eta}=(1+\gamma_{\tilde{c}})^t\tilde{N}_0,$$

so that the number of intermediate goods grows at the same rate than consumption and, from (7.4), the same will be true for output: $\gamma_{\tilde{Y}}=\gamma_{\tilde{N}}=\gamma_{\tilde{c}}.$[8] But, from (7.6), consumption grows at rate $\gamma_{\tilde{c}}$ at all time periods, so that the main variables in the economy either stay constant, as in the case of x_t or r_t, or grow at a constant rate at all time periods. Hence, the economy displays no transition, jumping to the new steady-state immediately after any perturbation or policy intervention.

On the other hand, we have just shown that the rate of growth happens to be the same for all positive growth variables, so that the steady state takes the form of a balanced growth trajectory characterized by

$$1+\gamma_{\tilde{Y}_t}=1+\gamma_{\tilde{N}}=1+\gamma_{\tilde{c}}=\beta^{1/\sigma}\left(1+\frac{1}{\eta}LA^{\frac{1}{1-\alpha}}\alpha^{\frac{2}{1-\alpha}}\frac{1-\alpha}{\alpha}\right)^{1/\sigma},$$

---

[8] The constant labour supply of L, together with the assumption of a unit endowment of labour for each consumer which is supplied inelastically, imply that we are dealing with a constant population. Per-capita and aggregate consumption then grow at the same rate, since $\tilde{C}_t=L\tilde{c}_t$, and the same is true for per-capita and aggregate output, since $\tilde{Y}_t=L\tilde{y}_t$.

$$x = LA^{\frac{1}{1-\alpha}} \alpha^{\frac{2}{1-\alpha}},$$

$$r = \frac{1}{\eta} LA^{\frac{1}{1-\alpha}} \alpha^{\frac{2}{1-\alpha}} \frac{1-\alpha}{\alpha},$$

$$\tilde{N}_t = \left[\beta^{1/\sigma} \left(1 + \frac{1}{\eta} LA^{\frac{1}{1-\alpha}} \alpha^{\frac{2}{1-\alpha}} \frac{1-\alpha}{\alpha} \right)^{1/\sigma} \right]^t \tilde{N}_0,$$

$$\tilde{C}_t = \tilde{N}_t \left\{ LA^{\frac{1}{1-\alpha}} \alpha^{\frac{2\alpha}{1-\alpha}} \left(1 - \alpha^2 \right) \right.$$

$$\left. - \eta \left[\beta \left(1 + \frac{1}{\eta} LA^{\frac{1}{1-\alpha}} \alpha^{\frac{2}{1-\alpha}} \frac{1-\alpha}{\alpha} \right) \right]^{1/\sigma} + \eta \right\},$$

$$\tilde{Y}_t = \frac{1}{\alpha^2} x \tilde{N}_t.$$

As shown above, the rate of growth depends on the two preference parameters: the intertemporal elasticity of substitution of consumption, and the rate of time discount. A greater willingness to save, in the form of either a lower σ or a higher discount rate β, will increase growth. The same is the case for a higher level of aggregate technology, as reflected in the value of the constant A. By raising the rate of return r, a decrease in the cost of innovation, η, will also lead to faster growth. Since there is no limitation to the use of a new product by all firms in the economy, beyond the one that came up with the innovation, the larger the economy, the lower the economy-wide unit cost of innovation, η/L. That is reflected in the presence of L in the expression for the growth rate, γ.

7.2.2 The Inefficiency of the Equilibrium Allocation

A benevolent social planner in this economy would maximize the level of welfare of the representative household, subject to the global constraint of resources (7.7).

The Lagrangian for this problem would be

$$\max_{\tilde{c}_t, x_t, \tilde{N}_{t+1}} \sum_{t=0}^{\infty} \beta^t \left\{ \frac{\tilde{c}_t^{1-\sigma} - 1}{1-\sigma} + \lambda_t \left[\tilde{N}_{t+1} - \frac{1}{\eta} \left(AL^{1-\alpha} \tilde{N}_t x_t^\alpha - L\tilde{c}_t + \eta \tilde{N}_t - \tilde{N}_t x_t \right) \right] \right\},$$

with first order conditions

$$\tilde{c}_t^{-\sigma} = \frac{1}{\eta} \lambda_t L,$$

$$\alpha AL^{1-\alpha} \tilde{N}_t x_t^{\alpha-1} = \tilde{N}_t,$$

$$\beta^t \lambda_t = \beta^{t+1} \lambda_{t+1} \left(\frac{1}{\eta} AL^{1-\alpha} x_{t+1}^\alpha + 1 - \frac{1}{\eta} x_{t+1} \right),$$

which imply that the optimal production of each of the intermediate goods is the same across goods and constant over time,[9]

$$x^* = LA^{\frac{1}{1-\alpha}} \alpha^{\frac{1}{1-\alpha}},$$

and it is larger than the equilibrium production of intermediate goods, since $\alpha < 1$.

The optimum level of output is

$$\tilde{Y}_t^* = AL^{1-\alpha} \tilde{N}_t^* (x^*)^\alpha = LA^{\frac{1}{1-\alpha}} \alpha^{\frac{\alpha}{1-\alpha}} \tilde{N}_t^*, \qquad (7.11)$$

which increases with the number of product varieties.

The optimal rate of growth is

$$1 + \gamma_{\tilde{c}}^* = \frac{\tilde{c}_{t+1}^*}{\tilde{c}_t^*} = \beta^{1/\sigma} \left(\frac{1}{\eta} AL^{1-\alpha} (x_t^*)^\alpha + 1 - \frac{1}{\eta} x_t^* \right)^{1/\sigma}$$

$$= \beta^{1/\sigma} \left(1 + \frac{1}{\eta} LA^{\frac{1}{1-\alpha}} \alpha^{\frac{\alpha}{1-\alpha}} (1 - \alpha) \right)^{1/\sigma},$$

which is easy to show that it is higher than the one implied in equilibrium.

An argument similar to the one we made in the previous section, together with (7.11) implies that aggregate consumption and output grow at the same rate than the number of intermediate goods, so that: $1 + \gamma_{\tilde{c}}^* = 1 + \gamma_{\tilde{Y}}^* = 1 + \gamma_{\tilde{N}}^*$. So, starting from a same initial condition $\tilde{N}_0$, the Pareto-efficient number of varieties of intermediate goods is always above the one obtained in equilibrium, and the same happens with the levels of consumption and output.

Therefore, the decentralized competitive equilibrium mechanism devotes less resources to the production of intermediate goods than the solution to the social planner and hence, obtains a lower level of output each time period. Furthermore, the rate of growth along the equilibrium solution is also lower than that obtained from the social planner solution. The reason is that the social rate of return,

$$r^* = \frac{1}{\eta} LA^{\frac{1}{1-\alpha}} \alpha^{\frac{\alpha}{1-\alpha}} (1 - \alpha),$$

is higher than the private rate of return on R&D.

In this economy, the inefficiency comes about because of the monopoly rights, which introduce a gap between the private and the social rates of return, because the price of the monopoly goods is above their marginal cost of production. Efficiency could be achieved through a tax-subsidy policy leading to marginal cost pricing without eliminating the incentives to innovate. These could take the form of either a subsidy to the purchase of all intermediate goods, or a subsidy to the final product. If the government subsidizes a proportion $1 - \alpha$ of the purchase of all intermediate goods the equilibrium quantity of intermediate goods becomes optimal, in spite of monopoly pricing. This comes about because the price of x, net of public subsidies,

---

[9] We denote by asterisks the solution to the benevolent planner's problem.

is equal to 1. An alternative would be to subsidize production of the final good by $\frac{1-\alpha}{\alpha}$, so that producers then receive $1/\alpha$ units of revenue for each unit of goods produced.

On the other hand, Barro and Sala-i-Martin [6] show that efficiency cannot be achieved by a subsidy to R&D expenditures. Such policy can lead to a rate of return and a rate of growth equal to those of the social planner, but the number of product varieties would still be short of optimal due to monopoly pricing.

7.2.3 A Stochastic Version of the Economy with a Variety of Intermediate Goods

7.2.3.1 The Producer of the Final Good

Maintaining the same structure described for the economy in previous sections, we now assume that the level of technology $A_t = \theta_t A$ is random. We assume that $\ln \theta_t$ evolves according to an autoregressive process with random innovation, ε_t:

$$\ln \theta_t = \phi \ln \theta_{t-1} + \varepsilon_t, \; \varepsilon_t \underset{iid}{\sim} N(0, \sigma_\varepsilon^2).$$

The technology available to the single producer of the final good is

$$\tilde{Y}_t = \theta_t A L^{1-\alpha} \int_0^{\tilde{N}_t} x_{jt}^\alpha dj, \quad 0 < \alpha < 1,$$

with the same interpretation as in the deterministic case. We maintain the assumption of a constant labor supply, $L_t = L, \forall t$.

The profit maximization problem of the firm

$$\max_{\{L, x_{jt}\}} E \left[\tilde{Y}_t - w_t L - \int_0^{\tilde{N}_t} P_{jt} x_{jt} dj \right],$$

where w_t is the wage rate and P_{jt} the price of the j-th intermediate good. Competitive behavior on the part of the producer of the final good leads to profit maximizing conditions

$$x_{jt} = L \left(\frac{\theta_t A \alpha}{P_{jt}} \right)^{\frac{1}{1-\alpha}}, \quad j \in [0, \tilde{N}_t], \; t = 0, 1, 2, \ldots,$$

$$w_t = (1 - \alpha) \frac{\tilde{Y}_t}{L}, \quad t = 0, 1, 2, \ldots.$$

Again, the nondurable nature of the intermediate goods, and the absence of any intertemporal features in the demand for intermediate goods, leads to the monopolist producing each intermediate good to maximize profit at a single point in time, taking the aggregate demand for the intermediate good as given

$$\max_{P_{jt}} (P_{jt}(x_{jt}) - 1) x_{jt},$$

where x_{jt} is the demand of the j-th intermediate good by the firm producing the final good, leading to the same mark-up as in the deterministic case

$$P_{jt} = P = \frac{1}{\alpha} > 1.$$

Symmetry again implies that monopoly prices for all intermediate goods are the same, and constant over time. With these monopoly prices, the demand for each intermediate goods is

$$x_{jt} = x_t = L\left(\theta_t A\alpha^2\right)^{\frac{1}{1-\alpha}}, \quad j \in [0, \tilde{N}_t], \quad t = 0, 1, 2, \dots$$

so that the output of the final good becomes

$$\tilde{Y}_t = \theta_t A L^{1-\alpha} \int_0^{\tilde{N}_t} \left(L\theta_t^{\frac{1}{1-\alpha}} A^{\frac{1}{1-\alpha}} \alpha^{\frac{2}{1-\alpha}} \right)^{\alpha} dj$$

$$= \theta_t A L^{1-\alpha} \tilde{N}_t L^{\alpha} \theta_t^{\frac{\alpha}{1-\alpha}} A^{\frac{\alpha}{1-\alpha}} \alpha^{\frac{2\alpha}{1-\alpha}}$$

$$= L\tilde{N}_t \theta_t^{\frac{1}{1-\alpha}} A^{\frac{1}{1-\alpha}} \alpha^{\frac{2\alpha}{1-\alpha}} = \frac{1}{\alpha^2} \tilde{N}_t x_t$$

so that for fixed L, output grows at the same rate than $\tilde{N}_t$.

7.2.3.2 Producers of Intermediate Goods

Under the maintained assumptions of perpetual monopoly rights over the production and sale of the intermediate good, and a unit cost of production, the present value of the returns from discovering the j-th intermediate good is

$$V_t = \sum_{s=t}^{\infty} \frac{1}{\prod_{l=0}^{s-t} (1 + r_{t+l})} (P_{js} - 1) x_{js},$$

where x_{jt} is the quantity produced at time t.

Solving the model now would require making explicit considerations regarding the attitude of private agents towards risk, and analytical considerations quickly become unfeasible. Following Barro and Sala-i-Martin [6], we make the assumption that, at each point in time, potential innovators just care about their conditional expectations of the present value of future returns,[10]

$$E_t V_t = L\alpha^{\frac{2}{1-\alpha}} \frac{1-\alpha}{\alpha} A^{\frac{1}{1-\alpha}} E_t \left(\sum_{s=t}^{\infty} \frac{\theta_s^{\frac{1}{1-\alpha}}}{\prod_{l=0}^{s-t}(1+r_{t+l})} \right).$$

The fixed cost of discovering a new good can then be recovered only if the sales price is greater than the unit marginal cost of production. Together with the assumption we have just made on the treatment of risk, the same considerations as in the deterministic model lead to: $E_t V_t = \eta$.

Writing this conditional expectation at time taking conditional expectations at time $t+1$ and taking conditional expectations as of time t, as of time t, we have: $E_t(E_{t+1}V_{t+1}) = E_t\eta$, which implies: $E_t V_{t+1} = \eta$, so we have

$$L\alpha^{\frac{2}{1-\alpha}} \frac{1-\alpha}{\alpha} A^{\frac{1}{1-\alpha}} E_t \left(\sum_{s=0}^{\infty} \frac{\theta_{t+1+s}^{\frac{1}{1-\alpha}}}{\prod_{j=0}^{s}(1+r_{t+1+j})} \right) = \eta,$$

and we have the relationship

$$E_t V_{t+1} = \left[E_t V_t - L\alpha^{\frac{2}{1-\alpha}} \frac{1-\alpha}{\alpha} A^{\frac{1}{1-\alpha}} E_t \left(\frac{\theta_t^{\frac{1}{1-\alpha}}}{1+r_t} \right) \right] (1+r_t)$$

and, using again: $E_t V_t = E_t V_{t+1} = \eta$, we finally get

$$r_t = \frac{1}{\eta} L\alpha^{\frac{2}{1-\alpha}} \frac{1-\alpha}{\alpha} A^{\frac{1}{1-\alpha}} \theta_t^{\frac{1}{1-\alpha}} = \frac{\pi_t}{\eta} = \frac{1-\alpha}{\alpha} \frac{x_t}{\eta},$$

where π_t denotes the static monopolistic profit. Interest rates are now time varying together with θ_t in a random fashion.

7.2.3.3 Household Decisions

We maintain the assumptions on consumers we made in the deterministic version of the model. The representative household maximizes the expected value of discounted, time aggregate utility over an infinite horizon,

---

[10] This is clearly a restrictive assumption, which neglects any consideration regarding the appropriate treatment of uncertainty under risk aversion.

$$\max_{\{\tilde{c}_t, \tilde{a}_{t+1}\}} E_0 \sum_{t=0}^{\infty} \beta^t \frac{\tilde{c}_t^{1-\sigma} - 1}{1 - \sigma},$$

who save at time t an amount $\tilde{a}_{t+1}$ of resources at a time varying rate of return r_t, and it is supplied with 1 unit of labor each period. For simplicity, we assume zero population growth, $n = 0$. The single period budget constraint is

$$\tilde{c}_t + \tilde{a}_{t+1} = w_t + (1 + r_t)\tilde{a}_t,$$

given $\tilde{a}_0$.

The Lagrangian is

$$L(\tilde{c}_t, \tilde{a}_{t+1}, \lambda_t) = \sum_{t=0}^{\infty} \beta^t \left(\frac{\tilde{c}_t^{1-\sigma} - 1}{1 - \sigma} - \lambda_t \left[\tilde{c}_t + \tilde{a}_{t+1} - w_t - (1 + r_t)\tilde{a}_t \right] \right),$$

with utility maximizing conditions

$$\frac{\partial L}{\partial \tilde{c}_t} = 0 \Rightarrow \tilde{c}_t^{-\sigma} = \lambda_t, \quad t = 0, 1, 2, \ldots,$$

$$\frac{\partial L}{\partial \tilde{k}_{t+1}} = 0 \Rightarrow -\beta^t \lambda_t + \beta^{t+1} E_t \left[(1 + r_{t+1})\lambda_{t+1} \right] = 0, \quad t = 0, 1, 2, \ldots,$$

Transversality Condition: $\lim_{T \to \infty} \beta^{t+T} E_t \tilde{c}_{t+T}^{-\sigma} \tilde{a}_{t+T+1} = 0,$

leading to

$$\tilde{c}_t^{-\sigma} = \beta E_t \left[(1 + r_{t+1})\tilde{c}_{t+1}^{-\sigma} \right]$$

$$= \beta E_t \left[\left(1 + \frac{1}{\eta} L \alpha^{\frac{2}{1-\alpha}} \frac{1-\alpha}{\alpha} A^{\frac{1}{1-\alpha}} \theta_{t+1}^{\frac{1}{1-\alpha}} \right) \tilde{c}_{t+1}^{-\sigma} \right], \quad t = 0, 1, 2, \ldots.$$

In equilibrium, total savings must be equal to the resources needed to put in place the varieties of intermediate goods

$$\tilde{a}_{t+1} = \eta \frac{\tilde{N}_{t+1}}{L}.$$

Introducing this condition into the consumer budget constraint, and taking into account the identity $L\tilde{c}_t = \tilde{C}_t$ and the demand for labor equation, we can write the global constraint of resources in per-capita terms

$$\tilde{c}_t + \frac{\eta}{L} \left(\tilde{N}_{t+1} - \tilde{N}_t \right) = \tilde{y}_t - \tilde{N}_t \frac{x_t}{L_t}$$

$$= \theta_t^{\frac{1}{1-\alpha}} A^{\frac{1}{1-\alpha}} \alpha^{\frac{2\alpha}{1-\alpha}} \tilde{N}_t - \theta_t^{\frac{1}{1-\alpha}} A^{\frac{1}{1-\alpha}} \alpha^{\frac{2}{1-\alpha}} \tilde{N}_t$$

$$= \theta_t^{\frac{1}{1-\alpha}} A^{\frac{1}{1-\alpha}} \alpha^{\frac{2\alpha}{1-\alpha}} \left(1 - \alpha^2 \right) \tilde{N}_t.$$

7.2.3.4 Analogy with the AK Model

The AK model with $n = 0$, $\delta = 0$, $\tau^c = \tau^y = 0$ and a production technology: $\tilde{Y}_t = A^* \tilde{K}_t$, has a global constraint of resources:

$$\tilde{k}_{t+1} = (1 + \theta_t A^*) \tilde{k}_t - \tilde{c}_t,$$

and an Euler equation:

$$\tilde{c}_t^{-\sigma} = \beta E_t \left[(1 + \theta_{t+1} A^*) \tilde{c}_{t+1}^{-\sigma} \right],$$

and leads to an interest rate:

$$r_t = \theta_t A^*.$$

On the other hand, introducing the change of variables: $\mu_t \equiv \theta_t^{\frac{1}{1-\alpha}}$, $A' \equiv \frac{A^{\frac{1}{1-\alpha}} \alpha^{\frac{\alpha}{1-\alpha}} (1-\alpha)}{\eta/L}$, $\tilde{q}_t \equiv \frac{\eta}{L} \tilde{N}_t$, in the planner solution to the model with varieties of intermediate goods, the global constraint of resources, the Euler condition and the rate of return can be written

$$\tilde{q}_{t+1} = \left[1 + \mu_t A' (1 + \alpha) \alpha^{\frac{\alpha}{1-\alpha}} \right] \tilde{q}_t - \tilde{c}_t,$$

$$\tilde{c}_t^{-\sigma} = \beta E_t \left[(1 + \mu_{t+1} A') \tilde{c}_{t+1}^{-\sigma} \right],$$

$$r_t^* = \mu_t A',$$

a system with strong similarity with the one obtained for the AK economy.

On the other hand, the equilibrium solution in the model with varieties of intermediate goods is characterized by the system

$$\tilde{q}_{t+1} = \left[1 + \mu_t A' (1 + \alpha) \alpha^{\frac{\alpha}{1-\alpha}} \right] \tilde{q}_t - \tilde{c}_t,$$

$$\tilde{c}_t^{-\sigma} = \beta E_t \left[(1 + \mu_{t+1} A' \alpha^{\frac{1}{1-\alpha}}) \tilde{c}_{t+1}^{-\sigma} \right],$$

$$r_t = \mu_t A' \alpha^{\frac{1}{1-\alpha}}.$$

The Euler equation for the equilibrium solution differs from the Euler equation for the planner solution in the presence of the $\alpha^{\frac{1}{1-\alpha}}$ term. Without that term the two Euler equations would be identical, leading to the same allocation of resources. So the $\alpha^{\frac{1}{1-\alpha}}$ term can be seen as the degree of inefficiency of the equilibrium solution to the model with varieties of intermediate goods. In any case, the equilibrium solution still has some similarity with the system characterizing the solution to the AK economy, which can be exploited when designing the algorithm to produce a numerical solution to the model in the next section.

7.2.3.5 Numerical Characterization of the Equilibrium Solution

To generate a sample realization for the numerical solution to this model, we define the auxiliary variable $z_t = \tilde{c}_t / \tilde{q}_t$.[11] The global constraint of resources can be written

$$\frac{\tilde{q}_{t+1}}{\tilde{q}_t} = 1 + \mu_t A'(1+\alpha)\alpha^{\frac{\alpha}{1-\alpha}} - z_t, \qquad (7.12)$$

while from the Euler condition we get

$$\left(\frac{\tilde{c}_t}{\tilde{q}_t}\right)^{-\sigma} \tilde{q}_t^{-\sigma} = \beta E_t \left[\left(\frac{\tilde{c}_{t+1}}{\tilde{q}_{t+1}}\right)^{-\sigma} \tilde{q}_{t+1}^{-\sigma}\left(1+\mu_{t+1}A'\alpha^{\frac{1}{1-\alpha}}\right)\right], \qquad (7.13)$$

$\tilde{N}_{t+1}$ is the period-t decision on the number of varieties available for production next period, which implies the expectations condition: $E_t\tilde{q}_{t+1} = \tilde{q}_{t+1}$. Taking this to (7.13) we finally get

$$\left[1+\mu_t A'(1+\alpha)\alpha^{\frac{\alpha}{1-\alpha}} - z_t\right]^{\sigma} = \beta E_t \left[\frac{z_{t+1}^{-\sigma}}{z_t^{-\sigma}}\left(1+\mu_{t+1}A'\alpha^{\frac{1}{1-\alpha}}\right)\right]. \qquad (7.14)$$

Steady-State

Steady-state is characterized by: $\mu_t = 1, \forall t$, and constant growth rates for per-capita variables and for $\tilde{N}_t$, so that from (7.12)

$$1+\gamma_q \equiv \frac{\tilde{q}_{t+1}}{\tilde{q}_t} = 1+A'(1+\alpha)\alpha^{\frac{\alpha}{1-\alpha}} - z_t, \qquad (7.15)$$

which implies that z_t must be constant in steady-state, i.e., that $\tilde{c}_t$ and $\tilde{q}_t$ grow at the same rate. Since $\tilde{q}_t = \frac{\eta}{L}\tilde{N}_t$, that means that the number of varieties of intermediate goods also grows at the same rate than these two variables: $\gamma_{\tilde{N}} = \gamma_{\tilde{c}} = \gamma_{\tilde{q}} = \gamma$.

Then, from the Euler condition, with $z_t = \tilde{c}_t/\tilde{q}_t$ constant and $\mu_t = 1, \forall t$, so that the rate of growth is

$$(1+\gamma)^{\sigma} = \beta\left(1+A'\alpha^{\frac{1}{1-\alpha}}\right) \Rightarrow 1+\gamma = \left[\beta\left(1+A'\alpha^{\frac{1}{1-\alpha}}\right)\right]^{\frac{1}{\sigma}},$$

and the steady-state value of z_t is readily obtained from (7.15)

$$z = A'(1+\alpha)\alpha^{\frac{\alpha}{1-\alpha}} - \gamma.$$

In what follows, we will consider values for structural parameters such that: $\gamma > 0$, $z > 0$. We will see in a numerical exercise below that such a region of the parameter space is non-empty.

---

[11] A similar ratio was used as auxiliary variable when solving the discrete-time AK model.

Log-Linear Approximation

The obtain the log-linear approximation to the model, we start by writing the Euler equation (7.14) as

$$0 = -e^{-\sigma \ln z_t} \left(e^{\ln \mu_t} A'(1+\alpha)\alpha^{\frac{\alpha}{1-\alpha}} + 1 - e^{\ln z_t} \right)^{\sigma}$$
$$+ \beta E_t \left[e^{-\sigma \ln z_{t+1}} \left(e^{\ln \mu_{t+1}} A'\alpha^{\frac{1}{1-\alpha}} + 1 \right) \right],$$

and introducing variables in logged differences with respect to steady-state: $\hat{z}_t = \ln(z_t/z)$, $\hat{\mu}_t = \ln(\mu_t)$, we have the approximation:

$$0 \simeq \sigma z^{-\sigma}(1+\gamma)^{\sigma}\hat{z}_t - \sigma z^{-\sigma}(1+\gamma)^{\sigma-1}A'(1+\alpha)\alpha^{\frac{\alpha}{1-\alpha}}\hat{\mu}_t$$
$$+ \sigma z^{-\sigma}(1+\gamma)^{\sigma-1}z\hat{z}_t$$
$$+ \beta E_t \left[-\sigma z^{-\sigma}\left(1+A'\alpha^{\frac{1}{1-\alpha}}\right)\hat{z}_{t+1} + z^{-\sigma}A'\alpha^{\frac{1}{1-\alpha}}\hat{\mu}_{t+1} \right].$$

Notice that $\ln\mu_t = \frac{1}{1-\alpha}\ln\theta_t \Rightarrow E_t\hat{\mu}_{t+1} = \frac{1}{1-\alpha}E_t(\ln\theta_{t+1}) = \frac{1}{1-\alpha}\phi\ln\theta_t = \phi\hat{\mu}_t$. Hence, the approximation above can be written

$$0 \simeq \sigma z^{-\sigma}\frac{(1+\gamma)^{\sigma}}{\beta}\left(1+\frac{z}{1+\gamma}\right)\hat{z}_t - \cdots$$
$$- \left[\sigma z^{-\sigma}\frac{(1+\gamma)^{\sigma-1}}{\beta}A'(1+\alpha)\alpha^{\frac{\alpha}{1-\alpha}} \right.$$
$$\left. - z^{-\sigma}A'\alpha^{\frac{\alpha}{1-\alpha}}\phi \right]\hat{\mu}_t - \sigma z^{-\sigma}\frac{(1+\gamma)^{\sigma}}{\beta}E_t\hat{z}_{t+1},$$

and solving for $\hat{z}_t$[12]:

$$\hat{z}_t = \varphi_1 E_t\hat{z}_{t+1} + \varphi_2\hat{\mu}_t,$$

with: $\varphi_1 = \frac{1+\gamma}{1+A'(1+\alpha)\alpha^{\frac{\alpha}{1-\alpha}}}$, $\varphi_2 = A'\alpha^{\frac{\alpha}{1-\alpha}}\frac{\sigma(1+\gamma)^{\sigma-1}(1+\alpha)-\beta}{\sigma(1+\gamma)^{\sigma}}\frac{1}{\varphi_1}$, where it is important to notice that the equality $1+\gamma = A'(1+\alpha)\alpha^{\frac{\alpha}{1-\alpha}}+1-z_{ss}$ implies: $0 < \varphi_1 < 1$. Therefore, we can solve this autoregression forwards, applying the law of iterated expectations as we have done in previous occasions, to obtain

$$\hat{z}_t = \frac{\varphi_2}{1-\varphi_1\phi}\hat{\mu}_t.$$

We can now proceed as follows:

1. Given a sample realization for $\{\varepsilon_t\}_{t=0}^T$, where $\varepsilon_t \underset{iid}{\sim} \tilde{N}(0,\sigma_\varepsilon^2)$, we can obtain a sample realization for $\{\theta_t\}_{t=0}^T$ and then for $\{\mu_t\}_{t=0}^T : \mu_t = \ln\mu_t = \frac{1}{1-\alpha}\ln\theta_t$.

---

[12] Using the equality: $1 + \frac{z_{ss}}{1+\gamma_{ss}} = \frac{1+\gamma_{ss}}{1+A'}$.

2. Given $\{\mu_t\}_{t=0}^T$, we compute $\{z_t\}_{t=0}^T : z_t = z\,e^{z_t}$, with $\hat{z}_t = \frac{\varphi_2}{1-\varphi_1\phi}\hat{\mu}_t$.
3. The initial value of $\tilde{q}_t$, $\tilde{q}_0$ is known through the initial condition on the number of varieties, $\tilde{N}_0$ by $\tilde{q}_0 = \frac{\eta}{L}\tilde{N}_0$. Then, given $\{\mu_t, z_t\}_{t=0}^T$, we compute $\{q_t\}_{t=0}^T$, and $\{\tilde{q}_t\}_{t=0}^T$ by iterating on $\tilde{q}_{t+1} = \left(1 + \mu_t A'(1+\alpha)\alpha^{\frac{\alpha}{1-\alpha}} - z_t\right)\tilde{q}_t$ and using: $q_t = \tilde{q}_t\,(1+\gamma)^{-t}$.
4. We compute $\{c_t\}_{t=0}^T$, and $\{\tilde{c}_t\}_{t=0}^T$ using the identities: $c_t = z_t q_t$, $\tilde{c}_t = z_t\tilde{q}_t$.
5. The number of varieties $\tilde{N}_t$ is obtained from $\tilde{N}_t = \frac{L}{\eta}\tilde{q}_t$.
6. Interest rates $\{r_t\}_{t=0}^T$ are obtained from $r_t = \mu_t A'\alpha^{\frac{\alpha}{1-\alpha}}$.
7. Per-capita output $\{\tilde{y}_t\}_{t=0}^T$ is obtained from $\tilde{y}_t = \theta_t^{\frac{1}{1-\alpha}}A^{\frac{1}{1-\alpha}}\alpha^{\frac{2\alpha}{2-\alpha}}\tilde{N}_t$, while aggregate output is $\tilde{Y}_t = L\tilde{y}_t$.
8. Real wages $\{\tilde{w}_t\}_{t=0}^T$ are obtained from $\tilde{w}_t = (1-\alpha)\tilde{y}_t$.

7.3 Technological Diffusion and Growth

The model of technological diffusion by Barro and Sala-i-Martin [5] considers two countries. The leading country, which we will label as country 1, is an economy with a variety of intermediate goods, like the one analyzed in the previous sections. So, for the leading country, we have a number of varieties, a level of output and a real interest rate given by

$$x_{1,j,t} = L_1\alpha^{\frac{2}{1-\alpha}}A_1^{\frac{1}{1-\alpha}}\theta_{1,t}^{\frac{1}{1-\alpha}} = x_{1,t}, \quad \forall j \in \left[0,\tilde{N}_{1,t}\right],$$

$$\tilde{Y}_{1,t} = L_1\alpha^{\frac{2\alpha}{1-\alpha}}A_1^{\frac{1}{1-\alpha}}\theta_{1,t}^{\frac{1}{1-\alpha}}\tilde{N}_{1,t} = \frac{1}{\alpha^2}\tilde{N}_{1,t}x_{1,t},$$

$$r_{1,t} = \frac{1}{\eta_1}\frac{1-\alpha}{\alpha}L_1\alpha^{\frac{2}{1-\alpha}}A_1^{\frac{1}{1-\alpha}}\theta_{1,t}^{\frac{1}{1-\alpha}},$$

$$\gamma_{\tilde{c},1} = \gamma_{\tilde{y},1} = \gamma_{\tilde{N},1} = \left[\beta\left(A_1'\alpha^{\frac{\alpha}{1-\alpha}}+1\right)\right]^{1/\sigma} - 1.$$

The follower country, or country 2, can either innovate and develop its own intermediate goods, or copy those that have already been invented in country 1. Copying or adapting an intermediate good from the leading country to be used in country 2, has a fixed cost $\upsilon_{2,t}$. Imitation differs from innovation in that the number of commodities that can be copied at any point in time is limited by the number of commodities already discovered in country 1 at that point, $\tilde{N}_{1,t}$ that have not been copied yet by country 2. The cost of imitation $\upsilon_{2,t}$ increases with the proportion of country 1 commodities that have been copied by country 2

$$\upsilon_{2,t} = \upsilon_2\left(\tilde{N}_{2,t-1}/\tilde{N}_{1,t-1}\right), \quad \upsilon_2' > 0.$$

Specifically, we take as specification for the imitation cost

$$\upsilon_{2,t} = \eta_2\left(\frac{\tilde{N}_{2,t-1}}{\tilde{N}_{1,t-1}}\right)^b, \quad \tilde{N}_{2,t} \leq \tilde{N}_{1,t}, \quad b > 0, \tag{7.16}$$

where η_2 being the cost of innovation,

which implies that whenever $\tilde{N}_{2,t-1} < \tilde{N}_{1,t-1}$, the cost of imitation will be lower than the cost of innovation: $\upsilon_{2,t} < \eta_2$.[13]

It makes sense to assume that the follower country starts with a number of intermediate goods well below that in the leading country: $\tilde{N}_{2,0} < \tilde{N}_{1,0}$. That implies that the cost of copying intermediate goods is initially lower than that of innovating: $\upsilon_{2,0} < \eta_2$, so country 2 will take the former option.

7.3.1 The Problem of the Follower Country

An agent in country 2 pays $\upsilon_{2,t}$ to imitate the j-th variety of the intermediate good from country 1. We assume that such agent would then obtain a perpetual monopoly on the use of that intermediate good for production in country 2, which leads to a monopoly price: $P_{j,2} = P_2 = \frac{1}{\alpha}$, as in country 1. Expressions for the quantity produced of the intermediate good $x_{2,j,t}$ and of total output $\tilde{Y}_{2,t}$, as well as that for the flow of monopoly profits are similar to those in country 1

$$x_{2,j,t} = x_{2,t} = L_2 A_2^{\frac{1}{1-\alpha}} \alpha^{\frac{2}{1-\alpha}} \theta_{2,t}^{\frac{1}{1-\alpha}}, \ j \in \left[0, \tilde{N}_{2,t}\right],$$

$$\tilde{Y}_{2,t} = L_2 A_2^{\frac{1}{1-\alpha}} \alpha^{\frac{2\alpha}{1-\alpha}} \theta_{2,t}^{\frac{1}{1-\alpha}} \tilde{N}_{2,t} = \tilde{N}_{2,t} \frac{x_{2,t}}{\alpha^2},$$

$$\pi_{2,t} = \frac{1-\alpha}{\alpha} L_2 A_2^{\frac{1}{1-\alpha}} \alpha^{\frac{2}{1-\alpha}} \theta_{2,t}^{\frac{1}{1-\alpha}},$$

so that the ratio of output per capita in both countries is

$$\frac{\tilde{Y}_{2,t}/L_2}{\tilde{Y}_{1,t}/L_1} = \frac{\tilde{y}_{2,t}}{\tilde{y}_{1,t}} = \left(\frac{A_2}{A_1}\right)^{\frac{1}{1-\alpha}} \left(\frac{\theta_{2,t}}{\theta_{1,t}}\right)^{\frac{1}{1-\alpha}} \frac{\tilde{N}_{2,t}}{\tilde{N}_{1,t}}.$$

7.3.1.1 Producers of Intermediate Goods

The present value from imitating the j-th intermediate good in country 2 is[14]

$$E_t V_{2,t} = L_2 \alpha^{\frac{2}{1-\alpha}} \frac{1-\alpha}{\alpha} A^{\frac{1}{1-\alpha}} E_t \left(\sum_{s=t}^{\infty} \frac{\theta_{2,s}^{\frac{1}{1-\alpha}}}{\prod_{l=0}^{s-t} (1 + r_{2,t+l})} \right).$$

---

[13] The cost of innovation, $\upsilon_{2,t}$, could be allowed to exceed from η_2 even when $N_{2,t-1} < N_{1,t-1}$ to capture a situation in which the yet uncopied goods from country 1 are hard to adapt for use in country 2. The proposed function does not allow for that possibility.

[14] Interest rates may be different in both countries due to the fact that we do not consider international borrowing and lending.

If there is free entry in the imitation business in country 2, firms will open to the point where $E_t V_{2,t} = v_{2,t}$. That implies: $E_{t+1} V_{2,t+1} = v_{2,t+1}$, and taking conditional expectations as of time $t : E_t V_{2,t+1} = E_t (E_{t+1} V_{2,t+1}) = E_t v_{2,t+1} = v_{2,t+1}$, where the last equality is obtained form the fact that both, $\tilde{N}_{2,t+1}$ and $\tilde{N}_{1,t+1}$ are decisions made at time t.

Therefore

$$E_t V_{2,t} - E_t V_{2,t+1} = v_{2,t} - v_{2,t+1}.$$

Since $E_t V_{2,t+1}$ can be written

$$E_t V_{2,t+1} = E_t (E_{t+1} V_{2,t+1})$$

$$= L_2 \alpha^{\frac{2}{1-\alpha}} \frac{1-\alpha}{\alpha} A^{\frac{1}{1-\alpha}} E_t \left(\sum_{s=t+1}^{\infty} \frac{\theta_{2,s}^{\frac{1}{1-\alpha}}}{\prod_{l=0}^{s-t-1} \left(1 + r_{2,t+l+1}\right)} \right),$$

we have: $E_t V_{2,t+1} = (1 + r_{2,t}) E_t V_{2,t} - \theta_{2,t}^{\frac{1}{1-\alpha}} L_2 \alpha^{\frac{2}{1-\alpha}} \frac{1-\alpha}{\alpha} A^{\frac{1}{1-\alpha}}$. So, we get, after simple manipulation

$$r_{2,t} = L_2 \alpha^{\frac{2}{1-\alpha}} \frac{1-\alpha}{\alpha} A^{\frac{1}{1-\alpha}} \frac{\theta_{2,t}^{\frac{1}{1-\alpha}}}{v_{2,t}} + \frac{v_{2,t+1} - v_{2,t}}{v_{2,t}} \qquad (7.17)$$

$$= \frac{1-\alpha}{\alpha} \frac{x_{2,t}}{v_{2,t}} + \frac{v_{2,t+1} - v_{2,t}}{v_{2,t}}.$$

7.3.1.2 Households

By the same argument made for country 1, the problem of the representative consumer in country 2 solves the optimization problem

$$\max_{\{\tilde{c}_{2,t}, \tilde{a}_{2,t+1}\}} E_0 \sum_{t=0}^{\infty} \beta^t \frac{\tilde{c}_{2,t}^{1-\sigma} - 1}{1 - \sigma},$$

subject to the sequence of single period budget constraints

$$\tilde{c}_{2,t} + \tilde{a}_{2,t+1} = \tilde{w}_{2,t} + (1 + r_{2,t}) \tilde{a}_{2,t},$$

given $\tilde{a}_{2,0}$, with optimality conditions

$$\tilde{c}_{2,t}^{-\sigma} = \beta E_t \left[(1 + r_{2,t+1}) \tilde{c}_{2,t+1}^{-\sigma} \right], \quad t = 0, 1, 2, \ldots$$

$$\lim_{T \to \infty} \beta^{t+T} E_t \tilde{c}_{2,t+T}^{-\sigma} \tilde{a}_{2,t+T+1} = 0.$$

In equilibrium, total savings must be equal to the resources needed to put in place the varieties of intermediate goods, all of them copied from country 1

$$\tilde{a}_{2,t} = v_{2,t}\frac{\tilde{N}_{2,t}}{L_2},$$

and the global constraint of resources can be written

$$
\begin{aligned}
\tilde{c}_{2,t} + v_{2,t+1}\frac{\tilde{N}_{2,t+1}}{L_2} &= \tilde{w}_{2,t} + (1+r_{2,t})v_{2,t}\frac{\tilde{N}_{2,t}}{L_2} \\
&= (1-\alpha)\tilde{y}_t \\
&\quad + \left(1 + \frac{1-\alpha}{\alpha}\frac{x_{2,t}}{v_{2,t}} + \frac{v_{2,t+1}-v_{2,t}}{v_{2,t}}\right)v_{2,t}\frac{\tilde{N}_{2,t}}{L_2} \\
&= (1-\alpha)\tilde{y}_t + \frac{1-\alpha}{\alpha}x_{2,t}\frac{\tilde{N}_{2,t}}{L_2} + v_{2,t+1}\frac{\tilde{N}_{2,t}}{L_2} \\
&= \left((1-\alpha^2)\,\theta_{2,t}^{\frac{1}{1-\alpha}}A_2^{\frac{1}{1-\alpha}}\alpha^{\frac{2\alpha}{1-\alpha}} + \frac{v_{2,t+1}}{L_2}\right)\tilde{N}_{2,t}\,,
\end{aligned}
$$

and the Euler condition

$$
\begin{aligned}
\tilde{c}_{2,t}^{-\sigma} &= \beta E_t\left[(1+r_{2,t+1})\tilde{c}_{2,t+1}^{-\sigma}\right] \\
&= \beta E_t\left[\tilde{c}_{2,t+1}^{-\sigma}\left(1 + L_2\alpha^{\frac{2}{1-\alpha}}\frac{1-\alpha}{\alpha}A^{\frac{1}{1-\alpha}}\frac{\theta_{2,t+1}^{\frac{1}{1-\alpha}}}{v_{2,t+1}}\right.\right. \\
&\qquad\left.\left. + \frac{v_{2,t+2}-v_{2,t+1}}{v_{2,t+1}}\right)\right].
\end{aligned}
$$

The presence of time-varying terms in the real rate of return (7.17) implies that the rate of growth of per-capita consumption will also change over time, displaying *a nontrivial transition* to steady-state. This runs contrary to the characteristics of the leader country, that lacks transitional dynamics, as shown in the previous section.

7.3.2 Deterministic Steady-State

In the deterministic steady-state, $\theta_{1,t} = \theta_{2,t} = 1, \forall t$, and the cost of imitation must be constant: $v_{2,t} = v_{2,ss}$. We already know that the leader country has a balanced growth path type of steady-state, without any transitional dynamics. So, per-capita variables in country 1 grow at the same rate γ_1 in all time periods. But the cost of imitation can remain constant in steady-state only if $\tilde{N}_{1,t}$ and $\tilde{N}_{2,t}$ grow at the same rate, so that: $1 + \gamma_{\tilde{N}_2} = 1 + \gamma_1 = \left[\beta\left(1 + A_1'\frac{\alpha}{1+\alpha}\right)\right]^{1/\sigma}$, with $A_1' = \dfrac{A_1^{\frac{1}{1-\alpha}}\alpha^{\frac{2\alpha}{1-\alpha}}(1-\alpha^2)}{\eta_1/L_1}$.

Since $v_{2,t}$ and the rates of growth of the number of intermediate goods in both countries are constant in steady-state we get, from the global constraint of resources

$$\frac{\tilde{c}_{2,t}}{\tilde{N}_{2,t}} = \left[(1-\alpha^2)A_2^{\frac{1}{1-\alpha}}\alpha^{\frac{2\alpha}{1-\alpha}} + \frac{v_2}{L_2}\right] - \frac{v_2}{L_2}(1+\gamma_2), \qquad (7.18)$$

which implies that $\frac{\tilde{c}_{2,t}}{\tilde{N}_{2,t}}$ must also be constant in steady-state. This implies: $1+\gamma_{2,\tilde{c}} = 1+\gamma_{2,\tilde{N}_2} = 1+\gamma_1$. Finally, since

$$\frac{\tilde{y}_{2,t}}{\tilde{y}_{1,t}} = \frac{\tilde{Y}_{2t}/L_2}{\tilde{Y}_{1t}/L_1} = \frac{\tilde{N}_{2,t}}{\tilde{N}_{1,t}}\left(\frac{A_2}{A_1}\right)^{\frac{1}{1-\alpha}},$$

we have that the common growth rate of the number of intermediate commodities in both countries implies that, in steady-state, the relative levels of per-capita income will remain constant. In other words, income per capita will also grow at the same rate in both countries. However, which country achieves the highest income per capita in steady-state will depend on the relative values of the number of intermediate goods, and the levels of productivity. To discuss this important issue, we advance that the transitional dynamics analysis of the model in the next section shows that if equilibrium is well-determined, the problem will have a saddle path structure, with a single stable eigenvalue. That means that all variables will experience monotone convergence to their steady state levels. Hence, if the number of intermediate commodities in country 2 is initially below that in country 1, $\tilde{N}_{2,0} < \tilde{N}_{1,0}$, their ratio $\tilde{N}_{2,t}/\tilde{N}_{1,t}$ will start from below 1 at $t = 0$, converging monotonically to its steady-state level.

Let us assume that the steady-state ratio is also below one: $\tilde{N}_2/\tilde{N}_1$. From the specification for the imitation cost function, we see that this would be the case of a country for which the cost of adapting commodities from country 1 remains, from the initial time, always below the cost of innovation, so the latter option is never exercised. If this country is relatively highly productive, i.e., if the A_2/A_1 ratio is sufficiently above 1, then it could be the case that the imitating country would end up above country 1 in terms of income per-capita, a phenomenon known as *leapfrogging*. It could be the case of countries which have been closed to technological developments for a number of years and at some point get admitted to an existing economic union of countries which enjoy a wide variety of commodities. If the first country has been very careful in maintaining a high level of human capital, it might have higher productivity than countries in the union, and experience a fast progress in terms of income per-capita, as goods form the union are adapted for use in the initially underdeveloped country. On the other hand, high productivity should be expected to create incentives for innovation, making unlikely that such a country would not develop its own goods, unless restricted in such process by political reasons.

Since utility maximization leads to $1+\gamma_{i,\tilde{c}} = [\beta(1+r_i)]^{1/\sigma}, i = 1,2$, in both countries, then the fact that the steady-state rate of growth of consumption per capita in both countries is the same implies that steady-state interest rates are also the same in both countries: $r_1 = r_2$

$$r_1 = r_2 \Rightarrow L_2\alpha^{\frac{2}{1-\alpha}}\frac{1-\alpha}{\alpha}A_2^{\frac{1}{1-\alpha}}\frac{1}{v_2} = L_1\alpha^{\frac{2}{1-\alpha}}\frac{1-\alpha}{\alpha}A_1^{\frac{1}{1-\alpha}}\frac{1}{\eta_1},$$

an equality that help us to determine the *equilibrium cost of imitation*

$$v_2 = \left(\frac{A_2}{A_1}\right)^{\frac{1}{1-\alpha}}\frac{L_2}{L_1}\eta_1. \tag{7.19}$$

Finally, the steady-state ratio $\left(\frac{\tilde{c}_{2,t}}{\tilde{N}_{2,t}}\right)_{ss}$ can be obtained by taking (7.19) to (7.18).

7.3.3 Computing the Numerical Solution by Log-Linear Approximations and Numerical Derivatives

We start by characterizing the transitional dynamics of the economy. For that we introduce auxiliary variables: $\tilde{q}_{2,t} = \frac{v_{2,t+1}\tilde{N}_{2,t}}{L_2}$, $z_{2,t} = \frac{\tilde{c}_{2,t}}{\tilde{q}_{2,t}}$, while maintaining those already defined for country 1: $\tilde{q}_{1,t} = \frac{\eta_1\tilde{N}_{1,t}}{L_1}$, $z_{1,t} = \frac{\tilde{c}_{1,t}}{\tilde{q}_{1,t}}$, which allow us to write the global constraint of resources

$$z_{2,t} + \frac{v_{2,t+1}}{v_{2,t+2}}\frac{\tilde{q}_{2,t+1}}{\tilde{q}_{2,t}} = \left[(1-\alpha^2)\,\theta_{2,t}^{\frac{1}{1-\alpha}}A_2^{\frac{1}{1-\alpha}}\alpha^{\frac{2\alpha}{1-\alpha}}\frac{L_2}{v_{2,t+1}} + 1\right],$$

and with the change of variables: $A_2' = (1-\alpha^2)A_2^{\frac{1}{1-\alpha}}\alpha^{\frac{2\alpha}{1-\alpha}}L_2$, $\mu_{2,t} = \theta_{2,t}^{\frac{1}{1-\alpha}}$, becomes

$$z_{2,t} + \frac{v_{2,t+1}}{v_{2,t+2}}\frac{\tilde{q}_{2,t+1}}{\tilde{q}_{2,t}} = \left(A_2'\mu_{2,t}\frac{1}{v_{2,t+1}} + 1\right),$$

while from the Euler condition, we get

$$z_{2,t}^{-\sigma}\left[\left(A_2'\mu_{2,t}\frac{1}{v_{2,t+1}} + 1 - z_{2,t}\right)\frac{v_{2,t+2}}{v_{2,t+1}}\right]$$
$$= \beta E_t\left[z_{2,t+1}^{-\sigma}\left(1 + \frac{\alpha}{1+\alpha}\frac{A_2'\mu_{2,t+1}}{v_{2,t+2}} + \frac{v_{2,t+2} - v_{2,t+1}}{v_{2,t+1}}\right)\right]. \tag{7.20}$$

The function describing the cost of imitation (7.16) can be written in terms of these new variables:

$$v_{2,t+1} = \eta_2\left(\frac{\tilde{N}_{2,t}}{\tilde{N}_{1,t}}\right)^b$$

$$\Rightarrow v_{2,t+1} = \eta_2\left(\frac{\tilde{N}_{2,t}v_{2,t+1}/L_2}{\tilde{N}_{1,t}\eta_1/L_1}\right)^b\left(\frac{\eta_1L_2}{L_1}\right)^b v_{2,t+1}^{-b}$$

$$\Rightarrow v_{2,t+1}^{1+b} = \eta_2 \left(\frac{\eta_1 L_2}{L_1} \right)^b \left(\frac{\tilde{q}_{2,t}}{\tilde{q}_{1,t}} \right)^b$$

$$\Rightarrow \frac{\tilde{q}_{2,t}}{\tilde{q}_{1,t}} = \frac{v_{2,t+1}^{(1+b)/b}}{\eta_2^{1/b} \eta_1 L_2/L_1}.$$

This expression can be used to write the global constraint of resources as

$$z_{2,t} + \frac{v_{2,t+1}}{v_{2,t+2}} \frac{\tilde{q}_{2,t+1}/\tilde{q}_{1,t+1}}{\tilde{q}_{2,t}/\tilde{q}_{1,t}} \frac{\tilde{q}_{1,t+1}}{\tilde{q}_{1,t}} = \left(A_2' \mu_{2,t} \frac{1}{v_{2,t+1}} + 1 \right).$$

But in the leader country: $\frac{\tilde{q}_{1,t+1}}{\tilde{q}_t} = \mu_{1,t} A_1' (1 + \alpha) \alpha^{\frac{\alpha}{1-\alpha}} + 1 - z_{1,t}$, so that we finally get

$$\left(\frac{v_{2,t+2}}{v_{2,t+1}} \right)^{1/b} = \frac{A_2' \mu_{2,t} \frac{1}{v_{2,t+1}} + 1 - z_{2,t}}{\mu_{1,t} A_1' (1 + \alpha) \alpha^{\frac{\alpha}{1-\alpha}} + 1 - z_{1,t}}. \tag{7.21}$$

We have a system of two dynamic equations (7.20), (7.21) in a control variable, z_2, and a state variable, v_2, so that to have a determinate equilibrium we should find one stable and one unstable eigenvalue in the log-linear approximation to the system. It is important to notice that $\{\mu_{1,t}\}$ and $\{z_{1,t}\}$ are obtained in the leader country, but they affect the follower country, as it is clear in (7.21). Hence, shocks in the leading country influence the follower country, while shocks in the follower country do not affect the leading country.

Once we get time series for $\{v_{2,t+2}\}_{t=0}^T$ and $\{z_{2,t}\}_{t=0}^T$, we can use the $\{\tilde{q}_{1,t}\}_{t=0}^T$ sequence obtained in the leading country to obtain the time series for $\{\tilde{q}_{2,t}\}_{t=0}^T$. Given $\{\tilde{q}_{2,t}\}_{t=0}^T$ and $\{z_{2,t}\}_{t=0}^T$, we can compute $\{\tilde{c}_{2,t}\}_{t=0}^T$. Given $\{\tilde{q}_{2,t}\}_{t=0}^T$ and $\{v_{2,t}\}_{t=0}^T$, we can compute $\{\tilde{N}_{2,t}\}_{t=0}^T$. Finally, given $\{\tilde{N}_{2,t}\}_{t=0}^T$, we can compute $\{\tilde{Y}_{2,t}\}_{t=0}^T$.

7.3.3.1 The Log-Linear Approximation and Numerical Derivatives

We now depart from the analysis we have made in previous models. Once we obtain the log-linear approximation to the model, we will use numerical derivatives rather than analytical derivatives, to compute the Jacobian to the system. Using analytical derivatives to compute the solution, as in previous models, is proposed as an exercise at the end of the chapter. On the other hand, the numerical approach we use here does not require partial derivatives and it can be adapted to all other models we have discussed throughout the book.

The system made up by (7.20), (7.21) can be written

$$E_t \left[F_1 \left(z_{2,t+1}, z_{2,t}, v_{2,t+2}, v_{2,t+1}; \mu_{2,t+1}, \mu_{2,t}; z_{1,t}, \mu_{1,t} \right) \right] = 0, \tag{7.22}$$

$$E_t \left[F_2 \left(z_{2,t+1}, z_{2,t}, v_{2,t+2}, v_{2,t+1}; \mu_{2,t+1}, \mu_{2,t}; z_{1,t}, \mu_{1,t} \right) \right] = 0. \tag{7.23}$$

Using the notation $\hat{\xi}_t = \ln(\xi_t/\xi_{ss})$, $\xi_t = z_{2,t}, \upsilon_{2,t+1}, \mu_{2,t}, z_{1,t}, \mu_{1,t}$, and denoting the partial derivatives of these two functions by: $J_{i,k} = \frac{\partial F_i}{\partial \xi_k}$, $i = 1,2$; $k = 1,2,\dots,8$, where: $\hat{\xi}_1 = \hat{z}_{2,t+1}$, $\hat{\xi}_2 = \hat{z}_{2,t}$, $\hat{\xi}_3 = \hat{\upsilon}_{2,t+2}$, $\hat{\xi}_4 = \hat{\upsilon}_{2,t+1}$, $\hat{\xi}_5 = \hat{\mu}_{2,t+1}$, $\hat{\xi}_6 = \hat{\mu}_{2,t}$, $\hat{\xi}_7 = \hat{z}_{1,t}$, $\hat{\xi}_8 = \hat{\mu}_{1,t}$, the log-linear approximation to $(7.22),(7.23)$ can be written

$$\Gamma_0 \begin{pmatrix} E_t\hat{z}_{2,t+1} \\ \hat{\upsilon}_{2,t+2} \end{pmatrix} + \Gamma_1 \begin{pmatrix} \hat{z}_{2,t} \\ \hat{\upsilon}_{2,t+1} \end{pmatrix} + \Gamma_2 \begin{pmatrix} \hat{\mu}_{2,t} \\ \hat{z}_{1,t} \\ \hat{\mu}_{1,t} \end{pmatrix} = \begin{pmatrix} 0 \\ 0 \end{pmatrix},$$

where

$$\Gamma_0 = \begin{pmatrix} J_{1,1} & J_{1,3} \\ 0 & J_{2,3} \end{pmatrix}, \quad \Gamma_1 = \begin{pmatrix} J_{1,2} & J_{1,4} \\ J_{2,2} & J_{2,4} \end{pmatrix},$$

$$\Gamma_2 = \begin{pmatrix} J_{1,5}\phi_1 + J_{1,6} & 0 & 0 \\ J_{2,6} & J_{2,7} & J_{2,8} \end{pmatrix},$$

where ϕ_1 is the autoregressive parameter of stochastic process for $\theta_{1,t}$, which leads to

$$\begin{pmatrix} E_t\hat{z}_{2,t+1} \\ \hat{\upsilon}_{2,t+2} \end{pmatrix} = \Gamma_3 \begin{pmatrix} \hat{z}_{2,t} \\ \hat{\upsilon}_{2,t+1} \end{pmatrix} + \Gamma_4 \begin{pmatrix} \hat{\mu}_{2,t} \\ \hat{z}_{1,t} \\ \hat{\mu}_{1,t} \end{pmatrix}, \tag{7.24}$$

where $\Gamma_3 = -\Gamma_0^{-1}\Gamma_1$, $\Gamma_4 = -\Gamma_0^{-1}\Gamma_2$.

As mentioned above, a well-determined equilibrium arises when Γ_3 has one stable and one unstable eigenvalues, which we will assume to be the case. The problem would then have the familiar saddle-path structure we have seen in other models throughout the book. The unstable direction will be eliminated by setting to zero each period the product of the eigenvector associated to the unstable eigenvalue by the vector made up by the control and state variables. That condition in turn, will give us the way to choose the control variable each period, as a function of the state variable, to have a stable solution. Without loss of generality, let us assume: $|\lambda_1| < 1$, $|\lambda_2| > 1$. We would then have the spectral decomposition:

$$\Gamma_3 = M\Lambda M^{-1}, \quad \Lambda = \begin{pmatrix} \lambda_1 & 0 \\ 0 & \lambda_2 \end{pmatrix}, \quad M^{-1} = \begin{pmatrix} m_{11} & m_{12} \\ m_{21} & m_{22} \end{pmatrix}.$$

Premultiplying (7.24) by M^{-1} and denoting by Q the product: $Q = M^{-1}\Gamma_4 = \begin{pmatrix} Q_{11} & Q_{12} & Q_{13} \\ Q_{21} & Q_{22} & Q_{23} \end{pmatrix}$, we have

$$m_{11}E_t\hat{z}_{2,t+1} + m_{12}\hat{\upsilon}_{2,t+2} = \lambda_1 (m_{11}\hat{z}_{2,t} + m_{12}\hat{\upsilon}_{2,t+1})$$
$$+ Q_{11}\hat{\mu}_{2,t} + Q_{12}\hat{z}_{1,t} + Q_{13}\hat{\mu}_{1,t},$$
$$m_{21}E_t\hat{z}_{2,t+1} + m_{22}\hat{\upsilon}_{2,t+2} = \lambda_2 (m_{21}\hat{z}_{2,t} + m_{22}\hat{\upsilon}_{2,t+1})$$
$$+ Q_{21}\hat{\mu}_{2,t} + Q_{22}\hat{z}_{1,t} + Q_{23}\hat{\mu}_{1,t},$$

which, using the results obtained from the leading country

$$\hat{z}_{1,t} = \frac{\varphi_2}{1 - \varphi_1 \phi_1} \hat{\mu}_t,$$

can be written

$$m_{11} E_t \hat{z}_{2,t+1} + m_{12} \hat{v}_{2,t+2} = \lambda_1 \left(m_{11} \hat{z}_{2,t} + m_{12} \hat{v}_{2,t+1} \right) + Q_{11} \hat{\mu}_{2,t}$$

$$+ \left(Q_{13} + Q_{12} \frac{\varphi_2}{1 - \varphi_1 \phi_1} \right) \hat{\mu}_{1,t}, \qquad (7.25)$$

$$m_{21} E_t \hat{z}_{2,t+1} + m_{22} \hat{v}_{2,t+2} = \lambda_2 \left(m_{21} \hat{z}_{2,t} + m_{22} \hat{v}_{2,t+1} \right) + Q_{21} \hat{\mu}_{2,t}$$

$$+ \left(Q_{23} + Q_{22} \frac{\varphi_2}{1 - \varphi_1 \phi_1} \right) \hat{\mu}_{1,t}. \qquad (7.26)$$

Defining now auxiliary variables: $f_{2,t}^0 = m_{21} \hat{z}_{2,t} + m_{22} \hat{v}_{2,t+1}$, we have $E_t f_{2,t+1}^0 = m_{21} E_t \hat{z}_{2,t+1} + m_{22} \hat{v}_{2,t+2}$, and the second equation becomes a first order autoregression with an unstable coefficient, which can be solved forwards, to obtain

$$f_{2,t}^0 = \frac{Q_{23} + Q_{22} \frac{\varphi_2}{1 - \varphi_1 \phi_1}}{\phi_1 - \lambda_2} \hat{\mu}_{1,t} + \frac{Q_{21}}{\phi_2 - \lambda_2} \hat{\mu}_{2,t},$$

where ϕ_2 is the autoregressive parameter of stochastic process for $\theta_{2,t}$, and finally

$$\hat{z}_{2,t} = \frac{1}{m_{21}} \left(\frac{Q_{23} + Q_{22} \frac{\varphi_2}{1 - \varphi_1 \phi_1}}{\phi_1 - \lambda_2} \hat{\mu}_{1,t} + \frac{Q_{21}}{\phi_2 - \lambda_2} \hat{\mu}_{2,t} - m_{22} \hat{v}_{2,t+1} \right), \qquad (7.27)$$

which is the *stability or control equation*.

Substituting (7.27) into (7.25) we get

$$E_t \left[\frac{m_{11}}{m_{21}} \left(\frac{Q_{23} + Q_{22} \frac{\varphi_2}{1 - \varphi_1 \phi_1}}{\phi_1 - \lambda_2} \hat{\mu}_{1,t+1} + \frac{Q_{21} \hat{\mu}_{2,t+1}}{\phi_2 - \lambda_2} - m_{22} \hat{v}_{2,t+2} \right) \right] + m_{12} \hat{v}_{2,t+2}$$

$$= \lambda_1 \frac{m_{11}}{m_{21}} \left(\frac{Q_{23} + Q_{22} \frac{\varphi_2}{1 - \varphi_1 \phi_1}}{\phi_1 - \lambda_2} \hat{\mu}_{1,t} + \frac{Q_{21}}{\phi_2 - \lambda_2} \hat{\mu}_{2,t} - m_{22} \hat{v}_{2,t+1} \right)$$

$$+ \lambda_1 m_{12} \hat{v}_{2,t+1} + \left(Q_{13} + Q_{12} \frac{\varphi_2}{1 - \varphi_1 \phi_1} \right) \hat{\mu}_{1,t} + Q_{11} \hat{\mu}_{2,t},$$

which can be written

$$\left(m_{12} - \frac{m_{11}}{m_{21}} m_{22} \right) \hat{v}_{2,t+2} = \lambda_1 \left(m_{12} - \frac{m_{11}}{m_{21}} m_{22} \right) \hat{v}_{2,t+1}$$

$$+ \left[\left(Q_{13} + Q_{12} \frac{\varphi_2}{1 - \varphi_1 \phi_1} \right) + (\lambda_1 - \phi_1) \right.$$

$$\left. \times \frac{m_{11}}{m_{21}} \frac{Q_{23} + Q_{22} \frac{\varphi_2}{1 - \varphi_1 \phi_1}}{\phi_1 - \lambda_2} \right] \hat{\mu}_{1,t}$$

$$+ \left[Q_{11} + (\lambda_1 - \phi_2) \frac{m_{11}}{m_{21}} \frac{Q_{21}}{\phi_2 - \lambda_2} \right] \hat{\mu}_{2,t},$$

and finally

$$\hat{v}_{2,t+2} = \lambda_1 \hat{v}_{2,t+1} + \frac{1}{m_{12} - \frac{m_{11}}{m_{21}} m_{22}} \left(S_1 \hat{\mu}_{1,t} + S_2 \hat{\mu}_{2,t} \right),$$

where $S_1 = \left(Q_{13} + Q_{12} \frac{\varphi_2}{1 - \varphi_1 \phi_1} \right) + (\lambda_1 - \phi_1) \frac{m_{11}}{m_{21}} \frac{Q_{23} + Q_{22} \frac{\varphi_2}{1 - \varphi_1 \phi_1}}{\phi_1 - \lambda_2}$, $S_2 = Q_{11} + (\lambda_1 - \phi_2) \frac{m_{11}}{m_{21}} \frac{Q_{21}}{\phi_2 - \lambda_2}$, which is the *state equation*.

We are now ready to compute the numerical solution to the model:

1. Given initial values $\{\tilde{N}_{2,0}, \tilde{N}_{1,0}\}$ we compute $\hat{v}_{2,1}$, and given sample realizations for $\{\hat{\mu}_{1,t}\}_{t=0}^{T}$ and $\{\hat{\mu}_{2,t}\}_{t=0}^{T}$, we obtain $\{\hat{v}_{2,t+1}\}_{t=1}^{T}$ from the state equation.
2. Given sample realizations for $\{\hat{\mu}_{1,t}\}_{t=0}^{T}$, $\{\hat{\mu}_{2,t}\}_{t=0}^{T}$ and $\{\hat{v}_{2,t+1}\}_{t=1}^{T}$, we obtain $\{\hat{z}_{2,t}\}_{t=0}^{T}$ from the control equation.

7.3.4 Numerical Exercise: Solving the Model with Varieties of Intermediate Goods, and the Diffusion Growth Model

The *simul_diffus.m* Matlab file computes a sample realization from the technological diffusion model. Sample realizations are obtained for all variables in the leader and the follower countries. The set of time series obtained for the leader country can be taken as a realization from the solution to the model with varieties of intermediate goods, discussed in the previous section. The model could easily be extended to compute an arbitrary number of sample realizations for the solution, the same way it is done when solving Growth models in other chapters.

The same program can also be used to compute impulse responses in both countries to a productivity shock in the leader country. In that case, rather than starting from sample realizations for the stochastic productivity shocks in both countries, a time series for the productivity shock in the leader country is chosen with a single non-zero value at a pre-specified point in time, as indicated in the comments in the program. The size of the shock can be changed as desired. The time series for the productivity shock in the follower country is set to zero at all points in time.[15] The program then computes a graph with the impulse responses in the leader country.

It is interesting to see that all detrended variables experience permanent effects from the purely transitory, single-period shock in productivity. This is a consequence of these variables having a unit root, even after discounting their deterministic growth component. Consumption and output increase, and so do the number of intermediate goods and the real wage. The first three variables show the fastest adjustment to their new steady-state levels, while the number of varieties, a cumulative state variable, increases more gradually. Real interest rates experience a sudden increase with the productivity shock, gradually returning to their level before the shock, a reflection of the fact that this variable does not contain a unit root. The relative persistence in the real rate of return is a mere consequence of the autoregressive structure of the productivity shock. Detrended variables in the follower country experience even more gradual adjustments to their new, higher steady-state levels, reflecting the nontrivial transition to the new-steady-state in this country. That is, in turn, a consequence of the fact that the number of intermediate commodities in this country adjust gradually to the increase in the number of intermediate commodities in the leader country. It is interesting to see the sharp decrease in real interest rates in the follower country, adjusting to their level prior to the shock with some overshooting. A second graph shows rates of growth in some key, detrended variables, showing those in the follower country to be more persistent. A last graph overlays graphs for both countries. It also shows the time evolution of the cost of imitation, that experiences an initial decrease as the number of intermediate varieties in the leader country increases faster than the one in the follower country, to gradually return to its level, prior to the productivity shock.

7.4 Schumpeterian Growth

We present in this section a stylized discrete time model under uncertainty where endogenous growth is driven by attempts to increase the quality of goods by innovation, in order to obtain a flow of monopoly profits (see [2, 37, 83] or [6, Chap. 7]). In this model, innovation creates a new intermediate commodity, which is more productive than the previously available, making them obsolete.[16]

---

[15] It is also straightforward to adapt the program to compute impulse responses to a shock in the follower country. The reader will see that the leader country does not react to such a shock, and that responses in the follower country are as expected.

[16] Our presentation follows Howitt and Aghion [42], in discrete time and in a stochastic setup.

7.4.1 The Economy

7.4.1.1 The Final Good Sector

The consumption commodity is produced in a competitive market. Work is represented by a continuous mass of L workers, who offer their labor supply inelastically. The intermediate commodities are produced by M industries, $x_{i,t}$ being the supply of the i-ith intermediate commodity at time t. The production for the final good is

$$\tilde{Y}_t = \theta_t L^{1-\alpha} \sum_{i=1}^{M} \tilde{A}_{i,t} x_{i,t}^{\alpha} , \qquad (7.28)$$

where θ_t denotes a productivity shock following a stochastic process

$$\ln \theta_t = \phi \ln \theta_{t-1} + \varepsilon_t, \quad \varepsilon_t \underset{iid}{\sim} N(0, \sigma_\varepsilon^2),$$

and $\tilde{A}_{i,t}$, $i = 1, \ldots, M$ is the productivity coefficient for each industry.

Each firm maximizes profits period by period taking wages w_t and prices of each intermediate good, $P_{i,t}$ as given

$$\max_{\left\{ L, \left\{ x_{i,t} \right\}_{i=1}^{M} \right\}} \theta_t L^{1-\alpha} \sum_{i=1}^{M} \tilde{A}_{i,t} x_{i,t}^{\alpha} - w_t L - \sum_{i=1}^{M} P_{i,t} x_{i,t},$$

with optimality conditions

$$P_{i,t} = \alpha \theta_t L^{1-\alpha} \tilde{A}_{i,t} x_{i,t}^{\alpha-1}, \quad i = 1, 2, \ldots, M, \qquad (7.29)$$

$$w_t = (1-\alpha) \theta_t L^{-\alpha} \sum_{i=1}^{M} \tilde{A}_{i,t} x_{i,t}^{\alpha}. \qquad (7.30)$$

7.4.1.2 Sector of Intermediate Goods

Private agents in the economy have an incentive to innovate with the hope of obtaining monopoly profits from producing on of the intermediate goods with a technology which is $1 + \gamma$ times ($\gamma > 0$) as productive as the previous one. For simplicity, we assume that the researcher who is successful in innovating in the sector of the i-th intermediate good at time t, will enjoy monopoly rights on the production of that good just over that period. No other producers can produce, at time t the i-th intermediate good with the improved technology, either because it can be kept secret, or because of the existence of a patent. After that, any agent will have access to the improved technology under a competitive market structure, until another researcher may be successful in obtaining a further technological improvement. When that happens, this new researcher will be able to enjoy monopoly profits for the period in which the new technology has been found.

In this section we compute the equilibrium profit of a successful innovator who becomes a monopolist in the i-th intermediate sector for one period. The innovator's monopoly profit π is determined as follows: The only input in the production of each intermediate good is physical capital, at the rate of $\tilde{A}_{i,t}$ units of physical capital for each unit of the i-th intermediate good at time t. The evolution of the productivity coefficient, $\tilde{A}_{i,t}$, is determined in the research sector. Capital is rented in a perfectly competitive market at a rate ζ_t. Hence, the unit cost of producing the ith intermediate good is $\zeta_t \tilde{A}_{i,t}$, and the price of that good is given by (7.29).

The monopoly rent for ith intermediate good is therefore

$$\tilde{\pi}_{i,t} = \max_{\{x_{i,t}\}_{i=1}^M} \left[P_{i,t}(x_{i,t})x_{i,t} - \zeta_t \tilde{A}_{i,t}x_{i,t} \right],$$

subject to (7.29), where we have made explicit the dependence of the monopoly price from the quantity being produced.

The optimality condition is

$$x_{i,t} = \left(\frac{\alpha^2 \theta_t}{\zeta_t} \right)^{\frac{1}{1-\alpha}} L. \tag{7.31}$$

Since the right-hand side of (7.31) does not depend on i, we have: $x_{i,t} = x_t$, $\forall i = 1, 2, \ldots, M$.

Substituting (7.31) into (7.29) we get

$$P_{i,t} = \frac{1}{\alpha} \tilde{A}_{i,t} \zeta_t, \tag{7.32}$$

so that the price of each intermediate good depends on the productivity on its own sector, but it does not depend on the productivity shock on the final commodity sector.

The monopolist profit is obtained by taking (7.32) and (7.31) to the profit function, to obtain

$$\tilde{\pi}_{i,t} = (1-\alpha)\alpha\theta_t L^{1-\alpha}\tilde{A}_{i,t}x_{i,t}^\alpha = (1-\alpha)\alpha\theta_t L^{1-\alpha}\tilde{A}_{i,t}x_t^\alpha. \tag{7.33}$$

Aggregate demand for physical capital is

$$\sum_{i=1}^M \tilde{A}_{i,t}x_{i,t} = x_t \sum_{i=1}^M \tilde{A}_{i,t} = x_t M \tilde{A}_t,$$

where $\tilde{A}_t = \frac{1}{M}\sum_{i=1}^M \tilde{A}_{i,t}$ is the average technology level among industries.

In equilibrium, we have equality between aggregate demand and supply of capital:

$$x_t M \tilde{A}_t = \tilde{K}_t. \tag{7.34}$$

7.4.1.3 Research Sector

The innovation effort at time t in industry i may have as a result an improvement in the corresponding intermediate good, whose productivity becomes, if research is successful:

$$\tilde{A}_{i,t} = (1+\gamma)\tilde{A}_{i,t-1},$$

for some $\gamma > 0$, which we assume to be constant over time and across industries. Otherwise, productivity remains invariant: $\tilde{A}_{i,t} = \tilde{A}_{i,t-1}$. When research is successful in some t period, the innovator is able to become a monopolist in the production of the i-th intermediate good for that t period.

We assume that the probability of time t research to be successful is given by

$$\lambda \left(\frac{\tilde{N}_{i,t}}{(1+\gamma)\tilde{A}_{i,t-1}} \right)^{b} \in (0,1), \quad 0 < b < 1.$$

This probability depends positively on the investment effort, given by the number of units invested in research, $\tilde{N}_{i,t}$. It also depends inversely on the level of productivity: improving productivity is harder the higher level of productivity, making less likely that some research becomes successful. The b parameter indicates that an increase in $\frac{\tilde{N}_{i,t}}{(1+\gamma)\tilde{A}_{i,t-1}}$ raises the probability of success in research less than proportionally. Finally, λ is an indicator of productivity in the R&D sector that guarantees the probability of success to be between 0 and 1.

Therefore, the level of productivity $\tilde{A}_{i,t}$ follows a Bernoulli distribution

$$\tilde{A}_{i,t} = (1+\gamma)\tilde{A}_{i,t-1}, \text{ with probability } p_{i,t|t-1} = \lambda \left(\frac{\tilde{N}_{i,t}}{(1+\gamma)\tilde{A}_{i,t-1}} \right)^{b}$$

$$= \tilde{A}_{i,t-1}, \text{ with probability } 1 - p_{i,t|t-1} = 1 - \lambda \left(\frac{\tilde{N}_{i,t}}{(1+\gamma)\tilde{A}_{i,t-1}} \right)^{b}.$$

The intermediate producer chooses her R&D level of investment $\tilde{N}_{i,t}$ to maximize the expected revenue from innovation minus the cost of R&D. The expected revenue is the probability of an innovation $\lambda \left(\frac{\tilde{N}_{i,t}}{(1+\gamma)\tilde{A}_{i,t-1}} \right)^{b}$ times the profit $\pi_{i,t}$, while the cost is just $\tilde{N}_{i,t}$. Therefore, the entrepreneur solves

$$\max_{\tilde{N}_{i,t}} \left\{ \lambda \left(\frac{\tilde{N}_{i,t}}{(1+\gamma)\tilde{A}_{i,t-1}} \right)^{b} \pi_{i,t} - \tilde{N}_{i,t} \right\},$$

where $\pi_{i,t}$ is given by (7.33).

The first order condition for this maximization yields the research-arbitrage equation

$$\frac{\tilde{N}_{i,t}}{(1+\gamma)\tilde{A}_{i,t-1}} = \left[b\lambda(1-\alpha)\alpha\theta_t L^{1-\alpha}x_t^\alpha\right]^{1/(1-b)}, \tag{7.35}$$

where x_t is given by (7.31).

Since the right-hand side of (7.35) does not depend on i, we have: $\frac{\tilde{N}_{i,t}}{(1+\gamma)\tilde{A}_{i,t-1}} = n_t, \forall i = 1,2,\ldots,M$, and we will refer to n_t as the productivity-adjusted effort in R&D.

We are now in condition to determine the behavior of average productivity across the intermediate goods sectors. Assuming a large number of intermediate goods, we can use the strong law of large numbers to approximately substitute the sample average by the mathematical expectation

$$\begin{aligned}
\tilde{A}_t &= \frac{1}{M}\sum_{i=1}^M \tilde{A}_{i,t} \underset{\substack{\text{strong law} \\ \text{of large numbers}}}{\simeq} \frac{1}{M}\sum_{i=1}^M E(\tilde{A}_{i,t}) \\
&= \frac{1}{M}\sum_{i=1}^M \left\{ \lambda\left(\frac{\tilde{N}_{i,t}}{(1+\gamma)\tilde{A}_{i,t-1}}\right)^b (1+\gamma)\tilde{A}_{i,t-1} \right. \\
&\quad \left. + \left[1 - \lambda\left(\frac{\tilde{N}_{i,t}}{(1+\gamma)\tilde{A}_{i,t-1}}\right)^b\right]\tilde{A}_{i,t-1} \right\} \\
&= \frac{1}{M}\sum_{i=1}^M \left[\lambda n_t^b (1+\gamma)\tilde{A}_{i,t-1} + (1-\lambda n_t^b)\tilde{A}_{i,t-1}\right] \\
&= \frac{1}{M}\left(1+\lambda\gamma n_t^b\right)\sum_{i=1}^M \tilde{A}_{i,t-1} = \left(1+\lambda\gamma n_t^b\right)\tilde{A}_{t-1}
\end{aligned}$$

so that the rate of growth of aggregate productivity is

$$\frac{\tilde{A}_t}{\tilde{A}_{t-1}} = 1 + \lambda\gamma n_t^b. \tag{7.36}$$

Let us write x_t in terms of *capital per efficiency unit*: if we denote k_t the $\tilde{K}_t/(M\tilde{A}_{t-1})$ ratio[17] then, using (7.36) in (7.34) we obtain

$$x_t = \frac{\tilde{K}_t}{M\tilde{A}_t} = \frac{k_t}{1+\lambda\gamma n_t^b}. \tag{7.37}$$

We can now write monopolist profits in terms of capital per efficiency unit. From (7.33) and (7.37), we have

$$\tilde{\pi}_{i,t} = (1-\alpha)\alpha\theta_t L^{1-\alpha}\tilde{A}_{i,t}k_t^\alpha\left(1+\lambda\gamma n_t^b\right)^{-\alpha}.$$

Finally, from (7.29) and (7.32), together with (7.37) we obtain the equilibrium cost of renting physical capital

$$\zeta_t = \alpha^2\theta_t L^{1-\alpha}k_t^{\alpha-1}\left(1+\lambda\gamma n_t^b\right)^{1-\alpha}. \tag{7.38}$$

---

[17] Note that the natural definition involves the ratio of physical capital by the level of productivity, both variables taken at the beginning of the period.

7.4.1.4 Market for Physical Capital

The owner of capital obtains ζ_t per unit. This amount must be enough to cover the cost of capital, which includes the interest rate, r_t, and the rate of depreciation, δ. Therefore, the absence of arbitrage condition in this market is

$$r_t + \delta = \alpha^2 \theta_t L^{1-\alpha} k_t^{\alpha-1} \left(1 + \lambda \gamma n_t^b\right)^{1-\alpha}. \tag{7.39}$$

7.4.2 Computing Equilibrium Trajectories

The law of motion for aggregate capital is

$$\tilde{K}_{t+1} = \tilde{Y}_t - \tilde{C}_t - \tilde{N}_t + (1-\delta)\tilde{K}_t, \tag{7.40}$$

where $\tilde{N}_t = \sum_{i=1}^{M} \tilde{N}_{i,t}$. If we divide through (7.40) by $M\tilde{A}_{t-1}$, we get

$$\frac{\tilde{K}_{t+1}}{M\tilde{A}_t} \frac{M\tilde{A}_t}{M\tilde{A}_{t-1}} = \frac{\tilde{Y}_t}{M\tilde{A}_{t-1}} - \frac{\tilde{C}_t}{M\tilde{A}_{t-1}} - \frac{\tilde{N}_t}{M\tilde{A}_{t-1}} + (1-\delta)\frac{\tilde{K}_t}{M\tilde{A}_{t-1}}. \tag{7.41}$$

Taking into account (7.36), (7.37) we have

$$\frac{\tilde{Y}_t}{M\tilde{A}_{t-1}} = \frac{\theta_t L^{1-\alpha} x_t^\alpha \tilde{A}_t M}{M\tilde{A}_{t-1}} = \theta_t L^{1-\alpha} k_t^\alpha \left(1 + \lambda \gamma n_t^b\right)^{1-\alpha},$$

$$\frac{\tilde{N}_t}{M\tilde{A}_{t-1}} = \frac{\sum_{i=1}^{M} \tilde{N}_{i,t}}{\sum_{i=1}^{M} \tilde{A}_{i,t-1}} = \frac{\sum_{i=1}^{M} n_t(1+\gamma)\tilde{A}_{i,t-1}}{\sum_{i=1}^{M} \tilde{A}_{i,t-1}} \tag{7.42}$$
$$= (1+\gamma)n_t,$$

that allow us to write (7.41) as

$$k_{t+1}\left(1 + \lambda \gamma n_t^b\right) = \theta_t L^{1-\alpha} k_t^\alpha \left(1 + \lambda \gamma n_t^b\right)^{1-\alpha} - c_t - (1+\gamma)n_t + (1-\delta)k_t.$$

From the standard optimization problem for the typical consumer, under a CRRA utility function with parameter σ, we get the familiar Euler condition

$$\tilde{C}_t^{-\sigma} = \beta E_t \left[\tilde{C}_{t+1}^{-\sigma}(1+r_{t+1})\right]. \tag{7.43}$$

If we write (7.43) in efficiency units and use the equilibrium condition in the market for physical capital (7.39) we get

$$c_t^{-\sigma}\left(1 + \lambda \gamma n_t^b\right)^\sigma = \beta E_t \left[c_{t+1}^{-\sigma}\left(\alpha^2 \theta_{t+1} L^{1-\alpha} k_{t+1}^{\alpha-1}\left(1 + \lambda \gamma n_{t+1}^b\right)^{1-\alpha} + 1 - \delta\right)\right]. \tag{7.44}$$

Hence, we have the following dynamic, stochastic system summarizing the model:

$$n_t = \left[b\lambda(1-\alpha)\alpha\theta_t L^{1-\alpha} \left(\frac{k_t}{1+\lambda\gamma n_t^b} \right)^{\alpha} \right]^{1/(1-b)}, \quad (7.45)$$

$$k_{t+1}\left(1+\lambda\gamma n_t^b\right) = \theta_t L^{1-\alpha} k_t^\alpha \left(1+\lambda\gamma n_t^b\right)^{1-\alpha} - c_t$$
$$- (1+\gamma)n_t + (1-\delta)k_t, \quad (7.46)$$

$$c_t^{-\sigma}\left(1+\lambda\gamma n_t^b\right)^\sigma = \beta E_t \left[c_{t+1}^{-\sigma}\left(\alpha^2\theta_{t+1}L^{1-\alpha}k_{t+1}^{\alpha-1}\right.\right.$$
$$\left.\left. \times \left(1+\lambda\gamma n_{t+1}^b\right)^{1-\alpha} + 1 - \delta\right)\right], \quad (7.47)$$

together with

$$\ln\theta_t = \phi\ln\theta_{t-1} + \varepsilon_t, \quad (7.48)$$

given parameter values $\{\alpha, L, \lambda, \gamma, \delta, \sigma, b\}$, and initial conditions $\{\theta_0, \tilde{K}_0, \tilde{A}_{-1}\}$.

Let us know see how can we solve this system following the Blanchard–Kahn approach: First, steady state values k, c, n, can be obtained from evaluating (7.45)–(7.47) at steady-state[18]

$$n = \left[b\lambda(1-\alpha)\alpha L^{1-\alpha} \left(\frac{k}{1+\lambda\gamma n^b} \right)^{\alpha} \right]^{1/(1-b)},$$

$$k\left(1+\lambda\gamma n^b\right) = L^{1-\alpha}k^\alpha\left(1+\lambda\gamma n^b\right)^{1-\alpha} - c - (1+\gamma)n + (1-\delta)k,$$

$$\left(1+\lambda\gamma n_t^b\right)^\sigma = \beta\left(\alpha^2 L^{1-\alpha}k^{\alpha-1}\left(1+\lambda\gamma n^b\right)^{1-\alpha} + 1 - \delta\right).$$

Let us now denote system (7.45)–(7.47) by

$$E_t\left[F_i(z_{t+1})\right] = 0, \quad i = 1, 2, 3,$$

where[19] $z_{t+1} = [\ln k_{t+1}, \ln c_{t+1}, \ln n_{t+1}, \ln\theta_{t+1}, \ln k_t, \ln c_t, \ln n_t, \ln\theta_t]'$ and

$$E_t\left[F_1(z_{t+1})\right] = n_t - \left[b\lambda(1-\alpha)\alpha\theta_t L^{1-\alpha}\left(\frac{k_t}{1+\lambda\gamma n_t^b}\right)^{\alpha}\right]^{1/(1-b)} = 0,$$

$$E_t\left[F_2(z_{t+1})\right] = \theta_t L^{1-\alpha}k_t^\alpha\left(1+\lambda\gamma n_t^b\right)^{1-\alpha} - c_t - (1+\gamma)n_t$$
$$+ (1-\delta)k_t - k_{t+1}\left(1+\lambda\gamma n_t^b\right) = 0,$$

---

[18] Using the steady state version of (7.42), we see that any value of λ such that: $\lambda(Mn)^b < 1$ in the definition of the probability of research success is admissible.

[19] Remember that any variable x can be represented by $e^{\ln x}$.

$$E_t\left[F_2\left(z_{t+1}\right)\right] = \beta E_t\left[c_{t+1}^{-\sigma}\left(\alpha^2\theta_{t+1}L^{1-\alpha}k_{t+1}^{\alpha-1}\left(1+\lambda\gamma n_{t+1}^b\right)^{1-\alpha}+1-\delta\right)\right]$$
$$-c_t^{-\sigma}\left(1+\lambda\gamma n_t^b\right)^{\sigma} = 0.$$

Let $J_{i,j} = \frac{\partial F_i}{\partial z_j}\big|_z$, $i = 1,2,3$; $j = 1,2,\ldots,8$. Sea $\hat{k}_t \equiv \ln(k_t/k)$, $\hat{c}_t \equiv \ln(c_t/c)$, $\hat{n}_t \equiv$ $\ln(n_t/n)$, $\hat{\theta}_t \equiv \ln(\theta_t)$, where k,c,n denote steady-state values of k_t, c_t, n_t.

The log-linear approximation to (7.45) will allow us to obtain the control variable $\hat{n}_t$ as a function of the states $\hat{k}_t$ and $\hat{\theta}_t$

$$\hat{n}_t = -\frac{J_{1,5}}{J_{1,7}}\hat{k}_t - \frac{J_{1,8}}{J_{1,7}}\hat{\theta}_t. \tag{7.49}$$

From (7.49), we get

$$E_t\hat{n}_{t+1} = -\frac{J_{1,5}}{J_{1,7}}\hat{k}_{t+1} - \frac{J_{1,8}}{J_{1,7}}\phi\hat{\theta}_t. \tag{7.50}$$

since $\hat{k}_{t+1}$ is determined at time t, so that $E_t\hat{k}_{t+1} = \hat{k}_{t+1}$.

Taking into account (7.49) and (7.50), the system that arises by log-linearizing (7.46) and (7.47) is

$$\Gamma_0\begin{bmatrix}\hat{k}_{t+1}\\E_t\hat{c}_{t+1}\end{bmatrix} = \Gamma_1\begin{bmatrix}\hat{k}_t\\\hat{c}_t\end{bmatrix} + \Gamma_2\hat{\theta}_t, \tag{7.51}$$

where

$$\Gamma_0 = \begin{bmatrix}J_{2,1} & 0\\J_{3,1}+J_{3,3}\frac{J_{1,5}}{J_{1,7}} & J_{3,2}\end{bmatrix},$$

$$\Gamma_1 = -\begin{bmatrix}J_{2,5}+J_{2,7}\frac{J_{1,5}}{J_{1,7}} & J_{2,6}\\J_{3,7}\frac{J_{1,5}}{J_{1,7}} & J_{3,6}\end{bmatrix},$$

$$\Gamma_2 = -\begin{bmatrix}J_{2,8}+J_{2,7}\frac{J_{1,8}}{J_{1,7}}\\J_{3,4}\phi+(J_{3,3}\phi+J_{3,7})\frac{J_{1,8}}{J_{1,7}}\end{bmatrix}.$$

that leads to the system

$$\begin{bmatrix}\hat{k}_{t+1}\\E_t\hat{c}_{t+1}\end{bmatrix} = \Gamma_3\begin{bmatrix}\hat{k}_t\\\hat{c}_t\end{bmatrix} + \Gamma_4\hat{\theta}_t, \tag{7.52}$$

with $\Gamma_3 = \Gamma_0^{-1}\Gamma_1$, $\Gamma_4 = \Gamma_0^{-1}\Gamma_2$.

We expect matrix Γ_3 to have one stable and one unstable eigenvalue, so that a well-determined equilibrium may exist.[20] Without loss of generality, let us assume: $|\lambda_1| < 1$, $|\lambda_2| > 1$. We would then have the spectral decomposition

---

[20] When, as in this model, an analytical proof does not exist, this supposed eigenvalue structure needs to be explored numerically, and may hold only in some region of the parameter space.

$$\Gamma_3 = \Upsilon \Lambda \Upsilon^{-1}, \quad \Lambda = \begin{pmatrix} \lambda_1 & 0 \\ 0 & \lambda_2 \end{pmatrix}, \quad \Upsilon^{-1} = \begin{pmatrix} \tilde{\Upsilon}_{11} & \tilde{\Upsilon}_{12} \\ \tilde{\Upsilon}_{21} & \tilde{\Upsilon}_{22} \end{pmatrix}.$$

Premultiplying (7.52) by Υ^{-1} and denoting by Q the product: $Q = \Upsilon^{-1}\Gamma_4 = \begin{pmatrix} Q_1 \\ Q_2 \end{pmatrix}$, we have

$$\tilde{\Upsilon}_{11}\hat{k}_{t+1} + \tilde{\Upsilon}_{12}E_t\hat{c}_{t+1} = \lambda_1\left(\tilde{\Upsilon}_{11}\hat{k}_t + \tilde{\Upsilon}_{12}\hat{c}_t\right) + Q_1\hat{\theta}_t, \tag{7.53}$$

$$\tilde{\Upsilon}_{21}\hat{k}_{t+1} + \tilde{\Upsilon}_{22}E_t\hat{c}_{t+1} = \lambda_2\left(\tilde{\Upsilon}_{21}\hat{k}_t + \tilde{\Upsilon}_{22}\hat{c}_t\right) + Q_2\hat{\theta}_t. \tag{7.54}$$

Defining now auxiliary variables: $f^0_{2,t} = \tilde{\Upsilon}_{21}\hat{k}_t + \tilde{\Upsilon}_{22}\hat{c}_t$, we have $E_t f^0_{2,t+1} = \tilde{\Upsilon}_{21}\hat{k}_{t+1} + \tilde{\Upsilon}_{22}E_t\hat{c}_{t+1}$, and the second equation becomes a first order autoregression with an unstable coefficient: $E_t f^0_{2,t+1} = \lambda_2 f^0_{2,t} + Q_2\hat{\theta}_t$, which can be solved forwards, to obtain

$$f^0_{2,t} = \frac{Q_2}{\phi - \lambda_2}\hat{\theta}_t,$$

and finally

$$\hat{c}_t = \frac{1}{\tilde{\Upsilon}_{22}}\left(\frac{Q_2}{\phi - \lambda_2}\hat{\theta}_t - \tilde{\Upsilon}_{21}\hat{k}_t\right), \tag{7.55}$$

which is the *stability or control equation.*

Substituting (7.55) into (7.53) we get

$$\hat{k}_{t+1} = \lambda_1\hat{k}_t + \frac{1}{\tilde{\Upsilon}_{11} - \frac{\tilde{\Upsilon}_{12}\tilde{\Upsilon}_{21}}{\tilde{\Upsilon}_{22}}}\left[Q_1 + \frac{Q_2\tilde{\Upsilon}_{12}/\tilde{\Upsilon}_{22}}{\rho - \lambda_2}(1 - \phi)\right]\hat{\theta}_t, \tag{7.56}$$

which is the *state equation.*

Hence, given initial conditions $\left\{\tilde{K}_0, \theta_0, \tilde{A}_{-1}\right\}$, we can compute $k_0 = \tilde{K}_0/(M\tilde{A}_{-1})$ and $\hat{k}_0 = \ln(k_0/k)$. Given a time series realization for the structural innovation $\{\varepsilon_t\}_{t=1}^T$, we use the law of motion for θ_t to compute the $\{\theta_t\}_{t=1}^T$ time series. We can then compute the time series for $\{\hat{k}_t\}_{t=1}^T$ using the state equation (7.56). Given time series $\{\hat{k}_t, \hat{\theta}_t\}_{t=0}^T$, and using (7.49) and (7.55) we can compute $\{\hat{n}_t, \hat{c}_t\}_{t=0}^T$. Obtaining now time series for $\{k_t, \theta_t, n_t, c_t\}_{t=0}^T$ is straightforward. We can also compute $\{y_t\}_{t=0}^T$ from $y_t = \theta_t L^{1-\alpha} k_t^\alpha \left(1 + \lambda\gamma n_t^b\right)^{1-\alpha}$.

Given $\{\hat{n}_t\}_{t=0}^T$ and $\tilde{A}_{-1}$, we can compute $\{\tilde{A}_t\}_{t=0}^T$ from (7.36). Given $\{\tilde{A}_t\}_{t=0}^T$, we can compute $\left\{\tilde{K}_{t+1}, \tilde{C}_t, \tilde{N}_t, \tilde{Y}_t\right\}_{t=0}^T$ from the $\{k_{t+1}, c_t, n_t, y_t\}_{t=0}^T$ time series.

Programming this recursive solution either as a Matlab program or in an Excel book is left as an exercise.

7.4.3 Deterministic Steady-State

In this section, we characterize the deterministic steady-state for this economy, and show that it takes the form of a balanced growth path. The deterministic steady state is a trajectory along which: (1) $\theta_t = 1$, $\forall t$, (2) variables $\tilde{A}_t, \tilde{Y}_t, \tilde{C}_t, \tilde{K}_t, \tilde{N}_t$ grow at a constant rate $(\gamma_{\tilde{A}}, \gamma_{\tilde{Y}}, \gamma_{\tilde{C}}, \gamma_{\tilde{K}}, \gamma_{\tilde{N}})$, and (3) $x_t = x$ remains constant $\forall t$.

If we substitute the equilibrium value of $x_{i,t}$ ($x_{i,t} = x_t = \tilde{K}_t/(M\tilde{A}_t)$) in the aggregate production function at steady-state, we get the usual specification with labour-augmented technological growth already discussed in Chap. 3

$$\tilde{Y}_t = M^{1-\alpha}\left(\tilde{A}_t L\right)^{1-\alpha} \tilde{K}_t^{\alpha}.$$

From (7.43) we obtain in steady-state[21]

$$(1+\gamma_{\tilde{C}})^{\sigma} = \beta(1+r_{t+1}),$$

showing that interest rate will also be constant in steady-state: $r_t = r$, $\forall t$.

In steady-state, the rate of growth of productivity will be

$$\gamma_{\tilde{A}} = \lambda \gamma n_t^b.$$

Since $\gamma_{\tilde{A}}$, λ and γ are constant in steady-state, then n_t will also be constant: $n_t = n$, $\forall t$, and $\tilde{N}_t$ must grow at the same rate than $\tilde{A}_t$. Since the rate of interest, r, and the research effort adjusted for the level of technology, n, are constant in steady-state, we get from (7.39) that k_t will also be constant in steady-state. This implies that the stock of physical capital $\tilde{K}_t$ also grows at the same rate than productivity.

Since in steady-state: $\gamma_{\tilde{A}} = \gamma_{\tilde{K}}$, from the production function, written in steady-state, we get in steady-state

$$1+\gamma_{\tilde{Y}} = (1+\gamma_{\tilde{A}})^{1-\alpha}(1+\gamma_{\tilde{K}})^{\alpha} = 1+\gamma_{\tilde{A}} = 1+\lambda \gamma n^b,$$

so that output of the final good also grows at the same rate than productivity. From the global constraint of resources we get the same result for aggregate consumption. Hence, the steady-state takes the form of a balanced growth path. The steady-state level of the interest rate is

$$r = \frac{\left(1+\lambda \gamma n^b\right)^{\sigma}}{\beta}.$$

Outside steady-state, the different variables in the economy will grow at their own rates, converging all of them to the same steady-state rate, that we have characterized above.

7.5 Endogenous Growth with Accumulation of Human Capital

We now present a model economy with two sectors, for human capital and the consumption commodity, that presents a nontrivial transition. It is a generalization of Uzawa [95] and Lucas [60], including leisure as an argument in the utility function,

---

[21] Since we assume a constant number of consumers, we can equivalently use per-capita or aggregate consumption.

and physical capital as an input in the production of new human capital. At a difference of Lucas [60], we do not consider aggregate human capital[22] as a positive externality in the production of the single final good in the economy. That would give raise to a nontrivial discussion on optimality which does not apply to our model, in which the competitive equilibrium allocation is Pareto optimum.

7.5.1 The Economy

7.5.1.1 The Final Good Sector

The first sector produces the final good, which is perishable and can either be consumed, or accumulated in the form of physical capital. The second sector produces human capital, for which we do not consider an explicit market. When we introduce distortionary taxes in the model as we did in the Cass–Koopmans economy, we will only tax the income obtained by private agents from devoting part of their time to the production of the final consumption good as well as for renting some of the physical capital they own in that same production sector. Since the human capital market lacks an explicit market, income obtained from devoting time and physical capital to the production of human capital will not be subject to taxes.

The economy is populated by a set of households who live for infinite periods. The number of households in each generation is $\tilde{N}_t$, growing at a rate n. Each household has a unit of time available. We denote by u_t the fraction of time that is devoted to the production of the final consumption good, while l_t denotes the fraction devoted to leisure, the remaining time, $1 - u_t - l_t$, being devoted to education, i.e., to human capital accumulation.

There is also a set of firms that behave competitively. The technology used in the production of the single physical commodity in the economy, that we will denote by Y_t, is represented by a production function $F(\tilde{K}_{1t}, \tilde{H}_{1t})$, where $\tilde{K}_{1t}$ denotes the stock of physical capital used in this sector, and $\tilde{H}_{1t}$ denotes the hours of qualified labor used in production. We will assume that the production technology is of Cobb–Douglas type:

$$Y_t = F(\tilde{K}_{1t}, \tilde{H}_{1t}) = \theta_t A (v_t \tilde{K}_t)^{\alpha_1} (u_t \tilde{H}_t)^{\alpha_2}, \qquad (7.57)$$

where v_t is the percentage of total physical capital, $\tilde{K}_t$, devoted to the production of the final good, u_t is the fraction of time that the consumer/worker devotes to working in this sector, $\tilde{H}_t$ is the aggregate stock of human capital, A is the level of technology, and θ_t is a random perturbation in technology that obeys the stochastic process:

$$\ln \theta_t = \phi_1 \ln \theta_{t-1} + \varepsilon_{1t}, \quad \varepsilon_{1t} \underset{iid}{\sim} N(0, \sigma_1^2), \quad |\phi_1| < 1. \qquad (7.58)$$

---

[22] That is, the socially available stock of human capital.

7.5.1.2 The Educational Sector

The educational sector produces new human capital using a technology represented by the production function[23] $G(\tilde{k}_{2t}, \tilde{h}_{2t})$, where $\tilde{k}_{2t}$ is the stock of effective physical capital used in this sector, and $\tilde{h}_{2t}$ is effective labor used in this sector, all in per capita terms. We will assume that the only way to obtain qualified labor is through education.[24] Furthermore, we assume that human capital depreciates at a constant rate $\delta_h \in (0,1)$. Hence, unless new human capital is produced, the level of education deteriorates. The level of education each period is determined by the accumulation law

$$\tilde{h}_{t+1} = G(\tilde{k}_{2t}, \tilde{h}_{2t}) + (1 - \delta_h)\tilde{h}_t = \eta_t B \left[(1 - v_t)\tilde{k}_t \right]^{\varsigma_1} \tag{7.59}$$
$$\times \left[(1 - u_t - l_t)\tilde{h}_t \right]^{\varsigma_2} + (1 - \delta_h)\tilde{h}_t$$

where B is the level of technology in this sector, $\tilde{h}_t$ is the stock of human capital per worker, $1 - v_t$ is the fraction of physical capital used in the production of human capital, $1 - u_t - l_t$ is the fraction of time devoted to the educational sector. η_t is a random technology shock in this sector, that evolves over time according to

$$\ln \eta_t = \phi_2 \ln \eta_{t-1} + \varepsilon_{2t}, \quad \varepsilon_{2t} \underset{iid}{\sim} N(0, \sigma_2^2), \quad |\phi_2| < 1. \tag{7.60}$$

We denote economy-wide aggregates with upper case letters, while we denote by lower case letters the same variables, divided by population. So, $X_t = \tilde{x}_t L_t$, $X = \tilde{C}, \tilde{K}, \tilde{H}, \tilde{Y}$. Besides, we maintain the convention from previous sections to denote with tildes, $\tilde{c}_t, \tilde{k}_t, \tilde{h}_t, \tilde{y}_t$, per-capita variables that grow in steady-state while denoting without tildes, c_t, k_t, h_t, y_t, the variables obtained after taking out from the former their growth trends. We will not use this convention with Lagrange multipliers.

Notice that in this model we could also define output in a broad sense, denoted by $\tilde{Q}_t$, by adding to final output the production of new human capital, evaluated in units of the final good:

$$\tilde{Q}_t = \tilde{Y}_t + (\tilde{\mu}_t / \tilde{\lambda}_t) G\left((1 - v_t)\tilde{k}_t, (1 - u_t - l_t)\tilde{h}_t \right) L_t,$$

where $\tilde{\mu}_t / \tilde{\lambda}_t$ is the shadow price of human capital in terms of the final good. The size of the public sector might then be defined more appropriately as the ratio between government expenditures and this broader output concept.

We describe in the next section the more general version of this model economy, that includes leisure in the utility function, physical capital in the educational sector, taxes on consumption as well as on labor and capital income, in a stochastic setup, and we show the necessary conditions for endogenous growth to arise. After that, we describe how to obtain a numerical solution to a simpler version of the model, that excludes taxes, leisure and physical capital as an input in the production

---

[23] Without loss of generality, we will assume a production function in per capita terms.

[24] We do not consider the experience in the job position as a way to obtain qualified work.

of new human capital. We leave as an exercise the computation of the numerical solution in a more complex setup, which is a straightforward extension of the solution procedure we present. That way, the reader will be able to address fiscal policy issues similar to those we examined in the chapter devoted to the Cass–Koopmans economy.

7.5.1.3 The Household Problem

Each individual in this economy derives utility from consuming $\tilde{c}_t$ $(\equiv \frac{\tilde{C}_t}{L_t})$ units of the produced commodity, as well as from leisure l_t. Total time available is normalized to one unit. Consumer preferences are represented by a continuous utility function $U(\tilde{c}_t, l_t)$, with continuous partial derivatives. Interpreting both arguments in the utility function as an homogeneous composite good, we assume a constant intertemporal elasticity of substitution $1/\sigma$

$$U(\tilde{c}_t, l_t) = \frac{\left(\tilde{c}_t^p, l_t^{1-p}\right)^{1-\sigma} - 1}{1 - \sigma}, \quad \sigma > 0, \quad p \in (0,1).$$

The representative consumer maximizes the discounted expected value of current and future utility

$$\max_{\left\{\tilde{c}_t, \tilde{i}_t, u_t, v_t, l_t, \tilde{k}_{t+1}, \tilde{h}_{t+1}\right\}} E_0 \sum_{t=0}^{\infty} \beta^t \frac{\left(\tilde{c}_t^p, l_t^{1-p}\right)^{1-\sigma} - 1}{1 - \sigma}, \tag{7.61}$$

subject to a sequence of budget constraints,[25] together with the laws of motion of physical and human capital:

$$(1 + \tau^c)\tilde{c}_t + \tilde{i}_t = (1 - \tau^r)r_t v_t \tilde{k}_t + \tau^r \delta_k v_t \tilde{k}_t + (1 - \tau^w)w_t u_t \tilde{h}_t, \tag{7.62}$$

$$t = 0, 1, 2, \ldots,$$

$$(1 + n)\tilde{k}_{t+1} = \tilde{i}_t + (1 - \delta_k)\tilde{k}_t, \quad t = 0, 1, 2, \ldots, \tag{7.63}$$

$$\tilde{h}_{t+1} = G\left((1 - v_t)\tilde{k}_t, (1 - u_t - l_t)\tilde{h}_t\right) + (1 - \delta_h)\tilde{h}_t, \tag{7.64}$$

$$t = 0, 1, 2, \ldots, \quad \tilde{k}_0, \tilde{h}_0, \text{ given,}$$

$$\tilde{c}_t, \tilde{k}_{t+1}, \tilde{h}_{t+1} \geq 0, \quad u_t, v_t, l_t \in (0,1), \quad u_t + l_t \in (0,1),$$

together with (7.58) and (7.60)

where $\tilde{i}_t$ denotes investment in physical capital, r_t is the return obtained from lending part of the physical capital for the production of the consumption good, w_t denotes the payment for working on that sector, τ^c, τ^r, and τ^w denote the tax rates on

---

[25] We assume that the consumer pays taxes on capital and labour rents obtained from the sector producing the final consumption good.

consumption, capital income and labor income. The presence of the $\tau^r \delta_k v_t \tilde{k}_t$ term in the budget constraint is due to depreciation allowances.

The Lagrangian for this optimization problem is

$$
\mathcal{L}(\tilde{c}_t, u_t, v_t, l_t, \tilde{k}_{t+1}, \tilde{h}_{t+1}, \lambda_t, \mu_t)
$$

$$
= E_0 \left[\sum_{t=0}^{\infty} \beta^t \frac{\left(\tilde{c}_t^p, l_t^{1-p}\right)^{1-\sigma} - 1}{1-\sigma} + \beta^t \lambda_t \left(-(1+\tau^c)\tilde{c}_t - (1+n)\tilde{k}_{t+1} \right. \right.
$$

$$
+ (1-\delta_k)\tilde{k}_t + (1-\tau^r)r_t v_t \tilde{k}_t + \tau^r \delta_k v_t \tilde{k}_t + (1-\tau^w)w_t u_t \tilde{h}_t \Big)
$$

$$
\left. + \beta^t \mu_t \left(-\tilde{h}_{t+1} + G\left((1-v_t)\tilde{k}_t, (1-u_t - l_t)\tilde{h}_t\right) + (1-\delta_h)\tilde{h}_t\right) \right],
$$

with first order conditions

$$
p\tilde{c}_t^{p(1-\sigma)-1} l_t^{(1-p)(1-\sigma)} = (1+\tau^c)\lambda_t, \tag{7.65}
$$

$$
(1-p)\tilde{c}_t^{p(1-\sigma)} l_t^{(1-p)(1-\sigma)-1} = \mu_t \eta_t B\varsigma_2 \left((1-v_t)\tilde{k}_t\right)^{\varsigma_1} \tag{7.66}
$$
$$
\times (1-u_t-l_t)^{\varsigma_2-1}\tilde{h}_t^{\varsigma_2},
$$

$$
(1-\tau^w)w_t\lambda_t = \mu_t \eta_t B\varsigma_2 \left((1-v_t)\tilde{k}_t\right)^{\varsigma_1} \left((1-u_t-l_t)\tilde{h}_t\right)^{\varsigma_2-1}, \tag{7.67}
$$

$$
[(1-\tau^r)r_t + \tau^r \delta_k]\lambda_t = \mu_t \eta_t B\varsigma_1 \left((1-v_t)\tilde{k}_t\right)^{\varsigma-1} \tag{7.68}
$$
$$
\times \left((1-u_t-l_t)\tilde{h}_t\right)^{\varsigma},
$$

$$
\lambda_t(1+n) = \beta E_t \left[\lambda_{t+1}\left((1-\tau^r)r_{t+1}v_{t+1} + \tau^r \delta_k v_{t+1} + 1 - \delta_k\right) \right. \tag{7.69}
$$
$$
+ \mu_{t+1}(1-v_{t+1})\eta_{t+1}B\varsigma_1 \left((1-v_{t+1})\tilde{k}_{t+1}\right)^{\varsigma_1-1}
$$
$$
\left. \times \left((1-u_{t+1}-l_{t+1})\tilde{h}_{t+1}\right)^{\varsigma_2}\right],
$$

$$
\mu_t = \beta E_t \left\{\lambda_{t+1}(1-\tau^w)w_{t+1}u_{t+1} + \mu_{t+1}\left[\eta_{t+1}B\varsigma_2\left((1-v_{t+1})\tilde{k}_{t+1}\right)^{\varsigma_1} \right.\right. \tag{7.70}
$$
$$
\left.\left. \times (1-u_{t+1}-l_{t+1})^{\varsigma_2-1}\tilde{h}_{t+1}^{\varsigma_2} + 1 - \delta_h\right]\right\},
$$

$$
\lim_{j\to\infty} E_t \left(\beta^t \lambda_{t+j}\tilde{k}_{t+j+1}\right) = 0, \tag{7.71}
$$

$$
\lim_{j\to\infty} E_t \left(\beta^t \mu_{t+j}\tilde{h}_{t+j+1}\right) = 0. \tag{7.72}
$$

7.5.1.4 The Firm's Problem

The representative firm working in the production of the final good maximizes profits each period

$$\max_{\{\tilde{K}_{1t},\tilde{H}_{1t}\}} F(\tilde{K}_{1t},\tilde{H}_{1t}) - w_t\tilde{H}_{1t} - r_t\tilde{K}_{1t}$$

subject to

$$F(\tilde{K}_{1t},\tilde{H}_{1t}) = \theta_t A \tilde{K}_{1t}^{\alpha_1} \tilde{H}_{1t}^{\alpha_2},$$

where $\tilde{K}_{1t} = v_t\tilde{K}_t$, $\tilde{H}_{1t} = u_t\tilde{H}_t$. First order conditions are

$$w_t = \alpha_2\theta_t A(v_t\tilde{K}_t)^{\alpha_1}(u_t\tilde{H}_t)^{\alpha_2-1}, \tag{7.73}$$
$$r_t = \alpha_1\theta_t A(v_t\tilde{K}_t)^{\alpha_1-1}(u_t\tilde{H}_t)^{\alpha_2}. \tag{7.74}$$

7.5.1.5 The Government's Problem

The government raises taxes on consumption, capital rents and labor rents obtained by households in the sector producing the final good, and uses the proceeds to finance an exogenously given process of government expenditures, G_t. These are 'thrown to the sea', i.e., they do not affect the level of utility or the technologies producing either the final good or human capital. Tax rates are chosen so as to balance the budget every period

$$\tilde{g}_t = \tau^w w_t u_t\tilde{h}_t + \tau^r r_t v_t\tilde{k}_t - \tau^r \delta_k v_t\tilde{k}_t + \tau^c \tilde{c}_t. \tag{7.75}$$

We denote the ratio of government expenditures to output, an indicator of the size of the public sector, as[26]

$$\xi_t = \tilde{g}_t/\tilde{y}_t, \quad \xi_t \in (0,1). \tag{7.76}$$

7.5.2 The Competitive Equilibrium

Given tax rates: $\{\tau^c,\tau^r,\tau^w\}$, the competitive equilibrium is a vector sequence $\{\tilde{c}_t,u_t,v_t,l_t,\tilde{k}_{t+1},\tilde{h}_{t+1},r_t,w_t,\tilde{g}_t\}_{t=0}^\infty$, satisfying the profit maximizing conditions (7.74), (7.73), the optimization conditions for the consumer's problem (7.65)–(7.72), the household's budget constraints (7.62)–(7.63), the law of accumulation of human capital (7.64), the government budget constraint (7.75)–(7.76) and the market clearing conditions

---

[26] Alternatively, we could consider a random ratio of government expenditures to output $\xi_t = \xi + \varepsilon_{3t}$, $\varepsilon_{3t} \sim N(0,\sigma_3^2)$, with σ_3^2 small enough so that ξ_t would fluctuate inside the (0,1) interval with probability one. That would introduce an additional source of randomness that could be interpreted as a possible error in controlling the level of government expenditures. We would then need at least a time varying tax rate so that the government budget constraint balances every period.

$$\tilde{C}_t + \tilde{K}_{t+1} - (1 - \delta_k)\tilde{K}_t + G_t = \theta_t A \tilde{K}_{1t}^{\alpha_1} \tilde{H}_{1t}^{\alpha_2} \tag{7.77}$$

that guarantees that the global constraint of resources in the economy also holds.

Thus, the conditions characterizing the competitive equilibrium can be summarized as follows. We first eliminate prices $(r_t, w_t, \lambda_t, \mu_t)$ from (7.67), (7.68), (7.74) and (7.73) to obtain

$$\frac{(1 - \tau^w)\alpha_2 \theta_t A \left(v_t \tilde{k}_t\right)^{\alpha_1} \left(u_t \tilde{h}_t\right)^{\alpha_2 - 1} L_t^{\alpha_1 + \alpha_2 - 1}}{(1 - \tau^r)\alpha_1 \theta_t A \left(v_t \tilde{k}_t\right)^{\alpha_1 - 1} \left(u_t \tilde{h}_t\right)^{\alpha_2} L_t^{\alpha_1 + \alpha_2 - 1} + \tau^r \delta_k} = \frac{\varsigma_2}{\varsigma_1} \frac{(1 - v_t)\tilde{k}_t}{(1 - u_t - l_t)\tilde{h}_t}, \tag{7.78}$$

showing that the marginal rate of transformation between labor and capital in the final good sector, net of taxes, must be equal in equilibrium, to that in the educational sector.

From (7.65), (7.66) and (7.73) we get

$$\frac{\left(\frac{p}{1-p}\right) l_t}{\tilde{c}_t(1 + \tau^c)} = \frac{1}{(1 - \tau^w)\alpha_2 \theta_t A \left(v_t \tilde{k}_t\right)^{\alpha_1} \left(u_t \tilde{h}_t\right)^{\alpha_2 - 1} \tilde{h}_t L_t^{\alpha_1 + \alpha_2 - 1}}, \tag{7.79}$$

showing that the marginal rate of substitution between consumption and leisure must be equal to the marginal product of labor, all net of taxes.

From (7.65), (7.69), (7.68) and (7.74), we get

$$\tilde{c}_t^{p(1-\sigma)-1} l_t^{(1-p)(1-\sigma)} = \beta E_t \left\{ \tilde{c}_{t+1}^{p(1-\sigma)-1} l_{t+1}^{(1-p)(1-\sigma)} \right. \tag{7.80}$$
$$\times \left[(1 - \tau^r)\alpha_1 \theta_{t+1} A \left(v_{t+1} \tilde{k}_{t+1}\right)^{\alpha_1 - 1} \right.$$
$$\times \left. \left(u_{t+1} \tilde{h}_{t+1}\right)^{\alpha_2} L_{t+1}^{\alpha_1 + \alpha_2 - 1} + 1 - (1 - \tau^r)\delta_k \right] \right\},$$

showing that the marginal utility of giving up one unit of consumption today must be equal to the expected marginal utility of future consumption multiplied by the return obtained from investing that unit of commodity for one period which is, in turn, equal to the marginal product of physical capital, net of depreciation and taxes.

From (7.65), (7.70), (7.67) and (7.73), we obtain

$$\tilde{c}_t^{p(1-\sigma)-1} l_t^{(1-p)(1-\sigma)} \frac{\theta_t \left(v_t \tilde{k}_t\right)^{\alpha_1} \left(u_t \tilde{h}_t\right)^{\alpha_2 - 1} L_t^{\alpha_1 + \alpha_2 - 1}}{\eta_t \left((1 - v_t)\tilde{k}_t\right)^{\varsigma_1} (1 - u_t - l_t)^{\varsigma_2 - 1} \tilde{h}_t^{\varsigma_2 - 1}}$$
$$= \beta E_t \left\{ \tilde{c}_{t+1}^{p(1-\sigma)-1} l_{t+1}^{(1-p)(1-\sigma)} \right.$$
$$\times \frac{\theta_{t+1} \left(v_{t+1} \tilde{k}_{t+1}\right)^{\alpha_1} \left(u_{t+1} \tilde{h}_{t+1}\right)^{\alpha_2 - 1} L_{t+1}^{\alpha_1 + \alpha_2 - 1}}{\eta_{t+1} \left((1 - v_{t+1})\tilde{k}_{t+1}\right)^{\varsigma_1} (1 - u_{t+1} - l_{t+1})^{\varsigma_2 - 1} \tilde{h}_{t+1}^{\varsigma_2 - 1}}$$
$$\times \left[B v_2 \eta_{t+1} \left((1 - v_{t+1})\tilde{k}_{t+1}\right)^{\varsigma_1} (1 - u_{t+1} - l_{t+1})^{\varsigma_2 - 1} \right.$$
$$\times \left. \tilde{h}_{t+1}^{\varsigma_2 - 1} (1 - l_{t+1}) + 1 - \delta_h \right] \right\}, \tag{7.81}$$

which is an Euler condition similar to the previous one, but this time associated to the educational sector.

From (7.77) and (7.76)

$$\tilde{c}_t + (1+n)\tilde{k}_{t+1} - (1-\delta_k)\tilde{k}_t = (1-\xi)A\theta_t(v_t\tilde{k}_t)^{\alpha_1}(u_t\tilde{h}_t)^{\alpha_2}L_t^{\alpha_1+\alpha_2-1}, \qquad (7.82)$$

which is the global constraint of resources in the economy.

Finally, from (7.64) we get

$$\tilde{h}_{t+1} = B\eta_t\left((1-v_t)\tilde{k}_t\right)^{\varsigma_1}(1-u_t-l_t)^{\varsigma_2-1}\tilde{h}_t^{\varsigma_2-1} + (1-\delta_h)\tilde{h}_t, \qquad (7.83)$$

the law of accumulation for human capital.

7.5.3 Analyzing the Deterministic Steady-State

In consistency with previous models, we define a deterministic steady-state in this economy as that situation in which the random shocks take their expected values at all time periods: $\theta_t = \eta_t = 1, \forall t$, and variables u_t, v_t, l_t remain constant at u, v, l, while $\tilde{c}_t, \tilde{k}_t, \tilde{h}_t, \tilde{y}_t$, all grow at constant rates $\gamma_{\tilde{c}}, \gamma_{\tilde{k}}, \gamma_{\tilde{h}}, \gamma_y$, respectively, and the ratio $\tilde{Y}_t/\tilde{K}_t$ stays constant,[27] which implies that $\gamma_{\tilde{K}} = \gamma_{\tilde{Y}}$.

Proposition 1. *The following are necessary conditions for endogenous growth to arise in the model economy:*

$$\varsigma_1\ln(1+\gamma_{\tilde{k}})+(\varsigma_2-1)\ln(1+\gamma_{\tilde{h}})=0, \qquad (7.84)$$

$$(\alpha_1-1)\ln(1+\gamma_{\tilde{k}})+\alpha_2\ln(1+\gamma_{\tilde{h}})=(1-\alpha_1-\alpha_2)\ln(1+n). \qquad (7.85)$$

Notice that if we solve this system for $\ln(1+\gamma_{\tilde{k}})$ and $\ln(1+\gamma_{\tilde{h}})$, we get

$$\ln(1+\gamma_{\tilde{k}}) = \frac{(1-\varsigma_2)(1-\alpha_1-\alpha_2)}{\varsigma_1\alpha_2-(1-\alpha_1)(1-\varsigma_2)}\ln(1+n),$$

$$\ln(1+\gamma_{\tilde{h}}) = \frac{\varsigma_1(1-\alpha_1-\alpha_2)}{\varsigma_1\alpha_2-(1-\alpha_1)(1-\varsigma_2)}\ln(1+n).$$

If $n \neq 0$, then the rates of growth for physical and human capital are positive whenever $\frac{(1-\varsigma_2)(1-\alpha_1-\alpha_2)}{\varsigma_1\alpha_2-(1-\alpha_1)(1-\varsigma_2)} > 0$ and $\frac{\varsigma_1(1-\alpha_1-\alpha_2)}{\varsigma_1\alpha_2-(1-\alpha_1)(1-\varsigma_2)} > 0$, so that (1) if there are increasing returns in the final good sector $(1 < \alpha_1 + \alpha_2)$ then positive growth arises if $\frac{1-\alpha_1}{\alpha_2} > \frac{\varsigma_1}{1-\varsigma_2}$; (2) if there are decreasing returns to scale in the final good sector $(1 > \alpha_1 + \alpha_2)$ then $\frac{1-\alpha_1}{\alpha_2} < \frac{\varsigma_1}{1-\varsigma_2}$ is needed for positive growth, while (3) in the presence of constant returns to scale $(1 = \alpha_1 + \alpha_2)$, then there is positive growth

---

[27] This latter condition is needed only when we do not assume constant returns to scale in either sector. In fact, that is the only case we will consider when solving the model. Then, the condition does not need to be imposed, since it will hold in equilibrium.

in the cumulative inputs if $\frac{1-\alpha_1}{\alpha_2} = \frac{\varsigma_1}{1-\varsigma_2}$, that is, if $\varsigma_1 + \varsigma_2 = 1$. If $n = 0$, then the rates of growth of physical and human capital can be strictly positive only if $\varsigma_1\alpha_2 > (1-\alpha_1)(1-\varsigma_2)$.

We will consider the latter case, in which there are constant returns to scale in both sectors, as a reference. Then the steady state will take the form of a *balanced growth path*, with per capita variables growing at constant, non-zero rates, except for hours worked, which will remain constant. Furthermore, it is easy to show that $\tilde{c}_t$, $\tilde{k}_t$, $\tilde{h}_t$, $\tilde{y}_t$ all grow at the same rate in steady-state.

Now, we will show that the conditions given in the previous proposition in fact guarantee non-zero growth in steady-state. Evaluating (7.83) at steady-state, we have

$$\frac{(1+\gamma_{\tilde{h}})-(1-\delta_h)}{B(1-v)^{\varsigma_1}(1-u-l)^{\varsigma_2}} = \tilde{k}_t^{\varsigma_1}\tilde{h}_t^{\varsigma_2-1}. \tag{7.86}$$

Since the left-hand side in this expression is constant, then dividing by the same expression lagged one period and taking logs, we get (7.84).

We now evaluate (7.82) at steady-state, obtaining

$$\frac{\tilde{c}_t}{\tilde{k}_t} + (1+n)(1+\gamma_{\tilde{k}}) - (1-\delta_k) = (1-\xi)Av^{\alpha_1}u^{\alpha_2}\tilde{k}_t^{\alpha_1-1}\tilde{h}_t^{\alpha_2}L_t^{\alpha_1+\alpha_2-1}, \tag{7.87}$$

while from the global constraint of resources we get: $\tilde{C}_t/\tilde{K}_t + \tilde{K}_{t+1}/\tilde{K}_t - (1-\delta_k) = (1-\xi)\tilde{Y}_t/\tilde{K}_t$, which can also be written as: $\frac{\tilde{c}_t}{\tilde{k}_t} = -(1+n)(1+\gamma_{\tilde{k}})+(1-\delta_k)+(1-\xi)\frac{\tilde{Y}_t}{\tilde{K}_t}$. Since $\tilde{Y}_t/\tilde{K}_t$ must remain constant in steady-state then, all terms on the right-hand side are constant, and hence, $\frac{\tilde{c}_t}{\tilde{k}_t}$ must also be constant. But then, moving all constant terms to the right-hand side, dividing by the same expression lagged one period, and taking logs, we obtain (7.85).

We now show that if these two conditions hold, then the rest of the equations characterizing the competitive equilibrium will also hold in steady-state. It is important to notice that if the two conditions in the proposition hold, then the products $\tilde{k}_t^{\varsigma_1}\tilde{h}_t^{\varsigma_2-1}$ and $\tilde{k}_t^{\alpha_1-1}\tilde{h}_t^{\alpha_2}L_t^{\alpha_1+\alpha_2-1}$ remain constant in steady-state, i.e., along the *balanced growth path*.

Evaluating (7.78) at steady-state, we get

$$\frac{(1-\tau^w)\alpha_2Av^{\alpha_1}u^{\alpha_2-1}\left[\tilde{k}_t^{\alpha_1-1}\tilde{h}_t^{\alpha_2}L_t^{\alpha_1+\alpha_2-1}\right]}{(1-\tau^r)\alpha_1Av^{\alpha_1-1}u^{\alpha_2}\left[\tilde{k}_t^{\alpha_1-1}\tilde{h}_t^{\alpha_2}L_t^{\alpha_1+\alpha_2-1}\right]+\tau^r\delta_k} = \frac{\varsigma_2}{\varsigma_1}\frac{(1-v)}{(1-u-l)}.$$

Since the expression in square brackets are constant and the other terms are either parameters or variables that remain constant in steady-state, this expression is compatible with the existence of a balanced growth path.

Evaluating (7.79) at steady-state, we have

$$\frac{p}{1-p}\frac{l}{(\tilde{c}_t/\tilde{k}_t)(1+\tau^c)} = \frac{1}{(1-\tau^w)\alpha_2Av^{\alpha_1}u^{\alpha_2-1}\left[\tilde{k}_t^{\alpha_1-1}\tilde{h}_t^{\alpha_2}L_t^{\alpha_1+\alpha_2-1}\right]}.$$

As before, the terms in brackets remain constant in steady-state, and the remaining terms are either parameters or variables that remain constant in steady-state, so this expression is consistent with the existence of a balanced growth path.

Evaluating (7.80) at steady-state, we have

$$(1+\gamma_{\tilde{c}})^{1-p(1-\sigma)} = \beta \left[(1-\tau^r)\alpha_1 A v^{\alpha_1-1} u^{\alpha_2} \right.$$
$$\left. \times \left(\tilde{k}_t^{\alpha_1-1} \tilde{h}_t^{\alpha_2} L_t^{\alpha_1+\alpha_2-1} \right) + 1 - (1-\tau^r)\delta_k \right],$$

where we can repeat the same analysis, the expression being then consistent with the existence of a balanced growth path.

Finally, evaluating (7.81) at steady-state, we get

$$(1+\gamma_{\tilde{c}})^{1-p(1-\sigma)}(1+\gamma_{\tilde{h}})^{\varsigma_2-\alpha_2}(1+\gamma_{\tilde{k}})^{\varsigma_1-\alpha_1}$$
$$= \beta \left[B\upsilon_2(1-v)^{\varsigma_1}(1-u-l)^{\varsigma_2-1}(1-l)\left(\tilde{k}_t^{\varsigma_1} \tilde{h}_t^{\varsigma_2-1} \right) + 1 - \delta_h \right],$$

where we can repeat the previous analysis. The proposition is thereby shown.

The steady-state of this economy can only be computed numerically. Let us assume that we have constant returns to scale in both sectors, so that the two conditions for existence of a balanced growth path in the previous proposition hold. Hence, $\alpha_1 = \alpha$, $\alpha_2 = 1-\alpha$, $\varsigma_1 = \varsigma$, $\varsigma_2 = 1-\varsigma$. In this case, it is very simple to show that $\tilde{c}_t$, $\tilde{k}_t$, $\tilde{h}_t$, $\tilde{y}_t$ all grow at the same rate, that we will denote by γ. Let us now define auxiliary variables:

$$z_t = \frac{\tilde{k}_t}{\tilde{h}_t}; \quad x_t = \frac{\tilde{c}_t}{\tilde{k}_t}; \quad 1+\gamma_{\tilde{h}} = \frac{\tilde{h}_{t+1}}{\tilde{h}_t},$$

which will remain constant in steady-state: $z_t = z$; $x_t = x$; $\gamma_{\tilde{h}} = \gamma$.

The equations characterizing steady-state come from (7.78)–(7.83), together with (7.75), under the constant returns to scale assumption:

$$\frac{(1-\tau^w)(1-\alpha)A v^{\alpha} u^{-\alpha} z^{\alpha}}{(1-\tau^r)\alpha A v^{\alpha-1} u^{1-\alpha} z^{\alpha-1} + \tau^r \delta_k} = \frac{1-\varsigma}{\varsigma} \frac{(1-v)z}{1-u-l},$$

$$\frac{p}{1-p} \frac{l}{x(1+\tau^c)} = \frac{1}{(1-\tau^w)(1-\alpha)A v^{\alpha} u^{-\alpha} z^{\alpha-1}},$$

$$(1+\gamma)^{1-p(1-\sigma)} = \beta \left[(1-\tau^r)\alpha A v^{\alpha-1} u^{1-\alpha} z^{\alpha-1} + 1 - (1-\tau^r)\delta_k \right],$$

$$(1+\gamma)^{1-p(1-\sigma)} = \beta \left[B(1-\varsigma)(1-v)^{\varsigma}(1-u-l)^{-\varsigma}(1-l)z^{\varsigma} + 1 - \delta_h \right],$$

$$[(1-\tau^r)\alpha + (1-\tau^w)(1-\alpha)]A v^{\alpha} u^{1-\alpha} z^{\alpha-1} = (1+\tau^c)x + (1+n)(1+\gamma)$$
$$- (1-\delta_k) - \tau^r \delta_k v,$$

$$1+\gamma = B(1-v)^{\varsigma}(1-u-l)^{1-\varsigma} z^{\varsigma} + 1 - \delta_h.$$

This system of equations can be solved for: z, c, u, v, l, γ. The time path of government expenditures along the steady-state is then obtained through the value of the ξ-parameter:

$$\xi = [(1 - \tau^r)\alpha + (1 - \tau^w)(1 - \alpha)] - \tau^r \delta_k v \left(\frac{\tilde{k}_t}{\tilde{y}_t} \right)_{ss} + \tau^c \left(\frac{\tilde{c}_t}{\tilde{y}_t} \right)_{ss},$$

where $\left(\frac{\tilde{k}_t}{\tilde{y}_t} \right)_{ss} = \frac{1}{Av^\alpha u^{1-\alpha} z^{\alpha-1}}$, $\left(\frac{\tilde{c}_t}{\tilde{y}_t} \right)_{ss} = \frac{x}{Av^\alpha u^{1-\alpha} z^{\alpha-1}}$.

7.5.4 Numerical Exercise: Steady-State Effects of Fiscal Policy

Matlab files *lucas_ss_c.m, lucas_ss_r.m* and *lucas_ss_w.m* compute the effects that different tax rates have on the steady-state values of the growth rate, the size of the public sector and the remaining variables in the economy. In all cases, parameter values are: $A = 1.0$, $B = 0.03942$, $\beta = 0.99$, $\sigma = 1.5$, $n = 0.0035$, $\delta_k = 0.025$, $\delta_h = 0.008$, $\alpha = 0.36$, $\varsigma = 0.15$, $p = 1/3$. These are standard in models calibrated in the literature. The time unit is supposed to represent one quarter, so that the 0.99 discount rate would be consistent with an approximate 4% real rate of interest. Annual depreciation of physical capital would then be around 10%, while that of human capital is lower, around 3.2%. Leisure receives a weight of 1/3 in the utility function, with consumption receiving a 2/3-weight. The elasticity of physical capital in the production of the final good is as we have used in previous chapters, while it is widely agreed that the role of physical capital in the accumulation of human capital is lower. Finally, the degree of risk aversion is taken to be 1.5.

Graphs displayed by these programs seem to contain a rugged response of some variables to tax changes. That is the case of effects of changes in consumption taxes on steady state values for u, v, l, for instance. In fact, the vertical axis shows that such effects are just a visual artifact, and what we see are just minor approximation errors from solving the nonlinear system of equations that characterizes steady-state. The right interpretation is that steady-state values of those variables are unaffected by changes in tax rates.

It is important that the values of the structural parameters are chosen so that the steady state rate of growth, as well as the values of variables u, l, v can fall inside the $(0, 1)$ interval. Furthermore, transversality conditions must also hold in steady-state. In particular

$$\lim_{t \to \infty} \beta^t \lambda_t \tilde{k}_{t+1} = 0$$

$$\Rightarrow \lim_{t \to \infty} \left(\beta (1 + \gamma)^{p(1-\sigma)} \right)^t \tilde{c}_0^{p(1-\sigma)-1} l_0^{(1-p)(1-\sigma)} (1 + \gamma) \tilde{k}_0 = 0$$

$$\Rightarrow \beta (1 + \gamma)^{p(1-\sigma)} \in (0, 1).$$

The $\beta (1 + \gamma)^{p(1-\sigma)} \in (0, 1)$ condition also implies that the discounted sum of current and future utility remains bounded. In particular, execution of the *lucas_ss_w.m* program shows that the steady-state is not defined for tax rates on labor income above 0.50, which does not leave aside any realistic situation, anyway.

An increase in consumption taxes does not affect the allocation of time among the different activities or the allocation of physical capital between the two sectors, while lowering the $x_t = \frac{\tilde{c}_t}{k_t}$ ratio. There is no effect on the rate of growth. In spite of the decrease in the tax base, tax revenues also increase, as a percentage of output.

An increase in labor income taxes leads to a substitution of leisure for hours worked, as expected, while the fraction of physical capital devoted to the education sector decreases, since there is less incentive to accumulate productive human capital. So, physical capital substitutes for labor in the production of the final good. The $\frac{\tilde{k}_t}{h_t}$ ratio increases, while the $\frac{\tilde{c}_t}{k_t}$ decreases. The productivity of capital decreases, in terms of the broader output concept, and the rate of growth of the economy decreases for higher labor taxes. Tax revenues increase for higher tax rates on labor income.

An increase in capital income taxes produces an increase in hours worked, and again a decrease in hours devoted to education. The reason for this is the desire to increase income from working in the production of the final good, to compensate for the higher taxes. The opportunity cost of accumulating physical capital is now lower, and the $\frac{\tilde{c}_t}{k_t}$ ratio increases, while the $\frac{k_t}{h_t}$ decreases. A higher fraction of physical capital is devoted to the educational sector as capital income taxes increase. So, at a difference of the response to labor income taxes, when capital income taxes increase, labor substitutes for physical capital in the production of the final good. The economy grows more slowly as capital income taxes increase.

7.5.5 Computing Equilibrium Trajectories in a Stochastic Setup Under the Assumption of Rational Expectations

We describe in this section how to produce numerical solutions out of the model with human capital accumulation. We consider a simplified version of the model economy considered above, with no taxes and without externalities, with human capital being produced without the use physical capital, and without leisure in the utility function. In terms of the parameters in the previous sections: $p = 1, \varsigma = 0, \tau^c = \tau^w = \tau^r = 0$. Extending the discussion to a more general model incorporating one or more of these features is an interesting, recommended exercise that can be solved following the lines outlined below. Unfortunately, as explained in the previous section, the steady-state will have to be found numerically in most cases, as we did above.

In the absence of externalities and distortionary taxation, the competitive equilibrium allocation is Pareto optimum. Therefore, we can characterize it by solving the social planner's problem

$$\max_{\{\tilde{c}_t, u_t, \tilde{k}_{t+1}, \tilde{h}_{t+1}\}} E_0 \sum_{t=0}^{\infty} \beta^t \frac{\tilde{c}_t^{1-\sigma} - 1}{1-\sigma}, \tag{7.88}$$

subject to

$$(1+n)\tilde{k}_{t+1} = A\tilde{k}_t^{\alpha} \left(u_t \tilde{h}_t\right)^{1-\alpha} \theta_t + (1-\delta_k)\tilde{k}_t - \tilde{c}_t, \tag{7.89}$$

$$\tilde{h}_{t+1} = \eta_t B(1-u_t)\tilde{h}_t + (1-\delta_h)\tilde{h}_t, \tag{7.90}$$

$$\ln \theta_t = \phi_1 \ln \theta_{t-1} + \varepsilon_{1t},$$

$$\ln \eta_t = \phi_2 \ln \eta_{t-1} + \varepsilon_{2t},$$

given $\tilde{h}_0, \tilde{k}_0$, where (7.89) is the global constraint of resources in the economy and (7.90) is the law of accumulation of human capital, both in per capita terms.

The Lagrangian for this problem is

$$L = E_0 \left\{ \sum_{t=0}^{\infty} \beta^t \frac{\tilde{c}_t^{1-\sigma} - 1}{1-\sigma} + \beta^t \lambda_t \left[A\tilde{k}_t^{\alpha} \left(u_t \tilde{h}_t\right)^{1-\alpha} \theta_t \right.\right.$$

$$\left. + (1-\delta_k)\tilde{k}_t - \tilde{c}_t - (1+n)\tilde{k}_{t+1} \right]$$

$$\left. + \beta^t \mu_t \left[\eta_t B(1-u_t)\tilde{h}_t + (1-\delta_h)\tilde{h}_t - \tilde{h}_{t+1} \right] \right\},$$

with first order conditions

$$\tilde{c}_t : \tilde{c}_t^{-\sigma} = \lambda_t, \tag{7.91}$$

$$u_t : \lambda_t(1-\alpha)A\tilde{k}_t^{\alpha}\tilde{h}_t^{1-\alpha}u_t^{-\alpha}\theta_t = \mu_t B\tilde{h}_t \eta_t, \tag{7.92}$$

$$\tilde{k}_{t+1} : \lambda_t(1+n) = \beta E_t \left[\lambda_{t+1} \left(A\alpha \left(\frac{\tilde{k}_{t+1}}{\tilde{h}_{t+1}} \right)^{\alpha-1} u_{t+1}^{1-\alpha} \theta_{t+1} + 1 - \delta_k \right) \right], \tag{7.93}$$

$$\tilde{h}_{t+1} : \mu_t = \beta E_t \left\{ \mu_{t+1} \left[B(1-u_{t+1})\eta_{t+1} + 1 - \delta_h \right] \right.$$

$$\left. + \lambda_{t+1}(1-\alpha)A \left(\frac{\tilde{k}_{t+1}}{\tilde{h}_{t+1}} \right)^{\alpha} u_{t+1}^{1-\alpha} \theta_{t+1} \right\}. \tag{7.94}$$

But (7.92) can be written

$$\mu_t = \lambda_t(1-\alpha)\frac{A}{B}\frac{\theta_t}{\eta_t} \left(\frac{\tilde{k}_t}{\tilde{h}_t} \right)^{\alpha} u_t^{-\alpha},$$

which taken to (7.94), allows us to write

$$\lambda_t \frac{\theta_t}{\eta_t} \left(\frac{\tilde{k}_{t+1}}{\tilde{h}_{t+1}}\right)^\alpha u_{t+1}^{-\alpha} = \beta E_t \left[\lambda_{t+1} \left(\frac{\tilde{k}_{t+1}}{\tilde{h}_{t+1}}\right)^\alpha u_{t+1}^{-\alpha} \frac{\theta_{t+1}}{\eta_{t+1}} (B\eta_{t+1} + 1 - \delta_h)\right].$$

After eliminating the Lagrange multipliers, the optimality conditions become

$$\tilde{c}_t^{-\sigma}(1+n) = \beta E_t \left[\tilde{c}_{t+1}^{-\sigma} \left(A\alpha \left(\frac{\tilde{k}_{t+1}}{\tilde{h}_{t+1}}\right)^{\alpha-1} u_{t+1}^{1-\alpha} \theta_{t+1} + 1 - \delta_k\right)\right], \qquad (7.95)$$

$$\tilde{c}_t^{-\sigma} \frac{\theta_t}{\eta_t} \left(\frac{\tilde{k}_{t+1}}{\tilde{h}_{t+1}}\right)^\alpha u_{t+1}^{-\alpha} = \beta E_t \left[\tilde{c}_{t+1}^{-\sigma} \left(\frac{\tilde{k}_{t+1}}{\tilde{h}_{t+1}}\right)^\alpha u_{t+1}^{-\alpha} \frac{\theta_{t+1}}{\eta_{t+1}} \qquad (7.96) \right.$$
$$\left. \times (B\eta_{t+1} + 1 - \delta_h)\right],$$

$$(1+n)\tilde{k}_{t+1} = A\tilde{k}_t^\alpha \left(u_t \tilde{h}_t\right)^{1-\alpha} \theta_t + (1-\delta_k)\tilde{k}_t - \tilde{c}_t, \qquad (7.97)$$

$$\tilde{h}_{t+1} = \eta_t B(1-u_t)\tilde{h}_t + (1-\delta_h)\tilde{h}_t, \qquad (7.98)$$

which is, each period, a system of four equations with four unknowns: $\{\tilde{c}_t, u_t, \tilde{k}_{t+1}, \tilde{h}_{t+1}\}_{t=0}^\infty$, given initial values for state variables, $\tilde{k}_0, \tilde{h}_0$, and a realization for $\{\theta_t\}_{t=0}^\infty$, $\{\eta_t\}_{t=0}^\infty$.

7.5.5.1 The Steady State as a Balanced Growth Path

We again define a deterministic steady-state in this economy as that situation in which the random shocks take their expected values at all time periods: $\theta_t = \eta_t = 1, \forall t$, and variable u_t, remain constant at u, while $\tilde{c}_t, \tilde{k}_t, \tilde{h}_t, \tilde{y}_t$, all grow at constant rates $\gamma_{\tilde{c}}, \gamma_{\tilde{k}}, \gamma_{\tilde{h}}, \gamma_y$, respectively, and the ratio $\tilde{Y}_t/\tilde{K}_t$ stays constant.

Now we show that the rates of growth for $\tilde{c}_t, \tilde{k}_t, \tilde{h}_t$, are the same. Since the ratio $\tilde{y}_t/\tilde{k}_t$, as well as hours worked u_t must remain constant in steady state then, from the transformed production function: $\frac{y_t}{\tilde{k}_t} = A\left(\frac{\tilde{k}_t}{\tilde{h}_t}\right)^{\alpha-1} u^{1-\alpha}$, we get that the ratio $\tilde{k}_t/\tilde{h}_t$ must also remain constant in steady state, which can only happen if both types of capital, $\tilde{k}_t$ and $\tilde{h}_t$, grow at the same rate: $\gamma_{\tilde{k}} = \gamma_{\tilde{h}}$.

Dividing through in (7.98) by $\tilde{h}_t$ we obtain the steady-state rate of growth for human capital:

$$1 + \gamma_{\tilde{h}} = B(1-u_t) + (1-\delta_h), \qquad (7.99)$$

while dividing by $\tilde{c}_t$ in (7.96), we get the steady-state rate of growth of consumption:

$$\left(\frac{\tilde{c}_{t+1}}{\tilde{c}_t}\right)^\sigma \left(\frac{\tilde{k}_{t+1}}{\tilde{k}_t}\right)^{-\alpha} \left(\frac{\tilde{h}_{t+1}}{\tilde{h}_t}\right)^{-\alpha} = \beta (B+1-\delta_h),$$

which implies

$$(1+\gamma_{\tilde{c}})^{\sigma} = \beta\,(B+1-\delta_h),\tag{7.100}$$

and finally, from (7.97)

$$(1+n)\frac{\tilde{k}_{t+1}}{\tilde{k}_t} = A\left(\frac{\tilde{k}_t}{\tilde{h}_t}\right)^{\alpha-1}u^{1-\alpha}+(1-\delta_k)-\frac{\tilde{c}_t}{\tilde{k}_t},\tag{7.101}$$

which can hold only if the ratio $\frac{\tilde{c}_t}{\tilde{k}_t}$ remains constant, implying that $\gamma_{\tilde{c}} = \gamma_{\tilde{k}}$. Hence, consumption, physical capital and human capital all grow at the same rate along the deterministic steady-state: $\gamma_{\tilde{c}} = \gamma_{\tilde{k}} = \gamma_{\tilde{h}} = \gamma$.

To characterize steady-state we can use $(7.95),(7.99),(7.100)$ and (7.101) to get the system

$$\gamma = [\beta\,(B+1-\delta_h)]^{1/\sigma}-1,\tag{7.102}$$

$$u = 1-\frac{\gamma+\delta_h}{B},\tag{7.103}$$

$$\left(\frac{\tilde{k}_t}{\tilde{h}_t}\right)_{ss} = \left[\frac{\frac{(1+n)(1+\gamma)^{\sigma}}{\beta}-(1-\delta_k)}{A\alpha u^{1-\alpha}}\right],\tag{7.104}$$

$$\left(\frac{\tilde{c}_t}{\tilde{k}_t}\right)_{ss} = A\left(\frac{\tilde{k}_t}{\tilde{h}_t}\right)_{ss}^{\alpha-1}u^{1-\alpha}+\left(1-\delta_{\tilde{k}}\right)-(1+n)(1+\gamma),\tag{7.105}$$

which can be recursively solved for: $\gamma, u, \left(\tilde{k}_t/\tilde{h}_t\right)_{ss}, \left(\tilde{c}_t/\tilde{k}_t\right)_{ss}$.

7.5.5.2 Log-Linear Approximation

To simulate the simplified model, we construct a log-linear approximation in $\left(\left(\tilde{k}_t/\tilde{h}_t\right)_{ss}, \left(\tilde{c}_t/\tilde{k}_t\right)_{ss}, u\right)$. We work with ratios because, as we have just seen, they have a well defined steady state. Any transitory perturbation will take the $\left(\left(\tilde{k}_t/\tilde{h}_t\right)_{ss}, \left(\tilde{c}_t/\tilde{k}_t\right)_{ss}\right)$ ratios to the same steady-state, no matter what the sign and the size of the perturbation might be. However, the steady-state is not determined for variables c_t, k_t, h_t, with $c_t = (1+\gamma)^{-t}\tilde{c}_t, k_t = (1+\gamma)^{-t}\tilde{k}_t, h_t = (1+\gamma)^{-t}\tilde{h}_t$, obtained after eliminating from $\tilde{c}_t, \tilde{k}_t, \tilde{h}_t$ the deterministic long-run growth components. That means that if the economy is initially on steady-state for initial values $\tilde{c}_0, \tilde{k}_0, \tilde{h}_0$, a purely transitory perturbation will take it to a new steady state with $\lim_{t\to\infty} w_t \neq w_0$, $w = \tilde{c}, \tilde{k}, \tilde{h}$, although $\lim_{t\to\infty}\frac{\tilde{c}_t}{\tilde{k}_t} = \frac{\tilde{c}_0}{\tilde{k}_0}, \lim_{t\to\infty}\frac{\tilde{k}_t}{\tilde{h}_t} = \frac{\tilde{k}_0}{\tilde{h}_0}$, which means that $\tilde{c}_t, \tilde{k}_t, \tilde{h}_t$ all have a unit root. Therefore, $\tilde{c}_t, \tilde{k}_t, \tilde{h}_t$ have a deterministic trend as well as a stochastic trend. This is a characteristic of endogenous growth models, as opposed to exogenous growth models, which can only posses deterministic trends.

Defining auxiliary variables, $z_t = \frac{\tilde{k}_t}{\tilde{h}_t}, x_t = \frac{\tilde{c}_t}{\tilde{k}_t}$, and using: $\frac{\tilde{h}_{t+1}}{\tilde{h}_t} = B(1-u_t)\eta_t+1-\delta_h$, we can write the optimality conditions in terms of ratios

$$x_t^{-\sigma} z_t^{-\sigma}(1+n)\left[B(1-u_t)+1-\delta_h\right]^\sigma = \beta E_t \left[x_{t+1}^{-\sigma} z_{t+1}^{-\sigma}\right.$$
$$\left. \times \left(A\alpha z_{t+1}^{\alpha-1} u_{t+1}^{1-\alpha}\theta_{t+1}+1-\delta_k\right)\right],$$

$$x_t^{-\sigma} z_t^{\alpha-\sigma}\frac{\theta_t}{\eta_t}u_t^{-\alpha}\left[B(1-u_t)+1-\delta_h\right]^\sigma = \beta E_t \left[x_{t+1}^{-\sigma} z_{t+1}^{\alpha-\sigma}\right.$$
$$\left. \times u_{t+1}^{-\alpha}\frac{\theta_{t+1}}{\eta_{t+1}}\left(B\eta_{t+1}+1-\delta_h\right)\right],$$

$$(1+n)\frac{z_{t+1}}{z_t}\left[B(1-u_t)+1-\delta_h\right] = Az_t^{\alpha-1} u_t^{1-\alpha}\theta_t+(1-\delta_k)-x_t,$$

which can be expressed, in terms of logged variables

$$0 = -e^{-\sigma\ln x_t}e^{-\sigma\ln z_t}(1+n)\left[B(1-e^{\ln u_t})e^{\ln \eta_t}+1-\delta_h\right]^\sigma$$
$$+\beta E_t\left[e^{-\sigma\ln x_{t+1}}e^{-\sigma\ln z_{t+1}}\left(A\alpha e^{(\alpha-1)\ln z_{t+1}}e^{(1-\alpha)\ln u_{t+1}}e^{\ln \theta_{t+1}}+1-\delta_k\right)\right],$$

$$0 = -e^{-\sigma\ln x_t}e^{(\alpha-\sigma)\ln z_t}e^{\ln \theta_t-\ln \eta_t}e^{-\alpha\ln u_t}\times\left[B(1-e^{\ln u_t})e^{\ln \eta_t}+1-\delta_h\right]^\sigma$$
$$+\beta E_t\left[e^{-\sigma\ln x_{t+1}}e^{(\alpha-\sigma)\ln z_{t+1}}e^{\ln \theta_{t+1}-\ln \eta_{t+1}}e^{-\alpha\ln u_{t+1}}\left(Be^{\ln \eta_{t+1}}+1-\delta_h\right)\right],$$

$$0 = -e^{-\ln z_{t+1}}\left[B(1-e^{\ln u_t})e^{\ln \eta_t}+1-\delta_h\right]$$
$$+Ae^{\alpha\ln z_t}e^{(1-\alpha)\ln u_t}e^{\ln \theta_t}+(1-\delta_k)e^{\ln z_t}-e^{\ln z_t}e^{\ln x_t}.$$

We now introduce logged deviations with respect to steady-state: $\hat{z}_t = \ln(z_t/z)$, $\hat{x}_t = \ln(x_t/x)$, $\hat{u}_t = \ln(u_t/u)$, $\hat{\theta}_t = \ln\theta_t$, $\hat{\eta}_t = \ln\eta_t$. Using the forecasting expressions: $E_t\hat{\theta}_{t+1} = \phi_1\hat{\theta}_t$, $E_t\hat{\eta}_{t+1} = \phi_2\hat{\eta}_t$, we can approximate the previous system by

$$0 \simeq \frac{\sigma(1+n)(1+\gamma)^\sigma}{\beta}(\hat{x}_t+\hat{z}_t)+\frac{\sigma(1+n)(1+\gamma)^{\sigma-1}}{\beta}Bu\hat{u}_t$$
$$-\frac{\sigma(1+n)(1+\gamma)^{\sigma-1}}{\beta}B(1-u)\hat{\eta}_t-\frac{\sigma(1+n)(1+\gamma)^\sigma}{\beta}E_t\hat{x}_{t+1}$$
$$+(1-\alpha)\left[\frac{(1+n)(1+\gamma)^\sigma}{\beta}-(1-\delta_k)\right]E_t\hat{u}_{t+1}$$
$$-\left[(1-\alpha+\sigma)\frac{(1+n)(1+\gamma)^\sigma}{\beta}-(1-\alpha)(1-\delta_k)\right]\hat{z}_{t+1}$$
$$+\left[\frac{(1+n)(1+\gamma)^\sigma}{\beta}-(1-\delta_k)\right]\phi_1\hat{\theta}_t,$$

$$0 \simeq \frac{\sigma(1+\gamma)^\sigma}{\beta}\hat{x}_t - (\alpha-\sigma)\frac{(1+\gamma)^\sigma}{\beta}\hat{z}_t$$

$$+\frac{\alpha(1+\gamma)^\sigma + \sigma(1+\gamma)^{\sigma-1}Bu}{\beta}\hat{u}_t - \frac{(1+\gamma)^\sigma}{\beta}(1-\phi_1)\hat{\theta}_t$$

$$+\left[\frac{(1+\gamma)^\sigma}{\beta} - \frac{\sigma(1+\gamma)^{\sigma-1}B(1-u)}{\beta} - (1-\delta_h)\phi_2\right]\hat{\eta}_t$$

$$-\frac{\sigma(1+\gamma)^\sigma}{\beta}E_t\hat{x}_{t+1} + (\alpha-\sigma)\frac{(1+\gamma)^\sigma}{\beta}\hat{z}_{t+1} - \alpha\frac{(1+\gamma)^\sigma}{\beta}E_t\hat{u}_{t+1},$$

$$0 \simeq -z(1+n)(1+\gamma)\hat{z}_{t+1} + \left[zBu(1+n) + A(1-\alpha)z^\alpha u^{1-\alpha}\right]\hat{u}_t$$

$$-z(1+n)B(1-u)\hat{\eta}_t + Az^\alpha u^{1-\alpha}\hat{\theta}_t$$

$$+\left[\frac{(1+n)(1+\gamma)^\sigma}{\beta} - x\right]z\,\hat{z}_t - zx\,\hat{x}_t.$$

This system has a matrix representation

$$\Gamma_0\begin{pmatrix}\hat{z}_{t+1}\\ E_t\hat{x}_{t+1}\\ E_t\hat{u}_{t+1}\end{pmatrix} = \Gamma_1\begin{pmatrix}\hat{z}_t\\ \hat{x}_t\\ \hat{u}_t\end{pmatrix} + \Gamma_2\begin{pmatrix}\hat{\theta}_t\\ \hat{\eta}_t\end{pmatrix},$$

with

$$\Gamma_0(1,1) = (1-\alpha+\sigma)\frac{(1+n)(1+\gamma)^\sigma}{\beta} - (1-\alpha)(1-\delta_k),$$

$$\Gamma_0(1,2) = \frac{\sigma(1+n)(1+\gamma)^\sigma}{\beta},$$

$$\Gamma_0(1,3) = -(1-\alpha)\left[\frac{(1+n)(1+\gamma)^\sigma}{\beta} - (1-\delta_k)\right],$$

$$\Gamma_0(2,1) = -(\alpha-\sigma)\frac{(1+\gamma)^\sigma}{\beta}, \quad \Gamma_0(2,2) = \frac{\sigma(1+\gamma)^\sigma}{\beta},$$

$$\Gamma_0(2,3) = \alpha\frac{(1+\gamma)^\sigma}{\beta}; \quad \Gamma_0(3,1) = z(1+n)(1+\gamma),$$

$$\Gamma_0(3,2) = \Gamma_0(3,3) = 0,$$

$$\Gamma_1(1,1) = \Gamma_1(1,2) = \frac{\sigma(1+n)(1+\gamma)^\sigma}{\beta},$$

$$\Gamma_1(1,3) = \frac{\sigma(1+n)(1+\gamma)^{\sigma-1}Bu}{\beta},$$

$$\Gamma_1(2,1) = -(\alpha-\sigma)\frac{(1+\gamma)^\sigma}{\beta}, \quad \Gamma_1(2,2) = \frac{\sigma(1+\gamma)^\sigma}{\beta},$$

$$\Gamma_1(2,3) = \alpha \frac{(1+\gamma)^\sigma}{\beta} + \frac{\sigma(1+\gamma)^{\sigma-1}B(1-u)}{\beta},$$

$$\Gamma_1(3,1) = \left(\frac{(1+n)(1+\gamma)^\sigma}{\beta} - x\right)z, \quad \Gamma_1(3,2) = -zx,$$

$$\Gamma_1(3,3) = \left[zBu(1+n) + A(1-\alpha)z^\alpha u^{1-\alpha}\right]$$

$$\Gamma_2(1,1) = \left[\frac{(1+n)(1+\gamma)^\sigma}{\beta} - (1-\delta_k)\right]\phi_1,$$

$$\Gamma_2(1,2) = -\frac{\sigma(1+n)(1+\gamma)^{\sigma-1}}{\beta}B(1-u),$$

$$\Gamma_2(2,1) = -\frac{(1+\gamma)^\sigma}{\beta}(1-\phi_1),$$

$$\Gamma_2(2,2) = \frac{(1+\gamma)^\sigma}{\beta} - \frac{\sigma(1+\gamma)^{\sigma-1}B(1-u)}{\beta} - (1-\delta_h)\phi_2,$$

$$\Gamma_2(3,1) = Az^\alpha u^{1-\alpha}, \quad \Gamma_2(3,2) = -z(1+n)B(1-u),$$

and we have

$$\begin{pmatrix} z_{t+1} \\ E_t\hat{x}_{t+1} \\ E_t\hat{u}_{t+1} \end{pmatrix} = \Gamma_3 \begin{pmatrix} z_t \\ \hat{x}_t \\ \hat{u}_t \end{pmatrix} + \Gamma_4 \begin{pmatrix} \hat{\theta}_t \\ \hat{\eta}_t \end{pmatrix},$$

with

$$\Gamma_3 = \Gamma_0^{-1}\Gamma_1; \quad \Gamma_4 = \Gamma_0^{-1}\Gamma_2.$$

The solution to this system will be determinate if two of the eigenvalues of matrix Γ_3 have modulus above 1, the third one being below 1. This is because we have two control variables, consumption and hours worked, which must be determined each period as a function of the state variables. The two unstable eigenvalues will give raise to two unstable directions which need to be eliminated. As in other model economies considered in previous chapters, that is achieved by setting to zero each period the product of the eigenvectors associated to the unstable eigenvalues, times the vector of variables in the autoregressive process, $\hat{z}_t, \hat{x}_t, \hat{u}_t$. That will give us two equations to set the values of $\hat{x}_t$ and $\hat{u}_t$ as a function of the state, $\hat{z}_t$. Furthermore, we will also be able to solve for the two conditional expectations, $E_t\hat{x}_{t+1}, E_t\hat{u}_{t+1}$. Later on, we present a model economy with accumulation of human capital and an externality in the production of the final good in which, for a region of the parameter space, the solution is indeterminate, as reflected in two of the three eigenvalues of the autoregressive matrix being below 1 in modulus.

Without loss of generality, let us denote by λ_1 the stable eigenvalue of Γ_3, and by λ_2, λ_3 the unstable eigenvalues. We have the decomposition of Γ_3:

$$\Gamma_3 = M\Lambda M^{-1} \text{ with } \Lambda = \begin{pmatrix} \lambda_1 & 0 & 0 \\ 0 & \lambda_2 & 0 \\ 0 & 0 & \lambda_3 \end{pmatrix}, \quad M = \begin{pmatrix} M_{11} & M_{12} & M_{13} \\ M_{21} & M_{22} & M_{23} \\ M_{31} & M_{32} & M_{33} \end{pmatrix}.$$

We denote the inverse of M by

$$
M^{-1} = \begin{pmatrix} m_{11} & m_{12} & m_{13} \\ m_{21} & m_{22} & m_{23} \\ m_{31} & m_{32} & m_{33} \end{pmatrix},
$$

where $M_{\bullet j}, j = 1,2,3$ denote the right eigenvectors associated to $\lambda_j, j = 1,2,3$, while $m_{j\bullet}$ are the left eigenvectors associated to $\lambda_j, j = 1,2,3$.

With this decomposition, we have

$$
M^{-1} \begin{pmatrix} \hat{z}_{t+1} \\ E_t \hat{x}_{t+1} \\ E_t \hat{u}_{t+1} \end{pmatrix} = \Lambda M^{-1} \begin{pmatrix} \hat{z}_t \\ \hat{x}_t \\ \hat{u}_t \end{pmatrix} + \underbrace{M^{-1}\Gamma_4}_{Q} \begin{pmatrix} \hat{\theta}_t \\ \hat{\eta}_t \end{pmatrix},
$$

where $Q = M^{-1}\Gamma_4$ is a 3×2 matrix. This system can be written in more detail, as

$$
m_{11}\hat{z}_{t+1} + m_{12}E_t\hat{x}_{t+1} + m_{13}E_t\hat{u}_{t+1} = \lambda_1 \left(m_{11}\hat{z}_t + m_{12}\hat{x}_t + m_{13}\hat{u}_t \right)
$$
$$
+ Q_{11}\hat{\theta}_t + Q_{12}\hat{\eta}_t,
$$

$$
m_{21}\hat{z}_{t+1} + m_{22}E_t\hat{x}_{t+1} + m_{23}E_t\hat{u}_{t+1} = \lambda_2 \left(m_{21}\hat{z}_t + m_{22}\hat{x}_t + m_{23}\hat{u}_t \right)
$$
$$
+ Q_{21}\hat{\theta}_t + Q_{22}\hat{\eta}_t,
$$

$$
m_{31}\hat{z}_{t+1} + m_{32}E_t\hat{x}_{t+1} + m_{33}E_t\hat{u}_{t+1} = \lambda_3 \left(m_{31}\hat{z}_t + m_{32}\hat{x}_t + m_{33}\hat{u}_t \right)
$$
$$
+ Q_{31}\hat{\theta}_t + Q_{32}\hat{\eta}_t.
$$

To simplify notation, we define vector $f_t^0 = \begin{pmatrix} m_{11}\hat{z}_t + m_{12}\hat{x}_t + m_{13}\hat{u}_t \\ m_{21}\hat{z}_t + m_{22}\hat{x}_t + m_{23}\hat{u}_t \\ m_{31}\hat{z}_t + m_{32}\hat{x}_t + m_{33}\hat{u}_t \end{pmatrix}$ which

allows us to write the system above as

$$
E_t f_{1,t+1}^0 = f_{1,t}^0 + Q_{11}\hat{\theta}_t + Q_{12}\hat{\eta}_t,
$$
$$
E_t f_{2,t+1}^0 = f_{2,t}^0 + Q_{21}\hat{\theta}_t + Q_{22}\hat{\eta}_t,
$$
$$
E_t f_{3,t+1}^0 = f_{3,t}^0 + Q_{31}\hat{\theta}_t + Q_{32}\hat{\eta}_t.
$$

If we apply the law of iterated expectations to solve forwards the last two equations in this system, as we have done in previous chapters, we get

$$
f_{2,t}^0 = \frac{Q_{21}}{\phi_1 - \lambda_2}\hat{\theta}_t + \frac{Q_{22}}{\phi_2 - \lambda_2}\hat{\eta}_t,
$$
$$
f_{3,t}^0 = \frac{Q_{31}}{\phi_1 - \lambda_3}\hat{\theta}_t + \frac{Q_{32}}{\phi_2 - \lambda_3}\hat{\eta}_t,
$$

which lead to

$$\underbrace{\begin{pmatrix} m_{21} \\ m_{31} \end{pmatrix}}_{S_0} \hat{z}_t + \underbrace{\begin{pmatrix} m_{22} & m_{23} \\ m_{32} & m_{33} \end{pmatrix}}_{S_1} \begin{pmatrix} \hat{x}_t \\ \hat{u}_t \end{pmatrix} = \underbrace{\begin{pmatrix} \frac{Q_{21}}{\phi_1 - \lambda_2} & \frac{Q_{22}}{\phi_2 - \lambda_2} \\ \frac{Q_{31}}{\phi_1 - \lambda_3} & \frac{Q_{32}}{\phi_2 - \lambda_3} \end{pmatrix}}_{S_2} \begin{pmatrix} \hat{\theta}_t \\ \hat{\eta}_t \end{pmatrix},$$

which leads to the system, of *control equations* or *stability conditions*:

$$\begin{pmatrix} \hat{x}_t \\ \hat{u}_t \end{pmatrix} = -S_1^{-1} S_0 \hat{z}_t + S_1^{-1} S_2 \begin{pmatrix} \hat{\theta}_t \\ \hat{\eta}_t \end{pmatrix} = S_3 \hat{z}_t + S_4 \begin{pmatrix} \hat{\theta}_t \\ \hat{\eta}_t \end{pmatrix}, \qquad (7.106)$$

with $S_3 = \begin{pmatrix} S_{31} \\ S_{32} \end{pmatrix}, S_4 = \begin{pmatrix} S_{4,11} & S_{4,12} \\ S_{4,21} & S_{4,22} \end{pmatrix}.$

From this system, we get

$$E_t \hat{x}_{t+1} = S_{31} \hat{z}_{t+1} + S_{4,11} \phi_1 \hat{\theta}_t + S_{4,12} \phi_2 \hat{\eta}_t,$$
$$E_t \hat{u}_{t+1} = S_{32} \hat{z}_{t+1} + S_{4,21} \phi_1 \hat{\theta}_t + S_{4,22} \phi_2 \hat{\eta}_t,$$

and we finally get the *state equation*

$$\hat{z}_{t+1} = \lambda_1 \hat{z}_t + \frac{Q_{11} + (\lambda_1 - \phi_1)(S_{4,11} m_{12} + S_{4,21} m_{13})}{m_{11} + m_{12} S_{31} + m_{13} S_{32}} \hat{\theta}_t$$
$$+ \frac{Q_{12} + (\lambda_1 - \phi_2)(S_{4,12} m_{12} + S_{4,22} m_{13})}{m_{11} + m_{12} S_{31} + m_{13} S_{32}} \hat{\eta}_t. \qquad (7.107)$$

The model can be simulated following two different approaches. The first one is easier, but it involves a larger approximation error.

First Simulation Approach

1. Given realizations for $\{\varepsilon_{1t}, \varepsilon_{2t}\}_{t=1}^T$ for two independent Normal distributions with standard deviations σ_1 and σ_2, respectively. Given initial conditions $(\hat{\theta}_0, \hat{\eta}_0)$, we use the laws of motion $\ln \theta_t = \phi_1 \ln \theta_{t-1} + \varepsilon_{1t}$, $\eta_t = \phi_2 \ln \eta_{t-1} + \varepsilon_{2t}$ to compute a time series realization $\{\hat{\theta}_t, \hat{\eta}_t\}_{t=0}^T$.
2. Given initial conditions $\tilde{k}_0, \tilde{h}_0$ we compute z_0 and $\hat{z}_0 = \ln(z_0/z)$.
3. Given $\hat{z}_0$ and $\{\hat{\theta}_t, \hat{\eta}_t\}_{t=0}^T$, we use (7.107) to obtain a realization $\{\hat{z}_t\}_{t=0}^T$. We also compute $z_t = z e^{\hat{z}_t}, t = 0, 1, 2, \ldots, T$.
4. Given $\{z_t\}_{t=0}^T$, $\{\hat{\theta}_t, \hat{\eta}_t\}_{t=0}^T$, we use (7.106) to compute $\{\hat{x}_t, \hat{u}_t\}_{t=0}^T$, and $x_t = x e^{\hat{x}_t}, u_t = u e^{\hat{u}_t}, t = 0, 1, 2, \ldots, T$.
5. We compute $\gamma_{\tilde{h},t} = B(1 - u_t)\eta_t + (1 - \delta_h) - 1, t = 0, 1, 2, \ldots T$.

6. From the definition $\frac{\tilde{h}_{t+1}}{\tilde{h}_t} = 1 + \gamma_{\tilde{h},t}$, we get $\frac{h_{t+1}(1+\gamma)^{t+1}}{h_t(1+\gamma)^t} = 1 + \gamma_{\tilde{h},t}$, and a time series realization for h_{t+1} from $h_{t+1} = \frac{1+\gamma_{\tilde{h},t}}{1+\gamma} h_t$. Hence, given $h_0 = \tilde{h}_0$, we can obtain the time path for human capital, net of the deterministic trend, $\{h_{t+1}\}_{t=0}^T$.

7. We compute the time series for physical capital $\{k_t\}_{t=0}^T$ using the fact that $\frac{k_t}{\tilde{h}_t} = z_t$ implies $\frac{k_t}{\tilde{h}_t} = z_t$, so that: $k_t = h_t z_t$.

8. We compute the time series for consumption $\{c_t\}_{t=0}^T$ from $c_t = x_t h_t, t = 0, 1, 2, \ldots$

9. Given the time series $\{k_t\}_{t=0}^T$, $\{h_t\}_{t=0}^T$, $\{c_t\}_{t=0}^T$, we can obtain $\{\tilde{k}_t, \tilde{h}_t, \tilde{c}_t\}_{t=0}^T$ from $\tilde{k}_t = (1+\gamma)^t k_t, \tilde{h}_t = (1+\gamma)^t h_t, \tilde{c}_t = (1+\gamma)^t c_t$.

10. Given time series for $\{\tilde{k}_t, \tilde{h}_t\}_{t=0}^T$, we compute $\gamma_{\tilde{k}}, \gamma_{\tilde{c}}$: $1 + \gamma_{\tilde{k}} = \frac{\tilde{k}_{t+1}}{\tilde{k}_t}, 1 + \gamma_{\tilde{c}} = \frac{\tilde{c}_{t+1}}{\tilde{c}_t}$.

Second Simulation Approach

Steps 1 and 2 are the same as in the first simulation approach:

- Given $\{\hat{z}_0, k_0, \hat{\theta}_0, \hat{\eta}_0\}$, we can use (7.106) to obtain $\{\ln c_0, \hat{u}_0\}$. Taking into account that $\hat{x}_t = \ln c_t - \ln k_t - \ln x$, we get

$$\ln c_0 = \ln k_0 + \ln x + S_{31}\hat{z}_0 + S_{4,11}\hat{\theta}_0 + S_{4,12}\hat{\eta}_0, \qquad (7.108)$$

$$\hat{u}_0 = S_{32}\hat{z}_0 + S_{4,21}\hat{\theta}_0 + S_{4,22}\hat{\eta}_0, \qquad (7.109)$$

and we can finally compute $c_0 = e^{\ln c_0}, u_0 = u e^{\hat{u}_0}$.

- Given $\{k_0, h_0, \hat{\theta}_0, \hat{\eta}_0, c_0, u_0\}$, we use the fact that $\hat{w}_t = (1+\gamma)^t w_t, w = c, k, h$, into the global constraint of resources and the accumulation law for human capital to obtain $\{k_1, h_1\}$

$$k_1 = \frac{1}{(1+n)(1+\gamma)} \left[Ak_0^\alpha (u_0 h_0)^{1-\alpha} \theta_0 + (1 - \delta_k)k_0 - c_0 \right]$$

and

$$h_1 = \frac{1}{1+\gamma} \left[B(1 - u_0)\eta_0 h_0 + (1 - \delta_h)h_0 \right].$$

- Given $\{k_1, h_1, \hat{\theta}_1, \hat{\eta}_1\}$, we obtain $z_1 = \frac{k_1}{h_1}$ and we can use (7.108), (7.109) to compute $\{c_1, u_1\}$.
- Repeat the last two steps to produce time series of length T : $\{c_t, u_t, k_t, h_t\}_{t=0}^T$. Once we have these time series, we compute time series for $\{\tilde{c}_t, \tilde{k}_t, \tilde{h}_t, \gamma_{\tilde{c}}, \gamma_{\tilde{k}}, \gamma_{\tilde{h}}\}_{t=0}^T$.

What is interesting in this second algorithm is that we obtain the variables in levels directly, using the restrictions without any approximation, so that the approximation error is smaller than that made when following the first approach.

7.5.6 Indeterminacy of Equilibria

We consider in this section the possibility that there might exist multiple trajectories taking the economy into the balanced growth path, which we will refer to as *indeterminacy of equilibria*. One situation where indeterminacy of equilibria may arise is in the endogenous growth model with human capital accumulation we have analyzed in previous sections, when we include a positive externality in the form of the stock of human capital entering as an input in the production of the final good. This is a very relevant situation that may arise in different growth models and strongly conditions the procedure that can be followed to obtain a numerical solution to the model.

We illustrate this using a discrete time, stochastic version of Lucas [60] model. Benhabib and Perli [9] and Xie [98] characterize a range of parameter values for a continuum of equilibria to exist in the continuous time, deterministic, endogenous growth Lucas [60] economy, incorporating the mentioned externality. These authors show that a high intertemporal elasticity of consumption together with a sufficiently strong externality are necessary conditions for indeterminacy in that model.

Indeterminacy of equilibria in endogenous growth models has important implications:

1. It may be consistent with optimality that two economies with identical initial endowment of physical and human capital decide to consume, save and allocate labor among sectors in different fashion. In the long-run, these economies will converge in terms of rates of growth, but not in terms of the level of output, physical and human capital.[28]
2. As a corollary, a country with lower endowments of physical and human capital than other can surpass[29] the latter in terms of the levels of output, physical and human capital, by just initially allocating to education a higher fraction of time.
3. Initial sacrifices of income due to an initially higher dedication of time to education lead to higher rates of growth during the transition, and higher future levels of income, thereby contributing to increase welfare. The long-run effect may well compensate for the initial loss of utility.

7.5.6.1 A Brief Introduction to the Local Indeterminacy of Equilibria

Global indeterminacy refers to the fact that a dynamic general equilibrium model may present multiple steady-states or, more generally, that models implying steady-state growth, might give raise to multiple *balanced growth paths*. In contrast, *local indeterminacy* arises when given a steady-state or a balanced growth path, there might exist a continuum of trajectories converging to it. We focus here on local indeterminacy using Lucas [60] model as an illustration.

---

[28] The ratios between growing variables will be the same in both economies, but not the levels of those variables.

[29] Which is known as *leapfrogging*.

In deterministic setups, indeterminacy of equilibria implies the existence of multiple *equilibrium trajectories* that can be indexed by different initial conditions for some control variables. As explained below, in an stochastic setup, indeterminacy is handled by introducing exogenous processes for some expectations errors, whose statistical characteristics are not restricted by the structure of the model.[30] The sample realizations for these processes select one among the continuum of solutions, and they gradually overcome the effect of the initial conditions that might be imposed on some control variables in determining the time evolution of the main variables.

Local indeterminacy can be explained analytically as follows: Let us assume that we have solved for the equilibrium of a dynamic growth model having in its deterministic version,[31] a unique balanced growth path. The set of Euler equations, budget constraints, laws of motion for structural shocks and market clearing conditions, all can be jointly represented as

$$0 = E_t\left[f\left(u_t, u_{t+1}, x_t, x_{t+1}; \theta_t, \theta_{t+1}\right)\right], \tag{7.110}$$

$$\hat{\theta}_{t+1} = \Psi\hat{\theta}_t + \varepsilon_{t+1}, \quad \varepsilon_{t+1} \underset{iid}{\sim} N(0, \Sigma), \tag{7.111}$$

where u_t denotes the $(m \times 1)$ vector of control or time t decision variables, x_t is the $(n \times 1)$ vector of state or predetermined variables, θ_t is the $(p \times 1)$ vector of structural shocks and policy variables, whose logged deviations with respect to steady-state follow a stable VAR process.[32] Furthermore, we assume a complete system, i.e., $f : \mathbb{R}^{n+m} \to \mathbb{R}^{n+m}$. If there are further lags in the system, they are accommodated by considering some of them as additional control variables, in a standard strategy followed in representations of time series models. Eventually, any dynamic model can be represented as a VAR(1) system, as above.

If we log-linearize system (7.110) and use the expectations condition $E_t\hat{\theta}_{t+1} = \Psi\hat{\theta}_t$, we get a new system in deviations of logged variables with respect to steady-state

$$\Gamma_0 \begin{bmatrix} \hat{x}_{t+1} \\ E_t\hat{u}_{t+1} \end{bmatrix} + \Gamma_1 \begin{bmatrix} \hat{x}_t \\ \hat{u}_t \end{bmatrix} + \Gamma_2\hat{\theta}_t = 0,$$

where Γ_0, Γ_1 and Γ_2 have the appropriate dimensions. Remember that, with our usual convention on notation, time $t + 1$ state variables, x_{t+1}, are determined at time t, so that $E_t\hat{x}_{t+1} = \hat{x}_{t+1}$.

Assuming that Γ_0 is a full rank matrix, the previous system can be represented as

$$\begin{bmatrix} \hat{x}_{t+1} \\ E_t\hat{u}_{t+1} \end{bmatrix} = \Gamma_3 \begin{bmatrix} \hat{x}_t \\ \hat{u}_t \end{bmatrix} + \Gamma_4\hat{\theta}_t, \tag{7.112}$$

where $\Gamma_3 = -\Gamma_0^{-1}\Gamma_1$, $\Gamma_4 = -\Gamma_0^{-1}\Gamma_2$.

---

[30] Beyond satisfying the restrictions imposed by rationality of expectations, if that is a maintained assumption.

[31] That is, the version of the model without any random shock.

[32] That is, the roots of the characteristic equation of the transition matrix Ψ of the vector AR(1) model in (7.111) are inside the unit circle.

If matrix Γ_3 has m unstable roots, then the rational expectations equilibrium is uniquely defined. We can then represent the system in logged variables in state-space form

$$\begin{bmatrix} \hat{x}_{t+1} \\ \hat{\theta}_{t+1} \end{bmatrix} = \begin{bmatrix} \Gamma_5 & \Gamma_6 \\ 0 & \Psi \end{bmatrix} \begin{bmatrix} \hat{x}_t \\ \hat{\theta}_t \end{bmatrix} + \begin{bmatrix} 0 \\ I_p \end{bmatrix} \varepsilon_{t+1}, \tag{7.113}$$

$$\hat{u}_t = \Gamma_7 \begin{bmatrix} \hat{x}_t \\ \hat{\theta}_t \end{bmatrix}. \tag{7.114}$$

where (7.113) is the state equation and (7.114) is the control equation, which is obtained after eliminating the unstable trajectories associated to the unstable eigenvalues of Γ_3.

Given initial conditions for state variables, together with a sample realization for each of the exogenous shocks and the policy variables, we could use the representation above to uniquely compute approximate equilibrium trajectories for state variables $\hat{x}_{t+1}$, and control variables $\hat{u}_t$. So, when equilibrium is uniquely determined, we are able to solve for the m conditional expectations for each of the control variables[33] by eliminating the unstable trajectories associated to the unstable eigenvalues of Γ_3. In addition to having the representation of control variables as functions of state variables and exogenous shocks, in a determinate equilibrium we can also write the errors associated to the control variables as linear combinations of innovations to the stochastic processes for the exogenous shocks, i.e., as functions of the model's fundamentals.

To see this, we write (7.112) as

$$\begin{bmatrix} \hat{x}_{t+1} \\ \hat{u}_{t+1} \\ \hat{\theta}_{t+1} \end{bmatrix} = \begin{bmatrix} & \Gamma_3 & \Gamma_4 \\ 0_{p \times (n+m)} & & \Psi \end{bmatrix} \begin{bmatrix} \hat{x}_t \\ \hat{u}_t \\ \hat{\theta}_t \end{bmatrix}$$
$$+ \begin{bmatrix} D_{(n+m) \times m} & 0_{(n+m) \times p} \\ 0_{p \times m} & I_{p \times p} \end{bmatrix} \begin{bmatrix} a_{t+1} \\ \varepsilon_{t+1} \end{bmatrix},$$

where $D = [0_{n \times m}, I_{m \times m}]$, and $a_{t+1} = \hat{u}_{t+1} - E_t \hat{u}_{t+1}$. Then, eliminating the unstable trajectories can be seen in two alternative ways: (1) as setting up to zero the product of premultiplying vector $[\hat{x}_t, \hat{u}_t, \hat{\theta}_t]$ by the matrix made up with the left eigenvectors associated to the unstable eigenvalues of the autoregressive matrix above. That allows us to write control variables as functions of state variables and exogenous shocks. Alternatively, (2) as setting up to zero the product of that matrix of eigenvectors by matrix

$$\begin{bmatrix} D_{(n+m) \times m} & 0_{(n+m) \times p} \\ 0_{p \times m} & I_{p \times p} \end{bmatrix} \begin{bmatrix} a_{t+1} \\ \varepsilon_{t+1} \end{bmatrix},$$

---

[33] Notice that the conditional expectations of highly nonlinear functions that initially appear in the optimality equations transform into conditional expectations of single variables when a linear or log-linear approximation is performed.

which allows us to write forecast errors a_{t+1} as functions of innovations in exogenous stochastic processes.

On the other hand, if Γ_3 has $m-q$ unstable roots ($m>q$), then we will be able to represent only $m-q$ control variables as a function of the other q control variables as well as the state variables, the structural shocks and the policy variables. Eliminating the unstable trajectories we will only be able to solve for the conditional expectations of only $m-q$ control variables. We can only solve for the remaining q conditional expectations by drawing exogenous sample realizations for the associated expectations errors. These expectations are treated as exogenous, since the model does not restrict them. That is, only $m-q$ forecast errors in control variables can be written as a function of the exogenous innovations. For each stochastic characterization chosen for the q expectations errors, we will obtain a different equilibrium. Summarizing, whenever the number of unstable eigenvalues of the transition matrix is smaller than the number of control variables, system (7.112) can be represented as

$$
\begin{bmatrix} \hat{x}_{t+1} \\ \hat{u}_{1,t+1} \\ \hat{\theta}_{t+1} \end{bmatrix} = \begin{bmatrix} \Phi_1 & \Phi_2 & \Phi_3 \\ \Phi_6 & \Phi_5 & \Phi_4 \\ 0 & 0 & \Psi \end{bmatrix} \begin{bmatrix} \hat{x}_t \\ \hat{u}_{1,t} \\ \hat{\theta}_t \end{bmatrix} \tag{7.115}
$$
$$
+ \begin{bmatrix} 0 & \Phi_7 \\ 0 & \Phi_8 \\ I_p & 0 \end{bmatrix} \begin{bmatrix} \varepsilon_{t+1} \\ a_{t+1} \end{bmatrix},
$$
$$
\hat{u}_{2,t} = \Phi_0 \begin{bmatrix} \hat{x}_t \\ \hat{u}_{1,t} \\ \hat{\theta}_t \end{bmatrix}, \tag{7.116}
$$

where $\hat{u}_{1,t}$ is the $(q \times 1)$ vector of control variables that we have to take initially as given because of the indeterminacy of equilibria, $\hat{u}_{2,t}$ is the $((m-q) \times 1)$ vector of control variables whose expectations were solved for by eliminating the unstable trajectories associated to the unstable eigenvalues of Γ_3. Finally, a_{t+1} is the $(q \times 1)$ vector of forecast errors for the $\hat{u}_1$ variables: $a_{t+1} = \hat{u}_{1,t+1} - E_t \hat{u}_{1,t+1}$. Being rational forecast errors, they must have a white noise structure, besides being conditionally uncorrelated with variables in the information set available to agents at time t. If we choose an (arbitrary) value for their variance-covariance matrix, and arbitrary values for the correlations between these forecast errors and the innovations in the exogenous structural processes, we will be able to obtain a realization of those errors which, together with an initial condition for $\hat{u}_{1,0}$ will allow us to obtain one of the multiple equilibrium trajectories, for given initial values for state variables ($\hat{x}_0$) and for the exogenous random shocks ($\hat{\theta}_0$), and given a sample realization for the exogenous innovations.

Notice that, under indetermination of equilibria, at each point in time there is the need to choose values for some control variables. The problem is that the choice at time t does not condition the choice made at any other point in time, so that the economy can be displaying significant jumps which can sometimes be interpreted as cycles. In essence, the situation is as if each of this subset of control variables is drawn each period from a given probability distribution. Indeterminacy can also give raise to self-fulfilling prophecies: as an example if, for some reason, consumers believe that future tax rates will rise, they will attempt to reduce the tax base, which may well lead the government to the need to effectively, increase tax rates so as to maintain the same revenue. That would be a case in which one among the continuum of possible equilibria is being chosen on the basis of a purely speculative behavior on the part of consumers. This situation will not arise when the equilibrium is well determined, since agents then use past information on expectation errors to update their views on the future of the economy, leaving no role for any unjustified, sudden change in expectations.[34]

7.5.6.2 Simulating the Model with Human Capital Accumulation Under Indeterminacy of Equilibria

In the absence of distortionary taxation, we can solve for the competitive equilibrium of the two-sector endogenous growth model with human capital accumulation when there is an externality in the form of the average stock of human capital $\tilde{h}_{a,t}$, as a productive input for the final good.

The representative consumer solves the problem

$$\max_{\{\tilde{c}_t, u_t, \tilde{k}_{t+1}, \tilde{h}_{t+1}\}} E_0 \sum_{t=0}^{\infty} \beta^t \frac{\tilde{c}_t^{1-\sigma} - 1}{1 - \sigma}, \tag{7.117}$$

subject to

$$\tilde{k}_{t+1} = \frac{1}{1+n} \left[A\tilde{k}_t^{\alpha} \left(u_t \tilde{h}_t \right)^{1-\alpha} \tilde{h}_{a,t}^{\psi} \theta_t + (1 - \delta_k) \tilde{k}_t - \tilde{c}_t \right], \tag{7.118}$$

$$\tilde{h}_{t+1} = \eta_t B(1 - u_t) \tilde{h}_t + (1 - \delta_h) \tilde{h}_t, \tag{7.119}$$

$$\ln \theta_t = \phi_1 \ln \theta_{t-1} + \varepsilon_{1t}, \quad |\phi_1| < 1, \quad \varepsilon_{1t} \underset{iid}{\sim} N(0, \sigma_1^2), \tag{7.120}$$

$$\ln \eta_t = \phi_2 \ln \eta_{t-1} + \varepsilon_{2t}, \quad |\phi_2| < 1, \quad \varepsilon_{2t} \underset{iid}{\sim} N(0, \sigma_2^2), \tag{7.121}$$

given $\tilde{h}_0, \tilde{k}_0$, where (7.118) is the global constraint of resources in the economy and (7.119) is the law of accumulation of human capital, both in per capita terms.

In equilibrium, we must have: $\tilde{h}_{a,t} = \tilde{h}_t$. Since all private agents are identical to each other, this condition just states that the average stock and the individual stock of human capital are equal. Once we eliminate the Lagrange multipliers and impose this equilibrium condition, optimality conditions for this problem can be summarized

$$\tilde{c}_t^{-\sigma}(1+n) = \beta E_t \left[\tilde{c}_{t+1}^{-\sigma} \left(A\alpha \tilde{k}_{t+1}^{\alpha-1} \tilde{h}_{t+1}^{1-\alpha+\psi} u_{t+1}^{1-\alpha} \theta_{t+1} + 1 - \delta_k \right) \right], \tag{7.122}$$

---

[34] This is because under determinacy of equilibria, there is a one-to-one mapping between expectations errors and structural innovations to the model, while under indeterminacy, some expectations errors are left free.

$$\tilde{c}_t^{-\sigma}\frac{\theta_t}{\eta_t}\left(\frac{\tilde{k}_{t+1}^{\alpha}}{\bar{h}_{t+1}^{\alpha-\psi}}\right)u_{t+1}^{-\alpha} = \beta E_t\left[\tilde{c}_{t+1}^{-\sigma}\left(\frac{\tilde{k}_{t+1}^{\alpha}}{\bar{h}_{t+1}^{\alpha-\psi}}\right)u_{t+1}^{-\alpha}\right. \tag{7.123}$$

$$\left. \times\frac{\theta_{t+1}}{\eta_{t+1}}(B\eta_{t+1}+1-\delta_h)\right],$$

$$(1+n)\tilde{k}_{t+1} = A\tilde{k}_t^{\alpha}\tilde{h}_t^{1-\alpha+\psi}u_t^{1-\alpha}\theta_t + (1-\delta_k)\tilde{k}_t - \tilde{c}_t, \tag{7.124}$$
$$\tilde{h}_{t+1} = \eta_t B(1-u_t)\tilde{h}_t + (1-\delta_h)\tilde{h}_t, \tag{7.125}$$

together with transversality conditions

$$\lim_{j\to\infty}E_t\beta^{t+j}\tilde{\lambda}_{t+j}\tilde{k}_{t+j+1} = 0,$$

$$\lim_{j\to\infty}E_t\beta^{t+j}\tilde{\mu}_{t+j}\tilde{h}_{t+j+1} = 0.$$

Deterministic Steady-State

In the deterministic steady-state, exogenous shocks take a value equal to their mathematical expectations at all time periods, $\theta_t = 1, \eta_t = 1, \forall t$, per capita variables $\tilde{c}_t, \tilde{k}_t, \tilde{h}_t$, grow at constant rates, $\gamma_c, \gamma_k, \gamma_h$, which is zero in the case of $u_t : u_t = u, \forall t$.
Then evaluating (7.122) at steady-state, we get

$$\tilde{k}_{t+1}^{\alpha-1}\tilde{h}_{t+1}^{1-\alpha+\psi} = \frac{\frac{(1+n)(1+\gamma_c)^{\sigma}}{\beta} - (1-\delta_k)}{A\alpha u^{1-\alpha}}, \tag{7.126}$$

which implies that $\tilde{k}_{t+1}^{\alpha-1}\tilde{h}_{t+1}^{1-\alpha+\psi}$ is constant in steady-state which, in turn, implies $1+\gamma_k = (1+\gamma_h)^{\frac{1-\alpha+\psi}{1-\alpha}}$. Notice that in this model with externalities, the long-term growth rates of the stocks of physical and human capital are different.
Since $\tilde{k}_{t+1}^{\alpha-1}\tilde{h}_{t+1}^{1-\alpha+\psi}$ is constant in steady-state, then $\tilde{y}_t/\tilde{k}_t$ must be constant in steady-state, since $\tilde{y}_t/\tilde{k}_t = A\tilde{k}_t^{\alpha-1}\tilde{h}_t^{1-\alpha+\psi}u^{1-\alpha}$. Therefore, $1+\gamma_k = 1+\gamma_y$.
Evaluating (7.124) at steady-state, we get

$$\frac{\tilde{c}_t}{\tilde{k}_t} = \tilde{y}_t/\tilde{k}_t + (1-\delta_k) - (1+n)(1+\gamma_k). \tag{7.127}$$

Therefore, since the right-hand side at (7.127) is constant, the $\frac{\tilde{c}_t}{\tilde{k}_t}$ ratio will also be constant in steady-state, i.e., $1+\gamma_c = 1+\gamma_k = 1+\gamma_y = 1+\gamma$.
Evaluating (7.123) at steady-state, we have

$$(1+\gamma_c)^{\sigma}(1+\gamma_k)^{-\alpha}(1+\gamma_h)^{\alpha-\psi} = \beta(B+1-\delta_h). \tag{7.128}$$

Using (7.128) together with the relationships $1 + \gamma_k = (1+\gamma_h)^{\frac{1-\alpha+\psi}{1-\alpha}}$ and $1 + \gamma_c$ $= 1 + \gamma_k = 1 + \gamma$, we can obtain the steady-state rate of economic growth

$$1 + \gamma = [\beta(B+1-\delta_h)]^{\frac{1-\alpha+\psi}{\sigma(1-\alpha+\psi)-\psi}}. \tag{7.129}$$

Evaluating (7.125) in steady-state, we can obtain u:

$$u = 1 - \frac{\gamma_h - \delta_h}{B}, \tag{7.130}$$

where $\gamma_h = (1+\gamma)^{\frac{1-\alpha}{1-\alpha+\psi}} - 1$, and $1 + \gamma$ is given by (7.129).

Let us now denote: $z = \left(\tilde{k}_{t+1}/\tilde{h}_{t+1}^{\frac{1-\alpha+\psi}{1-\alpha}}\right)_{ss}$, and $x = \left(\frac{\tilde{c}_t}{\tilde{k}_t}\right)_{ss}$. From (7.126) and (7.127), we get steady state values for z and x:

$$z = \left[\frac{A\alpha u^{1-\alpha}}{\frac{(1+n)(1+\gamma)^{\sigma}}{\beta} - (1-\delta_k)}\right]^{\frac{1}{1-\alpha}}, \tag{7.131}$$

$$x = Az^{\alpha-1}u^{1-\alpha} + (1-\delta_k) - (1+n)(1+\gamma). \tag{7.132}$$

Simulation

We first write optimality conditions as functions of z, x and u, where $z_t = \tilde{k}_{t+1}/\tilde{h}_{t+1}^{\frac{1-\alpha+\psi}{1-\alpha}}$, and $x_t = \frac{\tilde{c}_t}{\tilde{k}_t}$. Using (7.122)–(7.125) we have

$$x_t^{-\sigma}z_t^{-\sigma}(1+n)\left[B(1-u_t)\eta_t + 1 - \delta_h\right]^{\frac{\sigma(1-\alpha+\psi)}{1-\alpha}}$$
$$= \beta E_t\left[x_{t+1}^{-\sigma}z_{t+1}^{-\sigma}\left(A\alpha z_{t+1}^{\alpha-1}u_{t+1}^{1-\alpha}\theta_{t+1} + 1 - \delta_k\right)\right], \tag{7.133}$$

$$x_t^{-\sigma}z_t^{\alpha-\sigma}\frac{\theta_t}{\eta_t}u_t^{-\alpha}\left[B(1-u_t)\eta_t + 1 - \delta_h\right]^{\frac{\sigma(1-\alpha+\psi)-\psi}{1-\alpha}}$$
$$= \beta E_t\left[x_{t+1}^{-\sigma}z_{t+1}^{\alpha-\sigma}u_{t+1}^{-\alpha}\frac{\theta_{t+1}}{\eta_{t+1}}\left(B\eta_{t+1} + 1 - \delta_h\right)\right], \tag{7.134}$$

$$(1+n)\frac{z_{t+1}}{z_t}\left[B(1-u_t)\eta_t + 1 - \delta_h\right]^{\frac{(1-\alpha+\psi)}{1-\alpha}}$$
$$= Az_t^{\alpha-1}u_t^{1-\alpha}\theta_t + (1-\delta_k) - x_t. \tag{7.135}$$

Log-linearizing around the uniquely defined steady-state of this system, we get

$$\Gamma_0\begin{pmatrix}\hat{z}_{t+1} \\ E_t\hat{x}_{t+1} \\ E_t\hat{u}_{t+1}\end{pmatrix} = \Gamma_1\begin{pmatrix}\hat{z}_t \\ \hat{x}_t \\ \hat{u}_t\end{pmatrix} + \Gamma_2\begin{pmatrix}\hat{\theta}_t \\ \hat{\eta}_t\end{pmatrix},$$

with

$$\Gamma_0(1,1) = (1 - \alpha + \sigma)\frac{(1+n)(1+\gamma)^\sigma}{\beta} - (1-\alpha)(1-\delta_k),$$

$$\Gamma_0(1,2) = \frac{\sigma(1+n)(1+\gamma)^\sigma}{\beta},$$

$$\Gamma_0(1,3) = -(1-\alpha)\left[\frac{(1+n)(1+\gamma)^\sigma}{\beta} - (1-\delta_k)\right],$$

$$\Gamma_0(2,1) = -(\alpha - \sigma)\frac{(1+\gamma)^\sigma}{\beta(1+\gamma_h)^{\frac{\psi}{1-\alpha}}},$$

$$\Gamma_0(2,2) = \frac{\sigma(1+\gamma)^\sigma}{\beta(1+\gamma_h)^{\frac{\psi}{1-\alpha}}}, \quad \Gamma_0(2,3) = \alpha\frac{(1+\gamma)^\sigma}{\beta(1+\gamma_h)^{\frac{\psi}{1-\alpha}}},$$

$$\Gamma_0(3,1) = z(1+n)(1+\gamma), \quad \Gamma_0(3,2) = \Gamma_0(3,3) = 0,$$

$$\Gamma_1(1,1) = \Gamma_1(1,2) = \frac{\sigma(1+n)(1+\gamma)^\sigma}{\beta},$$

$$\Gamma_1(1,3) = \frac{\tilde{\sigma}(1+n)(1+\gamma)^\sigma Bu}{\beta(1+\gamma_h)},$$

$$\Gamma_1(2,1) = -(\alpha - \sigma)\frac{(1+\gamma)^\sigma}{\beta(1+\gamma_h)^{\frac{\psi}{1-\alpha}}}, \quad \Gamma_1(2,2) = \frac{\sigma(1+\gamma)^\sigma}{\beta(1+\gamma_h)^{\frac{\psi}{1-\alpha}}},$$

$$\Gamma_1(2,3) = \alpha\frac{(1+\gamma)^\sigma}{\beta(1+\gamma_h)^{\frac{\psi}{1-\alpha}}} + (\tilde{\sigma} - \frac{\psi}{1-\alpha})\frac{(1+\gamma)^{\sigma-1}Bu}{\beta},$$

$$\Gamma_1(3,1) = \left(\frac{(1+n)(1+\gamma)^\sigma}{\beta} - x\right)z, \quad \Gamma_1(3,2) = -zx,$$

$$\Gamma_1(3,3) = zBu(1+n)\frac{1+\gamma}{1+\gamma_h}\frac{1-\alpha+\psi}{1-\alpha} + A(1-\alpha)z^\alpha u^{1-\alpha},$$

$$\Gamma_2(1,1) = \left[\frac{(1+n)(1+\gamma)^\sigma}{\beta} - (1-\delta_k)\right]\phi_1,$$

$$\Gamma_2(1,2) = -\frac{\tilde{\sigma}(1+n)(1+\gamma)^\sigma}{\beta(1+\gamma_h)}B(1-u),$$

$$\Gamma_2(2,1) = -\frac{(1+\gamma)^\sigma}{\beta(1+\gamma_h)^{\frac{\psi}{1-\alpha}}}(1-\phi_1),$$

$$\Gamma_2(2,2) = \frac{(1+\gamma)^\sigma}{\beta(1+\gamma_h)^{\frac{\psi}{1-\alpha}}} - (\tilde{\sigma} - \frac{\psi}{1-\alpha})\frac{(1+\gamma)^{\sigma-1}B(1-u)}{\beta} - (1-\delta_h)\phi_2,$$

$$\Gamma_2(3,1) = Az^\alpha u^{1-\alpha},$$

$$\Gamma_2(3,2) = -z(1+n)B(1-u)\frac{1+\gamma}{1+\gamma_h}\frac{1-\alpha+\psi}{1-\alpha},$$

where $\tilde{\sigma} \equiv \frac{\sigma(1-\alpha+\psi)}{1-\alpha}$, $\hat{\chi}_t = \ln(\chi_t/\chi)$, $\chi = x, z, u$.

Notice that if $\psi = 0$, i.e., in the absence of the externality, the previous system collapses to the one we had in previous sections. This system can be written

$$\begin{pmatrix} \hat{z}_{t+1} \\ E_t\hat{x}_{t+1} \\ E_t\hat{u}_{t+1} \end{pmatrix} = \Gamma_3 \begin{pmatrix} \hat{z}_t \\ \hat{x}_t \\ \hat{u}_t \end{pmatrix} + \Gamma_4 \begin{pmatrix} \hat{\theta}_t \\ \hat{\eta}_t \end{pmatrix}$$

with

$$\Gamma_3 = \Gamma_0^{-1}\Gamma_1, \quad \Gamma_4 = \Gamma_0^{-1}\Gamma_2.$$

Benhabib and Perli [9] and Xie [98] show that indeterminacy of equilibria arises in this economy for high values of ψ and low values of σ. Matrix Γ_3 then has two stable and one unstable eigenvalue. Without loss of generality, let us assume that $|\lambda_1|, |\lambda_2| < 1$ and $|\lambda_3| > 1$, and we have the decomposition of Γ_3:

$$\Gamma_3 = M\Lambda M^{-1} \text{ with } \Lambda = \begin{pmatrix} \lambda_1 & 0 & 0 \\ 0 & \lambda_2 & 0 \\ 0 & 0 & \lambda_3 \end{pmatrix}, \quad M = \begin{pmatrix} M_{11} & M_{12} & M_{13} \\ M_{21} & M_{22} & M_{23} \\ M_{31} & M_{32} & M_{33} \end{pmatrix}.$$

We denote the inverse of M by

$$M^{-1} = \begin{pmatrix} m_{11} & m_{12} & m_{13} \\ m_{21} & m_{22} & m_{23} \\ m_{31} & m_{32} & m_{33} \end{pmatrix},$$

where $M_{\bullet j}, j = 1,2,3$ denote the right eigenvectors associated to $\lambda_j, j = 1,2,3$, while $m_{j\bullet}$ are the left eigenvectors associated to $\lambda_j, j = 1,2,3$.

With this decomposition, we have

$$M^{-1} \begin{pmatrix} \hat{z}_{t+1} \\ E_t\hat{x}_{t+1} \\ E_t\hat{u}_{t+1} \end{pmatrix} = \Lambda M^{-1} \begin{pmatrix} \hat{z}_t \\ \hat{x}_t \\ \hat{u}_t \end{pmatrix} + \underbrace{M^{-1}\Gamma_4}_{Q} \begin{pmatrix} \hat{\theta}_t \\ \hat{\eta}_t \end{pmatrix},$$

where $Q = M^{-1}\Gamma_4$ is a 3×2 block matrix. This system can be written in more detail, as

$$m_{11}\hat{z}_{t+1} + m_{12}E_t\hat{x}_{t+1} + m_{13}E_t\hat{u}_{t+1}$$
$$= \lambda_1 (m_{11}\hat{z}_t + m_{12}\hat{x}_t + m_{13}\hat{u}_t) + Q_{11}\hat{\theta}_t + Q_{12}\hat{\eta}_t, \tag{7.136}$$

$$m_{21}\hat{z}_{t+1} + m_{22}E_t\hat{x}_{t+1} + m_{23}E_t\hat{u}_{t+1}$$
$$= \lambda_2 (m_{21}\hat{z}_t + m_{22}\hat{x}_t + m_{23}\hat{u}_t) + Q_{21}\hat{\theta}_t + Q_{22}\hat{\eta}_t, \tag{7.137}$$

$$m_{31}\hat{z}_{t+1} + m_{32}E_t\hat{x}_{t+1} + m_{33}E_t\hat{u}_{t+1}$$
$$= \lambda_3 (m_{31}\hat{z}_t + m_{32}\hat{x}_t + m_{33}\hat{u}_t) + Q_{31}\hat{\theta}_t + Q_{32}\hat{\eta}_t. \tag{7.138}$$

To simplify notation, we define vector $f_t^0 = \begin{pmatrix} m_{11}\hat{z}_t + m_{12}\hat{x}_t + m_{13}\hat{u}_t \\ m_{21}\hat{z}_t + m_{22}\hat{x}_t + m_{23}\hat{u}_t \\ m_{31}\hat{z}_t + m_{32}\hat{x}_t + m_{33}\hat{u}_t \end{pmatrix}$ which

allows us to write the system above as

$$E_t f_{1,t+1}^0 = \lambda_1 f_{1,t}^0 + Q_{11}\hat{\theta}_t + Q_{12}\hat{\eta}_t,$$
$$E_t f_{2,t+1}^0 = \lambda_2 f_{2,t}^0 + Q_{21}\hat{\theta}_t + Q_{22}\hat{\eta}_t,$$
$$E_t f_{3,t+1}^0 = \lambda_3 f_{3,t}^0 + Q_{31}\hat{\theta}_t + Q_{32}\hat{\eta}_t.$$

If we apply the law of iterated expectations to solve forwards the last equation in this system, as we have done in previous chapters, we get

$$f_{3,t}^0 = \frac{Q_{31}}{\phi_1 - \lambda_3}\hat{\theta}_t + \frac{Q_{32}}{\phi_2 - \lambda_3}\hat{\eta}_t,$$

which leads to

$$\hat{x}_t = \frac{1}{m_{32}}\left[\frac{Q_{31}}{\phi_1 - \lambda_3}\hat{\theta}_t + \frac{Q_{32}}{\phi_2 - \lambda_3}\hat{\eta}_t - m_{31}\hat{z}_t - m_{33}\hat{u}_t\right], \tag{7.139}$$

providing us with the *control equations* or *stability conditions*.

If we plug (7.139) into (7.136)–(7.137) and use the result: $E_t\hat{u}_{t+1} = \hat{u}_{t+1} - a_{t+1}$ we have

$$\begin{bmatrix} \hat{z}_{t+1} \\ \hat{u}_{t+1} \end{bmatrix} = S_1^{-1}\Lambda_{(1)}S_1\begin{bmatrix} \hat{z}_t \\ \hat{u}_t \end{bmatrix} + S_1^{-1}S_2\begin{bmatrix} \hat{\theta}_t \\ \hat{\eta}_t \\ a_{t+1} \end{bmatrix}, \tag{7.140}$$

where

$$S_1 = \begin{bmatrix} m_{11} - \frac{m_{12}m_{31}}{m_{32}} & m_{13} - \frac{m_{12}m_{33}}{m_{32}} \\ m_{21} - \frac{m_{22}m_{31}}{m_{32}} & m_{23} - \frac{m_{22}m_{33}}{m_{32}} \end{bmatrix},$$

$$\Lambda_{(1)} = \begin{bmatrix} \lambda_1 & 0 \\ 0 & \lambda_2 \end{bmatrix},$$

$$S_2(1,1) = Q_{11} + (\lambda_1 - \phi_1)\frac{m_{12}}{m_{32}}\frac{Q_{31}}{\phi_1 - \lambda_3},$$

$$S_2(1,2) = Q_{12} + (\lambda_1 - \phi_2)\frac{m_{12}}{m_{32}}\frac{Q_{32}}{\phi_2 - \lambda_3},$$

$$S_2(1,3) = m_{13} - \frac{m_{12}m_{33}}{m_{32}},$$

$$S_2(2,1) = Q_{21} + (\lambda_2 - \phi_1)\frac{m_{22}}{m_{32}}\frac{Q_{31}}{\phi_1 - \lambda_3},$$

$$S_2(2,2) = Q_{22} + (\lambda_2 - \phi_2)\frac{m_{22}}{m_{32}}\frac{Q_{32}}{\phi_2 - \lambda_3},$$

$$S_2(2,3) = m_{23} - \frac{m_{22}m_{33}}{m_{32}}.$$

Computing the Numerical Solution

1. Draw sample realizations for the $\{\varepsilon_{1t}, \varepsilon_{2t}\}_{t=1}^{T}$ innovations from two independent Normal distributions with standard deviations σ_1 and σ_2, respectively. Use initial conditions $(\hat{\theta}_0, \hat{\eta}_0)$ in the laws of motion $\ln\theta_t = \phi_1 \ln\theta_{t-1} + \varepsilon_{1t}$, $\eta_t = \phi_2 \ln\eta_{t-1} + \varepsilon_{2t}$ to compute a time series realization $\{\hat{\theta}_t, \hat{\eta}_t\}_{t=0}^{T}$.

2. Given initial conditions $\tilde{k}_0, \tilde{h}_0, u_0$ we compute $z_0 = \tilde{k}_0/\tilde{h}_0^{\frac{1-\alpha+\psi}{1-\alpha}}$, $\hat{z}_0 = \ln(z_0/z)$ and $\hat{u}_0 = \ln(u_0/u)$.

3. Draw a sample realization for $\{a_{t+1}\}_{t=0}^{T}$ from a Normal distribution with standard deviation σ_a, and chosen correlations[35] $\rho_{a,\varepsilon_1} = corr(a_t, \varepsilon_{1t})$, $\rho_{a,\varepsilon_2} = corr(a_t, \varepsilon_{2t})$.

4. Given $\hat{z}_0$, $\hat{u}_0$ and $\{\hat{\theta}_t, \hat{\eta}_t, a_{t+1}\}_{t=0}^{T}$, we use (7.140) to obtain a realization $\{\hat{z}_t, \hat{u}_t\}_{t=0}^{T}$. We also compute $z_t = ze^{\hat{z}_t}$, $u_t = ue^{\hat{u}_t}$, $t = 0,1,2,\ldots,T$.

5. Given $\{\hat{z}_t, \hat{u}_t\}_{t=0}^{T}$, $\{\hat{\theta}_t, \hat{\eta}_t\}_{t=0}^{T}$, we use (7.139) to compute $\{\hat{x}_t\}_{t=0}^{T}$, and $x_t = xe^{\hat{x}_t}$, $t = 0,1,2,\ldots,T$.

6. We compute $\gamma_{\tilde{h},t} = B(1 - u_t)\eta_t + (1 - \delta_h)$, $t = 0,1,2,\ldots,T$.

7. The definition of growth rate $\frac{\tilde{h}_{t+1}}{\tilde{h}_t} = 1 + \gamma_{\tilde{h},t}$ implies $\frac{h_{t+1}(1+\gamma_h)^{t+1}}{h_t(1+\gamma_h)^t} = 1 + \gamma_{h,t}$, which can be used to obtain a time series realization for h_{t+1} from $h_{t+1} = \frac{1+\gamma_{\tilde{h},t}}{1+\gamma_h}h_t$. Hence, given $h_0 = \tilde{h}_0$, we can obtain the time path for human capital net of the deterministic trend, $\{h_{t+1}\}_{t=0}^{T}$.

8. We compute the time series for physical capital $\{k_t\}_{t=0}^{T}$ using the fact that $\frac{\tilde{k}_t}{\tilde{h}_t} = z_t$ implies $\frac{k_t}{h_t} = z_t$, so that: $k_t = h_t z_t$.

9. We compute the time series for consumption $\{c_t\}_{t=0}^{T}$ from $c_t = x_t k_t$, $t = 0,1,2,\ldots$.

10. Given the time series $\{k_t\}_{t=0}^{T}$, $\{h_t\}_{t=0}^{T}$, $\{c_t\}_{t=0}^{T}$, we can obtain $\{\tilde{k}_t, \tilde{h}_t, \tilde{c}_t\}_{t=0}^{T}$ from $\tilde{k}_t = \gamma^t k_t$, $\tilde{h}_t = \gamma_h^t h_t$, $\tilde{c}_t = \gamma^t c_t$.

11. Given time series for $\{\tilde{k}_t, \tilde{c}_t\}_{t=0}^{T}$, we compute $\gamma_{\tilde{k},t}$, $\gamma_{\tilde{c},t}$: $1 + \gamma_{\tilde{k},t} = \frac{\tilde{k}_{t+1}}{\tilde{k}_t}$, $1 + \gamma_{\tilde{c},t} = \frac{\tilde{c}_{t+1}}{\tilde{c}_t}$.

The reader should be able to adapt to this model the second algorithm we specified in the solution of the model without externalities.

---

[35] Specify a process, $a_t = \alpha_1\varepsilon_{1t} + \alpha_2\varepsilon_{2t} + \xi_t$, with $\xi \sim N(0, \sigma_\xi^2)$, $Cov(\xi_t, \varepsilon_{1t}) = Cov(\xi_t, \varepsilon_{1t}) = 0$. From $Cov(a_t, \varepsilon_{1t}) = \alpha_1\sigma_{\varepsilon 1}^2$, $Cov(a_t, \varepsilon_{1t}) = \alpha_1\sigma_{\varepsilon 1}^2$, $Var(a_t) = \alpha_1^2\sigma_{\varepsilon 1}^2 + \alpha_2^2\sigma_{\varepsilon 2}^2 + \sigma_\xi^2$, we can use given values for ρ_{a,ε_1}, ρ_{a,ε_2}, $Var(a_t)$ to choose the values of α_1, α_2, σ_ξ^2.

7.5.7 Numerical Exercise: The Correlation Between Productivity and Hours Worked in the Human Capital Accumulation Model

As an application of the solution methods described above, we use the endogenous growth model with capital accumulation to analyze its implications regarding the linear correlation coefficient between productivity and hours worked, a relevant statistic in labor market analysis whose value in actual data cannot be easily replicated by exogenous growth models. Exogenous growth models display implausibly high correlations, because a productivity shock produces changes in the demand for labor with no change in the supply of labor. Hence, incorporating shocks on labor supply is a way to reduce the productivity-hours worked correlation. In two sector models of human capital accumulation, a productivity shock in the sector producing new human capital creates incentives to substitute human capital for output in order to make the productivity in both sectors equal to each other. The substitution of study hours for working hours produces changes in labor supply, and the relationship between productivity and hours worked gets lower.

The Matlab program *lucas_sim1.m* simulates the human capital accumulation model using the first approach described above, while *lucas_sim2.m* uses the second approach. Both programs compute a single realization of the solution to the simplified version of the model economy considered in Sect. 7.5.5, with no taxes and without externalities, with human capital being produced without the use physical capital, and without leisure in the utility function. In terms of the parameters in the previous sections: $p = 1, \upsilon = 0, \tau^c = \tau^w = \tau^r = 0$. Extending the programs to more general setups is left out as an exercise.

The *lucas_sim1.m* program solves an economy with an externality in the production of the final good through the presence of the average stock of human capital as an input in that technology, using the first approach discussed in the previous section. Any positive value of the ψ-parameter corresponds to the presence of that externality, while using a value of $\psi = 0$ in the program eliminates that externality. This program can also be used to generate a numerical solution to this type of economy in cases when there is indeterminacy of equilibria, as discussed in the next section. An alternative benchmark parameterization is provided in the program for that case. This program contains an additional block of instructions that computes the matrices for the log-linear approximation numerically, as it is done in the *simul_diffus.m* program described in Sect. 7.3.4. In the program, the reader is asked to check that the matrices obtained from this method and from the analytical derivatives which are also included, are exactly the same.

The *Human capital.xls* Excel spreadsheet performs the same exercise as the *lucas_sim1.m* program file but without the externality produced by the possible presence of the average stock of human capital in the production of the final good.

The *lucas_sim2.m* program computes a single realization of the numerical solution to the economy without externalities in the production of the final good, using the second approach discussed in the previous section. The trajectories followed by per-capita, detrended physical and human capital, as well as for consumption and output exhibit strong persistency, as a consequence of the presence of a unit root in them, as we explained when describing the structure of the *AK* model.

Both programs can also be used to compute impulse responses to a productivity shock in either sector by following the instructions laid out in the programs. Following a productivity shock in the final good sector, we see a decrease in detrended human capital, together with an increase in physical capital. The time devoted to production of the final good goes up, while decreasing the time devoted to education. Detrended output and consumption go up for a number of periods, gradually reverting to their initial levels. Detrended human capital ends up above its level before the shock. This is the *normal case*, in the terminology of Caballe and Santos [13].

After a productivity shock in the educational sector, the detrended stock of human capital goes up, while physical capital comes down initially. However, the detrended stock of physical capital eventually ends up above its level prior to the productivity shock. Time devoted to the production of the final good decreases, while that devoted to education increases. Both revert relatively quickly to their initial levels. Detrended output and consumption decrease, but they gradually recover the levels they had before the shock.

The *Mlucas_sim.m* program computes multiple realizations of the endogenous growth model with human capital accumulation. We again use the simplified version of the model described in Sect. 7.5.5. As explained in the program, a *corr*12 parameter allows for introducing some correlation between the innovations in the productivity processes in the two sectors. The default value is zero. The user may include or not externalities in the production of the final good, which can be chosen by setting in the program the value $\psi = 0$ when the externality is undesired. The program can also be used for the case of indeterminacy of equilibria, and two alternative benchmark parameterizations leading to either situation are again provided. The multiple realizations are used to present average values of a wide variety of statistics, together with their standard deviations across the set of simulations.

As explained in previous sections, the model is solved in logs of c_t, k_t, h_t, y_t and gross output q_t, but the detrended series in levels are obtained afterwards. As discussed above, detrended per-capita variables still contain a unit root so that, at a difference of the programs computing a single realization, we have applied the Hoddrick–Prescott filter to the series. After that, the program first computes the mean and standard deviation for each realization for these variables, as well as for u_t and for the growth rates. But, as usual in these simulation exercises, we have as many observations for each of these statistics as realizations we have obtained for the numerical solution, which could be used to approximate their probability distribution. As an approximation, the Matlab program computes the average and standard deviation of each statistic across the set of simulations. The first panel refers to the mean of the main per-capita variables, which should be very close to their steady-state levels. The second panel refers to their volatility, and the third panel shows their coefficient of variation, again in the form of average values and standard deviations across the set of simulations.

The final panel displays the linear correlation coefficients between pairs of variables. In the case of unit root variables, we use the filtered variables obtained by application of the Hoddrick–Prescott filter, when computing these correlation coefficients. As mentioned above, it is particularly interesting to pay attention to the low level of the linear correlation between productivity and hours worked. Finally, a graph presents some of the time series obtained in the last realization computed by the program.

7.6 Exercises

Exercise 1. Compute the analytical derivatives in the log-linear approximation to the technological diffusion model and describe how to use them to compute the numerical solution to the model as it is done in other models.

Exercise 2. Program the algorithm for the solution of the Schumpeterian growth model in an Excel spreadsheet as well as in a Matlab program.

Exercise 3. Compute the log-linear approximation to the equilibrium conditions for the Schumpeterian growth model. Describe the implementation of Blanchard–Kahn approach to solve this model using the approximation, and program the algorithm in Matlab and Excel.

Exercise 4. Program in an Excel file the computation of a single realization of the solution to the endogenous growth model with human capital accumulation, using the Second simulation approach described in Sect. 7.5.5.

Exercise 5. Write a Matlab program to compute a single realization to the to the endogenous growth model with human capital accumulation in the case when physical capital is used in the production of human capital, using the First simulation approach described in Sect. 7.5.5.

Exercise 6. Repeat Exercise 5 using the Second simulation approach of Sect. 7.5.5.

Exercise 7. Repeat Exercise 5 additionally including leisure in the utility function. Repeat the exercise using the Second simulation approach and compare the statistical properties of the main time series.

Chapter 8
Growth in Monetary Economies: Steady-State Analysis of Monetary Policy

8.1 Introduction

In spite of the importance of money in actual economies, explaining why consumers have a demand for an asset which is dominated in return by other assets in the economy has been a traditional challenge for economic theory. Among many other monetary theorists, Keynes [49] proposed a detailed list of reasons why a typical consumer might demand money, including a precautionary reason or its role as facilitating transactions, which capture the role of money as a store of value and as a medium of exchange, respectively.

To explain the role of money as a medium of exchange when it is a dominated asset requires some specific aspects to be incorporated into the model. Specifically, some structure is needed that may force money to be used in transactions. One way of doing that was proposed by Clower [20] through a cash-in-advance constraint for at least a necessary commodity.[1] In this latter framework, it is necessary to specify the order in which the different markets open and close, since for the cash-in-advance constraint to lead to a non-trivial demand for money function, the markets for money and for commodities cannot be open simultaneously. That way, the agent that needs money to purchase a given commodity will have to get it in the money market in the session that closed previously to the opening of the commodity market. Another possibility is to consider heterogeneous agents who do not coincide with each other in the same market, as in an overlapping generations economy.[2] There, money is held between periods just because each consumer knows that some other agent will need next period the money he/she now holds.

A different alternative is that of Sidrauski [84], who introduced real balances as an argument in the utility function of the representative consumer. In the absence of monetary illusion, it must be real balances, rather than nominal balances,

---

[1] A commodity whose marginal utility at the level of zero consumption is equal to infinity must be purchased with money.

[2] This type of economies is not studied in this textbook. A good textbook for overlapping generations models is: Champ and Freeman [25].

the variable entering as an argument in the utility function. Without money, the consumer would have to search for some other agent who might be willing to exchange physical commodities with her, which could take significant time and effort. Money saves purchasing time that the consumer can enjoy as leisure, which explains its appearance as an argument in the utility function. Money is then a medium of exchange, but the markets for commodities and for money can be opened at the same time, since it is not necessary to impose any constraint on the transactions that are being made.

This chapter starts with a theoretical discussion about a version of Sidrauski [84] model, to characterize optimal growth in a monetary economy.[3] After describing the economy, the representative agent's problem is solved, and the implied steady-state optimality conditions are used to analyze alternative designs for monetary policy. We introduce the concept of optimal steady-state rate of inflation, and characterize conditions under which Friedman's prescription for a zero nominal interest rate can be optimal. The welfare cost of inflation is analyzed, and a numerical exercise is presented to evaluate the welfare implications of alternative monetary policies. Two sections are devoted to modelling: the first one compares the treatment of nominal and real bonds in the economy, while the second one compares the results obtained when real balances either at the beginning of the period or at the end of the period, are entered as an argument in the utility function of the representative consumer. After that, we start considering the interaction between monetary and fiscal policies by examining monetary policy in an economy subject to income and consumption taxes. We use again steady-state optimality conditions to characterize the feasible combinations of monetary and fiscal policies. In a numerical exercise the reader will see the existence of a Laffer curve in this economy. The previous models have considered an inelastic labor supply, so the following section discusses the neutrality of monetary policy in an economy with an endogenous labor supply. Up to this point we have made a steady-state analysis, which was the standard way to proceed before the use of numerical solution methods became widespread. In the last section of this chapter we characterize optimal monetary policy solving what is known as a dynamic Ramsey model, which takes into consideration the short- as well as the long-run effects of a policy intervention. Nevertheless, the implementability constraint that we introduce in that section allows us to perform this analysis without need of characterizing the transitional dynamics of the economy, a question which is discussed in detail in Chap. 9.

8.2 Optimal Growth in a Monetary Economy: The Sidrauski Model

We start our theoretical presentation with Sidrauski [84] model, which can be seen as a monetary version of the Cass–Koopmans economy we studied in Chaps. 3 and 4. We only consider the discrete-time version of the model, that could also

---

[3] A discussion on alternative ways to generate a demand for money in growth models can be seen in Walsh [96].

be formulated in continuous time. We suppose the economy is made up of N_t identical individuals, all with the same preferences, and all having access to the same production technology. Population grows at a rate n, $N_t = (1+n)^t N_0$, N_0 being the initial number of individuals in the economy. There is a single good in the economy, which can either be consumed or saved in the form of productive capital. Investment at time t becomes productive at time $t+1$. As an alternative to investing in physical capital, the consumer can also hold money, or purchase government bonds. There is no uncertainty in the economy: the level of utility that can be achieved through consumption or holding real balances is known with certainty, as it is the level of output that can be produced with a given amount of physical capital and labor. The rate of return on bonds is also known in advance with certainty.

The government does not engage into any production activity, and it does not make any expenditure that could affect the utility of the representative consumer or influence factor productivity. It just takes care of its finances, by printing money, $M_{t+1}^* - M_t^*$, giving transfers T_t away to the private sector, and issuing real bonds, B_{t+1}, which are purchased with one unit of commodity, and entitle their owner to $1 + r_t$ units of commodity at time $t+1$, with r_{t+1} being known to agents when bonds were issued at time t. Transfers to the private sector could be negative, which could then be interpreted as lump-sum taxes. The government budget balances every period, with a budget constraint

$$\frac{M_{t+1}^* - M_t^*}{P_t} + B_{t+1} = (1+r_t) B_t + T_t, \quad \forall t, \qquad (8.1)$$

which in per capita terms becomes

$$\frac{(1+n)M_{t+1} - M_t}{P_t} + (1+n)b_{t+1} = (1+r_t) b_t + \zeta_t, \quad \forall t,$$

where per capita variables are denoted by $b_t = B_t/N_t$, $\zeta_t = T_t/N_t$ and $M_t = M_t^*/N_t$.[4]
If we denote $m_t = \frac{M_t}{P_t}$ and $1 + \pi_{t+1} = \frac{P_{t+1}}{P_t}$, then

$$\frac{(1+n)M_{t+1} - M_t}{P_t} = \frac{(1+n)M_{t+1}}{P_{t+1}} \frac{P_{t+1}}{P_t} - \frac{M_t}{P_t} = (1+n)m_{t+1}(1+\pi_{t+1}) - m_t,$$

so that the government budget constraint can be written in per capita terms

$$(1+n)m_{t+1}(1+\pi_{t+1}) - m_t + (1+n)b_{t+1} - (1+r_t)b_t = \zeta_t.$$

---

[4] This choice of notation is not arbitrary. Associating a lower case letter to T_t would produce an awkward notation, while the proposed use of M_t is needed, because we have another money ratio, M_t/P_t, for which we reserve the m_t-notation.

The aggregate budget constraint of the private sector is[5]

$$C_t + K_{t+1} + \frac{M^*_{t+1} - M^*_t}{P_t} + B_{t+1} \leq F(K_t, N_t) + (1 - \delta) K_t + (1 + r_t) B_t + T_t, \quad (8.2)$$

where, as in previous chapters, the stock of capital accumulated at the end of period t takes the time index $t + 1$, corresponding to the time period when it will become productive.[6] Analogously, money balances and bonds accumulated at the end of period t also take the $t + 1$ time index. All variables in (8.2) are aggregate variables.

Dividing through (8.2) by N_t we get

$$c_t + (1 + n)k_{t+1} + \frac{(1 + n)M_{t+1}}{P_t} + (1 + n)b_{t+1}$$

$$\leq f(k_t) + (1 - \delta)k_t + \frac{M_t}{P_t} + (1 + r_t) b_t + \zeta_t.$$

As in previous chapters, the $f(k_t)$ term can be explained by the assumption of a constant returns to scale technology $F(K_t, N_t)$ which is scaled down by the N_t-factor

$$Y_t = F(K_t, N_t) = N_t F(K_t/N_t, 1) = N_t f(k_t).$$

8.2.1 The Representative Agent's Problem

We assume throughout the chapter zero population growth, $n = 0$. Extending the arguments to an economy with population growth is a simple exercise which does not alter any of the qualitative results we present. The representative agent in this economy takes care of consumption, savings and production, choosing sequences $\{c_t, M_{t+1}, k_{t+1}, b_{t+1}\}_{t=0}^{\infty}$ to solve the problem

$$\max_{\{c_t, M_{t+1}, k_{t+1}, b_{t+1}\}_{t=0}^{\infty}} \sum_{t=0}^{\infty} \beta^t U\left(c_t, \frac{M_t}{P_t}\right),$$

---

[5] The private sector in the economy is made up by households and firms. The budget constraint of the private sector consolidates the exchanges between both types of agents. One part of households' income comes form their financial investments, here represented by a portfolio of government bonds. They also receive income from the firm as a return to physical capital, that they own, as well as from their working time. Consolidating these income flows, we get (8.2). In Chap. 3 we already discussed the concept of representative agent as a way of modelling jointly the whole private sector of the economy, as well as the difference between this representative agent and a benevolent planner.

[6] For simplicity, we will assume along this chapter that there is not technological growth.

for some time discount factor $0 < \beta < 1$, subject to the sequence of budget constraints

$$c_t + k_{t+1} + \frac{M_{t+1}}{P_t} + b_{t+1} \leq f(k_t) + (1-\delta)k_t + \frac{M_t}{P_t} + (1+r_t)b_t + \zeta_t, \quad \forall t,$$

and given k_0, M_0, b_0.

We have assumed that the utility function of the agent depends on the real balances at the beginning of the period t, although we could alternatively have assumed that it depends on the real balances at the end of the period. In Sect. 8.4.2 we develop this alternative formulation of preferences.

We also assume that the utility function has positive marginal utilities, $U_1, U_2 > 0$, where $U_1 = \frac{\partial U}{\partial c}, U_2 = \frac{\partial U}{\partial (M/P)}$, the Hessian of U being a negative definite, symmetric matrix. Furthermore, $U_1\left(0, \frac{M}{P}\right) = U_2(c,0) = \infty$, $U_1\left(\infty, \frac{M}{P}\right) = U_2(c,\infty) = 0$.

The Lagrangian for this problem is

$$L = \sum_{t=0}^{\infty} \beta^t \left[U\left(c_t, \frac{M_t}{P_t}\right) - \lambda_t \left(c_t + k_{t+1} + \frac{M_{t+1}}{P_t} + b_{t+1}\right. \right.$$
$$\left. \left. - f(k_t) - (1-\delta)k_t - \frac{M_t}{P_t} - (1+r_t)b_t - \zeta_t\right)\right],$$

with optimality conditions[7]

$$\frac{\partial L}{\partial c_t} = U_1(c_t, \frac{M_t}{P_t}) - \lambda_t \leq 0; \quad \text{and} \quad c_t \left[U_1\left(c_t, \frac{M_t}{P_t}\right) - \lambda_t \right] = 0, \quad \forall t \qquad (8.3)$$

$$\frac{\partial L}{\partial k_{t+1}} = -\lambda_t + \beta\lambda_{t+1}\left(f'(k_{t+1}) + (1-\delta)\right) \leq 0 \quad \text{and}$$
$$k_{t+1}\left[-\lambda_t + \beta\lambda_{t+1}\left(f'(k_{t+1}) + (1-\delta)\right)\right] = 0, \quad \forall t \qquad (8.4)$$

$$\frac{\partial L}{\partial M_{t+1}} = \beta U_2\left(c_{t+1}, \frac{M_{t+1}}{P_{t+1}}\right)\frac{1}{P_{t+1}} - \lambda_t \frac{1}{P_t} + \lambda_{t+1}\beta\frac{1}{P_{t+1}} \leq 0; \quad \text{and}$$
$$M_{t+1}\left[\beta U_2\left(c_{t+1}, \frac{M_{t+1}}{P_{t+1}}\right)\frac{1}{P_{t+1}} - \lambda_t \frac{1}{P_t} + \lambda_{t+1}\beta\frac{1}{P_{t+1}}\right] = 0, \quad \forall t \qquad (8.5)$$

$$\frac{\partial L}{\partial \lambda_t} = \beta^t \left[c_t + k_{t+1} + \frac{M_{t+1}}{P_t} + b_{t+1} - f(k_t)\right.$$
$$\left. - (1-\delta)k_t - \frac{M_t}{P_t} - (1+r_t)b_t - \zeta_t\right] = 0, \quad \forall t \qquad (8.6)$$

---

[7] We take into explicit account in this case the fact that we are dealing with nonnegativity restrictions in all choice variables, which leads to the type of optimality conditions below. That allows us to discuss the possibility of zero demands for money or bonds, for instance. However, the reader must be aware that the same type of discussion could have been made in all other optimization problems in the book.

$$\frac{\partial L}{\partial b_{t+1}} = -\lambda_t + \beta \left(1 + r_{t+1}\right) \lambda_{t+1} \leq 0, \quad \text{and}$$

$$b_{t+1} \left[\beta \left(1 + r_{t+1}\right) \lambda_{t+1} - \lambda_t\right] = 0, \quad \forall t \tag{8.7}$$

and transversality conditions

$$\lim_{T \to \infty} \beta^T \lambda_T \frac{M_{T+1}}{P_T} = 0, \tag{8.8}$$

$$\lim_{T \to \infty} \beta^T \lambda_T k_{T+1} = 0, \tag{8.9}$$

$$\lim_{T \to \infty} \beta^T \lambda_T b_{T+1} = 0, \tag{8.10}$$

which are obtained as usual, taking derivatives in the finite horizon version of the Lagrangian with respect to state variables, capital stock, bonds and real balances, indexed by $T + 1$, the last period in the maximization problem with horizon T. In these conditions, the powered discount factor tends to zero, while state variables accumulate over time. If the marginal utility of consumption stays stable, transversality conditions (8.8)–(8.10) imply that state variables accumulate at a rate lower than β. They also imply that, along the optimal paths, consumption cannot go to zero *too quickly*.

From (8.3), assuming an interior solution,[8] i.e., $c_t > 0 \; \forall t$, we get

$$\lambda_t = U_1 \left(c_t, \frac{M_t}{P_t}\right),$$

so that, using (8.4) and (8.7),

$$b_{t+1} > 0 \Rightarrow \frac{\lambda_t}{\beta \lambda_{t+1}} = \frac{U_1 \left(c_t, \frac{M_t}{P_t}\right)}{\beta U_1 \left(c_{t+1}, \frac{M_{t+1}}{P_{t+1}}\right)} = 1 + r_{t+1},$$

$$k_{t+1} > 0 \Rightarrow \frac{U_1 \left(c_t, \frac{M_t}{P_t}\right)}{\beta U_1 \left(c_{t+1}, \frac{M_{t+1}}{P_{t+1}}\right)} = f'(k_{t+1}) + (1 - \delta),$$

which have the standard interpretation. The first condition is the equality between the intertemporal marginal rate of substitution of consumption and the real rate of interest. To interpret the second condition, notice that saving one additional unit of the consumption commodity at time t will produce a utility loss of $U_1 \left(c_t, \frac{M_t}{P_t}\right)$. Saving that unit in the form of physical capital, we would obtain at time $t + 1$, $f'(k_{t+1}) + (1 - \delta)$ additional units of the commodity, which, multiplied by $U_1 \left(c_{t+1}, \frac{M_{t+1}}{P_{t+1}}\right)$ approximates the utility gain at time $t + 1$, which we need to multiply by β to compare it with time t utility. Along the optimum path, the representative consumer must be indifferent with respect to this trade-off between current and future utility.

---

[8] There will always be an interior solution because of our assumption that the marginal utility of consumption becomes infinite for zero consumption.

From the previous conditions, we have the equality at each point in time between the marginal rate of substitution of consumption over time, the rate of return on physical capital, and the return on real financial assets, r_{t+1}, which is known at time t

$$MRS_{t,t+1} \equiv \frac{U_1\left(c_t, \frac{M_t}{P_t}\right)}{\beta U_1\left(c_{t+1}, \frac{M_{t+1}}{P_{t+1}}\right)} = f'(k_{t+1}) + (1-\delta) = 1 + r_{t+1}, \qquad (8.11)$$

a standard equilibrium condition in non-monetary growth models as well, as we have seen in previous chapters.

From (8.3) and (8.5), we get

$$M_{t+1} > 0 \Rightarrow \beta \frac{U_2\left(c_{t+1}, \frac{M_{t+1}}{P_{t+1}}\right)}{P_{t+1}} = \frac{U_1\left(c_t, \frac{M_t}{P_t}\right)}{P_t} - \beta \frac{U_1\left(c_{t+1}, \frac{M_{t+1}}{P_{t+1}}\right)}{P_{t+1}}, \qquad (8.12)$$

and dividing through by $\beta U_1\left(c_{t+1}, \frac{M_{t+1}}{P_{t+1}}\right) \frac{1}{P_{t+1}}$:

$$\frac{U_2\left(c_{t+1}, \frac{M_{t+1}}{P_{t+1}}\right)}{U_1\left(c_{t+1}, \frac{M_{t+1}}{P_{t+1}}\right)} = \frac{U_1\left(c_t, \frac{M_t}{P_t}\right)}{\beta U_1\left(c_{t+1}, \frac{M_{t+1}}{P_{t+1}}\right)} \frac{P_{t+1}}{P_t} - 1. \qquad (8.13)$$

Since we just consider the existence of real bonds in the economy, we must think of the nominal interest rate, i_{t+1}, as being an artificial construct defined in gross terms as the product of the real rate of interest and the rate of inflation: $1 + i_{t+1} = (1 + r_{t+1})(1 + \pi_{t+1})$. Equation (8.13), using (8.11) leads to

$$\frac{U_2\left(c_{t+1}, \frac{M_{t+1}}{P_{t+1}}\right)}{U_1\left(c_{t+1}, \frac{M_{t+1}}{P_{t+1}}\right)} = (1 + r_{t+1})(1 + \pi_{t+1}) - 1 = (1 + i_{t+1}) - 1 = i_{t+1}. \qquad (8.14)$$

Along the optimal trajectory, the marginal rate of substitution between real balances and consumption must be equal to the nominal interest rate. We are more used to think in terms of defining the (gross) real rate of interest from that expression. In any event, we show in Sect. 8.4.1 that whenever real and nominal bonds exist together, we have the equality $(1 + r_{t+1})\frac{P_{t+1}}{P_t} = 1 + i_{t+1}$ every period as an equilibrium condition.

Equation (8.14) can be safely interpreted as a demand function for money, emerging from utility maximizing conditions, with no ad-hoc assumptions imposed. If we assume that the utility function is separable in its two arguments, as in $U\left(c_t, \frac{M_t}{P_t}\right) = \ln c_t + \theta \ln \frac{M_t}{P_t}$, $\theta > 0$, (8.14) becomes

$$\frac{\theta c_{t+1}}{M_{t+1}/P_{t+1}} = i_{t+1} \Leftrightarrow \frac{M_{t+1}}{P_{t+1}} = \frac{\theta c_{t+1}}{i_{t+1}}.$$

So, an increase in nominal interest rates will tend to come together with a decrease in the demand for real balances at the beginning of period t. Similar effects would be produced by an increase in either the real interest rate or the inflation rate. An increase in consumption expenditures will also tend to come together with an increase in the demand for real balances, capturing a transaction demand aspect of the demand for real balances. Of course, this is easy to see just if these *ceteris paribus*-type of exercises were justified, unlike what happens in a general equilibrium setup like the one we are analyzing.

Condition (8.14) can also be interpreted in the usual fashion: If we decided to hold one additional monetary unit at time t, we would have a utility gain at time $t+1$ of $\frac{1}{P_{t+1}} U_2 \left(c_{t+1}, \frac{M_{t+1}}{P_{t+1}} \right)$. In addition to the utility of just holding money, we could use it to buy $\frac{1}{P_{t+1}}$ of the consumption commodity at time $t+1$, with a utility of $\frac{1}{P_{t+1}} U_1 \left(c_{t+1}, \frac{M_{t+1}}{P_{t+1}} \right)$. To hold that additional unit of money at time t, we have to give up on some of the government bonds we would have purchased at time t. The unit of money invested in bonds would have allowed us to buy $1/P_t$ bonds, which would have entitled us to $(1 + r_{t+1})/P_t$ units of commodity at time $t+1$. Consumption of those units would have produced a utility of $(1 + r_{t+1}) \frac{1}{P_t} U_1 \left(c_{t+1}, \frac{M_{t+1}}{P_{t+1}} \right)$. The result of these two alternative strategies must be the same in equilibrium, which is what the previous condition is saying.

Note that the assumptions we have made on the utility function $U(c_t, \frac{M_t}{P_t})$ guarantee that $c_t, \frac{M_t}{P_t} > 0 \ \forall t$. Furthermore, the government and the representative agent constraints, taken together as we have done in previous models, lead to a global constraint of resources

$$c_t + k_{t+1} = f(k_t) + (1 - \delta) k_t,$$

every period.

8.2.2 Steady-State in the Monetary Growth Economy

Steady-state is a sustainable trajectory along which all per-capita variables in the economy grow at a constant rate, which could be zero for some variables. The same argument used in the chapter on the Solow–Swan model can now be used to show that, in the economy we are considering, with decreasing returns for the cumulative inputs, the production technology and the time evolution of the production factors cannot sustain positive growth forever. Hence, the only possible steady state is one in which per-capita variables stay constant.[9]

---

[9] With population growth and the same production technology, economic growth for economy wide aggregates at the same rate than population growth could be sustained, as it is the case in the nonmonetary economies considered in previous chapters. Adding technical growth, which is not done in this chapter, would lead to a growth rate equal to the growth rate of population plus the rate of technical growth.

So, it seems sensible to assume that the government follows fiscal and monetary policies with an inflation target as well as a target for the level of lump-sum transfers to consumers,

$$\zeta_t = \zeta_{ss}, \quad \forall t$$
$$\pi_t = \pi_{ss}, \quad \forall t$$

and we look for steady-state values of per capita variables, c_{ss}, k_{ss}, y_{ss}, r_{ss}, b_{ss}, all of them as functions of ζ_{ss}, π_{ss} and the set of structural parameters, satisfying all optimality conditions and budget constraints. Structural parameters are β, δ, and those entering the production and utility functions. We show below that, under this policy design, real balances are constant in steady state, and we denote their steady-state value by m_{ss}.

Taking these constant values to the system of conditions above, we get

$$f'(k_{ss}) + (1 - \delta) = 1/\beta,$$

which provides us with the steady-state level of physical capital. To compute it, we need to make some specific assumption on the functional form of the production function. Redefining the discount factor[10] as $\beta = \frac{1}{1+\rho}$, we have

$$f'(k_{ss}) = \rho + \delta, \tag{8.15}$$

an equality we already obtained in the Cass–Koopmans model,[11] which provides a uniquely defined value for k_{ss}. So, the presence of money and bonds in the economy does not perturb the capital accumulation process in the long-run.

From the global constraint of resources in the economy, we get

$$c_{ss} + k_{ss} = f(k_{ss}) + (1 - \delta)k_{ss},$$

which gives us the steady-state level of consumption

$$c_{ss} = f(k_{ss}) - \delta k_{ss},$$

a function of structural parameters like the depreciation rate of capital and the output elasticity of physical capital. Notice that under a quite general definition of preferences, steady-state consumption does not depend on preferences or on the presence of money in the economy. However, as it is the case with the steady-state stock of capital, it changes with the rate of time discount.

---

[10] This is a pure change of notation, and both expressions are used in economic modelling. The relationship can be approximated (through a Taylor series expansion) by: $\beta = 1 - \rho$, so that, for instance, $\beta = 0.95$ corresponds with $\rho = 0.05$.

[11] With the only difference that in the Cass–Koopmans chapter, the discount factor was denoted by θ, rather than ρ.

From the production function we get the constant steady-state level of output

$$y_{ss} = f(k_{ss}).$$

From (8.11) we get, with constant consumption and real balances

$$\frac{1}{\beta} = 1 + r_{ss},$$

which gives us the steady-state real interest rate as a function of the discount rate, a relationship that we already obtained in the non-monetary Cass–Koopmans model.

From (8.14) we get

$$\frac{U_2(c_{ss}, m_{ss})}{U_1(c_{ss}, m_{ss})} = (1 + r_{ss})(1 + \pi_{ss}) - 1 = \frac{1 + \pi_{ss}}{\beta} - 1, \tag{8.16}$$

which, for a specific functional form for the utility function, would provide us with a function $m_{ss} = m(\pi_{ss})$ for steady-state real balances since, as shown above, steady-state consumption depends just on structural parameters. Hence, at least for this type of monetary policy, real balances are constant in steady-state. Nominal money balances will not be constant, however, growing at a rate π_{ss}, the rate of growth of prices.

The steady-state nominal interest rate can be obtained from

$$i_{ss} = (1 + r_{ss})(1 + \pi_{ss}) - 1 = \frac{1 + \pi_{ss}}{\beta} - 1, \tag{8.17}$$

while the stock of bonds is obtained from the government budget constraint in steady-state form[12]

$$[m_{ss}(1 + \pi_{ss}) - m_{ss}] + [b_{ss} - (1 + r_{ss})b_{ss}] = \zeta_{ss}$$

$$\Rightarrow b_{ss} = \frac{\pi_{ss}m_{ss} - \zeta_{ss}}{r_{ss}} = \frac{\pi_{ss}m(\pi_{ss}) - \zeta_{ss}}{r_{ss}}. \tag{8.18}$$

The reader must be aware of the fact that although we can compute the steady state level of government debt, this level could well be unreachable, since unless some stability mechanism is incorporated into the design of fiscal policy, the stock of debt outstanding will either explode or fall to zero.

The *inflation tax* is defined as the product of real balances by the inflation rate, $\pi_{ss}m_{ss}$. It is the loss in the purchasing power of the stock of real balances maintained by the representative agent due to inflation. The steady-state relationship: $\pi_{ss}m_{ss} = r_{ss}b_{ss} + \zeta_{ss}$, reflects the fact that we must allow for a positive inflationary tax in order to finance the transfers of commodity from the government to the private sector, as

---

[12] In an economy where the government cannot use debt financing, we would have: $m_{ss}\pi_{ss} = \zeta_{ss}$, and the size of the lump-sum transfer would no longer be an independent policy target, being determined by the choice target for the rate of inflation.

well as interest payments on outstanding debt. Transfers to the private sector could be negative, then being interpreted as lump-sum taxes, which would alleviate or even eliminate the need to raise an inflationary tax. In fact, we will later see in numerical exercises that the transfer to the private sector will end up being negative, becoming then a lump-sum tax, in those cases when a negative rate of inflation produces a negative inflation tax.

The previous equations characterize the optimal steady-state, which under conditions similar to those in Chaps. 2 and 3 will be unique. That steady state is, however, conditional on the design of monetary and fiscal policy. It is therefore a second-best optimum. The so-called Ramsey problem attempts to characterize the choice of policy that leads to the optimum allocation of resources among all the second-best solutions. As an example, we could consider a Cobb–Douglas technology, $y = Ak^{\alpha}$, with preferences: $U(c, M/P) = \ln(c) + \theta \ln(M/P)$. We would then have: $m_{ss} = \frac{\beta \theta c_{ss}}{1 + \pi_{ss} - \beta}$, with steady state expressions:

$$k_{ss} = \left(\frac{A\alpha}{\frac{1}{\beta} - 1 + \delta} \right)^{1-\alpha} ; \quad c_{ss} = Ak_{ss}^{\alpha} - \delta k_{ss}; \quad b_{ss} = \frac{\pi_{ss} \frac{\beta \theta c_{ss}}{1 + \pi_{ss} - \beta} - \zeta_{ss}}{\frac{1}{\beta} - 1},$$

with the last equation describing the choices available to the policy maker in terms of choosing a possible mix of fiscal and monetary policies.

8.2.3 Golden Rule

As in previous chapters, we could again define the Golden Rule, as the particular steady-state characterized by allowing for the maximum level of consumption. We could collapse the budget constraints for the government and for private agents into the same global constraint of resources as in a non-monetary economy, having in steady-state

$$c_{ss} + k_{ss} - f(k_{ss}) - (1 - \delta)k_{ss} = 0,$$

so that

$$\frac{\partial c_{ss}}{\partial k_{ss}} = -1 + f'(k_{ss}) + (1 - \delta) = 0 \Rightarrow f'(k_{GR}) = \delta, \tag{8.19}$$

$$\frac{\partial^2 c_{ss}}{\partial k_{ss}^2} = f''(k_{ss}) < 0, \tag{8.20}$$

the same characterization we already obtained for a non-monetary economy under zero population growth and absence of technical growth. Comparing the characterization of the optimal level of the stock of capital (8.15), with (8.19), we see that

$$k_{ss} < k_{GR},$$

the Golden Rule implying too much capital accumulation, relative to the optimal steady state. Excessive capital accumulation is achieved by too little consumption earlier on, and it is due to giving too much weight to future utility (or to future generations, depending on the interpretation we give to the growth model).

8.3 Steady-State Policy Analysis

In the previous section, we have characterized steady-state above under a policy design that sets targets for the rate of inflation and the level of lump-sum transfers to consumers. It should be noticed that there could be feasible steady-state trajectories with π_t and ζ_t not being constant. In that case, real balances would not be necessarily constant in steady state, since they would to satisfy

$$\frac{U_2\left(c_{ss}, m_t\right)}{U_1\left(c_{ss}, m_t\right)} = \frac{1+\pi_t}{\beta} - 1,$$

while π_t and ζ_t would have to be linked every period by

$$\pi_t m(\pi_t) - \zeta_t = b_{ss} r_{ss}.$$

The analysis in the previous section also suggests three relevant characteristics of this monetary economy:

1. Under zero population growth, real balances are constant in steady-state, the rate of inflation is equal to the rate of growth of money balances, x_{ss}, so we have the result that the rate of growth of money does not have any real effect, showing the long-run *superneutrality* of money. When the analysis of monetary policy is restricted to the steady-state, as it is the case in this chapter, changes in money growth have the same effects than changes in the inflation rate target. So, from the point of view of policy design, choosing a target for the rate of inflation, π_{ss}, amounts to choosing the rate of growth of money, x_{ss}. With positive population growth n, we would have

$$1 + \pi_{ss} = \frac{1+x_{ss}}{1+n}.$$

The rate of inflation would then not be equal to the rate of money growth, but we would still have the one-to-one correspondence between both variables, used as policy targets.

2. Furthermore, the qualitative effects of a change in the nominal interest rate are also the same as those of a change in the inflation target. The reason is that

$$1 + i_{ss} = \frac{1+\pi_{ss}}{\beta}.$$

In actual economies, monetary authorities control the time evolution of either a monetary aggregate or a short-term nominal rate of interest. In the general equilibrium monetary economy described in this chapter, we just consider a single interest rate, although a simultaneous consideration of a long- and a short-rate would allow us to discuss the roles of the slope of the term structure of interest rates in the transmission of monetary policy effects.

3. Monetary policy *is neutral* in this economy in the long-run, since c_{ss}, k_{ss}, y_{ss} are determined with independence of the value of π_{ss} or m_{ss}.

Additional remarks on alternative policy choices are:

- Let us assume that the monetary authority can control the size of the steady-state stock of real balances, m_{ss}. The steady-state rate of inflation and the stock of government bonds would be obtained from

$$\pi_{ss} = \beta \left(1 + \frac{U_2\left(c_{ss}, m_{ss}\right)}{U_1\left(c_{ss}, m_{ss}\right)} \right) - 1 = \pi\left(m_{ss}\right),$$

$$b_{ss} = \frac{\pi\left(m_{ss}\right) m_{ss} - \zeta_{ss}}{r_{ss}},$$

steady-state values for all other variables being obtained as under the policy rule we examined above, when the government was choosing π_{ss}.

- As reflected in these exercises on alternative policy designs, the government cannot decide on monetary and fiscal policy targets, m_{ss}, π_{ss}, b_{ss}, ζ_{ss} independently, since (8.18) imposes a constraint among their values, showing the interrelationship between fiscal and monetary policy.

- The previous discussion shows that the government needs to design policy by deciding on a value of either π_{ss} or m_{ss} and additionally, a value of either b_{ss} or ζ_{ss}. Otherwise, the long-run trajectory of the economy would remain indeterminate. For instance, the government cannot simultaneously choose π_{ss} and m_{ss}, unless the chosen targets are constrained by (8.16). But even then, we would have a single equation to solve for b_{ss} and ζ_{ss}, which would render the equilibrium indeterminate.

- Still an alternative policy would consist of choosing π_{ss} and b_{ss}, leaving m_{ss} and ζ_{ss} free. We would then have

$$\zeta_{ss} = \pi_{ss} m\left(\pi_{ss}\right) - r_{ss} b_{ss},$$

all other variables being obtained as above.

- The policies defined by a choice of either m_{ss} and b_{ss}, m_{ss} and ζ_{ss}, or π_{ss} and ζ_{ss}, could be analyzed similarly to those above.

8.3.1 Optimal Steady-State Rate of Inflation

When the monetary aggregate considered is the monetary base, nominal return on money is zero, while real return is negative, because of inflation. Against that, nominal return and, often, real return on assets other than money, is positive. Therefore, money is an asset which is dominated in return.

We know as Friedman's rule the policy prescription: '*Optimal monetary policy is defined as making of money an asset which is not dominated in return*'.[13] The nominal return of assets other than money can be seen as the opportunity cost of holding money. The social marginal cost of producing money is negligible. There is therefore an inefficiency produced by the gap between the social and the private marginal costs of money, and the inefficiency goes away only when the opportunity cost of holding money is zero, i.e., when the nominal return on any other assets like government and private bonds is equal to zero, $i_{ss} = 0$. This is why Friedman's rule is usually linked to a zero nominal rate of interest.

We now analyze whether Friedman's rule holds in the general equilibrium monetary economy we have introduced, under two different monetary policy designs, depending on whether it is the rate of inflation or the size of real balances that are used as a control variable.

The general approach to characterizing optimal monetary policy in a general equilibrium model consists on solving a Ramsey's problem, a leader-follower game between the government and the representative agent. The government is the leader, choosing the monetary policy design it prefers, and the representative agent makes his decisions knowing the design chosen for monetary policy implementation. The equations characterizing the solution to the problem of the representative agent are the reaction functions of the 'follower' to change in the leader's decisions. When the government makes the choice of a monetary policy, it knows the reaction functions of the representative agent. In steady-state, such functions are the steady-state expressions for consumption, real balances, output, and so on. It is usually assumed that the government's objective when makes a policy choice is to maximize the welfare of private agents, which seems consistent with a government searching to be reelected.

Therefore, in steady-state, the government chooses the monetary policy design that maximizes the steady-state level of utility of the representative agent subject to its budget constraint. That is, the chosen policy needs to be feasible from the point of view of the government. On the other hand, it is not necessary to take explicitly into account the steady-state version of the government's budget constraint provided there is a non-distortionary policy instrument to make it to hold, as it will usually be the case.

First, we consider the rate of inflation as the control variable for monetary policy, while fiscal policy may have either a target for the real value of the stock of public debt or the size of lump-sum transfers, as described in previous sections, and define the *optimal* rate of inflation as the one maximizing steady-state utility

$$\pi_{opt} = \arg\max\{W(\pi)\} = \arg\max\{U(c_{ss}(\pi), m_{ss}(\pi))\}.$$

The optimal inflation rate will have to satisfy

$$\frac{\partial W(\pi)}{\partial \pi} = U_1(c_{ss}, m_{ss})\frac{\partial c_{ss}}{\partial \pi} + U_2(c_{ss}, m_{ss})\frac{\partial m_{ss}}{\partial \pi} = 0. \qquad (8.21)$$

---

[13] This policy prescription was first issued in Friedman [34].

But we have just seen how the steady-state level of consumption does not depend on the inflation rate, so that: $\frac{\partial c_{ss}}{\partial \pi} = 0$. On the contrary, real balances depend on inflation $\left(\frac{\partial m_{ss}}{\partial \pi} \neq 0 \right)$, so that (8.21) implies that the optimal rate of inflation would be the one satisfying: $U_2(c_{ss}, m_{ss}) = \frac{\partial U(c_{ss}, m_{ss}(\pi))}{\partial m} = 0$. Hence, real balances under the optimal monetary policy will only be finite if preferences have a satiation point in the level of real balances.[14]

Since (8.16) is a condition characterizing steady-state, we must have

$$\frac{U_2(c_{ss}, m_{ss}(\pi))}{U_1(c_{ss}, m_{ss}(\pi))} = i_{ss} = \frac{1 + \pi}{\beta} - 1,$$

and, since $U_2(c_{ss}, m_{ss}) = 0$ under the optimal inflation rate, the optimal steady-state rate of inflation is negative and equal to: $\pi^{opt} = \beta - 1$, implying a zero nominal interest rate $i_{ss} = 0$. So, being negative, the optimal rate of inflation produces a positive real return on money, with a zero nominal return rate ($i^{money} = 0$): $r_{ss}^{money} = \frac{1 + i^{money}}{1 + \pi^{opt}} - 1 = \frac{1}{1 + \beta - 1} - 1 = \frac{1}{\beta} - 1 > 0$. Under the optimal rate of inflation, the steady-state real return on money is the same as the real return on any other asset alternative to money. Since real returns on all assets[15] are the same under the optimal rate of inflation, they also offer the same nominal return, and Friedman's rule is valid.

Second, let us assume now that, instead of the rate of inflation as a control variable, the government chooses exogenously m_{ss} and ζ_{ss}.[16] Similarly, we can then define *Optimal monetary policy* as the level of real balances for which

$$m_{opt} = \arg\max\{W(m)\} = \arg\max\{U(c_{ss}(m), m)\}.$$

In this case, the optimality condition is

$$\frac{\partial W(m)}{\partial m} = U_1(c_{ss}, m)\frac{\partial c_{ss}}{\partial m} + U_2(c_{ss}, m) = 0,$$

which is satisfied only if $U_2(c_{ss}, m) = 0$, implying again $i_{ss} = 0$. The reader can easily check that this solution satisfies the second order condition for a maximum.

This approach to characterizing optimal monetary policy is open to two criticisms:

- It is just a steady-state analysis, while it would be important to characterize optimal monetary policy taking into account the dynamics of the economy.
- The result has been obtained under the assumption that the government has available lump-sum taxes, public debt issuance and seigniorage revenues to accommodate any exogenous shock. If, following a change in monetary policy, the

---

[14] Condition (8.21) characterizes a maximum since, under the optimal policy, $\frac{\partial^2 W(\pi)}{\partial \pi^2} = U_{22}(c_{ss}, m_{ss})\left(\frac{\partial m_{ss}}{\partial \pi} \right)^2 < 0$.

[15] Like physical capital, for instance.

[16] Results would be similar if the government would choose the target level for public debt as well as for real balances, with the level of the lump-sum transfer then being endogenously determined.

government could only modify distortionary taxes like an income tax, then a positive rate of inflation might be optimal. In that situation, the utility of the private agent depends negatively on the inflation rate *and* on the level of the tax rate. It would be preferable to use actively the instrument producing lower distortions on the economy while allowing for financing a given government expenditures, which may lead to the optimality of a positive inflation tax.

In Sect. 8.7 we characterize optimal monetary policy under distortionary taxes while taking into account the dynamics of the economy outside steady-state.

8.3.2 The Welfare Cost of Inflation

In the Sidrauski model analyzed above, inflation produces a welfare loss because the level of utility depends positively on the level of real balances, which decreases when inflation raises. Hence, the model should allow us to quantify the welfare cost of inflation. Traditionally, the cost of inflation has been measured as the area below the demand curve for money (Bailey [7]). To quantify the size of the distortion introduced by any instrument of economic policy in general equilibrium models, it is standard to compute the percent change in steady-state consumption needed as a compensation for the consumer to be indifferent between a given policy and the optimal policy. Therefore, the welfare cost of inflation would be the percent change in steady-state consumption needed as a compensation for the consumer to be indifferent between a given rate of inflation and optimal inflation. Let us denote by v the percent increase in steady-state consumption, c_{ss} the level of steady-state consumption under any inflation rate,[17] and $m_{ss}(\pi)$ the steady-state level of real balances as a function of the rate of inflation (so that $m_{ss}(opt)$ is the level of real balances when $\pi = \pi^{opt}$). We must have

$$U((1+v)c_{ss}, m_{ss}(\pi)) = U(c_{ss}, m_{ss}(opt)).$$

For instance, if the utility function is (Lucas [61])

$$U(c_t, m_t) = \frac{1}{1-\sigma} \left\{ \left[c_t \varphi \left(\frac{m_t}{c_t} \right) \right]^{1-\sigma} - 1 \right\}, \quad \text{where}$$

$$\varphi \left(\frac{m_t}{c_t} \right) = \frac{1}{1 + \varpi \left(\frac{m_t}{c_t} \right)^{-1}}, \quad \text{with } \varpi > 0.$$

The reader can easily check that the *partial equilibrium* demand for money mentioned in Sect. 8.2.1 is, in this case, $m_t = \varpi^{1/2} c_t (i_t)^{-1/2}$. Besides, using the approach described in the previous section, we have that the optimal rate of inflation

---

[17] Since we have already seen that, in our model, inflation does not have any effect on consumption.

is $\pi^{opt} = \beta - 1$ and, under that optimal inflation rate, real balances become infinite in steady-state. The steady-state level of utility under the optimal rate of inflation is: $U(c_{ss}, \infty) = \frac{1}{1-\sigma}\left(c_{ss}^{1-\sigma} - 1\right)$.

The cost of inflation, measured in terms of the welfare lost, is

$$\frac{1}{1-\sigma}\left[\left(\frac{(1+v)c_{ss}}{1+\varpi\left(\frac{m_{ss}(\pi)}{(1+v)c_{ss}}\right)^{-1}}\right)^{1-\sigma} - 1\right] = \frac{1}{1-\sigma}\left(c_{ss}^{1-\sigma} - 1\right),$$

from where we have

$$v = \frac{\varpi c_{ss}/m_{ss}(\pi)}{1 - \varpi c_{ss}/m_{ss}(\pi)} = \frac{\sqrt{\varpi i_{ss}}}{1 - \sqrt{\varpi i_{ss}}}.$$

Let us consider the utility function: $U(c_t, m_t) = \ln c_t + \theta \ln m_t$, $\theta > 0$. This is a standard assumption on preferences for which the optimal rate of inflation is again $\pi^{opt} = \beta - 1$ and, under such optimal inflation rate, real balances are infinite in steady-state. Nevertheless, at a difference from the previous case, under the optimal rate of inflation, the level of utility is now unbounded, and the proposed approach to measuring the cost of inflation is not appropriate, since that cost becomes infinite. In such situations, it is standard to use a zero rate of inflation as a reference with respect to which to compute the welfare cost of positive rates of inflation (Guillman [39]). The numerical cost of inflation thereby obtained will clearly be an undervaluation of the true cost of inflation. To illustrate this fact, if we compute the cost of inflation for negative inflation rates, but greater than $\beta - 1$, we would obtain negative values, reflecting the fact that a zero rate of inflation distorts agents' decisions relative to negative rates of inflation, reducing their level of welfare.

Under the utility function we just mentioned, if we denote by $m_{ss}(0)$ the steady-state level of real balances when the rate of inflation is zero, we have: $v = \left(\frac{m_{ss}(0)}{m_{ss}(\pi)}\right)^{\theta} - 1 = \left(\frac{1-\beta+\pi}{1-\beta}\right)^{\theta} - 1$. The welfare cost of inflation, as a percentage of output is

$$\frac{vc_{ss}}{y_{ss}} = \left[\left(\frac{1-\beta+\pi}{1-\beta}\right)^{\theta} - 1\right]\left(1 - \delta\frac{k_{ss}}{f(k_{ss})}\right),$$

where k_{ss} denotes the steady-state stock of capital which, as we have shown in the previous section, is independent of the rate of inflation.

In Sect. 8.6.1 we show that when the assumption of an inelastic labor supply is dropped and leisure, private consumption and real balances enter as nonseparable arguments in the utility function, the rate of inflation is not neutral. In that case, characterizing the cost of inflation analytically is somewhat more complex, but still feasible.

For a specific utility function, the numerical values obtained for the cost of inflation, for each possible rate of inflation, will depend on the numerical values assumed for the structural parameters. It is therefore convenient to choose such values so that the model is able to explain a number of empirical observations. This is known as *calibration* of the model. For instance, it is standard to assume a production function displaying constant returns to scale which, in per capita terms, would be: $f(k_t) = k_t^\alpha$, which satisfies: $\frac{f'(k_t)k_t}{f(k_t)} = \alpha$. We already known from Chap. 3 that, in equilibrium, $f'(k_t)$ is the real return on capital before depreciation. Therefore, α is the share of capital rents in production, while its complement, $1-\alpha$, is the share of labour rents in total income. Averaging over a wide set of actual economies, it can be thought that the labor rents share is of the order of 0.65 or 0.70. So, $\alpha \in [0.30; 0.35]$.

Another empirical regularity of actual economies is the fact that the annual real rate of interest oscillates around 2%. This is the level achieved in our model when the discount parameter is approximately equal to 0.98. On the other hand, the depreciation rate of physical capital is hard to estimate, since we would need of time series for the stock of capital, which do not exist except in a few countries. There is, however, a broad agreement in assuming an annual depreciation rate for capital around 10%.

A particularly important parameter in the computation of the welfare cost of inflation is θ, which determines the relative preference for consumption versus holding real balances. The value of this parameter is chosen so that the model can explain the velocity of circulation of money in the actual economy to which the theoretical results are to be applied. The expression for the velocity of money in steady-state is

$$Velocity = \frac{y_{ss}}{m_{ss}} = \frac{(1 + \pi - \beta)k_{ss}^\alpha}{\beta \theta c_{ss}}.$$

This is of course a general consideration that has already been taken into account when choosing parameter values for the simulation exercises in previous chapters. What we want to emphasize now is the fact that the numerical implication from the model relative to a given question will be a function of the parameterization chosen, so that this must sound convincing to the reader.

A numerical exercise on evaluating the welfare cost of inflation for different utility functions is performed in the next section.

8.4 Two Modelling Issues: Nominal Bonds and the Timing of Real Balances

We devote this section to discussing two topics on modelling. The first one compares optimality conditions emerging from economies with nominal or with real debt. We obtain the well known relationship between the nominal return on bonds, the rate of return on real bonds and the rate of inflation as an equilibrium condition. The second analysis deals with the comparison between including the real value of nominal balances at the beginning or at the end of the period, alternatively, as an argument in the utility function.

8.4.1 Nominal Bonds: The Relationship Between Real and Nominal Interest Rates

As in previous sections, the government gives consumers a lump-sum transfer of T_t units of the consumption commodity, which is financed by liquidity injections, $M_{t+1}^* - M_t^*$, as well as by issuing some public debt. In particular, we assume in this section that the government issues nominal bonds V_t^*. The consumer will receive from the government $1 + i_t$ money units at time $t + 1$ for each money unit invested in government bonds at time t. The government budget constraint becomes[18]

$$\frac{M_{t+1}^* - M_t^*}{P_t} + \frac{V_{t+1}^* - (1 + i_t) V_t^*}{P_t} = T_t,$$

which, in terms of per capita money, nominal bonds and transfers are: $M_t = \frac{M_t^*}{N_t}$, $V_t = \frac{V_t^*}{N_t}$, and $\zeta_t = \frac{T_t}{N_t}$ can be written

$$\frac{(1+n)M_{t+1} - M_t}{P_t} + \frac{(1+n)V_{t+1} - (1 + i_t) V_t}{P_t} = \zeta_t,$$

or

$$\frac{(1+n)M_{t+1} - M_t}{P_t} + (1+n)\bar{b}_{t+1} - \frac{1 + i_t}{1 + \pi_t}\bar{b}_t = \zeta_t, \qquad (8.22)$$

where $\bar{b}_{t+1} = \frac{V_{t+1}}{P_t}$ now denotes the value of the stock of nominal bonds per capita at the end of period t in units of the consumption commodity.[19]

We started the chapter by considering real bonds, which are purchased with one unit of the consumption commodity, and entitle their owner to $1 + r_t$ units of the consumption commodity at time $t + 1$. These financing instruments led to a government budget constraint, in per capita terms

$$\frac{(1+n)M_{t+1} - M_t}{P_t} + (1+n)b_{t+1} - (1 + r_t)b_t = \zeta_t,$$

which, by comparison with the government budget constraint for the case of real debt (8.22) illustrates the relationship between nominal and real interest rates: $\frac{1 + i_t}{1 + \pi_t} = 1 + r_t$.

---

[18] We leave to the reader to show that the relationship between nominal and real interest rates that is obtained in this section still holds if, in addition to transfers to consumers, the government needs to finance the purchase of the single good in the economy, whatever its use may happen to be.

[19] Notice that

$$\frac{(1+n)V_{t+1} - (1 + i_t) V_t}{P_t} = (1+n)\frac{V_{t+1}}{P_t} - (1 + i_t)\frac{V_t}{P_{t-1}}\frac{P_{t-1}}{P_t} = \bar{b}_{t+1} - \frac{1 + i_t}{1 + \pi_t}\bar{b}_t.$$

This relationship can also be seen in the representative agent budget constraint, which takes the form

$$c_t + (1+n)k_{t+1} - (1-\delta)k_t + \frac{(1+n)M_{t+1} - M_t}{P_t} + (1+n)b_{t+1} - (1+r_t)b_t$$

$$\leq f(k_t) + \zeta_t,$$

when we exchange consumption for capital at the rate of one-to-one, as it is the case with the trade-off between consumption and real bonds, and it becomes

$$c_t + (1+n)k_{t+1} - (1-\delta)k_t + \frac{(1+n)M_{t+1} - M_t}{P_t} + (1+n)\bar{b}_{t+1} - \frac{1+i_t}{1+\pi_t}\bar{b}_t$$

$$\leq f(k_t) + \zeta_t, \tag{8.23}$$

for the case of nominal bonds. It is clear that both constraints coincide if

$$(1+n)b_{t+1} - (1+r_t)b_t = (1+n)\bar{b}_{t+1} - \frac{1+i_t}{1+\pi_t}\bar{b}_t,$$

which would also make both representations of the government budget constraint coincide.

But these comparisons only show that the same resource allocation set can be attained under real debt than under nominal debt if and only if the relationship between nominal and real interest rates is as shown above. Let us now look at optimality conditions when both types of debt are present in the economy.

The optimality condition corresponding to a positive demand for nominal bonds would be

$$(1+n)\frac{\lambda_t}{P_t} = \beta(1+i_{t+1})\frac{\lambda_{t+1}}{P_{t+1}},$$

leading to

$$\frac{1+n}{\beta} \frac{U_1\left(c_t, \frac{M_t}{P_t}\right)}{U_1\left(c_{t+1}, \frac{M_{t+1}}{P_{t+1}}\right)} = (1+i_{t+1})\frac{P_t}{P_{t+1}} = \frac{1+i_{t+1}}{1+\pi_{t+1}},$$

while the optimality condition for a positive demand of real debt is (8.11), allowing for population growth:

$$\frac{1+n}{\beta} \frac{U_1\left(c_t, \frac{M_t}{P_t}\right)}{U_1\left(c_{t+1}, \frac{M_{t+1}}{P_{t+1}}\right)} = 1 + r_{t+1}.$$

So, if both types of debt exist in the economy, they will both be in positive demand if and only if they offer the same return, that is, if

$$1 + r_{t+1} = \frac{1+i_{t+1}}{1+\pi_{t+1}},$$

an equilibrium condition relating nominal to real interest rates.

8.4.2 Real Balances in the Utility Function: At the Beginning or at the End of the Period?

In the models analyzed in previous sections, the representative agent demands some money in spite of the fact that money is an asset which is dominated in return by productive capital and bonds. It does so because real balances enter as an argument in his utility function, together with consumption.[20] In particular, money balances increase utility by facilitating transactions, then the presence of real balances in the utility function is quite clear. There are, however, different possibilities depending on the opening and closing schedules for the real and financial markets.

Variables in this section are all in per capita terms, and we assume zero population growth. If liquidity injections take place while commodity markets are still opened, then the relevant variable is the real value $\frac{M_{t+1}}{P_t}$ of balances at the end of period t, $M_{t+1} = M_t + \Delta M_t$. If, on the other hand, commodity markets close before financial markets open and liquidity injections take place, then it is real balances available at the beginning of period t, $\frac{M_t}{P_t}$ that are relevant. We assume that the government makes a *monetary* transfer ζ_t to each consumer at the beginning of each period.[21] If commodity markets open only after financial markets have already closed and transfers have been made, then public debt V_{t+1} will be bought with money, and interest on bonds will also paid with cash $(1+i_t)V_t$, and the argument in the utility function should be: $\frac{M_t + \zeta_t - V_{t+1} + (1+i_t)V_t}{P_t}$, since that is the purchasing ability of the nominal balances available to consumers when commodity markets open.

In the case when monetary injections are received while commodity markets are still open, the utility function is of the form: $U\left(c_t, \frac{M_{t+1}}{P_t}\right)$, and the budget constraint is (8.23). After eliminating Lagrange multipliers, optimality conditions, are

$$U_1\left(c_t, \frac{M_{t+1}}{P_t}\right) = \beta U_1\left(c_{t+1}, \frac{M_{t+2}}{P_{t+1}}\right)(1+i_{t+1})/(1+\pi_{t+1}), \qquad (8.24)$$

$$U_1\left(c_t, \frac{M_{t+1}}{P_t}\right) = \beta U_1\left(c_{t+1}, \frac{M_{t+2}}{P_{t+1}}\right)\left(f'(k_{t+1})+1-\delta\right), \qquad (8.25)$$

$$\left[U_1\left(c_t, \frac{M_{t+1}}{P_t}\right) - U_2\left(c_t, \frac{M_{t+1}}{P_t}\right)\right]\frac{1}{P_t} = \beta U_1\left(c_{t+1}, \frac{M_{t+2}}{P_{t+1}}\right)\frac{1}{P_{t+1}}. \qquad (8.26)$$

---

[20] Unless agents had money illusion, it is real, and not nominal money balances, which must appear as an argument in preferences.

[21] We comment below on the changes to be introduced when ζ_t is a transfer of some units of the consumption commodity.

Dividing (8.26) by $U_1\left(c_t, \frac{M_{t+1}}{P_t}\right)\frac{1}{P_t}$ we get

$$\frac{U_2(c_t, \frac{M_{t+1}}{P_t})}{U_1\left(c_t, \frac{M_{t+1}}{P_t}\right)} = 1 - \frac{\beta U_1\left(c_{t+1}, \frac{M_{t+2}}{P_{t+1}}\right)}{U_1\left(c_t, \frac{M_{t+1}}{P_t}\right)}\frac{P_t}{P_{t+1}}$$

$$= \frac{i_{t+1}}{1 + i_{t+1}},$$

where we have used (8.24), the fact that $\pi_{t+1} = \frac{P_{t+1}}{P_t} - 1$.

Alternatively, if commodity markets open only after monetary transfers and financial trades have already taken place, the utility function is of the form $U\left(c_t, \frac{D_t}{P_t}\right)$ with $D_t = M_t + \zeta_t - V_{t+1} + (1 + i_t)V_t$, and the budget constraint for the representative consumer is

$$c_t + [k_{t+1} - (1 - \delta)k_t] + \frac{M_{t+1}}{P_t} \le f(k_t) + \frac{D_t}{P_t},$$

with first order conditions[22]:

$$\left[U_1\left(c_t, \frac{D_t}{P_t}\right) + U_2\left(c_t, \frac{D_t}{P_t}\right)\right]$$

$$= \beta\left[U_1\left(c_{t+1}, \frac{D_{t+1}}{P_{t+1}}\right) + U_2\left(c_{t+1}, \frac{D_{t+1}}{P_{t+1}}\right)\right]\frac{1 + i_{t+1}}{1 + \pi_{t+1}}, \qquad (8.27)$$

$$U_1\left(c_t, \frac{D_t}{P_t}\right) = \beta U_1\left(c_{t+1}, \frac{D_{t+1}}{P_{t+1}}\right)[f'(k_{t+1}) + 1 - \delta], \qquad (8.28)$$

$$\frac{U_2\left(c_t, \frac{D_t}{P_t}\right)}{U_1\left(c_t, \frac{D_t}{P_t}\right)} = i_{t+1}. \qquad (8.29)$$

In a more complex setup, Carlstrom and Fuerst [17] consider these two utility function specifications in a model with no production, where the monetary authority chooses the nominal rate of interest as a function of expected inflation, with the

---

[22] Still an alternative formulation could consider ζ_t as transfers of the consumption commodity. Then D_t would be defined by $D_t = M_t - V_{t+1} + (1 + i_t)V_t$, and the budget constraint for the representative consumer would be

$$c_t + [k_{t+1} - (1 - \delta)k_t] + \frac{M_{t+1}}{P_t} \le f(k_t) + \frac{D_t}{P_t} + \zeta_t,$$

and optimality conditions can be obtained without any difficulty.

implication that the specification chosen for the utility function is key to obtain indeterminacy in real variables.[23]

Qualitative results associated to either of these formulations are the same when the analysis is made in steady-state, although steady-state levels may differ. Furthermore, results may be different when analyzed along the transition between steady-states. As an example, we leave as an exercise for the reader to show that, once we introduce uncertainty into the economy,[24] a transitory and unexpected increase in the money supply lasting a single period, when the economy is outside steady-state, does not have real effects under the utility function: $U\left(c_t, \frac{M_{t+1}}{P_t}\right) = \frac{\left(c_t \left(\frac{M_{t+1}}{P_t}\right)^\theta\right)^{1-\sigma}}{1-\sigma}$

while under the utility function $U\left(c_t, \frac{M_t}{P_t}\right) = \frac{\left(c_t \left(\frac{M_t}{P_t}\right)^\theta\right)^{1-\sigma}}{1-\sigma}$, consumption and the stock of capital change at the time of the monetary shock. The intuitive explanation is that in the first case, the price level increases in the same proportion than the money supply, so that the relevant measure of real balances, $\frac{M_{t+1}}{P_t}$, remains unaltered. In the second case, the relevant real balances are $\frac{M_t}{P_t}$, so that the increase in the price level as a consequence of the monetary shock produces a fall in real balances, increasing the marginal utility of consumption and affecting the accumulation of physical capital. In the next section, we present a numerical exercise evaluating the implications of some policy choices under alternative specifications of preferences, depending on whether it is beginning or end of period real balances that enter as an argument in the utility function.

The specification chosen for the arguments in the utility function may affect the computation of steady-state, because the latter needs to be characterized in terms of the variables that are really relevant for private agents. When the real value of money balances at the end of the period enters as an argument in the utility function, then the steady state value of $\bar{m}_{t+1} = \frac{M_{t+1}}{P_t}$, and not that of $m_t = \frac{M_t}{P_t}$ is relevant for consumer's decisions. Both relate to each other by

$$\bar{m}_{t+1} = \frac{M_{t+1}}{P_t} = \frac{M_{t+1}}{M_t} \frac{M_t}{P_t} = (1+x_{t+1})m_t, \tag{8.30}$$

where x_{t+1} denotes the rate of growth of money supply at time t.

To characterize steady-state in such an economy, the optimality condition (8.16), characterizing the demand for money, needs to be replaced by

$$\frac{U_2(c_{ss}, \bar{m}_{ss})}{U_1(c_{ss}, \bar{m}_{ss})} = \frac{i_{ss}}{1+i_{ss}} = \frac{1+\pi_{ss}-\beta}{1+\pi_{ss}},$$

and we can solve for steady-state levels along the lines followed in Sect. 8.2.2. Steady-state values for real variables (consumption, physical capital, output, real

---

[23] Remember from Chap. 3 that indeterminacy arises whenever the number of explosive eigenvalues of the transition matrix in the linear approximation to the equations describing the dynamics of the model is less than the number of control (i.e., decision) variables.

[24] Such analysis is undertaken in Chap. 9.

interest rates) obey the same expressions as in Sect. 8.2.2, while real balances are obtained from (8.30), for given policy targets, π_{ss}, ζ_{ss}. The steady-state level for public debt can then be obtained form the government budget constraint, as usual.

8.4.3 Numerical Exercise: Optimal Rate of Inflation Under Alternative Assumptions on Preferences

We compare in this section the steady-state welfare cost of inflation in two economies, differing only in the specification of preferences. In the first case, the consumer is supposed to get utility from real balances at the beginning of the period, while in the second case, real balances at the end of the period enter as the argument in the utility function. In both economies, the welfare cost of inflation is increasing in the level of the inflation rate, so the lowest feasible inflation rate turns out to be optimum. Steady-state expressions for the main variables from Sect. 8.2.2 can be used in the first case, while the reader must work out from the discussion in the previous paragraph the analogous expressions for the second economy. These expressions are displayed in the spreadsheet. The *Timing real balances.xls* file presents steady-state computations for both economies for a wide range of values of the inflation rate.[25]

Steady-state levels of real variables: capital stock, output and consumption are unaffected by the rate of inflation, showing the *neutrality* of this policy target. The inflation tax is negative for negative rates of inflation, so it acts as a transfer to consumers, who benefit from a falling price level. Real balances then become large because of their increasing purchasing power. Associated to the negative inflation tax we have a negative lump-sum transfer ζ to consumers, so that the negative inflation tax is financed through a lump-sum tax. The opposite happens under positive inflation rates, the more natural case. With positive inflation, we have an actual lump-sum transfer to consumers, which is financed through the positive inflation tax. In the absence of bonds, the lump-sum transfer to consumers is always endogenous.

Real balances are negatively related to the rate of inflation, so it is unclear how the inflation tax will move with inflation. Numerical computations in the spreadsheet show that, starting from the lowest feasible inflation rate of $\pi = -5\%$,[26] real balances quickly fall as inflation increases, while the level of the inflation tax and hence, the level of the lump-sum transfer, both increase. For plausible inflation rates, the size of the lump-sum transfer reaches a level close to 0.30, which is about 20%

---

[25] The comparison is not completely fair in the sense that the θ parameter should be adjusted so that the velocity of money would remain the same in both cases, as a reflection of the fact that we are trying to match relevant characteristics of actual economies. However, this adjustment, that the reader can do as an exercise, is minor, and does not significantly change the results.

[26] Rates of inflation below this are not compatible with existence of a competitive equilibrium, since money would dominate physical capital and hence, the representative agent would not accumulate any of the latter, eventually leading to zero production and consumption.

of output. This ratio would stabilize for large inflation rates at about 40% of output. Graphs displaying the time evolution of the main variables are presented to the right of the time series data.

8.5 Monetary Policy Analysis Under Consumption and Income Taxes

We now review the model incorporating the assumption that, in addition to printing money, issuing real bonds and collecting lump-sum taxes (i.e., giving away a negative transfer of ζ_t units of the consumption commodity), the government also levies a proportional tax on income, at a rate τ_t^y and a consumption tax, at a rate τ_t^c. For simplicity, we will assume that the tax base of the income tax is production income, with no depreciation allowances. Financial income is not being taxed. Alternative tax possibilities could be analyzed similarly. For simplicity, we maintain the assumption of zero population growth. We assume a general utility function having consumption and beginning of period real balances as arguments.

The representative agent budget constraint will now be[27]

$$(1+\tau_t^c)c_t + k_{t+1} + \frac{M_{t+1}}{P_t} + b_{t+1} \leq (1-\tau_t^y)f(k_t) + (1-\delta)k_t + \frac{M_t}{P_t}$$

$$+(1+r_t)b_t + \zeta_t, \quad \forall t$$

solving the maximization problem

$$\max_{\{c_t,M_{t+1},k_{t+1},b_{t+1}\}_{t=0}^{\infty}} \sum_{t=0}^{\infty} \beta^t U\left(c_t, \frac{M_t}{P_t}\right),$$

subject to the above budget constraint, for given values of M_0, b_0, k_0 as well as for a given sequence of tax rates $\{\tau_t^c, \tau_t^y\}_{t=0}^{\infty}$. The Lagrangian for this problem is

$$L = \sum_{t=0}^{\infty} \beta^t \left[U\left(c_t, \frac{M_t}{P_t}\right) - \lambda_t \left((1+\tau_t^c)c_t + k_{t+1} + \frac{M_{t+1}}{P_t} + b_{t+1} \right.\right.$$

$$\left.\left. - (1-\tau_t^y)f(k_t) - (1-\delta)k_t - \frac{M_t}{P_t} - (1+r_t)b_t - \zeta_t\right)\right],$$

and if we assume non-zero demands for bonds, money and physical capital, and follow an argument similar to the one used in the model without income and consumption taxes to eliminate the Lagrange multiplier, we get the optimality conditions

---

[27] With depreciation allowances, the tax term in the budget constraint would be, $(1-\tau_t^y)[f(k_t) - \delta k_t]$.

$$\frac{1+\tau_{t+1}^c}{1+\tau_t^c} \frac{U_1\left(c_t, \frac{M_t}{P_t}\right)}{\beta U_1\left(c_{t+1}, \frac{M_{t+1}}{P_{t+1}}\right)} = 1 + r_{t+1}, \quad \forall t, \tag{8.31}$$

$$\frac{1+\tau_{t+1}^c}{1+\tau_t^c} \frac{U_1\left(c_t, \frac{M_t}{P_t}\right)}{\beta U_1\left(c_{t+1}, \frac{M_{t+1}}{P_{t+1}}\right)} = \left(1 - \tau_{t+1}^y\right) f'(k_{t+1}) + (1 - \delta), \quad \forall t, \tag{8.32}$$

$$\left(1 + \tau_{t+1}^c\right) \frac{U_2\left(c_{t+1}, \frac{M_{t+1}}{P_{t+1}}\right)}{U_1\left(c_{t+1}, \frac{M_{t+1}}{P_{t+1}}\right)} = \left(1 + r_{t+1}\right)\left(1 + \pi_{t+1}\right) - 1, \quad \forall t. \tag{8.33}$$

Equations (8.31) and (8.32) show how, along the optimal trajectory, the marginal rate of substitution of consumption over time, net of consumption taxes, must be equal to the real interest rate every period, and also equal to the marginal product of capital, net of taxes and depreciation. Hence, the last two are also equal to each other:

$$r_{t+1} = \left(1 - \tau_{t+1}^y\right) f'(k_{t+1}) - \delta.$$

Equation (8.33) implies that the marginal rate of substitution between real balances and consumption must be equal every period to the nominal interest rate discounted by the consumption tax rate, which is in turn, the relative price of money and consumption at time $t+1$. It can be interpreted as a demand for money function, as in the case without income and consumption taxes.

The representative agent budget constraint can be written in the form

$$(1 + \tau_t^c)c_t + k_{t+1} - (1 - \delta)k_t + \frac{M_{t+1} - M_t}{P_t} + b_{t+1} - (1 + r_t)b_t$$

$$\leq \left(1 - \tau_t^y\right) f(k_t) + \zeta_t,$$

which shows that consumption expenditures, including consumption taxes, plus investment on physical capital, together with changes in the real value of the portfolio made up by financial assets (money balances and bonds), must be equal to the net aggregate of disposable income and government transfers.

The government budget constraint is

$$\frac{M_{t+1} - M_t}{P_t} + b_{t+1} - (1 + r_t)b_t + \tau_t^y f(k_t) + \tau_t^c c_t = \zeta_t,$$

showing that transfers to consumers are financed by printing money, issuing debt and raising taxes.

The transversality conditions are the same as in the version without income and consumption taxes. The three optimality conditions and the two budget constraints for the government and the representative agent make up a system of five

equations,[28] from which we should be able to get sequences $\left\{ c_t, k_{t+1}, r_t, b_{t+1}, \right.$
$\left. \frac{M_{t+1}}{P_{t+1}} \right\}_{t=0}^{\infty}$, given paths for policy variables $\left\{ \tau_t^c, \tau_t^y, \zeta_t, \pi_t \right\}_{t=0}^{\infty}$.

The government and the representative agent constraints, taken together, imply a standard global constraint of resources

$$c_t + k_{t+1} = f(k_t) + (1 - \delta) k_t.$$

8.5.1 Steady-State

To compute steady-state levels, we again use the optimality conditions, government budget constraint and global resources constraint particularized to steady-state,[29]

$$\frac{1}{\beta} = (1 - \tau_{ss}^y) f'(k_{ss}) + (1 - \delta),$$

$$\frac{1}{\beta} = 1 + r_{ss},$$

$$(1 + \tau_{ss}^c) \frac{U_2(c_{ss}, m_{ss})}{U_1(c_{ss}, m_{ss})} = (1 + r_{ss})(1 + \pi_{ss}) - 1 = \frac{1 + \pi_{ss}}{\beta} - 1, \qquad (8.34)$$

$$c_{ss} = f(k_{ss}) - \delta k_{ss},$$

$$\pi_{ss} m_{ss}(\pi_{ss}) - r_{ss} b_{ss} + \tau_{ss}^y f(k_{ss}) + \tau_{ss}^c c_{ss} = \zeta_{ss}. \qquad (8.35)$$

This a system of five equations in nine variables: $c_{ss}, k_{ss}, m_{ss}, b_{ss}, r_{ss}, \pi_{ss}, \tau_{ss}^y,$ τ_{ss}^c, ζ_{ss}. To determine the steady-state equilibrium we will need to maintain four of these variables constant, the resulting steady-state then being a function of the chosen constant levels. The role of fiscal and monetary policy will be precisely to keep those variables constant, if possible. However, not any four variables will solve the system of steady-state equations.

One such possibility is that the government defines a combination of fiscal and monetary policies to keep $\tau_t^y, \tau_t^c, \zeta_t, \pi_t$ constant at levels $\tau_{ss}^y, \tau_{ss}^c, \zeta_{ss}, \pi_{ss}$. Decreasing returns to capital imply that the only feasible steady-state is one at which per-capita variables stay constant: $c_t = c_{ss}, k_t = k_{ss}$, implying in turn that the rest of per-capita variables will also be constant over time. This policy design allows for a single solution to the system, providing us with a single steady-state equilibrium. The first equation shows that the level of the tax rate negatively affects the steady-state level of physical capital which, in turn, affects the levels of output, $y_{ss} = f(k_{ss})$, and

---

[28] This a system of non-linear equations, whose solution may not exist, not be unique, or be unstable. In Chap. 9 we discuss numerical procedures for computing time series for the endogenous variables in economies like the one in this section.

[29] There is no need to impose the budget constraint for the representative agent since, as we already know, it is always satisfied, being a combination of the global constraint of resources and the government budget constraint.

consumption. Hence, *income tax rate is not neutral in this economy*. On the other hand, from (8.34) we would obtain m_{ss} as a function of π_{ss}, τ_{ss}^c and c_{ss} which, in turn, depends on the tax rate τ_{ss}^y through the value of k_{ss}. Hence, the steady-state level of real balances is a function of both, fiscal and monetary parameters, showing once again the interdependence of the two types of economic policy. Finally, (8.35) will give us the level of b_{ss} as a function of $\tau_{ss}^y, \tau_{ss}^c, \zeta_{ss}, \pi_{ss}$. Notice that the level of consumption does not depend on the tax rate on consumption.

Real interest rates are not affected by the income tax rate. With this policy choice, we have $m_{ss}\left(\pi_{ss}, \tau_{ss}^y, \tau_{ss}^c\right), b_{ss}\left(\pi_{ss}, \tau_{ss}^y, \tau_{ss}^c, \zeta_{ss}\right)$, so that, at a difference of what happened in the case without income and consumption taxes, now the real money supply will depend not only on the chosen level of inflation, but on the choice of both tax rates as well. In the economy without distortionary taxation we had the dependence: $m_{ss}\left(\pi_{ss}\right), b_{ss}\left(\pi_{ss}, \zeta_{ss}\right)$, so that the choice of targets for inflation and transfers would give us the levels of real balances and bonds. We have one such situation for each combination of tax rates, although some of them might lead to unfeasible solutions.

A similar analysis arises if the policy mix chooses target levels for $\tau_{ss}^y, \tau_{ss}^c, b_{ss}, \pi_{ss}$. We again obtain a recursive system, which can be solved with no much problem. The income tax rate again affects the level of capital and hence, the levels of consumption and output, with implications similar to those in the previous case. Choosing a target for either b_{ss} or for ζ_{ss} does not significantly change the problem.

If the government has policy targets on $\zeta_{ss}, b_{ss}, \tau_{ss}^y, \pi_{ss}$, the system can again be recursively solved as in the previous cases considered, with analogous results. Monetary policy remains to be neutral.

On the other hand, if the government chooses targets for $\zeta_{ss}, b_{ss}, \tau_{ss}^c, \pi_{ss}$, then the system needs to be solved simultaneously for $c_{ss}, k_{ss}, m_{ss}, r_{ss}, \tau_{ss}^y$, since we lose the recursiveness of the previous case. Not all target levels for $\zeta_{ss}, b_{ss}, \tau_{ss}^c, \pi_{ss}$ will lead to feasible solutions. The simultaneity of the system implies that the real variables in the economy: consumption, physical capital, output, will depend on the chosen levels for $\zeta_{ss}, b_{ss}, \tau_{ss}^c, \pi_{ss}$, showing that *monetary policy is not neutral in this economy under this policy design*. If policy targets are chosen for $\zeta_{ss}, b_{ss}, \tau_{ss}^y, m_{ss}$, a similar conclusion is reached, confirming the non-neutrality of monetary policy.

Finally, at a difference of the case without income and consumption taxes, a monetary policy that chooses steady-state levels for π_{ss} and m_{ss} can also be instrumented, provided fiscal policy controls the level of either outstanding debt or transfers (but not the tax rate). In this case, characterized by mixing an *active monetary policy* and a *passive fiscal policy* (Leeper [55]), fiscal and monetary policy are both non-neutral.

A rather different situation would be faced if we attempted to choose target levels for $\pi_{ss}, m_{ss}, \tau_{ss}^y, \tau_{ss}^c$. The problem is then that given τ_{ss}^y, we can directly compute the value of k_{ss} and c_{ss}. The money demand equation is then a relationship without any unknown, which may not hold. The model is overdetermined, and there is not a set of values for the endogenous variables that satisfies all the equations in the model. The model imposes too many restrictions, that turn out to be incompatible among them. On the other hand, if the policy mix chooses less than three targets, we would have an underidentified model, with a continuum of steady-state solutions.

8.5.2 Numerical Exercise: Computation of Steady-State Levels Under Alternative Policy Choices

The *Steady state fiscal policy.xls* file contains computations of steady-state levels for the main variables in the economy under alternative policy choices that include a proportional income tax. There are not consumption taxes. Preferences are represented by the utility function: $U(c_t, m_t) = \ln c_t + \theta \ln m_t$, while the production function is, in per capita terms: $y_t = Ak_t^\alpha$. Structural parameter values are quite standard: the output elasticity of capital is $\alpha = 0.36$, the discount rate is $\beta = 0.95$, the rate of depreciation of physical capital is 10%, and the level of technology is $A = 1.0$. Finally, the relative appreciation for real balances is set at $\theta = 0.50$.

In the Case 1 spreadsheet, the government is supposed to choose the income tax rate as well as the steady-state level of outstanding debt and the rate of inflation, while the steady-state levels of real balances and lump-sum transfers to consumers become endogenous, i.e., they are obtained as a function of the chosen policy targets. In fact, the exercise is repeated for a grid of values of the inflation rate between the lowest possible level of -5.0% and a high value of 100.0%. The income tax rate is fixed at $\tau_{ss}^y = 15.0\%$, while the stock of outstanding debt is supposed to be 5.0. All variables are in per-capita terms. The level of seigniorage, i.e., the size of the inflation tax is seen to be bounded from above, and the welfare cost of inflation is increasing in the rate of inflation. Furthermore, $\pi_{ss} = -5.0\%$ turns out to be optimal rate of inflation, leading to a nominal interest rate equal to zero. So, Friedman's rule is valid in this case. This is compensated by an equally large lump-sum tax, i.e., a negative transfer to consumers. In the Case 2 spreadsheet the government chooses an income tax rate $\tau = 15.0\%$ and the steady-state size of the transfer, $\zeta = 0.20$, leaving the steady-state stock of bonds to be endogenously determined. Again, the level of seigniorage is bounded and Friedman's rule is valid, optimal monetary policy leading to a nominal interest rate equal to zero.

In the Case 3 spreadsheet the government chooses a steady-state transfer of $\zeta = 0.25$ and a steady-state stock of per-capita debt equal to 5.0. For a grid of values of the income tax rate, we endogenously compute the steady-state rate of inflation as well as values for real variables. The stock of capital, output and consumption per capita all decrease when the tax rate increases. Real balances first increase but start decreasing for an income tax rate above $\tau = 52\%$. Income tax revenues also increase initially as the income tax increases, but they decrease when the tax rate increases from above $\tau = 64\%$. This is the so called *Laffer curve*, that captures the possibility that tax revenues may decrease for a sufficiently high tax rate because of an implied fall in the tax base. On the other hand, the inflation tax follows the opposite evolution, decreasing as the income tax rate increases towards $\tau = 64\%$, and increasing afterwards. Total revenues, the sum of the income tax and the inflation tax remain constant as the income tax changes, as it is easy to see from the government's budget constraint. In this case, the highest level of steady-state utility is achieved for an income tax rate: $\tau = 36\%$ and, consequently, a rate of inflation: $\pi = 0.66\%$.

Case 3 illustrates the fact that high rates of inflation may be associated with low income tax rates, but also with high income tax rates. This is because income tax revenues behave according to a Laffer curve, i.e., there exists a given tax rate above which tax increases lead to lower revenues because of reductions in the tax base. In that situation, the government must react to a tax raise by increasing inflation to compensate the reduced tax revenues with a higher level of seigniorage, so that its budget constraint can hold every period. These results also illustrate how the public financing mechanism may affect economic activity. In particular, it can be seen that along the increasing part of Laffer's curve, where an increase in the tax rate leads to an increase in revenues, an increase in inflation associated to a reduction in the income tax rate produces an increase in output, the stock of capital and consumption. With regards to the utility level, it is shown that there is a pair of values ($\pi_{ss} > 0$, $\tau_{ss} > 0$) for which steady-state utility is maximized.

We leave to the reader to check that, maintaining our assumptions on lump-sum transfers and public debt in Case 3, if the government chooses the rate of inflation and, hence, the income tax rate is endogenously determined, then the combination of tax rate and inflation maximizing the level of utility is the same as in the previous case. If there is any discrepancy in the numerical results, the analysis should be repeated increasing the exogenous instrument by a smaller amount. Since the inflation rate associated to the highest level of welfare is not the one that gives raise to a zero nominal rate of interest, then Friedman's rule does not hold. This analysis cannot be done in a spreadsheet, since it is not possible to solve the system of equations recursively, so a math computer package like Matlab will be needed.

8.6 Monetary Policy Under Endogenous Labor Supply

In previous sections we have considered an inelastic labor supply. Needless to say, an endogenous supply of labor opens the door to analyzing a variety of interesting issues. We start this section by discussing conditions characterizing the neutrality of monetary policy under endogenous labor supply. We then perform some numerical evaluation of steady-state policies, to end the section with a characterization of optimal policy under distortionary taxation and endogenous labor supply.

8.6.1 The Neutrality of Monetary Policy Under Endogenous Labor Supply

In the model economy considered in previous sections, with an exogenous labor supply, we have shown that monetary policy is neutral in steady-state. When the assumption of an inelastic labor supply is abandoned, monetary policy is no longer necessarily neutral, and there are specifications for preferences for which monetary policy has expansionary effects on production. There are also specifications of preferences for which monetary policy negatively affects output, and still others under which the rate of inflation is neutral. The requirement that a utility function must satisfy for monetary policy to be non-neutral in steady-state is that real balances enter as an argument in preferences in a non-separable way with one other argument, either consumption or leisure. If the final objective of a given model is to discuss the economic business cycle, allowing for an endogenous labor supply is crucial, since the variability of employment along the business cycle is one its most remarkable characteristics. For simplicity, we only consider lump sum transfers[30] ζ_t in this discussion.

The government budget constraint, in per capita terms, is

$$\frac{M_{t+1} - M_t}{P_t} + b_{t+1} = (1 + r_t) b_t + \zeta_t.$$

The representative agent in this economy solves the problem

$$\max_{\{c_t, l_t, h_t, M_{t+1}, k_{t+1}, b_{t+1}\}_{t=0}^{\infty}} \sum_{t=0}^{\infty} \beta^t U\left(c_t, \frac{M_t}{P_t}, h_t\right),$$

subject to its budget constraint

$$c_t + k_{t+1} + \frac{M_{t+1}}{P_t} + b_{t+1} \leq f(k_t, l_t) + (1 - \delta) k_t + \frac{M_t}{P_t} + (1 + r_t) b_t + \zeta_t,$$

given k_0, M_0, b_0. $h_t + l_t = 1$, h_t being the proportion of hours enjoyed as leisure, while l_t denotes the proportion of hours devoted to production. We assume that the utility function satisfies usual assumptions guaranteeing concavity. The aggregate production function in this economy is $Y_t = F(K_t, L_t l_t)$ which, in per capita terms can be written as $f(k_t, l_t)$.[31]

The Lagrangian for this problem is

$$L = \sum_{t=0}^{\infty} \beta^t \left[U\left(c_t, \frac{M_t}{P_t}, h_t\right) - \lambda_t \left(c_t + k_{t+1} + \frac{M_{t+1}}{P_t} + b_{t+1} \right. \right.$$
$$\left. \left. - f(k_t, l_t) - (1 - \delta) k_t - \frac{M_t}{P_t} - (1 + r_t) b_t - \zeta_t \right) \right],$$

with optimality conditions (allowing for corner solutions)

$$U_1\left(c_t, \frac{M_t}{P_t}, h_t\right) \leq \lambda_t; \text{ and } c_t \left[U_1\left(c_t, \frac{M_t}{P_t, h_t}\right) - \lambda_t \right] = 0, \quad \forall t \quad (8.36)$$

$$k_{t+1} \left[-\lambda_t + \beta \lambda_{t+1} \left(f_k(k_{t+1}, l_{t+1}) + (1 - \delta) \right) \right] = 0, \quad \forall t \quad (8.37)$$

$$M_{t+1} \left[\beta U_2\left(c_{t+1}, \frac{M_{t+1}}{P_{t+1}}, h_{t+1}\right) \frac{1}{P_{t+1}} - \lambda_t \frac{1}{P_t} + \lambda_{t+1} \beta \frac{1}{P_{t+1}} \right] = 0, \quad \forall t \quad (8.38)$$

[30] Or lump-sum taxes, if ζ_t is negative.

[31] As shown in Sect. 3.5.2 when analyzing the Cass–Koopmans economy.

$$U_3(C_t, \frac{M_t}{P_t}, h_t) \leq \lambda_t f_l(k_t, l_t); \quad \text{and}$$

$$l_t \left[-U_3\left(c_t, \frac{M_t}{P_t}, h_t\right) + \lambda_t f_l(k_t, l_t) \right] = 0 \qquad (8.39)$$

$$c_t + k_{t+1} + \frac{M_{t+1}}{P_t} + b_{t+1} - f(k_t, l_t) - (1-\delta)k_t - \frac{M_t}{P_t} - (1+r_t)b_t - \zeta_t = 0, \quad \forall t \tag{8.40}$$

$$\lambda_t \leq \beta(1+r_{t+1})\lambda_{t+1}, \quad \text{and} \quad b_{t+1}[\beta(1+r_{t+1})\lambda_{t+1} - \lambda_t] = 0, \quad \forall t \qquad (8.41)$$

and transversality conditions

$$\lim_{T \to \infty} \beta^T \lambda_T \frac{M_{T+1}}{P_T} = 0,$$

$$\lim_{T \to \infty} \beta^T \lambda_T k_{T+1} = 0,$$

$$\lim_{T \to \infty} \beta^T \lambda_T b_{T+1} = 0.$$

where $f_k(k_t, l_t)$ and $f_l(k_t, l_t)$ denote the marginal productivities of physical capital and labor, respectively.

All conditions except (8.39) are analogous to the optimality conditions obtained when leisure was not an argument in the utility function. Therefore, when the Lagrange multipliers are eliminated, we get relationships similar to those in previous sections

$$b_{t+1} > 0 \Rightarrow \frac{U_1(c_t, \frac{M_t}{P_t}, h_t)}{\beta U_1(c_{t+1}, \frac{M_{t+1}}{P_{t+1}}, h_{t+1})} = 1 + r_{t+1},$$

$$k_{t+1} > 0 \Rightarrow \frac{U_1(c_t, \frac{M_t}{P_t}, h_t)}{\beta U_1(c_{t+1}, \frac{M_{t+1}}{P_{t+1}}, h_{t+1})} = f_k(k_{t+1}, l_{t+1}) + (1-\delta),$$

$$M_{t+1} > 0 \Rightarrow \frac{U_2\left(c_{t+1}, \frac{M_{t+1}}{P_{t+1}}, h_{t+1}\right)}{U_1\left(c_{t+1}, \frac{M_{t+1}}{P_{t+1}}, h_{t+1}\right)} = (1+r_{t+1})(1+\pi_{t+1}) - 1$$

$$= (1+i_{t+1}) - 1 = i_{t+1}.$$

Additionally, we have in this model, from (8.36) and (8.39)

$$\frac{U_3\left(c_t, \frac{M_t}{P_t}, h_t\right)}{U_1\left(c_t, \frac{M_t}{P_t}, h_t\right)} = f_l(k_t, l_t),$$

which is the labor supply schedule. It shows that the representative agent is willing to increase his/her supply of labor up to the point at which the marginal rate of substitution between consumption and leisure is equal to the marginal product of labor.

The solution to the problem of the representative agent is a vector of prices and an allocation of resources satisfying the optimality conditions above, the government budget constraint and the global constraint of resources. Combining the budget constraints for the representative agent and for the government we obtain the global constraint of resources. Therefore, one of the three equations cannot be used in the characterization of equilibrium. We will not use the budget constraint for the private agent, but the reader can easily check that the same solution is reached by dropping any other equation.

Consequently, the equations characterizing steady-state when the government chooses a stationary policy with constant lump-sum transfers and inflation

$$\zeta_t = \zeta_{ss}, \quad \forall t$$
$$\pi_t = \pi_{ss}, \quad \forall t$$

are

$$1 + r_{ss} = \frac{1}{\beta}, \tag{8.42}$$

$$\frac{1}{\beta} = f_k(k_{ss}, l_{ss}) + (1 - \delta), \tag{8.43}$$

$$\frac{U_2(c_{ss}, m_{ss}, h_{ss})}{U_1(c_{ss}, m_{ss}, h_{ss})} = \frac{1 + \pi_{ss}}{\beta}, \tag{8.44}$$

$$\frac{U_3(c_{ss}, m_{ss}, h_{ss})}{U_1(c_{ss}, m_{ss}, h_{ss})} = f_l(k_{ss}, l_{ss}), \tag{8.45}$$

$$c_{ss} + \delta k_{ss} = f(k_{ss}, l_{ss}), \tag{8.46}$$

$$\pi_{ss} m_{ss} - r_{ss} b_{ss} = \zeta_{ss}, \tag{8.47}$$

the last two relationships coming from the global resources constraint and the government budget constraint.

Let us now discuss the implications for the neutrality of the rate of inflation of choosing a particular specification for the utility function:

1. If the utility function is separable in its three arguments: $U(c_t, \frac{M_t}{P_t}, h_t) = v(c_t) \cdot \eta\left(\frac{M_t}{P_t}\right) \cdot H(h_t)$ then, (8.45) is an equation in c_{ss}, k_{ss} and l_{ss} since $l_{ss} + h_{ss} = 1$. (8.45) together with (8.43) and (8.46) allows us to obtain c_{ss}, k_{ss} and l_{ss} with independence of the type of monetary and fiscal policies being implemented. Then, m_{ss} is determined from (8.44) and b_{ss} comes from (8.47). Monetary and fiscal policies are neutral. This neutrality result also holds for nonseparable albeit homogeneous utility functions.

2. If the utility function is separable in leisure: $U(c_t, \frac{M_t}{P_t}, h_t) = v\left(c_t, \frac{M_t}{P_t}\right) \cdot H(h_t)$, with $v(.)$ being a non-homogeneous function, then (8.45) is an equation in c_{ss}, k_{ss}, m_{ss}, and l_{ss}, using that $l_{ss} + h_{ss} = 1$. Then, these four variables are jointly determined from the system made up by (8.43)–(8.46). As a consequence, real variables will depend on the rate of inflation, although they will be independent

from the size of the lump-sum transfer. Therefore, the neutrality of the rate of inflation no longer holds. As in the previous case, b_{ss} is determined from (8.47).

3. If the utility function is non-homogeneous, and not separable in leisure and real balances, but it is separable in consumption: $U\left(c_t, \frac{M_t}{P_t}, h_t\right) = v(c_t) \cdot H\left(\frac{M_t}{P_t}, h_t\right)$ the situation is analogous to the previous case.

4. If the utility function is not separable in consumption and leisure, but it is separable in real balances: $U\left(c_t, \frac{M_t}{P_t}, h_t\right) = v(c_t, h_t) \cdot \eta\left(\frac{M_t}{P_t}\right)$ the situation is analogous to the one discussed in the first case, and we have again neutrality of monetary and fiscal policy.

Therefore, the neutrality of the rate of inflation arises whenever the utility function is separable in real balances, with independence of the possible separability between consumption and leisure. On the other hand, the rate of inflation affects economic activity in steady-state whenever real balances and leisure enter nonseparably in the utility function, or when preferences are nonseparable in real balances and consumption.

Let us now see two examples sharing the property that the rate of inflation is not neutral, although economic effects produced in both models are of the opposite sign. In both cases, the production function is: $y_t = f(k_t, l_t) = A k_t^\alpha l_t^{1-\alpha}$, $\alpha \in (0,1)$, and inflation leads to a loss of utility. As usual, we denote real balances by: $m_t = \frac{M_t}{P_t}$.

Case 1: If the utility function is of the form $U(c_t, m_t, h_t) = \ln(c_t + m_t^\theta) + \varpi \ln(h_t) = \ln(c_t + m_t^\theta) + \varpi \ln(1 - l_t)$ with $\varpi > 0, 0 < \theta < 1$, that guarantee $U_h > 0$ as well as the quasiconcavity of the utility function, we can obtain from (8.43), (8.44) and (8.46)

$$\left(\frac{k}{l}\right)_{ss} = \left[\frac{A\alpha}{1/\beta - (1-\delta)}\right]^{\frac{1}{1-\alpha}},$$

$$\left(\frac{c}{l}\right)_{ss} = A\left[\left(\frac{k}{l}\right)_{ss}\right]^\alpha - \delta\left(\frac{k}{l}\right)_{ss},$$

$$m_{ss} = \left[\frac{\beta\theta}{1 + \pi_{ss} - \beta}\right]^{\frac{1}{1-\theta}}.$$

Using the identity $c_{ss} = \left(\frac{c}{l}\right)_{ss} l_{ss}$ in (8.45), we get

$$\left(\frac{c}{l}\right)_{ss} l_{ss} = \frac{A(1-\alpha)}{\varpi}\left[\left(\frac{k}{l}\right)_{ss}\right]^\alpha - \frac{A(1-\alpha)}{\varpi}\left[\left(\frac{k}{l}\right)_{ss}\right]^\alpha l_{ss} - (m_{ss})^\theta,$$

which implies

$$l_{ss} = \frac{\frac{A(1-\alpha)}{\varpi}\left[\left(\frac{k}{l}\right)_{ss}\right]^\alpha - (m_{ss})^\theta}{\left(\frac{c}{l}\right)_{ss} + \frac{A(1-\alpha)}{\varpi}\left[\left(\frac{k}{l}\right)_{ss}\right]^\alpha}.$$

In the previous expressions we see that the capital/employment ratio does not depend on the rate of inflation. Furthermore, since $\theta < 1$, increases in the inflation rate lead to reductions in the level of real balances. This produces an increase in the marginal utility of consumption, creating an incentive to increase utility from consumption, rather than leisure, which leads to an increase in employment, output, consumption and the stock of capital.

Case 2: If the utility function is of the form: $U(c_t, m_t, h_t) = \ln(c_t) + \theta' \ln(h_t + m_t^\psi) = \ln(c_t) + \theta' \ln(1 - l_t + m_t^\psi)$ with $\theta' > 0, 0 < \psi < 1$, the value of $\left(\frac{k}{l}\right)_{ss}$ is the same as in the previous case. From (8.45), we have

$$\frac{c_{ss}}{1 - l_{ss} + (m_{ss})^\psi} = A\frac{1-\alpha}{\theta'}\left[\left(\frac{k}{l}\right)_{ss}\right]^\alpha, \tag{8.48}$$

which together with

$$\frac{c_{ss}}{1 - l_{ss} + (m_{ss})^\psi} = \frac{1 + \pi_{ss} - \beta}{\beta\theta'\psi(m_{ss})^{\psi-1}},$$

which is obtained from (8.44), lead to

$$m_{ss} = \left[\frac{\beta\psi A(1-\alpha)\left[\left(\frac{k}{l}\right)_{ss}\right]^\alpha}{1 + \pi_{ss} - \beta}\right]^{\frac{1}{1-\psi}}.$$

The value of $\left(\frac{c}{l}\right)_{ss}$ is the same as in the previous case. Furthermore, since (8.48) is equivalent to

$$\frac{\left(\frac{c}{l}\right)_{ss}}{\frac{[1+(m_{ss})^\psi]}{l_{ss}} - 1} = A\frac{1-\alpha}{\theta'}\left[\left(\frac{k}{l}\right)_{ss}\right]^\alpha,$$

we obtain

$$l_{ss} = \frac{1 + (m_{ss})^\psi}{1 + \frac{\theta'\left(\frac{c}{l}\right)_{ss}}{A(1-\alpha)\left[\left(\frac{k}{l}\right)_{ss}\right]^\alpha}}.$$

In this case, an increase in the rate of inflation reduces the level of real balances. This leads to an increase in the marginal utility of leisure, which gives raise to an increase in the relative preference for leisure, relative to consumption. As a consequence, employment, consumption, the stock of capital and output, all decrease.

8.6.2 Numerical Exercise: Evaluation of Steady-State Policies with an Endogenous Labour Supply

Five different policy situations are considered in the *SS inflation endogenous leisure.xls* file. In the Case 1 spreadsheet we have where the government realizes a lump-sum transfer to consumers, which is fully financed by increasing the money supply. Private agents have a unit of time as endowment every period. Part of that unit is used to work (l_t), while the rest is used up as leisure

$(1 - l_t)$. The production function is: $y_t = Ak_t^\alpha l_t^{1-\alpha}$, and the utility function: $U(c_t, m_t, 1 - l_t) = \eta \ln c_t + (1 - \eta)\ln(1 - l_t) + \theta \ln m_t$, $\eta \in (0, 1)$, $\theta > 0$ and $m_t = \frac{M_t}{P_t}$. The government has an inflation target. The steady-state of the model can be solved for recursively. For parameter values $\alpha = 0.36$, $\beta = 0.95$, $A = 1$, $\delta = 0.1$, $\eta = 0.35$, $\theta = 0.175$, we compute the steady-state welfare cost associated to different values of the rate of inflation. In this case, we see that changes in the rate of inflation do not affect real variables like consumption, employment, capital and output. On the contrary, real balances are affected, so that the level of utility also changes with the inflation target. We see that the highest steady-state level of utility is achieved for an inflation rate $\beta - 1$. When the welfare cost of inflation is computed relative to the case of zero inflation, we see that the cost is increasing in the level of infla- tion.[32] Seigniorage revenues are increasing in the level of inflation, so maximizing revenues goes in the opposite direction to maximizing steady-state utility. The last column shows that the increase in welfare cost is not proportional to the increase in inflation but rather, the welfare cost is higher for an increase from a low level of inflation.

Maintaining the same structural environment, Case 2 considers the utility func- tion: $U(c_t, m_t, 1 - l_t) = \ln(c_t + m_t^\theta) + \varpi \ln(1 - l_t)$, $\theta \in (0, 1)$, $\varpi > 0$. Under the pa- rameterization: $\alpha = 0.36$, $A = 1$, $\beta = 0.95$, $\delta = 0.1$, $\theta' = 0.005$, $\varpi = 0.5$ inflation is shown to be non-neutral. The lowest feasible rate of inflation is again the one maxi- mizing steady-state welfare. In agreement with our previous discussion, an increase in inflation leads to an increase in the level of consumption, but a fall in real balances and leisure. So, there are conflicting effects on utility, but our numerical evaluation shows that the aggregate effect of the higher rate of inflation is a loss in utility.

In the Case 3 spreadsheet we perform a similar exercise, this time for the utility function: $U(c_t, m_t, 1 - n_t) = \ln(c_t) + \theta' \ln\left(1 - n_t + m_t^\psi\right)$, $\psi \in (0, 1)$, $\theta' > 0$. Using the same parameter values as before, except for $\theta = 2$ and $\psi = 0.5$, we find again conflicting evidence regarding the welfare effects of a higher rate of inflation, but of a different type. Now, leisure increases while the level of consumption falls, following an increase in the rate of inflation. However, our numerical computations illustrate how, in spite of the higher level of leisure, the fall in consumption and real balances lead again in this case to a loss of steady-state utility.

In the Case 4 and Case 5 spreadsheets we consider economies where the gov- ernment realizes a lump-sum transfer to consumers, which is financed by increasing the money supply and by a tax on consumption. We maintain the same produc- tion function as in previous cases, while the utility function is now as in Case 1: $U(c_t, \frac{M_t}{P_t}, l_t) = \eta \ln c_t + (1 - \eta)\ln(1 - l_t) + \theta \ln \frac{M_t}{P_t}$, with $\eta \in (0, 1)$, $\theta > 0$. In Case 4 we show that if the government has an inflation target, the steady-state of the economy can be solved for recursively under a constant tax rate on consumption. We consider parameter values $\alpha = 0.36$, $A = 1$, $\beta = 0.95$, $\delta = 0.1$, $\eta = 0.35$, $\theta = 0.175$ and a tax rate on consumption of 15%. The inflation target is shown to be neutral, with the lowest feasible level of inflation being optimum. So Friedman's rule is valid in this economy.

---

[32] We already mentioned that, with these preferences, it is not possible to compute the welfare cost of inflation relative to the optimal rate of inflation.

The analysis is performed again in the Case 5 spreadsheet, with the assumption that the government has an inflation target and that it keeps constant the level of lump-sum transfers. In this case, the steady-state cannot be solved recursively. Under an exogenous rate of inflation and an endogenous consumption tax rate the equation determining the later turns out to be nonlinear, and the system cannot easily be solved in a spreadsheet. However, if the tax rate is taken as exogenous and we endogenously compute the rate of inflation, then solving the model in a spreadsheet becomes very simple. This is the situation solved in the Case 5 spreadsheet. Such calculations show, among other things, that inflation is not neutral. The nonneutrality arises because the increase in inflation allows for a reduction in the consumption tax. Consumption then becomes cheaper relative to leisure, which leads to an increase in employment, capital and output.

8.7 Optimal Monetary Policy Under Distortionary Taxation and Endogenous Labor

Optimal monetary policy has been approached from different perspectives. One of them is what is known as the *optimal inflation tax* analysis. The rate of inflation is then considered as a control variable of monetary policy, and the welfare maximizing level of inflation is calculated. The analysis is done under the assumption that the government implements an exogenous level of expenditures, which can be financed either through liquidity injections that produce inflation, or through some distortionary tax on consumption or on labor income. This type of analysis was carried out in Sect. 8.3.1 without distortionary taxes and just for the steady-state. Usually, the loss in purchasing power of monetary balances due to inflation is known as the *inflation tax*. The financing decision is seen as a choice among different distortions. It will be optimal to use the inflation tax, leading to Friedman's rule not being valid, whenever the alternative tax produces bigger distortions on economic agents than those produced by inflation, when both are taken to the level that allows for financing the same level of government expenditures.

The first papers on the optimal inflation tax were Phelps [70], Kimbrough [50], and Lucas and Stokey [58]. Each one of them used a different structural approach to generate a demand for money. Phelps [70] assumed that real money balances enter as an argument in the utility function, Kimbrough [50] assumed that real balances reduce transaction costs, while Lucas and Stockey [58] introduced a cash-in-advance constraint into the model. These analysis show that when the government cannot use a lump-sum tax to finance expenditures, and it has only distortionary taxes available, the way how consumers' demand for cash is modelled may condition the characterization of optimal monetary policy. Later on, Guidotti and Végh [38] shown that the nature of the tax which is considered as an alternative to the inflation tax can also be an important factor conditioning the results.

Finally, Chari et al. [26] simultaneously considered the three different ways we have mentioned in the previous paragraph to produce a demand for money, to characterize the properties of the utility and the transaction cost functions guaranteeing that Friedman's rule holds. Utility functions and transaction cost functions considered in the theoretical literature to address a variety of issues in monetary economies usually fulfill such conditions. However, to the light of previous work, it would seem reasonable to refer to numerical estimations for general specifications of the mentioned functions to obtain a definite conclusion in favor or against the inflation tax but, unfortunately, we lack enough empirical evidence regarding this point.

To characterize the optimal inflation tax in this economy, we compute a *Ramsey equilibrium*. This is a pair formed by an economic policy and a vector of prices and quantities satisfying the property that the economic policy maximizes the discounted aggregate value of current and future utility, subject to the sequence of government budget constraints and the fact that the set of prices and quantities constitutes a competitive equilibrium allocation. To solve Ramsey's problem, we assume that there is some sort of institutional commitment forcing the government to actually implement in the future the policy that is chosen at time 0. Each period, the government applies that policy, and consumers are assumed to choose quantities and prices through the competitive equilibrium mechanism. Hence, when designing current and future monetary policy in period 0, the government needs to take into account the relationships between quantities and prices that arise from Euler equations, the optimizing conditions characterizing a dynamic competitive general equilibrium.

8.7.1 The Model

8.7.1.1 The Private Sector

For simplicity, we characterize the optimal inflation tax in a model with no capital accumulation, so that the only commodity in the economy is produced from labor. We assume the aggregate constant returns to scale technology, in per capita terms

$$y_t = l_t,$$

where, as in the previous section, l_t denotes the proportion of hours devoted to working, with $h_t + l_t = 1$.

The amount of work chosen by the firm is determined by the equality between the marginal product of labor and the real wage. Given the assumed production function, that condition implies that the price of the consumption good is equal to the nominal wage, so the real wage is equal to 1.

Furthermore, we assume that the private agent demands some money because real balances *at the end of the period* enter as an argument in the utility function, together with the levels of consumption and leisure

$$U\left(c_t, \frac{M_{t+1}}{P_t}, h_t\right) = v\left(c_t, \frac{M_{t+1}}{P_t}\right) H(h_t), \tag{8.49}$$

which is separable in leisure and where $v\left(c_t, \frac{M_{t+1}}{P_t}\right)$ is homogeneous of degree φ. Function U is assumed to be strictly concave and to satisfy Inada's conditions. In this economy, monetary policy turns out to be neutral because the utility function is separable in leisure and homogeneous in the joint term involving consumption and real balances (see Sect. 8.6.1 for a detailed discussion on this issue).

Each period, the consumer has two possibilities for saving: money and nominal public debt. Salary income is taxed at a rate τ_t^y, so that his budget constraint is

$$P_t c_t + M_{t+1} + V_{t+1} = M_t + (1 + i_t) V_t + P_t (1 - \tau_t^y) l_t, \tag{8.50}$$

where we have already incorporated the profit maximizing condition: $w_t = P_t$. As in the rest of the chapter, M_t, V_t denote the per capita levels of money in circulation and nominal public debt at the beginning of period t. We assume constant population.

We assume that the stock of public debt, in real terms, satisfies $\bar{b}_{t+1} = \frac{V_{t+1}}{P_t} \leq \breve{b}$, $\breve{b}$ being an arbitrarily large constant and also that $\bar{m}_{t+1} = \frac{M_{t+1}}{P_t} \leq \breve{m}$, where $\breve{m}$ is a satiation level of real balances (that is, $\frac{\partial U}{\partial m}|_{\breve{m}} = 0$). Notice that we reserve the "$-$" notation for the real value of end-of-period variables like the money supply and the stock of nominal bonds. Unless such a bliss point exists, real balances under the optimal monetary policy become infinity and the Ramsey problem has no solution. It is to avoid this problem that we impose the bound on real balances through the satiation level $\breve{m}$.

In real terms, the budget constraint of the private agent is

$$c_t + \bar{m}_{t+1} + \bar{b}_{t+1} = \frac{\bar{m}_t}{1 + \pi_t} + \frac{(1 + i_t) \bar{b}_t}{1 + \pi_t} + (1 - \tau_t^y) l_t, \tag{8.51}$$

where $1 + \pi_t = \frac{P_t}{P_{t-1}}$.

The problem being solved by the representative agent is

$$\max_{\{c_t, \bar{m}_{t+1}, l_t, \bar{b}_{t+1}\}} \sum_{t=0}^{\infty} \beta^t U(c_t, \bar{m}_{t+1}, 1 - l_t)$$

subject to (8.51), and given M_0, B_0.

Conditions characterizing the competitive general equilibrium are, in addition to the budget constraint (8.51):

$$U_{c,t} - \lambda_t = 0, \tag{8.52}$$

$$M_{t+1} > 0 \Leftrightarrow U_{\bar{m},t+1} + \beta \frac{\lambda_{t+1}}{1 + \pi_{t+1}} - \lambda_t = 0, \tag{8.53}$$

$$\bar{b}_{t+1} > 0 \Leftrightarrow -\lambda_t + \beta \frac{\lambda_{t+1}}{1 + \pi_{t+1}} (1 + i_{t+1}) = 0, \tag{8.54}$$

$$-U_{1-l,t} + \lambda_t (1 - \tau_t^y) = 0, \tag{8.55}$$

with λ_t being the Lagrange multiplier associated to the budget constraint. $U_{c,t}, U_{m,t+1}, U_{1-l,t}$ denote marginal utilities.

Transversality conditions are

$$\lim_{T \to \infty} \lambda_T \beta^T \bar{m}_{T+1} = 0,$$

$$\lim_{T \to \infty} \lambda_T \beta^T \bar{b}_{T+1} = 0.$$

Substituting (8.52) into (8.54) we obtain the equation determining the level of interest rates

$$1 + i_{t+1} = \frac{U_{c,t}}{\beta U_{c,t+1}}(1 + \pi_{t+1}), \tag{8.56}$$

which we already obtained in the models in previous sections.

Substituting (8.52) into (8.53) and using (8.56)

$$\frac{U_{\bar{m},t+1}}{U_{c,t}} = 1 - \frac{1}{1 + i_{t+1}}. \tag{8.57}$$

This condition determines the partial equilibrium demand for money, as already mentioned in previous sections. The only difference is that rather than the nominal rate of interest, the equation now includes a positive function of that nominal rate.

Under utility function (8.49) the previous condition becomes

$$\frac{\partial v / \partial \bar{m}_{t+1}}{\partial v / \partial c_t} = 1 - \frac{1}{1 + i_{t+1}}. \tag{8.58}$$

Finally, substituting (8.52) into (8.55)

$$U_{1-l,t} = U_{c,t}(1 - \tau_t^y), \tag{8.59}$$

which indicates that the marginal rate of substitution between consumption and leisure is equal to the after-tax real wage.

8.7.1.2 The Government

The government purchases $G_t = g_t N_t$ units of the consumption commodity which are financed by liquidity injections, by issuing debt and by the proceeds of the income tax

$$P_t g_t = [M_{t+1} - M_t] + [V_{t+1} - (1 + i_t) V_t] + \tau_t^y P_t l_t. \tag{8.60}$$

Analogously,

$$g_t = \left[\bar{m}_{t+1} - \frac{\bar{m}_t}{1 + \pi_t} \right] + \left[\bar{b}_{t+1} - \frac{1 + i_t}{1 + \pi_t} \bar{b}_t \right] + \tau_t^y l_t. \tag{8.61}$$

8.7.1.3 The Representative Agent Solution

The representative agent solution, which coincides with the competitive equilibrium, as we already shown in Chap. 3, is a sequence of quantities and prices such that: (1) the representative agent behaves competitively, (2) the market for the single commodity in the economy clears and (3) the government budget constraint holds. Therefore, the equilibrium allocation is characterized by: (8.51), (8.56)–(8.59) and (8.61). These equations guarantee that the market for the consumption commodity clears, production being split between private and public consumption[33]:

$$c_t + g_t = l_t.$$

8.7.2 Implementability Condition

The implementability condition allows us to achieve important simplification by consolidating for all t the Euler conditions (8.52)–(8.55), which form part of the characterization of the dynamic general equilibrium. It is obtained in a sequence of steps:

1. Multiply the period t budget constraint (8.51) by the discounted Lagrange multiplier $\beta^t \lambda_t$, and add over t:

$$\sum_{t=0}^{\infty} \beta^t \lambda_t c_t + \sum_{t=0}^{\infty} \beta^t \lambda_t \bar{m}_{t+1} + \sum_{t=0}^{\infty} \beta^t \lambda_t \bar{b}_{t+1}$$
$$= \sum_{t=0}^{\infty} \beta^t \lambda_t \frac{\bar{m}_t}{1+\pi_t} + \sum_{t=0}^{\infty} \beta^t \lambda_t \frac{(1+i_t)\bar{b}_t}{1+\pi_t} + \sum_{t=0}^{\infty} \beta^t \lambda_t (1-\tau_t^y) l_t.$$

2. $\sum_{t=0}^{\infty} \beta^t \lambda_t c_t = \sum_{t=0}^{\infty} \beta^t U_{c,t}\, c_t$ from (8.52).

3. $\sum_{t=0}^{\infty} \beta^t \lambda_t \left(\bar{m}_{t+1} - \frac{\bar{m}_t}{1+\pi_t} \right) = \sum_{t=0}^{\infty} \beta^t (\lambda_t - \frac{\beta \lambda_{t+1}}{1+\pi_{t+1}}) \bar{m}_{t+1} - \lambda_0 \frac{\bar{m}_0}{1+\pi_0}$
   $= \sum_{t=0}^{\infty} \beta^t U_{\bar{m},t+1} \bar{m}_{t+1} - U_{c,0} \frac{\bar{m}_0}{1+\pi_0}$; where we have used (8.53).

4. $\sum_{t=0}^{\infty} \beta^t \lambda_t \bar{b}_{t+1} - \sum_{t=0}^{\infty} \beta^t \lambda_t \frac{(1+i_t)\bar{b}_t}{1+\pi_t} = \sum_{t=0}^{\infty} \beta^t (\lambda_t - \beta \lambda_{t+1} \frac{1+i_{t+1}}{1+\pi_{t+1}}) \bar{b}_{t+1} - \lambda_0 \frac{(1+i_0)\bar{b}_0}{1+\pi_0}$
   $= -U_{c,0} \frac{(1+i_0)\bar{b}_0}{1+\pi_0}$ because of (8.54).

5. $\sum_{t=0}^{\infty} \beta^t \lambda_t (1-\tau_t^y) l_t = \sum_{t=0}^{\infty} \beta^t U_{1-l,t} l_t$ from (8.55).

6. Substituting the results from steps 2–5 in the expression obtained in step 1, we get

$$\sum_{t=0}^{\infty} \beta^t U_{c,t} c_t + \sum_{t=0}^{\infty} \beta^t U_{\bar{m},t+1} \bar{m}_{t+1} - \sum_{t=0}^{\infty} \beta^t U_{1-l,t} l_t$$
$$= U_{c,0} \left(\frac{\bar{m}_0 + (1+i_0)\bar{b}_0}{1+\pi_0} \right), \tag{8.62}$$

---

[33] Remember that there is not capital accumulation in this model economy.

which is the *implementability condition*. Let us denote $a_0 = \left(\frac{\bar{m}_0 + (1+i_0)\bar{b}_0}{1+\pi_0}\right)$. To make the Ramsey problem interesting, it is usually assumed that $a_0 = 0$. If $a_0 > 0$, then the initial stock of nominal assets in consumer's portfolio, $M_0 + (1+i_0)V_0$, is positive and it is optimal to increase the initial level of prices to infinity. On the other hand, if $a_0 < 0$, then the initial stock of nominal assets is negative and it is optimal to reduce prices so that the government obtains the resources it needs without using any distortionary instrument.

8.7.3 The Ramsey Problem

The Ramsey problem solved by the government consists on finding the combination of nominal interest rate and tax rate on salary income, as well as the sequence of prices and quantities that: (1) maximize the discounted flow of current and future utility, (2) while being a competitive equilibrium. Therefore, the problem is

$$\max_{\{c_t,\bar{m}_{t+1},l_t\}} \sum_{t=0}^{\infty} \beta^t U(c_t, \bar{m}_{t+1}, 1 - l_t),$$

subject to[34]

$$\sum_{t=0}^{\infty} \beta^t \left[c_t U_{c,t} + \bar{m}_{t+1} U_{\bar{m},t+1} - l_t U_{1-l_t} \right] = 0,$$

$$c_t + g_t = l_t. \tag{8.63}$$

The solution to this problem characterizes the optimal allocation of resources. Then, optimal policy instruments can be obtained by substituting the optimal allocations into the conditions characterizing the competitive equilibrium.

It is convenient to introduce the function

$$\Phi(c_t, \bar{m}_{t+1}, l_t, \mu) = U(c_t, \bar{m}_{t+1}, 1 - l_t) + \mu \left(c_t U_{c,t} + \bar{m}_{t+1} U_{\bar{m},t+1} - l_t U_{1-l_t} \right),$$

where μ is the Lagrange multiplier associated to the implementability condition (a single intertemporal condition). This allows us to rewrite the previous problem

$$\max_{\{c_t,\bar{m}_{t+1},l_t\}} \sum_{t=0}^{\infty} \beta^t \Phi(c_t, \bar{m}_{t+1}, l_t, \mu),$$

subject to (8.63).

---

[34] Notice that the two restrictions that follow characterize the competitive equilibrium. Indeed, we have already shown that the implementability condition summarizes (8.52)–(8.55). Together with the global constraint of resources (8.63), these conditions characterize the competitive equilibrium. It is not hard to show that if all these equations hold, so does the government budget constraint.

The Lagrangian is

$$L^R(c_t, \bar{m}_{t+1}, l_t) = \sum_{t=0}^{\infty} \beta^t \left[\Phi(c_t, \bar{m}_{t+1}, l_t, \mu) - \Omega_t (c_t + g_t - l_t) \right].$$

First order conditions are

$$\frac{\partial L^R}{\partial c_t} = 0 \Leftrightarrow \Phi_{c,t} - \Omega_t = 0, \tag{8.64}$$

$$\frac{\partial L^R}{\partial \bar{m}_{t+1}} = 0 \Leftrightarrow \Phi_{\bar{m},t+1} = 0, \tag{8.65}$$

$$\frac{\partial L^R}{\partial l_t} = 0 \Leftrightarrow \Phi_{l,t} + \Omega_t = 0, \tag{8.66}$$

Since $v(c_t, \bar{m}_{t+1})$ is homogeneous of degree φ, $c_t \frac{\partial v}{\partial c_t} + \bar{m}_{t+1} \frac{\partial v}{\partial \bar{m}_{t+1}} = \varphi v$, so that function $\Phi(.)$ becomes

$$\Phi(c_t, \bar{m}_{t+1}, l_t, \mu) = U(c_t, \bar{m}_{t+1}, 1 - l_t) + \mu \left(c_t U_{c,t} + \bar{m}_{t+1} U_{\bar{m},t+1} - l_t U_{1-l,t} \right)$$

$$= v(.)H(.) + \mu \left(c_t \frac{\partial v}{\partial c_t} H(.) + \bar{m}_{t+1} \frac{\partial v}{\partial \bar{m}_{t+1}} H(.) - v(.) \frac{\partial H}{\partial (1 - l_t)} l_t \right)$$

$$= v(.)H(.) + \mu \left(\varphi v(.)H(.) - v(.) \frac{\partial H}{\partial (1 - l_t)} l_t \right)$$

$$= v(.) \left(H(.)(1 + \mu\varphi) - \mu \frac{\partial H}{\partial (1 - l_t)} l_t \right)$$

$$= v(c_t, \bar{m}_{t+1}) \Psi(l_t, \mu),$$

where $\Psi(l_t, \mu) = \left(H(.)(1 + \mu\varphi) - \mu \frac{\partial H}{\partial (1 - l_t)} l_t \right)$.

Therefore, under the utility function (8.49), condition (8.65) becomes

$$\frac{\partial v}{\partial \bar{m}_{t+1}} = 0, \tag{8.67}$$

and taking this condition to (8.58), we obtain $i_{t+1} = 0$. This implies that, under the optimal monetary policy, the nominal return on bonds and on money coincide, so that Friedman's rule is valid.

8.8 Exercises

Exercise 1. Let us suppose that the government finances its lump-sum transfers to consumers just by printing money, issuing debt and raising proportional taxes on consumption. Consider a production function $y_t = Ak_t^\alpha$, and preferences represented by a utility function: $U(c_t, \bar{m}_{t+1}) = \ln(c_t) + \theta \ln(\bar{m}_{t+1})$, where $\bar{m}_{t+1} = \frac{M_{t+1}}{P_t}$. Show that if the government has an inflation steady-state target π_{ss}, the model can be solved recursively to obtain the steady state values of transfers and real balances which are compatible with the inflation target. Find the expressions determining the steady state levels of all variables in the economy. Is the inflation target always neutral or does neutrality depend on the assumptions on endogenous variables, i.e., on the policy targets established by the government?

Starting from values: $\alpha = 0.36$, $A = 1$, $\theta = 0.5$, $\beta = 0.95$, $\delta = 0.10$.

(a) Choose any values you want for τ_{ss}^c and b_{ss}. Find numerical steady-state levels $c_{ss}, k_{ss}, m_{ss}, y_{ss}, r_{ss}, \zeta_{ss}$ as functions of π_{ss}, b_{ss} and τ_{ss}^c for a range of values of the latter. What is the welfare cost of inflation?

(b) Choose any values you want for τ_{ss}^c and ζ_{ss}. Find numerical steady-state levels $c_{ss}, k_{ss}, m_{ss}, y_{ss}, r_{ss}, b_{ss}$ as functions of π_{ss}, ζ_{ss} and τ_{ss}^c for a range of values of the latter. What is the welfare cost of inflation?

(c) Choose any values you want for ζ_{ss} and b_{ss}. Find numerical steady-state levels $c_{ss}, k_{ss}, m_{ss}, y_{ss}, r_{ss}, \tau_{ss}^c$ as functions of π_{ss}, ζ_{ss} and b_{ss} for a range of values of the latter. What is the welfare cost of inflation?

Exercise 2. Let us suppose the government finances its lump-sum transfers to consumers by printing money, issuing debt and raising proportional taxes on output and consumption. Consider a production function $y_t = Ak_t^\alpha$, and preferences represented by a utility function: $U(c_t, \bar{m}_{t+1}) = \dfrac{\left(c_t \left(\frac{M_{t+1}}{P_t}\right)^\theta\right)^{1-\sigma}}{1-\sigma}$, $\theta > 0, \sigma > 0, \sigma \neq 1$, where $\bar{m}_{t+1} = \frac{M_{t+1}}{P_t}$.

(a) Assuming that the government maintains a constant tax rate on output τ_{ss}^y, a constant tax rate on consumption τ_{ss}^c and a constant stock of bonds b_{ss}, and it has a steady-state inflation target π_{ss}, show that the model can be solved recursively to obtain the steady-state values of the variables in the economy, as well as the steady-state levels of real balances and transfers which are compatible with the inflation target. Find analytical expressions determining the steady-state values of all variables in the economy. Is the inflation target neutral? Starting from values: $\alpha = 0.36$, $A = 1$, $\theta = 0.5$, $\beta = 0.95$, $\delta = 0.10$, find steady-state levels $c_{ss}, k_{ss}, m_{ss}, y_{ss}, r_{ss}, \zeta_{ss}$ as functions of π_{ss}, for a range of values of the latter. Choose any values you want for τ_{ss}^y, τ_{ss}^c and b_{ss}.

(b) Repeat the exercise under the assumption that the government maintains a constant level of transfers ζ_{ss}, a constant tax rate on consumption τ_{ss}^c, and a constant stock of bonds b_{ss} and it has a steady-state inflation target π_{ss}. (Note: Now, the model cannot be solved recursively. If we consider that the rate of inflation is exogenous the equation determining the tax rate turns out to be nonlinear, complicating the solution of the system in a spreadsheet. However, if the tax rate is supposed to be exogenous and we endogenously compute the rate of inflation, then solving the model in a spreadsheet becomes very simple. Such calculations show, among other things, that inflation is not neutral.)

(c) Repeat the exercise under the assumption that the government maintains a constant level of transfers ζ_{ss}, a constant tax rate on output τ^y_{ss}, and a constant stock of bonds b_{ss} and it has a steady-state inflation target π_{ss}.

Exercise 3. Let us assume that the government realizes a lump-sum transfer to consumers, which is financed by printing money, issuing debt and raising proportional taxes on labour and capital income at the same rate and consumption. Assume now that private agents have a unit of time as endowment every period. Part of that unit is used to work (l_t), while the rest is used up as leisure ($1 - l_t$). The production function is: $y_t = Ak_t^\alpha l_t^{1-\alpha}$, and the utility function: $U(c_t, \bar{m}_{t+1}, l_t) = \dfrac{\left(c_t(1-l_t)^\Psi \bar{m}_{t+1}^\theta\right)^{1-\sigma} - 1}{1-\sigma}$,
$\Psi, \theta > 0$ and $\bar{m}_{t+1} = \dfrac{M_{t+1}}{P_t}$. The government has an inflation target.

(a) Write the optimization problems faced by the representative consumer and by the firm. Derive and interpret the first order conditions for each of those optimization problems. Which set of equations defines the competitive equilibrium? Which variables are determined in competitive equilibrium?

(b) Show that the equilibrium levels of consumption, real balances, employment, output and the stock of capital in the economy in the previous paragraph are the same as those obtained if the consumer is assumed to face the budget constraint:

$$(1+\tau^c)c_t + k_{t+1} + \frac{M_{t+1}}{P_t} + b_{t+1} \leq (1-\tau^y)f(k_t, l_t) + (1-\delta)k_t + \frac{M_t}{P_t} + \zeta_t + r_t b_t.$$

(c) Suppose that the government chooses the tax rates on consumption and income, as well as the level of government debt and the rate of inflation. Show that the steady-state of the model can be solved for recursively. Find analytical expressions to determine steady-state levels for all variables in the economy. Is the inflation target neutral? Which is the inflation rate maximizing welfare in steady-state? Is that the same as the rate of inflation maximizing seigniorage revenues? Check that the answer to these two questions does not depend on the value of σ.

(d) Assume $\alpha = 0.36$, $\beta = 0.95$, $A = 1$, $\delta = 0.1$, $\Psi = 2$, $\theta = 0.175$, $\tau^c = 0.15$, $\tau^y = 0.2$ and compute the welfare cost in steady-state for different values of the rate of inflation. Is the increase in welfare cost proportional to the increase in inflation? Check that these results do not depend on the value of σ.

(e) Change the tax rate on consumption and compute the welfare cost in steady-state for different values of the rate of inflation. Is the increase in welfare cost proportional to the increase in inflation? Check that these results do not depend on the value of σ. Compare these results with those obtained in paragraph d) Does the welfare cost of inflation depend on the value of the consumption tax rate?

(f) Change the value of the income tax rate and compute the welfare cost in steady-state for different values of the rate of inflation. Is the increase in welfare cost proportional to the increase in inflation? Check that these results do not depend on the value of σ. Compare these results with those obtained in paragraph (d). Does the welfare cost of inflation depend on the value of the income tax rate?

Exercise 4. Consider the economy described in Exercise 3. Consider the utility function:

$$U(c_t, m_t, l_t) = \frac{\left(c_t m_t^\theta\right)^{1-\sigma}}{1-\sigma} + \Psi \ln(1 - l_t) \quad \text{with} \quad m_t = \frac{M_t}{P_t}.$$

In particular, assume parameter values $A = 1$, $\alpha = 0.36$, $\beta = 0.95$, $\delta = 0.10$, $\theta = 0.005$, $\Psi = 1.7$. Suppose that the government keeps constant the values of the tax rates on consumption and income, as well as the level of public expenditures. Show that, in this case, inflation is not neutral. What is the rate of inflation maximizing welfare in steady-state? What is the rate of inflation that maximizes seigniorage revenues? What is the welfare cost in steady state of a given increase in inflation? Does the welfare cost increase proportionally to an increase in inflation? Does the welfare cost of inflation depend on the values of the consumption and income tax rates?

Exercise 5. Assume that the government purchases some units of the consumption commodity, that are 'thrown to the sea'. These are financed by increasing the money supply and by a tax on consumption. The representative private agent has an endowment of a unit of time every period. Part of it is devoted to working l_t), the rest being used as leisure ($1-l_t$). The production function is: $y_t = k_t^\alpha l_t^{1-\alpha}$, while the utility function is: $U(c_t, \frac{M_{t+1}}{P_t}, l_t) = \Psi \ln c_t + (1 - \Psi) \ln(1 - l_t) + \Phi \ln \frac{M_{t+1}}{P_t}$, with $\Psi \in (0,1)$, $\Phi > 0$. Show that if the government has an inflation target and keeps constant the level of public expenditures, the steady-state of the economy can not be solved for recursively since the government then does not keep constant the value of the tax rate on consumption.

Assume parameter values $\alpha = 0.36$, $\beta = 0.95$, $\delta = 0.1$, $\Psi = 0.35$, $\theta = 0.175$, and also that public consumption represents 20% of production. Calculate numerically the changes produced in the steady-state allocation of resources, as well as in the level of welfare, as the inflation target changes. Is the inflation target neutral? What is the rate of inflation maximizing the level of utility in steady-state?

Chapter 9
Transitional Dynamics in Monetary Economies: Numerical Solutions

9.1 Introduction

In the previous chapter we have characterized dynamic optimality conditions for monetary economies, but we have only evaluated the steady-state effects of monetary policy. To complete the analysis, this chapter is devoted to characterizing the transitional dynamics of a monetary economy, as it moves from the initial condition to the steady-state. In particular, we examine the evolution of a given economy following a monetary policy intervention. We start by discussing the possible instability of the stock of debt, an issue that conditions the set of feasible policies which needs to be taken into consideration in the type of policy analysis which is undertaken in this chapter. As an example, we saw in the previous chapter how a policy of choosing the rate of money growth and the lump-sum transfer to consumers would lead to a well-defined steady-state, with stable inflation and a finite stock of debt. That is a not trivial result, since interest payments on outstanding debt have a feedback effect on the deficit and hence, on financing requirements, producing a tendency for the stock of debt to increase over time. Hence, when the government changes the inflation rate or the size of the lump-sum transfer, the service of outstanding debt could take the stock of debt to diverge from its steady-state level along an explosive path. This possibility can be avoided by linking the size of the lump-sum transfer to the level of outstanding debt each period t. The implication is then that the government can only freely choose monetary policy, fiscal policy being constrained to satisfy the government budget constraint.

There is a debate on whether the monetary authority should control the interest rate or the money supply. In this respect, our second theme for discussion shows that the type of monetary policy being implemented may lead to nominal indeterminacy, defined as the possibility that there might not be a unique equilibrium price level. To proceed in an orderly fashion, we first consider a deterministic monetary economy in which we successively discuss the cases when the monetary authority chooses the rate of growth of money supply and leaves interest rates to be determined in the market or, alternatively, when it uses nominal rates as the control variable. We show how nominal indeterminacy arises when the monetary authority controls nominal rates.

A. Novales et al., *Economic Growth: Theory and Numerical Solution Methods*,
© Springer-Verlag Berlin Heidelberg 2009

After that, we devote a section to numerically characterizing the short-run effects of a change in either type of policy, control of money growth or of nominal rates, as the economy moves along the transition towards the new steady-state. We show that even though monetary policy may be neutral in the long-run, it may be non-neutral in the short-run. Furthermore, we show that monetary policy effects may be larger if the government changes policy gradually, relative to the possibility of a drastic policy change. We then move to the stochastic version of the monetary economy, and consider again the same two types of monetary policy. When the nominal rate of interest is the control variable, we will consider the monetary authority following different versions of Taylor's rule, alternatively including or excluding the rate of inflation from the policy rule.

This chapter ends with neokeynesian monetary models. At a difference with the rest of the chapter, these models incorporate some aspect of price rigidity, and we emphasize the similarities and differences with neoclassical monetary models with flexible prices. As in previous chapters, numerical solutions are implemented in EXCEL spreadsheets and MATLAB programs which are provided along with the book.

9.2 Stability of Public Debt

Let us consider an economy in which the government makes each period a lump-sum transfer to the representative agent, which is financed through liquidity injections and real bond issuing. A real bond is bought with one unit of commodity and, at maturity, it gives back to its owner that unit of commodity increased by the return. The government chooses exogenously an inflation target which, as shown in Sect. 8.2.2, in the absence of population growth, it is equal in steady-state to the rate of growth of money supply. As shown in that section, if the government also chooses exogenously a target for the size of the lump-sum transfer, the steady-state stock of public debt (b_{ss}) will be endogenously determined, jointly with the level of consumption (c_{ss}), the stock of capital (k_{ss}), the real return on public debt, (r_{ss}), and the level of real balances at the beginning of the period (m_{ss}).

In particular, the government budget constraint will be, in steady-state

$$\pi_{ss}m_{ss} = \zeta_{ss} + r_{ss}b_{ss},$$

where ζ_{ss} and π_{ss} denote the size of the lump-sum transfer and the rate of inflation, both exogenous and constant.

We now show that if the initial stock of debt, b_0, is above its steady-state level b_{ss}, then the time path for debt may easily explode, never converging to its steady-state level. To see that, let us assume that the government keeps constant the inflation rate and the size of the lump-sum transfer at their target levels, π_{ss}, ζ_{ss}. For simplicity, let us also assume that the stock of capital is also at its steady-state level. Then, so will be consumption, output, real balances and real interest rates, and the government budget constraint will determine the time evolution of public debt as

$$b_{t+1} = (1+r_{ss})b_t + \zeta_{ss} - \pi_{ss}m_{ss}$$
$$= (1+r_{ss})^{t+1}b_0 - r_{ss}b_{ss}\frac{(1+r_{ss})^{t+1}-1}{r_{ss}}$$
$$= (1+r_{ss})^{t+1}(b_0 - b_{ss}) + b_{ss}.$$

Since $1+r_{ss} = \frac{1}{\beta} > 0$, then, unless $b_0 \neq b_{ss}$, the time path for the stock of public debt will generally be explosive at a rate that will violate the corresponding transversality condition.[1] Hence, it is necessary to include in our analysis some additional condition excluding that possibility. A way out of this difficulty, proposed by Sims [85] and Leeper [55], is to assume that, being aware of this difficulty, the authority follows a policy of linking each period the amount of the lump-sum transfer made to consumers to the stock of outstanding debt

$$\zeta_t = \zeta - \eta b_t, \tag{9.1}$$

so that the transfer is a decreasing function of the stock of public debt each period. Under this assumption, the equilibrium level for public debt in period t is

$$b_{t+1} = (1+r_{ss}-\eta)b_t + \zeta - \pi_{ss}m_{ss}, \quad \forall t ,$$

which converges to its steady-state level b_{ss} $\left(b_{ss} = \frac{\zeta-\pi_{ss}m_{ss}}{\eta-r_{ss}}\right)$ for any initial level b_0 so long as $-1 < 1+r_{ss}-\eta < 1$,[2] i.e., provided $\eta \in \left(\frac{1}{\beta}-1, \frac{1}{\beta}+1\right)$. This relationship between the level of the transfer and the stock of debt will be extensively used in the next sections.

Condition (9.1), that links the size of the lump-sum transfer to the private sector to the stock of public debt each period, avoids the instability problems with the path for the public debt variable not only when monetary policy is designed to control the money supply, but also when the control variable is the nominal rate of interest. As we will see below, the same link between both variables also guarantees the stationarity of the path for public debt when the stock of capital is outside steady-state, or when it experiences continuous deviations from its steady state level, as it is the case in stochastic economies. For the argument above, it is also irrelevant whether public debt is made up by real or by nominal bonds, or whether consumers care about the real value of money held at the beginning or at the end of the period.[3]

---

[1] From Chap. 8, the transversality condition becomes, under these assumptions:

$$\lim_{T\to\infty}\frac{1}{(1+r_{ss})^T}\lambda_T b_T = \lim_{T\to\infty}\frac{1}{(1+r_{ss})^T}\lambda_T\left[(1+r_{ss})^T(b_0-b_{ss})+b_{ss}\right]$$
$$= \lim_{T\to\infty}\lambda_T(b_0-b_{ss}) + \lim_{T\to\infty}\frac{\lambda_T b_{ss}}{(1+r_{ss})^T}$$

which will not be zero, since from optimality conditions, the Lagrange multiplier is equal to the marginal utility of consumption, which will generally be bounded away from zero in steady state.

[2] Or $r_{ss} < \eta < 2+r_{ss}$, an expression that we will use below.

[3] Or whether we are in a monetary or in a non-monetary economy, for that matter.

Summarizing, the backfeeding character of the stock of public debt implies that when the government implements an *active monetary policy* like controlling the rate of growth of money or the nominal rate of interest, it is forced to use a *passive fiscal policy* regarding the time evolution of the stock of public debt and the amount of the transfers to the private sector, with the only objective that the government budget constraint holds each period.

9.3 Alternative Strategies for Monetary Policy: Control of Nominal Rates vs. Money Growth Control

We consider again the problem solved by the representative agent in a monetary economy described in Sect. 8.5. In addition to the tax revenues obtained from consumption and income taxes, the government uses bond and money issuing to finance its purchases of some units of the consumption commodity, which are returned to consumers in the form of a lump-sum transfer. The consumer/worker household unit takes as given income and consumption taxes τ_t^y, τ_t^c as well as government transfers, ζ_t, and solves the optimization problem:

$$\max_{\{c_t, M_{t+1}, k_{t+1}, b_{t+1}\}_{t=0}^{\infty}} \sum_{t=0}^{\infty} \beta^t U(c_t, M_t/P_t)$$

subject to

$$(1 + \tau_t^c)c_t + k_{t+1} - (1 - \delta)k_t + \frac{M_{t+1}}{P_t} + b_{t+1}$$

$$= (1 - \tau_t^y)A_t k_t^\alpha + \frac{M_t}{P_t} + (1 + r_t)b_t + \zeta_t, \quad t = 0, 1, 2, \ldots, \quad (9.2)$$

$$\text{given } k_0, M_0, b_0,$$

where r_t is the rate of return on real debt. We assume that the level of technology follows an exogenous, first order autoregressive process

$$\ln(A_t) = (1 - \rho_A)\ln(A_{ss}) + \rho_A \ln(A_{t-1}), \quad |\rho_A| < 1. \quad (9.3)$$

The government budget constraint is

$$\tau_t^c c_t + \frac{M_{t+1} - M_t}{P_t} + (b_{t+1} - (1 + r_t)b_t) + \tau_t^y A_t k_t^\alpha = \zeta_t, \quad t = 0, 1, 2, \ldots \quad (9.4)$$

Central governments use two types of strategies to try affect the time evolution of the economy: either controlling the amount of money in circulation, or controlling the nominal rate of interest. It is impossible to control both variable simultaneously. The mechanism by which monetary policy gets transmitted to real activity is different, depending on which strategy is adopted for monetary policy. The analytical framework we have introduced is used in the next two sections to rigorously characterize the differences between both transmission mechanisms.

Hence, we consider two alternative situations:

1. The government chooses the time path for nominal money $\{M_t\}_{t=0}^{\infty}$ and for the two tax rates: $\{\tau_t^c, \tau_t^y\}_{t=0}^{\infty}$, while interest rates $\{i_t\}_{t=0}^{\infty}$, the size of the lump-sum transfer and the stock of public debt $\{\zeta_t, b_t\}_{t=0}^{\infty}$ are endogenously determined.
2. The government chooses the time path for nominal interest rates, i.e., the nominal return on bonds: $\{i_t\}_{t=0}^{\infty}$ and for the two tax rates: $\{\tau_t^c, \tau_t^y\}_{t=0}^{\infty}$, while the money supply $\{M_t\}_{t=0}^{\infty}$ and the size of the lump-sum transfer and the stock of public debt $\{\zeta_t, b_t\}_{t=0}^{\infty}$ are endogenously determined.

For simplicity, we will assume in both cases a constant choice of tax rates, $\tau_t^c = \tau^c, \tau_t^y = \tau^y, \forall t$.

9.4 Deterministic Monetary Model with the Monetary Authority Choosing Money Growth

Let the time evolution of nominal money balances be: $M_{t+1} = (1 + x_{t+1})M_t$ from a given M_0, with a growth rate chosen according to

$$\ln(1 + x_{t+1}) = (1 - \rho_x)\ln(1 + x_{ss}) + \rho_x \ln(1 + x_t), \quad |\rho_x| < 1. \quad (9.5)$$

that converges to its long-run value x_{ss}, so long as $|\rho_x| < 1$. A value $\rho_x = 0$ would allow us to analyze the constant-x_t case. It is important to bear in mind that, in spite of the time index, the value of x_{t+1} is known at time t. If the government also chooses the time path for transfers $\{\zeta_t\}_{t=0}^{T}$ under a condition $\zeta_t = \zeta - \eta b_t$, with $2 + r_{ss} > \eta > r_{ss}$, the time path for bonds would remain stable, as discussed in 9.2. From (9.4) and denoting $m_t = \frac{M_t}{P_t}$, the time path for government debt will obey the difference equation[4]:

$$\begin{aligned} b_{t+1} &= (1 + r_t)b_t + \zeta - \eta b_t - \tau^y A_t k_t^{\alpha} - x_{t+1}m_t - \tau^c c_t \\ &= (1 + r_t - \eta)b_t + \zeta - \tau^y A_t k_t^{\alpha} - x_{t+1}m_t - \tau^c c_t. \end{aligned} \quad (9.6)$$

Following an argument similar to those used in the Chap. 8 we obtain the equations characterizing the solution to the representative agent's model:

$$U_c(c_t, m_t) = \beta \left[U_c(c_{t+1}, m_{t+1}) \left((1 - \tau^y)A_{t+1}\alpha k_{t+1}^{\alpha-1} + 1 - \delta \right) \right], \quad (9.7)$$

$$r_{t+1} = (1 - \tau^y)A_{t+1}\alpha k_{t+1}^{\alpha-1} - \delta, \quad (9.8)$$

---

[4] Notice that $\frac{M_{t+1} - M_t}{P_t} = \frac{M_{t+1} - M_t}{M_t}\frac{M_t}{P_t} = x_{t+1}m_t$. In the steady-state analysis in the previous chapter we made a different type of transformation, leaving segniorage revenues as a function of the rate of inflation. We now prefer that the rate of money growth may explicitly appear, since we consider an exogenous time path for it, while the rate of inflation is endogenously determined.

$$i_{t+1} = (1+\tau^c)\frac{U_m(c_{t+1}, m_{t+1})}{U_c(c_{t+1}, m_{t+1})}, \tag{9.9}$$

$$1 + i_{t+1} = (1 + r_{t+1})(1 + \pi_{t+1}), \tag{9.10}$$

$$c_t + k_{t+1} - (1 - \delta)k_t = A_t k_t^\alpha, \tag{9.11}$$

for all t, together with the government's budget constraint (9.6). Equation (9.12) is an identity that allows us to compute the rate of inflation:

$$1 + \pi_{t+1} = \frac{m_t}{m_{t+1}}(1 + x_{t+1}). \tag{9.12}$$

Equation (9.7) is Euler's condition for the stock of capital. Equation (9.8) points out that the private agent will demand government bonds as well as physical capital, provided the rate of return on bonds is equal to the return on capital, net of taxes and depreciation. Equation (9.9) defines the demand for money. Equation (9.10) shows the relationship between nominal and real rates of interest and the rate of inflation. Equation (9.11) is the global constraint of resources in the economy.

Plugging (9.10), (9.12), (9.8) into (9.9), we get

$$\left[(1-\tau^y)A_{t+1}\alpha k_{t+1}^{\alpha-1} + 1 - \delta\right]\frac{m_t(1+x_{t+1})}{m_{t+1}} = 1 + (1+\tau^c)\frac{U_m(c_{t+1}, m_{t+1})}{U_c(c_{t+1}, m_{t+1})}. \tag{9.13}$$

The numerical solution can be obtained by computing $\{k_{t+1}, m_t, c_t\}_{t=0}^\infty$ from (9.7), (9.11) and (9.13) for specific processes and parameters: $(\{x_t, A_t\}_{t=0}^\infty, k_0, \tau^y, \tau^c)$. Specific details are discussed in the next section. In doing so, we will pay special attention to stability conditions. Then, $\{r_{t+1}\}_{t=0}^\infty$, $\{\pi_{t+1}\}_{t=0}^\infty$, $\{i_{t+1}\}_{t=0}^\infty$ are obtained from (9.8), (9.12), (9.10), respectively. Given the value of m_0 we just obtained and the level of M_0, we can compute P_0, reflecting the fact that there is not nominal indeterminacy. Therefore, we can compute the whole price sequence using the time path we have obtained for the inflation rate, and there is not nominal indeterminacy. Finally, given (ζ, η, b_0), we can compute $\{b_{t+1}, \zeta_t\}_{t=0}^\infty$ from (9.6) together with the imposed relationship between the size of the lump-sum transfer and the stock of government bonds (9.1).

Let us assume a specific utility function: $U(c_t, M_t/P_t) = \frac{\left[c_t(M_t/P_t)^\theta\right]^{1-\sigma} - 1}{1-\sigma}$, $\sigma > 0$, $\theta > 0$. Under this specification of preferences, the marginal utility of consumption depends on real balances, at a difference of what happens with a logarithmic utility function. *It is precisely this dependence what leads monetary policy to be non-neutral in the short run, even though the implied effects might be close to negligible in some cases.* The production function is the same we have often used along the book, with productivity following an autoregressive process as specified in (9.3): $y_t = f(k_t) = A_t k_t^\alpha$. Then, (9.7) and (9.13) become

$$c_t^{-\sigma} m_t^{\theta(1-\sigma)} = \beta c_{t+1}^{-\sigma} m_{t+1}^{\theta(1-\sigma)} \left[\alpha (1-\tau^y) A_{t+1} k_{t+1}^{\alpha-1} + 1 - \delta \right], \quad \forall t \qquad (9.14)$$

$$\left[(1-\tau^y) A_{t+1} \alpha k_{t+1}^{\alpha-1} + 1 - \delta \right] \frac{m_t}{m_{t+1}} (1 + x_{t+1}) = 1 + (1+\tau^c) \frac{\theta c_{t+1}}{m_{t+1}} \quad \forall t \qquad (9.15)$$

9.4.1 Steady-State

Steady-state levels for the variables in the economy solving the system of equations that are obtained as steady-state versions of (9.14), (9.15), (9.8), (9.10)–(9.12), (9.6) and (9.1).

From (9.3) and (9.5): $A_t = A_{ss}$, $x_t = x_{ss}$.

$$k_{ss} = \left[\frac{(1-\tau^y) A_{ss} \alpha}{\frac{1}{\beta} - (1-\delta)} \right]^{\frac{1}{1-\alpha}}, \qquad (9.16)$$

$$c_{ss} = A_{ss} k_{ss}^{\alpha} - \delta k_{ss}, \qquad (9.17)$$

$$m_{ss} = (1+\tau^c) \theta \frac{c_{ss}}{i_{ss}}, \qquad (9.18)$$

$$1 + r_{ss} = \frac{1}{\beta}, \qquad (9.19)$$

$$1 + i_{ss} = \frac{1}{\beta}(1 + x_{ss}), \qquad (9.20)$$

$$\pi_{ss} = x_{ss}, \qquad (9.21)$$

$$b_{ss} = \frac{1}{r_{ss} - \eta} \left[\zeta - \tau^y A_{ss} k_{ss}^{\alpha} - x_{ss} m_{ss} - \tau^c c_{ss} \right], \qquad (9.22)$$

$$\zeta_{ss} = \zeta - \eta b_{ss}. \qquad (9.23)$$

The natural way to interpret this system of equations is under the assumption that the monetary authority chooses the steady-state rate of growth, x_{ss}. Steady-state inflation and nominal interest rates are then determined from (9.21) and (9.20). The real rate of interest, determined by (9.19), is also unaffected by monetary policy, even though the nominal rate of interest increases with the rate of growth of money supply. The first two equations determine the stock of capital and consumption, and steady-state output can be readily obtained. They are unaffected by the choice of steady-state growth of money and, in this sense, *monetary policy is neutral in the long-run*. The stock of physical capital and output can be seen to depend negatively from the income tax rate, as it would be the case in a non-monetary economy. Steady-state consumption will also be lower for a higher income tax. In this sense, fiscal policy is not neutral. However, the consumption tax does not have any real effect in the long-run. Steady-state real balances decrease for a higher rate of money growth, because the opportunity cost of holding real balances then increases. Real balances increase with the consumption tax, for transaction reasons, while decreasing with an increase in the income tax.

9.4.2 Solution Through a Log-Linear Approximation

In Sect. 9.4.1 we mentioned that $\{k_{t+1}, m_t, c_t\}_{t=0}^{\infty}$ are obtained from the system of equations (9.14), (9.15), (9.11), although we did not explain the specific details to do that. The remaining variables can be recursively obtained afterwards. We now explain how to obtain $\{k_{t+1}, m_t, c_t\}_{t=0}^{\infty}$.

To log-linearize this system, we rewrite (9.11) as

$$e^{\ln c_t} + e^{\ln k_{t+1}} - (1 - \delta)e^{\ln k_t} = e^{\ln A_t} e^{\alpha(\ln k_t)}, \tag{9.24}$$

(9.14) as

$$e^{-\sigma(\ln c_t)} e^{\theta(1-\sigma)(\ln m_t)} = \beta \left[e^{-\sigma(\ln c_{t+1})} e^{\theta(1-\sigma)(\ln m_{t+1})} \right.$$

$$\left. \times \left((1 - \tau^y)\alpha e^{\ln A_{t+1}} e^{(\alpha-1)(\ln k_{t+1})} + 1 - \delta \right) \right], \tag{9.25}$$

and (9.15) as

$$\left[(1 - \tau^y)\alpha e^{\ln A_{t+1}} e^{(\alpha-1)(\ln k_{t+1})} + 1 - \delta \right] e^{\ln m_t} e^{-\ln m_{t+1}} e^{\ln(1+x_{t+1})}$$

$$= 1 + (1 + \tau^c)\theta e^{\ln c_{t+1}} e^{-\ln m_{t+1}}. \tag{9.26}$$

Let us denote: $\hat{u}_t = \ln(u_t/u_{ss})$, $u = c, m, k$; $\hat{x}_t = \ln(1+x_t) - \ln(1+x_{ss})$. We then get, from (9.24)

$$0 = A_{ss}k_{ss}^{\alpha}\hat{A}_t + [A_{ss}\alpha k_{ss}^{\alpha} + (1 - \delta)k_{ss}]\hat{k}_t - c_{ss}\hat{c}_t - k_{ss}\hat{k}_{t+1}. \tag{9.27}$$

while from (9.25) we obtain

$$0 = \frac{\sigma}{\beta}\hat{c}_t - \frac{\theta(1-\sigma)}{\beta}\hat{m}_t - \frac{\sigma}{\beta}\hat{c}_{t+1} + \frac{\theta(1-\sigma)}{\beta}\hat{m}_{t+1} + \cdots$$

$$+ (\alpha - 1)\left(\frac{1}{\beta} - (1 - \delta) \right)\hat{k}_{t+1} + \left(\frac{1}{\beta} - (1 - \delta) \right)\rho_A\hat{A}_t, \tag{9.28}$$

where we have used (9.3), together with $\alpha(1 - \tau^y)A_{ss}k_{ss}^{\alpha-1} + 1 - \delta = \frac{1}{\beta}$.

From (9.26)

$$0 = (1+x_{ss})(1-\tau^y)A_{ss}\alpha k_{ss}^{\alpha-1}\rho_A\hat{A}_t$$

$$+(1+x_{ss})(1-\tau^y)A_{ss}\alpha(\alpha-1)k_{ss}^{\alpha-1}\hat{k}_{t+1} + \frac{1}{\beta}(1+x_{ss})\hat{m}_t$$

$$-\frac{1}{\beta}(1+x_{ss})\hat{m}_{t+1} + \frac{1}{\beta}(1+x_{ss})\hat{x}_{t+1} - \theta(1+\tau^c)\frac{c_{ss}}{m_{ss}}\hat{c}_{t+1}$$

$$+\theta(1+\tau^c)\frac{c_{ss}}{m_{ss}}\hat{m}_{t+1}, \tag{9.29}$$

where we have used (9.3), together with $\alpha(1-\tau^y)A_{ss}k_{ss}^{\alpha-1}+1-\delta = \frac{1}{\beta}$.
Equations (9.27)–(9.29) can be written in matrix form:

$$\underbrace{\begin{bmatrix} k_{ss} & 0 & 0 \\ (1-\alpha)\left(\frac{1}{\beta}-(1-\delta)\right) & \frac{\sigma}{\beta} & -\frac{\theta(1-\sigma)}{\beta} \\ A_{3,1} & \theta(1+\tau^c)\frac{c_{ss}}{m_{ss}} & 1 \end{bmatrix}}_{A} \underbrace{\begin{bmatrix} \hat{k}_{t+1} \\ \hat{c}_{t+1} \\ \hat{m}_{t+1} \end{bmatrix}}_{s_{t+1}}$$

$$= \underbrace{\begin{bmatrix} A_{ss}\alpha k_{ss}^{\alpha}+(1-\delta)k_{ss} & -c_{ss} & 0 \\ 0 & \frac{\sigma}{\beta} & -\frac{\theta(1-\sigma)}{\beta} \\ 0 & 0 & \frac{1}{\beta}(1+x_{ss}) \end{bmatrix}}_{B} \underbrace{\begin{bmatrix} \hat{k}_t \\ \hat{c}_t \\ \hat{m}_t \end{bmatrix}}_{s_t}$$

$$+ \underbrace{\begin{bmatrix} A_{ss}k_{ss}^{\alpha} & 0 \\ \rho_A\left(\frac{1}{\beta}-(1-\delta)\right) & 0 \\ (1+x_{ss})\rho_A\left(\frac{1}{\beta}-(1-\delta)\right) & \frac{(1+x_{ss})}{\beta} \end{bmatrix}}_{C} \underbrace{\begin{bmatrix} \hat{A}_t \\ \hat{x}_{t+1} \end{bmatrix}}_{a_t}, \tag{9.30}$$

where $A_{3,1} = (1-\alpha)\left(\frac{1}{\beta}-(1-\delta)\right)(1+x_{ss})$, which can be written as

$$As_{t+1} = Bs_t + Ca_t, \tag{9.31}$$

with vectors and matrices as defined in (9.30).
Solving for s_{t+1}:

$$s_{t+1} = A^{-1}Bs_t + A^{-1}Ca_t = Ds_t + Fa_t, \tag{9.32}$$

where matrix D being 3×3, has three eigenvalues. Since there are two control variables in s_{t+1}, we would need two relationships between control and state variables to be able to solve the model. These should come from stability conditions obtained in the usual fashion, as explained in the chapter on solution methods. For that to be the case, one of the eigenvalues of D must be stable, the other two being unstable. Then, given k_0, we would have two stability conditions that would allow us to determine the initial values of the two control variables: c_0, m_0, as functions of k_0, A_0, x_1. This would be a *determinate* equilibrium.

If the three eigenvalues were greater than one in absolute value or in modulus, the system would generally not have a solution, since we would then have more equations than variables to solve for. On the other hand, less than two unstable eigenvalues would lead to *indeterminacy* of equilibria, as discussed in the chapter on numerical solutions (Chap. 5), since at least one of the control variables could be arbitrarily chosen and still have a stable solution path.

The two stability conditions can be obtained as follows: let $D = M\Lambda M^{-1}$ denote the Jordan decomposition of matrix D. So, M is the matrix having as columns the right eigenvectors of D, while Λ is a diagonal matrix having as elements the eigenvalues of D. Diagonal elements in Λ and columns of M are ordered accordingly. Without loss of generality, let us assume that: $|\mu_1| < 1$, $|\mu_2| > 1$, $|\mu_3| > 1$. From (9.32)

$$M^{-1}s_{t+1} = \Lambda M^{-1}s_t + \underbrace{M^{-1}F}_{Q}a_t,$$

that is, if we denote by m_{ij} the elements in M^{-1}, we have

$$\underbrace{m_{11}\hat{k}_{t+1} + m_{12}\hat{c}_{t+1} + m_{13}\hat{m}_{t+1}}_{s^1_{t+1}} = \mu_1(m_{11}\hat{k}_t + m_{12}\hat{c}_t + m_{13}\hat{m}_t)$$

$$+ Q_{11}\hat{A}_t + Q_{12}\hat{x}_{t+1}, \tag{9.33}$$

$$\underbrace{m_{21}\hat{k}_{t+1} + m_{22}\hat{c}_{t+1} + m_{23}\hat{m}_{t+1}}_{s^2_{t+1}} = \mu_2(m_{21}\hat{k}_t + m_{22}\hat{c}_t + m_{23}\hat{m}_t)$$

$$+ Q_{21}\hat{A}_t + Q_{22}\hat{x}_{t+1}, \tag{9.34}$$

$$\underbrace{m_{31}\hat{k}_{t+1} + m_{32}\hat{c}_{t+1} + m_{33}\hat{m}_{t+1}}_{s^3_{t+1}} = \mu_3(m_{31}\hat{k}_t + m_{32}\hat{c}_t + m_{33}\hat{m}_t)$$

$$+ Q_{31}\hat{A}_t + Q_{32}\hat{x}_{t+1}. \tag{9.35}$$

Since μ_2 and μ_3 are unstable, we solve (9.34) and (9.35) forwards (see section on Blanchard–Kahn's solution method in the corresponding chapter)

$$s^2_t = \frac{Q_{21}}{\rho_A - \mu_2}\hat{A}_t + \frac{Q_{22}}{\rho_x - \mu_2}\hat{x}_{t+1}. \tag{9.36}$$

$$s^3_t = \frac{Q_{31}}{\rho_A - \mu_3}\hat{A}_t + \frac{Q_{32}}{\rho_x - \mu_3}\hat{x}_{t+1}. \tag{9.37}$$

which can be written in matrix form as

$$\underbrace{\begin{bmatrix} m_{22} & m_{23} \\ m_{32} & m_{33} \end{bmatrix}}_{G} \begin{bmatrix} \hat{c}_t \\ \hat{m}_t \end{bmatrix} = \underbrace{\begin{bmatrix} -m_{21} \frac{Q_{21}}{\rho_A - \mu_2} & \frac{Q_{22}}{\rho_x - \mu_2} \\ -m_{31} \frac{Q_{31}}{\rho_A - \mu_3} & \frac{Q_{32}}{\rho_x - \mu_3} \end{bmatrix}}_{H} \begin{bmatrix} \hat{k}_t \\ \hat{A}_t \\ \hat{x}_{t+1} \end{bmatrix}.$$

If we solve for vector $[\hat{c}_t, \hat{m}_t]'$, we obtain the two stability conditions

$$\hat{c}_t = J_{11}\hat{k}_t + J_{12}\hat{A}_t + J_{13}\hat{x}_{t+1}, \tag{9.38}$$

$$\hat{m}_t = J_{21}\hat{k}_t + J_{22}\hat{A}_t + J_{23}\hat{x}_{t+1}, \tag{9.39}$$

where $J = G^{-1}H$.

Finally, plugging (9.38) and (9.39) into the equation for the stable eigenvalue, (9.33), we get the stock of capital

$$\hat{k}_{t+1} = \mu_1 \hat{k}_t + \frac{1}{m_{11} + m_{12}J_{11} + m_{13}J_{21}}$$
$$\times \big[(Q_{11} + (m_{12}J_{12} + m_{13}J_{22})(\mu_1 - \rho_A))\hat{A}_t$$
$$+ (Q_{12} + (m_{12}J_{13} + m_{13}J_{23})(\mu_1 - \rho_x))\hat{x}_{t+1} \big]. \tag{9.40}$$

Therefore, given sequences $\left\{ \{\hat{A}_t\}_{t=0}^{T}, \{\hat{x}_{t+1}\}_{t=0}^{T}, k_0 \right\}$, we obtain the time path for the stock of capital $\{\hat{k}_{t+1}\}_{t=0}^{T}$ from (9.40). From (9.38) and (9.39) we obtain $\{\hat{c}_t, \hat{m}_t\}_{t=0}^{T}$. Given $\{M_t, \hat{m}_t\}_{t=0}^{T}$ we compute $\{P_t\}_{t=0}^{T}$, and hence, $\{\pi_{t+1}\}_{t=0}^{T-1}$. Notice that there is no nominal indeterminacy, since we can compute the initial price level P_0. Using $\{\hat{A}_t, \hat{k}_t\}_{t=0}^{T}$ and (9.8) we can compute $\{r_t\}_{t=0}^{T}$. From (9.9) we get $\{i_{t+1}\}_{t=0}^{T}$. Finally, we can compute the $\{b_{t+1}\}_{t=0}^{T}$-sequence from the budget constraint (9.6), and we can obtain $\{\zeta_t\}_{t=0}^{T}$ imposing a relationship of the type $\zeta_t = \zeta - \eta b_t$, with $\eta \in (\frac{1}{\beta} - 1, \frac{1}{\beta} + 1)$ for the reasons mentioned above.

9.4.3 Complex Eigenvalues

All the above goes through whenever unstable eigenvalues are real. However, it is frequent to find that the eigenvalues of the transition matrix in (9.32) turn out to be complex numbers. How should we deal with that situation? We start by writing (9.31) as

$$\tilde{A} \begin{bmatrix} \hat{k}_{t+1} \\ \hat{c}_{t+1} \\ \hat{m}_{t+1} \\ \hat{A}_{t+1} \\ \hat{x}_{t+2} \end{bmatrix} = \tilde{B} \begin{bmatrix} \hat{k}_t \\ \hat{c}_t \\ \hat{m}_t \\ \hat{A}_t \\ \hat{x}_{t+1} \end{bmatrix}, \tag{9.41}$$

with

$$\tilde{A} = \begin{bmatrix} A & 0_{3\times2} \\ 0_{2\times3} & I_2 \end{bmatrix}, \quad \tilde{B} = \begin{bmatrix} B & C \\ 0_{2\times3} & \begin{pmatrix} \rho_A & 0 \\ 0 & \rho_x \end{pmatrix} \end{bmatrix},$$

or

$$\begin{bmatrix} \hat{k}_{t+1} \\ \hat{c}_{t+1} \\ \hat{m}_{t+1} \\ \hat{A}_{t+1} \\ \hat{x}_{t+2} \end{bmatrix} = \tilde{D} \begin{bmatrix} \hat{k}_t \\ \hat{c}_t \\ \hat{m}_t \\ \hat{A}_t \\ \hat{x}_{t+1} \end{bmatrix}, \tag{9.42}$$

with $\tilde{D} = \tilde{A}^{-1}\tilde{B}$.

Let us assume, without loss of generality, that it is eigenvalues μ_4 and μ_5 of matrix $\tilde{D}$ that are complex conjugate numbers with modulus above 1. To have a well defined solution, matrix $\tilde{D}$ must have three stable and two unstable eigenvalues, so that we can solve for the two control variables as functions of the three state variables. Indeed, by construction, we have here two unstable eigenvalues, the same complex conjugate numbers as in the 3×3 matrix in the previous paragraph.

As shown in the Mathematical Appendix, the solution to (9.42) is of the form

$$\begin{bmatrix} \hat{k}_t \\ \hat{c}_t \\ \hat{m}_t \\ \hat{A}_t \\ \hat{x}_{t+1} \end{bmatrix} = \underbrace{\begin{bmatrix} M_{11} & \cdots & M_{14} & M_{15} \\ \cdots & \cdots & \cdots & \cdots \\ M_{51} & \cdots & M_{44} & M_{55} \end{bmatrix}}_{M} \begin{bmatrix} C_1\mu_1^t \\ C_2\mu_2^t \\ C_3\mu_3^t \\ C_4\mu_4^t \\ C_5\mu_5^t \end{bmatrix}, \tag{9.43}$$

where M is the matrix having as columns the right eigenvectors of $\tilde{D}$. The C_i values, $i = 1, 2, \ldots, 5$ come from multiplying the left eigenvectors by the vector of initial conditions for the state variables. We have ordered the columns of M so as to include the real eigenvectors in the first three columns, while elements in columns 4 and 5, $M_{.4}, M_{.5}$, are complex conjugate numbers:

$$M_{.4} = \begin{bmatrix} d_1 + if_1 \\ d_2 + if_2 \\ d_3 + if_3 \\ d_4 + if_4 \\ d_5 + if_5 \end{bmatrix}, \quad M_{.5} = \begin{bmatrix} d_1 - if_1 \\ d_2 - if_2 \\ d_3 - if_3 \\ d_4 - if_4 \\ d_5 - if_5 \end{bmatrix},$$

The solution (9.43) can also be written[5]

$$\begin{bmatrix} \hat{k}_t \\ \hat{c}_t \\ \hat{m}_t \\ \hat{A}_t \\ \hat{x}_{t+1} \end{bmatrix} = \begin{bmatrix} \tilde{M}_1 \\ \cdots \\ \tilde{M}_5 \end{bmatrix},$$

---

[5] See Mathematical Appendix (Chap. 10).

where

$$\tilde{M}_j = M_{j1}C_1\mu_1^t + M_{j2}C_2\mu_2^t + M_{j3}C_3\mu_3^t$$
$$+ C_4 q^t \left(d_j\cos(\vartheta t) - f_j\sin(\vartheta t)\right) + C_5 q^t \left(d_j\sin(\vartheta t) + f_j\cos(\vartheta t)\right),$$
$$j = 1,2,\ldots,5, \quad \mu_4 = \breve{\gamma} + i\varpi, \quad \mu_5 = \breve{\gamma} - i\varpi,$$
$$\vartheta = \arctan(\varpi/\breve{\gamma}), \quad q = \left(\breve{\gamma}^2 + \varpi^2\right)^{1/2}.$$

For $t = 0$, the previous system determines the values of constants $C_1,\ldots,C_5$ from initial conditions by

$$\begin{bmatrix} C_1 \\ C_2 \\ C_3 \\ C_4 \\ C_5 \end{bmatrix} = \underbrace{\begin{bmatrix} M_{11} & M_{12} & M_{13} & d_1 & f_1 \\ \cdots & \cdots & \cdots & \cdots & \cdots \\ M_{51} & M_{52} & M_{53} & d_5 & f_5 \end{bmatrix}^{-1}}_{Mm} \begin{bmatrix} \hat{k}_0 \\ \hat{c}_0 \\ \hat{m}_0 \\ \hat{A}_0 \\ \hat{x}_1 \end{bmatrix}.$$

Notice that we just know the initial values of state variables $\{\hat{k}_0, \hat{A}_0, \hat{x}_1\}$, but to solve the system we also need to know $\{\hat{m}_0, \hat{c}_0\}$. For the solution (9.43) to be stable, the coefficients C_4 and C_5 in the unstable eigenvalues must be equal to zero. Therefore, from the system above, we have

$$\begin{bmatrix} 0 \\ 0 \end{bmatrix} = \begin{bmatrix} m_{41} & m_{42} & m_{43} & m_{44} & m_{45} \\ m_{51} & m_{52} & m_{53} & m_{54} & m_{55} \end{bmatrix} \begin{bmatrix} \hat{k}_0 \\ \hat{c}_0 \\ \hat{m}_0 \\ \hat{A}_0 \\ \hat{x}_1 \end{bmatrix},$$

where the elements of matrix Mm are denoted by m_{ij}. Hence, we can write the two stability conditions as

$$\begin{bmatrix} \hat{c}_0 \\ \hat{m}_0 \end{bmatrix} = -\underbrace{\begin{bmatrix} m_{42} & m_{43} \\ m_{52} & m_{53} \end{bmatrix}^{-1} \begin{bmatrix} m_{41} & m_{44} & m_{45} \\ m_{51} & m_{54} & m_{55} \end{bmatrix}}_{\tilde{\Gamma}_1} \begin{bmatrix} \hat{k}_0 \\ \hat{A}_0 \\ \hat{x}_1 \end{bmatrix}.$$

As shown in the Mathematical Appendix, these conditions apply for all t, providing us with the *control equations*:

$$\begin{bmatrix} \hat{c}_t \\ \hat{m}_t \end{bmatrix} = \tilde{\Gamma}_1 \begin{bmatrix} \hat{k}_t \\ \hat{A}_t \\ \hat{x}_{t+1} \end{bmatrix}. \tag{9.44}$$

Plugging the stability conditions in system (9.42), we get

$$
\begin{bmatrix} \hat{k}_{t+1} \\ \hat{A}_{t+1} \\ \hat{x}_{t+2} \end{bmatrix} = \underbrace{\begin{bmatrix} \tilde{D}_{11} & \tilde{D}_{14} & \tilde{D}_{15} \\ \tilde{D}_{41} & \tilde{D}_{44} & \tilde{D}_{45} \\ \tilde{D}_{51} & \tilde{D}_{54} & \tilde{D}_{55} \end{bmatrix}}_{J} \begin{bmatrix} \hat{k}_t \\ \hat{A}_t \\ \hat{x}_{t+1} \end{bmatrix}
$$

$$
+ \underbrace{\begin{bmatrix} \tilde{D}_{12} & \tilde{D}_{13} \\ \tilde{D}_{42} & \tilde{D}_{43} \\ \tilde{D}_{52} & \tilde{D}_{53} \end{bmatrix}}_{L} \begin{bmatrix} \hat{c}_t \\ \hat{m}_t \end{bmatrix}
$$

$$
= (J + L\tilde{\Gamma}_1) \begin{bmatrix} \hat{k}_t \\ \hat{A}_t \\ \hat{x}_{t+1} \end{bmatrix} , \tag{9.45}
$$

which is the set of *state equations*, from which we produce time series for the three state variables.

Once we have the time path for the stock of capital, the level of productivity and the rate of growth of the money supply, we can compute the remaining variables. In particular, we compute control variables $\{\hat{c}_t, \hat{m}_t\}_{t=0}^{T}$ using (9.44). Given $\{M_t, \hat{m}_t\}_{t=0}^{T}$ we compute $\{P_t\}_{t=0}^{T}$, and hence, $\{\pi_{t+1}\}_{t=0}^{T-1}$. Notice that there is no nominal indeterminacy, since we can compute the initial price level P_0. Using $\{\hat{A}_t, \hat{k}_t\}_{t=0}^{T}$ and (9.8) we can compute $\{r_t\}_{t=0}^{T}$. From (9.9) we get $\{i_{t+1}\}_{t=0}^{T}$. Finally, we can compute the $\{b_{t+1}\}_{t=0}^{T}$-sequence from the budget constraint (9.6), and we can obtain $\{\zeta_t\}_{t=0}^{T}$ imposing a relationship of the type $\zeta_t = \zeta - \eta b_t$, with $\eta \in (\frac{1}{\beta} - 1, \frac{1}{\beta} + 1)$ for the reasons mentioned above.

Equation (9.45) shows that the stock of physical capital varies when there are changes in the rate of money growth. Hence, private consumption, as well as production will both be affected.

This policy analysis is implemented in MATLAB program *money_M_d_gradual. m.* Matrix names in the program are those used in the discussion above. Being a deterministic model, the program computes a single realization starting from initial conditions that deviate from steady-state levels for *at least one* state variable. These are: the stock of bonds, the money supply, the rate of growth of money balances, the stock of capital and the level of productivity, and the program computes the reactions of endogenous variables from that deviation in a single exogenous variable from steady state. The program can also be used to compute the reactions to a simultaneous deviation from steady state in more than one exogenous variable, but the obtained responses will not be so easy to interpret.[6] MATLAB programs solving models with complex eigenvalues, as the one above, have been written so that they can also be used for parameterizations for which all eigenvalues are real.

---

[6] In the MATLAB program it is explained how to choose the variables that deviate from their steady-state levels.

9.5 Deterministic Monetary Model with the Monetary Authority Choosing Nominal Interest Rates

We consider in this section the case when the monetary authority chooses nominal rates of interest each period according to

$$\ln(1+i_t) = (1-\rho_i)\ln(1+i_{ss}) + \rho_i\ln(1+i_{t-1}), \ |\rho_i| < 1. \tag{9.46}$$

and also that, as in the previous section, the level of technology follows an exogenous, first order autoregressive process

$$\ln(A_t) = (1-\rho_A)\ln(A_{ss}) + \rho_A\ln(A_{t-1}), \ |\rho_A| < 1.$$

As in the previous section, the system of equations characterizing the solution to the representative agent's problem is (9.7)–(9.11), (9.6), (9.12) and (9.1). To compute the time paths for the endogenous variables, we follow a similar approach to that in the previous section. From (9.7), (9.9) and (9.11) we obtain the time paths for the stock of capital, consumption and real balances. After that, we follow a recursive procedure to compute the remaining variables. At the end of the section we describe in detail this procedure.

We start computing time paths for $\{k_{t+1}, m_t, c_t\}_{t=0}^T$ from (9.11), (9.7) and (9.9), which can be particularized for the utility function $U(c_t, m_t) = \frac{(c_t\, m_t^\theta)^{1-\sigma}-1}{1-\sigma}$, $\theta > 0$, $\sigma > 0$, $m_t = \frac{M_t}{P_t}$, as

$$c_t + k_{t+1} - (1-\delta)k_t = A_t k_t^\alpha, \tag{9.47}$$

$$c_t^{-\sigma} m_t^{\theta(1-\sigma)} = \beta\left[c_{t+1}^{-\sigma} m_{t+1}^{\theta(1-\sigma)}\left((1-\tau^y)A_{t+1}\alpha k_{t+1}^{\alpha-1} + 1 - \delta\right)\right], \tag{9.48}$$

$$i_{t+1} = (1+\tau^c)\theta\frac{c_{t+1}}{m_{t+1}}. \tag{9.49}$$

Let us denote: $\hat{u}_t = \ln(u_t/u_{ss})$, $u = c, m, k$; $\hat{x}_t = \ln(1+x_t) - \ln(1+x_{ss})$; $\hat{i}_t = \ln(1+i_t) - \ln(1+i_{ss})$. We start by computing the log-linear approximation to this system:

$$0 = A_{ss}k_{ss}^\alpha\hat{A}_t + (A_{ss}\alpha k_{ss}^\alpha + (1-\delta)k_{ss})\hat{k}_t - c_{ss}\hat{c}_t - k_{ss}\hat{k}_{t+1}, \tag{9.50}$$

$$0 = \frac{\sigma}{\beta}\hat{c}_t - \frac{\theta(1-\sigma)}{\beta}\hat{m}_t - \frac{\sigma}{\beta}\hat{c}_{t+1} + \frac{\theta(1-\sigma)}{\beta}\hat{m}_{t+1} + \cdots \tag{9.51}$$

$$+(\alpha-1)\left(\frac{1}{\beta}-(1-\delta)\right)\hat{k}_{t+1} + \left(\frac{1}{\beta}-(1-\delta)\right)\rho_A\hat{A}_t,$$

$$\hat{m}_{t+1} = \hat{c}_{t+1} - \frac{(1+i_{ss})}{i_{ss}}\hat{i}_{t+1}, \tag{9.52}$$

where we have used (9.3).

Furthermore, from (9.46) we get

$$\hat{\imath}_{t+1} = \rho_i \hat{\imath}_t. \tag{9.53}$$

in this case, at a difference of what happens when the government controls the rate of growth of money supply, the equation defining the demand fore money is a relationship between variables taken at the same point in time. By using (9.52) to eliminate $\hat{m}_t$ from the other equations, we get a system that determines the time series for $\{c_t, k_t, i_t\}$ as functions of A_t:

$$\underbrace{\begin{bmatrix} 0 & k_{ss} & 0 \\ \frac{\sigma - \theta(1-\sigma)}{\beta} & (1-\alpha)\left(\frac{1}{\beta} - (1-\delta)\right) & \frac{\theta(1-\sigma)}{\beta}\frac{1+i_{ss}}{i_{ss}} \\ 0 & 0 & 1 \end{bmatrix}}_{A} \underbrace{\begin{bmatrix} \hat{c}_{t+1} \\ \hat{k}_{t+1} \\ \hat{\imath}_{t+1} \end{bmatrix}}_{s_{t+1}}$$

$$= \underbrace{\begin{bmatrix} -c_{ss} & \alpha A_{ss}k_{ss}^\alpha + (1-\delta)k_{ss} & 0 \\ \frac{\sigma - \theta(1-\sigma)}{\beta} & 0 & \frac{\theta(1-\sigma)}{\beta}\frac{1+i_{ss}}{i_{ss}} \\ 0 & 0 & \rho_i \end{bmatrix}}_{B} \underbrace{\begin{bmatrix} \hat{c}_t \\ \hat{k}_t \\ \hat{\imath}_t \end{bmatrix}}_{s_t}$$

$$+ \underbrace{\begin{bmatrix} A_{ss}k_{ss}^\alpha \\ \left(\frac{1}{\beta} - (1-\delta)\right)\rho_A \\ 0 \end{bmatrix}}_{C} \hat{A}_t. \tag{9.54}$$

that is

$$s_{t+1} = D\, s_t + F\, \hat{A}_t, \tag{9.55}$$

where $D = A^{-1}B$, $F = A^{-1}C$.

We get three eigenvalues from matrix D. One of them will have a norm greater than 1 while, for most parameterizations, the other two eigenvalues will have a norm less than 1 (one of these eigenvalues is ρ_i). Since we have a control variable and two state variables (the stock of capital and the nominal rate of interest) in system (9.55), we need one stability condition to determine the level of consumption as a function of the stock of capital, the nominal rate of interest and the level of technology. Therefore, the single unstable eigenvalue is appropriate.

Given the Jordan decomposition of matrix $D = M\Lambda M^{-1}$, we can write system (9.55) as

$$M^{-1}s_{t+1} = \Lambda M^{-1}s_t + \underbrace{M^{-1}F}_{Q}\hat{A}_t. \tag{9.56}$$

Let $M = \begin{bmatrix} M_{11} & M_{12} & M_{13} \\ M_{21} & M_{22} & M_{23} \\ M_{31} & M_{32} & M_{33} \end{bmatrix}$, $M^{-1} = \begin{bmatrix} m_{11} & m_{12} & m_{13} \\ m_{21} & m_{22} & m_{23} \\ m_{31} & m_{32} & m_{33} \end{bmatrix}$, and let us assume,

without loss of generality, that $\|\mu_1\|, \|\mu_2\| < 1, \|\mu_3\| > 1$. System (9.56) can then be written as we did in the previous section

$$m_{11}\hat{c}_{t+1} + m_{12}\hat{k}_{t+1} + m_{13}\hat{\imath}_{t+1} = \mu_1 \left(m_{11}\hat{c}_t + m_{12}\hat{k}_t + m_{13}\hat{\imath}_t \right) + Q_1\hat{A}_t, \qquad (9.57)$$

$$m_{21}\hat{c}_{t+1} + m_{22}\hat{k}_{t+1} + m_{23}\hat{\imath}_{t+1} = \mu_2 \left(m_{21}\hat{c}_t + m_{22}\hat{k}_t + m_{23}\hat{\imath}_t \right) + Q_2\hat{A}_t, \qquad (9.58)$$

$$\underbrace{m_{31}\hat{c}_{t+1} + m_{32}\hat{k}_{t+1} + m_{33}\hat{\imath}_{t+1}}_{z_{t+1}} = \mu_3 \Big(\underbrace{m_{31}\hat{c}_t + m_{32}\hat{k}_t + m_{33}\hat{\imath}_t}_{z_t} \Big) + Q_3\hat{A}_t. \qquad (9.59)$$

Equation (9.59), which contains the unstable eigenvalue, can in turn be written

$$z_t = \frac{1}{\mu_3}z_{t+1} - \frac{Q_3}{\mu_3}\hat{A}_t, \qquad (9.60)$$

which can be solved forwards

$$z_t = \frac{Q_3}{\rho_A - \mu_3}\hat{A}_t. \qquad (9.61)$$

Taking into account the definition of z_t, together with (9.61), we get the stability condition that solves for c_t as a function of the state variables $\{\hat{k}_t, \hat{A}_t, \hat{\imath}_t\}$ and $\hat{m}_t$:

$$\hat{c}_t = -\frac{m_{32}}{m_{31}}\hat{k}_t - \frac{m_{33}}{m_{31}}\hat{\imath}_t + \frac{Q_3/m_{31}}{\rho_A - \mu_3}\hat{A}_t, \qquad (9.62)$$

that is

$$\hat{c}_t = \left[-\frac{m_{32}}{m_{31}}, -\frac{m_{33}}{m_{31}}, \frac{Q_3/m_{31}}{\rho_A - \mu_3} \right] \begin{bmatrix} \hat{k}_t \\ \hat{\imath}_t \\ \hat{A}_t \end{bmatrix}, \qquad (9.63)$$

which is the *control equation*.

Using (9.57) and (9.62) we get

$$\left(m_{12} - m_{11}\frac{m_{32}}{m_{31}} \right) \hat{k}_{t+1} + \left(m_{13} - m_{11}\frac{m_{33}}{m_{31}} \right) \hat{\imath}_{t+1}$$
$$= \mu_1 \left(m_{12} - m_{11}\frac{m_{32}}{m_{31}} \right) \hat{k}_t + \mu_1 \left(m_{13} - m_{11}\frac{m_{33}}{m_{31}} \right) \hat{\imath}_t$$
$$+ \left(Q_1 + (\mu_1 - \rho_A)\frac{m_{11}}{m_{31}}\frac{Q_3}{\rho_A - \mu_3} \right) \hat{A}_t, \qquad (9.64)$$

while using (9.58) and (9.62), we get

$$\left(m_{22} - m_{21}\frac{m_{32}}{m_{31}} \right) \hat{k}_{t+1} + \left(m_{23} - m_{21}\frac{m_{33}}{m_{31}} \right) \hat{\imath}_{t+1}$$
$$= \mu_2 \left(m_{22} - m_{21}\frac{m_{32}}{m_{31}} \right) \hat{k}_t + \mu_2 \left(m_{23} - m_{21}\frac{m_{33}}{m_{31}} \right) \hat{\imath}_t$$
$$+ \left(Q_2 + (\mu_2 - \rho_A)\frac{m_{21}}{m_{31}}\frac{Q_3}{\rho_A - \mu_3} \right) \hat{A}_t. \qquad (9.65)$$

Equations (9.64) and (9.65) and equation $\hat{A}_{t+1} = \rho_A \hat{A}_t$ can be written in matrix form as

$$\begin{bmatrix} \hat{k}_{t+1} \\ \hat{\imath}_{t+1} \\ \hat{A}_{t+1} \end{bmatrix} = \Gamma \begin{bmatrix} \hat{k}_t \\ \hat{\imath}_t \\ \hat{A}_t \end{bmatrix}, \tag{9.66}$$

which is analogous to system (9.45) for the case when money growth was the control variable. Equation (9.66) is the *state equation*.

In this system, $\Gamma = \Gamma_1^{-1}\Gamma_2$, and

$$\Gamma_1 = \begin{bmatrix} m_{12} - m_{11}\frac{m_{32}}{m_{31}} & m_{13} - m_{11}\frac{m_{33}}{m_{31}} & 0 \\ m_{22} - m_{21}\frac{m_{32}}{m_{31}} & m_{23} - m_{21}\frac{m_{33}}{m_{31}} & 0 \\ 0 & 0 & 1 \end{bmatrix},$$

$$\Gamma_2 = \begin{bmatrix} \mu_1\left(m_{12} - m_{11}\frac{m_{32}}{m_{31}}\right) & \mu_1\left(m_{13} - m_{11}\frac{m_{33}}{m_{31}}\right) & \Gamma_2(1,3) \\ \mu_2\left(m_{22} - m_{21}\frac{m_{32}}{m_{31}}\right) & \mu_2\left(m_{23} - m_{21}\frac{m_{33}}{m_{31}}\right) & \Gamma_2(2,3) \\ 0 & 0 & \rho_A \end{bmatrix},$$

where $\Gamma_2(1,3) = Q_1 + (\mu_1 - \rho_A)\frac{m_{11}}{m_{31}}\frac{Q_3}{\rho_A - \mu_3}$, $\Gamma_2(2,3) = Q_2 + (\mu_2 - \rho_A)\frac{m_{21}}{m_{31}}\frac{Q_3}{\rho_A - \mu_3}$.

Therefore, given initial conditions for the state variables $\{k_0, A_0, i_0\}$:

- We obtain $\{\hat{k}_1, \hat{A}_1, \hat{\imath}_1\}$ from (9.66). Repeating this procedure at each time period, we obtain the set of time series $\{\hat{k}_{t+1}, \hat{A}_{t+1}, \hat{\imath}_{t+1}\}_{t=0}^{T}$.
- From time series $\{\hat{k}_{t+1}, \hat{A}_{t+1}, \hat{\imath}_{t+1}\}_{t=0}^{T}$, we obtain $\{\hat{c}_t\}_{t=0}^{T}$ using (9.63).
- Using the fact that $\hat{z}_t = \ln(z_t/z_{ss})$, we obtain $\{k_{t+1}, A_{t+1}, i_{t+1}, c_t\}_{t=0}^{T}$ from $\{\hat{k}_{t+1}, \hat{A}_{t+1}, \hat{\imath}_{t+1}, \hat{c}_t\}_{t=0}^{T}$.
- From time series $\{k_{t+1}, A_{t+1}, i_{t+1}, c_t\}_{t=0}^{T}$ we can compute the real rate of interest from the standard equality between after-tax real rates of return: $r_t = (1 - \tau^y)A_t \alpha k_t^{\alpha-1} - \delta$.
- While the inflation rate $\{\pi_{t+1}\}_{t=0}^{T}$ is obtained from $1 + i_t = (1 + r_t)(1 + \pi_t)$.
- From the first order condition: $m_{t+1} = \theta c_{t+1}(1 + \tau_c)/i_{t+1}$, we obtain the time path for real money balances: $\{m_{t+1}\}_{t=0}^{T}$. Notice that we have not been able to determine the initial level of real balances m_0, $m_0 = \frac{M_0}{P_0}$. Hence, given M_0, any change in the initial price level, P_0, is compatible with the dynamic equilibrium we have just described. Therefore, even though the inflation rate $\{\pi_{t+1}\}_{t=0}^{\infty}$ is well defined in equilibrium, the path for prices $\{P_t\}_{t=0}^{\infty}$ remains undetermined. This is known as *nominal indeterminacy* of the price level.
- From $\frac{m_t}{m_{t+1}}(1 + x_{t+1}) = (1 + \pi_{t+1})$ we obtain the time series for money growth $\{x_{t+1}\}_{t=0}^{T}$.

The way the numerical solution is calculated illustrates the fact that deviations of nominal interest rates from their steady-state level influence the time paths for real variables, so these are not exogenous with respect to fluctuations in nominal rates.[7]

This policy analysis is implemented in MATLAB program *money_i_d.m*. Matrix names in the program are the same used in the discussion above. Being a deterministic model, the program computes a single realization starting from initial conditions which deviate from steady-state levels for at least one state variable. These are: the stock of bonds, the money supply, the stock of capital, the level of productivity, and the nominal rate of interest. Graphs provided by the program can be interpreted as the reaction of endogenous variables to a deviation in one or more exogenous variables from their steady state levels.

9.6 Transitional Effects of Policy Interventions

The *Short-run nonneutrality.xls* file analyzes the effects of different monetary policy experiments. In all cases, the production function is $y_t = Ak_t^{\alpha}$, and the government issues public debt. Furthermore, to avoid an explosive stock of public debt, the amount of the transfer to private agents is made to depend on the stock of public debt each period as above

$$\zeta_t = \zeta - \eta b_t. \tag{9.67}$$

In the *Change nominal rates* spreadsheet it is assumed that a government finances a transfer to consumers by printing money, issuing debt and raising a proportional tax on income, while using nominal rates as a control variable for monetary policy. In the *Once and-for-all money change* and *Gradual money change* spreadsheets the government makes a lump-sum transfer to the representative agent, which is financed through seigniorage and bond issuing. In them, the government uses the rate of growth of money supply as policy variable. In the *Once and-for-all money change* spreadsheet the government increases money supply at a constant rate, and we consider the effects of an experiment by which the growth rate experiences a drastic, permanent increase. On the contrary, in the *Gradual money change* spreadsheet, we consider a permanent but gradual change in money growth.

To simulate the different policy experiments in this spreadsheet, there are two differences with respect to the solution method proposed in the previous section. There, we used a log-linear approximation to obtain the stability conditions as well as the state-space formulation of the model. That way, all endogenous variables are obtained from the log-linear approximation, losing to a large extent the nonlinear structure of the model. In the EXCEL file we use a linear approximation to the model, as an alternative. That produces a larger approximation error, although with

---

[7] Under this policy design, nominal interest rates are simultaneously determined with consumption and capital, while being exogenous relative to inflation and real balances. However, this could be consistent with real balances having significant explanatory power in regressions for consumption and capital using simulated data if we do not consider the nominal rate of interest as explanatory variable.

a smaller chance of finding complex eigenvalues in the transition matrix than under the log-linear approximation. Dealing with complex eigenvalues is not so much of a problem when working with programs like MATLAB, but cannot be easily handled with EXCEL.

Secondly, in the EXCEL file we use the original, nonlinear global constraint of resources of the economy to compute the time paths of the endogenous variables, rather than its log-linear approximation, which is used in the state space formulation in the previous section. That way, we preserve more of the nonlinear structure of the original model. Then, given values for state variables at any time period, stability conditions can be used to obtain the values for decision variables, while the global constraint of resources, together with laws of motion for exogenous variables, allows us to compute next period values for state variables. Using the original global constraint of resources we reduce the approximation error, relative to using a full state-space formulation, although the stability conditions estimated on the log-linear approximation should be more accurate. This dual approach to the solution of the model should be useful to the reader as additional practice.

We first describe the details of obtaining the solution to the model under each policy experiment through a linear approximation, to then discuss the qualitative effects of each policy experiment in a numerical exercise section.

9.6.1 Solving the Model with Nominal Interest Rates as Control Variable, Using a Linear Approximation

Preferences are represented by a utility function: $U(c_t, m_t) = \ln(c_t) + \theta \ln(m_t)$, where $m_t = \frac{M_t}{P_t}$. The system of equations analogous to (9.47)–(9.49), under the current utility function, without a consumption tax and with a constant productivity parameter, is[8]

$$c_t + k_{t+1} - (1 - \delta)k_t = Ak_t^\alpha, \tag{9.68}$$

$$c_t^{-1} = \beta \left[c_{t+1}^{-1} \left((1 - \tau^y)A\alpha k_{t+1}^{\alpha-1} + 1 - \delta \right) \right], \tag{9.69}$$

$$i_{t+1} = \theta \frac{c_{t+1}}{m_{t+1}}. \tag{9.70}$$

Under exogenous nominal rates, the third equation can be used to solve for real balances, once we have the level of consumption for a given time period. The linear approximation around steady-state for the first two equations:

$$(c_t - c_{ss}) + (k_{t+1} - k_{ss}) - \frac{1}{\beta}(k_t - k_{ss}) = 0, \tag{9.71}$$

---

[8] The same analysis could be conducted with the utility function in the previous section, a consumption tax and an autoregressive structure for productivity. Real balances would then enter in (9.69), which could be eliminated using (9.70). The nominal rate of interest would then appear in the transformed (9.69), but this is an exogenous variable in this policy experiment.

$$-(c_t - c_{ss}) = -(c_{t+1} - c_{ss}) + \beta (c_{ss}) (1 - \tau^y) \alpha A (\alpha - 1) (k_{ss})^{\alpha-2} (k_{t+1} - k_{ss}).$$

$$(9.72)$$

This system can be written in matrix form[9]

$$\begin{bmatrix} \hat{\rho} & 1 \\ 1 & 0 \end{bmatrix} \begin{bmatrix} (k_{t+1} - k_{ss}) \\ (c_{t+1} - c_{ss}) \end{bmatrix} = \begin{bmatrix} 0 & 1 \\ \frac{1}{\beta} & -1 \end{bmatrix} \begin{bmatrix} (k_t - k_{ss}) \\ (c_t - c_{ss}) \end{bmatrix},$$

where $\hat{\rho} \equiv -\beta c_{ss} \alpha (\alpha - 1) A (1 - \tau) (k_{ss})^{\alpha-2}$, which is of the form

$$\begin{bmatrix} (k_{t+1} - k_{ss}) \\ (c_{t+1} - c_{ss}) \end{bmatrix} = \begin{bmatrix} \frac{1}{\beta} & -1 \\ \Omega & 1 - \beta\Omega \end{bmatrix} \begin{bmatrix} (k_t - k_{ss}) \\ (c_t - c_{ss}) \end{bmatrix},$$

with $\Omega = c_{ss} \alpha (\alpha - 1) A (1 - \tau) (k_{ss})^{\alpha-2}$. This is the same dynamic system characterizing the equilibrium trajectories for the stock of capital and consumption in the Cass–Koopmans model. Therefore, the condition guaranteeing stability is the same we characterized in that chapter:

$$(c_0 - c_{ss}) + \left(\frac{1}{\beta} - \mu_2 \right) (k_0 - k_{ss}) = 0, \tag{9.73}$$

where μ_2 is the stable eigenvalue of the transition matrix

$$\mu_2 = \frac{\left(\frac{1}{\beta} + 1 - \beta\Omega \right) - \sqrt{\left(\frac{1}{\beta} + 1 - \beta\Omega \right)^2 - 4\frac{1}{\beta}}}{2}.$$

Hence, given k_0, (9.73) places the economy on the trajectory converging to steady-state, c_0 being the level of consumption in the initial period. Then, given k_0 and c_0, k_1 is obtained from (9.68) and, given k_1, the stability condition

$$(c_t - c_{ss}) + \left(\frac{1}{\beta} - \mu_2 \right) (k_t - k_{ss}) = 0, \tag{9.74}$$

is used to compute c_1. This process is repeated recursively. Remember that the stability condition (9.74) rather than (9.69) must be used to determine c_t since, as it was the case in the Cass–Koopmans model, the resulting solution would not be stable. Once we have $\{c_t, k_{t+1}\}_{t=0}^{\infty}$, $\{m_{t+1}, r_{t+1}, \zeta_t, \pi_{t+1}, x_{t+1}\}_{t=0}^{\infty}$ are obtained as explained for the log-linear approximation in Sect. 9.5.

---

[9] We could increase the dimension of the system by including the law of motion for the nominal rate of interest, as we have done in some other previous analysis. The difference is that the stability condition would then involve deviations of nominal rates around their steady state level. However, if the central bank follows a policy of maintaining constant interest rates, then there is no difference between both formulations.

9.6.2 Numerical Exercise: Changes in Nominal Interest Rates

In the *Change nominal rates* spreadsheet it is assumed that a government finances a transfer to consumers by printing money, issuing debt an raising proportional taxes on output. Furthermore, the government uses nominal rates as a control variable for monetary policy, while maintaining steady-state targets for lump-sum transfers to consumers, ζ_{ss}, and debt in real terms, b_{ss}. These two steady-state values are chosen as in Case 3 in *Steady-state fiscal policy.xls*. In that spreadsheet we obtained combinations (i, τ) allowing for financing a given level of government transfers while leading to the chosen steady state level of debt, b_{ss}. We guarantee that the stock of public debt in fact converges to b_{ss} by choosing the stock of debt outstanding each period from (9.67). For that, we first choose a value of η inside the range leading to stability (see Sect. 9.2), and choose the value of ζ so that the policy target values for ζ_{ss}, b_{ss}, satisfy that condition.

In this environment, the government decides at a given point in time to change the level of nominal rates from $i = 12.7\%$ to $i = 13.4\%$. Given the time discount factor $\beta = 0.95$, this implies a change in steady-state inflation from $\pi_0 = 7.06\%$ to $\pi_1 = 7.75\%$. From our steady-state analysis in *Steady-state fiscal policy.xls* we already know that these changes need of a once and-for-all adjustment in the income tax rate, from $\tau = 12.0\%$ to $\tau = 11.0\%$:

$$(i, \tau) = (i_0, \tau_0), \quad t < \tilde{t}$$

$$(i, \tau) = (i_1, \tau_1), \quad i_1 > i_0, \ \tau_1 < \tau_0, \ t \geq \tilde{t}$$

To compute the transition we need to use the right stability condition after the policy intervention takes place at $\tilde{t} = 10$. The vector autoregressive representation is obtained under the old and the new policy parameters, and the stabilizing constant (i.e., the stability condition) is updated after the policy intervention. We use that stability condition to compute the time series for consumption once we have the data for the stock of capital each period.

The calculations we present in this section show, among other things, that *the level of interest rates is not neutral in this economy*. The spreadsheet displays the transitional dynamics of consumption, the stock of capital, real balances, the level of utility, the level of transfers, the stock of government debt, the level of seigniorage, the level of income tax revenues, the rate of inflation, the real rate of interest, and the rate of money growth.

The reduction in the income tax rate increases the after-tax return on capital, which accumulates faster. Production does not react at the time of the policy intervention, increasing afterwards because of the higher stock of physical capital. Consumption falls at the time of the policy intervention, increasing afterwards to a steady state level above the one before the intervention. The initial fall in consumption is needed because of the higher investment, with output unaltered. In spite of the increase in production, the tax cut leads to a decrease in tax revenues. The faster accumulation of productive capital leads to higher output each period. Whether or not the new steady state level of consumption is above the old one will generally depend on the chosen parameterization. With the one used in the spreadsheet, consumption increases in the long-run, relative to its level before the tax cut.

By permanently increasing the nominal rate of interest, the policy intervention increases the opportunity cost of holding money, producing an instantaneous fall in the demand for real balances and in the rate of growth of money supply, which lead to a decrease in seigniorage revenues.[10] The rate of inflation increases because of the increased demand for the single commodity. This increase in inflation makes the after-tax real rate of interest adjusts less than completely to the raise in the nominal rate.

Because of the simultaneous, single-period fall in seigniorage and tax revenues, the government is forced to sharply increase the stock of debt outstanding initially. Through the stability condition for public debt, the size of the transfer to the private sector falls after the policy intervention. The rate of growth of money supply recovers immediately after the new rate of interest is in effect. This recovery dominates the fall in real balances, and revenues from seigniorage increase. This increase in revenues allows the government to retire some debt until it gradually returns to its level before the policy change, and the same behavior is followed by the transfer to consumers.

9.6.3 Solving the Model with Money Growth as Control Variable, Using a Linear Approximation

We want to show that a monetary policy intervention can be nonneutral if it is implemented gradually, while being neutral if the new policy target is achieved immediately. In order to do that, we need to know how to solve a monetary economy in which the government has a target on the rate of growth of the money supply, as we did in Sect. 9.4. We maintain a setup similar to those in the previous section, but we now assume that the government controls the rate of growth of the money supply at each point in time according to[11]

$$x_t = (1 - \rho_x)x_{ss} + \rho_x x_{t-1}, \tag{9.75}$$

where x_{ss} is its target for the rate of growth of the money supply in the long run, and $\rho_x \in [0, 1)$.

Relative to Sect. 9.4, the difference with the treatment in this section is that tax rates on consumption and income are now zero and the productivity parameter is

---

[10] Remember that seignoriage revenues SR can be written as the product of the rate of growth of money supply by the level of real balances: $SR = \frac{M_{t+1} - M_t}{P_t} = \frac{M_{t+1} - M_t}{M_t} \frac{M_t}{P_t} = x_{t+1} m_t$.

[11] Since $\ln(1 + x_t) \simeq x_t$ for small x_t, it is just appropriate that we specify the money growth autoregression for $\ln(1 + x_t)$ under the log-linear approximation and for x_t itself under the linear approximation.

constant.[12] System (9.14), (9.15), (9.11) that allows us to compute the time paths for consumption, the stock of capital and real balances can be particularized, under our assumptions on tax rates and productivity, into

$$c_t^{-\sigma}m_t^{\theta(1-\sigma)} = \beta c_{t+1}^{-\sigma}m_{t+1}^{\theta(1-\sigma)}\left[\alpha Ak_{t+1}^{\alpha-1}+1-\delta\right], \quad \forall t \tag{9.76}$$

$$\left[A\alpha k_{t+1}^{\alpha-1}+1-\delta\right]m_t(1+x_{t+1}) = m_{t+1}+\theta c_{t+1}, \quad \forall t \tag{9.77}$$

$$c_t+k_{t+1}-(1-\delta)k_t = Ak_t^{\alpha}. \tag{9.78}$$

The linear approximation to this system, using the fact that $[A\alpha k_{ss}^{\alpha-1}+1-\delta] = \frac{1}{\beta}$ is

$$-\sigma c_{ss}^{-\sigma-1}m_{ss}^{\theta(1-\sigma)}\left(c_{t+1}-c_{ss}\right)+\theta(1-\sigma)c_{ss}^{-\sigma}m_{ss}^{\theta(1-\sigma)-1}\left(m_{t+1}-m_{ss}\right)$$
$$= -\sigma c_{ss}^{-\sigma-1}m_{ss}^{\theta(1-\sigma)}\left(c_t-c_{ss}\right)+\theta(1-\sigma)c_{ss}^{-\sigma}m_{ss}^{\theta(1-\sigma)-1}\left(m_t-m_{ss}\right)$$
$$-\beta c_{ss}^{-\sigma}m_{ss}^{\theta(1-\sigma)}\alpha Ak_{ss}^{\alpha-2}(\alpha-1)\left(k_{t+1}-k_{ss}\right). \tag{9.79}$$

$$\left(m_{t+1}-m_{ss}\right)+\theta\left(c_{t+1}-c_{ss}\right)$$
$$= \alpha Ak_{ss}^{\alpha-2}(\alpha-1)m_{ss}(1+x_{ss})\left(k_{t+1}-k_{ss}\right)$$
$$+\frac{1}{\beta}(1+x_{ss})\left(m_t-m_{ss}\right)+\frac{1}{\beta}m_{ss}\left(x_{t+1}-x_{ss}\right) \tag{9.80}$$

$$\left(c_t-c_{ss}\right)+\left(k_{t+1}-k_{ss}\right)-\frac{1}{\beta}\left(k_t-k_{ss}\right) = 0. \tag{9.81}$$

Finally, from (9.75)

$$x_{t+2}-x_{ss} = \rho_x\left(x_{t+1}-x_{ss}\right). \tag{9.82}$$

The matrix representation for (9.79)–(9.82) is

$$\begin{bmatrix} a_{11} & a_{12} & a_{13} & 0 \\ a_{21} & -\theta & -1 & 0 \\ 1 & 0 & 0 & 0 \\ 0 & 0 & 0 & 1 \end{bmatrix}\begin{bmatrix} \tilde{k}_{t+1} \\ \tilde{c}_{t+1} \\ \tilde{m}_{t+1} \\ \tilde{x}_{t+2} \end{bmatrix} = \begin{bmatrix} 0 & b_{12} & b_{13} & 0 \\ 0 & 0 & b_{23} & b_{24} \\ 1/\beta & -1 & 0 & 0 \\ 0 & 0 & 0 & \rho_x \end{bmatrix}\begin{bmatrix} \tilde{k}_t \\ \tilde{c}_t \\ \tilde{m}_t \\ \tilde{x}_{t+1} \end{bmatrix},$$

where $\tilde{k}_t \equiv k_t-k_{ss}$, $\tilde{c}_t \equiv c_t-c_{ss}$, $\tilde{m}_t \equiv m_t-m_{ss}$, $\tilde{x}_{t+1} \equiv x_{t+1}-x_{ss}$,

$$a_{11} = \beta c_{ss}^{-\sigma}m_{ss}^{\theta(1-\sigma)}\alpha Ak_{ss}^{\alpha-2}(\alpha-1),$$
$$a_{12} = b_{12} = -\sigma c_{ss}^{-\sigma-1}m_{ss}^{\theta(1-\sigma)},$$
$$a_{13} = b_{13} = \theta(1-\sigma)c_{ss}^{-\sigma}m_{ss}^{\theta(1-\sigma)-1},$$
$$a_{21} = \alpha Ak_{ss}^{\alpha-2}(\alpha-1)m_{ss}(1+x_{ss}),$$
$$b_{24} = -\frac{1}{\beta}m_{ss}; \qquad b_{23} = -\frac{1}{\beta}(1+x_{ss}).$$

---

[12] A more general discussion could be made with non-zero tax rates and a non-constant productivity parameter, with the same qualitative results.

Hence, the system of equations can be written in matrix form:

$$Az_{t+1} = Bz_t,$$

with $z_t = \begin{bmatrix} k_{t+1} - k_{ss}; & c_{t+1} - c_{ss}; & m_{t+1} - m_{ss}; & x_{t+2} - x_{ss} \end{bmatrix}'$ being the vector of variables.

Let $\mu_1, \mu_2, \mu_3, \mu_4$ be the four eigenvalues for the transition matrix of the autoregressive representation: $z_{t+1} = Cz_t$, $C = A^{-1}B$. With two control variables in this economy, for a determinate solution to exist we need two unstable eigenvalues in the transition matrix. The inner product of the left eigenvectors $\begin{bmatrix} d_{11} & d_{12} & d_{13} & d_{14} \end{bmatrix}$, $\begin{bmatrix} d_{21} & d_{22} & d_{23} & d_{24} \end{bmatrix}$ associated to the unstable eigenvalues by vector z_t, provide us with the stability conditions we need to produce a numerical solution. Such products lead to expressions of the form:

$$d_{11}(k_0 - k_{ss}) + d_{12}(c_0 - c_{ss}) + d_{13}(m_0 - m_{ss}) + d_{14}(x_1 - x_{ss}) = 0,$$
$$d_{21}(k_0 - k_{ss}) + d_{22}(c_0 - c_{ss}) + d_{23}(m_0 - m_{ss}) + d_{24}(x_1 - x_{ss}) = 0,$$

which can be written in matrix form:

$$\begin{bmatrix} d_{12} & d_{13} \\ d_{22} & d_{23} \end{bmatrix} \begin{bmatrix} c_0 - c_{ss} \\ m_0 - m_{ss} \end{bmatrix} = - \begin{bmatrix} d_{11} & d_{14} \\ d_{21} & d_{24} \end{bmatrix} \begin{bmatrix} k_0 - k_{ss} \\ x_1 - x_{ss} \end{bmatrix},$$

from which we get

$$\begin{bmatrix} c_0 - c_{ss} \\ m_0 - m_{ss} \end{bmatrix} = - \begin{bmatrix} d_{12} & d_{13} \\ d_{22} & d_{23} \end{bmatrix}^{-1} \begin{bmatrix} d_{11} & d_{14} \\ d_{21} & d_{24} \end{bmatrix} \begin{bmatrix} k_0 - k_{ss} \\ x_1 - x_{ss} \end{bmatrix}$$
$$= \begin{bmatrix} e_{11}(k_0 - k_{ss}) + e_{12}(x_1 - x_{ss}) \\ e_{21}(k_0 - k_{ss}) + e_{22}(x_1 - x_{ss}) \end{bmatrix}.$$

Hence, for each period t, the two stability conditions, valid at each point in time, are

$$c_t = c_{ss} + e_{11}(k_t - k_{ss}) + e_{12}(x_{t+1} - x_{ss}), \quad t = 0, 1, 2, \ldots, \quad (9.83)$$
$$m_t = m_{ss} + e_{21}(k_t - k_{ss}) + e_{22}(x_{t+1} - x_{ss}), \quad t = 0, 1, 2, \ldots. \quad (9.84)$$

Summarizing, the solution to the representative agent model can be found following the steps:

1) Characterize the two stability conditions for the model.[13]
2) Given k_0, x_1, use stability condition (9.83) to compute c_0.
3) Once k_0 and c_0 are known, the global constraint of resources (9.78) allows us to obtain the value of k_1.
4) Given x_1, the policy rule (9.75) allows us to compute x_2.

---

[13] The transitional dynamics can be solved in a spreadsheet and, in fact, that is done in *Short-run nonneutrality.xls*. Eigenvalues are solved for by using Newton's method for finding the roots of a given equation.

5) To obtain the time path for $\{k_{t+1}, x_{t+2}, c_t\}_{t=1}^{\infty}$ we repeat steps 2–4 at every time period. From this description, it is clear that the time paths for the stock of capital and consumption will depend on the realization for the money growth process.

6) To obtain the time path $\{m_t\}_{t=0}^{\infty}$, we use stability condition (9.84) and the trajectories for $\{k_t, x_{t+1}\}_{t=0}^{\infty}$, which are already known. Notice that given M_0, and once $\{x_t\}_{t=1}^{\infty}$ is known, we can compute the $\{M_t\}_{t=0}^{\infty}$-path. Since $m_t = \frac{M_t}{P_t}$, once we know the trajectories for $\{M_t, m_t\}_{t=0}^{\infty}$, we can compute the time path for prices $\{P_t\}_{t=0}^{\infty}$. Therefore, in this case there is not *nominal indeterminacy*.

The remaining variables are computed as described in Sect. 9.4.

9.6.4 Numerical Exercise: Gradual vs. Drastic Changes in Money Growth

An once and-for-all change in the rate of growth of money supply is achieved by setting $\rho_x = 0$ in (9.75) and introducing a change in the long-run target at some time $\tilde{t}$:

$$x_t = x_{ss}, \quad \text{for } t < \tilde{t},$$
$$x_t = \tilde{x}_{ss}, \quad \text{for } t \geq \tilde{t}.$$

This is the policy experiment considered in the *Once and-for-all money change* spreadsheet. If the economy is in steady-state when the government changes policy, then consumption, the stock of capital and output are unaffected, while real balances adjust to their new steady-state level immediately. The size of the lump-sum transfer to the private sector and the stock of bonds would take a number of periods to reach their new steady-state levels. If, on the other hand, the economy is not at steady-state at the time of the policy change, then there are effects on the transition paths on all the variables in the economy. Therefore, monetary policy is non-neutral in the short-run.

The spreadsheet assumes that the stock of capital is initially (at $t = 0$) 1% below its steady-state level and we compute two sets of time series, the one to the left is obtained under the initial policy parameters, with a rate of money growth of 3% each period, while the one to the right is obtained under a change at $t = 10$, from a rate of money growth of 3% to a rate of growth of 4%. So, the left panel just describes the transition path followed by the economy from its initial position, outside steady state. The right panel, on the other hand, describes the trajectory followed after a policy intervention that permanently increases the rate of growth of money supply. The steady-state rate of inflation is equal to the rate of growth of the money supply, so inflation will converge to 3% and 4%, respectively, in each policy experiment. The transfer to consumers can be seen to be negative in both cases, acting therefore as a lump-sum tax. For this parameterization, interest payments on outstanding debt are being financed by the combination of seigniorage revenues and a lump-sum tax, as can easily be seen from the steady-state formulation of the government budget constraint. In fact, in steady state, seigniorage revenues are $\pi_{ss} m_{ss} = (0.03)(7.154) = 0.21$, and the lump-sum tax is 1.27, which allow for financing interest on debt: $r_{ss} b_{ss} = (0.0526)(28.170) = 1.48$.

The computations show that the policy intervention lacks any significant real effect, the time series for consumption, the stock of capital and output being essentially unaltered. There are in fact, some effects but they are small enough not to show up in the graphs. The rate of inflation and the nominal interest rate, both exhibit substantial peaks at the time of the policy intervention, falling back to their new steady state levels after a single period. Real balances experience a permanent fall, as it is the case with the stock of debt, while the size of the transfer to the private sector experiences a permanent increase. The level of utility falls permanently, due to the fall in real balances. The reader can also check that if initial capital is set at their steady-state levels before the policy change, then the effect of the change in the inflation target is zero.

Since the change in money growth does not affect the real return on capital, the convergence path of the demand for productive capital does not change. Hence, the time path for output is not affected either, and neither is the consumption time path, from the market clearing condition for the single commodity. The increase in money growth leads to higher inflation and hence, higher nominal interest rates. That, in turn, increases the opportunity cost of holding money, leading to a sharp decrease in the demand for real balances.

On the fiscal side, in steady-state the increase in inflation from the government intervention compensates the fall in real balances and seigniorage revenues increase $\pi_{ss} m_{ss} = (0.04)(6.359) = 0.25$, and the lump-sum tax can be reduced to 1.22, to finance interest on debt, which is barely changed: $r_{ss} b_{ss} = (0.0526)(28.056) = 1.47$.

A gradual intervention would be of the form

$$x_t = x_{ss}, \quad \text{for } t < \tilde{t},$$
$$x_t = (1 - \rho_x)\tilde{x}_{ss} + \rho_x x_{t-1}, \quad \text{for } t \geq \tilde{t},$$

with $x_{ss} \neq \tilde{x}_{ss}$. Then the levels of capital stock and consumption will not remain constant even if the economy is in steady-state at the time of the policy change. The qualitative effect will depend on whether $\sigma \lessgtr 1$. In the *Gradual money change* spreadsheet we perform this experiment for an increase in single period money growth (and steady-state inflation) from 3% to 4%. Contrary to the previous exercise, all variables are now supposed to be initially at their steady-state levels. Consumption, the stock of capital and output start a transition trajectory which eventually converges back to the same steady-state as before the policy intervention.

It is important to remark that the numerical solution we compute in the spreadsheet is obtained under the assumption that consumers know that the monetary authority is implementing a gradual change in the rate of growth of money supply, which will eventually end up at a constant level of $\tilde{x}_{ss}$. This is reflected in the fact that, in the first period when money growth starts to change, at $t = 10$, we impose a stability condition calculated under a rate of money growth of $\tilde{x}_{ss}$. The anticipation of a higher, permanent change in money growth makes the rate of inflation and the nominal rate of interest both experience a drastic one period increase, higher than should be expected on the basis of the first-period increase in money growth. After the initial reaction, both variables start adjusting to their new steady-state level which are above the ones before the policy intervention. The sharp increase in inflation drastically reduces the demand for real balances initially. They experiment an additional, smaller decrease afterwards and they stay permanently below their level at the initial steady state. From the point of view of the consumer, the described time path for real balances produces an initial increase in the marginal utility of consumption followed by an even larger increase in future periods. Hence, the consumer would like to increase consumption even more at later periods than at the first periods after the government intervention. The change in the marginal rate of substitution of consumption incentives faster capital accumulation early on, which allows for higher future output and consumption. At some point, the increased consumption leads to negative net investment, and the stock of capital gradually returns to its level before the policy intervention.

On the financing side, the lower demand for real balances leads to an initial fall in seigniorage revenues, requiring the government to initially increase the stock of debt outstanding. Seigniorage revenues start increasing after the initial period because the effect of higher growth dominates the lower real balances. One period after the intervention, the (9.67)-rule leads to a higher lump-sum tax. If the increased in aggregate revenues (seigniorage and lump-sum taxes) happens not to be enough to cover interest payments, the government will have to increase the stock of debt outstanding for a number of periods. The situation will reverse after a number of periods, allowing the government to retire some debt since, as the reader may easily check, the stability rule for debt implies that higher steady state seigniorage revenues come together with a lower stock of debt.

The reader can use *money_M_d.m* MATLAB file to compute a single realization (since the model is deterministic) that incorporates a purely transitory intervention, where the rate of growth of money supply starts from outside steady-state. That amounts to computing the responses of endogenous variables to a policy intervention that deviates money growth from its steady state value for a single period. Program *money_M_d_gradual.m* computes the effects of a permanent, gradual change in money growth. The effects of a drastic, permanent change in money growth can be obtained by setting $\rho_x = 0$.

9.7 The Stochastic Version of the Monetary Model

We will now consider an economy where the time evolution of the general level of productivity follows a given stochastic process. For convenience, we include the real value of money balances at the end of the period, rather than at the beginning, as an argument in the utility function.[14] The relevant variable for the private agent is then M_{t+1}/P_t which, as we did in Sect. 8.7, we denote by $\bar{m}_{t+1}$. Consumers can purchase discount government bonds offering a known nominal return. Bonds purchased at time t are denoted by V_{t+1}. They offer a nominal return i_t.

The representative agent solves the problem

$$\max_{\{c_t, M_{t+1}, k_{t+1}, V_{t+1}\}_{t=0}^{\infty}} E_0 \sum_{t=0}^{\infty} \beta^t U(c_t, M_{t+1}/P_t)$$

subject to

$$(1+\tau^c)c_t + k_{t+1} - (1-\delta)k_t + \frac{M_{t+1}}{P_t} + \left[\frac{V_{t+1}}{(1+i_t)P_t}\right] = (1-\tau^y)A_t k_t^{\alpha} + \frac{M_t}{P_t} + \frac{V_t}{P_t} + \zeta_t,$$

given k_0, M_0, V_0. The productivity shock is assumed to obey the stochastic process

$$\ln A_t = (1-\rho_A)\ln A_{ss} + \rho_A A_{t-1} + \varepsilon_{A,t}, \quad |\rho_A| < 1, \quad \varepsilon_{A,t} \underset{iid}{\sim} N(0,\sigma_A^2).$$

The government raises income and consumption taxes, prints money and issues nominal bonds, which are bought at price $1/(1+i_t)$. It also provides transfers ζ_t to the private sector. The government budget constraint is

$$\tau^c c_t + \tau^y A_t k_t^{\alpha} + \frac{M_{t+1} - M_t}{P_t} + \left[\frac{V_{t+1}}{(1+i_t)P_t} - \frac{V_t}{P_t}\right] = \zeta_t.$$

The fiscal authority chooses sequences $\{\tau^c, \tau^y\}$ and $\{\zeta_t\}_{t=0}^{\infty}$. To guarantee stability of the public debt trajectory, we will assume that

$$\zeta_t = \zeta - \eta \frac{V_t}{P_t}, \tag{9.85}$$

which implies

$$\bar{b}_{t+1} = (1+i_t)\left[\zeta - \tau^c c_t - \tau^y A_t k_t^{\alpha} - \bar{m}_{t+1} + \frac{\bar{m}_t}{1+\pi_t}\right]$$
$$+ (1-\eta)\frac{1+i_t}{1+\pi_t}\bar{b}_t, \tag{9.86}$$

where, as in previous chapter, $\bar{b}_{t+1} = \frac{V_{t+1}}{P_t}$, $\bar{m}_{t+1} = \frac{M_{t+1}}{P_t}$. Then, $\bar{b}_{t+1}$ will be stable so long as $\frac{2+r_{ss}}{1+r_{ss}} > \eta > \frac{r_{ss}}{1+r_{ss}}$, where: $1+r_{ss} = (1+i_{ss})/(1+\pi_{ss})$.

---

[14] If we used M_t/P_t as an argument in the utility function, as in previous sections, the demand for money equation would involve expectations of policy and control variables, and the analytical treatment of the model becomes more tedious.

9.7.1 The Monetary Authority Chooses Nominal Interest Rates

Additionally, we will assume that the monetary authority chooses the sequence of nominal interest rates $\{i_t\}_{t=0}^{\infty}$ according to a Taylor's rule:

$$\hat{i}_t = \rho_i \hat{i}_{t-1} + \rho_\pi \hat{\pi}_t + \rho_y \hat{y}_t + \varepsilon_{i,t}, \quad |\rho_i| < 1, \quad \varepsilon_{i,t} \underset{iid}{\sim} N(0, \sigma_i^2),$$

where $\hat{i}_t \equiv \ln\left(\frac{1+i_t}{1+i_{ss}}\right); \hat{\pi}_t \equiv \ln\left(\frac{1+\pi_t}{1+\pi_{ss}}\right); \hat{y}_t \equiv \ln\left(\frac{y_t}{y_{ss}}\right) \underset{y_t = A_t k_t^\alpha}{=} \hat{A}_t + \alpha \hat{k}_t, \hat{A}_t \equiv \ln\left(\frac{A_t}{A_{ss}}\right),$

$\hat{k}_t \equiv \ln\left(\frac{k_t}{k_{ss}}\right)$. A simple equation of this type can capture the central bank policy, as initially suggested by Taylor [92] with equation $i_t = 1.5\pi_t + 0.5y_t$. The central bank has policy targets for inflation and output, and moves nominal rates as a function of the deviations in inflation and output relative to their policy targets. This assumption aims to gaining generality over the assumption of a first order autoregression for nominal rates, which could be obtained as a special case of the rule above, setting $\rho_\pi = \rho_y = 0$.

9.7.1.1 Case 1: $\rho_\pi = 0$

If $\rho_\pi = 0$, the Taylor rule becomes

$$\hat{i}_t = \rho_i \hat{i}_{t-1} + \rho_y\left(\hat{A}_t + \alpha \hat{k}_t\right) + \varepsilon_{i,t}, \tag{9.87}$$

and there is nominal indeterminacy at two levels: first, since the initial price level, P_0, remains unknown, the price sequence is indeterminate. Second, we will show that we can only compute the expectations of inflation, but not the realized inflation rate. So, at a difference from previous indeterminacy situations, in which we could have computed a continuum of price sequences, all consistent with the previously obtained inflation trajectory, in this economy we are unable to compute any price sequence, since the time series for inflation cannot be obtained.

The Lagrangian of the representative agent is

$$L = E_0 \left\{ \sum_{t=0}^{\infty} \beta^t \left[U(c_t, M_{t+1}/P_t) + \lambda_t \left((1-\tau^y)A_t k_t^\alpha + \frac{M_t}{P_t} + \frac{V_t}{P_t} + \zeta_t \right. \right. \right.$$

$$\left. \left. \left. - (1+\tau^c)c_t - k_{t+1} + (1-\delta)k_t - \frac{M_{t+1}}{P_t} - \frac{V_t}{(1+i_t)P_t} \right) \right] \right\},$$

with first order conditions:

$$U_c(c_t, \bar{m}_{t+1}) = (1 + \tau^c)\lambda_t,$$

$$\lambda_t = \beta E_t \left[\lambda_{t+1} \left((1 - \tau^y)\alpha A_{t+1} k_{t+1}^{\alpha-1} + 1 - \delta \right) \right],$$

$$-U_m(c_t, \bar{m}_{t+1})\frac{1}{P_t} + \lambda_t \frac{1}{P_t} = \beta E_t \left(\lambda_{t+1} \frac{1}{P_{t+1}} \right),$$

$$\lambda_t \frac{1}{P_t(1 + i_t)} = \beta E_t \left(\lambda_{t+1} \frac{1}{P_{t+1}} \right),$$

where $\bar{m}_{t+1} = M_{t+1}/P_t$.

Plugging the first optimality condition into the other three conditions, we get

$$U_c(c_t, \bar{m}_{t+1}) = \beta E_t \left[U_c(c_{t+1}, \bar{m}_{t+2}) \left((1 - \tau^y)\alpha A_{t+1} k_{t+1}^{\alpha-1} + 1 - \delta \right) \right]. \qquad (9.88)$$

$$-U_m(c_t, \bar{m}_{t+1}) + \frac{U_c(c_t, \bar{m}_{t+1})}{(1 + \tau^c)} = \beta E_t \left[\frac{U_c(c_{t+1}, \bar{m}_{t+2})}{(1 + \tau^c)} \frac{1}{1 + \pi_{t+1}} \right]. \qquad (9.89)$$

$$U_c(c_t, \bar{m}_{t+1}) = \beta(1 + i_t) E_t \left[U_c(c_{t+1}, \bar{m}_{t+2}) \frac{1}{1 + \pi_{t+1}} \right]. \qquad (9.90)$$

From (9.89) and (9.90) we get

$$\frac{i_t}{1 + i_t} = (1 + \tau^c) \frac{U_m(c_t, \bar{m}_{t+1})}{U_c(c_t, \bar{m}_{t+1})}. \qquad (9.91)$$

For the utility function $U(c_t, M_{t+1}/P_t) = \frac{\left[c_t (M_{t+1}/P_t)^\theta \right]^{1-\sigma} - 1}{1 - \sigma}$, $\sigma > 0$, (9.91) becomes

$$\frac{i_t}{1 + i_t} = \theta(1 + \tau^c)\frac{c_t}{\bar{m}_{t+1}}. \qquad (9.92)$$

From the budget constraints for the representative agent and the government, we obtain the global constraint of resources in the economy:

$$c_t + k_{t+1} - (1 - \delta)k_t = A_t k_t^\alpha. \qquad (9.93)$$

Let us now recollect the set of optimality conditions that we are going to log-linearize in order to solve the model under the assumed utility function. From (9.88), (9.90), (9.92), (9.93), we get

$$c_t^{-\sigma} \bar{m}_{t+1}^{\theta(1-\sigma)} = \beta E_t \left[c_{t+1}^{-\sigma} \bar{m}_{t+2}^{\theta(1-\sigma)} \left((1 - \tau^y)\alpha A_{t+1} k_{t+1}^{\alpha-1} + 1 - \delta \right) \right], \qquad (9.94)$$

$$c_t^{-\sigma} \bar{m}_{t+1}^{\theta(1-\sigma)} = \beta(1 + i_t) E_t \left[c_{t+1}^{-\sigma} \bar{m}_{t+2}^{\theta(1-\sigma)} \frac{1}{1 + \pi_{t+1}} \right], \qquad (9.95)$$

$$\theta(1 + \tau^c)\frac{c_t}{\bar{m}_{t+1}} + \frac{1}{1 + i_t} - 1 = 0, \qquad (9.96)$$

$$c_t + k_{t+1} - (1 - \delta)k_t = A_t k_t^\alpha. \qquad (9.97)$$

Steady-State

From (9.94)–(9.97), we get

$$k_{ss} = \left[\frac{(1-\tau^y)\alpha A_{ss}}{\frac{1}{\beta} - (1-\delta)} \right]^{\frac{1}{1-\alpha}},$$

$$c_{ss} = A_{ss}k_{ss}^{\alpha} - \delta k_{ss},$$

$$\pi_{ss} = \beta(1+i_{ss}) - 1,$$

$$m_{ss} = \theta(1+\tau^c)c_{ss}\frac{1+i_{ss}}{i_{ss}}.$$

From (9.86) we get b_{ss}, while ζ_{ss} is obtained from (9.85).

Log-Linearization

To log-linearize this system (9.94)–(9.97), we rewrite the system as

$$e^{-\sigma \ln c_t}e^{\theta(1-\sigma)\ln \bar{m}_{t+1}} = \beta E_t \left[e^{-\sigma \ln c_{t+1}}e^{\theta(1-\sigma)\ln \bar{m}_{t+2}} \right. \tag{9.98}$$
$$\left. \times \left((1-\tau^y)\alpha e^{\ln A_{t+1}}e^{(\alpha-1)\ln k_{t+1}} + 1 - \delta \right) \right],$$

$$e^{-\sigma \ln c_t}e^{\theta(1-\sigma)\ln \bar{m}_{t+1}} = \beta e^{\ln(1+i_t)}E_t \left[e^{-\sigma \ln c_{t+1}}e^{\theta(1-\sigma)\ln \bar{m}_{t+2}}e^{-\ln(1+\pi_{t+1})} \right], \tag{9.99}$$

$$\theta(1+\tau^c)e^{\ln c_t - \ln \bar{m}_{t+1}} + e^{-\ln(1+i_t)} - 1 = 0, \tag{9.100}$$

$$e^{\ln c_t} + e^{\ln k_{t+1}} - (1-\delta)e^{\ln k_t} = e^{\ln A_t}e^{\alpha \ln k_t}. \tag{9.101}$$

Let us denote the deviations from steady-state by: $\hat{u}_t = \ln(u_t/u_{ss})$, $u = c, k, \bar{m}, A, 1+i, 1+\pi$. Using the fact that $E_t\hat{A}_{t+1} = \rho_A\hat{A}_t$, and also that $(1-\tau^y)\alpha A_{ss}k_{ss}^{\alpha-1} = \frac{1}{\beta} - (1-\delta)$, we obtain from (9.98)–(9.101)

$$0 = \frac{\sigma}{\beta}\hat{c}_t - \frac{\theta(1-\sigma)}{\beta}\widehat{m}_{t+1} - \frac{\sigma}{\beta}E_t\hat{c}_{t+1} + \frac{\theta(1-\sigma)}{\beta}E_t\widehat{m}_{t+2}$$
$$+ \left(\frac{1}{\beta} - (1-\delta) \right)\rho_A\hat{A}_t + \left(\frac{1}{\beta} - (1-\delta) \right)(\alpha-1)\hat{k}_{t+1}, \tag{9.102}$$

$$0 = \frac{\sigma}{\beta}\hat{c}_t - \frac{\theta(1-\sigma)}{\beta}\widehat{m}_{t+1} + \frac{1+i_{ss}}{1+\pi_{ss}}\hat{i}_t - \frac{\sigma}{\beta}E_t\hat{c}_{t+1}$$
$$+ \frac{\theta(1-\sigma)}{\beta}E_t\widehat{m}_{t+2} - \frac{1}{\beta}E_t\hat{\pi}_{t+1}, \tag{9.103}$$

$$\widehat{m}_{t+1} = \hat{c}_t - \frac{1}{i_{ss}}\hat{i}_t, \tag{9.104}$$

$$A_{ss}k_{ss}^{\alpha}\hat{A}_t + (A_{ss}\alpha k_{ss}^{\alpha} + (1-\delta)k_{ss})\hat{k}_t - c_{ss}\hat{c}_t - k_{ss}\hat{k}_{t+1} = 0, \tag{9.105}$$

where $\widehat{m}_{t+1}$ is known at time t.

Plugging (9.104) into (9.102) and (9.103), we get

$$0 = \frac{\sigma - \theta(1-\sigma)}{\beta}\hat{c}_t + \frac{\theta(1-\sigma)}{\beta i_{ss}}\hat{i}_t - \frac{\sigma - \theta(1-\sigma)}{\beta}E_t\hat{c}_{t+1}$$
$$- \frac{\theta(1-\sigma)}{\beta i_{ss}}E_t\hat{i}_{t+1} + \left(\frac{1}{\beta} - (1-\delta)\right)\left(\rho_A\hat{A}_t + (\alpha-1)\hat{k}_{t+1}\right), \tag{9.106}$$

$$0 = \frac{\sigma - \theta(1-\sigma)}{\beta}\hat{c}_t + \left(\frac{\theta(1-\sigma)}{\beta i_{ss}} + \frac{1+i_{ss}}{1+\pi_{ss}}\right)\hat{i}_t$$
$$- \frac{\sigma - \theta(1-\sigma)}{\beta}E_t\hat{c}_{t+1} - \frac{\theta(1-\sigma)}{\beta i_{ss}}E_t\hat{i}_{t+1} - \frac{1}{\beta}E_t\hat{\pi}_{t+1}. \tag{9.107}$$

We will now use the results, shown in Appendix 1, that in a log-linear approximation

$$E_t\hat{\pi}_{t+1} = \hat{i}_t - \hat{r}_t, \tag{9.108}$$

and also that

$$\hat{r}_t = \frac{1}{1+r_{ss}}(1-\tau^y)\alpha A_{ss}k_{ss}^{\alpha-1}\left[\rho_A\hat{A}_t + (\alpha-1)\hat{k}_{t+1}\right]. \tag{9.109}$$

From (9.87)

$$E_t\hat{i}_{t+1} = \rho_i\hat{i}_t + \rho_y\left(\rho_A\hat{A}_t + \alpha\hat{k}_{t+1}\right). \tag{9.110}$$

Using (9.108)–(9.110), we get from (9.106)

$$0 = \frac{\sigma - \theta(1-\sigma)}{\beta}\hat{c}_t + \frac{\theta(1-\sigma)}{\beta i_{ss}}(1-\rho_i)\hat{i}_t - \frac{\sigma - \theta(1-\sigma)}{\beta}E_t\hat{c}_{t+1}$$
$$+ \left[\left(\frac{1}{\beta} - (1-\delta)\right) - \frac{\theta(1-\sigma)}{\beta i_{ss}}\rho_y\right]\rho_A\hat{A}_t$$
$$- \left[(1-\alpha)\left(\frac{1}{\beta} - (1-\delta)\right) + \frac{\theta(1-\sigma)}{\beta i_{ss}}\alpha\rho_y\right]\hat{k}_{t+1}, \tag{9.111}$$

while from (9.107) we get

$$0 = \frac{\sigma - \theta(1-\sigma)}{\beta}\hat{c}_t + \frac{\theta(1-\sigma)}{\beta i_{ss}}(1-\rho_i)\hat{i}_t - \frac{\sigma - \theta(1-\sigma)}{\beta}E_t\hat{c}_{t+1}$$
$$+ \left[\left(\frac{1}{\beta} - (1-\delta)\right) - \frac{\theta(1-\sigma)}{\beta i_{ss}}\rho_y\right]\rho_A\hat{A}_t$$
$$- \left[(1-\alpha)\left(\frac{1}{\beta} - (1-\delta)\right) + \frac{\theta(1-\sigma)}{\beta i_{ss}}\alpha\rho_y\right]\hat{k}_{t+1}, \tag{9.112}$$

where we can see that (9.111) and (9.112) are the same equation. Hence, under (9.108) and (9.109) the Euler conditions on physical capital and bonds become the same. Equation (9.109) is a contemporaneous relationship that would allow us to compute the time path for real interest rates, once we know the time path for the stock of capital and for productivity.

Therefore, we can initially reduce the solution to the model to (9.105), (9.111) and (9.87), whose matrix representation is

$$
\underbrace{\begin{bmatrix} 0 & k_{ss} & 0 \\ \frac{\sigma - \theta(1-\sigma)}{\beta} & \tilde{\rho} & -\frac{\theta(1-\sigma)}{\beta i_{ss}}(1-\rho_i) \\ 0 & 0 & 1 \end{bmatrix}}_{D} \underbrace{\begin{bmatrix} E_t \hat{c}_{t+1} \\ \hat{k}_{t+1} \\ \hat{i}_t \end{bmatrix}}_{E_t v_{t+1}}
$$

$$
= \underbrace{\begin{bmatrix} -c_{ss} & \alpha A_{ss} k_{ss}^{\alpha} + (1-\delta) k_{ss} & 0 \\ \frac{\sigma - \theta(1-\sigma)}{\beta} & 0 & 0 \\ 0 & \alpha \rho_y & \rho_i \end{bmatrix}}_{G} \underbrace{\begin{bmatrix} \hat{c}_t \\ \hat{k}_t \\ \hat{i}_{t-1} \end{bmatrix}}_{v_t}
$$

$$
+ \underbrace{\begin{bmatrix} A_{ss} k_{ss}^{\alpha} \\ \left(\frac{1}{\beta} - (1-\delta)\right) - \frac{\theta(1-\sigma)}{\beta i_{ss}} \rho_y \\ \rho_y \end{bmatrix}}_{H} \rho_A \hat{A}_t + \underbrace{\begin{bmatrix} 0 \\ 0 \\ 1 \end{bmatrix}}_{J} \varepsilon_{i,t},
$$

where $\tilde{\rho} \equiv \left[(1-\alpha)\left(\frac{1}{\beta} - (1-\delta)\right) + \frac{\theta(1-\sigma)}{\beta i_{ss}} \alpha \rho_y \right]$, that is,

$$
D E_t v_{t+1} = G v_t + H \rho_A \hat{A}_t + J \varepsilon_{i,t},
$$

or

$$
E_t v_{t+1} = \Gamma_1 v_t + \Gamma_2 \hat{A}_t + \Gamma_3 \varepsilon_{i,t}, \tag{9.113}
$$

where $\Gamma_1 = D^{-1}G$, $\Gamma_2 = D^{-1}H\rho_A$, $\Gamma_3 = D^{-1}J$. Matrix Γ_1 is 3×3, with two stable and one unstable eigenvalues, whose associated eigenvector allows us to compute the value of the control variable (consumption) as a function of the two states $\left(\{\hat{k}_t, \hat{i}_{t-1}\}\right)$.

As in previous model economies, we now apply Blanchard and Kahn's approach to obtain the numerical solution: Let $\Gamma_1 = M\Lambda M^{-1}$, where Λ and M are the matrices of eigenvalues and eigenvectors, respectively. Without loss of generality, let us assume that $|\mu_1|, |\mu_2| < 1, |\mu_3| > 1$. Then, expression (9.113) will be equivalent to the system:

$$
m_{11} E_t \hat{c}_{t+1} + m_{12} \hat{k}_{t+1} + m_{13} \hat{i}_t = \mu_1 \left(m_{11} \hat{c}_t + m_{12} \hat{k}_t + m_{13} \hat{i}_{t-1} \right)
$$

$$
+ L_1 \hat{A}_t + Q_1 \varepsilon_{i,t}, \tag{9.114}
$$

$$m_{21}E_t\hat{c}_{t+1} + m_{22}\hat{k}_{t+1} + m_{23}\hat{i}_t = \mu_2\left(m_{21}\hat{c}_t + m_{22}\hat{k}_t + m_{23}\hat{i}_{t-1}\right)$$
$$+ L_2\hat{A}_t + Q_2\varepsilon_{i,t}, \tag{9.115}$$

$$m_{31}E_t\hat{c}_{t+1} + m_{32}\hat{k}_{t+1} + m_{33}\hat{i}_t = \mu_3\left(m_{31}\hat{c}_t + m_{32}\hat{k}_t + m_{33}\hat{i}_{t-1}\right)$$
$$+ L_3\hat{A}_t + Q_3\varepsilon_{i,t}, \tag{9.116}$$

where $L = (L_1, L_2, L_3)' = M^{-1}\Gamma_2$, $Q = (Q_1, Q_2, Q_3)' = M^{-1}\Gamma_3$. Expression (9.116) can be solved forwards applying the law of iterated expectations. Indeed, let $z_t = m_{31}\hat{c}_t + m_{32}\hat{k}_t + m_{33}\hat{i}_{t-1}$. Then

$$z_t = \frac{L_3}{\rho_A - \mu_3}\hat{A}_t - \frac{Q_3}{\mu_3}\varepsilon_{i,t},$$

that is,

$$\hat{c}_t = -\frac{m_{32}}{m_{31}}\hat{k}_t - \frac{m_{33}}{m_{31}}\hat{i}_{t-1} + \frac{L_3/m_{31}}{\rho_A - \mu_3}\hat{A}_t - \frac{Q_3}{\mu_3 m_{31}}\varepsilon_{i,t}, \tag{9.117}$$

which is the stability condition for the system in differences (9.113), that determines consumption as a function of the two state variables.

Plugging this stability condition in (9.114) and (9.115), we can write the two state variables as functions of their own past:

$$\left(m_{12} - \frac{m_{11}m_{32}}{m_{31}}\right)\hat{k}_{t+1} + \left(m_{13} - \frac{m_{11}m_{33}}{m_{31}}\right)\hat{i}_t$$
$$= \mu_1\left(m_{12} - \frac{m_{11}m_{32}}{m_{31}}\right)\hat{k}_t + \mu_1\left(m_{13} - \frac{m_{11}m_{33}}{m_{31}}\right)\hat{i}_{t-1}$$
$$+ \left(L_1 + \frac{L_3 m_{11}/m_{31}}{\rho_A - \mu_3}(\mu_1 - \rho_A)\right)\hat{A}_t$$
$$+ \left(Q_1 - \frac{Q_3 m_{11}\mu_1}{\mu_3 m_{31}}\right)\varepsilon_{i,t}, \tag{9.118}$$

$$\left(m_{22} - \frac{m_{21}m_{32}}{m_{31}}\right)\hat{k}_{t+1} + \left(m_{23} - \frac{m_{21}m_{33}}{m_{31}}\right)\hat{i}_t$$
$$= \mu_2\left(m_{22} - \frac{m_{21}m_{32}}{m_{31}}\right)\hat{k}_t + \mu_2\left(m_{23} - \frac{m_{21}m_{33}}{m_{31}}\right)\hat{i}_{t-1}$$
$$+ \left(L_2 + \frac{L_3 m_{21}/m_{31}}{\rho_A - \mu_3}(\mu_2 - \rho_A)\right)\hat{A}_t$$
$$+ \left(Q_2 - \frac{Q_3 m_{21}\mu_2}{\mu_3 m_{31}}\right)\varepsilon_{i,t}, \tag{9.119}$$

or, in matrix form:

$$
\begin{bmatrix}
m_{12} - \frac{m_{11}m_{32}}{m_{31}} & m_{13} - \frac{m_{11}m_{33}}{m_{31}} & -\kappa_{L_1} \\
m_{22} - \frac{m_{21}m_{32}}{m_{31}} & m_{23} - \frac{m_{21}m_{33}}{m_{31}} & -\kappa_{L_2} \\
0 & 0 & 1
\end{bmatrix}
\begin{bmatrix}
\hat{k}_{t+1} \\
\hat{\imath}_t \\
\hat{A}_t
\end{bmatrix}
$$
$$
=
\begin{bmatrix}
\mu_1\left(m_{12} - \frac{m_{11}m_{32}}{m_{31}}\right) & \mu_1\left(m_{13} - \frac{m_{11}m_{33}}{m_{31}}\right) & 0 \\
\mu_2\left(m_{22} - \frac{m_{21}m_{32}}{m_{31}}\right) & \mu_2\left(m_{23} - \frac{m_{21}m_{33}}{m_{31}}\right) & 0 \\
0 & 0 & \rho_A
\end{bmatrix}
\begin{bmatrix}
\hat{k}_t \\
\hat{\imath}_{t-1} \\
\hat{A}_{t-1}
\end{bmatrix}
$$
$$
+
\begin{bmatrix}
Q_1 - \frac{Q_3 m_{11}\mu_1}{\mu_3 m_{31}} & 0 \\
Q_2 - \frac{Q_3 m_{21}\mu_2}{\mu_3 m_{31}} & 0 \\
0 & 1
\end{bmatrix}
\begin{bmatrix}
\varepsilon_{i,t} \\
\varepsilon_{A,t}
\end{bmatrix},
\tag{9.120}
$$

where $\kappa_{L_1} \equiv \left(L_1 + \frac{L_3 m_{11}/m_{31}}{\rho_A - \mu_3}(\mu_1 - \rho_A)\right)$, $\kappa_{L_2} \equiv \left(L_2 + \frac{L_3 m_{21}/m_{31}}{\rho_A - \mu_3}(\mu_2 - \rho_A)\right)$.

Expression (9.120) is the system of state equations, while (9.117) is the control equation. Given initial values for the states $\{\hat{k}_0, \hat{\imath}_{-1}, \hat{A}_{-1}\}$ and realizations for the innovations $\{\varepsilon_{i,t}, \varepsilon_{A,t}\}_{t=0}^{\infty}$ we can obtain time series for $\{\hat{c}_t, \hat{k}_{t+1}, \hat{\imath}_t, \hat{A}_t\}_{t=0}^{\infty}$. Once this set of time series has been obtained, we can obtain series in levels: $\{c_t, k_{t+1}, i_t, A_t\}_{t=0}^{\infty}$. From (9.96) we obtain $\{\bar{m}_{t+1}\}_{t=0}^{\infty}$. From (9.109) we obtain $\{\hat{r}_t\}_{t=0}^{\infty}$. From (9.108) we obtain $\{E_t\hat{\pi}_{t+1}\}_{t=0}^{\infty}$. However, we cannot compute the levels of realized inflation and prices or the time series for nominal money balances. Therefore, as we mentioned above we have indeterminacy at two levels: (1) we do not know the initial price level, P_0, (2) we cannot compute the realized time paths for prices and inflation. The sequences for real or nominal government debt and transfers cannot be obtained either, since they are obtained as functions of the time paths for prices and inflation.

The numerical solution is implemented in the $S\_i\_npi\_s.m$ MATLAB file, that computes a single realization for the numerical solution.

9.7.1.2 Case 2: $\rho_\pi \neq 0$

It can be shown that if $\rho_\pi > 1$, we can determine the time path for the rate of inflation, although we will still not be able to compute the initial price level, so that nominal indeterminacy will still prevail. If $\rho_\pi > 1$, we can use (9.108) and Taylor's rule to obtain

$$
E_t\hat{\pi}_{t+1} = \hat{\imath}_t - \hat{r}_t = \rho_i\hat{\imath}_{t-1} + \rho_\pi\hat{\pi}_t + \rho_y\hat{y}_t + \varepsilon_{i,t} - \hat{r}_t,
$$

that is,

$$
\hat{\pi}_t = \frac{1}{\rho_\pi}E_t\hat{\pi}_{t+1} - \frac{1}{\rho_\pi}\underbrace{\left(\rho_i\hat{\imath}_{t-1} + \rho_y\hat{y}_t + \varepsilon_{i,t} - \hat{r}_t\right)}_{s_t},
$$

which has a single solution whenever $\rho_\pi > 1$:[15]

$$\hat{\pi}_t = -\frac{1}{\rho_\pi} \sum_{j=0}^{\infty} \left(\frac{1}{\rho_\pi}\right)^j E_t s_{t+j}.$$

To compute the numerical solution, we use the representation of the model (9.106), (9.107), (9.105) together with Taylor's rule

$$\hat{\imath}_t = \rho_i \hat{\imath}_{t-1} + \rho_\pi \hat{\pi}_t + \rho_y \hat{y}_t + \varepsilon_{i,t}, \tag{9.121}$$

written in state space form. Let $v_t = \left(\hat{c}_t, \hat{\pi}_t, \hat{k}_t, \hat{\imath}_{t-1}\right)'$. Then (9.121) can be written

$$\hat{\imath}_t = B v_t + \rho_y \hat{A}_t + \varepsilon_{i,t}, \tag{9.122}$$

where $B = \left(0, \rho_\pi, \rho_y \alpha, \rho_i\right)$. Furthermore

$$E_t \hat{\imath}_{t+1} = B E_t v_{t+1} + \rho_y \rho_A \hat{A}_t, \tag{9.123}$$

where $E_t v_{t+1} = \left(E_t \hat{c}_{t+1}, E_t \hat{\pi}_{t+1}, \hat{k}_{t+1}, \hat{\imath}_t\right)'$.

Equations (9.106), (9.107), (9.105) can be written in terms of v_t:

$$D\, E_t v_{t+1} + F\, E_t \hat{\imath}_{t+1} = G v_t + H \hat{\imath}_t + J \hat{A}_t, \tag{9.124}$$

where

$$D = \begin{bmatrix} \frac{\sigma - \theta(1-\sigma)}{\beta} & 0 & (1-\alpha)\left(\frac{1}{\beta} - (1-\delta)\right) & -\frac{\theta(1-\sigma)}{\beta i_{ss}} \\ \frac{\sigma - \theta(1-\sigma)}{\beta} & \frac{1}{\beta} & 0 & -\left(\frac{\theta(1-\sigma)}{\beta i_{ss}} + \frac{1+i_{ss}}{1+\pi_{ss}}\right) \\ 0 & 0 & k_{ss} & 0 \\ 0 & 0 & 0 & 1 \end{bmatrix};$$

$$F = \begin{bmatrix} \frac{\theta(1-\sigma)}{\beta i_{ss}} \\ \frac{\theta(1-\sigma)}{\beta i_{ss}} \\ 0 \\ 0 \end{bmatrix};$$

$$G = \begin{bmatrix} \frac{\sigma - \theta(1-\sigma)}{\beta} & 0 & 0 & 0 \\ \frac{\sigma - \theta(1-\sigma)}{\beta} & 0 & 0 & 0 \\ -c_{ss} & 0 & \alpha A_{ss} k_{ss}^\alpha + (1-\delta) k_{ss} & 0 \\ 0 & 0 & 0 & 0 \end{bmatrix}; \quad H = \begin{bmatrix} 0 \\ 0 \\ 0 \\ 1 \end{bmatrix};$$

---

[15] The solution is: $\hat{\pi}_t = \lim_{j \to \infty} \left(\frac{1}{\rho_\pi}\right)^j E_t \hat{\pi}_{t+j} - \frac{1}{\rho_\pi} \sum_{j=0}^{\infty} \left(\frac{1}{\rho_\pi}\right)^j E_t s_{t+j}$, although, whenever $\rho_\pi > 1$ the limit in the first term will be zero.

$$J = \begin{bmatrix} \left(\frac{1}{\beta} - (1-\delta)\right)\rho_A \\ 0 \\ A_{ss}k_{ss}^{\alpha} \\ 0 \end{bmatrix}.$$

Notice that the solution strategy in this case is different from the one followed in the section above or in the next one, in that now we have not only $E_t\hat{\pi}_{t+1}$, but also $\hat{\pi}_t$ in the reduced system that characterizes equilibrium. An equilibrium condition in most models in this chapter is $E_t\hat{\pi}_{t+1} = \hat{\iota}_t - \hat{r}_t$, so that when $E_t\hat{\pi}_{t+1}$, but not $\hat{\pi}_t$ appear in the reduced system, we can use that condition to completely eliminate inflation from the system. That is not possible in this model, and we are forced to retain the $E_t\hat{\pi}_{t+1} = \hat{\iota}_t - \hat{r}_t$ as part of the system, which has now dimension 4 rather than 3.

Plugging (9.122) and (9.123) into (9.124):

$$\underbrace{(D+FB)}_{L}E_tv_{t+1} = \underbrace{(G+HB)}_{N}v_t + \underbrace{\left(J+H\rho_A - F\rho_A\rho_y\right)}_{Q}\hat{A}_t + H\varepsilon_{i,t}, \qquad (9.125)$$

and, premultiplying this expression by L^{-1}:

$$E_tv_{t+1} = \Gamma_1 v_t + \Gamma_2 \hat{A}_t + \Gamma_3 \varepsilon_{i,t}, \qquad (9.126)$$

where $\Gamma_1 = L^{-1}N$; $\Gamma_2 = L^{-1}Q$; $\Gamma_3 = L^{-1}H$.

Notice that matrix Γ_1 has rank 3, since N has rank 3. Hence, one of its eigenvalues is equal to zero. Two of the other three eigenvalues will be above one, in absolute value whenever $\rho_\pi > 1$. The remaining eigenvalue will be below one in absolute value. Therefore, as we show next, we get two stability conditions from the two unstable eigenvalues, which will determine the two controls $(\hat{c}_t, \hat{\pi}_t)$ as functions of the states $(\hat{k}_t, \hat{\iota}_{t-1})$ at each time period t. Without loss of generality, let us assume that $|\mu_1| = 0$, $|\mu_2| < 1$, and $|\mu_3|$, $|\mu_4| > 1$. Jordan's decomposition of matrix Γ_1 is: $\Gamma_1 = M\Lambda M^{-1}$.

Let us denote

$$M = \begin{bmatrix} M_{11} & M_{12} & \cdots & M_{14} \\ M_{21} & M_{22} & \cdots & M_{24} \\ \cdots & \cdots & \cdots & \cdots \\ M_{41} & M_{42} & \cdots & M_{44} \end{bmatrix}; \quad M^{-1} = \begin{bmatrix} m_{11} & m_{12} & \cdots & m_{14} \\ m_{21} & m_{22} & \cdots & m_{24} \\ \cdots & \cdots & \cdots & \cdots \\ m_{41} & m_{42} & \cdots & m_{44} \end{bmatrix}.$$

If we multiply to the left of (9.126) by M^{-1}, we obtain

$$M^{-1}E_tv_{t+1} = \Lambda v_t + \underbrace{M^{-1}\Gamma_2}_{\Phi}\hat{A}_t + \underbrace{M^{-1}\Gamma_3}_{\Psi}\varepsilon_{i,t},$$

that is,

$$m_{11}E_t\hat{c}_{t+1} + m_{12}E_t\hat{\pi}_{t+1} + m_{13}\hat{k}_{t+1} + m_{14}\hat{\iota}_t = \Phi_1\hat{A}_t + \Psi_1\varepsilon_{i,t}, \qquad (9.127)$$

$$\begin{aligned} m_{21}E_t\hat{c}_{t+1} &+ m_{22}E_t\hat{\pi}_{t+1} + m_{23}\hat{k}_{t+1} + m_{24}\hat{\iota}_t \\ &= \mu_2\left(m_{21}\hat{c}_t + m_{22}\hat{\pi}_t + m_{23}\hat{k}_t + m_{24}\hat{\iota}_{t-1}\right) \\ &+ \Phi_2\hat{A}_t + \Psi_2\varepsilon_{i,t}, \end{aligned} \qquad (9.128)$$

$$\begin{aligned} m_{31}E_t\hat{c}_{t+1} &+ m_{32}E_t\hat{\pi}_{t+1} + m_{33}\hat{k}_{t+1} + m_{34}\hat{\iota}_t \\ &= \mu_3\left(m_{31}\hat{c}_t + m_{32}\hat{\pi}_t + m_{33}\hat{k}_t + m_{34}\hat{\iota}_{t-1}\right) \\ &+ \Phi_3\hat{A}_t + \Psi_3\varepsilon_{i,t}, \end{aligned} \qquad (9.129)$$

$$\begin{aligned} m_{41}E_t\hat{c}_{t+1} &+ m_{42}E_t\hat{\pi}_{t+1} + m_{43}\hat{k}_{t+1} + m_{44}\hat{\iota}_t \\ &= \mu_4\left(m_{41}\hat{c}_t + m_{42}\hat{\pi}_t + m_{43}\hat{k}_t + m_{44}\hat{\iota}_{t-1}\right) \\ &+ \Phi_4\hat{A}_t + \Psi_4\varepsilon_{i,t}. \end{aligned} \qquad (9.130)$$

Equations (9.129) and (9.130) can be solved forwards by application of the law of iterated expectations, since $|\mu_3|, |\mu_4| > 1$:

$$m_{31}\hat{c}_t + m_{32}\hat{\pi}_t + m_{33}\hat{k}_t + m_{34}\hat{\iota}_{t-1} = \frac{\Phi_3}{\rho_A - \mu_3}\hat{A}_t - \frac{\Psi_3}{\mu_3}\varepsilon_{i,t},$$

$$m_{41}\hat{c}_t + m_{42}\hat{\pi}_t + m_{43}\hat{k}_t + m_{44}\hat{\iota}_{t-1} = \frac{\Phi_4}{\rho_A - \mu_4}\hat{A}_t - \frac{\Psi_4}{\mu_4}\varepsilon_{i,t},$$

which are the two stability conditions. In matrix form:

$$\underbrace{\begin{bmatrix} \hat{c}_t \\ \hat{\pi}_t \end{bmatrix}}_{f_t} = \Theta \underbrace{\begin{bmatrix} \hat{k}_t \\ \hat{\iota}_{t-1} \end{bmatrix}}_{s_{t-1}} + \Xi\hat{A}_t + \Omega\varepsilon_{i,t}, \qquad (9.131)$$

where $\Theta = S^{-1}U$; $\Xi = S^{-1}V$; $\Omega = S^{-1}W$;

$$S = \begin{bmatrix} m_{31} & m_{32} \\ m_{41} & m_{42} \end{bmatrix}; \quad U = -\begin{bmatrix} m_{33} & m_{34} \\ m_{43} & m_{44} \end{bmatrix};$$

$$V = \begin{bmatrix} \frac{\Phi_3}{\rho_A - \mu_3} \\ \frac{\Phi_4}{\rho_A - \mu_4} \end{bmatrix}; \quad W = \begin{bmatrix} -\frac{\Psi_3}{\mu_3} \\ -\frac{\Psi_4}{\mu_4} \end{bmatrix}.$$

Expression (9.131) is the *control equation*. The state equation emerges from plugging the control equation in (9.127) and (9.128). If we write these two equations in matrix form

$$\underbrace{\begin{bmatrix} m_{11} & m_{12} \\ m_{21} & m_{22} \end{bmatrix}}_{\tilde{B}} E_t f_{t+1} + \underbrace{\begin{bmatrix} m_{13} & m_{14} \\ m_{23} & m_{24} \end{bmatrix}}_{\tilde{D}} s_t$$

$$= \underbrace{\begin{bmatrix} 0 & 0 \\ \mu_2 m_{21} & \mu_2 m_{22} \end{bmatrix}}_{\tilde{F}} f_t + \underbrace{\begin{bmatrix} 0 & 0 \\ \mu_2 m_{23} & \mu_2 m_{24} \end{bmatrix}}_{\tilde{G}} s_{t-1}$$

$$+ \underbrace{\begin{bmatrix} \Phi_1 \\ \Phi_2 \end{bmatrix}}_{\tilde{H}} \hat{A}_t + \underbrace{\begin{bmatrix} \Psi_1 \\ \Psi_2 \end{bmatrix}}_{\tilde{J}} \varepsilon_{i,t}.$$

Plugging the control equation in this equation, we get

$$s_t = \tilde{L}^{-1} \tilde{Q} \, s_{t-1} + \tilde{L}^{-1} \tilde{U} \hat{A}_t + \tilde{L}^{-1} \tilde{V} \varepsilon_{i,t}, \tag{9.132}$$

where $\tilde{L} = \tilde{B}\Theta + \tilde{D}$; $\tilde{Q} = \tilde{F}\Theta + \tilde{G}$; $\tilde{U} = \tilde{H} + (\tilde{F} - \tilde{B}\rho_A)\,\Xi$; $\tilde{V} = \tilde{J} + \tilde{F}\Omega$.

Using (9.132) and the law of motion for the productivity shock, we obtain the *state equation*:

$$\begin{bmatrix} s_t \\ \hat{A}_t \end{bmatrix} = \begin{bmatrix} \tilde{L}^{-1}\tilde{Q} & \rho_A \tilde{L}^{-1}\tilde{U} \\ [0\ 0] & \rho_A \end{bmatrix} \begin{bmatrix} s_{t-1} \\ \hat{A}_{t-1} \end{bmatrix}$$

$$+ \begin{bmatrix} \tilde{L}^{-1}\tilde{V} & \tilde{L}^{-1}\tilde{U} \\ 0 & 1 \end{bmatrix} \begin{bmatrix} \varepsilon_{i,t} \\ \varepsilon_{A,t} \end{bmatrix}. \tag{9.133}$$

Given realizations for the innovations $\{\varepsilon_{i,t}, \varepsilon_{A,t}\}_{t=0}^{\infty}$, together with initial values for the state variables $\{\hat{k}_0, \hat{\imath}_{-1}, \hat{A}_{-1}\}$, we obtain the time paths for the state variables $\{\hat{k}_{t+1}, \hat{\imath}_t, \hat{A}_t\}_{t=0}^{\infty}$. Given this set of time series, and using the control equation, we can obtain the control variables $\{\hat{c}_t, \hat{\pi}_t\}_{t=0}^{\infty}$. However, since we cannot compute the initial price level, the nominal indeterminacy will prevail. On the other hand, the rate of inflation can be solved for in this case. The time paths for nominal assets will then be undetermined under this policy design. Real money balances $\{\widehat{\bar{m}}_{t+1}\}_{t=0}^{\infty}$ can be obtained from (9.96), while interest rates $\{\hat{r}_t\}_{t=0}^{\infty}$ are obtained from (9.109). The time path for real government debt can be obtained using the government budget constraint, from an initial level of debt:

$$\underbrace{\bar{b}_{t+1}}_{\frac{V_{t+1}}{P_t}} = (1+i_t) \left[\zeta - \tau^c c_t - \tau^y A_t k_t^\alpha - \bar{m}_{t+1} + \frac{\bar{m}_t}{1+\pi_t} \right] + (1-\eta)\frac{1+i_t}{1+\pi_t}\bar{b}_t.$$

The numerical solution is implemented in the $S\_i\_pi\_s.m$ MATLAB file. Being a stochastic economy, we can now compute as many realizations as desired, since they will all be different from each other. This can be done with program $mS\_i.m$. These realizations can be used to calculate the value of any statistic, whose probability distribution can then be estimated over the set of simulations.

9.7.2 The Monetary Authority Chooses Money Supply Growth

We consider in this section the case when the government chooses money growth according to[16]

$$\ln(1+x_{t+1}) = (1-\rho_x)\ln(1+x_{ss}) + \rho_x \ln(1+x_t) + \varepsilon_{x,t},$$
$$|\rho_x| < 1, \quad \varepsilon_{x,t} \underset{iid}{\sim} N(0,\sigma_x^2), \tag{9.134}$$

or, equivalently

$$\hat{x}_{t+1} = \rho_x \hat{x}_t + \varepsilon_{x,t}, \tag{9.135}$$

so that the money supply evolves by

$$M_{t+1} = (1+x_{t+1})M_t, \quad \text{given } M_0. \tag{9.136}$$

The monetary authority is now choosing money growth as a policy control variable, in addition to the time path for the stock of bonds and the two tax rates, on consumption and income. From the discussion above, we know that[17]

$$E_t\hat{\pi}_{t+1} = \hat{\imath}_t - \hat{r}_t, \quad \text{where} \quad \hat{r}_t = \hat{\imath}_t - \frac{\delta+r_{ss}}{1+r_{ss}}\left(\rho_A\hat{A}_t + (\alpha-1)\hat{k}_{t+1}\right). \tag{9.137}$$

From (9.136) we have[18]

$$\hat{\pi}_{t+1} = \hat{x}_{t+2} + \widehat{\tilde{m}}_{t+1} - \widehat{\tilde{m}}_{t+2}, \tag{9.138}$$

so that

$$E_t\hat{\pi}_{t+1} = E_t\hat{x}_{t+2} + \widehat{\tilde{m}}_{t+1} - E_t\widehat{\tilde{m}}_{t+2}, \tag{9.139}$$

---

[16] For consistency with other variables, we denote by x_{t+1} the rate of growth of money supply at time t. So, the value of x_{t+1} is chosen at time t according to (9.134). Special cases include a deterministic rate of money growth (when $\sigma_x^2 = 0$), or even constant money growth, (if $\sigma_x^2 = \rho_x = 0$).

[17] In the Appendix to this chapter, we get

$$\hat{r}_t = \frac{1}{1+r_{ss}}(1-\tau^y)\alpha A_{ss}k_{ss}^{\alpha-1}\left[\rho_A\hat{A}_t + (\alpha-1)\hat{k}_{t+1}\right].$$

on the other hand, we have, in steady-state: $(1-\tau^y)\alpha A_{ss}k_{ss}^{\alpha-1} = \frac{1}{\beta} - (1-\delta)$, and $1+r_{ss} = \frac{1}{\beta}$.

Plugging both equalities into the first equation, we get

$$\hat{r}_t = \hat{\imath}_t - \frac{\delta+r_{ss}}{1+r_{ss}}\left(\rho_A\hat{A}_t + (\alpha-1)\hat{k}_{t+1}\right).$$

[18] Notice that:

$$M_{t+2} = (1+x_{t+2})M_{t+1},$$

which is analogous to

$$\frac{P_{t+1}}{P_t}\frac{M_{t+2}}{P_{t+1}} = (1+x_{t+2})\frac{M_{t+1}}{P_t} \Leftrightarrow (1+\pi_{t+1})\check{m}_{t+2} = (1+x_{t+2})\check{m}_{t+1},$$

and from the log-linear approximation to this equation, we get (9.138).

since $\widehat{m}_{t+1}$ is known at time t.

From (9.137) and (9.138)

$$\hat{\imath}_t = E_t\hat{x}_{t+2} + \widehat{m}_{t+1} - E_t\widehat{m}_{t+2} + \hat{r}_t. \qquad (9.140)$$

Hence, the equations making up the reduced form system that represents the dynamics of the model economy are:

(i) Equations (9.105) and (9.102), which we write again by convenience:

$$A_{ss}k_{ss}^{\alpha}\hat{A}_t + (A_{ss}k_{ss}^{\alpha} + (1-\delta)k_{ss})\hat{k}_t - c_{ss}\hat{c}_t - k_{ss}\hat{k}_{t+1} = 0, \qquad (9.141)$$

$$0 = \frac{\sigma}{\beta}\hat{c}_t - \frac{\theta(1-\sigma)}{\beta}\widehat{m}_{t+1} - \frac{\sigma}{\beta}E_t\hat{c}_{t+1} + \frac{\theta(1-\sigma)}{\beta}E_t\widehat{m}_{t+2}$$
$$+ \left(\frac{1}{\beta} - (1-\delta)\right)\rho_A\hat{A}_t + \left(\frac{1}{\beta} - (1-\delta)\right)(\alpha - 1)\hat{k}_{t+1}. \quad (9.142)$$

(ii) and an equation emerging from (9.103), (9.104), (9.139):

$$0 = \frac{\sigma + i_{ss}}{\beta}\hat{c}_t - \frac{\theta(1-\sigma) + (1+i_{ss})}{\beta}\widehat{m}_{t+1} - \frac{\sigma}{\beta}E_t\hat{c}_{t+1}$$
$$+ \frac{\theta(1-\sigma) + 1}{\beta}E_t\widehat{m}_{t+2} - \frac{\rho_x}{\beta}\hat{x}_{t+1}, \qquad (9.143)$$

where we have used the fact: $r_{ss} = \frac{1}{\beta}$.

If we write these equations in matrix form, we have

$$\underbrace{\begin{bmatrix} 0 & 0 & k_{ss} \\ \frac{\sigma}{\beta} & -\frac{\theta(1-\sigma)}{\beta} & \left(\frac{1}{\beta} - (1-\delta)\right)(1-\alpha) \\ \frac{\sigma}{\beta} & -\frac{\theta(1-\sigma)+1}{\beta} & 0 \end{bmatrix}}_{B} \underbrace{\begin{bmatrix} E_t\hat{c}_{t+1} \\ E_t\widehat{m}_{t+2} \\ \hat{k}_{t+1} \end{bmatrix}}_{E_t s_{t+1}^0}$$

$$= \underbrace{\begin{bmatrix} -c_{ss} & 0 & A_{ss}\alpha k_{ss}^{\alpha} + (1-\delta)k_{ss} \\ \frac{\sigma}{\beta} & -\frac{\theta(1-\sigma)}{\beta} & 0 \\ \frac{\sigma+i_{ss}}{\beta} & -\frac{\theta(1-\sigma)+1+i_{ss}}{\beta} & 0 \end{bmatrix}}_{D} \underbrace{\begin{bmatrix} \hat{c}_t \\ \widehat{m}_{t+1} \\ \hat{k}_t \end{bmatrix}}_{s_t^0}$$

$$+ \underbrace{\begin{bmatrix} A_{ss}k_{ss}^{\alpha} & 0 \\ \left(\frac{1}{\beta} - (1-\delta)\right)\rho_A & 0 \\ 0 & -\frac{\rho_x}{\beta} \end{bmatrix}}_{F} \underbrace{\begin{bmatrix} \hat{A}_t \\ \hat{x}_{t+1} \end{bmatrix}}_{a_t},$$

that is,

$$BE_t s^0_{t+1} = D s^0_t + F a_t,$$

or

$$E_t s^0_{t+1} = \Gamma_1 s^0_t + \Gamma_2 a_t, \tag{9.144}$$

where $\Gamma_1 = B^{-1}D$, $\Gamma_2 = B^{-1}F$.

It is easy to see that matrix Γ_1 has two unstable and one stable eigenvalues. The two unstable eigenvalues will allow us to compute, through their associated eigenvectors, the two stability conditions determining the control variables $\{\widehat{m}_{t+1}, \hat{c}_t\}$ as a function of the states $\{\hat{k}_t, \hat{A}_t, \hat{x}_{t+1}\}$.

For the parameterization assumed in the accompanying MATLAB program, the unstable eigenvalues are a pair of complex conjugate numbers, with norm above 1. Without loss of generality, we will assume that the eigenvalues of Γ_1 are: $|\mu_1| < 1$, $\mu_2 = a + bi$, $\mu_3 = a - bi$, such that $(a^2 + b^2)^{1/2} > 1$. Given k_0, we will have two stability conditions to determine $\{c_0, \bar{m}_1\}$. We now show how to compute the two stability conditions. To do so, it is convenient to write system (9.144) as

$$
\begin{bmatrix} \hat{c}_{t+1} \\ \widehat{m}_{t+2} \\ \hat{k}_{t+1} \\ \hat{A}_{t+1} \\ \hat{x}_{t+2} \end{bmatrix}
=
\underbrace{\begin{bmatrix} \Gamma_1 & \Gamma_2 \\ 0_{2\times3} & \Omega \end{bmatrix}}_{\Gamma_3}
\begin{bmatrix} \hat{c}_t \\ \widehat{m}_{t+1} \\ \hat{k}_t \\ \hat{A}_t \\ \hat{x}_{t+1} \end{bmatrix}
$$

$$
+ \underbrace{\begin{bmatrix} 1 & 0 \\ 0 & 1 \\ 0 & 0 \\ 0 & 0 \\ 0 & 0 \end{bmatrix}}_{\Gamma_4} \begin{bmatrix} \check{\eta}_{1,t+1} \\ \check{\eta}_{2,t+1} \end{bmatrix}
+ \underbrace{\begin{bmatrix} 0 & 0 \\ 0 & 0 \\ 0 & 0 \\ 1 & 0 \\ 0 & 1 \end{bmatrix}}_{\Gamma_5} \begin{bmatrix} \varepsilon_{A,t+1} \\ \varepsilon_{x,t+1} \end{bmatrix}, \tag{9.145}
$$

where we have added to system (9.144) the laws of motion for the technology variable $\hat{A}_{t+1}$ and that of the money growth process $\hat{x}_{t+2}$, and we have written the expectations of consumption and real balances as being equal to their realized values minus their respective prediction errors, $E_t \hat{c}_{t+1} = \hat{c}_{t+1} - \check{\eta}_{1,t+1}$, $E_t \widehat{m}_{t+2} = \widehat{m}_{t+2} - \check{\eta}_{2,t+1}$. Furthermore,

$$\Omega = \begin{bmatrix} \rho_A & 0 \\ 0 & \rho_x \end{bmatrix}.$$

Matrix Γ_3 has now five eigenvalues, the three already mentioned for Γ_1, together with ρ_A and ρ_x. Let us assume that we set up the diagonalization of matrix Γ_3 as

$$\Gamma_1 = M\Lambda M^{-1},$$

$$
\Lambda = \begin{bmatrix}
\mu_1 & 0 & 0 & 0 & 0 \\
0 & \rho_A & 0 & 0 & 0 \\
0 & 0 & \rho_x & 0 & 0 \\
0 & 0 & 0 & a+bi & 0 \\
0 & 0 & 0 & 0 & a-bi
\end{bmatrix};
$$

$$
M = \begin{bmatrix}
M_{11} & M_{12} & M_{13} & d_1 + f_1 i & d_1 - f_1 i \\
M_{21} & M_{22} & M_{23} & d_2 + f_2 i & d_2 - f_2 i \\
M_{31} & M_{32} & M_{33} & d_3 + f_3 i & d_3 - f_3 i \\
M_{41} & M_{42} & M_{43} & d_4 + f_4 i & d_4 - f_4 i \\
M_{51} & M_{52} & M_{53} & d_5 + f_5 i & d_5 - f_5 i
\end{bmatrix} .
$$

As shown in the Mathematical Appendix devoted to the solution of deterministic systems in finite order differences with complex eigenvalues, given a system of dimension 2:

$$
\begin{bmatrix} x_{1t} \\ x_{2t} \end{bmatrix} = \begin{bmatrix} A_{11} & A_{12} \\ A_{21} & A_{22} \end{bmatrix} \begin{bmatrix} x_{1t-1} \\ x_{2t-1} \end{bmatrix},
$$

if the eigenvalues associated to its transition matrix are complex conjugate numbers, we have

$$
\begin{bmatrix} A_{11} & A_{12} \\ A_{21} & A_{22} \end{bmatrix} = \underbrace{\begin{bmatrix} g_1 + h_1 i & g_1 - h_1 i \\ g_2 + h_2 i & g_2 - h_2 i \end{bmatrix}}_{P} \begin{bmatrix} \varpi + vi & 0 \\ 0 & \varpi - vi \end{bmatrix}
$$

$$
\times \begin{bmatrix} g_1 + h_1 i & g_1 - h_1 i \\ g_2 + h_2 i & g_2 - h_2 i \end{bmatrix}^{-1}
$$

and the general solution to this deterministic first order difference system can be written

$$
\begin{bmatrix} x_{1t} \\ x_{2t} \end{bmatrix} = \begin{bmatrix} s^t C_1 [g_1 \cos(\omega t) - h_1 \sin(\omega t)] + s^t C_2 [g_1 \sin(\omega t) + h_1 \cos(\omega t)] \\ s^t C_1 [g_2 \cos(\omega t) - h_2 \sin(\omega t)] + s^t C_2 [g_2 \sin(\omega t) + h_2 \cos(\omega t)] \end{bmatrix}
$$

$$
= \underbrace{\begin{bmatrix} g_1 & h_1 \\ g_2 & h_2 \end{bmatrix}}_{\tilde{P}} \begin{bmatrix} s^t [C_1 \cos(\omega t) + C_2 \sin(\omega t)] \\ s^t [-C_1 \sin(\omega t) + C_2 \cos(\omega t)] \end{bmatrix},
$$

where $s = (\varpi^2 + v^2)^{1/2}$ and $\omega = \arctan(v/\varpi)$, while C_1 and C_2 are two constants to be determined. Notice that $\tilde{P}$ is a two-column matrix: the first one is the real part of the right eigenvector of the transition matrix, while the second column is the imaginary part of that eigenvector.

Taking this result into account, the solution to the homogeneous version of system (9.145) is of the form:

$$
\begin{bmatrix} \hat{c}_t \\ \hat{m}_{t+1} \\ \hat{k}_t \\ \hat{A}_t \\ \hat{x}_{t+1} \end{bmatrix} = \tilde{M} \begin{bmatrix} \acute{C}_1 \mu_1^t \\ \acute{C}_2 \rho_A^t \\ \acute{C}_3 \rho_x^t \\ [\acute{C}_4 \cos(\theta t) + \acute{C}_5 \sin(\theta t)] q^t \\ [-\acute{C}_4 \sin(\theta t) + \acute{C}_5 \cos(\theta t)] q^t \end{bmatrix},
$$

$$\text{with } \tilde{M} = \begin{bmatrix} M_{11} & M_{12} & M_{13} & d_1 & f_1 \\ M_{21} & M_{22} & M_{23} & d_2 & f_2 \\ M_{31} & M_{32} & M_{33} & d_3 & f_3 \\ M_{41} & M_{42} & M_{43} & d_4 & f_4 \\ M_{51} & M_{52} & M_{53} & d_5 & f_5 \end{bmatrix},$$

where $q = (a^2 + b^2)^{1/2}$ and $\theta = \arctan(b/a)$. Since $q > 1$, this solution will be stable if and only if $\acute{C}_4$ and $\acute{C}_5$ are both equal to zero, which is the condition to eliminate the unstable trajectories. Besides setting the two constants to zero, we get the stability conditions determining the control variables at each point in time as a function of the states:

$$\tilde{M}^{-1} \begin{bmatrix} \hat{c}_t \\ \hat{m}_{t+1} \\ \hat{k}_t \\ \hat{A}_t \\ \hat{x}_{t+1} \end{bmatrix} = \begin{bmatrix} \acute{C}_1 \mu_1^t \\ \acute{C}_2 \rho_A^t \\ \acute{C}_3 \rho_x^t \\ 0 \\ 0 \end{bmatrix} \Rightarrow \begin{bmatrix} \tilde{M}_{1:3,:}^{-1} \\ \tilde{M}_{4:5,:}^{-1} \end{bmatrix} \begin{bmatrix} \hat{c}_t \\ \hat{m}_{t+1} \\ \hat{k}_t \\ \hat{A}_t \\ \hat{x}_{t+1} \end{bmatrix} = \begin{bmatrix} \acute{C}_1 \mu_1^t \\ \acute{C}_2 \rho_A^t \\ \acute{C}_3 \rho_x^t \\ 0 \\ 0 \end{bmatrix}$$

$$\Rightarrow \tilde{M}_{4:5,:}^{-1} \begin{bmatrix} \hat{c}_t \\ \hat{m}_{t+1} \\ \hat{k}_t \\ \hat{A}_t \\ \hat{x}_{t+1} \end{bmatrix} = \begin{bmatrix} 0 \\ 0 \end{bmatrix}, \tag{9.146}$$

where $\tilde{M}_{4:5,:}^{-1}$ denotes rows 4 and 5 in matrix $\tilde{M}^{-1}$. These correspond to columns 4 and 5 in $\tilde{M}$, which act are right "pseudo-eigenvectors" for matrix Γ_3.

From expression (9.146) we obtain the *control equation*:

$$\begin{bmatrix} \hat{c}_t \\ \hat{m}_{t+1} \end{bmatrix} = \underbrace{-[\tilde{M}_{4:5,1:2}^{-1}]^{-1} \tilde{M}_{4:5,3:5}^{-1}}_{\Psi_1} \begin{bmatrix} \hat{k}_t \\ \hat{A}_t \\ \hat{x}_{t+1} \end{bmatrix}, \tag{9.147}$$

where $\tilde{M}_{4:5,1:2}^{-1}$ denotes the submatrix of $\tilde{M}^{-1}$ made up by rows 4 and 5 and columns 1 and 2, while $\tilde{M}_{4:5,3:5}^{-1}$ denotes the submatrix of $\tilde{M}^{-1}$ made up by rows 4 and 5, and columns 3, 4 and 5.

If we multiply to the left through (9.145) by $\tilde{M}^{-1}$, we get

$$\tilde{M}^{-1} z_{t+1} = \tilde{M}^{-1} \Gamma_3 z_t + \tilde{M}^{-1} \Gamma_4 \check{\eta}_{t+1} + \tilde{M}^{-1} \Gamma_5 \varepsilon_{t+1}, \tag{9.148}$$

$$\text{where } z_{t+1} = \begin{bmatrix} \hat{c}_{t+1} \\ \hat{m}_{t+2} \\ \hat{k}_{t+1} \\ \hat{A}_{t+1} \\ \hat{x}_{t+2} \end{bmatrix}, \check{\eta}_{t+1} = \begin{bmatrix} \check{\eta}_{1,t+1} \\ \check{\eta}_{2,t+1} \end{bmatrix}, \varepsilon_{t+1} = \begin{bmatrix} \varepsilon_{A,t+1} \\ \varepsilon_{x,t+1} \end{bmatrix}.$$

Expression (9.148) can be written

$$\tilde{M}^{-1}z_{t+1} = \left(\tilde{M}^{-1}\Gamma_3\tilde{M}\right)\tilde{M}^{-1}z_t + \tilde{M}^{-1}\Gamma_4\breve{\eta}_{t+1} + \tilde{M}^{-1}\Gamma_5\varepsilon_{t+1}. \tag{9.149}$$

Notice that the structure of matrix $\left(\tilde{M}^{-1}\Gamma_3\tilde{M}\right)$ is as follows:

$$\tilde{\Lambda} = \left(\tilde{M}^{-1}\Gamma_3\tilde{M}\right) = \begin{bmatrix} \tilde{\Lambda}_{(1)} & \tilde{\Lambda}_{(2)} \\ \tilde{\Lambda}_{(3)} & \tilde{\Lambda}_{(4)} \end{bmatrix},$$

$$\text{where } \tilde{\Lambda}_{(1)} = \begin{bmatrix} \mu_1 & 0 & 0 \\ 0 & \rho_A & 0 \\ 0 & 0 & \rho_x \end{bmatrix}, \quad \tilde{\Lambda}_{(2)} = \begin{bmatrix} 0 & 0 \\ 0 & 0 \\ 0 & 0 \end{bmatrix}, \tag{9.150}$$

$$\tilde{\Lambda}_{(3)} = \begin{bmatrix} 0 & 0 & 0 \\ 0 & 0 & 0 \end{bmatrix}, \quad \tilde{\Lambda}_{(4)} = \begin{bmatrix} \mu_{44} & \mu_{45} \\ \mu_{54} & \mu_{55} \end{bmatrix}.$$

Hence, from system (9.149) we obtain

$$\underbrace{\tilde{M}^{-1}_{4:5,:}z_{t+1}}_{=0 \text{ by } (9.146)} = \underbrace{\tilde{\Lambda}_{(3)}\tilde{M}^{-1}_{1:3,:}z_t}_{=0 \text{ by } (9.150)} + \underbrace{\tilde{\Lambda}_{(4)}\tilde{M}^{-1}_{4:5,:}z_t}_{=0 \text{ by } (9.146)}$$

$$+ \tilde{M}^{-1}_{4:5,:}\Gamma_4\breve{\eta}_{t+1} + \tilde{M}^{-1}_{4:5,:}\Gamma_5\varepsilon_{t+1},$$

that is,

$$0 = \tilde{M}^{-1}_{4:5,:}\Gamma_4\breve{\eta}_{t+1} + \tilde{M}^{-1}_{4:5,:}\Gamma_5\varepsilon_{t+1}.$$

If we solve for the prediction errors we get their relationship with the innovations to the stochastic processes in the model:

$$\begin{bmatrix} \breve{\eta}_{1,t+1} \\ \breve{\eta}_{2,t+1} \end{bmatrix} = \underbrace{-[\tilde{M}^{-1}_{4:5,:}\Gamma_4]^{-1}[\tilde{M}^{-1}_{4:5,:}\Gamma_5]}_{\Psi_2} \begin{bmatrix} \varepsilon_{A,t+1} \\ \varepsilon_{x,t+1} \end{bmatrix}. \tag{9.151}$$

This is also a stability condition, since it has been obtained by imposing stability in the deterministic version of system (9.145) (i.e., in the homogeneous part of (9.145)).

Finally, substituting expressions (9.147) and (9.151) in system (9.145) we get the *state equation*:

$$\begin{bmatrix} \hat{k}_{t+1} \\ \hat{A}_{t+1} \\ \hat{x}_{t+2} \end{bmatrix} = \underbrace{[\Gamma_{3_{(3:5,1:2)}}\Psi_1 + \Gamma_{3_{(3:5,3:5)}}]}_{\Phi_1} \begin{bmatrix} \hat{k}_t \\ \hat{A}_t \\ \hat{x}_{t+1} \end{bmatrix}$$

$$+ \underbrace{[\Gamma_{5_{(3:5,:)}} + \Gamma_{4_{(3:5,:)}}\Psi_2]}_{\Phi_2} \begin{bmatrix} \varepsilon_{A,t+1} \\ \varepsilon_{x,t+1} \end{bmatrix}. \tag{9.152}$$

A single realization for the numerical solution for this model is implemented in
$S\_M\_s.m$ MATLAB file. An arbitrary number of realizations can be obtained using
the $mS\_M.m$ program. In this program we have labelled matrices Ψ_1 as 'MCONT1',
Ψ_2 as 'MCONT2', Φ_1 as 'MS1', and Φ_2 as 'MS2'.

Given initial conditions $k_0, \hat{A}_0, \hat{x}_1$, we obtain $\{\hat{k}_{t+1}, \hat{A}_{t+1}, \hat{x}_{t+2}\}_{t=0}^{T}$ from (9.152).
From (9.147) we compute the time paths $\{\hat{c}_t, \widehat{m}_{t+1}\}_{t=0}^{T}$. Given $\{M_t, \widehat{m}_{t+1}\}_{t=0}^{T}$ we
compute $\{P_t\}_{t=0}^{T}$, and hence, $\{\pi_{t+1}\}_{t=0}^{T-1}$. Notice that there is not nominal indeterminacy in the model, since we can compute P_0 as well as the whole time path for
inflation and for inflation expectations without any problem

$$\hat{\pi}_{t+1} = \hat{x}_{t+2} + \widehat{m}_{t+1} - E_t \widehat{m}_{t+2},$$

$$E_t \hat{\pi}_{t+1} = \rho_x \hat{x}_{t+1} + \widehat{m}_{t+1} - E_t \widehat{m}_{t+2},$$

where $E_t \widehat{m}_{t+2} = \Psi_1(2,1)\hat{k}_{t+1} + \Psi_1(2,2)\rho_A \hat{A}_t + \Psi_1(2,3)\rho_x \hat{x}_{t+1}$.

From (9.137) and (9.140) we can obtain the time path for nominal and real interest rates. From the government budget constraint

$$\underbrace{\bar{b}_{t+1}}_{\frac{V_{t+1}}{P_t}} = (1 + i_t)\left[\zeta - \tau^c c_t - \tau^y A_t k_t^\alpha - \bar{m}_{t+1} + \frac{\bar{m}_t}{1 + \pi_t}\right] + (1 - \eta)\frac{1 + i_t}{1 + \pi_t}\bar{b}_t.$$

we obtain $\{\bar{b}_{t+1}\}_{t=0}^{T}$ starting from and initial condition V_0 and the initial price level
P_0 (already determined) as a function of the time path for transfers $\{\zeta_t\}_{t=0}^{T}$, by
imposing a stability condition of the type $\zeta_t = \zeta - \eta \bar{b}_t$. Since we know the time
paths for prices and real bonds, computing that for the stock of nominal bonds is
straightforward. Finally, time series for level variables can be readily obtained from
time series for variables in differences to steady-state values.

9.8 A New Keynesian Monetary Model

In this section we present and solve a dynamic, stochastic, general equilibrium
model with real balances in the utility function, à la Sidrauski, that incorporates
price rigidity. We assume the economy is made up by 4 agents: a representative
household, a representative firm that produces the final good, a continuum of intermediate goods-producing firms, and a monetary authority. Since intermediate
commodities are imperfect substitutes in the production of the final good, the representative firm producing intermediate commodities sells its production under monopolistic competition, deciding on its output price as a function of the demand that
the final-good producing firm makes of each intermediate commodity. We assume
that the firm producing intermediate commodities faces quadratic costs for adjusting
nominal prices between periods, which are responsible for the price rigidity in this
model. In the absence of adjustment costs, the symmetric equilibrium of this model

would converge to that of an economy with flexible prices. The price rigidity in the model allows us to obtain, as one of the equilibrium conditions, a Phillips curve.

We are specially interested in presenting this monetary model with price rigidity so that the reader could clearly see the similarities and differences between price flexibility and price rigidity, as well as compare the structure of a neoclassical monetary model with that of a neo-keynesian model. We start by presenting a neo-keynesian monetary model that we can easily write in terms of standard IS, LM and Phillips curves, which departs from previous models in that it has an elastic labour supply function and the lack of capital accumulation. This latter assumption allows us to obtain the IS and LM equations in a very natural manner. Once we present this model, we will return to a specification where agents offer their units of labour inelastically and we allow for physical capital accumulation. Under this specification IS and LM curves are less evident, although we can solve the model very similarly to how we have solved neoclassical monetary models above.

The specification of the IS-LM-Phillips curve model with micro foundations we present next is taken from Ireland [45].

9.8.1 A Model Without Capital Accumulation: Ireland's (2004)

The Representative Household

The household is endowed with h_t units of labour which it dedicates to the different intermediate commodity-producing firms. Since there is a continuum of such firms, indexed by $j \in [0, 1]$, we have

$$h_t = \int_0^1 h_t(j)dj.$$

The household starts each period t with a stock of *nominal* government debt B_t and a money stock M_t. At the beginning of the period, the household receives a *nominal* lump-sum transfer T_t from the monetary authority. After receiving this transfer, government bonds mature, providing the household with B_t additional units of money. These monetary units are used in part to purchase new government bonds B_{t+1}, at a nominal cost $\frac{B_{t+1}}{1+i_t}$, where i_t denotes the nominal rate of interest. The remaining money is used to purchase the final good at a nominal price P_t. At the end of the period, the household receives D_t money units in the form of dividend payments from the different intermediate commodities producing firms. Money M_{t+1} and government bonds B_{t+1} are carried over to period $t + 1$, subject to the budget constraint:

$$c_t + \frac{M_{t+1}}{P_t} + \frac{B_{t+1}}{P_t(1+i_t)} \leq \frac{M_t}{P_t} + \frac{B_t}{P_t} + \frac{T_t}{P_t} + w_t h_t + \frac{D_t}{P_t}, \tag{9.153}$$

where w_t denotes the real wage.

The representative household solves the problem

$$\max_{\{c_t, M_{t+1}, B_{t+1}\}} E_0 \sum_{t=0}^{\infty} \beta^t a_t \left[U\left(c_t, \left(\frac{M_{t+1}}{P_t}\right)/e_t\right) - \psi h_t \right]$$

subject to (9.153) and given M_0, B_0, where a_t and e_t denote, respectively, a preference shock, which will end up showing as a perturbation in the IS equation, and a shock to money demand, following the stochastic processes:

$$\ln a_t = \rho_a \ln a_{t-1} + \varepsilon_{at}, \quad |\rho_a| < 1, \quad \varepsilon_{at} \underset{iid}{\sim} N(0, \sigma_a^2), \tag{9.154}$$

$$\ln e_t = \rho_e \ln e_{t-1} + \varepsilon_{et}, \quad |\rho_e| < 1, \quad \varepsilon_{et} \underset{iid}{\sim} N(0, \sigma_e^2). \tag{9.155}$$

First order conditions for this problem are

$$a_t U_1(c_t, \bar{m}_{t+1}/e_t) = \lambda_t, \tag{9.156}$$

$$\psi a_t = \lambda_t w_t, \tag{9.157}$$

$$\lambda_t = \beta(1 + i_t) E_t[\lambda_{t+1}/(1 + \pi_{t+1})], \tag{9.158}$$

$$(a_t/e_t) U_2(c_t, \bar{m}_{t+1}/e_t) = \lambda_t - \beta E_t[\lambda_{t+1}/(1 + \pi_{t+1})], \tag{9.159}$$

together with (9.153) written as an equality, for $t = 0, 1, 2, \ldots$, and the transversality condition:

$$\lim_{T \to \infty} E_t \left[\beta^{t+T} \lambda_{t+T} \left(\frac{M_{t+T+1}}{P_{t+T}} + \frac{B_{t+T+1}}{P_{t+T}(1 + i_{t+T})} \right) \right] = 0,$$

where $\bar{m}_{t+1} = \frac{M_{t+1}}{P_t}$, $\pi_{t+1} = \frac{P_{t+1}}{P_t} - 1$.

The Representative Finished Goods-Producing Firm

This firm produces y_t units of the final good using as inputs $y_t(j)$ units of each intermediate good, for $j \in [0, 1]$. Each intermediate commodity is purchased at price $P_t(j)$. The technology used by this firm is

$$\left[\int_0^1 y_t(j)^{(\varepsilon-1)/\varepsilon} dj \right]^{\varepsilon/(\varepsilon-1)} \geq y_t, \quad \varepsilon > 1. \tag{9.160}$$

and it solves the problem:

$$\max_{\{y_t(j)\}} \Pi_t = P_t y_t - \int_0^1 P_t(j) y_t(j) dj,$$

subject to (9.160).

First order conditions are

$$y_t(j) = [P_t(j)/P_t]^{-\varepsilon} y_t, \quad \forall j \in [0,1], \tag{9.161}$$

where ε measures the constant price elasticity of demand for each intermediate good.

Competition among firms in the market for the final good leads to zero profits. It is easy to show that the zero profit condition implies[19]

$$P_t = \left[\int_0^1 P_t(j)^{1-\varepsilon} dj \right]^{\frac{1}{1-\varepsilon}}. \tag{9.162}$$

The Representative Intermediate Goods-Producing Firm

Each period t the j-th firm producing intermediate goods hires $h_t(j)$ units of labour at a real wage w_t, to produce $y_t(j)$ units of the intermediate good using the technology

$$z_t h_t(j) \geq y_t(j), \tag{9.163}$$

where z_t is an aggregate technological shock, common to all firms, that obeys the stochastic process

$$\ln z_t = \rho_z \ln z_{t-1} + \varepsilon_{zt}, \quad |\rho_z| < 1, \quad \varepsilon_{zt} \underset{iid}{\sim} N(0, \sigma_z^2). \tag{9.164}$$

As mentioned above, intermediate goods substitute imperfectly to produce the final commodity. Hence, the representative intermediate commodity producing firm sells its production in a monopolistic competition market at a price that depends on the demand by the firm producing the final good, and facing a quadratic cost of changing nominal prices as specified in Rotemberg [79]:

$$\frac{\phi}{2} \left[\frac{P_t(j)}{(1+\pi_{ss})P_{t-1}(j)} - 1 \right]^2 y_t,$$

where $\phi \geq 0$ and π_{ss} denotes the steady state rate of inflation.

---

[19] To show that result:

$$\Pi_t = 0 \Rightarrow P_t y_t - \int_0^1 P_t(j) y_t(j) dj = 0 \underset{\text{using (9.161)}}{\Rightarrow} P_t y_t - P_t^{\varepsilon} y_t \int_0^1 P_t(j)^{1-\varepsilon} dj = 0$$

$$\Rightarrow P_t^{1-\varepsilon} = \int_0^1 P_t(j)^{1-\varepsilon} dj \Rightarrow (9.162).$$

This adjustment cost makes the market value maximization problem of the representative j-th firm producing intermediate commodities to be dynamic:

$$\max_{\{P_t(j)\}} E_0 \sum_{t=0}^{\infty} \beta^t \lambda_t \left[\frac{D_t(j)}{P_t}\right]$$

subject to: (9.161) and (9.163), where

$$\frac{D_t(j)}{P_t} = \frac{P_t(j)}{P_t} y_t(j) - w_t h_t(j) - \frac{\phi}{2}\left[\frac{P_t(j)}{(1+\pi_{ss})P_{t-1}(j)} - 1\right]^2 y_t$$

$$\underset{\text{using (9.161) and (9.163)}}{=} \left[\frac{P_t(j)}{P_t}\right]^{1-\varepsilon} y_t - \left[\frac{P_t(j)}{P_t}\right]^{-\varepsilon}\frac{w_t y_t}{z_t}$$

$$- \frac{\phi}{2}\left[\frac{P_t(j)}{(1+\pi_{ss})P_{t-1}(j)} - 1\right]^2 y_t, \tag{9.165}$$

$\forall t = 0, 1, 2, \ldots$, where $\beta^t \lambda_t / P_t$ measures the value for the representative household of the marginal utility of an additional monetary unit received as dividends in period t.

First order conditions are

$$0 = (1-\varepsilon)\lambda_t\left[\frac{P_t(j)}{P_t}\right]^{-\varepsilon}\frac{y_t}{P_t} + \varepsilon\lambda_t\left[\frac{P_t(j)}{P_t}\right]^{-1-\varepsilon}\frac{w_t y_t}{z_t P_t}$$

$$-\phi\lambda_t\left[\frac{P_t(j)}{(1+\pi_{ss})P_{t-1}(j)} - 1\right]\left[\frac{y_t}{(1+\pi_{ss})P_{t-1}(j)}\right]$$

$$+\beta\phi E_t\left\{\lambda_{t+1}\left[\frac{P_{t+1}(j)}{(1+\pi_{ss})P_t(j)} - 1\right]\left[\frac{y_{t+1}P_{t+1}(j)}{(1+\pi_{ss})P_t(j)^2}\right]\right\},$$

$$\forall t = 0, 1, 2, \ldots. \tag{9.166}$$

The Monetary Authority

The monetary authority implements policy adjusting the nominal rate of interest, i_t, in response to deviations of the final output, y_t, inflation, π_t, and money growth, x_t, with respect to their respective steady-state values: y_{ss}, π_{ss}, x_{ss}:

$$\ln\left(\frac{1+i_t}{1+i_{ss}}\right) = \rho_i \ln\left(\frac{1+i_{t-1}}{1+i_{ss}}\right) + \rho_y \ln(y_t/y_{ss})$$

$$+\rho_\pi \ln\left(\frac{1+\pi_t}{1+\pi_{ss}}\right) + \rho_x \ln\left(\frac{1+x_t}{1+x_{ss}}\right) + \varepsilon_{it}, \tag{9.167}$$

where

$$1 + x_t = M_t/M_{t-1}, \tag{9.168}$$

and $\varepsilon_{it} \underset{iid}{\sim} N(0, \sigma_i^2)$.

Equilibrium

We consider a symmetric equilibrium, in which all intermediate commodities producing firms take the same decisions, so that: $y_t(j) = y(t)$, $h_t(j) = h_t$, $P_t(j) = P_t$ and $d_t(j) = D_t(j)/P_t = D_t/P_t = d_t$, $\forall j \in [0,1]$, and $\forall t = 0,1,2,\ldots$. Furthermore, market clearing conditions $M_{t+1} = M_t + T_t$ and $B_{t+1} = B_t = 0$ hold for all $t = 0,1,2,\ldots$.

With these conditions, equilibrium is summarized in the following system, whose first equation is the global constraint of resources.

$$y_t = c_t + \frac{\phi}{2} \left[\frac{1+\pi_t}{(1+\pi_{ss})} - 1 \right]^2 y_t, \tag{9.169}$$

$$\ln a_t = \rho_a \ln a_{t-1} + \varepsilon_{at}, \tag{9.170}$$

$$\ln e_t = \rho_e \ln e_{t-1} + \varepsilon_{et}, \tag{9.171}$$

$$a_t U_1(c_t, \bar{m}_{t+1}/e_t) = \lambda_t, \tag{9.172}$$

$$\psi a_t = \lambda_t w_t, \tag{9.173}$$

$$\lambda_t = \beta(1+i_t)E_t[\lambda_{t+1}/(1+\pi_{t+1})], \tag{9.174}$$

$$(a_t/e_t)U_2(c_t, \bar{m}_{t+1}/e_t) = \lambda_t - \beta E_t[\lambda_{t+1}/(1+\pi_{t+1})], \tag{9.175}$$

$$y_t = z_t h_t, \tag{9.176}$$

$$\ln z_t = \rho_z \ln z_{t-1} + \varepsilon_{zt}, \tag{9.177}$$

$$d_t = y_t - \frac{w_t h_t}{z_t} - \frac{\phi}{2} \left[\frac{1+\pi_t}{(1+\pi_{ss})} - 1 \right]^2 y_t, \tag{9.178}$$

$$0 = (1-\varepsilon)\lambda_t + \varepsilon\lambda_t \frac{w_t}{z_t} - \phi\lambda_t \left[\frac{1+\pi_t}{1+\pi_{ss}} - 1 \right] \left[\frac{1+\pi_t}{1+\pi_{ss}} \right]$$
$$+ \beta\phi E_t \left\{ \lambda_{t+1} \left[\frac{1+\pi_t}{1+\pi_{ss}} - 1 \right] \left[\frac{y_{t+1}(1+\pi_{t+1})}{y_t(1+\pi_{ss})} \right] \right\}, \tag{9.179}$$

$$\bar{m}_t(1+x_{t+1}) = \bar{m}_{t+1}(1+\pi_t), \tag{9.180}$$

$$\ln\left(\frac{1+i_t}{1+i_{ss}}\right) = \rho_i \ln\left(\frac{1+i_{t-1}}{1+i_{ss}}\right) + \rho_y \ln(y_t/y_{ss})$$

$$+\rho_\pi \ln\left(\frac{1+\pi_t}{1+\pi_{ss}}\right) + \rho_x \ln\left(\frac{1+x_t}{1+x_{ss}}\right) + \varepsilon_{it}. \qquad (9.181)$$

This thirteen equations determine the equilibrium values for: y_t, π_t, $\bar{m}_t$, i_t, c_t, h_t, w_t, d_t, λ_t, x_t, a_t, e_t, z_t.

We can simplify the system by eliminating h_t, w_t, d_t, and λ_t, using (9.172), (9.173), (9.176) and (9.178):

$$y_t = c_t + \frac{\phi}{2}\left[\frac{1+\pi_t}{(1+\pi_{ss})} - 1\right]^2 y_t, \qquad (9.182)$$

$$\ln a_t = \rho_a \ln a_{t-1} + \varepsilon_{at}, \qquad (9.183)$$

$$\ln e_t = \rho_e \ln e_{t-1} + \varepsilon_{et}, \qquad (9.184)$$

$$a_t U_1(c_t, \bar{m}_{t+1}/e_t) = \beta(1+i_t)E_t[a_{t+1}U_1(c_{t+1}, \bar{m}_{t+2}/e_{t+1})/(1+\pi_{t+1})], \qquad (9.185)$$

$$U_2(c_t, \bar{m}_{t+1}/e_t) = \frac{i_t}{1+i_t}e_t U_1(c_t, \bar{m}_{t+1}/e_t), \qquad (9.186)$$

$$0 = (1-\varepsilon) + \varepsilon\frac{\psi}{z_t U_1\left(c_t, \frac{\bar{m}_{t+1}}{e_t}\right)} - \phi\left[\frac{\pi_t - \pi_{ss}}{1+\pi_{ss}}\right]\frac{1+\pi_t}{1+\pi_{ss}}$$

$$+\beta\phi E_t\left\{\frac{a_{t+1}U_1(c_{t+1}, \frac{\bar{m}_{t+2}}{e_{t+1}})}{a_t U_1(c_t, \frac{\bar{m}_{t+1}}{e_t})}\left[\frac{\pi_t - \pi_{ss}}{1+\pi_{ss}}\right]\frac{y_{t+1}(1+\pi_{t+1})}{y_t(1+\pi_{ss})}\right\}, \qquad (9.187)$$

$$\bar{m}_t(1+x_{t+1}) = \bar{m}_{t+1}(1+\pi_t), \qquad (9.188)$$

$$\ln z_t = \rho_z \ln z_{t-1} + \varepsilon_{zt}, \qquad (9.189)$$

$$\ln\left(\frac{1+i_t}{1+i_{ss}}\right) = \rho_i \ln\left(\frac{1+i_{t-1}}{1+i_{ss}}\right) + \rho_y \ln(y_t/y_{ss})$$

$$+\rho_\pi \ln\left(\frac{1+\pi_t}{1+\pi_{ss}}\right) + \rho_x \ln\left(\frac{1+x_t}{1+x_{ss}}\right) + \varepsilon_{it}. \qquad (9.190)$$

These nine equations determine the equilibrium values for: y_t, π_t, $\bar{m}_{t+1}$, i_t, c_t, x_{t+1}, a_t, e_t, z_t.

Steady State

In the absence of shocks, the economy will converge to steady state, with $y_t = y_{ss}$, $\pi_t = \pi_{ss}$, $\bar{m}_t = \bar{m}_{ss}$, $i_t = i_{ss}$, $c_t = c_{ss}$, $x_t = x_{ss}$, $a_t = 1$, $e_t = 1$, and $z_t = 1$. If the monetary authority chooses a nominal interest rate i_{ss}, we have, from (9.185)

$$\pi_{ss} = \beta(1 + i_{ss}) - 1,$$

while from (9.188), we get

$$x_{ss} = \pi_{ss}.$$

From (9.186) and (9.187) we obtain steady state values for c_{ss} and $\bar{m}_{ss}$, solving the system:

$$U_2(c_{ss}, \bar{m}_{ss}) = \frac{i_{ss}}{1 + i_{ss}} U_1(c_{ss}, \bar{m}_{ss}),$$

$$\varepsilon - 1 = \frac{\varepsilon \psi}{U_1(c_{ss}, \bar{m}_{ss})}.$$

Finally, from (9.182) we get

$$y_{ss} = c_{ss}.$$

Log-linear approximation

We can now compute the log-linear approximation of system (9.182)–(9.190) around the steady state we have just characterized. Using the notation: $\hat{y}_t = \ln(y_t/y_{ss})$, $\hat{\pi}_t = \ln[(1 + \pi_t)/(1 + \pi_{ss})]$, $\hat{m}_t = \ln(\bar{m}_t/\bar{m}_{ss})$, $\hat{i}_t = \ln[(1 + i_t)/(1 + i_{ss})]$, $\hat{c}_t = \ln(c_t/c_{ss})$, $\hat{x}_t = \ln[(1 + x_t)/(1 + x_{ss})]$, $\hat{a}_t = \ln a_t$, $\hat{e}_t = \ln e_t$, $\hat{z}_t = \ln z_t$, system (9.182)–(9.190) becomes

$$\hat{y}_t = \hat{c}_t, \tag{9.191}$$

$$\hat{a}_t = \rho_a \hat{a}_{t-1} + \varepsilon_{at}, \tag{9.192}$$

$$\hat{e}_t = \rho_e \hat{e}_{t-1} + \varepsilon_{et}, \tag{9.193}$$

$$\hat{y}_t = E_t \hat{y}_{t+1} - \varpi_1(\hat{i}_t - E_t \hat{\pi}_{t+1}) + \varpi_2(\widehat{\bar{m}}_{t+1} - E_t \widehat{\bar{m}}_{t+2})$$

$$- \varpi_2(\hat{e}_t - E_t \hat{e}_{t+1}) + \varpi_1(\hat{a}_t - E_t \hat{a}_{t+1}), \tag{9.194}$$

$$\widehat{\bar{m}}_{t+1} = \varpi_3 \hat{y}_t - \varpi_4 \hat{i}_t + \varpi_5 \hat{e}_t, \tag{9.195}$$

$$\hat{\pi}_t = \frac{1 + \pi_{ss}}{1 + i_{ss}} E_t \hat{\pi}_{t+1} + \frac{\varepsilon - 1}{\phi} \left[\frac{1}{\varpi_1} \hat{y}_t - \frac{\varpi_2}{\varpi_1} \widehat{\bar{m}}_{t+1} + \frac{\varpi_2}{\varpi_1} \hat{e}_t - \hat{z}_t \right], \tag{9.196}$$

$$\widehat{\bar{m}}_t + \hat{x}_{t+1} = \widehat{\bar{m}}_{t+1} + \hat{\pi}_t, \tag{9.197}$$

$$\hat{z}_t = \rho_z \hat{z}_{t-1} + \varepsilon_{zt}, \tag{9.198}$$

$$\hat{i}_t = \rho_i \hat{i}_{t-1} + \rho_y \hat{y}_t + \rho_\pi \hat{\pi}_t + \rho_x \hat{x}_t + \varepsilon_{it}, \tag{9.199}$$

where (9.191) has been used to obtain (9.194)–(9.196) and:

$$\varpi_1 = -\frac{U_1(y_{ss}, \bar{m}_{ss})}{y_{ss} U_{11}(y_{ss}, \bar{m}_{ss})},$$

$$\varpi_2 = -\frac{\bar{m}_{ss} U_{12}(y_{ss}, \bar{m}_{ss})}{y_{ss} U_{11}(y_{ss}, \bar{m}_{ss})},$$

$$\varpi_3 = \left(\frac{y_{ss}(1 + i_{ss})\varpi_2}{\bar{m}_{ss}\varpi_1} + \frac{i_{ss}}{\varpi_1} \right)\varpi_4,$$

$$\varpi_4 = \frac{1 + i_{ss}}{i_{ss}\bar{m}_{ss}} \left[\frac{U_2(y_{ss}, \bar{m}_{ss})}{i_{ss} U_{12}(y_{ss}, \bar{m}_{ss}) - (1 + i_{ss})U_{22}(y_{ss}, \bar{m}_{ss})} \right],$$

$$\varpi_5 = 1 - i_{ss}\varpi_4.$$

We can interpret (9.194), (9.195) and (9.196) as the IS curve augmented with real balances, the LM curve, and the Phillips curve augmented with real balances. So, these three curves can be obtained as the output from a stochastic, dynamic general equilibrium model with micro-foundations. The solution to this model, as well as its maximum likelihood estimation, can be read in Peter N. Ireland Web page: (http://www2.bc.edu/~irelandp).

However, we proceed to introduce a more general version of the model, incorporating capital accumulation and an inelastic labour supply which is allocated among the intermediate commodity producing firms. We will see that the solution to this model is very similar to that of the Sidrauski model, in spite of having introduced price rigidity in order to obtain the Phillips curve, which is also used to compute the solution.

9.8.2 A New Keynesian Monetary Model with Capital Accumulation

In this section, we formulate and solve a monetary growth model à la Sidrausky under the assumption of price rigidity. This economy is a simplified version of Ireland [44].

9.8.2.1 The Representative Household

The basic difference between the household problem in this economy and that in the previous section is that the household allocates its expenditures between consumption, c_t, and investment, inv_t. The law of motion for physical capital is

$$k_{t+1} = (1 - \delta)k_t + v_t inv_t, \tag{9.200}$$

where v_t is the shock to the marginal efficiency of investment, as specified in Greenwood et al. [36] and follows the stochastic process:

$$\ln v_t = \rho_v \ln v_{t-1} + \varepsilon_{vt}, \quad |\rho_z| < 1, \quad \varepsilon_{vt} \underset{iid}{\sim} N(0, \sigma_v^2). \qquad (9.201)$$

Furthermore, we assume that the household is endowed with a unit of labour that is inelastically offered to the different firms producing intermediate commodities, so that

$$1 = \int_0^1 h_t(j) dj, \quad j \in [0, 1]. \qquad (9.202)$$

Hence, the household faces the problem:

$$\max_{\{c_t, k_{t+1}, M_{t+1}, B_{t+1}\}} E_0 \sum_{t=0}^{\infty} \beta^t a_t U\left[c_t, \left(\frac{M_{t+1}}{P_t}\right)/e_t\right]$$

subject to

$$\frac{M_t}{P_t} + \frac{B_t}{P_t} + \zeta_t + (1 - \tau^w) w_t + (1 - \tau^q) q_t k_t + \frac{D_t}{P_t} \qquad (9.203)$$

$$\geq (1 + \tau^c) c_t + \frac{1}{v_t} k_{t+1} - (1 - \delta) k_t + \frac{M_{t+1}}{P_t} + \frac{B_{t+1}}{P_t(1 + i_t)}$$

$$\text{given } k_0, M_0, B_0,$$

where a_t and e_t are defined as in the previous model, q_t is the renting price of capital, and ζ_t denotes the real transfers received from the government and where we have included taxes on consumption and labor and capital income, as shown in the budget constraint (9.203).

The utility function $U(.)$ is similar to that in neoclassical monetary growth models analyzed in previous sections:

$$U\left[c_t, \left(\frac{M_{t+1}}{P_t}\right)/e_t\right] = \frac{\left[c_t \left(\frac{M_{t+1}}{P_t e_t}\right)^\theta\right]^{1-\sigma} - 1}{1 - \sigma}$$

leading to first order conditions:

$$a_t c_t^{-\sigma} \bar{m}_{t+1}^{\theta(1-\sigma)} e_t^{-\theta(1-\sigma)} = \lambda_t (1 + \tau^c), \qquad (9.204)$$

$$\lambda_t \frac{1}{v_t} = \beta E_t \left[\lambda_{t+1} \left((1 - \tau^q) q_{t+1} + (1 - \delta) \frac{1}{v_{t+1}}\right)\right], \qquad (9.205)$$

$$\lambda_t = \beta(1 + i_t) E_t[\lambda_{t+1}/(1 + \pi_{t+1})], \qquad (9.206)$$

$$(a_t/e_t) \theta c_t^{1-\sigma} \bar{m}_{t+1}^{\theta(1-\sigma)-1} e_t^{1-\theta(1-\sigma)} = \lambda_t - \beta E_t[\lambda_{t+1}/(1 + \pi_{t+1})], \qquad (9.207)$$

together with (9.203) written as an equality, for $t = 0, 1, 2, \ldots$, together with the transversality condition:

$$\lim_{T \to \infty} E_t \left[\beta^{t+T} \lambda_{t+T} \left(k_{t+1} + \frac{M_{t+T+1}}{P_{t+T}} + \frac{B_{t+T+1}}{P_{t+T}(1 + i_{t+T})} \right) \right] = 0.$$

If we eliminate λ_t, optimality conditions (9.204)–(9.207) can be summarized in the system:

$$a_t c_t^{-\sigma} \bar{m}_{t+1}^{\theta(1-\sigma)} e_t^{-\theta(1-\sigma)} \frac{1}{v_t} = \beta E_t \left[a_{t+1} c_{t+1}^{-\sigma} \bar{m}_{t+2}^{\theta(1-\sigma)} e_{t+1}^{-\theta(1-\sigma)} \right. \tag{9.208}$$
$$\left. \times \left((1 - \tau^q) q_{t+1} + (1 - \delta) \frac{1}{v_{t+1}} \right) \right],$$

$$a_t c_t^{-\sigma} \bar{m}_{t+1}^{\theta(1-\sigma)} e_t^{-\theta(1-\sigma)} = \beta (1 + i_t) E_t \left[\frac{a_{t+1} c_{t+1}^{-\sigma} \bar{m}_{t+2}^{\theta(1-\sigma)} e_{t+1}^{-\theta(1-\sigma)}}{1 + \pi_{t+1}} \right], \tag{9.209}$$

$$\theta (1 + \tau^c) c_t = \bar{m}_{t+1} \frac{i_t}{1 + i_t}. \tag{9.210}$$

9.8.2.2 The Representative Finished Goods-Producing Firm

The firm producing the final good solves the same problem as in the previous section.

9.8.2.3 The Representative Intermediate Goods-Producing Firm

Each period t the j-th firm producing intermediate commodities hires $h_t(j)$ units of labour from the representative household at a wage w_t, and $k_t(j)$ units of capital at a rental price q_t, in order to produce $y_t(j)$ units of the intermediate commodity, with technology:

$$A k_t(j)^\alpha (z_t h_t(j))^{1-\alpha} \geq y_t(j), \tag{9.211}$$

where z_t is an aggregate technology shock common to all firms that obeys the stochastic process:

$$\ln z_t = \rho_z \ln z_{t-1} + \varepsilon_{zt}, \quad |\rho_z| < 1, \quad \varepsilon_{zt} \underset{iid}{\sim} N(0, \sigma_z^2), \tag{9.212}$$

Intermediate commodities substitute imperfectly in the production of the final good. Therefore, the firm producing intermediate commodities sells them in a monopolistic competition market, at a price that depends on the demand received from the firm producing the final good, while facing a quadratic cost of changing the nominal price between periods:

$$\frac{\phi}{2}\left[\frac{P_t(j)}{(1+\pi_{ss})P_{t-1}(j)}-1\right]^2 y_t,$$

where $\phi \geq 0$ and π_{ss} denotes the steady state rate of inflation.

Because of the presence of the adjustment cost function, the j-th firm producing intermediate commodities solves the dynamics problem of maximizing its market value:

$$\max_{\{h_t(j),k_t(j),P_t(j)\}} E_0 \sum_{t=0}^{\infty} \beta^t \lambda_t \left[\frac{D_t(j)}{P_t}\right]$$

subject to: (9.211), where

$$\frac{D_t(j)}{P_t} = \frac{P_t(j)}{P_t}y_t(j) - w_t h_t(j) - q_t k_t(j) - \frac{\phi}{2}\left[\frac{P_t(j)}{(1+\pi_{ss})P_{t-1}(j)}-1\right]^2 y_t, \quad (9.213)$$

for all $t = 0, 1, 2, \ldots$, where $\beta^t \lambda_t / P_t$ measures the value for the representative household of the marginal utility of an additional monetary unit received as dividends during period t.

First order conditions are

$$w_t h_t(j)\lambda_t = \xi_t(1-\alpha)Ak_t(j)^{\alpha}(z_t h_t(j))^{1-\alpha} \quad (9.214)$$

$$q_t k_t(j)\lambda_t = \xi_t \alpha Ak_t(j)^{\alpha}(z_t h_t(j))^{1-\alpha} \quad (9.215)$$

$$\phi\lambda_t\left[\frac{P_t(j)}{(1+\pi_{ss})P_{t-1}(j)}-1\right]\frac{P_t}{(1+\pi_{ss})P_{t-1}(j)}$$
$$= \lambda_t(1-\varepsilon)\left(\frac{P_t(j)}{P_t}\right)^{-\varepsilon} + \xi_t\varepsilon\left(\frac{P_t(j)}{P_t}\right)^{-\varepsilon-1} + \beta\phi$$
$$\times E_t\left[\lambda_{t+1}\left(\frac{P_{t+1}(j)}{(1+\pi_{ss})P_t(j)}-1\right)\frac{y_{t+1}}{y_t}\frac{P_{t+1}(j)P_t}{(1+\pi_{ss})P_t(j)^2}\right], \quad (9.216)$$

where ξ_t is the Lagrange multiplier associated to the technological constraint in the profit maximization problem of the intermediate good-producing firm.

9.8.2.4 The Monetary Authority

The monetary authority implements policy by choosing the level of the nominal rate of interest, i_t, according to the same Taylor rule followed in the neoclassical monetary models in previous sections:

$$\ln\left(\frac{1+i_t}{1+i_{ss}}\right) = \rho_i \ln\left(\frac{1+i_{t-1}}{1+i_{ss}}\right) + \rho_y \ln(y_t/y_{ss}) + \rho_\pi \ln\left(\frac{1+\pi_t}{1+\pi_{ss}}\right) + \varepsilon_{it}, \quad (9.217)$$

where $\varepsilon_{it} \underset{iid}{\sim} N(0,\sigma_i^2)$. We leave as an exercise to the reader to specify and solve the model when the monetary authority chooses the rate of money growth, rather than nominal interest rates.

9.8.2.5 The Fiscal Authority

The fiscal authority raises taxes on labour and capital income, as well as on consumption. It also issues debt to finance its deficit, and it gives lump-sum transfers (taxes, if negative) to households according to the budget constraint:

$$\tau^c c_t + \tau^w w_t + \tau^q q_t k_t + \frac{M_{t+1} - M_t}{P_t} + \left(\frac{B_{t+1}}{P_t(1+i_t)} - \frac{B_t}{P_t} \right) = \zeta_t. \qquad (9.218)$$

We assume that the government chooses transfers, ζ_t, under the condition $\zeta_t = \zeta - \eta \frac{B_t}{P_t}$, that implies

$$\frac{B_{t+1}}{P_t} = (1+i_t) \left[\zeta - \tau^c c_t - \tau^w w_t - \tau^q q_t k_t - \frac{M_{t+1}}{P_t} + \frac{M_t}{P_{t-1}(1+\pi_t)} \right]$$

$$+(1-\eta)\frac{1+i_t}{1+\pi_t}\frac{B_t}{P_{t-1}}, \qquad (9.219)$$

where $\frac{B_{t+1}}{P_t}$ will be stable if $1 > \eta > \frac{r_{ss}}{1+r_{ss}}$, with $1 + r_{ss} = (1+i_{ss})/(1+\pi_{ss})$.

9.8.2.6 Symmetric Equilibrium

We consider a symmetric equilibrium, where all intermediate good producing firms make the same decisions: $y_t(j) = y(t)$, $k_t(j) = k_t$, $h_t(j) = 1$, $P_t(j) = P_t$, $d_t(j) = D_t(j)/P_t = D_t/P_t = d_t$, $\forall j \in [0,1]$, and $\forall t = 0,1,2,\dots$. If we apply the conditions for a symmetric equilibrium, substitute the government budget constraint into that of the household, and eliminate variables d_t and ξ_t, the equations characterizing the solution to the model are

$$a_t c_t^{-\sigma} \bar{m}_{t+1}^{\theta(1-\sigma)} e_t^{-\theta(1-\sigma)} \frac{1}{v_t} = \beta E_t \left[a_{t+1} c_{t+1}^{-\sigma} \bar{m}_{t+2}^{\theta(1-\sigma)} e_{t+1}^{-\theta(1-\sigma)} \right.$$

$$\left. \times \left((1-\tau^q)q_{t+1} + (1-\delta)\frac{1}{v_{t+1}} \right) \right], \qquad (9.220)$$

$$a_t c_t^{-\sigma} \bar{m}_{t+1}^{\theta(1-\sigma)} e_t^{-\theta(1-\sigma)} = \beta(1+i_t)E_t \left[\frac{a_{t+1} c_{t+1}^{-\sigma} \bar{m}_{t+2}^{\theta(1-\sigma)} e_{t+1}^{-\theta(1-\sigma)}}{1+\pi_{t+1}} \right], \qquad (9.221)$$

$$\theta(1+\tau^c)c_t = \bar{m}_{t+1}\frac{i_t}{1+i_t}.$$ (9.222)

$$\phi\left[\frac{1+\pi_t}{1+\pi_{ss}}-1\right]\frac{1+\pi_t}{1+\pi_{ss}} = (1-\varepsilon)+\varepsilon\frac{q_t k_t}{\alpha A k_t^\alpha z_t^{1-\alpha}}+\beta\phi$$

$$\times E_t\left[\frac{a_{t+1}c_{t+1}^{-\sigma}\bar{m}_{t+2}^{-\theta(1-\sigma)}e_{t+1}^{-\theta(1-\sigma)}}{a_t c_t^{-\sigma}\bar{m}_{t+1}^{-\theta(1-\sigma)}e_t^{-\theta(1-\sigma)}}\left(\frac{\pi_t-\pi_{ss}}{1+\pi_{ss}}\right)\frac{1+\pi_{t+1}}{1+\pi_{ss}}\frac{Ak_{t+1}^\alpha z_{t+1}^{1-\alpha}}{Ak_t^\alpha z_t^{1-\alpha}}\right],$$ (9.223)

$$Ak_t^\alpha z_t^{1-\alpha} = c_t + \frac{1}{v_t}[k_{t+1}-(1-\delta)k_t]+\frac{\phi}{2}\left[\frac{1+\pi_t}{1+\pi_{ss}}-1\right]^2 Ak_t^\alpha z_t^{1-\alpha}$$ (9.224)

$$\ln\left(\frac{1+i_t}{1+i_{ss}}\right) = \rho_i\ln\left(\frac{1+i_{t-1}}{1+i_{ss}}\right)+\rho_y\ln(y_t/y_{ss})$$

$$+\rho_\pi\ln\left(\frac{1+\pi_t}{1+\pi_{ss}}\right)+\varepsilon_{it},$$ (9.225)

together with the laws of motion for the shocks (9.201), (9.154), (9.155) and (9.164).

This system of 10 equations can be solve for variables k_{t+1}, π_t, $\bar{m}_{t+1}$, i_t, c_t, q_t, v_t, a_t, e_t, z_t. Notice that we once the system has been solved, we can also obtain the values of the following variables:

$$w_t = \frac{1-\alpha}{\alpha}q_t k_t,$$ (9.226)

$$\lambda_t = a_t c_t^{-\sigma}\bar{m}_{t+1}^{-\theta(1-\sigma)}e_t^{-\theta(1-\sigma)}/(1+\tau^c),$$ (9.227)

$$\xi_t = \frac{q_t k_t \lambda_t}{\alpha A k_t^\alpha z_t^{1-\alpha}},$$ (9.228)

$$y_t = Ak_t^\alpha z_t^{1-\alpha},$$ (9.229)

$$d_t = y_t - w_t - q_t k_t - \frac{\phi}{2}\left[\frac{1+\pi_t}{1+\pi_{ss}}-1\right]^2 y_t.$$ (9.230)

9.8.2.7 Steady State

In the absence of random shocks, the economy will converge to steady state $y_t = y_{ss}$, $\pi_t = \pi_{ss}$, $\bar{m}_t = \bar{m}_{ss}$, $k_t = k_{ss}$, $i_t = i_{ss}$, $c_t = c_{ss}$, $q_t = q_{ss}$, $v_t = 1$, $a_t = 1$, $e_t = 1$, $z_t = 1$. Once the monetary authority chooses a level of the nominal rate of interest i_{ss}, we get from (9.220)

$$q_{ss} = \left[\frac{1}{\beta}-(1-\delta)\right]\frac{1}{1-\tau^q},$$

while from (9.221), (9.223), (9.224) and (9.222) we get

$$\pi_{ss} = \beta(1 + i_{ss}) - 1.$$

$$k_{ss} = \left[A\alpha \frac{\varepsilon - 1}{\varepsilon} \frac{1}{q_{ss}} \right].$$

$$c_{ss} = Ak_{ss}^{\alpha} - \delta k_{ss}.$$

$$\bar{m}_{ss} = \frac{1 + i_{ss}}{i_{ss}} (1 + \tau^c) \theta (Ak_{ss}^{\alpha} - \delta k_{ss}).$$

and (9.226), (9.229) and (9.230) we get

$$w_{ss} = \frac{1 - \alpha}{\alpha} q_{ss} k_{ss},$$

$$y_{ss} = Ak_{ss}^{\alpha},$$

$$d_{ss} = Ak_{ss}^{\alpha} - \frac{1}{\alpha} \left[\frac{1}{\beta} - (1 - \delta) \right] \frac{1}{1 - \tau^q} k_{ss}.$$

9.8.2.8 Log-Linearization

Using the notation: $\hat{k}_t = \ln(k_t/k_{ss})$, $\hat{\pi}_t = \ln[(1 + \pi_t)/(1 + \pi_{ss})]$, $\widehat{\bar{m}}_t = \ln(\bar{m}_t/\bar{m}_{ss})$, $\hat{i}_t = \ln[(1 + i_t)/(1 + i_{ss})]$, $\hat{c}_t = \ln(c_t/c_{ss})$, $\hat{q}_t = \ln(q_t/q_{ss})$, $\hat{a}_t = \ln a_t$, $\hat{v}_t = \ln v_t$, $\hat{e}_t = \ln e_t$, $\hat{z}_t = \ln z_t$, (9.226)–(9.230), together with the stochastic processes for the shocks, log-linearized around steady state, become

$$0 = -\frac{1}{\beta}(1 - \rho_a)\hat{a}_t + \frac{1}{\beta}(1 - \rho_v)\hat{v}_t + \frac{\theta(1 - \sigma)}{\beta}(1 - \rho_e)\hat{e}_t + \frac{\sigma}{\beta}\hat{c}_t$$
$$- \frac{\theta(1 - \sigma)}{\beta}\widehat{\bar{m}}_{t+1} - \frac{\sigma}{\beta}E_t\hat{c}_{t+1} + \frac{\theta(1 - \sigma)}{\beta}E_t\widehat{\bar{m}}_{t+2} + (1 - \tau^q)E_t\hat{q}_{t+1},$$
$$\text{(9.231)}$$

$$0 = -\frac{1}{\beta}(1 - \rho_a)\hat{a}_t + \frac{\theta(1 - \sigma)}{\beta}(1 - \rho_e)\hat{e}_t + \frac{\sigma}{\beta}\hat{c}_t - \frac{\theta(1 - \sigma)}{\beta}\widehat{\bar{m}}_{t+1}$$
$$+ \frac{1}{1 + \pi_{ss}}\hat{i}_t - \frac{\sigma}{\beta}E_t\hat{c}_{t+1} + \frac{\theta(1 - \sigma)}{\beta}E_t\widehat{\bar{m}}_{t+2} - \frac{1}{\beta}E_t\hat{\pi}_{t+1}, \qquad \text{(9.232)}$$

$$\widehat{\bar{m}}_{t+1} = \hat{c}_t - \frac{\hat{i}_t}{i_{ss}}, \qquad \text{(9.233)}$$

$$0 = -\phi\hat{\pi}_t + (\varepsilon - 1)\hat{q}_t + (1 - \alpha)(\varepsilon - 1)\hat{k}_t - (1 - \alpha)(\varepsilon - 1)\hat{z}_t + \beta\phi E_t\hat{\pi}_{t+1}, \quad \text{(9.234)}$$

$$0 = -\left[\alpha A k_{ss}^{\alpha-1} + (1-\delta)\right] \hat{k}_t + \frac{c_{ss}}{k_{ss}} \hat{c}_t + \hat{k}_{t+1} - (1-\alpha) A k_{ss}^{\alpha-1} \hat{z}_t - \delta \hat{v}_t \quad (9.235)$$

$$\hat{\imath}_t = \rho_i \hat{\imath}_{t-1} + \rho_y \alpha \hat{k}_t + \rho_y (1-\alpha) \hat{z}_t + \rho_\pi \hat{\pi}_t + \varepsilon_{it}, \quad (9.236)$$

$$\hat{z}_t = \rho_z \hat{z}_{t-1} + \varepsilon_{zt}, \quad (9.237)$$

$$\hat{a}_t = \rho_a \hat{a}_{t-1} + \varepsilon_{at}, \quad (9.238)$$

$$\hat{e}_t = \rho_e \hat{e}_{t-1} + \varepsilon_{et}, \quad (9.239)$$

$$\hat{v}_t = \rho_v \hat{v}_{t-1} + \varepsilon_{vt}. \quad (9.240)$$

We can somewhat simplify the system by eliminating $\widehat{m}_{t+1}$. So, if we substitute (9.233) into (9.231) and (9.232), taking into account that, according to (9.233) $E_t \widehat{m}_{t+2} = E_t \hat{c}_{t+1} - \frac{E_t \hat{\imath}_{t+1}}{i_{ss}}$, while, according to (9.236) $E_t \hat{\imath}_{t+1} = \rho_i \hat{\imath}_t + \rho_y \alpha \hat{k}_{t+1} + \rho_y \rho_z (1-\alpha) \hat{z}_t + \rho_\pi E_t \hat{\pi}_{t+1}$, we get

$$
\begin{aligned}
0 = &-\frac{1}{\beta}(1-\rho_a)\hat{a}_t + \frac{1}{\beta}(1-\rho_v)\hat{v}_t + \frac{\theta(1-\sigma)}{\beta}(1-\rho_e)\hat{e}_t \\
&+ \left(\frac{\sigma}{\beta} - \frac{\theta(1-\sigma)}{\beta}\right)(\hat{c}_t - E_t \hat{c}_{t+1}) + \frac{\theta(1-\sigma)}{\beta i_{ss}}(1-\rho_i)\hat{\imath}_t \\
&+ (1-\tau^q) E_t \hat{q}_{t+1} - \frac{\theta(1-\sigma)}{\beta i_{ss}}\left(\rho_\pi E_t \hat{\pi}_{t+1} + \rho_y \alpha \hat{k}_{t+1} + \rho_y \rho_z (1-\alpha)\hat{z}_t\right),
\end{aligned}
$$

$$(9.241)$$

$$
\begin{aligned}
0 = &-\frac{1}{\beta}(1-\rho_a)\hat{a}_t + \frac{\theta(1-\sigma)}{\beta}(1-\rho_e)\hat{e}_t + \left(\frac{\sigma}{\beta} - \frac{\theta(1-\sigma)}{\beta}\right)\hat{c}_t \\
&+ \left[\frac{\theta(1-\sigma)}{\beta i_{ss}}(1-\rho_i) + \frac{1}{1+\pi_{ss}}\right]\hat{\imath}_t - \left(\frac{\sigma}{\beta} - \frac{\theta(1-\sigma)}{\beta}\right) E_t \hat{c}_{t+1} \\
&- \left(\frac{1}{\beta} + \frac{\theta(1-\sigma)}{\beta i_{ss}}\rho_\pi\right) E_t \hat{\pi}_{t+1} - \frac{\theta(1-\sigma)}{\beta i_{ss}}\left(\rho_y \alpha \hat{k}_{t+1} + \rho_y \rho_z (1-\alpha)\hat{z}_t\right).
\end{aligned}
$$

$$(9.242)$$

Therefore, we have a system of nine equations [(9.241), (9.242), (9.234)–(9.240)], to solve for $\hat{k}_{t+1}$, $\hat{\pi}_t$, $\hat{\imath}_t$, $\hat{c}_t$, $\hat{q}_t$, $\hat{a}_t$, $\hat{v}_t$, $\hat{e}_t$, $\hat{z}_t$. This system can be written in matrix form as

$$DE_t s_{t+1}^0 = G s_t^0 + H\Psi_t + J\varepsilon_{it}, \quad (9.243)$$

where

$$s_t^0 = \left[\hat{c}_t, \hat{\pi}_t, \hat{q}_t, \hat{k}_t, \hat{\imath}_{t-1}\right]',$$
$$\Psi_t = \left[\hat{z}_t, \hat{a}_t, \hat{e}_t, \hat{v}_t\right]',$$

$$D = \begin{bmatrix} \tilde{\sigma} & \frac{\theta(1-\sigma)}{\beta i_{ss}}\rho_\pi & -(1-\tau^q) & \frac{\theta(1-\sigma)}{\beta i_{ss}}\rho_y\alpha & -\frac{\theta(1-\sigma)}{\beta i_{ss}}(1-\rho_i) \\ \tilde{\sigma} & \frac{1}{\beta}+\frac{\theta(1-\sigma)}{\beta i_{ss}}\rho_\pi & 0 & \frac{\theta(1-\sigma)}{\beta i_{ss}}\rho_y\alpha & D_{2,5} \\ 0 & \beta\phi & 0 & 0 & 0 \\ 0 & 0 & 0 & 1 & 0 \\ 0 & 0 & 0 & 0 & 1 \end{bmatrix},$$

$$G = \begin{bmatrix} \tilde{\sigma} & 0 & 0 & & 0 & 0 \\ \tilde{\sigma} & 0 & 0 & & 0 & 0 \\ 0 & \phi & 1-\varepsilon & (1-\alpha)(1-\varepsilon) & 0 \\ -\frac{c_{ss}}{k_{ss}} & 0 & 0 & \alpha A k_{ss}^{\alpha-1}+(1-\delta) & 0 \\ 0 & \rho_\pi & 0 & \rho_y\alpha & \rho_i \end{bmatrix},$$

$$H = \begin{bmatrix} -\frac{\theta(1-\sigma)}{\beta i_{ss}}\rho_y\rho_z(1-\alpha) & -\frac{1}{\beta}(1-\rho_a) & \frac{\theta(1-\sigma)}{\beta}(1-\rho_e) & \frac{1}{\beta}(1-\rho_v) \\ -\frac{\theta(1-\sigma)}{\beta i_{ss}}\rho_y\rho_z(1-\alpha) & -\frac{1}{\beta}(1-\rho_a) & \frac{\theta(1-\sigma)}{\beta}(1-\rho_e) & 0 \\ (1-\alpha)(\varepsilon-1) & 0 & 0 & 0 \\ (1-\alpha)A k_{ss}^{\alpha-1} & 0 & 0 & \delta \\ \rho_y(1-\alpha) & 0 & 0 & 0 \end{bmatrix},$$

$$J = [0,0,0,0,1]',$$

where $\tilde{\sigma} \equiv \frac{\sigma}{\beta} - \frac{\theta(1-\sigma)}{\beta}$, $D_{2,5} \equiv -\frac{\theta(1-\sigma)}{\beta i_{ss}}(1-\rho_i) - \frac{1}{1+\pi_{ss}}$.

Expression (9.243) can be written as

$$E_t s_{t+1}^0 = \Gamma_1 s_t^0 + \Gamma_2 \Psi_t + \Gamma_3 \varepsilon_{it}, \tag{9.244}$$

where $\Gamma_1 = D^{-1}G$, $\Gamma_2 = D^{-1}H$, $\Gamma_3 = D^{-1}J$.

To characterize the stability of (9.244) we need to analyze the eigenvalues of Γ_1. For our parameterization,[20] which is the same for the parameters already appearing in the neoclassical monetary model, there is a pair of complex conjugate eigenvalues of Γ_1, so that we will write system (9.244) in state-space form following the steps already described for the neoclassical monetary model in the case when the monetary authority chooses money growth, rather than the nominal rate of interest. Without loss of generality, we will assume the eigenvalues of Γ_1 have been ordered decreasingly by norm. For our parameterization, such eigenvalues are: $\lambda_1 = 0$, $\lambda_2 < 1$, $\lambda_3 = a + bi$, $\lambda_4 = a - bi$, $\lambda_5 > 1$, with $(a^2+b^2)^{1/2} > 1$. Therefore, we have three unstable eigenvalues that we will use to compute the

---

[20] MATLAB program neokeyn.m computes a single realization that it presents in the form of graphics. Program nkeyprg.m presents standard statistics after simulating the model an arbitrary number of times, chosen by the user. This program calls function nkeyn.m, which it must either be placed in the same directory as the programs above, or the directory be included in the MATLAB path.

values of the three control variables $\{\hat{c}_t, \hat{\pi}_t, \hat{q}_t\}$ as function of the state variables $\{\hat{k}_t, \hat{\imath}_{t-1}, \hat{a}_t, \hat{v}_t, \hat{e}_t, \hat{z}_t\}$, leading therefore to a well-determined solution.[21]

To compute the control equation or stability conditions, it is convenient to write system (9.244) as

$$
\begin{bmatrix}
\hat{c}_{t+1} \\
\hat{\pi}_{t+1} \\
\hat{q}_{t+1} \\
\hat{k}_{t+1} \\
\hat{\imath}_t \\
\hat{z}_{t+1} \\
\hat{a}_{t+1} \\
\hat{e}_{t+1} \\
\hat{v}_{t+1}
\end{bmatrix}
=
\underbrace{\begin{bmatrix}
\Gamma_1 & \Gamma_2 \\
0_{4\times 5} & \Omega
\end{bmatrix}}_{\Gamma_4}
\begin{bmatrix}
\hat{c}_t \\
\hat{\pi}_t \\
\hat{q}_t \\
\hat{k}_t \\
\hat{\imath}_{t-1} \\
\hat{z}_t \\
\hat{a}_t \\
\hat{e}_t \\
\hat{v}_t
\end{bmatrix}
+
\underbrace{\begin{bmatrix}
1 & 0 & 0 \\
0 & 1 & 0 \\
0 & 0 & 1 \\
0 & 0 & 0 \\
0 & 0 & 0 \\
0 & 0 & 0 \\
0 & 0 & 0 \\
0 & 0 & 0 \\
0 & 0 & 0
\end{bmatrix}}_{\Gamma_5}
\begin{bmatrix}
\eta_{c,t+1} \\
\eta_{\pi,t+1} \\
\eta_{q,t+1}
\end{bmatrix}
$$

$$
+
\underbrace{\begin{bmatrix}
0_{5\times 4} & \Gamma_3 \\
I_{4\times 4} & 0_{4\times 1}
\end{bmatrix}}_{\Gamma_6}
\begin{bmatrix}
\varepsilon_{z,t+1} \\
\varepsilon_{a,t+1} \\
\varepsilon_{e,t+1} \\
\varepsilon_{v,t+1} \\
\varepsilon_{i,t+1}
\end{bmatrix},
\tag{9.245}
$$

where we have added to system (9.244) the laws of motion for $\{\hat{z}_t, \hat{a}_t, \hat{e}_t, \hat{v}_t,\}$, and we have written the expectations of consumption, inflation rental rate for capital as being equal to their realized values minus their respective prediction errors, $E_t\hat{c}_{t+1} = \hat{c}_{t+1} - \eta_{c,t+1}$, $E_t\hat{\pi}_{t+1} = \hat{\pi}_{t+1} - \eta_{\pi,t+1}$, $E_t\hat{q}_{t+1} = \hat{q}_{t+1} - \eta_{q,t+1}$. Furthermore,

$$
\Omega =
\begin{bmatrix}
\rho_z & 0 & 0 & 0 \\
0 & \rho_a & 0 & 0 \\
0 & 0 & \rho_e & 0 \\
0 & 0 & 0 & \rho_v
\end{bmatrix}.
$$

Matrix Γ_4 has now 9 eigenvalues, the five already mentioned for Γ_1, together with ρ_z, ρ_a, ρ_e and ρ_v. Let us assume that we set up the diagonalization of matrix Γ_4 as

---

[21] It is important to point out that the values of parameters ε and ϕ are crucial to determine whether the solution is determinate or indetermined. Remember that ε is the price elasticity of demand for intermediate goods on the part of the firm producing the final good, while ϕ measures the level of the adjustment cost of prices. The lower ε and ϕ may be, the easier will be to obtain four stable and one unstable eigenvalues, leading to an undetermined equilibrium, i.e., multiple equilibria path, all converging to the same steady state. Our MATLAB programs have been written to capture the case of determined equilibria, while in the second chapter on endogenous growth models we discussed in detail the implications of equilibrium indeterminacy and how a numerical solution can be obtained, if desired. Hence, the user must take into account the possibility that for different values of ε and ϕ we can get indeterminacy, and the provided program will not compute the right solution. The same approach used for endogenous growth models can be followed to write the program that computes the numerical solution under indeterminacy in this model.

$$\Gamma_4 = M\Lambda M^{-1},$$

$$\Lambda = \begin{bmatrix} 0 & 0 & 0 & 0 & 0 & 0 & 0 & 0 & 0 \\ 0 & \lambda_2 & 0 & 0 & 0 & 0 & 0 & 0 & 0 \\ 0 & 0 & \rho_z & 0 & 0 & 0 & 0 & 0 & 0 \\ 0 & 0 & 0 & \rho_a & 0 & 0 & 0 & 0 & 0 \\ 0 & 0 & 0 & 0 & \rho_e & 0 & 0 & 0 & 0 \\ 0 & 0 & 0 & 0 & 0 & \rho_v & 0 & 0 & 0 \\ 0 & 0 & 0 & 0 & 0 & 0 & a+bi & 0 & 0 \\ 0 & 0 & 0 & 0 & 0 & 0 & 0 & a-bi & 0 \\ 0 & 0 & 0 & 0 & 0 & 0 & 0 & 0 & \lambda_5 \end{bmatrix};$$

$$M = \begin{bmatrix} M_{11} & \cdots & M_{16} & d_1+f_1 i & d_1-f_1 i & M_{91} \\ \vdots & \ddots & \vdots & \vdots & \vdots & \vdots \\ M_{91} & \cdots & M_{96} & d_9-f_9 i & d_9-f_9 i & M_{99} \end{bmatrix}.$$

As shown in the section of the Mathematical Appendix devoted to the solution of deterministic systems in finite order differences if the eigenvalues associated to the transition matrix of the bivariate system:

$$\begin{bmatrix} x_{1t} \\ x_{2t} \end{bmatrix} = \begin{bmatrix} A_{11} & A_{12} \\ A_{21} & A_{22} \end{bmatrix} \begin{bmatrix} x_{1t-1} \\ x_{2t-1} \end{bmatrix},$$

are complex conjugate numbers, we have

$$\begin{bmatrix} A_{11} & A_{12} \\ A_{21} & A_{22} \end{bmatrix} = \underbrace{\begin{bmatrix} g_1+h_1 i & g_1-h_1 i \\ g_2+h_2 i & g_2-h_2 i \end{bmatrix}}_{P} \begin{bmatrix} \mu+vi & 0 \\ 0 & \mu+vi \end{bmatrix}$$

$$\times \begin{bmatrix} g_1+h_1 i & g_1-h_1 i \\ g_2+h_2 i & g_2-h_2 i \end{bmatrix}^{-1}$$

and the general solution to this deterministic first order difference system can be written

$$\begin{bmatrix} x_{1t} \\ x_{2t} \end{bmatrix} = \begin{bmatrix} s^t C_1 [g_1 \cos(\omega t) - h_1 \sin(\omega t)] + s^t C_2 [g_1 \sin(\omega t) + h_1 \cos(\omega t)] \\ s^t C_1 [g_2 \cos(\omega t) - h_2 \sin(\omega t)] + s^t C_2 [g_2 \sin(\omega t) + h_2 \cos(\omega t)] \end{bmatrix}$$

$$= \underbrace{\begin{bmatrix} g_1 & h_1 \\ g_2 & h_2 \end{bmatrix}}_{\tilde{P}} \begin{bmatrix} s^t [C_1 \cos(\omega t) + C_2 \sin(\omega t)] \\ s^t [-C_1 \sin(\omega t) + C_2 \cos(\omega t)] \end{bmatrix},$$

where $s = (\mu^2 + v^2)^{1/2}$ and $\omega = \arctan(v/\mu)$, while C_1 and C_2 are two constants to be determined. Notice that $\tilde{P}$ is a two-column matrix: the first one is the real part of the right eigenvector of the transition matrix, while the second column is the imaginary part of that eigenvector.

Taking this result into account, the solution to the homogeneous version of system (9.245) is of the form:

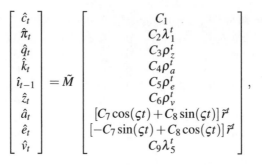

with

$$\tilde{M} = \begin{bmatrix} M_{11} & \cdots & M_{16} & d_1 & f_1 & M_{91} \\ \vdots & \ddots & \vdots & \vdots & \vdots & \vdots \\ M_{91} & \cdots & M_{96} & d_9 & f_9 & M_{99} \end{bmatrix},$$

where $\tilde{r} = (a^2 + b^2)^{1/2}$ and $\varsigma = \arctan(b/a)$. Since $\tilde{r} > 1$, this solution will be stable if and only if C_7, C_8 and C_9 are equal to zero, which is the condition to eliminate the unstable trajectories. Besides setting the three constants to zero, we get the stability conditions determining the control variables at each point in time as a function of the states:

$$\tilde{M}^{-1} \begin{bmatrix} \hat{c}_t \\ \hat{\pi}_t \\ \hat{q}_t \\ \hat{k}_t \\ \hat{\imath}_{t-1} \\ \hat{z}_t \\ \hat{a}_t \\ \hat{e}_t \\ \hat{v}_t \end{bmatrix} = \begin{bmatrix} C_1 \\ C_2 \lambda_1^t \\ C_3 \rho_z^t \\ C_4 \rho_a^t \\ C_5 \rho_e^t \\ C_6 \rho_v^t \\ 0 \\ 0 \\ 0 \end{bmatrix} \Rightarrow \begin{bmatrix} \tilde{M}_{1:6,:}^{-1} \\ \tilde{M}_{7:9,:}^{-1} \end{bmatrix} \begin{bmatrix} \hat{c}_t \\ \hat{\pi}_t \\ \hat{q}_t \\ \hat{k}_t \\ \hat{\imath}_{t-1} \\ \hat{z}_t \\ \hat{a}_t \\ \hat{e}_t \\ \hat{v}_t \end{bmatrix} = \begin{bmatrix} C_1 \\ C_2 \lambda_1^t \\ C_3 \rho_z^t \\ C_4 \rho_a^t \\ C_5 \rho_e^t \\ C_6 \rho_v^t \\ 0 \\ 0 \\ 0 \end{bmatrix}$$

$$\Rightarrow \tilde{M}_{7:9,:}^{-1} \begin{bmatrix} \hat{c}_t \\ \hat{\pi}_t \\ \hat{q}_t \\ \hat{k}_t \\ \hat{\imath}_{t-1} \\ \hat{z}_t \\ \hat{a}_t \\ \hat{e}_t \\ \hat{v}_t \end{bmatrix} = \begin{bmatrix} 0 \\ 0 \\ 0 \end{bmatrix}, \qquad (9.246)$$

where $\tilde{M}_{7:9,:}^{-1}$ denotes rows 7 to 9 in matrix $\tilde{M}^{-1}$. These correspond to columns 7 to 9 in $\tilde{M}$, which act are right "pseudo-eigenvectors" for matrix Γ_4.

From expression (9.246) we obtain the *control equation*:

$$
\begin{bmatrix} \hat{c}_t \\ \hat{\pi}_t \\ \hat{q}_t \end{bmatrix} = \underbrace{-[\tilde{M}^{-1}_{7:9,1:3}]^{-1}\tilde{M}^{-1}_{7:9,4:9}}_{\Psi_1} \begin{bmatrix} \hat{k}_t \\ \hat{\imath}_{t-1} \\ \hat{z}_t \\ \hat{a}_t \\ \hat{e}_t \\ \hat{v}_t \end{bmatrix}, \tag{9.247}
$$

where $\tilde{M}^{-1}_{7:9,1:3}$ denotes the submatrix of $\tilde{M}^{-1}$ made up by rows 7–9 and columns 1–3, while $\tilde{M}^{-1}_{7:9,4:9}$ denotes the submatrix of $\tilde{M}^{-1}$ made up by rows 7–9, and columns 4–9.

If we multiply to the left through (9.245) by $\tilde{M}^{-1}$, we get

$$
\tilde{M}^{-1}\tilde{z}_{t+1} = \tilde{M}^{-1}\Gamma_4\tilde{z}_t + \tilde{M}^{-1}\Gamma_5\eta_{t+1} + \tilde{M}^{-1}\Gamma_6\varepsilon_{t+1}, \tag{9.248}
$$

$$
\text{where } \tilde{z}_{t+1} = \begin{bmatrix} \hat{c}_t \\ \hat{\pi}_t \\ \hat{q}_t \\ \hat{k}_t \\ \hat{\imath}_{t-1} \\ \hat{z}_t \\ \hat{a}_t \\ \hat{e}_t \\ \hat{v}_t \end{bmatrix}, \quad \eta_{t+1} = \begin{bmatrix} \eta_{c,t+1} \\ \eta_{\pi,t+1} \\ \eta_{q,t+1} \end{bmatrix}, \quad \varepsilon_{t+1} = \begin{bmatrix} \varepsilon_{z,t+1} \\ \varepsilon_{a,t+1} \\ \varepsilon_{e,t+1} \\ \varepsilon_{v,t+1} \\ \varepsilon_{i,t+1} \end{bmatrix}.
$$

Expression (9.248) can be written

$$
\tilde{M}^{-1}\tilde{z}_{t+1} = \left(\tilde{M}^{-1}\Gamma_4\tilde{M}\right)\tilde{M}^{-1}\tilde{z}_t + \tilde{M}^{-1}\Gamma_5\eta_{t+1} + \tilde{M}^{-1}\Gamma_6\varepsilon_{t+1}. \tag{9.249}
$$

Notice that the structure of matrix $\left(\tilde{M}^{-1}\Gamma_3\tilde{M}\right)$ is as follows:

$$
\tilde{\Lambda} = \left(\tilde{M}^{-1}\Gamma_4\tilde{M}\right) = \begin{bmatrix} \tilde{\Lambda}_{(1)} & \tilde{\Lambda}_{(2)} \\ \tilde{\Lambda}_{(3)} & \tilde{\Lambda}_{(4)} \end{bmatrix},
$$

$$
\text{where } \tilde{\Lambda}_{(1)} = \begin{bmatrix} 0 & 0 & 0 & 0 & 0 & 0 \\ 0 & \lambda_2 & 0 & 0 & 0 & 0 \\ 0 & 0 & \rho_z & 0 & 0 & 0 \\ 0 & 0 & 0 & \rho_a & 0 & 0 \\ 0 & 0 & 0 & 0 & \rho_e & 0 \\ 0 & 0 & 0 & 0 & 0 & \rho_v \end{bmatrix},
$$

$$
\tilde{\Lambda}_{(2)} = 0_{6\times3}, \quad \tilde{\Lambda}_{(3)} = 0_{3\times6},
$$

$$
\tilde{\Lambda}_{(4)} = \begin{bmatrix} a & -b & 0 \\ b & a & 0 \\ 0 & 0 & \lambda_5 \end{bmatrix}. \tag{9.250}
$$

Hence, from system (9.249) we obtain

$$\tilde{M}_{7:9,:}^{-1} z_{t+1} = \underbrace{\tilde{\Lambda}_{(3)} \tilde{M}_{1:6,:}^{-1} z_t}_{=0 \text{ by } (9.247)} + \underbrace{\tilde{\Lambda}_{(4)} \tilde{M}_{7:9,:}^{-1} z_t}_{=0 \text{ by } (9.250)} + \underbrace{\tilde{M}_{7:9,:}^{-1} \Gamma_5 \eta_{t+1} + \tilde{M}_{7:9,:}^{-1} \Gamma_6 \varepsilon_{t+1}, 0}_{=0 \text{ by } (9.247)}$$

that is,

$$0 = \tilde{M}_{7:9,:}^{-1} \Gamma_5 \eta_{t+1} + \tilde{M}_{7:9,:}^{-1} \Gamma_6 \varepsilon_{t+1}.$$

If we solve for the prediction errors we get their relationship with the innovations to the stochastic processes in the model:

$$\begin{bmatrix} \eta_{c,t+1} \\ \eta_{\pi,t+1} \\ \eta_{q,t+1} \end{bmatrix} = \underbrace{-[\tilde{M}_{7:9,:}^{-1} \Gamma_5]^{-1} [\tilde{M}_{7:9,:}^{-1} \Gamma_6]}_{\Psi_2} \begin{bmatrix} \varepsilon_{z,t+1} \\ \varepsilon_{a,t+1} \\ \varepsilon_{e,t+1} \\ \varepsilon_{v,t+1} \\ \varepsilon_{i,t+1} \end{bmatrix}. \qquad (9.251)$$

This is also a stability condition, since it has been obtained by imposing stability in the deterministic version of system (9.245) (i.e., in the homogeneous part of (9.245)).

Finally, substituting expressions (9.247) and (9.251) in system (9.245) we get the *state equation*:

$$\begin{bmatrix} \hat{k}_{t+1} \\ \hat{\imath}_t \\ \hat{z}_{t+1} \\ \hat{a}_{t+1} \\ \hat{e}_{t+1} \\ \hat{v}_{t+1} \end{bmatrix} = \underbrace{[\Gamma_{4_{(4:9,1:3)}} \Psi_1 + \Gamma_{4_{(4:9,4:9)}}]}_{\Psi_3} \begin{bmatrix} \hat{k}_t \\ \hat{\imath}_{t-1} \\ \hat{z}_t \\ \hat{a}_t \\ \hat{e}_t \\ \hat{v}_t \end{bmatrix} + \underbrace{\Gamma_{6_{(4:9,:)}}}_{\Psi_4} \begin{bmatrix} \varepsilon_{z,t+1} \\ \varepsilon_{a,t+1} \\ \varepsilon_{e,t+1} \\ \varepsilon_{v,t+1} \\ \varepsilon_{i,t+1} \end{bmatrix}. \qquad (9.252)$$

A single realization for the numerical solution for this model is implemented in *neokeyn.m* MATLAB file. An arbitrary number of realizations can be obtained using the *nkeyprg.m* program.

Given a realization for $\{\varepsilon_{z,t+1}, \varepsilon_{a,t+1}, \varepsilon_{e,t+1}, \varepsilon_{v,t+1}, \varepsilon_{i,t+1}\}_{t=0}^T$, and initial conditions for $\{\hat{k}_0, \hat{\imath}_{-1}, \hat{z}_0, \hat{a}_0, \hat{e}_0, \hat{v}_0\}$, we get from (9.252) a realization for the state vector $\{\hat{k}_{t+1}, \hat{\imath}_t, \hat{z}_{t+1}, \hat{a}_{t+1}, \hat{e}_{t+1}, \hat{v}_{t+1}\}_{t=0}^T$. Given the realization for the state vector, we get from (9.247) the values of the control variables $\{\hat{c}_t, \hat{\pi}_t, \hat{q}_t\}_{t=0}^T$. From (9.233) we compute $\{\widehat{\bar{m}}_{t+1}\}_{t=0}^T$. Notice that, as in the neoclassical monetary model, there is nominal indeterminacy, since we cannot compute the price path unless we impose an initial price P_0. Once we have computed the values of $k_t, \pi_t, \bar{m}_t, i_t, c_t, q_t, v_t, a_t, e_t, z_t$, we can obtain the paths for the real wage, the marginal utility of consumption, the co-state variable ξ_t, output and dividends, using (9.226)–(9.230).

The reader will have noticed that there is a much larger variety of stochastic shocks in this model than in monetary and non-monetary models analyzed above and in previous chapters. Those models could also be extended to include some of the shocks that appear in this monetary model, an extension that could be used as interesting practice to gain expertise in the numerical solution of growth models of different kinds.

9.9 Appendix: In a Log-Linear Approximation, $E_t \hat{\pi}_{t+1} = \hat{\imath}_t - \hat{r}_t$

Let us consider the problem of the representative agent when the government issues real bonds:

$$\max_{\{c_t, M_{t+1}, k_{t+1}, b_{t+1}\}} E_0 \sum_{t=0}^{\infty} \beta^t U(c_t, M_{t+1}/P_t)$$

subject to

$$(1+\tau^c)c_t + k_{t+1} - (1-\delta)k_t + \frac{M_{t+1}}{P_t} + [b_{t+1}/(1+r_t)] = (1-\tau^y)A_t k_t^\alpha + \frac{M_t}{P_t} + b_t + \zeta_t,$$

for given values of k_0, M_0, b_0.

First order conditions for this optimization problem are

$$U_c(c_t, \bar{m}_{t+1}) = (1+\tau^c)\mu_t, \tag{9.253}$$

$$\mu_t = \beta E_t \left[\mu_{t+1} \left((1-\tau^y)\alpha A_{t+1} k_{t+1}^{\alpha-1} + 1 - \delta \right) \right], \tag{9.254}$$

$$-U_{\bar{m}}(c_t, \bar{m}_{t+1})\frac{1}{P_t} + \mu_t \frac{1}{P_t} = \beta E_t \left[\mu_{t+1} \frac{1}{P_{t+1}} \right], \tag{9.255}$$

$$\mu_t \frac{1}{(1+r_t)} = \beta E_t \left[\mu_{t+1} \right]. \tag{9.256}$$

Comparing this set of optimality conditions with that for the problem when the government issues nominal bonds, we get

1) $\mu_t = \lambda_t$.
2) From (9.90) and (9.256)

$$E_t \left[\lambda_{t+1} \left(\frac{1+i_t}{1+\pi_{t+1}} - (1+r_t) \right) \right] = 0.$$

It is easy to show that the log-linear approximation for this equation is

$$E_t \hat{\pi}_{t+1} = \hat{\imath}_t - \hat{r}_t.$$

3) From (9.254) and (9.256)

$$E_t \left\{ U_c(c_{t+1}, \bar{m}_{t+2}) \left[\left((1-\tau^y)\alpha A_{t+1} k_{t+1}^{\alpha-1} + 1 - \delta \right) - (1+r_t) \right] \right\} = 0,$$

with a log-linear approximation:

$$\hat{r}_t = \frac{1}{1+r_{ss}}(1-\tau^y)\alpha A_{ss} k_{ss}^{\alpha-1}\left[\rho_A \hat{A}_t + (\alpha-1)\hat{k}_{t+1}\right].$$

4) At steady-state:

$$1+\pi_{ss} = \frac{1+i_{ss}}{1+r_{ss}}, \ \ 1+r_{ss} = \frac{1}{\beta}, \ \ (1-\tau^y)\alpha A_{ss} k_{ss}^{\alpha-1} = r_{ss}+\delta. \qquad (9.257)$$

9.10 Exercises

Exercise 1. Let us suppose the government finances its lump-sum transfers to consumers by printing money, issuing debt and raising proportional taxes on output and consumption. Consider a production function $y_t = Ak_t^\alpha$, and preferences represented by a utility function: $U(c_t, m_{t+1}) = \dfrac{\left(c_t\left(\frac{M_{t+1}}{P_t}\right)^\theta\right)^{1-\sigma}}{1-\sigma}$, $\theta > 0, \sigma > 0, \sigma \neq 1.$, where $m_t = \frac{M_{t+1}}{P_t}$.

(a) Assuming that the government maintains a constant tax rate on output τ_{ss}^y, a constant level of transfers ζ_{ss}, and a constant stock of bonds b_{ss}, and it has a nominal interest rate i_{ss} as target. Starting from values: $\alpha = 0.36, A = 1, \theta = 0.5, \beta = 0.95, \delta = 0.10$, find steady-state levels $c_{ss}, k_{ss}, m_{ss}, y_{ss}, r_{ss}, \tau_{ss}^c$ as functions of i_{ss}, for two values of the latter: i_0, i_1. Choose any values you want for τ_{ss}^y, ζ_{ss} and b_{ss}.

(b) Assume a specific rule for transfers, as a function of the stock of government debt outstanding, to be compatible with the steady-state analysis in that paragraph. Assume the government changes monetary and fiscal policy from the first to the second of the pairs (i_0, τ_0^c), (i_1, τ_1^c) obtained in the previous paragraph:

$$(i, \tau^c) = (i_0, \tau_0^c) \quad t < t_{ss}.$$
$$(i, \tau^c) = (i_1, \tau_1^c) \quad t \geq t_{ss}.$$

Exercise 2. Characterize the transitional dynamics of consumption, the stock of capital, real balances, the level of utility, the level of transfers, the stock of government debt, the level of seigniorage, the level of income tax revenues, the rate of inflation, the real rate of interest, and the rate of money growth. Use four different approaches:

b1) under a log-linear approximation to the set of equations defining the model, and a state-space representation for the model's dynamics

b2) under a linear approximation to the set of equations defining the model, and a state-space representation for the model's dynamics b3) under a log-linear approximation to the set of equations defining the model, computing the time path for physical capital from the global constraint of resources, and consumption from the stability condition

b4) under a linear approximation to the set of equations defining the model, computing the time path for physical capital from the global constraint of resources, and consumption from the stability condition

Exercise 3. Assume that the government finances its lump-sum transfers to consumers by issuing money and debt, as well as with the revenues from consumption and income taxes. Consider a production function $y_t = Ak_t^\alpha l_t^{1-\alpha}$, and a utility function: $U(c_t, l_t, \bar{m}_{t+1}) = \psi \ln(c_t) + (1-\psi)\ln(1-l_t^{1-\alpha}) + \theta \ln(\bar{m}_{t+1})$, where $\bar{m}_{t+1} = \frac{M_{t+1}}{P_t}$. Consider parameter values $A = 1, \beta = 0.9, \alpha = 0.33, \delta = 0.07, \theta = 0.50, \psi = 0.35, \tau^c = 0.15, \tau^y = 0.20$, the autonomous component of transfers (ζ) is equal to 0.15 and the sensitivity of transfers to government debt is 0.40. Assume that the nominal rate of interest increases from 3% to 5%, while keeping constant the tax rates on consumption and income.

(a) Characterize the initial steady-state.
(b) Characterize the final steady-state.
(c) Under the assumption that the change takes place at a single point in time: $i_t = 0.03\ t < t_0$, $i_t = 0.05\ t \geq t_0$, with t_0 being the time of change, characterize the transitional dynamics of the economy from the initial to the final steady-state, using one of the solution approaches discussed in this chapter.
(d) Repeat the analysis in the previous paragraph under the assumption of a gradual change in nominal rates: starting from time $t_0, i_t = (1-\rho_i)i_{ss} + \rho_i i_{t-1}$. Make the analysis for different values of $\rho_i \in (0,1)$.
What would happen in paragraphs c) and d) if the government maintains constant nominal transfers in spite of the increase in the rate of inflation?

Exercise 4. Assume that the government finances transfers to consumers by issuing money and debt. Consider a production function $y_t = Ak_t^\alpha$, and a utility function:

$$U(c_t, m_{t+1}) = \frac{\left(c_t \left(\frac{M_{t+1}}{P_t}\right)^\theta\right)^{1-\sigma}}{1-\sigma}, \quad \theta > 0, \sigma > 0, \sigma \neq 1.$$

Also, assume that the size of nominal transfers depends on the stock of debt outstanding and consider parameter values: $A = 1, \beta = 0.95, \alpha = 0.35, \delta = 0.1, \theta = 0.5, \sigma = 1.2, \zeta = 10, \eta = 0.4$.

(a) Assume that the capital stock is initially at 99% of its steady-state level, under a money growth rate of 2%. The government modifies monetary policy so that the money supply grows at 3% from period $t = 10$ on. What effects has this change on the economy? Would the effects be different if $\sigma = 0.95$?
(b) Assume that the economy is initially at the steady-state associated to a money growth rate of 2%. Characterize the effects on the economy if the government changes its long-run money growth target to 3%, following the rule:

$$x_t = (1-\rho)x_{ss} + \rho x_{t-1}.$$

Exercise 5. Assume that the government finances its transfers to consumers by issuing money and debt, as well as using revenues from consumption and income taxes. Consider a production function $y_t = A_t k_t^\alpha l_t^{1-\alpha}$,

$$\ln(A_t) = (1-\rho_A)\ln(A_{ss}) + \rho_A \ln(A_{t-1}) + \varepsilon_{A,t}, \quad |\rho_A| < 1.$$

and a utility function: $U(c_t, l_t, \bar{m}_{t+1}) = \psi \ln(c_t) + (1-\psi)\ln(1-l_t) + \theta \ln(\bar{m}_{t+1})$, where $\bar{m}_{t+1} = \frac{M_{t+1}}{P_t}$. Consider parameter values $A = 1, \beta = 0.9, \alpha = 0.33, \delta = 0.07, \theta = 0.50, \psi = 0.35, \tau^c = 0.15, \tau^y = 0.20$, the autonomous component of transfers (ζ) is equal to 0.15 and the sensitivity of transfers to government debt is 0.40. Suppose that the monetary authority chooses the nominal rate of interest according to Taylor's rule:

$$\hat{i}_t = \rho_i \hat{i}_{t-1} + \rho_\pi \hat{\pi}_t + \rho_y \hat{y}_t + \varepsilon_{i,t}, \quad |\rho_i| < 1, \quad \varepsilon_{i,t} \underset{iid}{\sim} N(0, \sigma_i^2),$$

where $\hat{i}_t \equiv \ln\left(\frac{1+i_t}{1+i_{ss}}\right)$; $\hat{\pi}_t \equiv \ln\left(\frac{1+\pi_t}{1+\pi_{ss}}\right)$; $\hat{y}_t \equiv \ln\left(\frac{y_t}{y_{ss}}\right) \underset{y_t=A_t k_t^\alpha}{=} \hat{A}_t + \alpha \hat{k}_t, \hat{A}_t \equiv \ln\left(\frac{A_t}{A_{ss}}\right)$,

$\hat{k}_t \equiv \ln\left(\frac{k_t}{k_{ss}}\right).$

Choose values for the parameters in Taylor's rule, as well as for ρ_A, $\sigma_{\varepsilon,A}^2$, $\sigma_{\varepsilon,i}^2$. Compute a sample realization for the model's perturbations, for 200 observations. Obtain 100 such realizations and compute sample distributions for the average and the standard deviation for the main variables in the model. Do sample moments depend on the values chosen for the parameters in Taylor's rule?

Exercise 6. Consider the same economy described in Exercise 4. Suppose now that the monetary authority controls the rate of money growth, according to the law of motion:

$$\ln(1+x_t) = (1-\rho_x)\ln(1+x_{ss}) + \rho_x \ln(1+x_{t-1}) + \varepsilon_{t-1},$$

Choose values for parameters $\rho_A, \rho_x, \sigma_{\varepsilon,A}^2, \sigma_{\varepsilon,x}^2$. Compute a sample realization of size 200 for the perturbations in the model. Obtain 100 of such realizations, and compute the sample distribution of the average and standard deviation for each of the main variables in the model.

Chapter 10
Mathematical Appendix

10.1 The Deterministic Control Problem in Continuous Time

Let us consider the dynamic optimization problem,

$$\underset{v_t}{Max} \int_0^T f(x_t, v_t, t) dt$$

subject to the constraint,

$$\dot{x}_t = h(x_t, v_t, t)$$
$$\text{and given } x_0$$

where v_t is known as the *control* variable, x_t being the *state* variable. The constraint is in the form of a differential equation describing the time evolution of the state variable, as a function of the decision taken at each point in time, i.e., of the value of the control variable. Control and state could be vector variables, in which case we would have several restrictions like the one above, one for each state variable.

We write the *Hamiltonian* for this problem,

$$H(x_t, v_t, \mu_t, t) = f(x_t, v_t, t) + \mu_t h(x_t, v_t, t),$$

where μ_t are *co-state* variables, one for each restriction, having the interpretation of shadow prices, or the marginal value of one additional unit of the associated *co-state* variable at time t in units of utility at time 0.

Pontryagin's principle indicates that maximization of the Hamiltonian by choice of the v_t sequence leads to optimality conditions:

$$1) \ \frac{\partial H}{\partial v_t} = 0 \Leftrightarrow \frac{\partial f}{\partial v_t} + \mu_t \frac{\partial h}{\partial v_t} = 0,$$

A. Novales et al., *Economic Growth: Theory and Numerical Solution Methods*,
© Springer-Verlag Berlin Heidelberg 2009

which is the *state equation* (one for each control variable), also known as *order condition*, and

$$2) \; \dot{\mu}_t = -\frac{\partial H}{\partial x_t} \Leftrightarrow \dot{\mu}_t = -\frac{\partial f}{\partial x_t} - \mu_t \frac{\partial h}{\partial x_t},$$

known as the *co-state equation* (one for each state variable).

If the control variable v_t is restricted in sign, $v_t \geq 0$, the state equation becomes,

$$\frac{\partial H}{\partial v_t} = \frac{\partial f}{\partial v_t} + \mu_t \frac{\partial h}{\partial v_t} \leq 0 \;\; \text{together with} \;\; v_t \frac{\partial H}{\partial v_t} = 0,$$

Finally, we have the transversality condition.

10.1.1 Transversality Condition

Sometimes, the terminal value of the state variable, $x(T) = x_T$ is restricted in sign. This is usually the case in economic applications of the maximum principle, where a typical state variable is the stock of productive capital in the economy. We have as transversality condition,

$$x_T \geq 0, \;\; x_T \mu_T = 0,$$

which implies that either $x_T = 0$, or else, $\mu_T = 0$.

If, on the contrary, x_T is not restricted in value or sign, then we must have as transversality condition: $\mu_T = 0$.

If the planning problem has an infinite horizon, the transversality condition becomes,

$$\lim_{T \to \infty} x_T \geq 0, \;\; \lim_{T \to \infty} x_T \mu_T = 0,$$

when x_T is restricted in sign, and

$$\lim_{T \to \infty} \mu_T = 0,$$

when x_T is not restricted in sign or value.

10.1.2 The Discounted Problem

Let us now assume that, as it is the case in many economic applications and, specifically, in growth problems, the global intertemporal objective is the result of aggregating over time an instantaneous objective function, subject to some time discount θ. That is, function $f(x_t, v_t, t)$ is of the form,

$$f(x_t, v_t, t) = e^{-\theta t} g(x_t, v_t, t),$$

where the time discount makes the net contribution of a given level of the objective function $g(.)$ to be lower the farther it occurs into the future. If, for simplicity, we assume that $f(x_t, v_t, t)$, $g(x_t, v_t, t)$, $h(x_t, v_t, t)$ do not change with time t, we will have the control problem,

$$\underset{v_t}{Max} \int_0^T e^{-\theta t} g(x_t, v_t) dt \,,$$

subject to the constraint,

$$\dot{x}_t = h(x_t, v_t),$$
$$\text{and given } x_0,$$

with Hamiltonian,

$$H(x_t, v_t, \mu_t) = e^{-\theta t} g(x_t, v_t) + \mu_t h(x_t, v_t),$$

state equation or order condition,

$$\frac{\partial H}{\partial v_t} = \frac{\partial f}{\partial v_t} + \mu_t \frac{\partial h}{\partial v_t} = e^{-\theta t} \frac{\partial g}{\partial v_t} + \mu_t \frac{\partial h}{\partial v_t} = 0,$$

co-state equation,

$$\dot{\mu}_t = -\frac{\partial H}{\partial x_t} \Leftrightarrow \dot{\mu}_t = -\frac{\partial f}{\partial x_t} - \mu_t \frac{\partial h}{\partial x_t} = -e^{-\theta t} \frac{\partial g}{\partial x_t} - \mu_t \frac{\partial h}{\partial x_t}, \qquad (10.1)$$

and the same transversality condition as before.

All variables are discounted as of time $t = 0$. In particular, the multiplier μ_t converts the contribution of the state variable x_t to the Hamiltonian in units of the initial period, providing us with the value of the state variable at time t, in units of the initial period $t = 0$. However, it is more useful to write the problem in terms of utility units at time t. Besides, unless we do so, differential equations like (10.1) defining the optimality conditions would depend on time t, due to the presence of the $e^{-\theta t}$-factor.

To work in current values, we rewrite the Hamiltonian,

$$H(x_t, v_t, \mu_t) = e^{-\theta t} \left[g(x_t, v_t) + \mu_t e^{\theta t} h(x_t, v_t) \right],$$

and define the *current-value multiplier*,

$$\lambda_t = \mu_t e^{\theta t}, \qquad (10.2)$$

which provides us with the shadow price or marginal value of the state variable x_t at time t. We also define the *current value Hamiltonian, H^**,

$$H^* = e^{\theta t} H = g(x_t, v_t) + \mu_t e^{\theta t} h(x_t, v_t) = g(x_t, v_t) + \lambda_t h(x_t, v_t),$$

where it is easy to see that the choice of v_t maximizing the current value Hamiltonian H^* is the same as that maximizing the Hamiltonian H.

Furthermore, using (10.1) and (10.2), we get as optimality conditions for maximization of H,

1.

$$\frac{\partial H}{\partial v_t} = \frac{\partial \left(e^{-\theta t} H^*\right)}{\partial v_t} = e^{-\theta t} \frac{\partial H^*}{\partial v_t},$$

from which we get,

$$\frac{\partial H}{\partial v_t} = 0 \quad \Leftrightarrow \quad \frac{\partial H^*}{\partial v_t} = 0.$$

2.

$$\dot{\lambda}_t = \theta \lambda_t + e^{\theta t} \dot{\mu}_t = \theta \lambda_t - e^{\theta t} \frac{\partial H}{\partial x_t} = \theta \lambda_t - \frac{\partial g}{\partial x_t} - e^{\theta t} \mu_t \frac{\partial h}{\partial x_t} = \theta \lambda_t - \frac{\partial H^*}{\partial x_t}.$$

So the state and co-state equations can also be written,

$$\frac{\partial H^*}{\partial v_t} = \frac{\partial g}{\partial v_t} + \lambda_t \frac{\partial h}{\partial v_t} = 0,$$

$$\dot{\lambda}_t = \theta \lambda_t - \frac{\partial H^*}{\partial x_t} = \theta \lambda_t - \frac{\partial g}{\partial x_t} - \lambda_t \frac{\partial h}{\partial x_t}.$$

We can perform a similar transformation in the transversality conditions, to have for the infinite horizon case, in terms of the current-value multiplier,

$$\lim_{T \to \infty} x_T \geq 0, \quad \lim_{T \to \infty} e^{-\theta t} x_T \lambda_T = 0, \tag{10.3}$$

when x_T is restricted in sign, and

$$\lim_{T \to \infty} e^{-\theta T} \lambda_T = 0, \tag{10.4}$$

when x_T is not restricted in sign or value.

Summarizing, when there is a discount factor in the objective function, the Hamiltonian can be written in two alternative forms, depending on the way the multipliers are defined, and we need to be careful with using the appropriate expression for the optimality conditions.

10.1.3 Calculus of Variations

Let us now devote a few comments to the Calculus of Variations problem. This is a special case of the optimal control problem, when the control variables are, precisely, the changes to be introduced in the state variables. So, the laws of motion of the system take a simple form,

$$\dot{x}_t = v_t \ \text{ that is } \ h(x_t, v_t, t) = v_t,$$

where both variables are continuous at intervals, given an initial value x_0 and possibly, also a terminal value x_T.

Since it is a special case of the optimal control problem, it can be solved by direct application of Pontryagin's principle. The Hamiltonian for this problem is,

$$H = f(x_t, v_t, t) + \mu_t v_t,$$

so that the *state equation* is,

$$\frac{\partial H}{\partial v_t} = \frac{\partial f}{\partial v_t} + \mu_t = 0,$$

and the *co-state equation*,

$$\dot{\mu}_t = -\frac{\partial H}{\partial x_t} = -\frac{\partial f}{\partial x_t} - \mu_t \frac{\partial h}{\partial x_t} = -\frac{\partial f}{\partial x_t},$$

since, in the Calculus of Variations problem, the h-function does not depend on x_t.
From the state equation, we get,

$$\mu_t = -\frac{\partial f}{\partial v_t},$$

so that, taking derivatives,

$$\dot{\mu}_t = \frac{d}{dt}\left(-\frac{\partial f}{\partial x_t}\right),$$

and the *co-state equation* can be written in this case,

$$\frac{d}{dt}\left(\frac{\partial f}{\partial x_t}\right) = \frac{\partial f}{\partial x_t},$$

which is a differential equation of second order, known as *Euler's equation*.

10.2 The Deterministic Control Problem in Discrete Time

Let us consider the dynamic optimization problem in discrete time, with continuously differentiable functions:

$$\underset{\{v_t\}_0^T}{Max} \sum_{t=0}^{\infty} \beta^t f(x_t, v_t)$$

subject to the constraints,

$$x_{t+1} = h(x_t, v_t),$$
$$x_{t+1} \geqslant 0,$$
$$v_t \geqslant 0,$$

and given x_0,

where v_t is known as the *control* variable, x_t being the *state* variable. The first constraint is in the form of a difference equation describing the time evolution of the state variable, as a function of the decision taken at each point in time, i.e., of the value of the control variable. The other two constraints indicate that the variables cannot take negative values, a standard assumption in economic models.

We write the *Lagrangian* for this problem,

$$L(x_t, v_t, \mu_t) = \sum_{t=0}^{\infty} \beta^t \left[f(x_t, v_t) - \lambda_{1,t}(x_{t+1} - h(x_t, v_t)) - \lambda_{2,t} x_{t+1} - \lambda_3 v_t \right],$$

where $\lambda_{i,t}$ $i = 1, 2, 3$ are the Kuhn–Tucker multipliers, having the interpretation of shadow prices. Kuhn–Tucker multipliers in this type of problems are usually known as *Lagrange multipliers*.

The Kuhn–Tucker conditions allow us to solve the nonlinear optimization problem above:

$$\frac{\partial L}{\partial v_t} = \beta^t \left(\frac{\partial f}{\partial v_t} + \lambda_{1,t} \frac{\partial h}{\partial v_t} - \lambda_{3,t} \right) = 0, \tag{10.5}$$

$$\frac{\partial L}{\partial x_{t+1}} = \beta^{t+1} \left(\frac{\partial f}{\partial x_{t+1}} + \lambda_{1,t+1} \frac{\partial h}{\partial x_{t+1}} \right) - \beta^t (\lambda_{1,t} + \lambda_{2,t}) = 0, \tag{10.6}$$

$$\frac{\partial L}{\partial \lambda_{1,t}} = x_{t+1} - h(x_t, v_t) = 0, \tag{10.7}$$

$$\frac{\partial L}{\partial \lambda_{2,t}} = -x_{t+1} \leqslant 0, \text{ and } \lambda_{2,t} x_{t+1} = 0, \tag{10.8}$$

$$\frac{\partial L}{\partial \lambda_{3,t}} = -v_t \leqslant 0, \text{ and } \lambda_{3,t} v_t = 0. \tag{10.9}$$

Additionally, the Lagrange multipliers cannot be positive, that is,

$$\lambda_{i,t} \leqslant 0, \ i = 1, 2, 3. \tag{10.10}$$

Conditions (10.5)–(10.7) are known as primal feasibility conditions, (10.8)–(10.9) are the conditions for complementarity slackness and (10.10) are the dual feasibility conditions.

Solving for $\lambda_{3,t}$ and $\lambda_{2,t}$ in (10.5) and (10.6), respectively:

$$\lambda_{3,t} = \frac{\partial f}{\partial v_t} + \lambda_{1,t} \frac{\partial h}{\partial v_t},$$

$$\lambda_{2,t} = -\lambda_{1,t} + \beta \left(\frac{\partial f}{\partial x_{t+1}} + \lambda_{1,t+1} \frac{\partial h}{\partial x_{t+1}} \right),$$

and plugging these two expressions in (10.8)–(10.10), we obtain Kuhn–Tucker conditions:

$$\left[-\lambda_{1,t} + \beta \left(\frac{\partial f}{\partial x_{t+1}} + \lambda_{1,t+1} \frac{\partial h}{\partial x_{t+1}} \right) \right] x_{t+1} = 0, \qquad (10.11)$$

$$\left(\frac{\partial f}{\partial v_t} + \lambda_{1,t} \frac{\partial h}{\partial v_t} \right) v_t = 0, \qquad (10.12)$$

$$-\lambda_{1,t} + \beta \left(\frac{\partial f}{\partial x_{t+1}} + \lambda_{1,t+1} \frac{\partial h}{\partial x_{t+1}} \right) \leqslant 0, \qquad (10.13)$$

$$\frac{\partial f}{\partial v_t} + \lambda_{1,t} \frac{\partial h}{\partial v_t} \leqslant 0. \qquad (10.14)$$

equivalent to the ones initially described, which are the ones we use throughout the book.

In Economics, the objective function and the set of restrictions usually satisfy the conditions for an interior solution so that: $x_{t+1} > 0$, $v_t > 0$. Then, the previous conditions reduce to:

$$-\lambda_{1,t} + \beta \left(\frac{\partial f}{\partial x_{t+1}} + \lambda_{1,t+1} \frac{\partial h}{\partial x_{t+1}} \right) = 0,$$

$$\frac{\partial f}{\partial v_t} + \lambda_{1,t} \frac{\partial h}{\partial v_t} = 0.$$

These are the optimality conditions of the Lagrange theorem to solve dynamic, discrete time optimization problems under equality constraints. Finally, we have the transversality condition, which is analogous to the one for the continuous-time case.

The analysis we have described can be generalized to the case with multiple state and control variables.

10.3 First Order Differential Equations

10.3.1 1. First Order Differential Equations with Constant Coefficients

Case 1.1: Homogeneous, Lineal Equation, with Constant Coefficients: $\dot{y}_t = r y_t$,

with r being a known constant. The equation can be written,

$$\frac{dy_t}{dt} = ry_t \quad \Rightarrow \quad \frac{dy_t}{y_t} = rdt \quad \Rightarrow \quad \ln y_t = rt + C \quad \Rightarrow$$

$$y_t = e^{rt+C} = C'e^{rt}, \tag{10.15}$$

where the constant C' is determined from a boundary condition, like the value of y_t at time $t = 0$. If we particularize (10.15) at time 0, we get: $y_0 = C'$, and we end up with a solution,

$$y_t = y_0 e^{rt}.$$

Case 1.2: Non-Homogeneous, Lineal Equation, with Constant Coefficient:
$\dot{y}_t = ry_t + g_t$,

with r being a known constant. The general solution to this equation is constructed as the sum of the solution to the homogeneous equation (i.e., ignoring the presence of g_t in the equation), plus a particular solution to the non-homogeneous equation. The solution to the homogeneous equation is that found in Case 1, $y_t = y_0 e^{rt}$. To find a particular solution to the non-homogeneous equation, we substitute a function of time, u_t, for the constant in the equation, to have,

$$y_{1t} = u_t e^{rt} \quad \Rightarrow \quad \hat{y}_{1t} = \dot{u}_t e^{rt} + u_t r e^{rt},$$

which taken to the initial equation, gives us,

$$\dot{y}_{1t} = ry_{1t} + g_t \quad \Rightarrow \quad \dot{u}_t e^{rt} + u_t r e^{rt} = ru_t e^{rt} + g_t,$$

leading to,

$$\dot{u}_t = e^{-rt} g_t,$$

which can be integrated in two different ways:

- towards the past,

$$u_t = \int_0^t e^{-rs} g_s ds,$$

- or towards the future,

$$u_t = -\int_t^\infty e^{-rs} g_s ds$$

as can be checked by taking derivatives in each of them with respect to time t. To obtain those derivatives we use Leibniz's rule, which gives us the derivative with respect to the parameter t of a parametric integral function,

$$I(t) = \int_{a(t)}^{b(t)} f(x,t)dx,$$

as,

$$\frac{dI(t)}{dt} = \int_{a(t)}^{b(t)} \frac{\partial f(x,t)}{\partial t} dx + f(b(t),t)\frac{db}{dt} - f(a(t),t)\frac{da}{dt}.$$

The integral towards the future has interest in economic applications, but it is valid only if it converges, for which a necessary, although not necessarily sufficient, condition is,

$$\lim_{s \to \infty} e^{-rs} g_s \to 0.$$

If this condition holds, we will have the particular solution to the non-homogeneous equation,

$$y_{1t} = -e^{rt} \int_t^\infty e^{-rs} g_s ds.$$

Notice that since we look just for a particular solution, we can ignore the additive constants which are standard when solving differential equations.

Finally, the general solution to the non-homogeneous equation is obtained by adding up to the solution of the homogeneous case, the particular solution, y_{1t}.

$$y_t = Ce^{rt} - e^{rt} \int_t^\infty e^{-rs} g_s ds,$$

If we know the sequence $\{g_s\}_{s=0}^\infty$, and the value of the constant coefficient r, a boundary condition will allow us to determine the numerical value of the constant C.

For instance, in the case of a constant sequence $g_s = g \; \forall s$, then writing the general solution at time $t = 0$,

$$y_0 = C - \int_0^\infty e^{-rs} g ds = C - \frac{g}{r} \Rightarrow C = y_0 + \frac{g}{r},$$

and finally,

$$y_t = \left(y_0 + \frac{g}{r}\right) e^{rt} - e^{rt} \int_t^\infty e^{-rs} g ds = \left(y_0 + \frac{g}{r}\right) e^{rt} - \frac{g}{r}.$$

To gain some familiarity with differential equations, let us now follow an alternative argument: The particular solution to the homogeneous equation is of type (10.15): $y_t = Ce^{rt}$. To obtain a particular solution to the non-homogeneous equation, we try,

$$y_t = u_t e^{rt},$$

and substituting in the differential equation, we get,

$$\dot{u}_t e^{rt} + u_t r e^{rt} = r u_t e^{rt} + g \Rightarrow \dot{u}_t = g e^{-rt},$$

which leads to,

$$u_t = -\frac{1}{r} g e^{-rt}.$$

So, the general solution to the non-homogeneous, first-order differential equation is,

$$y_t = Ce^{rt} - \frac{g}{r}.$$

At time 0 we would have,

$$y_0 = C - \frac{g}{r} \Rightarrow C = y_0 + \frac{g}{r}$$

and, finally, the solution,

$$y_t = \left(y_0 + \frac{g}{r}\right)e^{rt} - \frac{g}{r}.$$

10.3.2 2. First Order Differential Equations with Variable Coefficients

Case 2.1: Homogeneous, Lineal Equation, with Variable Coefficients: $\dot{y}_t = r_t y_t$.

The equation can be written,

$$\frac{dy_t}{dt} = r_t y_t \ \Rightarrow \ \frac{dy_t}{y_t} = r_t dt \ \Rightarrow \ \ln y_t = \int_0^t r_s ds + C \ \Rightarrow$$

$$y_t = e^{\int_0^t r_s ds + C} = C' e^{\int_0^t r_s ds}, \tag{10.16}$$

and, again, the constant C' is determined from a boundary condition, like the value of variable y_t at time $t = 0$, which implies,

$$y_t = y_0 e^{\int_0^t r_s ds}.$$

Example: In the main text, we face the differential equation

$$\dot{q}_t / q_t = n + \theta - r_t,$$

which following the argument above, can be integrated to,

$$q_t = q_0 e^{-\int_0^t (r_s - (n+\theta))ds}.$$

Case 2.2: Non-Homogeneous, Variable Coefficient, Lineal Equation: $\dot{y}_t = r_t y_t + g_t$.

The general solution to this equation is made up by adding to the solution to the homogeneous equation (i.e., ignoring the presence of g_t in the equation), a particular solution to the non-homogeneous equation. The solution to the homogeneous equation is that found in Case 1. To find a particular solution to the non-homogeneous equation, we substitute a function of time u_t for the constant in the equation, to have,

$$y_{1t} = u_t e^{\int_0^t r_s ds} \ \Rightarrow \ \dot{y}_{1t} = \dot{u}_t e^{\int_0^t r_s ds} + u_t r_t e^{\int_0^t r_s ds},$$

which taken to the initial equation, $\dot{y}_{1t} = r_t y_{1t} + g_t$, gives us:

$$\dot{u}_t e^{\int_0^t r_s ds} + u_t r_t e^{\int_0^t r_s ds} = r_t u_t e^{\int_0^t r_s ds} + g_t,$$

leading to,

$$\dot{u}_t = e^{-\int_0^t r_s ds} g_t,$$

and integrating towards the future, we obtain a particular solution to the non-homogeneous differential equation,

$$u_t = -\int_t^\infty e^{-\int_0^z r_s ds} g_z dz,$$

as can be checked by taking derivatives with respect to time t.

Finally, the general solution to the non-homogeneous equation is,

$$y_t = Ce^{\int_0^t r_s ds} - e^{\int_0^t r_s ds}\int_t^\infty e^{-\int_0^z r_s ds} g_z dz,$$

as it can be seen by taking derivatives with respect to t.

But, since $z > t$, we can write,

$$-\int_0^z r_s ds = -\int_0^t r_s ds - \int_t^z r_s ds,$$

which allows us to decompose the integral at the far right in the solution to the differential equation, to obtain,

$$y_t = Ce^{\int_0^t r_s ds} - e^{\int_0^t r_s ds}\int_t^\infty e^{-\int_0^t r_s ds} e^{-\int_t^z r_s ds} g_z dz,$$

where the first exponential factor, which does not depend on the integration variable, can be taken out of the integral, simplifying with the factor outside the integral. We finally have,

$$y_t = Ce^{\int_0^t r_s ds} - \int_t^\infty e^{-\int_t^z r_s ds} g_z dz,$$

as the solution to the non-homogeneous equation.

The constant can be found from a known initial condition, like the value of y_0. Making $t = 0$ in the previous equation,

$$t = 0 \Rightarrow y_0 = Ce^{\int_0^0 r_s ds} - \int_0^\infty e^{-\int_0^z r_s ds} g_z dz \Rightarrow C = y_0 + \int_0^\infty e^{-\int_0^z r_s ds} g_z dz,$$

so that,

$$
\begin{aligned}
y_t &= \left[y_0 + \int_0^\infty e^{-\int_0^z r_s ds} g_z dz\right] e^{\int_0^t r_s ds} - \int_t^\infty e^{-\int_t^z r_s ds} g_z dz \\
&= y_0 e^{\int_0^t r_s ds} + \int_0^\infty e^{-\int_t^z r_s ds} g_z dz - \int_t^\infty e^{-\int_t^z r_s ds} g_z dz = \\
&= y_0 e^{\int_0^t r_s ds} + \int_0^t e^{\int_z^t r_s ds} g_z dz.
\end{aligned}
$$

Example: Let us consider the special case: $g_s = g, r_s = r \ \forall s$. Then,

$$y_t = y_0 e^{\int_0^t r ds} + \int_0^t e^{\int_z^t r ds} g dz = y_0 e^{rt} + g \int_0^t e^{r(t-z)ds} dz$$

$$= y_0 e^{rt} - \frac{g}{r}(1 - e^{rt}) = \left(y_0 + \frac{g}{r}\right) e^{rt} - \frac{g}{r}$$

the same solution as we obtained above for first order, nonhomogeneous, constant coefficient differential equations [Case 1.2].

Example: In the main text, we face the differential equation,

$$\dot{a}_t + c_t + \tau_t = \omega_t + (r_t - n) a_t,$$

which, following the argument in this section, integrates to,

$$a_t = a_0 e^{\int_0^t (r_s - n) ds} + \int_0^t e^{\int_z^t (r_s - n) ds} \left(\omega_z - c_z - \tau_z\right) dz$$

$$= \left[a_0 + \int_0^t e^{-\int_0^z (r_s - n) ds} \left(\omega_z - c_z - \tau_z\right) dz\right] e^{\int_0^t (r_s - n) ds}.$$

10.4 Matrix Algebra

For a square matrix A, an eigenvalue is a (possibly complex) number μ for which there is a vector x such that,

$$Ax = \mu x.$$

Vector x is then called the right eigenvector associated to the eigenvalue μ of A. The left eigenvector associated to the eigenvalue μ is a vector x such that,

$$x'A = \mu x'.$$

To compute the eigenvalues of matrix A, we solve the determinant equation: $|A - \mu I| = 0$, which is known as the characteristic equation of matrix A.

Let Λ be the diagonal matrix having as elements the eigenvalues of A. Then, if Γ is the matrix having as columns the right–eigenvectors of A, we have, $A\Gamma = \Gamma\Lambda$. If $\tilde{\Gamma}$ is the matrix having as rows the left-eigenvectors of A, then $\tilde{\Gamma}A = \Lambda\tilde{\Gamma}$. The *spectral decomposition* of a square matrix A is defined as the factor product $A = \Gamma\Lambda\Gamma^{-1}$, where Λ is a diagonal matrix with elements equal to the eigenvalues of A, and Γ is the matrix which has as columns the right eigenvectors of A.

Furthermore, the *spectral decomposition* of the exponential of a square matrix A is defined as the factor product $e^A = \Gamma e^\Lambda \Gamma^{-1}$, where, again, Λ is a diagonal matrix with elements equal to the eigenvalues of A, and Γ is the matrix which has as columns the right eigenvectors of A.

Lemma 1. *The left eigenvectors of a square matrix A are the right eigenvectors of matrix A'. A matrix and its transpose have the same eigenvalues.*

Proof. Let $\tilde{\Gamma}$ be the matrix having as rows the left-eigenvectors of a square matrix A. Then, $\tilde{\Gamma}A = \Lambda\tilde{\Gamma}$ which implies $A'\tilde{\Gamma}' = \tilde{\Gamma}'\Lambda' = \tilde{\Gamma}'\Lambda$, since Λ is a diagonal matrix. This equality shows that $\tilde{\Gamma}'$ has as columns the right eigenvectors of matrix A', and also that the eigenvalues of A and A' are the same. But each column of $\tilde{\Gamma}'$ is clearly a row of $\tilde{\Gamma}$, which shows the result.   □

When characterizing stability as part of the numerical solution of a model, we will extensively use the following result:

Lemma 2. *Let A be a square, invertible matrix.*

(a) A and A^{-1} have the same right eigenvectors.
(b) If Γ is the matrix having as columns the right eigenvectors of A, then the rows of Γ^{-1} are the left eigenvectors of A^{-1}.
(c) A and A^{-1} have the same left eigenvectors

Proof. (a) From the spectral decomposition for $A : A = \Gamma\Lambda\Gamma^{-1}$, and inverting both sides: $A^{-1} = \Gamma\Lambda^{-1}\Gamma^{-1}$, where Λ^{-1} is the diagonal matrix having along the diagonal the inverse of the eigenvalues of A. Hence, when A is invertible, the eigenvalues of A^{-1} are the inverse of the eigenvalues of A, and both matrices, A and A^{-1}, have the same right eigenvectors.
(b) According to the definition of Γ, $A\Gamma = \Gamma\Lambda$ so that inverting at both sides: $\Gamma^{-1}A^{-1} = \Lambda^{-1}\Gamma^{-1}$. We again see that the eigenvalues of A^{-1} are the inverse of the eigenvalues of A, and also that the rows of Γ^{-1} are the left eigenvectors of A^{-1}.
(c) Putting together both results, we get that both matrices also share the same left eigenvectors.   □

To simplify notation, in what follows we will normalize eigenvectors to have a first component equal to one.
We will sometimes face the spectral decomposition of the power t of a matrix, A^t.

Lemma 3. *If matrix A admits the spectral decomposition: $A = \Gamma\Lambda\Gamma^{-1}$, then the spectral decomposition of A^t is: $A^t = \Gamma\Lambda^t\Gamma^{-1}$, where Λ^t is the diagonal matrix having as elements the power t of the elements of Λ.*

Proof. We proceed by induction. The result holds for $t = 2 : A^2 = AA = \left(\Gamma\Lambda\Gamma^{-1}\right)\left(\Gamma\Lambda\Gamma^{-1}\right) = \Gamma\Lambda\Gamma^{-1}\Gamma\Lambda\Gamma^{-1} = \Gamma\Lambda^2\Gamma^{-1}$, and also for $t = 3 : A^3 = A^2A = \left(\Gamma\Lambda^2\Gamma^{-1}\right)\left(\Gamma\Lambda\Gamma^{-1}\right) = \Gamma\Lambda^3\Gamma^{-1}$. Now, let us assume that the proposition holds for $t - 1, i.e. : A^{t-1} = \Gamma\Lambda^{t-1}\Gamma^{-1}$. Then, we have: $A^t = A^{t-1}A = \left(\Gamma\Lambda^{t-1}\Gamma^{-1}\right)\left(\Gamma\Lambda\Gamma^{-1}\right) = \Gamma\Lambda^t\Gamma^{-1}$. This completes the proof.   □

Let us now consider the power function e^A of an $nxn-$matrix A admitting a spectral decomposition as above. Using the matrix version of McLaurin's power expansion:

$$e^A = I_n + A + \frac{1}{2!}A^2 + \frac{1}{3!}A^3 + ... = I_n + \Gamma\Lambda\Gamma^{-1} + \frac{1}{2!}\left(\Gamma\Lambda\Gamma^{-1}\right)^2$$

$$+\frac{1}{3!}\left(\Gamma\Lambda\Gamma^{-1}\right)^3+... = I_n+\Gamma\Lambda\Gamma^{-1}+\frac{1}{2!}\Gamma\Lambda^2\Gamma^{-1}+\frac{1}{3!}\Gamma\Lambda^3\Gamma^{-1}+...$$

$$= \Gamma\left(I_n+\Lambda+\frac{1}{2!}\Lambda^2+\frac{1}{3!}\Lambda^3+...\right)\Gamma^{-1} =$$

$$= \Gamma e^{\Lambda}\Gamma^{-1}.$$

10.4.1 The 2×2 Case

Let A denote the 2×2 matrix of coefficients in system $\dot{z}_t = Az_t$, with $z_t = (z_{1t}, z_{2t})'$

$$A = \begin{pmatrix} a_{11} & a_{12} \\ a_{21} & a_{22} \end{pmatrix},$$

whose characteristic equation is,

$$\mu^2 - (a_{11}+a_{22})\mu + (a_{11}a_{22} - a_{12}a_{21}) = 0,$$

with roots,

$$\mu_1 = \frac{(a_{11}+a_{22})+\sqrt{(a_{11}+a_{22})^2 - 4(a_{11}a_{22}-a_{12}a_{21})}}{2},$$

$$\mu_2 = \frac{(a_{11}+a_{22})-\sqrt{(a_{11}+a_{22})^2 - 4(a_{11}a_{22}-a_{12}a_{21})}}{2}.$$

The right eigenvector corresponding to the μ_1 eigenvalue is the vector $x = (x_1, x_2)$ satisfying,

$$\begin{pmatrix} a_{11} & a_{12} \\ a_{21} & a_{22} \end{pmatrix}\begin{pmatrix} x_1 \\ x_2 \end{pmatrix} = \mu_1\begin{pmatrix} x_1 \\ x_2 \end{pmatrix},$$

that is,

$$a_{11}x_1 + a_{12}x_2 = \mu_1 x_1,$$
$$a_{21}x_1 + a_{22}x_2 = \mu_1 x_2,$$

which lead to,

$$x_2 = \frac{\mu_1 - a_{11}}{a_{12}}x_1,$$

$$x_2 = \frac{a_{21}}{\mu_1 - a_{22}}x_1,$$

two equations that turn out to be the same, precisely because of μ being a root to the characteristic equation.

Normalizing $x_1 = 1$, we get the eigenvector,

$$x = \begin{pmatrix} x_1 \\ x_2 \end{pmatrix} = \begin{pmatrix} 1 \\ \frac{\mu_1 - a_{11}}{a_{12}} \end{pmatrix}.$$

In a similar fashion, we would get the eigenvector associated to the μ_2 *eigenvalue*,

$$y = \begin{pmatrix} y_1 \\ y_2 \end{pmatrix} = \begin{pmatrix} 1 \\ \frac{\mu_2 - a_{11}}{a_{12}} \end{pmatrix},$$

with a factor product:

$$x'y = x_1 y_1 + x_2 y_2 = 1 + \frac{\mu_1 - a_{11}}{a_{12}} \frac{\mu_2 - a_{11}}{a_{12}}$$

$$= 1 + \frac{\mu_1 \mu_2 - a_{11}(\mu_1 + \mu_2) + a_{11}^2}{a_{12}^2} = 1 - \frac{a_{21}}{a_{12}}.$$

If A is symmetric, then x and y are orthogonal to each other because its product is zero.

Let us now compute the spectral decomposition of matrix A, $A = \Gamma \Lambda \Gamma^{-1}$, where Λ is a diagonal matrix with elements given by the eigenvalues of A, $\Lambda = \begin{pmatrix} \mu_1 & 0 \\ 0 & \mu_2 \end{pmatrix}$, and the columns of Γ are the right–eigenvectors of A, so that, $\Gamma = \begin{pmatrix} x_1 & y_1 \\ x_2 & y_2 \end{pmatrix}$ and its inverse matrix has the form:

$$\begin{pmatrix} u_1 & v_1 \\ u_2 & v_2 \end{pmatrix} = \Gamma^{-1} = \begin{pmatrix} x_1 & y_1 \\ x_2 & y_2 \end{pmatrix}^{-1} = \frac{1}{x_1 y_2 - x_2 y_1} \begin{pmatrix} y_2 & -y_1 \\ -x_2 & x_1 \end{pmatrix}$$

$$= \frac{a_{12}}{\mu_2 - \mu_1} \begin{pmatrix} \frac{\mu_2 - a_{11}}{a_{12}} & -1 \\ -\frac{\mu_1 - a_{11}}{a_{12}} & 1 \end{pmatrix},$$

so that,

$$A = \frac{a_{12}}{\mu_2 - \mu_1} \begin{pmatrix} 1 & 1 \\ \frac{\mu_1 - a_{11}}{a_{12}} & \frac{\mu_2 - a_{11}}{a_{12}} \end{pmatrix} \begin{pmatrix} \mu_1 & 0 \\ 0 & \mu_2 \end{pmatrix} \begin{pmatrix} \frac{\mu_2 - a_{11}}{a_{12}} & -1 \\ -\frac{\mu_1 - a_{11}}{a_{12}} & 1 \end{pmatrix}.$$

In some cases, we will be interested in imposing orthogonality between the left eigenvector x associated to one of the eigenvalues, μ_1, say, and the vector of variables z_t. That would imply,

$$z_{1t} + \frac{\mu_1 - a_{11}}{a_{12}} z_{2t} = 0.$$

But the two roots of the characteristic equation satisfy: $\mu_1\mu_2 = a_{11}a_{22} - a_{12}a_{21}$; $\mu_1 + \mu_2 = a_{11} + a_{22}$, so that $-\frac{a_{21}}{\mu_2 - a_{11}} = \frac{\mu_1 - a_{11}}{a_{12}}$, and the previous condition can also be written,

$$z_{1t} - \frac{a_{21}}{\mu_2 - a_{11}} z_{2t} = 0.$$

10.4.2 Systems with a Saddle Path Property

A 2×2 system with a characteristic equation of the form,

$$\mu^2 - \left(1 + \frac{1}{\beta} + A\right)\mu + \frac{1}{\beta} = 0,$$

has a *saddle path* structure, with an eigenvalue above $1/\beta$, and the other below 1. To show this property, notice that the two roots of the characteristic equation satisfy,

$$\mu_1 + \mu_2 = 1 + \frac{1}{\beta} + A, \ \mu_1\mu_2 = \frac{1}{\beta},$$

so that,

$$\mu_1 + \frac{1}{\beta\mu_1} = 1 + \frac{1}{\beta} + A.$$

The function $f(\mu_1) = \mu_1 + \frac{1}{\beta\mu_1}$ describing the sum of the two roots is continuous on the positive real line. It takes the same value at $\mu_1 = 1$ and at: $\mu_1 = \frac{1}{\beta}$: $f(1) = f(\frac{1}{\beta}) = 1 + \frac{1}{\beta}$, and has a minimum at $\mu_1 = \sqrt{1/\beta}$, between the previous two points. Since $1 + \frac{1}{\beta} + A > 1 + \frac{1}{\beta}$, then the two possible values of μ_1 satisfying the equation $f(\mu_1) = 1 + \frac{1}{\beta} + A$ are one below $\mu_1 = 1$, and the other above $\mu_1 = \frac{1}{\beta}$.

10.4.3 Imposing Stability Conditions Over Time

We show in this section that imposing stability conditions on a linear or loglinear approximation to a dynamic system at time $t = 0$ amounts to imposing the conditions at each point in time. Linear or log-linear approximations to nonlinear dynamic systems of difference equations are often computed throughout the book, in order to compute a numerical solution. That approximation can always be written as a first order autoregressive process for an extended vector of variables that includes all control and state variables in the system. If the model exhibits long dynamics, the vector may include lags of state and control variables. That representation is known as *state-space representation*.

Proposition 2. *In the state-space formulation of any dynamic economy, imposing the stability condition at $t = 0$ amounts to imposing it $\forall t$.*

Consider the dynamic system:

$$\begin{bmatrix} s_{t+1} \\ c_{t+1} \end{bmatrix} = \underbrace{\begin{bmatrix} \Gamma_{11} & \Gamma_{12} \\ \Gamma_{21} & \Gamma_{22} \end{bmatrix}}_{\Gamma} \begin{bmatrix} s_t \\ c_t \end{bmatrix}, \text{ dado } s_0,$$

where s_t is a vector of state variables of order $k \times 1$, and c_t is a $r \times 1$ vector of control variables. So, Γ_{11} is a matrix of order $k \times k$, Γ_{22} is a $r \times r$ matrix, Γ_{12} is a $k \times r$ matrix, while Γ_{21} is a $r \times k$ matrix.

Let us diagonalize Γ :

$$\underbrace{\begin{bmatrix} M_{11} & M_{12} \\ M_{21} & M_{22} \end{bmatrix}}_{M} \underbrace{\begin{bmatrix} \Lambda_1 & 0_{k \times r} \\ 0_{r \times k} & \Lambda_2 \end{bmatrix}}_{\Lambda} \underbrace{\begin{bmatrix} m_{11} & m_{12} \\ m_{21} & m_{22} \end{bmatrix}}_{M^{-1}} = \begin{bmatrix} \Gamma_{11} & \Gamma_{12} \\ \Gamma_{21} & \Gamma_{22} \end{bmatrix}.$$

where we assume Λ_1 to be the diagonal matrix made up by the stable eigenvalues (those with norm below 1) while Λ_2 is the diagonal matrix made up by the unstable eigenvalues (eigenvalues with norm above 1). Therefore, the submatrix $[M_{12} \ M_{22}]$ contains as columns the unstable right eigenvectors, while the $[m_{21} \ m_{22}]$ contains, as rows, the unstable left eigenvectors. Notice that matrix Λ_2 must be of order $r \times r$ to guarantee that the solution is determinate.

If we eliminate the unstable paths, we will have that, given the initial conditions for the state variables, the solution to the dynamic system will be stable, having a saddle path solution. Eliminating the unstable directions implies obtaining initial values for the control variables as functions of the initial values for the state variables that eliminate the explosive trajectories:

$$m_{21}s_0 + m_{22}c_0 = 0 \Rightarrow c_0 = -m_{22}^{-1}m_{21}s_0.$$

If we substitute this expression in the transition matrix for $t = 1$, we will have, on the one hand:

$$s_1 = \Gamma_{11}s_0 - \Gamma_{12}m_{22}^{-1}m_{21}s_0$$
$$= \left[\Gamma_{11} - \Gamma_{12}m_{22}^{-1}m_{21}\right]s_0,$$

that is,

$$s_0 = \left[\Gamma_{11} - \Gamma_{12}m_{22}^{-1}m_{21}\right]^{-1}s_1, \tag{10.17}$$

and, on the other,

$$c_1 = \Gamma_{21}s_0 + \Gamma_{22}c_0$$
$$= \Gamma_{21}s_0 - \Gamma_{22}m_{22}^{-1}m_{21}s_0$$
$$= \left[\Gamma_{21} - \Gamma_{22}m_{22}^{-1}m_{21}\right]s_0, \tag{10.18}$$

where, plugging expressions (10.17) into (10.18), we have:

$$c_1 = \left[\Gamma_{21} - \Gamma_{22} m_{22}^{-1} m_{21}\right] \left[\Gamma_{11} - \Gamma_{12} m_{22}^{-1} m_{21}\right]^{-1} s_1. \qquad (10.19)$$

Therefore, all we need is to show that: $\left[\Gamma_{21} - \Gamma_{22} m_{22}^{-1} m_{21}\right] \times \left[\Gamma_{11} - \Gamma_{12} m_{22}^{-1} m_{21}\right]^{-1}$ $= -m_{22}^{-1} m_{21}$. Once this has been shown, it is easy to conclude that the stability condition is satisfied for all t, since the same argument used for $t = 1$ can be used for all future t.

First, we know that:

$$\begin{bmatrix} \Lambda_1 & 0_{k \times r} \\ 0_{r \times k} & \Lambda_2 \end{bmatrix} \begin{bmatrix} m_{11} & m_{12} \\ m_{21} & m_{22} \end{bmatrix} = \begin{bmatrix} m_{11} & m_{12} \\ m_{21} & m_{22} \end{bmatrix} \begin{bmatrix} \Gamma_{11} & \Gamma_{12} \\ \Gamma_{21} & \Gamma_{22} \end{bmatrix}$$

$$\Rightarrow \begin{bmatrix} \Lambda_1 m_{11} & \Lambda_1 m_{12} \\ \Lambda_2 m_{21} & \Lambda_2 m_{22} \end{bmatrix} = \begin{bmatrix} m_{11}\Gamma_{11} + m_{12}\Gamma_{21} & m_{11}\Gamma_{12} + m_{12}\Gamma_{22} \\ m_{21}\Gamma_{11} + m_{22}\Gamma_{21} & m_{21}\Gamma_{12} + m_{22}\Gamma_{22} \end{bmatrix}$$

we have two alternative expressions for Λ_2:

$$\Lambda_2 = m_{21}\Gamma_{11} m'_{21} (m_{21} m'_{21})^{-1} + m_{22}\Gamma_{21} m'_{21} (m_{21} m'_{21})^{-1}$$
$$\Lambda_2 = m_{21}\Gamma_{12} m_{22}^{-1} + m_{22}\Gamma_{22} m_{22}^{-1} \qquad (10.20)$$

where we allow for m_{12} not being a square matrix.

Making these expressions equal to each other, and multiplying on the right by $m_{21} m'_{21}$:

$$m_{21}\left[\Gamma_{11} m'_{21}(m_{21} m'_{21})^{-1} m_{21} m'_{21} - \Gamma_{12} m_{22}^{-1} m_{21} m'_{21}\right]$$
$$= -m_{22}\left[\Gamma_{21} m'_{21}(m_{21} m'_{21})^{-1} m_{21} m'_{21} - \Gamma_{22} m_{22}^{-1} m_{21} m'_{21}\right]$$

$$\Rightarrow m_{21}\left[\Gamma_{11} m'_{21} - \Gamma_{12} m_{22}^{-1} m_{21} m'_{21}\right]$$
$$= -m_{22}\left[\Gamma_{21} m'_{21} - \Gamma_{22} m_{22}^{-1} m_{21} m'_{21}\right]$$

$$\Rightarrow m_{21}\left[\Gamma_{11} - \Gamma_{12} m_{22}^{-1} m_{21}\right] m'_{21}$$
$$= -m_{22}\left[\Gamma_{21} - \Gamma_{22} m_{22}^{-1} m_{21}\right] m'_{21}$$

$$\Rightarrow m_{21}\left[\Gamma_{11} - \Gamma_{12} m_{22}^{-1} m_{21}\right] = -m_{22}\left[\Gamma_{21} - \Gamma_{22} m_{22}^{-1} m_{21}\right]$$

$$\Rightarrow -m_{22}^{-1} m_{12} = \left[\Gamma_{21} - \Gamma_{22} m_{22}^{-1} m_{21}\right] \left[\Gamma_{11} - \Gamma_{12} m_{22}^{-1} m_{21}\right]^{-1}.$$

$\square$

10.5 Some Notes on Complex Numbers

Let $\{\mu_1 = a + bi,\ \mu_2 = a - bi\}$ two complex conjugate numbers. If we transform these two numbers to polar coordinates we get: $\mu_1 = q\cos(\theta) + i\,q\sin(\theta)$, $\mu_2 = q\cos(\theta) - iq\sin(\theta)$, where $\theta = \arctan(b/a)$ and $q = \|\mu_1\| = \|\mu_2\| = (a^2 + b^2)^{1/2}$.

Proposition 3. $e^{i\theta} = \cos(\theta) + i\sin(\theta)$.

Proof. Step 1: we describe the McLaurin's series expansions of $\sin(\theta)$, $\cos\theta$ and e^x:

$$\sin(\theta) = \sin 0 + \theta\cos 0 - \frac{1}{2!}\theta^2\sin 0 - \frac{1}{3!}\theta^3\cos 0 + \frac{1}{4!}\theta^4\sin 0 + \dots$$

$$= \theta - \frac{\theta^3}{3!} + \frac{\theta^5}{5!} - \frac{\theta^7}{7!} + \frac{\theta^9}{9!} - \dots$$

$$\cos(\theta) = \cos 0 - \theta\sin 0 - \frac{1}{2!}\theta^2\cos 0 + \frac{1}{3!}\theta^3\sin 0 + \frac{1}{4!}\theta^4\cos 0 - \dots$$

$$= 1 - \frac{\theta^2}{2!} + \frac{\theta^4}{4!} - \frac{\theta^6}{6!} + \frac{\theta^8}{8!} - \dots$$

$$e^x = 1 + x + \frac{x^2}{2!} + \frac{x^3}{3!} + \frac{x^4}{4!} + \dots$$

If $x = i\theta$, then:

$$e^{i\theta} = 1 + i\theta - \frac{\theta^2}{2!} - i\frac{\theta^3}{3!} + \frac{\theta^4}{4!} + i\frac{\theta^5}{5!} - \frac{\theta^6}{6!} - i\frac{\theta^7}{7!} + \dots$$

$$= \left(1 - \frac{\theta^2}{2!} + \frac{\theta^4}{4!} - \frac{\theta^6}{6!} + \frac{\theta^8}{8!} - \dots\right) + i\left(\theta - \frac{\theta^3}{3!} + \frac{\theta^5}{5!} - \frac{\theta^7}{7!} + \frac{\theta^9}{9!} - \dots\right)$$

$$= \cos(\theta) + i\sin(\theta).$$

$\square$

Corollary 1. $e^{-i\theta} = \cos(\theta) - i\sin(\theta)$

$$e^{-i\theta} = 1 - i\theta - \frac{\theta^2}{2!} + i\frac{\theta^3}{3!} + \frac{\theta^4}{4!} - i\frac{\theta^5}{5!} - \frac{\theta^6}{6!} + i\frac{\theta^7}{7!} + \dots$$

$$= \left(1 - \frac{\theta^2}{2!} + \frac{\theta^4}{4!} - \frac{\theta^6}{6!} + \frac{\theta^8}{8!} - \dots\right) - i\left(\theta - \frac{\theta^3}{3!} + \frac{\theta^5}{5!} - \frac{\theta^7}{7!} + \frac{\theta^9}{9!} - \dots\right)$$

$$= \cos(\theta) - i\sin(\theta).$$

Corollary 1. *Given two complex conjugate numbers* $\mu_1 = a + ib = q[\cos(\theta) + i\sin(\theta)] = qe^{i\theta}$, $\mu_2 = a - ib = q[\cos(\theta) - i\sin(\theta)] = qe^{-i\theta}$, *where q and θ are defined as above, we have:*

$$e^{i\theta t} = \cos(\theta t) + i\sin(\theta t)$$
$$\mu_1^t = (a+ib)^t = q^t \left[\cos(\theta t) + i\sin(\theta t)\right] = q^t e^{i\theta t}$$
$$\mu_2^t = (a-ib)^t = q^t \left[\cos(\theta t) - i\sin(\theta t)\right] = q^t e^{-i\theta t}$$

Proof. The reader may easily check these expressions by arguments similar to those used for previous results.   □

10.6 Solving a Dynamic Two-Equation System with Complex Roots

Let us consider the system:

$$\begin{bmatrix} x_{1t} \\ x_{2t} \end{bmatrix} = \underbrace{\begin{bmatrix} a & b \\ c & d \end{bmatrix}}_{\Gamma} \begin{bmatrix} x_{1t-1} \\ x_{2t-1} \end{bmatrix}. \tag{10.21}$$

The solution, provided the two roots of Γ are different, is:

$$\begin{bmatrix} x_{1t} \\ x_{2t} \end{bmatrix} = \begin{bmatrix} A_1 \mu_1^t + A_2 \mu_2^t \\ B_1 \mu_1^t + B_2 \mu_2^t \end{bmatrix}, \tag{10.22}$$

where A_1, A_2, B_1, B_2 are constants to be determined.

Let us assume that the transition matrix Γ in expression (10.21) has complex roots. Then,

$$\mu_1 = \alpha + \beta i,$$
$$\mu_2 = \alpha - \beta i,$$
$$A_1 = \gamma + \delta i, \ A_2 = \gamma - \delta i,$$
$$B_1 = \varpi + \eta i, \ B_2 = \varpi - \eta i. \tag{10.23}$$

We will first show that: $\begin{Bmatrix} A_1 \mu_1^t + A_2 \mu_2^t \\ B_1 \mu_1^t + B_2 \mu_2^t \end{Bmatrix}$ are real solutions if and only if A_1, A_2 are, in fact, complex conjugate numbers and B_1, B_2 are also complex conjugate numbers.

$\Rightarrow$): Let $A_1 = \gamma_1 + \delta_1 i$, $A_2 = \gamma_2 + \delta_2 i$. If $A_1 \mu_1^t + A_2 \mu_2^t$ is a real number $\forall t$, then it will also be real for $t=0 \Rightarrow A_1 + A_2$ must be real $\Rightarrow \gamma_1 + \delta_1 i + \gamma_2 + \delta_2 i$ must be real $\Rightarrow \delta_1 = -\delta_2$. Let us denote from now on: $\delta = \delta_1$. If $A_1 \mu_1^t + A_2 \mu_2^t$ is real $\forall t$, then, at time $t=1 \Rightarrow A_1 \mu_1 + A_2 \mu_2$ must be real $\Rightarrow (\gamma_1 + \delta i)(\alpha + \beta i) + (\gamma_2 - \delta i)(\alpha - \beta i) = (\gamma_1 \alpha - 2\delta\beta + \gamma_2 \alpha) + \beta i(\gamma_1 - \gamma_2)$ which will be real if $\gamma_1 = \gamma_2$. Let us denote from now on, $\gamma = \gamma_1$. Hence, $A_1 = \gamma + \delta i$, $A_2 = \gamma - \delta i$, are complex conjugate numbers. The same proof can be used for B_1 and B_2.

$\Rightarrow$): If A_1, A_2 are complex conjugate numbers and B_1, B_2 are complex conjugate numbers, then the solution $\begin{Bmatrix} A_1 \mu_1^t + A_2 \mu_2^t \\ B_1 \mu_1^t + B_2 \mu_2^t \end{Bmatrix}$ is real. We can write: $A_1 = \gamma + \delta i = s$

$e^{i\omega} = s\left[\cos(\omega) + i\sin(\omega)\right]$, $A_2 = \gamma - \delta i = s \, e^{-i\omega} = s\left[\cos(\omega) - i\sin(\omega)\right]$, where $s = (\gamma^2 + \delta^2)^{1/2}$, $\omega = \arctan(\delta/\gamma)$. Let $\mu_1 = \alpha + \beta i = q \, e^{i\vartheta} = q\left[\cos(\vartheta) + i\sin(\vartheta)\right]$, $\mu_2 = \alpha - \beta i = q \, e^{-i\vartheta} = q\left[\cos(\vartheta) - i\sin(\vartheta)\right]$, where $q = (\alpha^2 + \beta^2)^{1/2}$, $\vartheta = \arctan(\beta/\alpha)$.

Therefore, $A_1\mu_1^t + A_2\mu_2^t = s \, e^{i\omega} q^t \, e^{i\vartheta t} + s \, e^{-i\omega} q^t \, e^{-i\vartheta t} = sq^t\left[e^{i(\omega+\vartheta t)} + e^{-i(\omega+\vartheta t)}\right] = sq^t\left[\cos(\omega + \vartheta t) + i\sin(\omega + \vartheta t) + \cos(\omega + \vartheta t) - i\sin(\omega + \vartheta t)\right] = 2sq^t \cos(\omega + \vartheta t) = 2sq^t\left[\cos(\omega)\cos(\vartheta t) - \sin(\omega)\sin(\vartheta t)\right] = $

$$2q^t\left[\underbrace{s\cos(\omega)}_{\gamma}\cos(\vartheta t) - \underbrace{s\sin(\omega)}_{\delta}\sin(\vartheta t)\right] = 2q^t\left[\gamma\cos(\vartheta t) - \delta\sin(\vartheta t)\right], \quad \text{which}$$

is real.[1]

Therefore, the solution to the system can also be written:

$$\begin{bmatrix} x_{1t} \\ x_{2t} \end{bmatrix} = \begin{bmatrix} 2q^t\left[\gamma\cos(\vartheta t) - \delta\sin(\vartheta t)\right] \\ 2q^t\left[\varpi\cos(\vartheta t) - \eta\sin(\vartheta t)\right] \end{bmatrix}, \tag{10.24}$$

with $\gamma, \delta, \varpi, \eta$ being constants to be determined.

We show next that the solution can also be written:

$$\begin{bmatrix} x_{1t} \\ x_{2t} \end{bmatrix} = \begin{bmatrix} q^t c_1[d_1\cos(\vartheta t) - f_1\sin(\vartheta t)] + q^t c_2[d_1\sin(\vartheta t) + f_1\cos(\vartheta t)] \\ q^t c_1[d_2\cos(\vartheta t) - f_2\sin(\vartheta t)] + q^t c_2[d_2\sin(\vartheta t) + f_2\cos(\vartheta t)] \end{bmatrix}, \tag{10.25}$$

with only two constants, c_1, c_2 to be determined. d_1, d_2 come from the real part of the eigenvector associated to μ_1 or μ_2, since they share the same real part, and f_1, f_2 are real numbers from the imaginary part of the eigenvector associated to μ_1. Therefore, this presentation of the solution is more convenient since, given initial conditions (x_{10}, x_{20}), we can only compute two constants. That means that when presenting the solution in the form (10.21)–(10.24), A_1, B_1 must be proportional to each other, and so must be the pairs (A_2, B_2), (γ, ϖ) and (δ, η), with the proportionality constant being a function of the components of the transition matrix Γ.

Let us now show that the solution can be written as in (10.25). To do so, notice that we could solve the system of difference equations as:

$$\begin{bmatrix} x_{1t} \\ x_{2t} \end{bmatrix} = \begin{bmatrix} a & b \\ c & d \end{bmatrix}^t \begin{bmatrix} x_{10} \\ x_{20} \end{bmatrix}$$

$$= \underbrace{\begin{bmatrix} M_{11} & M_{12} \\ M_{21} & M_{22} \end{bmatrix}}_{M} \underbrace{\begin{bmatrix} \mu_1^t & 0 \\ 0 & \mu_2^t \end{bmatrix}}_{\Lambda^t} \underbrace{\begin{bmatrix} m_{11} & m_{12} \\ m_{21} & m_{22} \end{bmatrix}}_{M^{-1}} \begin{bmatrix} x_{10} \\ x_{20} \end{bmatrix}$$

$$= \begin{bmatrix} M_{11} & M_{12} \\ M_{21} & M_{22} \end{bmatrix} \begin{bmatrix} \mu_1^t C_1 \\ \mu_2^t C_2 \end{bmatrix} = \begin{bmatrix} C_1 M_{11}\mu_1^t + C_2 M_{12}\mu_2^t \\ C_1 M_{21}\mu_1^t + C_2 M_{22}\mu_2^t \end{bmatrix}, \tag{10.26}$$

where $C_1 = m_{11}x_{10} + m_{12}x_{20}$, $C_2 = m_{21}x_{10} + m_{22}x_{20}$.

---

[1] Where we have applied the property of the cosine of the sum: $\cos(a + b) = \cos(a)\cos(b) - \sin(a)\sin(b)$.

Let M, m be the matrices:

$$M = \begin{bmatrix} d_1 + if_1 & d_1 - if_1 \\ d_2 + if_2 & d_2 - if_2 \end{bmatrix}; \ m = \begin{bmatrix} g_1 + ih_1 & g_2 + ih_2 \\ g_1 - ih_1 & g_2 - ih_2 \end{bmatrix}.$$

Notice that matrix M has as columns the complex conjugate right eigenvectors, while the rows in m are the complex conjugate left eigenvectors. Given matrices M and m, it is easy to show that the constants C_1 and C_2 are also complex conjugate numbers:

$$C_1 = \underbrace{(g_1 x_{10} + g_2 x_{20})}_{C_r} + \underbrace{(h_1 x_{10} + h_2 x_{20})i}_{C_i},$$

$$C_2 = (g_1 x_{10} + g_2 x_{20}) - (h_1 x_{10} + h_2 x_{20})i.$$

Comparing (10.26) and (10.22), we have:

$$\{C_1 M_{11} = A_1; \ C_2 M_{12} = A_2; \ C_1 M_{21} = B_1; \ C_2 M_{22} = B_2\} \Rightarrow$$

$$\{(C_r + iC_i)(d_1 + if_1) = \gamma + i\delta; \ (C_r + iC_i)(d_2 + if_2) = \varpi + i\eta\} \Rightarrow$$

$$\gamma = (C_r d_1 - C_i f_1); \ \delta = (C_i d_1 + C_r f_1);$$
$$\varpi = (C_r d_2 - C_i f_2); \ \eta = (C_i d_2 + C_r f_2). \tag{10.27}$$

so that, using (10.27) in (10.24), we get:

$$\begin{bmatrix} x_{1t} \\ x_{2t} \end{bmatrix} = \begin{bmatrix} 2q^t \left[(C_r d_1 - C_i f_1) \cos(\vartheta t) - (C_i d_1 + C_r f_1) \sin(\vartheta t) \right] \\ 2q^t \left[(C_r d_2 - C_i f_2) \cos(\vartheta t) - (C_i d_2 + C_r f_2) \sin(\vartheta t) \right] \end{bmatrix}$$

$$= \begin{bmatrix} 2q^t \left[C_r (d_1 \cos(\vartheta t) - f_1 \sin(\vartheta t)) - C_i (d_1 \sin(\vartheta t) + f_1 \cos(\vartheta t)) \right] \\ 2q^t \left[C_r (d_2 \cos(\vartheta t) - f_2 \sin(\vartheta t)) - C_i (d_2 \sin(\vartheta t) + f_2 \cos(\vartheta t)) \right] \end{bmatrix}$$

$$= \begin{bmatrix} q^t c_1 \left[d_1 \cos(\vartheta t) - f_1 \sin(\vartheta t) \right] + q^t c_2 \left[d_1 \sin(\vartheta t) + f_1 \cos(\vartheta t) \right] \\ q^t c_1 \left[d_2 \cos(\vartheta t) - f_2 \sin(\vartheta t) \right] + q^t c_2 \left[d_2 \sin(\vartheta t) + f_2 \cos(\vartheta t) \right] \end{bmatrix},$$

where: $c_1 = 2C_r$, $c_2 = -2C_i$.

References

1. Adda, J. and R.W. Cooper (2003), *Dynamic Economics: Quantitative Methods and Applications*, MIT, Cambridge.
2. Aghion, P. and P. Howitt (1992), "A model of growth through creative destruction", *Econometrica*, 80(2), 323–351.
3. Aghion, P. and P. Howitt (1999), *Endogenous Growth Theory*, MIT, Cambridge.
4. Barro, R.J. (1990), "Government spending in a simple model of endogenous growth", *Journal of Political Economy*, 98(5), S103–S126.
5. Barro, R.J. and X. Sala-i-Martin (1997), "Technological diffusion, convergence, and growth", *Journal of Economic Growth*, 2(1), 1–26.
6. Barro, R. and X. Sala-i-Martin (2003), *Economic Growth*, 2nd edition, MIT, Cambridge.
7. Bailey, M.J. (1956), "The welfare cost of inflationary finance", *Journal of Political Economy*, 64, 93–110.
8. Bayoumi, T., D. Laxton, and P. Pesenti (2004), "Benefits and spillovers of greater competition in Europe: A macroeconomic assessment", ECB Working Paper, No. 341, European Central Bank.
9. Benhabib, J. and R. Perli (1994), "Uniqueness and indeterminacy: Transitional dynamics with multiple equilibria", *Journal of Economic Theory*, 63, 113–142.
10. Blanchard, O. and C.M. Kahn (1980), "The solution of linear difference models under rational expectations", *Econometrica*, 48(5), 1305–1311.
11. Blanchard, O. and S. Fischer (1989), *Lectures on Macroeconomics*, MIT, Cambridge.
12. Brock, W.A. and L.J. Mirman (1972), "Optimal economic growth and uncertainty: The discounted case", *Journal of Economic Theory*, 4, 479–513.
13. Caballe, J. and M. Santos (1993), "On endogenous growth with physical and human capital", *Journal of Political Economy*, 101, 1042–1067.
14. Cagan, P. (1956), "The monetary dynamics of hyperinflation", in M. Friedman (ed.) *Studies in the Quantity Theory of Money*, University of Chicago Press, Chicago, pp. 25–117.
15. Calvo, G. (1983), "Staggered prices in a utility maximizing framework", *Journal of Monetary Economics*, 12, 383–398.
16. Canova, F. (2007), *Methods for Applied Macroeconomic Research*, Princeton University Press, Princeton.
17. Carlstrom, C.T. and T.S. Fuerst (2001), "Timing and real indeterminacy in monetary models", *Journal of Monetary Economics*, 47(2), 285–298.
18. Cass, D. (1965), "Optimum growth in an aggregative model of capital accumulation", *Review of Economic Studies*, 32, 233–240.
19. Castañeda, A., J. Diaz-Gimenez, and J.V. Rios-Rull (1998), "Exploring the income distribution business cycle dynamics", *Journal of Monetary Economics*, 42, 93–130.
20. Clower, R.W. (1967), "A reconsideration of the microfoundations of monetary theory", *Western Economic Journal*, 6(1), 1–9.

21. Coenen, G. and V. Wieland (2000), "A small estimated euro area model with rational expectations and nominal rigidities", *European Economic Review*, 49, 1081–1104.
22. Coenen, G. and R. Straub (2005), "Does government spending crowd in private consumption? Theory and empirical evidence for the Euro area", *International Finance*, 8, 435–470.
23. Coenen, G., P. McAdam and R. Straub, (2008), "Tax reform and Labour-Market Performance in the Euro Area: A Simulation-Based Analysis Using the New Area-Wide Model", Journal of Economic Dynamics and Control, 32, 8, 2543–2583.
24. Cooley, T.F. (1995), *Frontiers of Business Cycle Research*, Princeton University Press, Princeton.
25. Champ, B. and S. Freeman (2001), *Modelling Monetary Economies*, Cambridge University Press, Cambridge.
26. Chari, V.V., L. Christiano, and P. Kehoe (1996), "Optimality of the Friedman rule in economies with distorting taxes", *Journal of Monetary Economics*, 37, 203–223.
27. De Jong, D.N. and C. Dave (2007), *Structural Macroeconometrics*, Princeton University Press, Princeton.
28. Den Haan, W. and A. Marcet (1990), "Solving the stochastic growth model by parameterized expectations", *Journal of Business and Economic Statistics*, 8, 31–34.
29. Den Haan, W. and A. Marcet (1994), "Accuracy in Simulations", *Review of Economic Studies*, 61, 3–17.
30. Díaz-Giménez, J. (1999), "Linear quadratic approximations", in Ramon Marimon and Andrew Scott (eds.), *Computational Methods for the Study of Dynamic Economics*, chap. 1, Oxford University Press, New York, 13–29.
31. Dixit, A.K. and J. Stiglitz (1977), "Monopolistic competition and optimum product diversity", *American Economic Review* 67, 297–308.
32. Erceg, C.J., L. Guerrieri and C. Gust, (2005), "*SIGMA: A New Open Economy Model for Policy Analysis*", International Finance Discussion Papers No. 835, Board of Governors of the Federal Reserve System, July.
33. Ethier, W.J. (1982), "National and international returns to scale in the modern theory of international trade", *American Economic Review* 72, 389–405.
34. Friedman, M. (1969), "The Optimum Quantity of Money", in *The Optimum Quantity of Money and other Essays*, Aldine, Chicago.
35. Gali, J. and M. Gertler (1999), "Inflation dynamics: A structural econometric analysis", *Journal of Monetary Economics*, 44(2), 195–222.
36. Greenwood, J., Z. Hercowitz, Z. and G.W. Huffman (1988), "Investment, capacity utilization, and the real business cycle", *American Economic Review*, 78, 402–417.
37. Grossman, G.M. and E. Helpman (1991), *Innovation and Growth in the Global Economy*, MIT, Cambridge.
38. Guidotti, P.E. and C.A. Végh (1993), "The optimal inflation tax when money reduces transactions costs. A reconsideration", *Journal of Monetary Economics*, 31, 189–205.
39. Guillman, M. (1993), "The welfare cost of inflation in a cash-in-advance economy with costly credit", *Journal of Monetary Economics*, 31(1), 97–115.
40. Hansen, L.P. and T.J. Sargent (2005), *Recursive Methods of Linear Dynamic Economies*, manuscript, New York University.
41. Heer, B. and A. Maussner (2005), *Dynamic General Equilibrium Modelling: Computational Methods and Applications*, Springer, Berlin.
42. Howitt, P. and P. Aghion (1998), "Capital accumulation and innovation as complementary factors in long-run growth", *Journal of Economic Growth* 3, 111–130.
43. Ireland, P.N. (1994), "Supply-side economics and endogenous growth", *Journal of Monetary Economics*, 33, 559–572.
44. Ireland, P.N. (2003), "Endogenous money or sticky prices?", *Journal of Monetary Economics*, 50, 1623–1648.
45. Ireland, P.N. (2004), "Money's role in the monetary business cycle", *Journal of Money, Credit, and Banking*, 36(6), 969–983.
46. Ireland, P.N. (2004), "A method for taking models to the data", *Journal of Economic Dynamics and Control*, 28(6), 1205–1226.

47. Jones, L.E. and R. Manuelli (1990), "A convex model of economic growth", *Journal of Political Economy*, 98(5), 1008–1038.
48. Judd, K.L. (1998), *Numerical Methods in Economics*, MIT, Cambridge.
49. Keynes, J.M. (1936), *The General Theory of Employment, Interest and Money*, Reprinted Harbinger, Hardcourt Brace and World, 1964.
50. Kimbrough, K. (1986), "The optimum quantity of money rule in the theory of public finance", *Journal of Monetary Economics*, 18, 277–284.
51. King, R.G, C.I. Plosser, and S. Rebelo (1988), "Production, growth, and business cycles: II. New directions", *Journal of Monetary Economics* 21, 309–341.
52. Koopmans, T.C. (1965), "On the concept of optimal economic growth", in *The Economic Approach to Development Planning*, North-Holland, Amsterdam.
53. Kydland, F.E. and E.C. Prescott (1982), "Time to build and aggregate fluctuations", *Econometrica*, 50, 1345–1370.
54. Kydland, F.E. and E.C. Prescott (1996), "The computational experiment: An econometric tool", *Journal of Economic Perspectives*, 10(1), 69–85.
55. Leeper, E.M. (1991), "Equilibria under 'active' and 'passive' monetary and fiscal policies", *Journal of Monetary Economics*, 27, 129–147.
56. Ljunqvist, L. and T. Sargent (2004), *Recursive Macroeconomic Theory*, 2nd edition, MIT, Cambridge.
57. Lucas, R.E. (1976), *Econometric Policy Evaluation: A Critique*, Carnegie-Rochester Conference Series on Public Policy.
58. Lucas, R.E. and N.L. Stokey (1983), "Optimal fiscal and monetary policy in an economy without capital", *Journal of Monetary Economics*, 12, 55–93.
59. Lucas, R.E. (1987), *Models of Business Cycles*, Blackwell, Oxford.
60. Lucas, R.E. (1988), "On the mechanism of economic development", *Journal of Monetary Economics*, 122, 3–42.
61. Lucas, R.E. (1994), *The Welfare Cost of Inflation*, CEPR Publication no. 394, Stanford University, Stanford.
62. Marcet, A. and W.J. den Haan (1990), "Solving nonliear stochastic models by parameterizing expectations", *Journal of Business and Economic Statistics*, 8, 31–34.
63. Marcet, A. and G. Lorenzoni (1999), "Parameterized expectations approach: some practical issues", in R. Marimon and A. Scott (eds.), *Computational Methods for the Study of Dynamic Economics*, Oxford University Press, Oxford, pp. 143–171.
64. Marimon, R. and A. Scott (eds.) (1999), *Computational Methods for the Study of Dynamic Economics*, Oxford University Press, Oxford.
65. McCallum, B.T. (1989), "Real business cycle models", in R.J. Barro (ed.), *Modern Business Cycle Theory*, Harvard University Press, Cambridge.
66. McCandless, G. (2008), *ABCs of RBCs: An Introduction to Dynamic Macroeconomic Models*, Harvard East Asian Monographs, Cambridge.
67. McGrattan, E.R. (1999), "Application of weighted residual methods to dynamic economic models", in R. Marimon and A. Scott (eds.), *Computational Methods for the Study of Dynamic Economies*, Oxford University Press, Oxford.
68. Miranda, M.J. and P.L. Fackler (2002), *Applied Computational Economics and Finance*, MIT, Cambridge.
69. Novales, A. and J. Ruiz (2002), "Dynamic Laffer effects", *Journal of Economic Dynamics and Control*, 27, 181–206.
70. Phelps, E.S. (1973), "Inflation in the theory of public finance", *Swedish Journal of Economics*, 75, 67–82.
71. Poole, W. (1970), "Optimal choice of monetary policy instruments in a simple stochastic macro model", *Quarterly Journal of Economics*, 84(2), 197–216.
72. Press, W.H., B.P. Flannery, S.A. Teukolsky, and W.T. Vetterling (1986), *Numerical Recipes: The Art of Scientific Computing*, Cambridge University Press, Cambridge.
73. Ramsey, F. (1928), "A mathematical theory of saving", *Economic Journal*, 38, 543–559.
74. Rebelo, S. (1991), "Long-run policy analysis and long-run growth", *Journal of Political Economy*, 99(3), 500–521.

75. Rios-Rull, J.V. (1996), "Life-cycle economies and aggregate fluctuations", *Review of Economic Studies*, 63, 465–490.
76. Romer, P.M. (1986), "Increasing returns and long-run growth", *Journal of Political Economy*, 94(5), 1002–1037.
77. Romer, P.M. (1987), "Growth based on increasing returns due to specialization", *American Economic Review*, 77(2), 56–62.
78. Romer, P.M. (1990), "Endogenous technological change", *Journal of Political Economy*, 98(5), part II, S71–S102.
79. Rotemberg, J.J. (1982), "Sticky prices in the United States", *Journal of Political Economy*, 39, 173–196.
80. Sargent, T.J. (1979), *Macroeconomic Theory*, Academic, New York.
81. Sargent, T.J. (1987), *Dynamic Macroeconomic Theory*, Harvard University Press, Cambridge.
82. Schumpeter, J.A. (1934), *The Theory of Economic Development*, Harvard University Press, Cambridge.
83. Segerstrom, P.S., T.C.A Anant, and E. Dinopoulos (1990), "A Schumpeterian model of the product life cycle", *American Economic Review*, 80, 1077–1091.
84. Sidrauski, M. (1967), "Rational choice and patterns of growth in a monetary economy", *American Economic Revenue*, 57(2), 534–544.
85. Sims, C.A. (1994), "A simple model for study of the determination of the price level and the interaction of monetary and fiscal policy", *Economic Theory*, 4, 381–399.
86. Sims, C.A. (2001), "Solving linear rational expectations models", *Journal of Computational Economics*, 20, 1–20.
87. Smets, F. and R. Wouters (2003), "An estimated dynamic stochastic general equilibirum model of the Euro area", *Journal of the european economic association*, 1(5), 1123–1175.
88. Solow, R.M. (1956), "A contribution to the theory of economic growth", *Quarterly Journal of Economics*, 70(1), 65–94.
89. Spence, M. (1976), "Product selection, fixed costs, and monopolistic competition", *Review of Economic Studies*, 43(2), 217–235.
90. Stokey, N.L. and R.E. Lucas (1989), *Recursive Methods in Dynamic Economies*, Harvard University Press, Cambridge.
91. Swan, T.W. (1956), "Economic growth and capital accumulation", *Economic Record*, 32, 334–361.
92. Taylor, J.B. (1993), "Discretion versus policy rules in practice", *Carnegie–Rochester Conferences Series on Public Policy*, 39(December), 195–214.
93. Turnovsky, S. (2000), *Methods of Macroeconomic Dynamics*, MIT, Cambridge.
94. Uhlig, H. (1999), "A toolkit for analyzing nonlinear dynamic stochastic models easily", in R. Marimon and A. Scott (eds.), *Computational Methods for the Study of Dynamic Economics*, Oxford University Press, Oxford, pp. 30–61.
95. Uzawa, H. (1964), "Optimal growth in a two sector model of capital accumulation", *Review of Economic Studies*, 31(1), 1–24.
96. Walsh, C.E. (1998), *Monetary Theory and Policy*, MIT, Cambridge.
97. Whiteman, C.H. (1983), *Linear Rational Expectations Models: A User's Guide*, University of Minnesota Press, Minneapolis.
98. Xie, D. (1994), "Divergence in economic performance: transitional dynamics with multiple equilibria", *Journal of Economic Theory* 63, 97–112.

Index